Dynamic Models of
International Conflict

Dynamic Models of International Conflict

edited by
Urs Luterbacher and
Michael D. Ward

Lynne Rienner Publishers, Inc.
Boulder, Colorado

Published in the United States of America by
Lynne Rienner Publishers, Inc.
948 North Street, Boulder, Colorado 80302

Library of Congress Cataloging in Publication Data

Main entry under title:

Dynamic models of international conflict.

   Bibliography: p.
   Includes index.
   1. International relations--Research. I. Luterbacher,
Urs. II. Ward, Michael Don, 1948-
JX1291.D93   327'.072   85-26710
ISBN 0-931477-18-2 (lib. bdg.)

Distributed outside of North and South America and Japan by
Frances Pinter (Publishers) Ltd, 25 Floral Street,
London WC2E 9DS England. UK ISBN: 0-86187-558-3

Printed and bound in the United States of America

ERRATA   Dynamic Models of International Conflict, edited by Urs Luterbacher and Michael D. Ward

Chapter 2

p. 12, Fig. 2.1: insert the line "Column" on the right side of the figure, above the line that reads "Cooperate (C)" and "Do not cooperate $(\bar{C})$"

p. 13, ll. 42-45: "Although Row would 'win' in this case by getting his best outcome, Column would not 'lose' in the usual sense by getting his worst outcome, but rather his next worse."

p. 14, l. 20: "preemptory" should read "preemptive"

p. 14, ll. 26-27: "Thus r_4 and c_4 signify the highest payoffs for Row and Column, respectively, r_1 and c_1 the lowest, etc."

p. 15, key to Fig. 2.2: line 1 should read "(r_i, r_j) = (payoff to Row, payoff to Column)"

p. 16, ll. 2-3: delete "(1)" and "(2)"

p. 18, ll. 27-28: should read "from a preemption equilibrium"

p. 20, Eq. 3: should read "(s = 1, q = 1; t = 0, p = p_0)"

p. 21, l. 4: the equation in line 4 should begin $\frac{\partial E_c}{\partial t}$

p. 22, l. 21: "[because $1p + 0(1 - p) = p < c_3$]."

Chapter 3

p. 27, l. 29: should read "definition of individual rationality, for the"

p. 28, second line from the bottom: "U" should read "U"

p. 29, l. 2: should read "$v_k(u(i, j)) = v_k(i, j)$ for $k = 1$ and 2."

p. 30: the caption for Figure 3.2 should be "Notation for Determination of Stability for Player 1"

p. 31, l. 16: "matrix U" should read "matrix U"

p. 31, l. 27: should begin "j)) = v_{ij}^1, $\bar{i} \neq i$)"

p. 31, l. 29: "U" should read "U"

p. 32, l. 12: "V(i, j)" should read "$v_1(i, j)$"

p. 35, l. 5: "metartational" should read "metarational"

p. 36, heading: "SYMMETRIC METARATIONALITY" should be a second-level, rather than a first-level, heading

p. 36, l. 30: "minmax$_1$" should read "Minmax$_1$"

p. 38, ll. 21-22: should read "1 anticipates 2's choosing

1

the one (j_q) most harmful to 1."

p. 38, l. 25: should begin "while 1 guards against 2 hurting him"

p. 38, missing text at end of page: "to represent a player's exact choice as a function of his anticipation matrix. More specifically, 1 always assumes that 2 will act exactly in 2's own best interests (as 1 perceives them), and assumes that 2 makes the same assumption about 1, etc. These assumptions are captured by iterating T_1 and T_2."

p. 45, l. 10: "option" should read "notion"

p. 45, l. 14: should begin "$T_{21}^{\infty} U = X^r$"

p. 49, l. 4: should end "then $v_1(y(i, j)) \geq$ "

p. 49. l. 6: should read "any strategy for 1 satisfying"

p. 50, l. 7: "Similarly, (1, j)" should read "Similarly, (i, j)"

Chapter 4

p. 55, l. 1: should read "To demonstrate that mutual deterrence is both stable and"

p. 62, l. 8: "because of" should read "due to"

p. 65, l. 17: "This" should read "Thus"

Chapter 7

p. 135, Eq. 4: "V_A" should read "v_A"

p. 136, l. 18: "F_A" should read "f_A"

p. 137, l. 3: should read "decisions on both sides regarding targeting, $\alpha'(t)$, $\beta'(t)$;"

p. 140, Eq. 8: ">" should read "$\geq$"; "V_A" should read "v_A"

p. 140, l. 18: "C_B" should read "$\bar{C}_B$"

p. 140, tenth line from bottom: should read "$(\beta = \bar{\beta}, \beta' = 0)$"

p. 141, Eq. 9: replace "<" with "$\leq$"

p. 141, Eq. 10: replace ">" with "$\geq$"

p. 141, l. 9: replace "C_A" with "$\hat{C}_A$"

p. 142, Fig. 7.1: intersection of "A ATTACKS" and "B ATTACKS" lines should be labeled "I"

p. 145, Eq. 13: in the denominator, replace "α" with "$\bar{\alpha}$"

p. 146, Eq. 16: replace "a" with "α"

p. 147, l. 5: should read "if the target is βM_A"

p. 147, l. 22: should read "(and nonmilitary net investment)"

2

p. 147, l. 30: should read "the welfare integral at time τ"

p. 148, Eq. 21: should begin "$D_A(M_A^*(M_B) - M_A) = 0$"

p. 148, Eq. 25: should begin "$\dot{P}_A$"

p. 149, Eq. 27: replace second "=" sign with a "+" sign

p. 149, l. 10: "P_A" should read "$\dot{P}_A$"

p. 149, l. 14: "M_A" should read "$\dot{M}_A$"

p. 149, Eq. 33: "δ" should read "$-\delta$"

pp. 153, 155, 156: In Figures 7.3, 7.4, and 7.5, the intersection of the lines "A deters" and "B deters" should be labeled "D," and the intersection of the lines "A attacks" and "B attacks" should be labeled "I." The figure titles should be as follows: Figure 7.3--"A Stable Equilibrium at the Point of Minimal Mutual Deterrence"; Figure 7.4--"An Unstable Arms Race Trap"; Figure 7.5--"An Asymmetric Arms Race Trap."

p. 160, n. 12: in the matrix, "$- k_B$" should read "$-k_B$"

p. 160, n. 12, three lines below the matrix: "are alternative" should read "alternate"

Chapter 8

p. 161: the author's name should carry the superscript "1"

p. 162, ll. 40-42: should read "but most specialists probably would agree that if England eventually did not go under, it was by a small margin."

p. 163, Fig. 8.1: remove the two "2's" from the left side of the diagram; the figure caption should read "Peacefulness and Agressiveness in Arms Races"

p. 166, l. 3: "gewolt" should read "gewollt"

p. 173, l. 6: "decisions" should read "divisions"

p. 174, n. 15: should read "Not excepting the half dozen or so models for which this writer is wholly or partly responsible. On this point, see Allan (1983, pp. 64-65)."

Chapter 10

p. 220, l. 9: "Jarvis" should read "Jervis"

Chapter 11

p. 235, l. 22: "greater took" should read "greater too"

p. 236, bottom of the page: should read

$$^{BP}A,B = R_{A,B}\frac{PC_{A,B}}{PC_{B,A}}$$

3

p. 241, ll. 12-13: should read "If Caplow's A > B > C, B + C > A triad is considered"

p. 241: the functions displayed on the bottom third of the page should read

$$U_{AC} = (BP_{CB/AC} - E)(F - BP_{CA})$$
$$U_{BC} = (BP_{CA/BC} - H)(K - BP_{CB})$$
$$U_C = (BP_{CB} - I)(J - BP_{CA})$$

p. 243, Eq. 2: the numerator of the partial of U_C w.r.t. should read "$-2BP_C + J\ BP_A + I\ BP_B$

p. 244, Eq. 3: X_{BC} should read $\dot{X}_{BC}$

p. 245, Eq. 4: K_{CB}^* should read $\ddot{K}_{CB}^*$

p. 245, l. 31: "treadic" should read "triadic"

Chapter 12

p. 263, ninth line from bottom of page: "satisfying" should read "satisficing"

p. 266, Eq. 3: "FGG" should read "FGC"

Chapter 15

p. 354, second paragraph: the paragraph should begin "Mao Tse-tung developed operational conceptions for both types. In his essay of 1936 he describes the conception of revolutionary warfare. A detailed description of the national guerrilla warfare can be found in his 1938 study." The paragraph should end "in his study about the lengthy war (Mao, 1938)."

p. 357, ll. 4-5: should read "unit of 2 against the units of 1, and b is the destruction rate of a unit of 1 against the units of 2."

p. 357, l. 30: "flight" should read "fight"

p. 358, l. 3: "destroyed" should read "hit"

p. 363, l. 13: "the other hand" should read "the other side"

Chapter 17

p. 409: in the last box of Figure 17.1, "at t + t" should read "at t + +"

p. 416, bottom of page: the formulae should read

(FOR ALL x) {REVOLTS-FROM(x, ATHENS)
IMPLIES BESIEGES (ATHENS, x)}
(FOR ALL x) {REVOLTS-FROM(x, ATHENS)
AND NOT (SURRENDER-TO(x, ATHENS))

```
    IMPLIES DESTROYED (x)}
    (FOR ALL x) {REVOLTS-FROM(x, ATHENS)
    IMPLIES BESIEGES (ATHENS, x)}
    (FOR ALL x) {BESIEGES (ATHENS, x)
    IMPLIES INCURS-COST (ATHENS)}
```

P. 417, 11. 20-21: should read "AND ((REVOLTS-FROM(z, ATHENS)
AND NOT (REVOLTS-FROM(y, ATHENS))) OR ENEMIES-OF(y, z))"

p. 417, last line: should end "(x, ATHENS))}"

p. 418, 11. 40-41: "n = 0 and m = 0" should read "n >= 0 and m
>= 0"

p. 419, 11. 7-8: should read "If n = 0 then write it as [ ] and
interpret it as a sentence which is always false."

p. 419, 11. 13 & 20: "m = 1" should read "m >= 1"

p. 420, 1. 34: delete the reference to Figures 17.5 and 17.6

References

Add the following entries:

Allan, Pierre and Albert A. Stahel (1983). "Tribal Guerilla
Warfare Against a Colonial Power: Analyzing the War in
Afghanistan." Journal of Conflict Resolution 27:590-617.

Halin, J. (1974). MIMIC-Handbuch des Instituts für
Reaktortechnik. Zurich: ETH.

Laqueur, Walter (1977). Guerilla, A Historical and Critical
Study. London: Weidenfeld and Nicolson.

Mao Tsetung (1936). "Strategische Probleme des revolutionaren
Krieges in China." In Ausgewählte Militärische Schriften.
Beijing: Verlag für fremdsprachige Literatur, 1969. S. 87-
177.

Mao Tsetung (1938). "Strategische Probleme des Partisanenkriegs
gegen die japanische Aggression." In Ausgewählte
Militärische Schriften. Beijing: Verlag für fremdsprachige
Literatur, 1969. S. 179-221.

Mao Tsetung. "Ueber den langwierigen Krieg." In Ausgewählte
Militärische Schriften. Beijing: Verlag für fremdsprachige
Literatur, 1969. S. 223-325.

Stahel, Albert A. (1973). Die Anwendung der numerischen Mathe-
matik und der Simulationstechnik bei der Darstellung des
Ablaufs einer internationalen Krise. Frauenfeld: Huber & Co.

Stahel, Albert A. (1980). Simulationen sicherheitspolitischer
Prozesse, anhand von Beispielen und Problemen der

schweizerischen Sicherheitspolitik. Zürcher Beiträge zur
Politischen Wissenschaft, Band 2. Frauenfeld: Huber & Co.

Stahel, Albert A. and P. Bucherer (1984). "Afghanistan, 5
Jahre Widerstand und Kleinkrieg." In Allgemeinen
Schweizerischen Militärzeitschrift, ASMZ, No. 12.
Frauenfeld: Huber & Co.

Volterra, U. (1931). Leçons sur la théorie mathématique de la
lutte pour la vie. Paris: Gauthier-Villars et Cie.

Contents

PART 5
ARTIFICIAL INTELLIGENCE

PART 7
COMMENTARY

Preface

In early summer of 1983 an announcement of U.S. cooperative science programs sponsored by the Division of International Programs at the U.S. National Science Foundation crossed my desk. At that point, I alerted Urs Luterbacher and raised with him the possiblity of convening a seminar focused on dynamic approaches to modeling international conflict. At that time I also explored the receptivity of the Division of International Programs to receiving a proposal from social scientists. Drs. Warren Thompson and Henryk Uznanski, both with the NSF's International Programs office, were extremely helpful and supportive in encouraging us to pursue our idea.

Through the helpfulness of the University of Colorado's dean of the College of Arts and Science, Everly B. Fleischer, and the dean of the Graduate School and vice-chancellor for research, Bruce Ekstrand, it was possible for me to stop in Geneva during a visit to the International Institute for Applied Systems Analysis in Austria. During this stop-over in Geneva, I was able to work out the major outline of the seminar with Professor Luterbacher. One short month later, in October 1983, Luterbacher was in the United States, and once again, Dean Fleischer, in collaboration with the director of our then newly founded Center for International Relations, Manus I. Midlarsky, provided funds, this time to bring Luterbacher from the East Coast to Boulder, where for two days we worked further on what were to become our separate proposals to the U.S. and Swiss National Science Foundations. By August 1984 the review process had been completed, and we received word that the U.S. and Swiss National Science Foundations would sponsor our Joint Seminar on Dynamic Approaches to Modeling International Conflict, to be held in Boulder some ten weeks hence.

Through the wonderful support of the program on Political and Economic Change at the University of

Colorado's Institute of Behavioral Science, the planning
and local arrangements proceeded smoothly. Richard Jessor
and Ed Greenberg were especially accommodative of our
demands during the conference and subsequently. We are
grateful to Jean Umbreit, our project secretary, for
helping to ensure that it all got done. Through the good
offices of Dr. Lewis L. House of the High Altitude
Observatory and Dr. Wilmont Hess, director of the National
Center for Atmospheric Research, a magnificent setting was
provided and our meetings were held in the Damon Seminar
Room, looking out on the Flatirons. I believe that the
community and supportiveness this provided the visiting
scientists contributed in a major way to the success of
the seminar.

Each scholar who attended the conference made a major
contribution to our joint understanding of the dynamics of
international conflict. In particular, Steven Brams and
Michael Intriligator got our deliberations off to a
splendid beginning on the first day.

The editorial work involved in assembling,
organizing, and editing the volume was done in Boulder.
Support for this was provided by the U.S. NSF grant.

Lynne Rienner and her able staff, especially Pat
Jensen, have been very supportive of the production and
editorial process, understanding of the complexities of
international collaboration, and committed to making this
publication happen with a maximum of style and a minimum
of hassle.

The conference was supported by the U.S. National
Science Foundation under Grant No. INT-8405145 and by a
grant for Swiss participation from the Fonds national
suisse de la recherche scientifique. As is customary, the
normal disclaimers apply; any opinions, findings, and
conclusions or recommendations expressed in this
publication are those of the individual authors and do not
necessarily reflect the views of the U.S. or Swiss
National Science Foundations. However, both foundations
deserve a large amount of credit for facilitating and
financing the conference and the collection of results,
findings, conclusions, and opinions that appear on the
following pages.

Michael D. Ward
Boulder, Colorado
August 1985

1 Perspectives on Modeling International Conflict

For many, international conflict is a timeless process. Or so it seems. It is present often, and in a myriad of locales, on our small globe. The major premise of this book, however, is that international conflict is not a timeless process. It is not timeless in the sense that it need not be ever present, and it is not timeless in the important sense that it is difficult to understand unless one examines its dynamic properties. Both convective storms and international crises may appear to many to burst magically into existence. But both need dynamic approaches to their understanding, especially insofar as they may represent highly unstable phenomena.

For decades, realist analysts of world politics have depended upon a relatively stable, static analysis of the so-called primary forces of the international system. Such a formulation is not consonant with the episodic outbreaks of interstate disputes, nor with the recurrent crises that tend to characterize the historical record, as well as the contemporary period.

Recent advances have promoted a variety of perspectives on how to model and ultimately understand international conflict behavior. It is only lately that these frameworks have begun to focus on the properties of change in the international system and, more specifically, in the evolution of political-economic structures and processes.

In 1982 Michael Intriligator published a survey of research on conflict theory that appeared in the Journal of Conflict Resolution. In that survey, eight analytic approaches, ranging from differential equations to organization theory, and eight substantive areas of application, such as arms races and crisis behavior, were cross-classified. This volume and most of the chapters in it attempt to add a third dimension to that 8 by 8 cross-classification: namely, a temporal dimension.

The first section of the book focuses on game-theoretic and utility approaches. Beginning with the generalization of the rational decision-making paradigm, a

1

variety of empirically testable propositions and theoretical insights have been accumulated based on these techniques. Of course, neither game theory nor utility theory are sparkling new techniques. What is new is their focus in this book on the dynamics of the conflict situation.

It is only recently that game-theoretical perspectives have been enlarged by the representations of anticipations and expectations, as well as by the long-term strategic calculations that may be exemplified, for example, by non-myopic equilibrium (Brams and Wittman, 1983; Zagare, 1983). In a similar vein, utility theory is beginning to be expanded to focus on the dynamics of optimization as applied to political decision problems as they relate to international conflict.

The importance of strategic calculations in world politics has been long-standing. Steven Brams and D. Marc Kilgour's chapter, "The Path to Stable Deterrence," takes this so-called holy grail of contemporary world politics and utilizes a two-person, non-constant-sum game to analyze it. This game is one in which quantitative choices and the possibility of retaliation are analyzed. It is illustrated that a rational dynamic path exists for two different kinds of Nash equilibria--deterrence and preemption--each of which is Pareto-superior. A dynamic path is shown to exist that will lead from a preemptive to a deterrent equilibrium; however, it entails certain risks. Brams and Kilgour conclude that deterrence, even when based on a variety of probabilistic choices, can be justified on dynamic rational-choice grounds. This entails making the ultimate threat, but in their opinion also tends to stabilize the deterrence equilibrium.

D. Marc Kilgour, a mathematician, contributes some fascinating and novel results in Chapter 3. Providing a definition of anticipation in a decision framework, he analyzes decision makers' choices as a function of the consequences that they anticipate their actions to entail. Such a dynamic analysis of look-ahead rules leads to interesting results for the two-person game, and for international conflict as well. In contrast to most static analysis, Kilgour proves that the status quo may not be stable for certain horizons. Within this dynamic framework of anticipated opportunities and constraints, Kilgour proposes that new concepts of non-myopic stability will be clarified and developed. He also discusses how far ahead it is rational to look. This creative piece of work adds significantly to our growing retinue of conceptual devices for dealing with one of the very important aspects of "real-life, real-time" decision making: namely, what is waiting for me down the road in three months, if I take this particular juncture.

Chapter 4, by Frank Zagare, comes from the same game-theoretic tradition as that applied to political decision making. He also is probing its frontiers insofar as he utilizes a "theory-of-moves" to explore the dynamics of unilateral deterrence. Four prototypic situations are analyzed in which a satisfied status quo power is pitted against an unsatisfied revisionist power. Each situation is shown to lack a non-myopic equilibrium. By incorporating the notion of holding power, or the ability of one actor to remain at a Pareto-inferior outcome while absorbing its costs, an equilibrium is shown to exist, so long as the so-called threat remains credible. In contrast to Brams and Kilgour, Zagare finds that the absence of limitations on players moving from one outcome to another tends to foster the possibility that a single player can impose a stable unilateral deterrence. In general, Zagare's conclusions are at odds with those of Brams, especially insofar as they suggest that nuclear weapons add little to the stability of the deterrence. For Zagare, credible threat is neither necessary nor sufficient for a stable strategic balance.

In Chapter 5, Zeev Maoz adds a game-theoretic effort to study the evolution of international conflicts over time. Taking the cost-benefit model of Bueno de Mesquita as a point of departure, Maoz derives the notion of tangible and intangible costs and suggests that mixed strategies of conflict management may be superior to pure conflict strategies since they have the dynamic potential of transforming the expected outcomes and of creating incentives for negotiations that did not previously exist. He also suggests how these novel ideas may be empirically probed with measurement strategies and data analysis.

James D. Morrow's chapter seeks to help game-theoretic and utility approaches "move forward in time." His starting point is that "existing applications of utility theory to explain international conflict are almost entirely static in nature; an observation that seems paradoxical, given the inherent dynamic nature of empirically estimated utilities." In attempting to resolve and illuminate this paradox, Morrow points out the dynamic facets of the Bueno de Mesquita model and its derivatives. In terms of suggested developments, Morrow suggests that an adaptive, "enlightened Cournot rationality" should be useful in evaluating alliance behavior. The main idea of this is the evaluation of moves and strategy during policy implementation and evaluation. This of course entails the ability to forecast and learn from the anticipated behavior of potential collaborators and opponents in a conflict situation. Despite the importance of this line of reasoning and the optimistic directions pointed to by

Morrow, his essay ends on a slightly pessimistic note that
points out the considerable difficulties in obtaining
reliable quantitative information about the time-
dependent utility schedules of decision makers.

In sum Part 1 presents the leading edge of game-
theory and rational-choice research aimed at probing
deeply the dynamic consequences of decisions in the realm
of international conflict behavior. Although a variety of
differing conclusions are reached, overall the lines of
reasoning are promising for future developments.

The second section of the book focuses on an
explicit consideration of the escalation process as it
relates to arms races and international conflict
processes. In a provocative and thorough article, Michael
Intriligator and Dagobert L. Brito pose a dynamic model of
war fighting and arms races that can be used as a
decision-making heuristic in strategic planning and
defense procurement. They illustrate that there are a
variety of arms race traps that are unstable. A
fundamental distinction between stability of the arms race
and stability of deterrence is drawn and teased out
mathematically. In suggesting the instability of the arms
race as it may be coupled with the stability of
deterrence, Intriligator and Brito promote an intense and
careful consideration of the potential for accidental or
non-intentional war initiation.

In a similar vein, Jean-Christian Lambelet poses the
question of whether arms races can be "good things." He
reaches conclusions similar to those of Intriligator and
Brito, but ends with a set of policy recommendations
distinct from their "optimal package": namely, dumping of
the MX programs, withdrawal of the Pershings, a general,
time-limited freeze on nuclear production and deployment,
and renunciation of the so-called star wars scenario.

Thomas Mayer's chapter on transform methods and
dynamic models tackles two important problems. First, it
is a study of the arms accumulation process currently
underway in the US and Soviet Union. Second, it probes
the considerable promise and value of transform methods,
such as the Laplace transform and Fourier transformations.
These, he argues, provide an effective and relatively
simple approach to obtaining both continuous and discrete
analytical solutions for a wide range of dynamic models.
His sober note of caution about the narrow focus on model
prediction at the expense of model development and
analytic exploration buttresses the focus on explicit
dynamic models of international conflict and cooperation
that served as the main organizing theme of the Boulder
conference.

A slightly different tack is taken by Barry O'Neill.
His focus is not so much on the arms race, but on
escalatory processes generally. The dollar auction,

wherein undergraduates may be induced into escalating
their bidding to the extent that they will pay over three
dollars for a one dollar bill, is probed to determine if
there is a rational "winning" strategy. One is developed,
and it is illustrated that a rational approach to the
dollar auction would never entrap players. An examination
of the similarities and differences between the dollar
auction and escalation in world politics suggests why the
latter is often entrapping.

The third major dynamic theme that is presented in
this volume deals with simulation approaches to modeling
international conflict. Urs Luterbacher and Pierre Allan
describe a dynamic theory of conflict and coalition
formation in Chapter 11. Building on the rational choice
approach, they propose a modified version of Allan's
earlier work on bargaining power in 2 by 2 games. A
preliminary attempt at validation is undertaken and is
presented in the context of US, Chinese, and Soviet
interrelations as represented in the SIMPEST simulation
model.

Another important contribution from Switzerland
comes from T. Michael Clarke. Clarke's discussion of the
SIMSWISS model is itself a model of clarity and precision.
In the context of presenting actual results from the
validation of the model, he develops a variety of
hypotheses about the evolution of "small countries."

Claudio Cioffi-Revilla also presents a multitude of
simulation results, which are based on his exploration of
the analytical properties of his theory of political
reliability. For Cioffi-Revilla, reliability varies with
political structure, the two main variants of which are
serial structures (independence) and parallel structures
(redundancy). His results suggest that political
reliability is a highly volatile process sensitive to both
the number and the redundancy of political decision units.

Part 4 concentrates on dynamic models of war
fighting. Long a bastion of research in the area of
military science, mathematical models of actual war
fighting are also finding their way into the literature on
international relations. Unlike the seminal work of
Intriligator on war fighting in a nuclear environment, the
two pieces in this section concentrate on nonnuclear
engagements. The first, by Martin McGuire, takes aim at
extending the Lanchester model. McGuire's conclusions
suggest that two battlefield "design principles" should be
dispersion and decentralization in order to maximize
survival. To reach these conclusions he develops an
extension of production theory.

Albert Stahel's chapter describes the general
characteristics of one frequent and important form of
international conflict, guerrilla war. Stahel's analysis
of Afghani resistance to the Soviet invasion and

occupation is combined with an overview of other historical cases, including the war in South Sudan in 1956 and the partisan war in Yugoslavia during 1941-1944. His simulation model accurately predicts the evolution of guerrilla wars, particularly in Afghanistan. The dynamic, endogenous nature of his models, as well as their success, suggests a major improvement over Lanchester models for this particular form of international conflict.

The fifth division of the book explores dynamic approaches that eschew the use of mathematics and concentrate instead on the application of so-called artificial intelligence. Chapter 16, by Philip A. Schrodt, provides an especially lucid overview of the shortcomings of the rational-choice theory as applied to international relations, even when it is dynamic. Schrodt's dynamic model of precedent and pattern matching, as applied to international event-interaction data, is a major departure. The adaptive, precedent-based logic he develops emerges from one of the much heralded research frontiers in the cognitive and computer sciences. Dwain Mefford's chapter, also written from the "AI" tradition and departing from a mathematical basis, marks a departure from quantitative information bases, as well. Using the logic-processing language known as PROLOG, Mefford analyzes a political argument. His program tracks the changes in political imagination and reasoning that Thucydides documented in his history of the Peloponnesian War. Mefford offers a relatively rigorous, qualitative, and dynamic analysis of the political reasoning and argumentation associated with international conflict.

Part 6 is the "now for something completely different" section. Building on the image-processing techniques developed in satellite technology, Michael Ward and Lewis House illustrate their visual approach to the display and analysis of international conflict and cooperation. This paper is based on a color 16mm movie that was generated through a high-resolution computer graphics system. The kernel of the idea is that a visual presentation of quantitative, evolving data on international conflicts not only highlights the temporal characteristics of the conflict process, but also features the multilateral characteristics of world politics.

William Thompson's chapter analyzes the long sweep of history as it relates to cycles of general, hegemonic, and global war. The importance of cycles of war and peace point Thompson, and others in the world systems tradition, toward the analysis of social chronographs. Social processes, in this view, proceed according to their own clock, which is calibrated by major systemic power shifts at the global level.

Dieter Ruloff concludes this section with his own analysis of periodicities, using spectral analysis to forecast the diplomatic climate between the East and West. According to his analysis and data, there is strong evidence of cycles in US-Soviet conflict behaviors. For example, Ruloff suggests the existence of a ten-year cycle in US conflict with the Soviet Union.

The final chapter in the book has been contributed by Charles Tilly, who attended the Boulder conference in order to help us understand the conference results from a slightly different perspective from that which generated them. His chapter accomplishes this goal. Not only does he suggest the importance of dynamic conflict models as they could be applied to other areas, such as domestic conflict, but he also "returns the favor."

_____ **Part 1**

Game Theoretic and
Utility Approaches

2 The Path to Stable Deterrence

In a previous paper (Brams and Kilgour, 1985a), we showed that the Nash equilibria (Nash, 1951), or stable outcomes, of a two-person, nonconstant-sum "Deterrence Game" could be grouped into three categories: deterrence, preemption, and naive. The deterrence equilibrium (DE) provided a cooperative solution to the Deterrence Game (DG), whereas the preemption equilibria (PE), of which there were essentially two, led to one player's prevailing over the other.

We dismissed the naive equilibrium (NE) as unsatisfactory, not only because it was worse for both players than the deterrence equilibrium, and hence Pareto-inferior, but also because it entailed the possibility of the players' suffering their mutually worst outcome in the Deterrence Game. We shall not consider it further in the present analysis.

The deterrence equilibrium is sustained by the players' never preempting but retaliating, if preempted, with a probability above a certain threshold. by contrast, a preemption equilibrium involves one player's always preempting and the other player's never retaliating, always suffering from being preempted.

The first question we address in this paper is the following: if the players are at one of the two preemption equilibria, are there strategy changes that the preempted player can initiate to induce the preemptor to switch his own strategy so that the outcome of the game shifts to the deterrence equilibrium? If there are paths to this equilibrium, which is least costly to the preempted player, and what is the risk?

Steven J. Brams gratefully acknowledges the financial support of the Ford Foundation under Grant No. 845-034 and the National Science Foundation under Grant No. SES84-08505. D. Marc Kilgour gratefully acknowledges the financial support of the Natural Sciences and Engineering Research Council of Canada under Grant No. A8974.

Our main result is that, while there are multiple paths to stable deterrence, only one minimizes the preempted player's expected cost. However, that player must risk the possibility of inducing the worst outcome-- inferior, even, to being preempted--if the preemptor ignores the threat of retaliation which is the first step of this path. But this outcome is also the preemptor's worst, so it is not rational for the preemptor to ignore the threat. We shall interpret this result in the case of both conventional and nuclear conflict between states.

THE DETERRENCE GAME[1]

The Deterrence Game is based on the two-person game of Chicken, which we shall first describe and briefly analyze. In Chicken, each player can choose between two strategies: cooperate (C) and not cooperate ($\bar{C}$), which in the context of deterrence may be thought of as "not attack" and "attack," respectively. These strategies lead to four possible outcomes, which the players are assumed to rank from best (4) to worst (1). These rankings are shown as ordered pairs in the outcome matrix of Figure 2.1, with the first number indicating the rank assigned by the row player (called "Row"), and the second number indicating the rank assigned by the column player (called "Column"). Chicken is defined by the following outcome ranking of the strategy combinations of the two players:

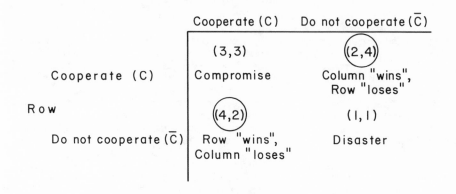

	Cooperate (C)	Do not cooperate ($\bar{C}$)
Cooperate (C)	(3,3) Compromise	(2,4) Column "wins", Row "loses"
Do not cooperate ($\bar{C}$)	(4,2) Row "wins", Column "loses"	(1,1) Disaster

Row

Key: (x,y) = (rank of Row, rank of Column)
4 = best; 3 = next best; 2 = next worst; 1 = worst
Circled outcomes are Nash equilibria

Figure 2.1   Outcome Matrix of Chicken

1.   Both players cooperate (CC)--next best outcome for both players: (3,3).

2.   One player cooperates and the other does not (CC̄ and C̄C)--best outcome for the player who does not cooperate and next-worst outcome for the player who does: (2,4) and (4,2).

3.   Both players do not cooperate (C̄C̄)--worst outcome for both players: (1,1).

Outcomes (2,4) and (4,2) in Figure 2.1 are circled to indicate that they are <u>Nash equilibria</u>: neither player (Row nor Column) would have an incentive unilaterally to depart from these outcomes because he would do worse if he did. For example, from (2,4) Row would do worse if he moved to (1,1), and Column would do worse if he moved to (3,3). By contrast, from (3,3) Row would do better if he moved to (4,2), and Column would do better if he moved to (2,4).

The shorthand verbal descriptions given for each outcome in Figure 2.1 suggest the vexing problem that players confront in choosing between C and C̄: by choosing C̄, each can "win" but risks disaster; by choosing C, each might benefit from compromise but could also "lose." Each of the Nash equilibria shown in Figure 2.1 favors one player over the other, and the stability of these equilibria as such says nothing about which of the two--if either--will be chosen.

Other concepts of equilibrium distinguish (3,3) as a stable outcome, but the rules of play that render compromise stable presume that the players (1) act nonmyopically or farsightedly, and (2) cannot threaten each other (Brams and Wittman, 1981; Kilgour, 1984, 1985; Zagare, 1984). If threats are possible in repeated play of Chicken under still different rules, the stability of (3,3) is undermined (Brams and Hessel, 1984).

The effect that threats may have in Chicken is not hard to grasp. If one player (say, Row) threatens the other player (Column) with the choice of C̄, and this threat is regarded as credible, Column's best response is C, leading to (4,2).

Clearly, the player with the credible threat--if there is one--can force the other player to back down in order to avoid (1,1). Although Row would "win" in this case by getting the best outcome, Column would not "lose" in the usual sense by getting the worst outcome, but rather the next worst.

This illustrates that Chicken is not a <u>constant-sum</u> game, in which what one player wins the other player loses. That is why we have set "win" and lose" in quotation marks. In nonconstant-sum games like Chicken, the sum of the players' payoffs at each outcome (if measured cardinally by utilities rather than ordinally by ranks) is not constant but variable. This means that both players may do better at some outcomes [e.g., (3,3)] than at others [e.g., (1,1)]. Outcomes, such as (1,1) in Chicken, which are inferior for both players to some other outcome(s) in the game, are called Pareto-inferior; those outcomes which are not Pareto-inferior are Pareto-superior, as are the other three outcomes in Chicken.

The Deterrence Game is based on Chicken but adds two refinements: (1) the players can make quantitative choices of levels of cooperation (or noncooperation), not just qualitative choices of C or C̄; (2) once these initial choices, which we shall interpret as levels of nonpreemption (or preemption) are made, each player's choice of a subsequent level of retaliation comes into play, provided the opponent's initial choice was regarded as preemptory and the player's own was not. More formally, the Deterrence Game is defined by the following rules:

1. The final outcome will be one of the four outcomes of Chicken. The payoffs are the same as those of Chicken, except that cardinal utilities replace ordinal rankings. Thus r4 and c4 signify the highest payoffs for Row and Column, respectively, r1 and c1 the lowest, etc.

2. The players do not choose initially between C and C̄, as in Chicken, but instead choose (unspecified) actions that are associated with a nonpreemption probability (s for Row and t for Column) and a complementary preemption probability (1-s for Row and 1-t for Column). With these probabilities, the actions will be interpreted as cooperative (C) and noncooperative (C̄) strategy choices, respectively.

3. If both players' initial choices are perceived as the same, the game ends at that position (i.e., CC or C̄C̄). If one player's choice is perceived as C and the other's as C̄, the former player chooses a subsequent action with an associated nonretaliation probability (p for Column and q for Row) and a complementary retaliation probability (1-p for Column and 1-q for Row). With the retaliation probability, the conflict is escalated to the final outcome C̄C̄; otherwise it remains (at CC̄ or C̄C).

4. The players choose their preemption probabilities and retaliation probabilities before play of the game. Play commences when each player simultaneously

chooses initial actions that may be interpreted as either C or $\bar{C}$, with associated preemption probabilities. One player may then choose subsequent actions, according to Rule 3, with the associated retaliation probability specified at the beginning of play.

The Deterrence Game is represented in Figure 2.2. Note that besides the fact that the initial strategy choices of the two players are probabilities (with assumed underlying actions), rather than actions (C and $\bar{C}$) themselves, this representation differs from the Figure 2.1 outcome matrix in having expected payoffs rather than (certain) payoffs in its off-diagonal entries. This is because we assume that if one player is perceived to preempt, the other player's (probabilistic) retaliation will be virtually instantaneous, so it is proper to include in the off-diagonal entries a combination of payoffs—reflecting both possible retaliation and possible nonretaliation—by means of an expected value.

We assume, of course, that $0 \leqslant s$, t, p, $q \leqslant 1$ because they represent probabilities. To simplify subsequent calculations, we normalize the payoffs of the players so that the best and worst payoffs are 1 and 0, respectively.

Column

	t	1-t
s	(r_3, c_3)	$q(r_2, c_4) + (1-q)(r_1, c_1)$ $= (qr_2, q)$
1-s	$p(r_4, c_2) + (1-p)(r_1, c_1)$ $= (p, pc_2)$	$(r_1, c_1) = (0, 0)$

Row

Key: (r_i, c_j) = (payoff to Row, payoff to Column)
r_4, c_4 = best; $r_3 c_3$ = next-best; r_2, c_2 = next-worst; r_1, c_1 = worst
s, t = probabilities of nonpreemption; p, q = probabilities of nonretaliation
Normalization: $0 = r_1 < r_2 < r_3 < r_4 = 1$; $0 = c_1 < c_2 < c_3 < c_4 = 1$

Figure 2.2   Representation of Deterrence Game

Hence,

$$0 = r_1 < r_2 < r_3 < r_4 = 1 \tag{1}$$

$$0 = c_1 < c_2 < c_3 < c_4 = 1 \tag{2}$$

Because we assume that the preemption and retaliation probabilities are chosen independently by the players, the expected payoffs for Row and Column are simply the sums of the four payoffs (expected payoffs) in the Figure 2.2 matrix, each multiplied by the probability of its occurrence:

$$E_R(s,q;t,p) = str_3 + (1-s)tp + s(1-t)qr_2 \tag{1}$$

$$E_C(t,p;s,q) = stc_3 = s(1-t)q + (1-s)tpc_2 \tag{2}$$

Besides the Pareto-inferior naive equilibrium in mixed strategies, which we dismissed earlier, there are effectively three Nash equilibria in the Deterrence Game. They can be grouped into two classes:

1. Deterrence Equilibrium (DE): $s = 1$, $q \leqslant c_3$; $t = 1$, $p \leqslant r_3$. This equilibrium is one in which the players never preempt ($s = t = 1$), but Row retaliates with probability $1-p > r_3$ and Column retaliates with probability $1-q > c_3$. Essentially, these inequalities ensure that a player's expected payoff as the sole preemptor—p for Row and q for Column, as shown in the off-diagonal entires in Figure 2.2—is not greater than what is obtained from the cooperative outcomes of the underlying Chicken game, with payoffs (r_3, c_3).

2. Preemption Equilibria (PE_C and PE_R: (1) $s = 1$, $q = 1$; $t = 0$, p arbitrary; (2) $s = 0$, q arbitrary; $t = 1$, $p = 1$. The first equilibrium is certain preemption by Column and no retaliation by Row; because Row is deterred by Column's initiative, Column's retaliation probability is arbitrary since it never comes into play. The second equilibrium is analogous, with the roles of Column and Row switched. At these equilibria, the outcomes of the Deterrence Game are the outcomes of the underlying Chicken game associated with wins for Column and Row, with payoffs $(r_2,1)$ and $(1,c_2)$, respectively.

Of the three Pareto-superior Nash equilibria, only the deterrence equilibrium (Class 1) depends on the possibility of retaliation--specifically, precommitted threats to respond (at least probabilistically) to a provocation when it is viewed as equivalent to the choice of $\bar{C}$. Such threats distinguish the Deterrence Game from the underlying game of Chicken, in which retaliation against the choice of $\bar{C}$ is not permitted.

Note that the two preemption equilibria in Class 2 occur only when retaliatory threats are never used ($p = 1$ or $q = 1$ or both). They correspond precisely to the two pure-strategy Nash equilibria in Chicken and so introduce no new elememt into the analysis of deterrence beyond what was earlier provided by Chicken. However, when a threat structure is added to Chicken that yields the Deterrence Game, a qualitatively different equilibrium (the deterrence equilibrium) emerges in the latter game. This equilibrium demonstrates how threats can work to the advantage of both players to stabilize the Pareto-superior cooperative outcome (r_3, c_3), which is unstable in Chicken

without the possibility of retaliation.

Because the deterrence equilibrium depends fundamentally on threats that would be costly for the threatener to implement, it is neither perfect nor subgame-perfect in the sense of Selten (1975).[3] Nevertheless, the deterrence equilibrium possesses a dynamic-stability property that should, once the equilibrium forms, contribute to its persistence in repeated play. That is to say, given that the players are at the deterrence equilibrium, if one player (say, Column) for any reason suspects that the other player (Row) may contemplate preemption, thereby rendering $s < 1$, Row can still do no better than continue to choose $t = 1$.

In other words, even should Row think he might be preempted, he should nonetheless continue to refuse to preempt in order to keep his expected payoff at its maximum. This obviates the problem that Schelling (1960, Ch. 7) called "the reciprocal fear of surprise attack" that leads inexorably to preemption.

Our proof (Brams and Kilgour, 1985a, Appendix) of this dynamic-stability property of the deterrence equilibrium shows, in effect, that any perceived departures by the players of s or t from 1 will not initiate an escalatory process whereby they are motivated to move closer and closer toward preemption for certain. The fact that the deterrence equilibrium is impervious to perturbations in s or t means that the players, instead of being induced to move up the escalation ladder, will have an incentive to move down should one player deviate from s $= t = 1$.

The restoration of the deterrence equilibrium depends on probabilistic threats of retaliation that satisfy

$$0 < q < c_3; \; 0 < p < r_3$$

But note that if deterrence for any reason should fail, it is irrational to retaliate, even on a probabilistic basis, because retaliation leads to a worse outcome for the retaliator, as well as for the player who preempted and thereby provoked retaliation.

The apparent irrationality of retaliating in the Deterrence Game is precisely what makes the deterrence equilibrium imperfect. Despite its imperfectness, it, like the preemption equilibria, has the essential equilibrium property of "mutually fulfilled expectations": if either player anticipates that the opponent will choose an equilibrium strategy--associated with one of the three equilibria--he can never do better than choose his corresponding equilibrium strategy (associated with this same equilibrium) to maximize his payoff.[4]

The problem of imperfection crops up again when we try to chart a path from one of the two preemption equilibria to the deterrence equilibrium. The player who is preempted must risk moving from his next-worst to his worst outcome in order to induce the preemptor to switch from preemption to nonpreemption, as we shall next show.

A RATIONAL PATH FROM PREEMPTION TO DETERRENCE

To shift the equilibrium outcome of the Deterrence Game from preemption by one player to deterrence by both, we ask how the cycle of expectation-fulfillment can be broken through unilateral action. We are particularly interested in what paths, or trajectories, from the preemption equilibrium to the deterrence equilibrium can be induced through the use of threats.

It is worth noting that players would never have the opposite incentive--to move from the deterrence equilibrium to a preemption equilibrium. For once at the deterrence equilibrium, it is not rational for either player ever to preempt (by departing from $s = 1$ or $t = 1$), because the preemptor's resulting expected payoff would be lower, assuming the nonretaliation probabilities are fixed. Moreover, even if one player departed from the strategy of nonpreemption, the other player still would not be induced to move because of this equilibrium's dynamic stability property. True, a player (say, Row, by choosing $q > c_3$) can make it rational for the opponent

(Column) to preempt him, but destabilizing the deterrence equilibrium to suffer a worse outcome hardly is rational.

On the other hand, it may be rational for Row, once at the preemption equilibrium where he suffers his next-worst outcome (r_2), to threaten retaliation [to $(0,0)$] unless Column pledges never to preempt ($t = 1$)--if this pledge can be made rational for Column. How to induce Column to backtrack from preemption, where he obtains a payoff of 1, to nonpreemption, where his payoff is less (c_3), is the main question we analyze in this section.

Before analyzing this question in the Deterrence Game, however, it is useful to consider the question in a more general context. Suppose a game is at some equilibrium A, and one player can credibly announce that he is changing his strategy so that it is no longer consistent with A but is instead consistent with another equilibrium, B. Assuming that his announcement is believed (in practice, this may require that the new strategy actually be chosen in one or more plays), one would expect that the other player will eventually adjust his strategy so as to achieve equilibrium B.

Naturally, a player would not be interested in making such an announcement unless he received a greater payoff at B than at A. The problem, however, is that the initiating player may incur a cost, albeit temporary, after he chooses his new strategy while his opponent continues with his old strategy. Presumably, the price to the initiating player of this change of equilibria will depend on both the magnitude of the temporary cost (in any single play) and the length of time it takes the responding player to switch to the new equilibrium.

We assume that the initiating player seeks to find a move away from equilibrium A that sets off a "chain reaction" of rational moves that eventually result in equilibrium B. Subsequent moves are rational if they serve, in turn, to maximize the mover's payoff. Although in general it will be (temporarily) costly for the initiating player to move from an equilibrium, there are games in which there are no temporary costs at all for the initiator.[5]

Consider now the possible trajectories in the Deterrence Game from the preemption equilibrium in which Column preempts Row (PE_C) to the deterrence equilibrium (DE). (The analysis for paths from PE_R, in which Row preempts Column, to DE is analogous because of the symmetry of the Deterrence Game, so it need not be considered separately.) A move from PE_C to DE would yield Row a net increase in payoff of $r_3 - r_2$ and Column a net decrease of $1 - c_3$, so it is obviously Row who would have the incentive to initiate this change in equilibria.

Suppose the initial strategy choices of the players are

$$(s = 1, 1 = 1; t = 0, p = p_0) \qquad (3)$$

where p_0 is arbitrary. This means that Row never preempts but column always does; since Row nevr retaliates after being preempted, these strategies define a PE_C.[6]

Next suppose that Row changes his nonretaliation probability to $q = q_0 < 1$. The game is now at

$$(s = 1, q = q_0; t = 0, p = p_0) \qquad (4)$$

with payoffs $q_0 r_2$ to Row and q_0 to Column. Thus, Row incurs a temporary cost of $r_0 - q_0 r_2 = (1 - q_0) r_2$ in making the change from (3) to (4).

Column's expected payoff by (2) is

$$E_C(t, p; 1, q_0) = t c_3 + (1-t) q_0 = q_0 + t(c_3 - q_0)$$

It is easy to see that Column maximizes E_C by choosing $t = 1$, provided that $q_0 < c_3$.

Assume $q_0 < c_3$. Then Column is motivated to choose $t = 1$, resulting in

$$(s = 1, q = q_0; t = 1, p = p_0) \qquad (5)$$

But this is a DE, given that Column takes the additional step of changing p_0, if necessary, so that $p_0 \le r_3$ in (5).

(This step offers no immediate benefit to Column, but it does deter possible future defections by Row.)

So far we have shown that Row can initiate a trajectory from the preemption equilibrium where he is preempted to the deterrence equilibrium by changing his nonretaliation probability from $q = 1$ to $q = q_0 < c_3$.

Because Row's temporary cost in making this change is $(1-q_0) r_2$, Row would have an incentive to choose a value of q_0 as large as possible (subject to $q_0 < c_3$). If $q_0 = c_3 - \varepsilon$, where ε is a small positive number, then Row's temporary cost is minimized at $(1-c_3) r_2 + \varepsilon r_2$.

We shall next demonstrate that the choice of $s = 1$, $q = c_3 - \varepsilon$ is the most cost-effective way for Row to trigger a trajectory from PE_C to DE. By (2),

$$\frac{\partial E_C}{\partial t} = sc_3 - sq + (1-s) \, p_0 c_2$$

It follows immediately that $\frac{\partial E_C}{\partial t} > 0$ if and only if either one of two conditions is met:

(a) $q < c_3$; or

(b) $p_0 > 0$, $q \geqslant c_3$, and $s < \dfrac{p_0 c_2}{p_0 c_2 + q - c_3}$

In other words, given that either condition (a) or (b) holds, it would be rational for Column to choose $t = 1$ because by so doing he would maximize his expected payoff E_C.

We shall now demonstrate that the temporary cost to Row of inducing Column to choose $t = 1$ is always greater than $(1-c_3)r_2$ by showing that the initial payoff to Row must be less than $c_3 r_2$. That is, we will prove that before Column is induced to switch from $t = 0$ to $t = 1$, Row's expected payoff [see (1)] ,

$$E_R(s,q;0,p) = sqr_2$$

will always be less than $c_3 r_2$.

First, since $q < c_3$ under condition (a),

$$sqr_2 \leqslant qr_2 < c_3 r_2$$

Under condition (b)

$$sq < \frac{qp_0 c_2}{p_0 c_2 + q - c_3}$$

The right side of this inequality has a maximum, for values of q satisfying $c_3 \leqslant q \leqslant 1$ (as assumed), at $q = c_3$.

Hence,

$$sq < \frac{p_0 c_2 c_3}{p_0 c_2 + c_3 - c_3} = c_3$$

and necessarily $sqr_2 < c_3r_2$. Thus, Row's expected payoff will drop by more than $r_2 - c_3r_2$ when he chooses any new strategy that induces Column to switch from $t = 0$ to $t = 1$.

This demonstrates that no possible trajectory from PE_C to DE has a smaller temporary cost than that which Row induces by choosing $s = 1$, $q = c_3 - \varepsilon$.[7] We conclude that the "cheapest" way for the preempted player (Row in our analysis) to set in motion a chain of events leading from PE_C to DE is simply to change his nonretaliation probability from $q = 1$ to $q = c_3 - \varepsilon$.

Essentially, then, Row upsets PE_C by threatening to retaliate with a probability just sufficient to make it more costly for Column to continue to preempt (not cooperate) than not to preempt (cooperate). Of course, Row risks the possibility of his worst outcome if Column does not accede to this threat, but Column also faces this risk, making it advantageous for him to accept his next-best payoff (c_3) rather than an expected payoff-- reflecting the threat--that mixes his best (1) and worst (0) payoffs and is less desirable than cooperation [because $1 + 0(1-p) = p < c_3$]. In short, the preempted player must take a chance to topple a preemption equilibrium and replace it with the deterrence equilibrium, but at least there is a rational response on the part of the opponent that he can trigger, and at a calculable minimum cost.

CONCLUSIONS

We previously argued (Brams and Kilgour, 1985a) that the deterrence equilibrium had substantial appeal because it stabilized the cooperative outcome in Chicken when quantitative levels of preemption and retaliation were introduced via the Deterrence Game. Yet, all was not sweetness and light because the one-sided preemption equilibria also had the same claim to stability and Pareto-superiority (unlike the naive equilibrium).

Now we have shown that there is a rational path from each preemption equilibrium to the deterrence equilibrium, though it is not without potential cost to the initiator. For the preemptor to ignore a credible threat of the preempted player, however, is irrational, though in reality, of course, it may occur.

Thus, for example, Iraq's threat to retaliate against shipping to Iran unless Iran negotiates an end to their costly and bitter conflict seems to have been ignored, though the threat has been made quite palpable through actual retaliation (with counter-retaliation by Iran). It might, perhaps, be better to model this conflict by a repeated game in which it is rational to carry out threats in any single play, leading to a Pareto-inferior "breakdown outcome," if one side thinks it possesses "threat power" over the long run (Brams and Hessel, 1984). In this model, there would be nothing irrational about both sides' suffering temporarily if there is uncertainty about which side has threat power and will eventually prevail.

In conflicts between nuclear powers, on the other hand, there will surely be less willingness to test the limits of each other's strengths, especially if, out of desperation, one side could introduce nuclear weapons that might be devastating to all. In such situations, escape from a preemption equilibrium through nuclear threats may be easier because the frightening consequences of refusal to cooperate will be stunningly evident.

It is heartening to find that though both deterrence and preemption lead to equilibrium outcomes in the Deterrence Game, the deterrence equilibrium is in a sense more stable because there is a rational path that can be taken to it, but not from it (assuming the players are fixed in their determination to retaliate). This result echoes what we found in the so-called Deescalation Game based on Prisoners' Dilemma (Brams and Kilgour, 1985b): there is a rational path from the "Escalation Equilibrium" to the "Deescalation Equilibrium" which, even more auspiciously, is costless to initiate (in part because the latter equilibrium is Pareto-superior to the former).

The ability to retaliate seems to be the key to the cooperative solutions of both the Deterrence Game and the Deescalation Game. Unlike Axelrod (1984), we do not assume that retaliation can occur only through repetition of play, with success measured by scores in a tournament comprising many different players. We also differ in allowing probabilistic threats immediately known to both players--not just inferred from repeated play--which may be considered to have certain equivalents at lower levels of retaliation. Particularly in nuclear conflict, we think the ambiguity of probabilistic threats may not only be sufficient to deter an opponent--with partial escalation or preemption possible--but an ambiguous threat may also be a good deal more credible than the certain threat of retaliation suggested by a policy of "tit-for-tat" (with the only options being cooperation or noncooperation).

In conclusion, we think a policy of deterrence--including nuclear--that is rooted in probabilistic choices can be justified on rational-choice grounds. To be sure, one may have to threaten to do the untoward, and take steps that may not be immediately rational so that the threat is taken seriously. But such a policy is justified, we think, if these threats help to achieve or preserve the deterrence equilibrium.

NOTES

1.   This section is based in part on Brams and Kilgour (1985a).

2.   There is a third Nash equilibrium in Chicken, but it is not in pure strategies, or specific strategies that players would choose with certainty. Rather, it is mixed strategies, which are defined as probability distribution over a player's pure strategies. The calculation of equilibria involving mixed strategies requires that payoffs be given in cardinal utilities--not just ordinal ranks--which we shall introduce when we define the Deterrence Game later in this section.

3.   See also Shubik (1982, pp. 265-270) for a recent discussion of perfect equilibria and related concepts.

4.   We underscore "corresponding" because equilibrium strategies in the Deterrence Game are not interchangeable (Luce and Raiffa, 1957, p. 106). Specifically, one player's choice of his deterrence equilibrium strategy combined with the other player's choice of his preemption equilibrium strategy does not constitute an equilibrium. The lack of interchangeability is important in the subsequent analysis.

5.   An example of such a game called the Deescalation Game and based on Prisoners' Dilemma, is given in Brams and Kilgour (1985b). We show that there is a unilateral move from the so-called escalation equilibrium that is not only costless to the initiator but also sets in motion subsequent rational moves that result in the Pareto-superior deescalation equilibrium. Whether deterrence is better modeled by the underlying games of Chicken or Prisoners' Dilemma is discussed in, among other places, Zagare (1985), Brams (1985, Ch. 1), and Brams and Hessel (1984).

6.   Technically, there are infinitely many such equilibria, one for each value of p_0, but this

nonretaliation probability of Column's is irrelevant to the outcome because he preempts. However, it is not irrelevant in the subsequent dynamic analysis, for p_0 must be below a particular threshold if the trajectory that Row triggers by his unilateral departure is to be held on course--through subsequent deterrence of Row by Column--as noted in the text below.

7.   To ensure that this trajectory terminates at DE rather than continuing to PE_R, Column would have to choose

a nonretaliation probability of $p < r_3$, thereby making it

unprofitable for Row to preempt him in turn at (r_3, c_3).

3 Anticipation and Stability in Two-Person Non-Cooperative Games

The most basic axiom of game theory is the postulate of individual rationality. As phrased by Luce and Raiffa (1957, p. 50), it is assumed that "of two alternatives which would give rise to outcomes, a player will choose the one which yields the preferred outcome." Unfortunately this postulate can seldom be applied directly in non-cooperative models, for it is rare that an individual player's choice determines the final outcome, and rarer still that a player who has such power can make full use of it. However a modification of the postulate of individual rationality can be applied directly in a broad class of non-cooperative models. It will be assumed here that a rational player will choose the alternative which yields the preferred <u>anticipated</u> outcome. Thus, an individual's rational choice is assumed to depend fundamentally on the various consequences that he anticipates his alternative actions yielding. This study, then, focuses on the way that what is anticipated determines what is chosen, and, in particular, on how anticipation determines when a status quo is stable in a conflict situation.

A status quo position is called stable for a player when that player has no incentive to deviate from it unilaterally. In non-cooperative game theory, the fundamental notion of stability is embodied in the Nash (1950) equilibrium, which is simply an outcome from which no player can achieve an immediate gain by departing unilaterally. This straightforward concept has had impressive success in describing stability; yet, despite its wide acceptance as both a descriptive and a normative principle, a number of alternatives have been proposed. These alternatives depend on the players' ability at least to contemplate responding to each other's choices. Thus, they do not apply to conflicts which end abruptly when the players' strategies have been selected--rather, they model those political, economic, and other conflicts in which the players have some freedom to change their initial strategies, and in which any outcomes through which the game passes prior to stabilizing contribute negligibly to the final payoffs. These alternative definitions therefore require that the traditional normal-form game of von Neumann and Morgenstern (1953, pp. 79-84) be reinterpreted, specifying a status quo position and allowing the players to change their "strategies." This reinterpretation will be formalized below.

Within the class of finite two-person non-cooperative games (or an appropriate subclass), the alternative stability concepts[1] that have been proposed include the stability definitions of von Stackelberg (1934) (see also Henderson and Quandt, 1971; Howard, 1971; Fraser and Hipel, 1979 and 1984; Brams and Wittman, 1981; Zagare, 1984; and Kilgour, 1984). Besides their orientation toward description of behavior in real-world applications, these alternative concepts share other features: they depend only on ordinal information about players' preferences, they avoid mixed strategies entirely, and they model the actions of players whose patterns of foresight are more sophisticated than those in the Nash model. All can be evaluated according to the various criteria for "robustness" suggested by Shubik (1981). But all differ in the assumed patterns of play foreseen by a player. It will be shown below that these patterns, which implicitly define models of play, can be represented conveniently by anticipations.

The definition of rationality used here is a definition of individual Roman rationality, for the rational player acts on a personal understanding of the situation. An outcome is stable for a player if, when that outcome is the status quo, he would prefer to stay there rather than to depart unilaterally. By assumption, a rational player bases this decision on his evaluation of the anticipated consequences of his available actions. In particular, the player might anticipate some response by the coplayer, possibly even a counterresponse. Which of the coplayer's available responses is anticipated may depend on the player's perception (which might or might not be accurate) of the coplayer's preferences and understanding of the conflict. Thus the property of stability exists entirely on the individual level. A position which both players find stable will be called an equilibrium--it is conventional to interpret the equilibria as the outcomes likely to result from the conflict.

The objectives of this paper are to present a conflict model within which the various stability definitions, and the concept of anticipation, can be understood, to represent each stability definition by an appropriate pattern of anticipation, and to generalize, compare, and interrelate the various definitions. This will be accomplished in the context of two-person conflicts.

THE CONFLICT MODEL, ANTICIPATION, AND STABILITY

A conflict model appropriate to the study of the stability definitions referred to above will now be formulated. It is simply the finite two-person non-cooperative game, with certain special conventions adopted for the present purpose. The rows and columns of the finite game matrix will be called "strategies" in conformity with conventional usage, but is should be noted that a "strategy" is better interpreted as a (policy) position than as a specific action, since a player can change his current strategy whenever he wishes. Both players' current strategy selections determine the current game position; only if a specific game position persists will it be taken to correspond to an outcome of the conflict. Finally, if both players are indifferent between two outcomes, the outcomes are considered identical.

Let the two players in the game model be denoted 1 and 2, and let U denote the set of all possible outcomes of the conflict.[3] For $k = 1$ or 2 and $u \in U$, let $v_k(u)$ measure the worth[4] of outcome u to Player k. The payoff functions $v_k(\cdot)$ are assumed to contain only ordinal information, so that player k prefers $u_1 \in U$ to $u_2 \in U$, or is indifferent between u_1 and u_2, iff $v_k(u_1) \geqslant v_k(u_2)$. If $v_k(u_1) = v_k(u_2)$ for $k = 1$ and 2, then $u_1 = u_2$, so that different outcomes have different payoffs for at least one player. We shall sometimes assume that U is strict ordinal, which means that $u_1 = u_2$ if $v_k(u_1) = v_k(u_2)$ for either $k = 1$ or $k = 2$; in other words different outcomes have different payoffs for both players.

The set U of possible final outcomes must now be related to the play of the game. Let Player 1's set of available strategies be $M = \{1, 2, \ldots, m\}$ and let Player 2's be[5] $N = \{1, 2, \ldots, n\}$. If Player 1's current strategy is $i \in M$ and 2's is $j \in N$, then the current **game position** is (i, j). If the position (i, j) persists indefinitely, the model specifies an outcome $u(i, j) \in U$ which is the result (or final outcome) of the conflict. Denote by U the $m \times n$ matrix with $u(i, j)$ as its (i, j) entry, and note that $U \in U_{m \times n}$, the set of all m x n matrices with entries from U. For convenience, let $v_k(u(i, j)) = v_k(i, j)$ for $k = 1$ and 2. This model can then be represented as the $m \times n$ bimatrix with $(v_1(i, j),$ $v_2(i, j))$ as its (i, j) entry. In this representation, it "looks like" a conventional two-person non-cooperative (bimatrix) game.

In order to assess the stability of a particular game position from the viewpoint of Player 1, the consequences Player 1 anticipates should he unilaterally move the game position from that status quo must also be included in the model. Suppose that, for $i \in M$ and $j \in N$, Player 1 believes that the eventual outcome which will arise should he move the game position to (i, j) is $x(i, j) \in U$. Note that $x(i, j)$ does not depend on the game position prior to 1's unilateral strategy shift. Denote by X the $m \times n$ matrix with $x(i, j)$ as its (i, j) entry, and note that $X \in U_{m \times n}$. The matrix X will be called 1's **anticipation matrix**. Again, X is unambiguously represented by the $m \times n$ bimatrix with $(v_1(x(i, j)),$ $v_2(x(i, j))$ as its (i, j) entry.

Figure 3.1 shows explicitly Player 1's decision problem in the simple situation when he can remain at the status quo $(1, 1)$ or shift unilaterally to either $(2, 1)$ or $(3, 1)$. The outcomes among which he chooses are $u(1, 1)$, $x(2, 1)$, and $x(3, 1)$. Figure 3.2 shows the general representation of both the underlying matrix and the anticipation matrix U which will be used below in describing examples. Note that the specification of an anticipation matrix amounts to the specification of the results of all possible future plays. When the underlying matrix is given and the Player with the initiative (opportunity to move first) has been designated, knowledge of the anticipation matrix permits the (rational) Player's action to be predicted at each possible status quo position, simply by solving an extensive game like the one in Figure 3.1.

Given a status quo game position (i, j), the actions of a rational Player 1 under the anticipation matrix X will now be examined explicitly. Player 1 must decide whether to stay at (i, j), leading to the outcome $u(i, j)$, or to depart unilaterally. The greatest payoff that Player 1 can achieve by departing unilaterally from (i, j) is

$$v_{ij}^1 = \max\{v_1(x(i', j)): i' \neq i\}.$$

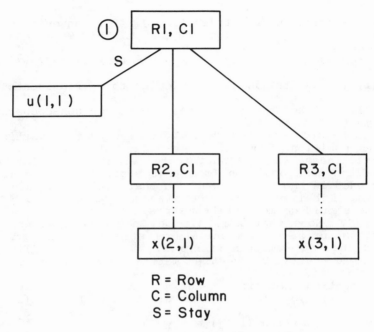

R = Row
C = Column
S = Stay

Figure 3.1   Player 1's Decision Problem

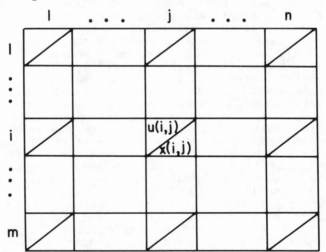

Key: u(i,j) = status quo outcome
      x(i,j) = 1's anticipated
              eventual outcome

Figure 3.2   Notation of Determination of Stability for Player 1

Since Player 1's payoff if he stays at (i, j) is $v_1(i, j)$, rationality implies that (i, j) is stable for 1 under

$$X \text{ iff } v_1(i, j) \geqslant v_{ij}^1 \tag{1}$$

Note that (1) includes the assumption of inertia: a Player will stay at a status quo unless he perceives a positive incentive to depart.

While relation (1) formally defines stability for Player 1, it will be useful below to describe precisely what action 1 takes when the status quo position (i, j) is not stable for 1. For example, Player 2 might wish to predict 1's departure moves, and 1 might wish to predict 2's predictions, etc. The principle of rationality implies that, if (i, j) is not stable for 1 under X, then 1 will unilaterally change his strategy to some $\bar{i} \neq i$ satisfying $v_1(x(\bar{i}, j)) = v_{ij}^-$. Assume for the moment

that U is strict ordinal and that the underlying matrix U is fixed. Then it is possible to define a transformation T_1 giving, for each possible status quo position, the outcome (or anticipated outcome) 1 would choose. Formally, define T_1: $U_{m \times n} \to U_{m \times n}$ such that, if 1's

anticipation matrix is X and $Y = T_1X$, then the (i, j)-entry of Y is

$$y(i, j) = \begin{cases} u(i, j) & \text{if } v_1(i, j) \geqslant v_{ij}^1 \\ x(\bar{i}, j) & \text{if } v_1(i, j) < v_{ij}^1 \end{cases} \tag{2}$$

Observe that, if (i, j) is not stable for 1 under X, the new row $(\bar{i})$ chosen by 1 may not be well-defined (because there might be two or more solutions to $v_1(x(\bar{i}, j)) = v_{ij}^1, \bar{i} \neq i)$, but that the anticipated outcome selected by 1 is always uniquely determined as a consequence of the assumption that U is strict ordinal. Thus $y(i, j)$ is always the outcome (or anticipated outcome) selected by 1 when the status quo position is (i, j). Below, relations (1) and (2) will be used to trace the play of action, reaction, and counterreaction from a status quo position.

It is still possible to define the transformation T_1 when U is not strict ordinal, providing some

additional postulate on 1's behavior is made. Briefly, a problem arises when 1 must choose among two or more positions, each of which maximizes his own anticipated payoff, but among which 2 is not indifferent. (Such a choice could not arise if U were strict ordinal, for if the anticipated outcomes were valued equally by 1, they would be identical and thus 2 would have no preference either.) An example of an appropriate postulate and the resulting definition of T_1 is now given. Assume that,

when 1 moves unilaterally, he does so to minimize the payoff he anticipates 2 will receive, subject to the constraint of maximizing his own. If this calculation were being performed by 2, then this assumption would amount to a defensive posture on 2's part, for 2 really has no way to predict 1's choice when 1 is genuinely indifferent. Formally, if $V(i, j) < v_{ij}^1$, let

$$I_{ij}^1 = \{i' \neq i: v_1(x(i', j)) = v_{ij}^1\}$$

so that $\bar{i} \in I_{ij}^1$ can be defined as any solution of

$$v_2(x(\bar{i}, j)) = \min \{v_2(x(i', j)): i' \in I_{ij}^1\}. \qquad (3)$$

Observe that $\bar{i}$ may not be uniquely determined by (3), but that any other value $\bar{i}' \in I_{ij}^1$ also satisfying (3) corresponds to the same anticipated eventual outcome, i.e., $x(\bar{i}, j) = x(\bar{i}', j)$. Thus (2) can again be employed to define $Y = T_1 X$ unambiguously. Again (1) and (2) imply that a status quo position (i, j) is stable for 1 under X if and only if $y(i, j) = u(i, j)$.

Below, analogous definitions for Player 2 of v_{ij}^2, I_{ij}^2, $\bar{j}$, and T_2 will be assumed. Also, Player 1's minimax and maximin values are given by

$$\text{Minmax}_1 = \min_j \ \max_i \ v_1(i, j)$$

$$\text{Maxmin}_1 = \max_i \ \min_j \ v_1(i, j)$$

respectively. It is well known that $\text{Maxmin}_1 \leq \text{Minmax}_1$. Player 2's minimax and maximin values are analogous.

REPRESENTATION OF SELECTED STABILITY DEFINITIONS

Now a variety of different concepts of stability will be represented as stability for player 1 under an

	1	2	3
1	3,5	8,2	4,4
2	9,1	7,7	2,3
3	6,8	5,9	1,6

Figure 3.3   Example Game

appropriate anticipation matrix. To illustrate, the game shown in Figure 3.3 will be fully analyzed in accordance with the anticipation matrix representation of each stability type.

Nash Stability

Following Nash (1950), the game position (i, j) is Nash-stable for 1 iff $v_1(i, j) \geq v_1(i', j)$ for all i' ε M. Let Player 1's anticipation matrix be $X = U$. Then $v_{ij}^1 = \max\{v_1(i', j): i' \neq i\}$ and it is clear that (i, j) is stable for 1 under X iff (i, j) is Nash-stable for 1. Thus, Nash stability corresponds to a player's anticipation that a unilateral departure would not be followed by any further moves.

In Figure 3.4, the game of Figure 3.3 is analyzed for Nash stability for Player 1. Note that $x(i, j) = u(i, j)$ for each i and j.

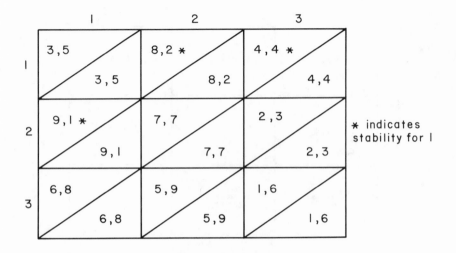

Figure 3.4   Representation of Nash-stability for Player 1

General Metarationality

Howard 1971 (see also Kilgour et al., 1984) defined general metarationality as follows: the game position (i, j) is general metarational for i iff for every i' ε M such that $v_1(i', j) > v_1(i, j)$, there exists j' ε N such that $v_1(i', j') \leqslant v_1(i, j)$. It turns out that general metarationality can be represented as stability under many different anticipation matrices. A relatively transparent representation is obtained by defining $\dot{j}(i)$ to be any value of j' minimizing $v_1(i, j')$, and then setting $x(i, j) = u(i, \dot{j}(i))$. To demonstrate that (i, j) is general metarational for 1 iff it is stable for 1 under the anticipation matrix X just defined, assume first the former. If, for some i' $\neq$ i, $v_1(i, j) \geqslant v_1(i', j)$ then $v_1(i, j) \geqslant v_1(x(i', j))$ since $v_1(x(i', j)) \leqslant v_1(i', j)$. If, for some i' $\neq$ i and j' $\neq$ j, $v_1(i', j) > v_1(i, j)$ and $v_1(i', j') \leqslant v_1(i, j)$, then again, since $v_1(i', j') \geqslant v_1(i', \dot{j}(i'))$, it follows that

$v_1(i, j) \geqslant v_1(x(i', j))$. Thus $v_1(i, j) \geqslant v_{ij}^1$, and (i, j) is stable for 1 under X. Conversely, if (i, j) is stable for 1 under X and $i' \neq i$ satisfies $v_1(i', j) >$ $v_1(i, j)$, then $v_1(i', \dot{\jmath}(i')) = v_1(x(i', j)) \leqslant v_1(i, j)$ so that (i, j) is general metartational for 1.

Observe that in the foregoing representation of general metarationality as stability under the anticipation matrix X, Player 1 anticipates that his unilateral move would induce 2 to shift the strategy so as to harm 1 as much as possible, and that this countermove would end the sequence. Since 1 anticipates that any unilateral shift of his strategy would trigger the "immediate worst" that his coplayer can deliver, it is hardly surprising that 1 becomes exceedingly cautious about moving. Indeed, Kilgour et al. (1984) found that any game position stable according to any of the other stability concepts they examined is also general metarational.

Figure 3.5 shows the determination of Player 1's general metarational game positions in the game of Figure 3.3, using the anticipation matrix X presented above.

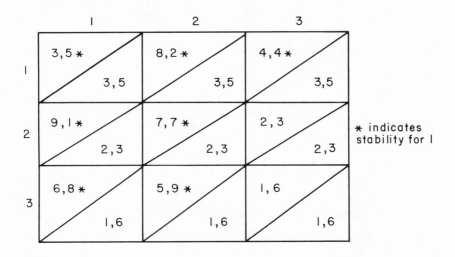

Figure 3.5   First Representation of General Metarationality for Player 1

An alternative, and perhaps not so graphic, representation of general metarationality is given by $x(i, j) = u(i_m, j_m)$, where (i_m, j_m) is any game position satisfying $u(i_m, j_m) = \text{Maxmin}_1$. That the anticipation matrix so defined also represents general metarationality is easily proven using the Characterization Theorem of Howard (1971, p. 103), which shows that a game position (i, j) is general metarational for 1 iff $v_1(i, j) \geq \text{Maxmin}_1$.

SYMMETRIC METARATIONALITY

Howard (1971) (see also Kilgour et al., 1984) identified an important special case of general metarationality--the game position (i, j) is symmetric metarational for 1 iff there exists $j* \; \varepsilon \; N$ such that $v_1(i', j*) \leq v_1(i, j)$ for every $i' \; \varepsilon \; M$. Again, Howard (1971, p. 105) characterized symmetric metarationality quite simply, finding that (i, j) is symmetric metarational for 1 iff $v_1(i, j) \geq \text{Minmax}_1$. It is therefore easy to verify that (i, j) is symmetric metarational for 1 iff it is stable for 1 under the anticipation matrix X with (i, j) entry $x(i, j) = u(i^m, j^m)$, where (i^m, j^m) is any game position satisfying $v_1(i^m, j^m) = \text{Minmax}_1$.

A more interesting representation of symmetric metarationality can also be given. Let $\tilde{j} \; \varepsilon \; N$ be any strategy of 2 satisfying

$$\min_{j} \max_{i} v_1(i, j) = \max_{i} v_1(i, j) = \text{Minmax}_1$$

and set $x(i, j) = u(i, \tilde{j})$ for each i and j. If it should happen that there is a unique $i_1 \varepsilon$ M, such that $v_1(i_1, \tilde{j})$ = minmax$_1$, choose any $i_2 \; \varepsilon \; M - i_1$ and redefine $x(i_2, j) = u(i_1, \tilde{j})$. The matrix X thus obtained satisfies $v_{ij}^1 = \text{Minmax}_1$ for every i and j, so that (1) shows immediately that a game position (i, j) is symmetric metarational for

1 iff it is stable for 1 under X. In this representation of symmetric metarationality, 1 anticipates that 2 will respond to 1's unilateral change of strategy with 2's "uniform response" $\tilde{j}$, from which 2 will never deviate. However, 1 may have the opportunity (if he has shifted to i_2) to make his best counter-response (i_1) to j.

Figure 3.6 shows the determination of Player 1's symmetric metarational game positions in the game of Figure 3.3, using the anticipation matrix X given above (with $\tilde{j} = 3$, $i_1 = 1$, and $i_2 = 2$). Using this example, it can be verified that the redefinition $x(i_2, j) = u(i_1, \tilde{j})$ is essential to the representation.

Sequential Stability

Fraser and Hipel (1979 and 1984) (see also Kilgour et al., 1984), defined a game position (i, j) to be sequentially stable for Player 1 iff for every i' ε M such that $v_1(i', j) > v_1(i, j)$, there exists j' ε N such

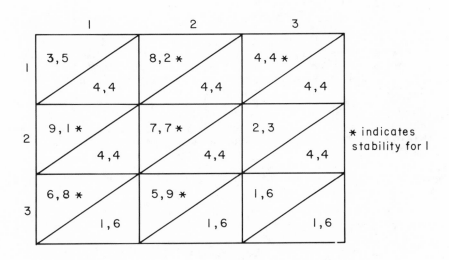

Figure 3.6   Second Representation for Symmetric Metarationality for Player 1

that $v_2(i', j') > v_2(i', j)$ and $v_1(i', j') \leqslant v_1(i, j)$.

This stability condition is similar to general metarationality, but admits only those "sanctions" (j') which are "credible" ($v_2(i', j') > v_2(i', j)$).

An anticipation matrix representing sequential stability is not difficult to construct. For i ε M and j ε N, set

$$Q = j \cap \{j' \in N: v_2(i, j') > v_2(i, j)\} \ .$$

If it should happen that $v_1(i, j) = \min \{v_1(i, j'): j' \in Q\}$ let $j_q = j$; otherwise let $j_q \in Q$ be any solution of

$$v_1(i, j_q) = \min \{v_1(i, j'): j' \in Q\} \ .$$

Finally, put $x(i, j) = u(i, j_q)$. The matrix X so defined indeed yields sequential stability, since $v_{ij}^1 = \max \{v_1(x(i', j)): i' \neq i\} \leqslant v_1(i, j)$ iff for every i' ε M satisfying $v_1(i', j) > v_1(i, j)$, there exists j_q ε N satisfying $v_2(i', j_q) > v_2(i', j)$ and $v_1(i', j_q) \leqslant v_1(i, j)$.

This anticipation matrix X is not difficult to interpret, for $x(i, j) = u(i, j)$ unless 2 has a strategy (j' ε Q - j) which both improves 2's position and harms 1's. If 2 has more than one such strategy, 1 anticipates choosing the one (j_q) most harmful to 1. This interpretation supports the view that sequential stability is a blend of caution and realism, because, while 1 guards against 2, he assumes that 2 will not hurt himself in the process.

Figure 3.7 illustrates how the game positions which are sequentially stable for 1 are determined in the game of Figure 3.3.

LIMITED-MOVE STABILITIES

The examples of the previous section show a rough progression in the extent of Player 1's foresight in anticipating future moves and the extent to which Player 1 takes into account player 2's preferences. The stability concepts presented next extend this trend. They make explicit use of the transformations T_1 and T_2

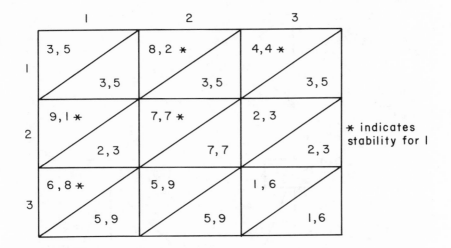

Figure 3.7   Representation of Fraser-Hipel Sequential Stability for Player 1

In the context of strict ordinal 2 x 2 games, Zagare (1984) suggested a form of stability in which a player's horizon of foresight is a parameter to be supplied by the modeler. A player's actions are determined under the assumption that subsequent moves, which alternate between the players, are always made in the best interest of the mover, who takes into account all the possible courses for future moves (up to the horizon). Stability of this type, for a player whose horizon is h moves distant (where h is a positive integer), is referred to here as L_h stability. Below, L_h stability will be defined by applying these ideas to models in the broad class described in section 2; this definition extends Zagare's since the two coincide for strict ordinal 2 x 2 games.

Figures 3.8 and 3.9 illustrate these ideas by showing the direct method of assessing the L_2 and L_3 stability of the (1, 1) position in the game of Figure 3.3. Comparison with Figure 3.1 shows that, for L_2 stability, $x(2, 1) = (2, 2)$ and $x(3, 1) = (3, 2)$, whereas for L_3 stability, $x(2, 1) = (1, 3)$ and $x(3, 1) = (3, 1)$.

40

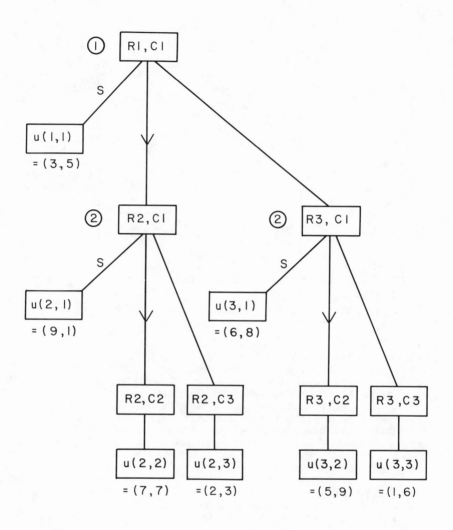

Figure 3.8   Player 1's Decision Problem with Two-step Horizon

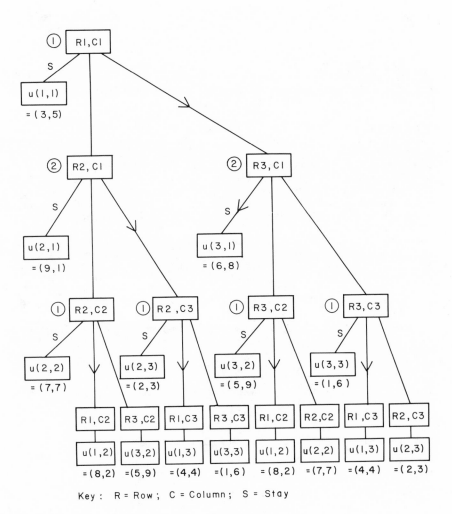

Key : R = Row ; C = Column ; S = Stay

Figure 3.9   Player 1's Decision Problem with Three-step Horizon

3.3. Comparison with Figure 3.1 shows that, for L_2 stability, $x(2, 1) = (2, 2)$ and $x(3, 1) = (3, 2)$, whereas for L_3 stability, $x(2, 1) = (1, 3)$ and $x(3, 1) = (3, 1)$.

L_h Stability

We proceed now to a more formal representation of L_h stability. It is clear that L_1 stability is Nash stability, for the focal player can see nothing beyond his own (potential) move. Under L_2 stability, however, the player anticipates that, should he move unilaterally, his coplayer will have the opportunity to do likewise. If either player chooses not to move, the sequence ends and the current game position is final. Thus, the generalization of Zagare's definition of L_2 stability for Player 1 must include 1's anticipation that 2 will have the opportunity to move after 1, and that no further moves by either player will be permitted; in other words, 1's anticipation matrix must be $X^2 = T_2 U$.

Similarly, 1's horizon is three moves distant in L_3 stability, so 1 anticipates that 2 will anticipate that 1 will have an additional opportunity to move after 2's move. Thus, for L_3 stability 1's anticipation matrix is $X^3 = T_2 T_1 U$. In general, game position (i, j) is L_h stable for 1 iff it is stable for 1 under the anticipation matrix $X^{h-1} = T_{21}^{h-1} U$, where, for non-negative integers g, the transformation $T_{21}^g : U_{m \times n} \to U_{m \times n}$ is defined by $T_{21}^0 U = U$, $T_{21}^1 U = T_2 U$, and $T_{21}^g U = T_2 T_1 T_{21}^{g-2} U$ for $g = 2, 3, 4, \ldots$. Thus, 1's anticipation matrix for L_h stability is $X^{h-1} = T_2 T_1 T_2 \ldots T_k U$, where $k = 1$ if h is odd and $k = 2$ if h is even. Define the transformation T_{12}^g analogously to T_{21}^g. Then (i, j) is L_h stable for 1 iff $u(i, j)$ is fixed under T_{12}^h; i.e., the (i, j) entry of $T_{12}^h U$ is precisely $u(i, j)$.[6]

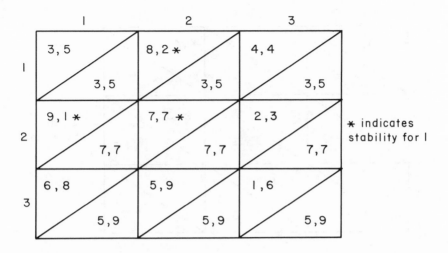

Figure 3.10   Limited-move, Horizon 2 Stability for Player 1

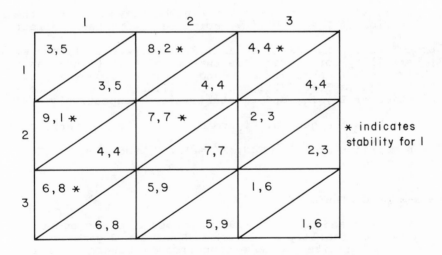

Figure 3.11   Limited-move, Horizon 3 Stability for Player 1

44

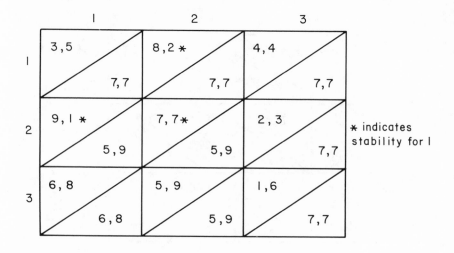

Figure 3.12   Limited-move, Horizon 4 Stability for Player 1

It is easy to verify inductively that the definition of L_h stability coincides with the direct procedure of Figures 3.8 and 3.9. One way to interpret L_h stability for Player i is that 1 believes that 2 has a horizon h - 1 moves distant, and simply goes one better.

Figures 3.10, 3.11, and 3.12 illustrate the determination of L_2, L_3, and L_4 stabilities, respectively, for Player 1 in the game of Figure 3.3. Player 1's anticipation matrices are $X^2 = T_2U$, $X^3 = T_2T_1U$, and $X^4 = T_2T_1T_2U$, respectively.

NON-MYOPIC STABILITY

Brams and Wittman (1981) proposed the concept of non-myopic stability in strict ordinal 2 x 2 games. This principle utilized a move-countermove sequence, as did limited-move stability, but with a horizon extending just far enough that one player would have the opportunity to stay at his most preferred outcome should the sequence continue all the way to the horizon. In general 2 x 2 games, Kilgour (1984) broadened this idea by endowing the players with sufficient foresight to envision the outcomes of arbitrarily long move-countermove sequences. If all sufficiently long sequences have the same outcome, then the result of a departure by a "foresightful" player is determined. The status quo is stable when the foresightful player chooses not to depart unilaterally from it.

The concepts of non-myopic stability are easy to generalize to the finite two-person model of the second section using the option of stability under an anticipation matrix. Consider the sequence of matrices $X^{h-1} = T_{21}^{h-1}U$ for h = 1, 2, 3, ... If it should happen that $X^r = X^{r+1} = X^{r+2} = ...$ for some $r \geqslant 1$, set $X^\infty = T_{21}^\infty U = X^r$. Define a game position (i, j) to be non-myopically (L_∞) stable for 1 iff it is stable for 1 under the anticipation matrix X^∞. Observe that no game position (i, j) can be L_∞ stable for 1 unless the sequence $T_{21}^0 U$, $T_{21}^1 U$, $T_{21}^2 U$, ... is eventually constant. If so, the game is called determinate (Kilgour, 1984). Note that $T_{12}U = T_1 T_{21}^{h-1}U$ for h = 1, 2, 3, ..., so that a game is determinate with respect to player 2's anticipations iff it is determinate with respect to player 1's. Finally, note that (i, j) is L_∞ stable for 1 iff u(i, j) is fixed under $T_{12}^\infty = T_1 T_{21}^\infty$; i.e., the (i, j) entry of $T_{12}^\infty U$ is precisely u(i, j).

For the game of Figure 3.13, the sequence $X^{h-1} = T_{21}^{h-1}U$, because h = 1, 2, 3, ... is eventually constant. The minimum value of r for which $X^r = X^{r+1} = ... = X^\infty$ is r = 9. The determination of the game positions which are L_∞ stable for Player 1 is shown in Figure 3.13, using the anticipation matrix $X = X^\infty$.

EQUILIBRIA

All of the stability concepts considered above are individual stability concepts in that they model a specific player's decision to stay at or depart unilaterally from a status quo game position. A game position is an equilibrium iff both players find it stable. (Kilgour et al.[1984] refer to an equilibrium as a "group stable" outcome.) While most of the definitions of equilibrium appearing in the literature are symmetric

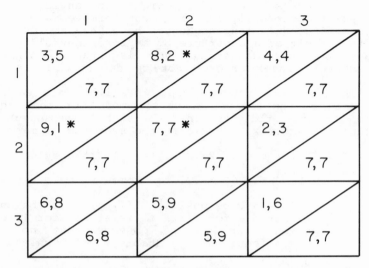

* indicates stability for I

Figure 3.13   Non-Myopic Stability for Player 1

in the sense that they postulate the same individual stability type for both players, this need not be the case.[7] It may well be appropriate to use an asymmetric equilibrium model if the capacities or psychologies of the players are different, or if they are under different constraints. One asymmetric equilibrium definition is given now.

In the context of strict ordinal two-person games, von Stackelberg (1934) (see also Henderson and Quandt, 1971) proposed what amounted to a definition of equilibrium with an unusual feature. In this definition, both players understand that, whatever the status quo, one specific player (the "leader") has the first opportunity to depart unilaterally; then, whether the leader has moved or not, the other player (the "follower") has the opportunity to move. It follows that a game position is stable in the sense of von Stackelberg iff it is L_2 stable for the leader and Nash (or L_1) stable for the follower.[8]

The definition of L_2 stability given above thus permits von Stackelberg's equilibrium concept to be applied to any finite two-person game.

Figures 3.14, 3.15, and 3.16 show the determination of Stackelberg equilibria in the game of Figure 3.3.

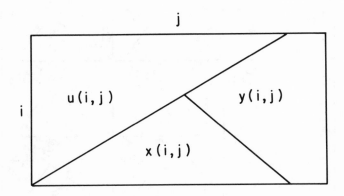

Figure 3.14　　Notation for the Determination of Equilibria

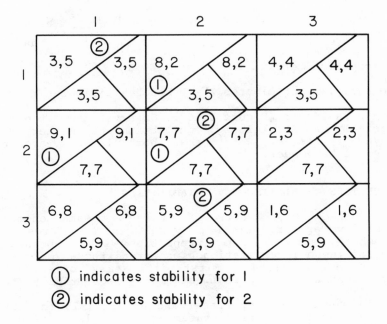

Figure 3.15　　Stackelberg Equilibrium for Player 1 Leader, Player 2 Follower

48

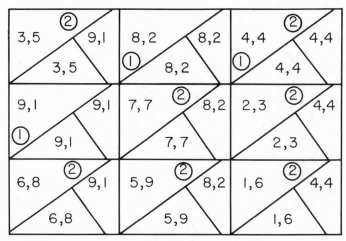

③ indicates stability for I

② indicates stability for 2

Figure 3.16   Stackelberg Equilibrium for Player 2 Leader, Player 1 Follower

When Player 1 is leader (Figure 3.15), note that 1's

anticipation matrix is $X = T_2U$ and 2's is $Y = U$.

Similarly, 1 anticipates $X = U$ and 2 anticipates $Y = T_1U$

when 2 is leader (Figure 3.16). Observe that there is
precisely one Stackelberg equilibrium no matter which
player is leader, but that both players prefer that
Player 1 be leader.

PROPERTIES OF LIMITED-MOVE STABILITIES

Since the concepts of limited-move and non-myopic
stability appear here in more general forms than
elsewhere, some of their properties will be presented.
Some of these interrelationships extend those reported by
Kilgour et al. (1984). First, it is easy to verify that
a game position which is L_2 stable is sequentially-stable

in the sense meant by Fraser and Hipel (1979 and 1984).
The converse of this statement is false; also the
statement fails for L_h stability whenever $h > 2$.
Nonetheless, a Stackelberg equilibrium (as defined above)
is a sequential equilibrium.

Other relations of limited-move and non-myopic stabilities to other stability types are consequences of the following properties of the transformations T_1 and T_2:

Theorem 1: For any $h \geq 1$, if $Y = T_{12}^h U$, then $v_1(y(i, j))$ Maxmin$_i$ for every $i \in M$ and $j \in N$.

Proof: Let $i_m \in M$ be any strategy for satisfying

$$\min_j v_1(i_m, j) = \max_i \min_j v_1(i, j) = \text{Maxmin}_1.$$

If $h = 1$, note that $v_1(y(i, j)) \geq v_1(u(i_m, j)) \geq$ Maxmin$_1$ for every i and j. If $h \geq 2$, let $S = T_{12}^{h-2} U$ and $W = T_2 S$ so that $Y = T_1 W$. Observe first that, for every j, $v_1(s(i_m, j)) \geq v_1(u(i_m, j)) \geq$ Maxmin$_1$. If for some j, $w(i_m, j) = u(i_m, j)$, then $v_1(w(i_m, j)) \geq$ Maxmin$_1$. If $w(i_m, j) \neq u(i_m, j)$, then $w(i_m, j) = s(i_m, j')$ for some $j' \neq j$ so that, again, $v_1(w(i_m, j)) \geq$ Maxmin$_1$. Finally, $v_1(y(i_m, j)) \geq v_1(u(i_m, j)) \geq$ Maxmin$_1$ for every j, and, if $i \neq i_m$, then $v_1(y(i, j)) \geq v_1(w(i_m, j)) \geq$ Maxmin$_1$, completing the proof.

Theorem 2: If $h \geq 1$ is odd and $Y = T_{12}^h U$, then $v_1(y(i, j)) \geq$ Minmax$_1$ for every $i \in M$ and $j \in N$.

Proof: Since Minmax$_1 = \min_j \max_i v_1(u(i, j))$, there exists for each j an $i = i^*(j)$ satisfying $v_1(u(i^*(j), j)) \geq$ Minmax$_1$. If $h = 1$, note that $v_1(y(i, j)) \geq v_1(u(i^*(j), j)) \geq$ Minmax$_1$ for every i and j.

Assume that the theorem holds for $h - 2$ and define $S = T_{12}^{h-2} U$ and $W = T_2 S$ so that $Y = T_1 W$. For any j, if $i = i^*(j)$, then $v_1(y(i^*(j), j)) \geq v_1(u(i^*(j), j)$, so the proof is complete. Otherwise $v_1(y(i, j)) \geq v_1(w(i^*(j),$

j)); again the proof is complete if $w(i^*(j), j) = u(i^*(j), j)$. If $w(i^*(j), j) = s(i^*(j), j')$ for some $j' \neq j$, then $v_1(y(i, j)) = v_1(s(i^*(j), j')) \geqslant \text{Minmax}_1$ by induction. Theorems 1 and 2 apply to limited-move stability because a game position (i, j) is L_h stable for 1 iff the (i, j) entry of $T_{12}^h U$ is $u(i, j)$; in other words, iff T_{12}^h fixes $u(i, j)$. Similarly, $(1, j)$ is L_∞ stable for 1 only if T_{12}^h fixes $u(i, j)$ for all sufficiently large h. It follows from Theorem 1 that any game position which is L_h stable for 1 pays 1 at least Maxmin_1; if h is odd, Theorem 2 implies that any game position which is L_h stable for 1 pays 1 at least Minmax_1, as does any game position which is L_∞ stable for 1. From other facts noted above, it follows that any game position which is L_h stable for 1 is general metarational for 1, and any game position which is L_h stable for 1 when h is odd, or which is L_∞ stable for 1, is symmetric metarational for 1. In particular, a Stackelberg equilibrium is always general metarational for the leader and symmetric metarational for the follower.

CONCLUSIONS

The objective of this work has been to bring to bear the principle of rational choice on the problem of describing and assessing the stability of outcomes in a non-cooperative conflict. This goal was accomplished through the notion of anticipation applied to an appropriate conflict model. The anticipation matrix was demonstrated to be a convenient device for classifying and comparing stability concepts, and provided useful and workable generalizations when they were needed. It is likely that new stability concepts will be developed within this framework, and that the relationships among new and existing stability definitions will be clarified.

NOTES

1. Many of these alternatives, as well as Nash stability, are compared and evaluated by Kilgour et al.

(1984), who also give references to a great variety of applications of these concepts.

2. The stability definitions and relationships given below are applicable to conflict models which are much more general than those described in the text. For example, certain features of hypergame models (Bennett, 1980; Takahashi et al., 1983) incorporating misperception and deception can be included. Other notes below will indicate how the conflict model developed here can be broadened far beyond the usual non-cooperative game. Nonetheless, conventional terminology will be used whenever possible.

3. To construct a more general conflict model with a view to assessing stability of game positions for Player 1, U can be taken to be the set of all possible outcomes of the conflict as perceived by 1. Members of U need not all correspond to specific game positions, but may include such additional possibilities as a player escalating or prematurely terminating the conflict.

4. With reference to Note 3, $v_2(u)$ can be taken to be Player 1's perception of the worth of outcome u to Player 2.

5. With reference to Note 3, N can be taken to be the set of strategies available to Player 2, as perceived by Player 1.

6. Determination of $T_{12}^h U$ is equivalent to the solution of mn extensive games of length h. The games of Figures 3.8 and 3.9 have lengths 2 and 3 respectively. These games have a special form which enables them to be "collapsed" into positional games not unlike those described by Shubik (1982, pp. 48-51). Because it exploits this special form, solution by alternate iteration of T_1 and T_2 is more efficient than the direct method.

7. In fact, as indicated in Notes 3, 4, and 5, stability for a player depends on his personal perception of the conflict in which he is engaged. Not only might the players' behaviors be described by different stability types, but their perceptions of each other's strategies and preferences might not agree.

8. This generalization to non-strict ordinal games differs from that of Kilgour et al. (1984), who follow Basar and Olsder (1982). Their definition cannot be "decomposed" into individual stabilities.

9. This phenomenon occurs in any strict ordinal game. It is reported by Kilgour et al. (1984), whose results on Stackelberg equilibria in strict ordinal games apply here, despite the differences described in Note 8.

4 The Pathologies of Unilateral Deterrence

In a recent paper I argued (Zagare, 1984c) that the theory of mutual deterrence could be restated in a more satisfying, logically consistent, and parsimonious manner when the rules of play implicitly assumed by deterrence theorists--i.e., sequential and conditional strategy choices--are formalized and integrated into a dynamic game-theoretic framework recently developed by Brams (1983) and others. In that paper, not only were the conditions sufficient for the successful operation of mutual deterrence in its prototypical form identified (as summarized below) but the ramifications of some reasonable and empirically meaningful deviations from the ideal type were explored. The purpose of this chapter is to extend the previous analysis to the case of unilateral deterrence. Curiously, this extension is not as straight-forward as might be expected. In the case of unilateral deterrence, an instability problem not present in a relationship of mutual deterrence arises unexpectedly. As a result, the ability of a satisfied status quo nation to deter an unsatisfied revisionist power in these games is rendered problematic.

To demonstrate this problem, and to offer an understanding of the conditions under which it might be circumvented, I will first describe the prototypical relationship of mutual deterrence and the "theory of moves" framework that is useful in analyzing it. A brief discussion of the Falkland/Malvinas crisis of 1982 then highlights the problem unique to deterrence in the unilateral case. In the third section, three sets of conditions that alter somewhat the conclusions of section two are presented. And finally, in the last section, this analysis is summarized and its implications for the theory of deterrence explored.

STABLE MUTUAL DETERRENCE AND THE THEORY OF MOVES

To illustrate the structural characteristics of a relationship of mutual deterrence, consider for now the abstract representation of a deterrence game depicted in

Figure 4.1. In this representation, each of two players is assumed to have two strategies, one that supports the status quo, and one that upsets it. As argued more extensively in Zagare (1984c), the fact that each player in such a relationship is attempting to deter the other from moving away from the status quo implies the following rank ordering of three of the four outcomes in the deterrence game of Figure 4.1:

$$\begin{aligned} &\text{a.}\quad \text{For A, } u(a_2,b_1) > u(a_1,b_1) > u(a_1,b_2) \text{ and} \\ &\text{b.}\quad \text{For B, } u(a_1,b_2) > u(a_1,b_1) > u(a_2,b_1). \end{aligned} \qquad (1)$$

In words, this ranking implies that, certis paribus, each player would prefer to upset the status quo unilaterally, and would prefer that the other player not upset it.

		PLAYER B:	
		b_1	b_2
PLAYER A:	a_1	Status Quo (a_1, b_1)	Victory For B (a_1, b_2)
	a_2	Victory For A (a_2, b_1)	Mutual Loss (a_2, b_2)

Figure 4.1 Abstract Representation of a 2 x 2 Deterrence Game

To complete this ordering, and hence, to fully determine the nature of the deterrence game, it is necessary to specify the preference relationship of these three outcomes to (a_2,b_2). (a_2,b_2) represents the outcome that would be induced if one player upset the status quo in order to gain a unilateral advantage, and the other player resisted and attempted to punish the first and deny him these benefits. Put differently, (a_2,b_2) represents the threat upon which the deterrence relationship rests.

Patently, each player's evaluation of the threatened outcome is a function of the capability of the other; and each player's perception of the other's evaluation of this outcome depends upon the credibility of the other player's threat. Thus, if capability is defined as the ability to hurt, A will prefer (a_2,b_1) to (a_2,b_2) if and only if B is capable, and B will prefer (a_1,b_2) to (a_2,b_2) if and only if A is capable. And if credibility is defined as a player's willingness (or preference) to carry out a deterrent threat if the other player takes the proscribed action, A's threat will be credible if and only if B perceives that A prefers (a_2,b_2) to (a_1,b_2); similarly, B will have a credible threat if A perceives that B prefers (a_2,b_2) to (a_2,b_1). Of course, the nature of the mutual deterrence relationship, and ultimately whether it succeeds or fails, depends upon the capability and credibility of both players. (As will be seen, this is not necessarily the case in unilateral deterrence.) Still, deterrence theorists almost uniformly assert that mutual deterrence is most likely to be stable when the threat of both players is both credible and capable. Significantly, there is strong support for this proposition in the mathematical theory of games.

To see this, consider for now the mutual deterrence game depicted in Figure 4.2. In this representation, the (ordinal) payoffs of the two players are ranked from 1 to 4, with 4 representing each player's best outcome, 3 each player's next-best outcome, and so on. As is easily seen, the rank ordering of the four outcomes for each player in this game satisfies the restrictions implied by equation (1) and the requirements implicit in the notion of a credible and capable threat (see above). The alert reader will recognize that this ordering defines this particular game as a Prisoners' Dilemma. Thus, the Prisoners' Dilemma game represents the relationship of mutual deterrence in its prototypical form.

PLAYER B:

b₁ b₂

	b₁	b₂
a₁	Status Quo (3 , 3)	Victory For B (1 , 4)
a₂	Victory For A (4 , 2)	Mutual Loss (2 , 2)

PLAYER A:

Figure 4.2 The Mutual Deterrence Game (Prisoner's Dilemma)

To demonstrate that mutual deterrence is both and (farsightedly) rational when both players have credible and capable threat, a "theory of moves" analysis will be used. As developed by Brams (1983, p. 184) and others, "the theory of moves describes optimal strategic calculations in normal-form games in which the players can move and countermove from an initial outcome in sequential play."

At the heart of the theory-of-moves framework is the concept of a **nonmyopic equilibrium** (Brams and Wittman, 1981), a concept that significantly mirrors the decisional setting assumed by deterrence theorists. Unlike the concept of a Nash (1951) equilibrium--the standard game-theoretic measure of stability--the concept of a nonmyopic equilibrium assumes that each player can make conditional and sequential moves from an initial outcome in a game, and is able to evaluate the long-term consequences of such a departure. More specifically, the concept of a nonmyopic equilibrium assumes that the following rules of play operate in a 2 x 2 ordinal game:

1. Both players simultaneously choose strategies, thereby defining an **initial outcome** of the game or, alternately, in the interpretation given in this essay, an initial outcome (or status quo) is imposed on the players by empirical circumstances.

2. Once at an initial outcome, either player can
    unilaterally switch strategies and change the
    outcome to a subsequent outcome.

3. The other player can respond by unilaterally
    switching strategies, thereby changing the
    subsequent outcome to a new subsequent outcome.

4. These strictly alternating moves continue
    until the player with the next move chooses not
    to switch strategies. When this happens, the
    game terminates, and the outcome reached is the
    final outcome (Brams and Hessel, 1982).

Given these rules, and the ability of the players
to calculate the consequences of a departure from an
initial outcome, two conditions must be met for an
initial outcome to be considered a nonmyopic equilibrium:
first, neither player must perceive an advantage in
departing from it, and second, there must be **termination**
of the move-countermove sequence, that is, the sequence of
moves and countermoves must not cycle back to the initial
outcome. Brams and Wittman (1981) assume that
termination will occur if an outcome is reached in the
sequential move process whereby the player with the next
move can ensure his best outcome by staying at it.[1]

It is easy to show that the status quo outcome in
the mutual deterrence (Prisoners' Dilemma) game of Figure
4.2 satisfies both of these requirements. (For a more
formal demonstration, see Zagare, 1984a.) This is
significant because it suggests that in its prototypical
form, when both players have credible and capable
threats--save for one proviso mentioned below--mutual
deterrence constitutes a stable relationship.

To see this, consider for now the chain of events
that would be touched off if one player, say A, departed
from the status quo outcome (3,3) in the game of Figure
4.2. A's initial incentive to depart unilaterally in a
mutual deterrence relationship is assumed to exist (see
equation 1). This is reflected in A's preference for
(a_2,b_1) over the status quo, (a_1b_1). But what would occur

if A acted unilaterally to induce the assumed advantages?
Given B's ability to respond to A's move, and B's
preference for (a_2,b_2) over (a_2,b_1), i.e., a credible

threat, B would rationally move from (a_2,b_1) to (a_2,b_2),

the next-worst outcome for both players, rather than
accept the worst outcome at (a_2,b_1). Once at (a_2,b_2),

however, neither player would rationally choose to move

again since such a move would induce termination of the game at the outcome that is worst for the player who moves and best for the player who does not move from (a_2,b_2).

Given a departure by A from the next-best outcome (3,3), then, implies A's next-worst outcome (2,2) as the final outcome in a sequence of moves and countermoves. Clearly, A has no incentive to move from (3,3) if it anticipates that B will respond rationally. And, by symmetry, neither does B. Consequently, the status quo (3,3) in a mutual deterrence game in which both players have a credible and capable threat is both stable and farsightedly rational, provided, of course, that A's move from the status quo does not circumvent B's capability by depriving B of the ability to carry out the deterrent threat, as would be the case if A possessed a first-strike capability.[2]

THE PATHOLOGIES OF UNILATERAL DETERRENCE

In the previous section it was demonstrated that mutual deterrence is stable (and rational) when both players have a capable and credible threat. One of the purposes of this essay is to demonstrate that the above statement is not necessarily true when the deterrence relationship is unilateral rather than mutual.

Rather than demonstrate this pathology with an abstract example, however, it would perhaps be more instructive to highlight the problems implicit in a relationship of unilateral deterrence with a discussion of an actual, real-world game. To this end, consider for now the representation of the strategic situation, as the Galtieri regime probably perceived it, immediately preceding the Falkland/Malvinas crisis of 1982. The strategies, outcomes, and player preferences of the putative games the Argentine leadership thought it was playing with the British are summarized in Figure 4.3. In this representation, the British are assumed to have two major options, either to fortify and defend the Falkland Islands or not to fortify them and leave the Islands exposed to possible military action by Argentina. For their part, the Argentines are assumed to have the choice of accepting the preinvasion status quo (i.e., continuing British sovereignty), taking de facto control if a leasing arrangement or some other face-saving device could be negotiated, or using force to upset the long-standing British control of the Malvinas.

Two of the assumptions implicit in this representation of the Falkland/Malvinas crisis deserve comment. First, since the Galtieri regime clearly did not want to fight for the Malvinas, and since it did not expect the British to "go to war for such a small problem as these few rocky islands" (Haig, 1984), the outcome

58

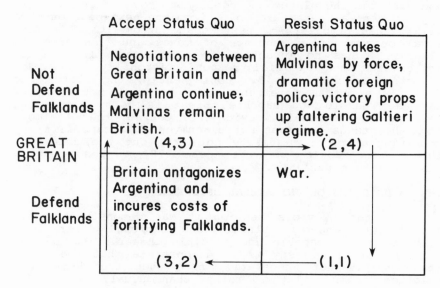

ARGENTINA

	Accept Status Quo	Resist Status Quo
Not Defend Falklands	Negotiations between Great Britain and Argentina continue; Malvinas remain British. (4,3)	Argentina takes Malvinas by force; dramatic foreign policy victory props up faltering Galtieri regime. (2,4)
Defend Falklands	Britain antagonizes Argentina and incures costs of fortifying Falklands. (3,2)	War. (1,1)

GREAT BRITAIN

Figure 4.3   Falklands/Malvinas Crisis of 1982

associated with the execution of the deterrent threat
(i.e., war) is assumed to be worst for both states. In
terms of the previously postulated definitions, this
means that neither state is assumed to have a credible
threat.   (Later, this assumption will be shown to be
inconsequential to the analysis of this game.)   Second,
note that in this representation Britain is assumed to
most prefer the existent status quo, rendering this a
game of unilateral, rather than mutual, deterrence.
     The major pathology of unilateral deterrence is
manifest in the Falkland/Malvinas game of Figure 4.3:   the
status quo (4,3) is not stable in the longer-term sense of
Brams and Wittman, or even the short-term sense of Nash.
The fundamental instability of the status quo outcome,
therefore, renders problematic unilateral deterrence in
this and--as will be seen--similar games.
     The reason why the status quo is not a nonmyopic
equilibrium in this game is that there is no termination
of the sequence of moves and countermoves, as there was
in the mutual deterrence game of Figure 4.2.   Put in a
slightly different way, the move and countermove process
is cyclic;   that is, at least one player has an
incentive to move from every outcome in this game, as
indicated by the arrows in Figure 4.3.   Moreover, the lack
of any nonmyopic equilibrium in this game also renders

problematic any explanations and predictions about it. In other words, this game, as presently formulated, is essentially **indeterminate**. It should be pointed out that (2,4) is a Nash equilibrium in the Falkland/Malvinas game of Figure 4.3. However, the ability of Nash's equilibrium concept to explain either the dynamics or the eventual outcome of this game is clearly inadequate.

Significantly, this conclusion would not be affected in any way if the credibility assumptions reflected in Figure 4.3--where neither player's threat is assumed to be credible--are altered. The status quo outcomes in both of the games listed in Figure 4.4, 64(48) and 15(21), in which the revisionist player is assumed to have a credible threat, are also not nonmyopic or Nash equilibria, and the same is true of the two games, 76(72) and 65(55), listed in Figure 4.5, wherein the revisionist player is assumed not to have a credible threat.[4] (Ignore, for now, the arrows in these four figures.) Moreover, no outcome in all four of these games is a nonmyopic equilibrium.[5]

THREE SETS OF STABILITY CRITERIA

In the previous section, an essential indeterminacy was shown to characterize four typical unilateral deterrence games. Without additional assumptions, therefore, not only is it difficult to say whether deterrence will succeed (i.e., is stable) in these games, but it is also difficult to specify what outcome will eventually evolve if it fails.[6] Moreover, it is especially important to note that this indeterminacy can be directly attributed to the fact that one player in each game prefers the status quo to all other outcomes. To wit, were the preference ranking of the status quo players' two best outcomes simply reversed, making each game a game of mutual deterrence, one outcome in each game would be singled out as a nonmyopic equilibrium. Interestingly, in two of the four transformed games, 64(48) and 65(55), deterrence is stable, since it is the status quo outcome that is a nonmyopic equilibrium. By contrast, in the two remaining games, in which only one player has a credible threat, 15(21) and 76(72), deterrence is not stable. In each of these games, the unique nonmyopic equilibrium is associated with the best outcome of the player with, and the next-worst outcome of the player without, a credible threat.

At this point, there are two obvious questions. First, what additional assumptions are necessary to render the four games of unilateral deterrence determinate? And second, given that such conditions can be identified, will deterrence succeed or fail? In what follows, three different sets of stability criteria, drawn from the

Two Unilateral Deterrence Games. The threat of the Revisionist (column) player is assumed to be credible.

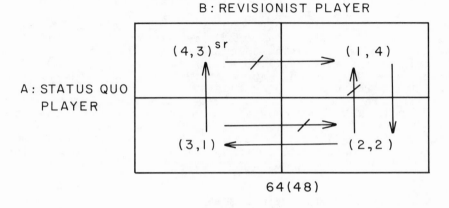

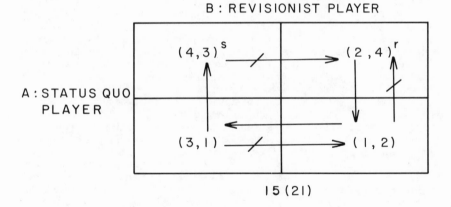

Key:
    s = holding power outcome when the status quo player has holding power.
    r = holding power outcome when the revisionist player has holding power.

Figure 4.4   Two Unilateral Deterrence Games

Two Unilateral Deterrence Games. The threat of the Revisionist (column) player is assumed not to be credible.

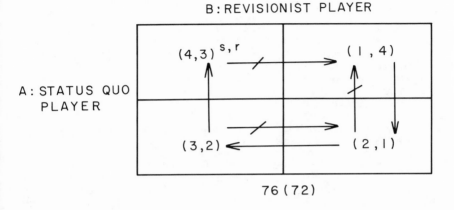

76 (72)

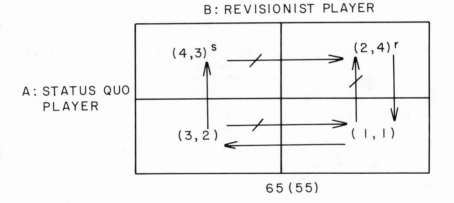

65 (55)

Key:
s = holding power outcome when the status quo player has holding power.
r = holding power outcome when the revisionist player has holding power.

Figure 4.5   Two Unilateral Deterrence Games

theory of moves, will be discussed and their implications for the success of deterrence in the unilateral case explored.

The Absorbing Criteria and Attitudes Toward Risk

One set of conditions sufficient to induce a determinate outcome in each of the four archetypical games of unilateral deterrence is associated with the notion of an **absorbing outcome** because of Brams and Hessel (1982). The concept of an absorbing outcome rests upon the supposition that, in 2 x 2 games without nonmyopic equilibria, where at least one player has an incentive to move away from every outcome, the incentive to move away from some outcomes will be stronger than the incentive to move away from others. As will be seen, the nature of these incentives has some important implications for the stability of deterrence in the unilateral case.

To demonstrate this, assume (1) that players will always move away from their worst and next-worst outcomes, and (2) that when there is a conflict between these two principles a player will not move from that outcome that leads to a better outcome than the other. Given these two assumptions, at least one outcome in 33 of the 41 2 x 2 games without a nonmyopic equilibrium is considered to be an absorbing outcome. As its name suggests, such an outcome, even if it is not an initial outcome, will, like a black hole, attract movement toward itself. Consequently, if an absorbing outcome is either the initial outcome or is reached in a sequence of moves and countermoves, it will exhibit a degree of stability absent in outcomes that are not absorbing. For this reason, Brams and Hessel (1982, p. 394) characterize absorbing outcomes as "'conditionally' or 'almost nonmyopically' stable."

The two assumptions at the beginning of the preceding paragraph are not sufficient to induce an absorbing outcome in any of the four unilateral deterrence games discussed herein. Moreover, as the arrows in Figures 4.4 and 4.5 indicate (ignore for now the slashes indicating the deletion of some of the arrows), a cycle would still exist among the four outcomes in each game even if it were assumed (3) that a player would move from his next-best outcome (i.e., 3). In other words, given assumptions (1) through (3), the process of moves and countermoves remains intransitive in these four games.

In order for an absorbing outcome to be induced in the four unilateral deterrence games, assumption (3) must be relaxed and replaced with the assumption (4) that a player will consider moving from his next-best outcome unless, by not moving, he can break the cycle and thereby assure himself an outcome that exceeds his security level, that is, an outcome at least as good as his next-best. For each of the four games, then, assumption (4) is both necessary and sufficient to render one outcome--significantly, the status quo outcome--an absorbing outcome. Moreover, underscoring the essential relationship among these four games is the fact that, given assumption (4), they uniquely comprise one of the four distinct categories of 2 x 2 games with an absorbing outcome.

In order to demonstrate the above, consider for now the arrows in game 64(48) in Figure 4.4. The six arrows in this and the remaining games of Figures 4.4 and 4.5 are implied by assumptions (1) through (3): that players will move from their worst, next-worst, and next-best outcomes. As the arrows reveal, these assumptions lead to a cycle among the four outcomes.

Now, assume that the revisionist player would be satisfied with its next-best outcome rather than risk cycling in order to obtain its best outcome. In this case, the arrow from (4,3) to (1,4) can be deleted. Deleted arrows are indicated by a slash through them. The deletion of this arrow, however, logically implies the deletion of both the arrow from (3,1) to (2,2) and the deletion of the arrow from (2,2) to (1,4).

Briefly, the rationale for the deletion of these two additional arrows is as follows. Suppose the process of moves and countermoves reaches (3,1). At (3,1), as the arrows indicate, both players have an incentive to move. But the fact that (4,3) is acceptable to the revisionist player means that the revisionist player would prefer not to move to (2,2) in order to induce (1,4), but instead would prefer that the status quo player be the one to move--from (3,1) to (4,3)--and thereby induce the next-best outcome of the revisionist player. Hence, given the deletion of the arrow at (4,3), the deletion of the arrow from (3,1) to (2,2) is implied.

Similar logic leads to the deletion of the arrow from (2,2) to (1,4). Given the deletion of the arrow from (4,3), the status quo player would prefer a move by the revisionist player to (3,1) that would, in turn, lead rationally to its best outcome at (4,3) rather than a move from (2,2) that would lead to its worst outcome at (1,4).

Notice that with the deletion of these two additional arrows, the remaining arrows all lead to, or **converge upon,** (4,3). Thus, if one assumes that the revisionist player has an aversion to cycling, then the outcome implied by a sequence of moves and countermoves is the original status quo. Put in another way, the assumption that the revisionist player prefers not to cycle is sufficient to induce the stability of the status quo outcome in this and the other three unilateral deterrence games.

How reasonable is this assumption? It is difficult to say, especially given the ordinal framework assumed in this analysis. Under some circumstances, cycling may indeed be rational, in an expected value sense, depending on each player's cardinal valuation of the outcomes and its estimation of the probability that each outcome will occur. On the other hand, depending on these same factors, cycling might produce a lower payoff than that associated with the certain selection of the status quo outcome.

Patently, in such a situation, cycling will have a higher expected payoff, _ceteris_ _paribus_, the more intense the preferences of the revisionist player for the best outcome. Conversely, the expected value of cycling will be diminished for a player who places a relatively low valuation on its worst or next-worst outcome. This suggests that the attitude of the revisionist player toward risk can be considered a key determinant of the stability of deterrence in the unilateral case. Risk-averse actors with deflated valuations of their best outcome will most likely find the status quo acceptable. By contrast, unilateral deterrence is more problematic when the revisionist player, with more intense preference, is risk-acceptant. Unfortunately, the failure of deterrence that produced the brief war between Britain and Argentina is probably testimony to this fact.

Power Asymmetries

Implicit in the discussion of the previous section, in which deterrence was shown to be stable when the revisionist player is risk-averse, was the assumption of power parity; neither player was posited to have any advantages outside those implied by the preferences that defined the structure of the game. Clearly, the assumption of parity limits the empirical applicability of these conclusions, for it is frequently the case that deterrence relationships, unilateral or mutual, occur under asymmetric power conditions. What is less clear, however, are the implications of such an asymmetric distribution on the stability of unilateral deterrence. In this section, this question will be addressed.

Although several distinct notions of power have been developed within the theory-of-moves framework (for a discussion and synthesis, see Brams, 1983), the notion of **holding power** is most relevant to a discussion of deterrence in one-shot games. Underlying this concept is the idea that one player, the player with holding power

(H), has the capability of remaining at an outcome in a sequential game longer than the player without holding power (NH). Thus, depending upon the preferences of the two players, H might be able to force NH to backtrack and terminate a game at an outcome advantageous to H. In other words, the range of choices open to a player with holding power is assumed to be expanded. While NH, as before, can choose either to stay at or move from each outcome when it is his turn to move, H is assumed to be able to stay, move, or hold.

As reflected in the game tree of Figure 4.6 in which the revisionist player B is assumed to have holding power, and in which (4,3) is assumed to be the initial outcome in game 65(55), a player with holding power is also assumed to be able to make the first move, or to pass and allow the player without holding power to make the first move, from an initial outcome in a sequential game. This, unlike the notion of **staying power** developed by Brams and Hessel (1983), in which the more powerful player is assumed to move second, the concept of holding power does not unnecessarily restrict the domain of choices available to a player who possesses it.

There are two additional assumptions about the players associated with the definition of holding power. First, consistent with the theory-of-moves framework adopted herein, is the assumption of **nonmyopic calculation**: players are assumed to make their decision to move or not move from an initial outcome in full anticipation of how each will respond to the other. Second is the **inertia principle**: a player will not move from any outcome unless a better outcome is anticipated as the final outcome. Among other things, this implies that a player without holding power will not move from an outcome if he anticipates that H will hold and force him to rationally return to it.

The inertia principle has important implications not only for the rational choices each player makes when it is his turn to move, but also for the length of the tree itself. For instance, the right side of the tree of Figure 4.6, commencing with B's (i.e., H's) move from (4,3), is extended by four moves, or the number of moves necessary to cycle back to the initial outcome. If the sequence of moves and countermoves leads back to (4,3), given nonmyopic choices by the players, B will be assumed to pass at the initial outcome.

Similarly, given that B passes, the left side of the tree is also extended by four moves from A's (i.e., NH's) choice at (4,3). In this case, though, since it would be up to B to move and complete the cycle or to hold and force A to make the next move, A is assumed to be able to respond, should B choose to hold.

It is important to point out that implicit in the inertia principle is an aversion to cycling on the part of the players. Perforce, this assumption induces a unique holding power outcome from every initial outcome and thus does not necessarily address the indeterminacy problem associated with games, like those in Figures 4.4 and 4.5, without nonmyopic equilibria.[7] Nevertheless, the assumptions associated with the concept of holding power do seem reasonable enough to explore their implications for the stability of the status quo outcome in games of unilateral deterrence.

To this end, the holding power outcome in the game in Figure 4.6, i.e., 65(55), given that (4,3) is the initial outcome and that B is the player with holding power, will be identified by using a backwards induction process similar to the algorithm associated with the determination of nonmyopic equilibria. The holding power outcome in this game can be determined by simply working backwards up the game tree and asking what the rational strategy choice of each player is at each node or decision point. For reasons that will become apparent shortly, the right side of the tree that commences with B's decision to move from (4,3) will be analyzed first.

At the lowest level of this game tree, given that B either holds or moves at the previous level, A's choice will terminate the game. Should B hold at the previous level, A will induce the worst outcome (1,1) by staying and the next-worst outcome (2,4) by moving. Hence, if A is rational, he would not stay at (1,1)--indicated by a slash through this branch--but would move to (2,4). Similarly, if B had decided to move from (1,1) at the previous level, A's choices would be to stay at (3,2), the next-best outcome, or to move to (4,3), the best outcome. Again, if A is rational, he will move to (4,3) and complete the cycle.

Given the rational choices of A at each of these nodes, what should B do at the previous level? As the player with holding power, B is assumed to be able to stay, move, or hold. By staying at (1,1), B's worst outcome is induced as the final outcome of the game. If B moves to (3,2), the process of moves and countermoves would return to the original status quo--B's next best outcome--since, as just illustrated, A's rational choice at (3,2) would also be to move and complete the cycle. Finally, if B holds at (1,1), his best outcome is induced since A's rational choice at the subsequent node would be to move to (2,4). Clearly, B should hold at (1,1).

But would the process ever rationally get to this point? At the previous node, A's choice would be between staying at (2,4)--his next-worst outcome--and moving to (1,1). But, as just demonstrated, a move to (1,1) also implies (2,4) as the final outcome of the game. By the

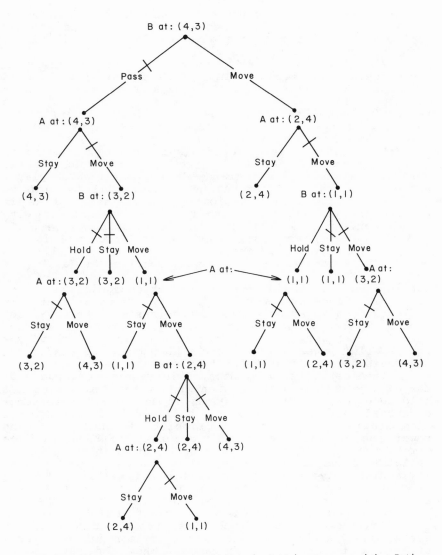

Game tree of game 65(55), given that (4,3) is the initial outcome and that B (the Revisionist player) has Holding Power.

Figure 4.6   Game Tree of Game 65(55)

inertia principle, therefore, A would rationally stay at
(2,4). Consequently, B's best outcome (2,4) is implied
as the final outcome of the game should B move initially
from the previous node (4,3).

A similar analysis of the left side of the tree
would reveal that (4,3) is implied as the final outcome if
B passes initially. A will always stay at the best
outcome. Thus, since B prefers (2,4) to (4,3), his
rational choice, given that he has holding power, is to
move and induce his best outcome as the final (holding
power) outcome of this game.

By contrast, (4,3) is the holding power outcome in
game 65(55) if A is assumed to be H. This means that in
this game successful deterrence depends upon which player
has holding power. A status quo player will be able to
successfully deter a revisionist player as long as it
retains the ability to absorb the costs associated with
mutual punishment longer than the revisionist player. On
the other hand, as just illustrated, deterrence is not
stable when the revisionist player is H. Still, even
under these conditions, prolonged conflict at (a_2, b_2) is

not implied. If the status quo player recognizes the fact
that the balance of power favors the revisionist state, it
would rationally accept, rather than resist, the new order
implied by the imbalance of (holding) power. Of course,
since it may not always be patently obvious which player
has superior power, war may occur when both the status quo
and revisionist player think they possess it.

Interestingly, as indicated in Figures 4.4 and 4.5,
the status quo is stable, when the status quo player has
holding power, in all four games of unilateral deterrence
discussed herein. Moreover, unilateral deterrence is
also stable, even if the revisionist player has holding
power, as long as the status quo player has a credible
threat, that is, prefers to resist rather than accept a
unilateral departure from the status quo by the
revisonist player--see games 64(48) and 76(22). Thus, a
credible threat is a sufficient though not necessary
condition for stable deterrence in a unilateral
deterrence game characterized by asymmetries of power.

Conversely, the absence of a credible threat by the
status quo player is a necessary condition for unilateral
deterrence to fail in such games. When the revisionist
player has holding power, and the status quo player's
threat is not credible--as in games 15(21) and
65(55)--the revisionist player has an incentive,
unilaterally, to move from the status quo, since his
holding power enables him to induce his best outcome as
the final (holding power) outcome.

Move Limitations

A third set of conditions that can affect the stability of a deterrence relationship is rooted in the notion of a **limited-move equilibrium** recently developed by Zagare (1984b). Underlying this concept is the idea that particular features of some real-world conflicts might restrict the ability of players in a sequential game to make all of the logically possible moves and countermoves. For instance, given the current political situation within Great Britain, it is probably not possible for the British government to restore the <u>status quo</u> <u>ante</u> by withdrawing the garrison on the Falkland Islands, even should it become convinced that the present Argentine leadership has no intention of reoccupying them.[8] Thus, in some games, it may not be possible to return to an outcome once it has been left. In other games, depending upon circumstances, it may not be possible to get through one outcome, or to even get to another. In these and similar situations where the sequential move process is fettered, the concept of a limited-move equilibrium is an appropriate measure of outcome stability.

The essentially idiosyncratic nature of such constraints, of course, makes it virtually impossible to survey all of the logical possibilities. Nevertheless, in deterrence games at least, five empirically plausible sets of move limitations suggest themselves for systematic analysis.

<u>Both Players Possess First-Strike Capability</u>. When both players possess a first-strike capability, each player is, in effect, limited to a single, unilateral deviation from the status quo, and the stability requirements reduce to those associated with the concept of a Nash equilibrium. The Nash criteria, therefore, define one extreme on the continuum of move limitations, wherein each player can make the minimum number of moves in a game, that is, one each. By contrast, the criteria that define a nonmyopic equilibrium represent the other extreme: each player can make the maximum number of moves and countermoves--two each--before cycling back to an initial outcome.

As already noted, the status quo outcome in each of the four unilateral deterrence games is neither a Nash nor a nonmyopic equilibrium. There is, therefore, no stability at either extreme. At least one player (i.e., the revisionist player) will always have an incentive, unilaterally, to depart from the status quo. But when both players have a first-strike capability, even the status quo player will have such an incentive. By preempting the move of the revisionist player, and moving from its best outcome (a_1, b_1) to its next-best outcome

(a_2,b_1), the status quo player is able to avoid suffering
either its worst or next-worst outcome, which would be
induced should the revisionist player strike first.
Clearly,   deterrence   is   extremely   unstable--and
unlikely--under these conditions.

The Revisionist Player has a First- and Second-
Strike Capability. The   revisionist player's first-strike
capability--which precludes a second-strike capability for
the status quo player--means that it can preempt the
status quo player and end the game at (a_1,b_2). Its

second-strike capability--which precludes a first-strike
capability for the status quo player--means that it can
respond to a unilateral departure from (a_1,b_1) by the

by the status   quo   player   and induce--if it
prefers-- (a_2,b_2).

Unilateral deterrence is no less unstable when the
revisionist player has both a first- and second-strike
capability than when both players have a first-strike
capability. The revisionist player will always have an
incentive to preempt, although the motivation of the
status quo player to preempt is somewhat different. The
status quo player, as before, will have an incentive to
move from its best outcome, in order to avoid its worst
and next-worst outcomes, in the two games, 65(55) and
76(72), in which the revisionist player's threat to
retaliate is not credible, and also in the one game,
64(48), in which it prefers mutual punishment to the
victory of the revisionist player. But in game 15(21),
when the status quo player prefers the victory of the
revisionist player to mutual punishment, and when the
revisionist player's threat is credible, the status quo
player would prefer not to upset the status quo first.
In effect, under these conditions, the status quo player
would surrender.

The Status Quo Player has a First- and Second-Strike
Capability. The complete instability manifest in the
previous two cases is altered when it is the status quo
player, and not the revisionist player, that has first-
and   second-strike   capabilities.   The   most   obvious
historical analogue is the US-USSR strategic relationship
in the early 1960s. Under these conditions, a credible
threat by the status quo player is both necessary and
sufficient for successful deterrence--see games 64(48) and
76(72). In the absence of this condition--as in games
15(21) and 65(55)--the revisionist player will have an
incentive to move from (a_1,b_1) in order to induce its best

outcome at (a_1, b_2); similarly, the status quo player will also have an incentive to preempt in order to avoid its next-worst outcome should the revisionist player move from the status quo first.

Mutual Assured Destruction. Under this set of constraints, both players are assumed to be able to move to but not through (a_2, b_2), as might be the case in a conflict between two nuclear powers who anticipate that any confrontation will escalate into a nuclear war and termination of the game. Such a situation differs from the previous case only by assuming that the revisionist player also has a second-strike capability. Interestingly, however, save for one small exception, the strategic situation is almost identical in both cases. A credible threat on the part of the status quo player remains a necessary and sufficient condition for stable deterrence, since the revisionist player retains an incentive to move from the status quo in the absence of these conditions. But the status quo player's incentive to preempt (i.e., game 15[21]) is removed when the revisionist player's threat to retaliate is credible. In this one game, the victory of the revisionist player is implied by the rules that limit the ability of the players to move or countermove. All in all, however, a second-strike capability for a revisionist player has a negligible effect on the dynamics of unilateral deterrence.

War Fighting. Under this set of constraints, both players are assumed to have a war fighting capability, that is, the ability to get through (a_2, b_2), the outcome associated with mutual punishment, but are not assumed to be able to return to (a_1, b_1), the original status quo.[10]

Hence, movement from the status quo implies, depending upon the preferences of the players, a victory for one player or the other after a brief confrontation, or prolonged conflict at (a_2, b_2).

Notice that when these conditions are satisfied, either player is limited to an initial move from the status quo and a single response to the countermove of the other. Thus, the choice of whether the sequential process moves to (a_2, b_2) rests with the player who does not choose, initially, to upset the status quo; and the choice of whether the process moves through (a_2,b_2) is up to the player who moves first from the status quo. Significantly, the ability of both players to get through (a_2,b_2), coupled with an inability to return to (a_1,b_1), renders deterrence stable in three of the four games of unilateral deterrence examined herein. A credible threat by the status quo player is no longer a necessary condition for stable unilateral deterrence, though it remains a sufficient condition. The lack of a credible threat by the revisionist player is also a sufficient condition for stability in these games. Unilateral deterrence is unstable only in game 15(21), wherein the revisionist player, but not the status quo player, has a credible threat. In this game, the victory of the revisionist player at (a_1,b_2) is implied by the rules that preclude movement back to the status quo, regardless of which player upsets it first.

SUMMARY AND CONCLUSION

A theory-of-moves framework is used in this essay to explore the dynamics of unilateral deterrence, wherein a satisfied status quo state is pitted against an unsatisfied revisionist power. Four games typical of this type of relationship are identified. Since each of these games lacks a nonmyopic equilibrium, it is argued that they are essentially indeterminate. Consequently, without qualifying assumptions, little can be said about either the probability that unilateral deterrence will succeed, or the likely consequences of a breakdown of deterrence in these games.

To induce more determinate results, three sets of stability criteria drawn from the theory of moves were introduced, and their impact on the stability of deterrence in the unilateral case examined. Each set of postulates is shown to have a variable impact on the unilateral deterrence relationship.

The stability criteria associated with the notion of an absorbing outcome were examined first. The status quo outcome in each of these games is rendered stable in the absorbing sense if the revisionist player is assumed to be risk-averse, that is, prefers to accept the next-best outcome rather than risk a cycle in order to induce the best outcome. In the absence of this assumption, however, the four unilateral deterrence games examined herein remain indeterminate.

The impact of holding power, or the ability of one player to stay at and absorb the costs of a Pareto-inferior outcome longer than another player, was also examined. When such an asymmetric distribution of power is assumed, deterrence is shown to be stable as long as the status quo power has either holding power or a credible threat. Conversely, in the absence of these conditions, when the revisionist player has holding power and the deterrent threat of the status quo state is not credible, deterrence is unstable. Nevertheless, even under these conditions, prolonged conflict is not implied, since the revisionist player's holding power, if recognized, provides an incentive for the status quo player to accept, rather than resist, the new order induced by the breakdown of the deterrent relationship.

The final set of rationality postulates explored in this essay is associated with the concept of a limited-move equilibrium or an outcome that is rendered stable when environmental conditions preclude players in a sequential game from making all of the logically possible moves and countermoves. Given the essentially idiosyncratic nature of such move limitations, only a selected number of empirically plausible constraints were examined. In general, the analysis revealed that the lack of limitations on the ability of the players to move from one outcome to another tended to foster, rather than destroy, the possibility of stable unilateral deterrence. At the most extreme end of the continuum, when either the revisionist player, or both players, have a first-strike capability, deterrence is very unstable. Under these conditions, in all but one possible situation, both players have an incentive to launch a preemptive assault on the other. Stability begins to emerge in these games when the status quo player has both a second-strike capability and a credible retaliatory threat. Finally, provided that a return to the status quo ante is not possible, unilateral deterrence is stable in three of the four games when the players have the ability to pass through the outcome associated with mutual punishment, as might be the case when both sides have an ability to fight a limited war.

One interesting conclusion that can be drawn from an analysis of the ramifications of move limitations on the unilateral deterrence relationship concerns the overall destabilizing impact of nuclear weapons. To the extent that nuclear weapons are associated with a first-strike capability, or to the extent that they preclude carefully controlled levels of escalation (i.e., a war fighting capability), nuclear weapons add little to, and in some cases detract from, the possibility of unilateral deterrence.

The overall picture of unilateral deterrence that emerges from this study is one of complexity and fragility. Slight alterations in risk-taking propensi-

ties, power asymmetries, and the ability of players to
move to, pass through, or return to, certain outcomes were
shown to have important implications for the possibility
of unilateral deterrence. Moreover, while a credible
threat was seen to be an important part of the deterrence
equation, it is, in general, neither a necessary nor a
sufficient condition for the emergence of strategic
balance. Unilateral deterrence remains stable, even when
the status quo player lacks a credible
retaliatory threat, as long as it possesses holding power
or is faced with a risk-averse revisionist opponent.

Finally, this analysis is consistent with the power
transition theory of Organski and Kugler (1980)--that
power imbalances do not imply war--and may shed some
light on the conditions necessary for peaceful power
transitions. As already noted, a status quo power, faced
with a revisionist state with holding power, should
accede to, rather than resist, an attempt by its opponent
to institute a new order. Moreover, to the extent that
conditions of power parity contribute to misperceptions
about the possession of holding power, one would
logically expect transition periods of approximately
equal power to be associated with the outbreak of major
conflict. Note that Organski and Kugler's (1980, chapter
1) empirical data support this conclusion. This is
precisely why Quester (1982) has listed just this type of
pernicious misperception among the major causes of
international war.

NOTES

1. For a related termination condition, called
rational termination, that defines a player's "staying
power," see Brams and Hessel (1983).
2. For a further discussion of this point, see
Zagare (1984a).
3. For a more extensive discussion of this point,
see Brams and Wittman (1981).
4. The two numbers for each game given in these two
figures are the numbers assigned by Brams (1977) (the
first number) and by Rapoport and Guyer (1966) (the
number in parentheses).
5. Game 65(55) in Figure 4.5 is the same as the
Falklands/Malvinas game of Figure 4.3. It is reproduced
here to facilitate the subsequent discussion.
6. It is important to note that the (2,4) outcomes
associated with a victory for the revisionist player in
both games 15(24) and 65(55) are Nash equilibria, since
neither player has an _immediate_ incentive to move,
unilaterally, from it. Thus, even though both of these
equilibrium concepts coincide in their evaluation that

unilateral deterrence is unstable in these games, Nash's equilibrium concept predicts a victory for the revisionist player. By contrast, the concept of a nonmyopic equilibrium admits the possibility of a move to an immediately less attractive outcome, i.e., (a_2, b_2), by the status quo player in order to ultimately induce an outcome better than (2,4) for the status quo player. In other words, the concept of a nonmyopic equilibrium reveals a "long-term" instability in the (2,4) outcomes in both of these games.

    7. The inertia principle should be contrasted with the termination condition associated with both the concept of a nonmyopic equilibrium and the assumption of **rational termination** associated with the concept of "staying power" (Brams and Hessel, 1983). Since a player with staying power, S, is assumed to make the second move in a sequential game, S will always be the player in the position to complete the cycle. Rational termination assumes (1) that S will always complete the cycle unless he obtains his best outcome by staying, and (2) that the player without staying power will not move unless he can obtain a better outcome before the cycle is completed.

    8. For another possible empirical constraint during the Falkland/Malvinas crisis, see Zagare (1984b). And for another empirical example, see Zagare (1981).

    9. Zagare (1984b) calls outcomes stable under this set of constraints Type II equilibria.

    10. Zagare (1984b) calls outcomes stable under this set of constraints Type III equilibria.

5 Decision-Theoretic and Game-Theoretic Models of International Conflict

This chapter outlines a game-theoretic model that attempts to account for the transition of international relations from peace to war and from war to peace through several stages of the conflict process. The point of departure in this model is Bueno de Mesquita's (1980, 1981, 1985) expected-utility theory of international conflict, which constitutes the decision-theoretic foundation of the game-theoretic approach outlined below. The utility and probability concepts developed in the original study allow for a basic set of measures upon which the present model relies. A preliminary version of the game-theoretic model (Maoz, 1982, 1984b) dealt essentially with conflict initiation processes. The present study expands this version in three important ways. First, it incorporates a recent innovation of the decision-theoretic model (Bueno de Mesquita, 1985) which introduces measures of risk-disposition into the expected utility calculations of the parties. Second, I develop measures of combat-related costs and incorporate them into the expected-utility equations. I also develop measures of intangible (moral and diplomatic) costs associated with aggression. The concepts of tangible and intangible costs are instrumental both for the transformation of the decision-theoretic model into a game-theoretic one and for the conversion of both models into more dynamic terms. Third, and most important, the game-theoretic model is expanded here in a way allowing derivation of deductions concerning the unfolding of the conflict process over time

---

This study was supported by a grant from the Fund for Basic Research, the Israeli Academy of Sciences. I have benefited immensely from numerous discussions with Steven J. Brams in the preparation of the study. Neither the Academy nor Professor Brams is responsible for any errors or other problems that may be contained in what follows.

and across its various stages. In particular, this expansion consists of a systematic explanation concerning the evolution of international conflicts from their initiation (the pre-conflict stage and the initial outbreak of hostilities), the management of their violent-prone and violent-ridden incidents, as well as the stages of conflict resolution and termination. The logic of this particular extension follows closely that of Wittman (1979) and, to a lesser extent, Pillar's (1983) work on war termination.

The following section outlines briefly the basic game-theoretic model and shows how it is derived from Bueno de Mesquita's decision-theoretic approach. The third section derives endogenously the cost terms outlined above, as well as various probability terms which depict estimates of victory and defeat in different types of wars. These terms were not part of the decision-theoretic model, but their inclusion is justified on both decision-theoretic terms (independent choice) and game-theoretic terms (interdependent choice). The fourth section extends the game-theoretic framework to conflict management and conflict escalation processes, and the fifth section discusses conflict resolution or other forms of conflict termination as a bargaining process.

THE INITIATION GAME

Despite its unquestionably profound contribution to the study of international conflict, Bueno de Mesquita's decision-theoretic approach possesses several notable weaknesses. Some of these weaknesses (such as the problem of interpersonal comparison of utilities, or the zero-sum property of the original model), which were pointed out by critics (e.g., Zagare, 1982; Maoz, 1984a), were rectified innovatively in subsequent work (Bueno de Mesquita, 1985), but other problems have yet to be resolved. In order to show the relationship between the game-theoretic model to be developed below and the decision-theoretic approach and to illustrate the improvement in the rational choice theory of conflict that the former entails, I will briefly discuss some of the remaining difficulties in the expected-utility model.

The expected-utility approach as presented by Bueno de Mesquita conceives conflict-related calculations within the framework of independent choice. However, one of the fundamental characteristics of international conflicts is their interdependent nature. The decision calculus of rational actors operating in a conflictual (or even in a cooperative) environment must be based on their perceptions of the alternatives open to other actors and their preferences over those alternatives. Although the revised expected-utility model has made some progress toward the incorporation of interdependence, it has not come full circle in this regard. For example, the noninitiation alternative is analyzed in terms of a probability distribution over the future course of relations between an actor and its opponent. Yet the model does not acknowledge that the opponent faces an identical choice between initiation and noninitiation, and hence misses the strategic logic underlying this kind of interaction.

The expected-utility model also completely ignores cost calculations. Elsewhere, Bueno de Mesquita (1983) treats the costs of combat as an outcome variable that is a function of expected-utility calculations rather than an integral part of them. Yet, in conflict games, as in other ordinary lotteries, both winners and losers have to pay some price to enter and stay in the game, and this price must be deduced from their expected profits.

Finally, the expected-utility theory is highly static in nature. Since it lacks propositions regarding changes in expected utilities over time and under different circumstances, it is difficult to show how it can account for the unfolding of the conflict processes through their various stages. The main theme of the present study is that all of these problems can be overcome by the construction of a game-theoretic model based on the expected-utility approach, and builds upon it in a manner enriching the original theory without a significant loss of parsimony.

To derive the game-theoretic model I start with a modified version of the conflict initiation problem as viewed from the perspective of a single actor. For the sake of simplicity, I assume that conflict initiation occurs within a strictly bilateral setting and that no additional actors are expected to intervene. This is a working assumption which can be relaxed in subsequent research without changing the basic logic of the argument. Figure 5.1 depicts the decision tree of the conflict initiation problem.

As is evident from this figure, the major differences between this and Bueno de Mesquita's model consist of the unpacking of the noninitiation alternative in a manner that takes into account the alternatives available to the opponent, and of the addition of cost-related concepts. The unpacking of the noninitiation alternative creates a two-step choice process in which i's resistance decision depends upon j's initiation decision. While this description of the decision problem is more sensitive to the strategic nature of initiation calculuses and taps the interdependence lacking from the original version, it nonetheless contains two important problems. First, it is predicated on an implicit assumption of

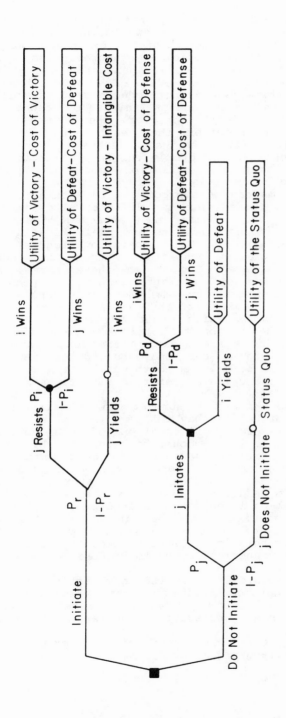

Figure 5.1   The Initiator's Decision Problem

Legend: P_r = Probability of j's resistance to i's initiative; P_i = Probability of i winning a unilaterally-initiated war; P_j = Probability of j's initiation; P_d = Probability of i winning a self-defensive war.

sequential choice. Second, it ignores the possibility of simultaneous initiation. These two points constitute serious impediments to a game-theoretic extension because they seemingly violate the basic game-theoretic assumption of parties making their choices independently--though not in ignorance of--each other. If each actor has an initiative alternative, and if both choose simultaneously, then reciprocal and simultaneous initiation cannot be ruled out as a possibility. Moreover, the assumption of simultaneous choice requires that each actor have a complete strategy before the game starts. Hence the resist or yield choices of Actor j, given i's initiation, and of Actor i, given j's initiation, must be selected before the game is played.

These problems can be overcome if the noninitiation alternative is decomposed into two distinct alternatives: "don't initiate but resist if attacked" (labeled self-defense), and "don't initiate and yield if attacked" (the yield alternative). This operation renders the sequential choice problem consistent with a game theory conception of a strategy. Seen in these terms, the interdependent nature of initiation calculuses can be depicted as the extensive-form game shown in Figure 5.2.

Some of the payoffs attached to the tree-branches are expected utilities while other payoffs are strict utility terms. The reason for this differentiation is that all war situations are risky in the sense that the identity of the winner can only be "determined" in probabilistic terms before its outbreak. On the other hand, the U_w, U_y, and U_q terms refer to situations in which the parties know for sure--given the issues at stake--what kind of values they imply.[1]

The extensive-form presentation of the conflict initiation game takes into account both the possibility of a simultaneously initiated war and the preselection of strategies by the parties independently from one another. Yet the essentially interdependent nature of the initiation problem is due to two important aspects of this game. First, real-world outcomes posited by this game are results of joint decisions by the parties. Second, the nonobvious aspect of interdependence stems from the ability to reduce this game into a simple 2 x 2 binary-choice game. This reduction is due to Proposition 1.

Proposition 1: Regardless of the opponent's expected choice, and regardless of preference ordering of alternatives, one of the noninitiation strategies (i.e., Yield or Self-Defense) necessarily dominates the other.

Proof: To facilitate the proof of this proposition, consider the normal-form game as derived from Figure 5.3.

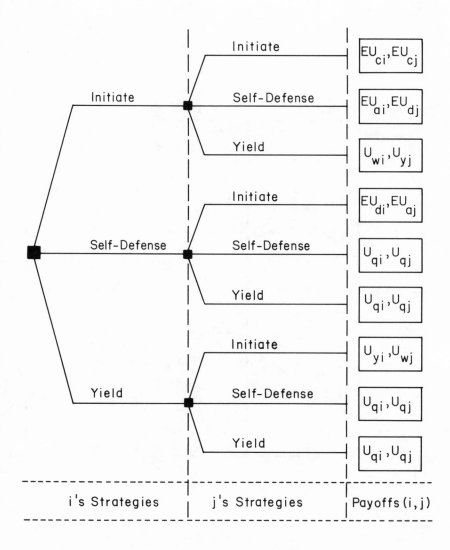

Legend: EU_c = The expected Utility to be derived by an actor from a simultaneously-initiated war; EU_a = The expected utility to be derived from an aggressive (unilaterally-initiated) war; EU_d = the expected utility to be derived from a self-defensive war; U_w = The utility of a nonviolent victory due to the opponent's decision to give in; U_y = The utility of unconditional fulfillment of the initiator's demands; U = The utility to be derived from the status quo; i, j = actors.

Figure 5.2   The Conflict Initiation Game in Extensive Form

		j	
	INITIATE	SELF-DEFENSE	YIELD
INITIATE	EU_{cj} EU_{ci}	EU_{dj} EU_{ai}	U_{yj} U_{wi}
SELF-DEFENSE	EU_{aj} EU_{di}	U_{qj} U_{qi}	U_{qj} U_{qi}
i YIELD	U_{wj} U_{yi}	U_{qj} U_{qi}	U_{qj} U_{qi}

Notes: 1) i's payoffs are given at the lower-left corner of each box; j's payoffs are at the upper-right corner

2) Legend in Figure 2.

Figure 5.3 The Conflict Initiation Game in Normal Form

This game, viewed from i's perspective, suggests that i would be indifferent between self-defense and yielding whenever j selects either self-defense or yield strategies: in each of these four outcomes the status quo is preserved. Hence, i's preference of one noninitiation alternative over the other will depend strictly on the preference order of EU_{di} and U_{yi}. i would prefer self-defense to yielding iff $EU_{di} > U_{yi}$, and i would prefer yielding to self-defense iff $U_{yi} > EU_{di}$. The same applies, of course, to j's calculus. Since both actors determine their preference orderings of outcomes before the game is played, each of them can determine in advance which of the noninitiation strategies dominates the other and thereby eliminate the dominated strategy from the admissible strategy set. This reduces the conflict game to its basic form, as depicted in Figure 5.4.

The second meaning of interdependence in this game is that each actor's payoff at one of the off-diagonal outcomes depends on the previous choice made by the opponent. Whether i's payoff in the upper-right box will be EU_{ai} or U_{wi} depends on whether j prefers EU_{dj} to U_{yj}.

This raises a number of interesting possibilities of deception and misperception in games of incomplete information, where opponents do not know each other's entire preference ordering.

As it is, however, Proposition 1 raises a number of interesting ideas. Initiation-related calculations (that is, those concerning the questions of whether to initiate or not) are undominated and hence nondeterministic in the sense that they depend to a large extent on the opponent's choices. However, noninitiation calculations express fundamental policy orientations which are independent of the environmental context. Thus, preferences regarding the precise nature of the noninitiation alternative are clearly deterministic. If that is the case, several counterintuitive propositions about strategic behavior in international relations can be made at this early stage.

Proposition 2: A state preferring deterministically the yield alternative to the self-defense one would not necessarily prefer the yield alternative to the initiation alternative. Put differently, there are cases in which a defeatist state (preferring yield to self-defense) will initiate conflict.

Although a formal proof of this proposition must be deferred to the next section, in which the various game payoffs will be formally defined, an intuitive explication

	INITIATE j	DON'T INITIATE
INITIATE i	EU_{cj} EU_{ci}	EU_{dj} or U_{yj} EU_{ai} or U_{wi}
DON'T INITIATE	EU_{aj} or U_{wj} EU_{di} or U_{yi}	U_{qj} U_{qi}

Notes: 1) If i is indifferent between EU_{di} and U_{yi}, either team could be inserted at the southwest box. If i has a preference order of $EU_{di} > .U_{yi}$ then only EU_{di} will be inserted. Otherwise, U_{yi} will be inserted. The same applies to j's payoffs at the northeast box.

2) Legend in Figure 2.

Figure 5.4   The Reduced Conflict Game

can be given at this point. Comparing the two noninitiation alternatives in Figure 5.3, we have seen that a nation whose preference ordering is of the $U_y > EU_d$

variety would unconditionally prefer to yield if attacked. However, comparing the noninitiation and initiation strategies in Figure 5.4, we can easily see that EU_c might

be preferred to U_y and EU_a might be preferred to the

status quo. In a nuclear conflict environment, for example, a state might think it fruitless to strike back if attacked because issuing a second strike might breed eventual catastrophe. Given the nuclear balance between itself and the opponent it is clear it would lose everything in such an exchange. Thus, it may be rational to yield at the outset if attacked. Nonetheless, if i commits itself to striking first, it can gain considerable advantage and possibly secure a better outcome than by awaiting a first strike by its opponent. One possible version of such a situation is illustrated in Figure 5.5.

Without knowing anything about nation j's payoffs, i's self-defense strategy is dominated by the yield strategy. Although the status quo is the best outcome from i's perspective, i has two undominated strategies in the reduced game (which in our case is a game of incomplete information); initiate if j is expected to initiate, and don't initiate otherwise. If i's payoffs are treated as ordinal preferences, and irrespective of j's preference ordering of outcomes, it can be easily seen that neither of the two off-diagonal outcomes will be a Nash equilibrium of a perfect information game where one actor has i's preference ordering.² From an expected-utility perspective, assuming an underlying utility function for these ordinal preferences, i would initiate conflict iff:

$$EU(I) \geqslant EU(\bar{I}) \tag{1}$$

Where I and $\bar{I}$ are "initiate" and "don't initiate" alternatives, respectively, and

$$EU(I) \geqslant P_j U_{ij} + (1-P_j)U_{ij} \tag{2.1}$$

$$EU(I) \geqslant P_j U_{\bar{i}j} + (1-P_j)U_{\overline{ij}} \tag{2.2}$$

where P_j is the probability of j initiating, and the

subscripted utility terms are i's payoffs in the intersected game outcomes. Substituting equations (2.1) and (2.2) into inequality (1) and solving for P_j, we get:

I. THE EXTENDED GAME

	j		
	Initiate	Self-Defense	Yield
Initiate	3	4	5
i Self-Defense	1	6	6
Yield	2	6	6

2. THE BASIC (REDUCED) GAME

	j	
	Initiate	Don't Initiate
Initiate	3	4 or 5
i Don't Initiate	2	6

Notes: Numbers represent row's payoffs
6 = Best outcome; 5 = Next-best outcome; .... 2 = Next-worst outcome; 1 = Worst outcome

Figure 5.5   A Game Where A Defeatist State May be Committed to Conflict Initiation

$$P_j \geq \frac{U_{\overline{ij}} - U_{\overline{ij}}}{U_{ij} + U_{\overline{ij}} - U_{i\overline{j}} - U_{\overline{ij}}} \tag{3}$$

Using standardized utilities for our game example in which the best outcome ($U_{\overline{ij}}$ in this case) is assigned a utility of 1, the worst outcome ($U_{\overline{ij}}$ in our example) is assigned a utility of zero, and the two intermediate outcomes are defined as $0 \leq U_{ij} \leq U_{i\overline{j}} \leq 1$, we get for equation (3):[3]

$$P_j \geq \frac{1 - U_{i\overline{j}}}{1 + U_{ij} - U_{i\overline{j}}} \tag{4}$$

Equation (4) suggests that the threshold probability of j's initiation that renders i indifferent between initiation and noninitiation has in this game a range of real values, such that:

$$P_j = 0 \qquad \text{iff} \quad U_{ij} = U_{i\overline{j}} = 1 \tag{5.1}$$

$$P_j = 1 \qquad \text{iff} \quad U_{ij} = U_{i\overline{j}} = 0 \tag{5.2}$$

$$0 < P_j < 1 \qquad \text{iff} \quad U_{i\overline{j}} < 1 \ \text{ and } \ U_{ij} > 0 \tag{5.3}$$

The implication of this analysis is that there exists some probability of attack on a defeatist state that would render it highly motivated to initiate conflict and thus unwilling to exercise its defeatist disposition. This point logically supports Bueno de Mesquita's original focus on a single passively cooperative alternative to conflict initiation (Bueno de Mesquita, 1981). If the two noninitiation alternatives in Figures 5.2 and 5.3 are seen as boundary cases on a passive cooperation continuum (where the yield alternative is the most cooperative and the self-defense alternative is the least cooperative) then the logic of reducing the continuum to a single cooperative strategy via the elimination of dominated alternatives would apply to the continuum as a whole. In the event of noninitiation by j the status quo will become the outcome of all cooperative strategies, and hence the final selection of the dominant cooperative strategy will depend on their preference ranking in the event of a conflict initiated by j.

Yet the very same logic also suggests that treating the conflict initiation problem strictly within the confines of decision theory is also flawed, because whether or not a nation would actually initiate depends inherently on its estimates and expectations concerning the initiation-related behavior of its opponent.[4]

MEASURING PAYOFFS IN THE INITIATION GAME

In order to understand the interdependent calculus of conflict initiation, it is necessary to explicate how the parties define their payoffs in the conflict initiation game. This requires exploring the substantive features of the situations that are captured by the various game outcomes, and what costs and benefits they entail for each of the parties.

From the point of view of each individual participant, the initiation game entails three different types of war and three short-of-war situations. The war types are (1) a simultaneously initiated war, (2) an aggressive war (where the actor is the unilateral initiator, and (3) a self-defensive war (where the actor is initiated against). The non-war outcomes are (1) the status quo, (2) the win condition (where the opponent yields to the actor's demands at the outset), and (3) the yield condition (which is the opposite of the win condition). As noted above, the payoffs in each of the war types are expected utilities due to the uncertain results of the war.

These war types resemble each other in the sense that their expected utilities are composed of the same set of factors: probability of winning (or losing), political utility of winning (or losing), and costs of war. Yet each type of war differs from the others in the sense that the values of the probabilities and costs would differ across war types. Let us try to capture the similarities and differences among war types by formally defining the components of the expected utility of war.

In general, the expected utility an actor, i, derives from a war of type x is given as:

$$EU_{xi} = P_x U_{sx} + (1-P_x)U_{fx} - C_x \qquad (6.1)$$

where P_x is the probability of victory, U_s is the utility of success, U_f is the utility of failure, and C_x is the cost term. This term can also be presented as:

$$EU_x = P_x(U_s - C_s) + (1-P_x)(U_f - C_f) \qquad (6.2)$$

From equation (6.2) it is obvious that the cost term is
defined as:

$$C_x = P_x C_s + (1-P_x)C_f \qquad\qquad (6.3)$$

In general, and following Bueno de Mesquita's
definitions, U_s will assume, for a given actor, the same
value across all war types. The same applies to the U_f
term. This is due to the notion that, politically, a
victory in a war means imposing the winner's will on the
loser (Clausewitz, 1832, p. 1). Thus, regardless of
whether the winner is the initiator or the defender (if
they are distinguishable), the political payoff is the
same. We now have a basic expected-utility equation that
preserves its basic structure across all war types, as
well as two political utility terms with identical values
across all war types.[5] This exhausts the similarities
shared by all war payoffs.

Let us start outlining the differences among wars by
defining probabilities.[6] First, the baseline probability
of victory is the one estimated by an actor in the
simultaneous war case. This term, P_c (P_i in Bueno de

Mesquita's terminology) represents an estimate of success
in war which is based strictly on structural factors and
attributes of the parties (specifically, on their relative
military capabilities). The reason for using it as a
baseline probability is that in a simultaneously initiated
war none of the parties enjoys any situational advantages
(such as surprise). Hence the baseline probability of
success in such a war will depend primarily on the balance
of capabilities.

How will an actor's estimate of its chances to win a
defensive war differ from this baseline estimate? The
answer to this question requires exploring the strategic
implications of absorbing a first strike. The defender
faces three important situationally induced disadvantages.
First, there is the possibility of being surprised which
puts the defender in a psychologically inferior
situation.[7] Second, even if the defender is not surprised
by the timing of the initial attack, it is always faced by
a series of faits accomplis concerning its locus and
scope, which are chosen by the initiator.[8] Third, and
most important, the first strike enables the initiator to
wipe out some portion of the defender's retaliatory
capability, thereby altering the basic balance of forces,
since the defender is left only with a portion of the
initial capability. Taken together, these points suggest
that an actor's probability of victory in a self-
defensive war will be marginally smaller than the

probability of victory in a simultaneous war. Therefore, I define the former probability, P_{di}, as:

$$P_{di} = P_{ci} - D_i \qquad (7.1)$$

where D_i is the damage caused to the defender by the initiator's first strike and is defined as:

$$D_i = P_c - P_c^2 = P_c(1-P_c) \qquad (7.2)$$

The reason for this definition of the damage term is the not implausible assumption that the higher the initial capability of the defender, the smaller the effects of a first strike upon capability. Thus, substituting D_i from equation (7.2) into equation (7.1) we get:

$$P_{di} = P_c - P_c(1-P_c) = P_c^2 \qquad (7.3)$$

which satisfies the logic of the defender's probability calculus as described above.[10] The probability of victory in an aggressive war is based on the application of the same substantive principles to the initiator. Facing the advantages of a potential surprise, being able to dictate the scope, timing, and locus of the first strike, and being able to wipe out some of the opponent's retaliatory capability, the initiator of an aggressive war would perceive the probability of victory as marginally higher than the baseline probability. Thus, the probability of victory in an aggressive war is defined by Actor i to be:

$$P_i = P_{ci} + D_j \qquad (8.1)$$

where D_j is defined as $D_j = P_{cj} - P_{cj}^2$, and P_{cj} is defined as $P_{cj} = (1-P_{ci})$. Hence:

$$D_j = 1 - P_{ci} - (1-P_{ci})^2 = P_{ci}(1-P_{ci}) \qquad (8.2)$$

Substituting the value of D_j from equation (8.2) into equation (8.1), we have:

$$P_i = P_{ci} + P_{ci}(1-P_{ci}) = P_{ci}(2-P_{ci}) \qquad (8.3)$$

Having defined the probabilities of victory in the three types of war payoffs, we can now proceed to the definition of costs. In general, the way actors determine their costs of war is basically identical in different types, though each war adds something to this definition. As we have seen in equations (6.1) - (6.3) above, the costs of war can be treated as a global sum which is deduced from the expected-utility calculations, or be decomposed into costs of winning and costs of losing. The global costs of war are, of course, the expected value of their decomposed parts. Let us start with the tangible costs of war, consisting of number of fatalities, dollar value of destroyed or otherwise damaged equipment, direct and indirect economic damages, and so forth. While estimates of the expected costs are constantly made by decision makers (Blainey, 1973), the real problem is to convert these real-valued costs into abstract concepts such as utiles that can be incorporated into the politico-strategic calculus depicted in Bueno de Mesquita's equations. In order to enable such a conversion, I assume that cost estimates vary with the extent to which decision makers are unsure of their ability to win the war. Since decision makers define the probability of victory primarily on the basis of the balance of power between their state and the opponent's, a very powerful state contemplating war against a weak opponent will perceive its probability of victory as very high. At the same time, the costs of conducting such a war will be perceived as very low because of the expectation of a brief and decisive war and because of the opponent's lack of sufficient power to inflict heavy damages. Viewed from the perspective of the weak state, such a war would be characterized by a low probability of victory and by an excessively high cost estimate, given the unfavorable balance of power. This assumption seems reasonable because it corresponds to and in fact taps the essential logic of force deployment, weapons acquisition, and conventional or nuclear arms race processes. This assumption suggests that the costs of war could be conceptualized in terms of a discount rate (or percent depreciation) in the political value of winning (V_s) due to risk or uncertainty surrounding its actual realization.[11] Stated formally, the tangible costs of a war of type x (excluding a self-defensive war) are defined as:

$$TC_x = \frac{V_s - }{V_s} = \frac{V_s - P_x V_x - (1 - P_x)V_f}{V_s} \qquad (9.1)$$

Using Bueno de Mesquita's definitions, we have

$$V_s = (U_{ii} - U_{ij}); \qquad V_f = (U_{ij} - U_{ii}) \qquad (9.2)$$

Substituting the terms from equation (9.2) into (9.1), we get:

$$TC_x = \frac{(U_{ii} - U_{ij}) - P_x(U_{ii} - U_{ij}) - (1-P_x)(U_{ij} - U_{ii})}{(U_{ii} - U_{ij})}$$

$$= 2(1-P_x) \tag{9.3}$$

Thus, the tangible costs of war are defined very simply as twice the probability of defeat in that war; the higher this probability, the higher the costs.[12] Now, let us see what kind of twist this baseline definition receives in each kind of war. For one thing, it is obvious that cost estimates vary among war types as a function of variations in probabilities of defeat. Yet there is more. In a simultaneous war the total cost estimates will equal the baseline calculus of tangible costs because neither actor can take advantage of situational factors in order to reduce his own costs or to increase those of the opponent. In addition, intangible costs (such as diplomatic sanctions, loss of friendship with external actors, international condemnation of aggression, and so forth) do not exist in this kind of war, because of simultaneous initiation. To the extent that they are expected, they will be cancelled out by the lack of a clear aggressor.

The situation is somewhat different in calculating self-defense costs. Although in a self-defensive war the defender does not expect to incur intangible costs, his tangible cost estimate would be marginally higher than his cost estimate in a simultaneous war for two reasons. First, his probability of defeat is marginally higher. Second, given the underlying logic of probability calculations, which stresses the expectation of some initial damage due to the absorption of a first strike, the defender must add this damage to the subsequent cost of the war's conduct. Thus, formally stated, the cost of self-defense TC_d is:

$$TC_d = 2(1-P_d) + D = 2(1-P_c^2) + P_c(1-P_c) = 2 + P_c(1-3P_c) \tag{10}$$

On the face of it, it seems that the initiation game suggests strong incentives for aggression: by becoming a unilateral initiator, an actor can both increase the probability of victory and--consequently--cut down on tangible costs. This is so because, given equation (9.3), the tangible costs of the initiator would be:

$$TC_a = 2(1-P_i) = 2[1 - P_c(2-P_c)] = 2(1-P_c)^2 \tag{11}$$

so that there seems to be a cost-related as well as a probability-related premium on aggression. If that were the case, international relations would have been a

Hobbesian state of nature, constantly engulfed in violence, because every state would have been pushed to conflict by this escalatory logic (Jervis, 1979). However, despite its basically anarchical nature, the international system has developed a set of norms and institutions designed to check and condemn outright aggression. For example, the only legitimate war according to the United Nations Charter is a self-defensive war. And, although diplomatic or economic sanctions are difficult to implement and by and large ineffective, rational actors contemplating initiation must take into account that some intangible costs will have to be incurred as a result of their aggression. Thus the costs of an aggressive war consist of two components, between which there is a trade-off relationship: tangible costs that are smaller than the tangible costs in any other type of war ($TC_a \leqslant TC_c \leqslant TC_d$) and intangible costs

that assume meaningful values only in an aggressive war.

The definition of intangible costs is based on two assumptions regarding the relative acceptability of aggression in international relations or, more precisely, regarding the ability of an actor to justify aggressive acts on moral terms. The first assumption is that strong actors would find it more difficult to justify aggression against weak states than vice versa. Attacks on weak states evoke moral outrage because of the violation of fairness or equity norms of international conduct (something like: "Why don't you pick on someone your own size?") and because of their exploitative connotation. The occupation of Belgium by Germany in 1914, the Italian invasion of Ethiopia in 1935, the Russo-Finnish war of 1939, and, more recently, the Israeli invasion of Lebanon are good cases in point. The second assumption is that an attack on a traditional enemy is more "acceptable" (or "justifiable") than an attack on a friendly or neutral state. Because neutrality and friendship are rare qualities in an anarchical international system, their brutal violation seems to be morally unacceptable. Moreover, initiation of war against traditional enemies can be justified on grounds of preemption or prevention of an impending attack which the opponent has presumably been planning. However, such claims (which are designed to translate aggression into the more legitimate language of self-defense), are difficult to make if the opponent is a friendly or neutral state.

This logic suggests that the highest intangible costs will be incurred by a powerful state attacking a weak friendly or neutral state, and the lowest intangible costs will be incurred by a weak state attacking a strong traditional enemy. Formally,[13] then, intangible costs of aggression are defined as:

$$IC_i = P_i(1+U^*_{ij}) \tag{12.1}$$

and the total costs of the initiator of an aggressive war are given as:[14]

$$C_a = TC_i + IC_i = 2(1-P_c)^2 + P_c(2-P_c)(1+U^*_{ij}) \tag{12.2}$$

The tradeoff between tangible and intangible costs in an aggressive war is now apparent. The larger the difference between the probability of victory in an aggressive war and the baseline probability (P_c), the higher the incentive to initiate in order to cut down on the tangible costs of war. At the same time, the more constraints are imposed on the initiator due to increasingly large intangible costs.

As Appendix 2 shows, these measures allow us to derive cardinal payoffs for the initiation game and thereby explain why a certain dyad would be engaged in conflict while another dyad would not. Likewise, if conflict is to be a rational outcome in a game, they help explain which actor is likely to be the initiator, and whether the opponent is going to defend itself or yield at the outset.

In contrast to the game-theoretic studies that attempt to find equilibria solutions to games that presumably characterize aspects of international relations (Brams and Hessel, 1984; Brams, 1985; Zagare, 1983), my approach is to set forth a set of a priori rules that would specify the conditions under which the outbreak of conflict is to be expected. Because, as in Bueno de Mesquita's model, we are dealing with necessary but not sufficient conditions, these rules will be stated in a somewhat qualified form. In general, the starting point of the initiation game is the status quo outcome. This is so because the calculus depicted by the game is performed prior to any action by the parties. I also assume that the normal state of affairs in international relations is nonviolent, that is, the status quo is seen as some sort of prior equilibrium. Deviations from this equilibrium will occur when changes in the expected utility calculations of the parties will lead one or both of them to conclude that they will be better off by shifting their strategies. This is, of course, the concept of Nash equilibrium. Stated in game-theoretic terms, the initiation game suggests that conflict would be observed if one or more of the following conditions is met:

(1) One or both parties have a dominant initiation strategy.

(2) One party has a dominant initiation strategy and the other prefers self-defense over yielding.

(3) The status quo outcome is not a Nash equilibrium of the game.[15]

(4) If the game contains no Nash equilibrium but one of the parties has a maximin initiation strategy.

(5) If the game contains no Nash equilibrium and none of the parties has a maximin strategy, conflict will be observed with a probability of $1-(1-q)(1-r)$, where q and r are the mixed conflict strategies of i and j, respectively.

Conditions 4 and 5 are illustrated by the games in Figure 5.6.

Of course, these conditions vary in terms of determinism of conflict occurrence. Thus, to make them compatible with Bueno de Mesquita's (1985) hypotheses, they must be respecified in the following way (see also Maoz, 1984a):

(1) Conflict is most likely when both parties have a dominant initiation strategy. In this case the game will have a unique Nash equilibrium at the initiate_i - initiate_j outcome.

(2) Conflict is highly likely when one party has a dominant initiation strategy and the other prefers self-defense to yielding. In this case, the outcome can be either a simultaneous war or an aggressive self-defensive war.

(3) Conflict is likely if none of the Nash equilibria of the game is the status quo outcome. In this case the precise form of conflict depends on which of the conflict outcomes is a Nash equilibrium.

(4) There is a variable likelihood of conflict in cases without Nash equilibria (conditions 4 and 5 above) depending on maximin strategies or mixed strategy probabilities.

(5) The likelihood of conflict ranges between low and zero when:
(a) Maximin strategies clash with Nash equilibria (such as in Chicken).
(b) Mixed strategies yield a high probability of cooperation.
(c) The status quo is one of the Nash equilibria of the game.
(d) One party has a dominant noninitiation strategy and the other prefers yielding to self-defense.

1. A Game that Satisfies Condition 4

j

	Initiate	Don't Initiate
Initiate	0.8 1	1 0.5
Don't Initiate	0.3 0	0 0.8

i

This game contains <u>no</u> Nash equilibrium. However, j has a maximum initiation strategy which forces i to initiate. Hence the outcome is simultaneous initiation.

2. A Game that Satisfies Condition 5

j

	Initiate	Don't Initiate
Initiate	0 1	1 0.5
Don't Initiate	0.8 0	0.3 0.8

i

This game contains <u>no</u> Nash equilibrium.
The parties would therefore mix their strategies as follows: i would initiate with a probability of q = .615, and j would initiate with a probability of r = .467. Since conflict occurs in all but the status quo (mutual noninitiation) outcome, its probability is 1-(1-q) (1-r) = 1-(1-.615)(1-.467) = .795. The reason for that is that mixed-strategy payoffs are higher than minimax payoffs for both parties.

Figure 5.6   Examples of Games that Satisfy Conditions 4 and 5

(e) Both parties have a dominant noninitiation
strategy.

These deductions can be expanded in several ways. First,
one can incorporate expectations regarding third party
intervention as has been done in the expected-utility
research. Second, one can try to model the initiation
process in more dynamic terms by showing how the
preferences and calculations of the parties change over
time as a function of changes in their relative
capabilities or in their alignment patterns, which
constitute the empirical referents of the probability and
utility terms. Third, one can examine the vulnerability
of certain games to deception and miscalculation by
viewing them as games of either incomplete information or
partial information of the sort contained in some of Bueno
de Mesquita's (1985) new expected-utility equations.[16]
While all these undertakings are of indisputable
importance, they are beyond the scope of the present
study. Instead, in the remainder of the paper I will
develop several theoretical ideas concerning a dynamic
theory of conflict management and conflict termination.

THE CONFLICT MANAGEMENT GAME

In contrast to the initiation game, the starting
point of the management game is the eruption of an overt
conflict between the parties. As Schelling (1960) and
Kahn (1965) pointed out, conflict management is a
"competition in risk-taking." The object of this
competition is to force the opponent into accepting one's
demands while minimizing one's costs. Since both parties
pursue the same thing, their goals, once the conflict
begins, seem to be totally opposed. Thus, resolution of
the conflict would seemingly occur only when one of them
decides that he is better off by yielding to the
opponent's demands than by continuing to fight. Yet, even
in games of complete information, conflict management
seems to be of profound importance. To illustrate this
point, consider Figure 5.7.

The conflict starts with each party expecting a
certain payoff but no costs. This is denoted by points
EU_{ci0} and EU_{cj0}, respectively. As time passes, this

expected payoff declines at a certain rate (b) due to the
costs of combat. Each party has certain expectations
regarding the duration of the conflict. Specifically, the
expected duration of conflict is the time span during
which an actor's payoffs decline from EU_{c0} to EU_c.

However, even if this expected time span expires prior to

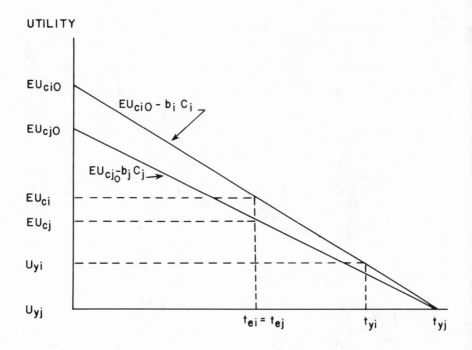

UTILITY

EU_{ciO}

$EU_{ciO} - b_i\,C_i$

EU_{cjO}

$EU_{cj_O} - b_j\,C_j$

EU_{ci}

EU_{cj}

U_{yi}

U_{yj}

$t_{ei} = t_{ej}$ t_{yi} t_{yj}

TIME (months of conflict)

Where: EU_{cO} = Expected utility from conflict at time 0 (without cost).
EU_c = Expected utility from conflict with cost.
t_e = Expected duration of conflict.
t_y = Maximum time-span for which fighting is rational
U_y = Utility of yielding.
C = Cost of fighting.

Note: Linear decline functions are assumed for illustrative purposes only.

Figure 5.7   The Conflict Management Problem

a clear-cut outcome of the conflict, it is still rational
for each party to continue fighting as long as its
conflict payoff at time t exceeds its yield payoff, such
that $EU_{ct} \geq U_y$. The maximum time during which fighting is
rational (t_y) depends for each party on the initial
(no-cost) conflict payoff, and on the rate of decline (b).
To formalize this idea, we can define for each party the
rate of decline (assuming it is linear) as:

$$EU_{ct} = EU_{c0} - btC_c \qquad (13.1)$$

$$\frac{dEU_c}{dt} = b; \qquad b = \frac{EU_{c0} - EU_c}{EU_{c0} - U_y}$$

The expected and maximum time of fighting are given as:

$$t_e = \frac{EU_{c0} - EU_c}{bc} ; \qquad t_y = \frac{EU_{c0} - U_y}{bc} \qquad (13.2)$$

According to Figure 5.7, j can hold out longer than
i despite the fact that the latter started with a higher
payoff for conflict. Thus we could reasonably expect j to
be the winner of that conflict because after t_{yi} days of
fighting i would surrender. But if information is
complete, conflict should not break out in the first
place. This is so because, knowing how long each party
can hold out fighting, both should be able to exchange an
amount equal to the utility they expect to derive at t_{yi},
at the outset. Now, the big puzzle is how could we talk
about conflict initiation and conflict management given
this model?

One can argue that the assumption of complete
(perfect) information is implausible. The rate with which
an actor's expected utility declines over time depends,
among other things, on willingness to take risks; the more
risk-acceptant an actor, the smaller the rate of decline.
Whereas utilities and probabilities could, in principle,
be estimated quite accurately by the opponents, since they
are based on hard and quantifiable data, the
risk-propensity exponent is a psychological construct
which is difficult, if not impossible, to estimate
objectively. Thus, if information is incomplete there is
room for deception and a distinct possibility of
miscalculation. Each actor can expect to hold out longer
than the opponent, and as long as such expectations obtain
conflict is rational. Although this is an important and
possibly correct point, it implies that conflict arises
from human imperfection, which disables decision makers

from reaching negotiated solutions to their problems. It further implies that conflict could have been totally abolished as a form of international behavior had we been able to find ways to correct these estimation problems. But clearly, beyond being a generally naive implication, this idea contradicts not only the rational basis of conflict but also most of the empirical and substantive knowledge about this phenomenon (Waltz, 1958).

Another--and, I think, more appealing--resolution of the problem of the seeming irrationality of international conflict lies in the idea that strategy matters and that its application is what conflict management is all about. Simply stated, i--knowing that he is bound to lose--finds himself in a precarious situation. The problem is how to use or display force in a manner that would minimize the decline rate in the expected utility over time. Moreover, if such a strategy of force employment could be found, it would presumably increase j's decline rate by increasing the latter's costs of combat. However, j--knowing that i is engaged in search for an optimal conflict management strategy--would also look for measures that would offset i's possible management strategies and--at the same time--be optimal for him in that they would minimize his own decline rate. Given this mutually expected search for optimal conflict management strategies, each party wants to make his optimal strategy insensitive to whatever management strategy the opponent chooses to employ. This, in game-theoretic terms, is the notion of mixed strategies. To model this process, let us now construct the management game in normal form, as depicted in Figure 5.8.

Let e represent a level of escalation ranging between zero and one (Brams, 1984). When e = 1, it would mean that an actor throws all his military capability into the war effort at the outset of fighting. By doing that he does not affect his conflict payoff function or his win payoff (U_w). But he can reduce the yield payoff to zero,

thereby increasing his willingness to resist (and consequently increasing the time span of rational fighting). However, one could do better. By choosing a level of escalation such that $0 < e < 1$, one can reduce the decline rate in the conflict payoff function over time, while simultaneously increasing one's resistance ability by discounting the yield payoff by $(1 - e)$. These management strategies enable an actor to raise his fighting time in a manner not possible if he were to use a simple-minded management strategy of the form e = 1, $(1 - e) = 0$. But, knowing that the opponent is engaged in a similar calculus, an actor would search for an optimal randomization of force employment (i.e., a given mixture of e and 1-e), such that, irrespective of his opponent's

	e_j	j	$(1-e_j)$
e_i	$\dfrac{EU_{cjO}}{e_j} - b_j C_j$		U_{yj}
i	$\dfrac{EU_{ciO}}{e_i} - b_i C_i$	U_{wi}	
$(1-e_i)$	U_{wj}		U_{qj}
	U_{yi}		U_{qi}

Where: e = Level of conflict escalation: $0 \leqslant e \leqslant 1$

Notes: The conflict payoff function ($EU_{cO} - b$) is changed in the manner shown in the matrix because the initial conflict payoff at time zero is unaffected by the level of escalation an actor selects. Thus, for any given level of escalation, e, the conflict payoff function is always: $EU_{cO} - eb_C$.

The omission of time in the conflict payoff function is somewhat problematic. In fact, one may want to consider the time-dependent effects of conflict management strategies. In such a case e would be a variable function of time, denoted e_t and $1-e_t$, respectively. Obviously e_t would decrease over time and the conflict payoff function will be asymptotic to the time axis. However, this complicates matter because it requires to consider how the probability of success (P_c) varies as a function of a certain mixture of e_t and $1-e_t$. What this game suggests is that parties want to select a management strategy at the outset which is independent of the particular point in time they are in.

Figure 5.8   The Conflict Mangement Game in Normal Form

strategies, he would be assured of at least a minimum expected payoff of V. This suggests:

$$e \left[\frac{EU_{c0}}{e} - bC \right] + (1-e)U_y \geqslant V \tag{14.1}$$

$$eU_w + (1-e)U_q \geqslant V \tag{14.2}$$

Treating both as equalities yields

$$EU_{c0} - eb \pm (1-e)U_y = eU_w + (1-e)U_q \tag{14.3}$$

$$e = \frac{U_q - U_y - EU_{c0}}{U_q - U_y - bC - U_w}$$

Thus e is an optimal management strategy of an actor, and, as long as $b > 0$ and $U_w > EU_{c0}$ (which are satisfied by definition), it will be always smaller than one. However, e would have a meaningful value (i.e., it would be higher than zero) iff $EU_{c0} = U_q - U_y$. This important constraint suggests that the preference order of payoffs in the conflict management must be $U_w \geqslant EU_{c0} \geqslant U_q \geqslant U_y$, that is, the conflict payoff at time zero must be pareto-optimal. The reason for this puzzling constraint is quite interesting. If the preference ordering of outcomes by the parties were such that $U_q > EU_{c0}$, then the parties would be locked into an infinite war of attrition because they would then adopt a strategy of $e \to 0$. By such a strategy they would reduce their rate of utility decline to a level so small they could afford almost infinite fighting time. But then the parties must lose all hope of terminating the conflict either by defeating the opponent in the battlefield or through negotiation Moreover, a strategy of $e \to 0$ would make each party extremely vulnerable to a sudden escalation by the opponent and thus highly likely to lose.

Let us see graphically what strategy can do to the conflict management game. This is shown in Figure 5.9. As this figure suggests, by employing an optimal management strategy--based essentially on force economy--Actor i can improve his situation considerably as long as j uses suboptimal management strategies. In fact, as long as this is the case, i can well hope to win this conflict.

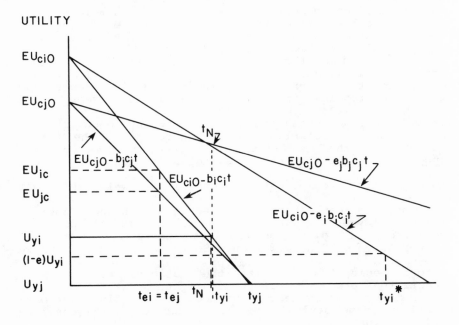

Figure 5.9   A Graphical Illustration of the Management Game

On the other hand, if only j uses optimal management strategies, he can hope at point t_{yi} to get better terms of surrender than was originally the case. However, being rational means that neither party can rely on the irrationality of the opponent. Hence, each actor selects an optimal management strategy while controlling for whatever counterstrategies the opponent may employ.

The combined use of optimal management strategies does not alter the basic conflict picture beyond the fact that it provides the parties additional fighting time. Actor i is still the expected loser of the conflict. Yet, an important structural change in the conflict process may indeed occur. The time span of $t_0 - t_N$ can be seen as a period during which the parties probe each other's strategies and establish estimates regarding the future course of the conflict. The closer the conflict approaches point t_N, the more reliably can the actors forecast its outcome. At t_N, Actor i can well see that the most he can hope to achieve through optimal force employment is additional time, but at this point he realizes that he may be able to secure for himself a better outcome by negotiation. So t_N is the point where actors begin to realize the rational basis for a negotiated termination of the conflict.

Thus, management strategies in international conflict serve several important functions. To conclude this section, let us briefly summarize them:

(1) They enable an actor to transform an unfavorable expected outcome by the combined use of force and cooperative moves (Schelling, 1966; George et al., 1972).

(2) Without optimal employment of strategy the actor is undoubtedly worse off, because he can be outmaneuvered by the optimal management strategies of the opponent.

(3) Management strategies provide the actor more fighting time and increase his ability to resist the opponent's pressure during most of the conflict process.

(4) The optimal use of management strategies may create a mutually recognized rational basis for negotiation where none has existed previously.

This last point brings us directly to the last stage of the theory, dealing with the various forms of conflict termination.

THE NEGOTIATION GAME

Conflict resolution games can actually begin when the parties arrive at complementary expectations regarding the unnegotiated outcome of the conflict. Such a meeting of minds is most likely to be observed at point t_N of the management game (which is not an equilibrium), because at this point it becomes obvious that using mixed escalation/de-escalation strategies is not sufficient for a mutually optimal (pareto-superior) outcome of the conflict. Since each party realizes that the opponent uses an optimal management strategy, the most he can do is prolong the duration of the conflict but not alter its expected substantive outcome. It is also at this point in time that the parties become aware that, by varying the U_q payoff for their opponent through settlement offers, they may be able to terminate the conflict sooner and at a lower cost than by continued fighting.

Not all conflicts end by agreement or even reach the negotiation stage. Pillar (1983, pp. 16-30) found that only 48% of all wars during the 1816-1979 period ended by negotiated settlements. Maoz (1984c) found a comparable figure (44%) for serious interstate disputes during the 1816-1976 time span. In terms of our game-theoretic model there may be several reasons for this fact. First, the conflict may reach a military conclusion before or immediately after its expected termination (t_e). Recall that the conflict payoff function represents only utility-related expectations of the parties, not actual outcomes. Especially in cases where payoffs are expected utilities their revision may be a function of actual battlefield occurrences. Thus, it may well be possible that the actual decline in the conflict payoff is faster than expected, and that one of the parties--despite the adoption of optimal management strategies--will find itself in a situation where $EU_c < U_y$, making it rational to yield. Second, a meeting of minds in terms of the intersection of expected utilities may not necessarily occur even after adoption of optimal management strategies. Thus, the most actors can do is revise their management strategies over time by reducing e such that the level of actual conflict diminishes over time to insignificant magnitudes. This is the kind of outcome defined by Maoz (1984c) as a stalemate.

Nonetheless, if a meeting of minds occurs, the parties realize that they can secure a better outcome by making offers and counteroffers that alter sequentially the utility of the cooperative outcome. In general, these offers will make U_q (which is now seen as the post-conflict status quo) a variable whose range is U_y $\leqslant U_q \leqslant U_w$. This development, with the actual decline of e and EU_{ct}, would ultimately render a cooperative solution optimal for both parties. The modeling of this process, although beyond the scope of the present study, would follow closely the abstract logic suggested by Wittman (1979) and generally supported by Pillar's (1983) case studies of wartime negotiations.

CONCLUSION

This study presented several formal ideas concerning a game-theoretic approach to the evolution of international conflicts over time. Although the discussion was in generally abstract terms which yield some quite interesting ideas, this process model is empirically testable. The concepts introduced in this study are measurable (as shown in the appendixes), and the data for their analysis is readily available. Thus, the next step in this project will be to complete the modeling of the negotiation game and to test the entire set of game models empirically.

APPENDIX 1

The purpose of this appendix is to simplify the transformation of values derived from Bueno de Mesquita (1981) into utilities by incorporating his risk-propensity index (Bueno de Mesquita, 1985).
The original value equations are:

$$V_{si} = U_{ii} - U_{ij}; \qquad V_{fi} = U_{ij} - U_{ii}$$

These equations are transformed by Bueno de Mesquita (1985) into utilities as follows:

$$U_{si} = 2 - 4 \left[(2 - (U_{ii} - U_{ij}))/4 \right]^{ri}$$

$$U_{fi} = 2 - 4 \left[(2 - (U_{ij} - U_{ii}))/4 \right]^{ri}$$

The problem with this particular value-entity transformation is twofold. First, it is very complex.

There are four constants (excluding the ri exponent) required to avoid exponentiation of negative numbers. Second, this transformation conflicts with classic utility theory in that, for example, the utility of a gain is higher than the value of a gain for a risk-averse actor, and lower than the value of gain for a risk-acceptant actor. Likewise, the utility of a loss is smaller than the value of loss for risk-averting actors and higher than the value of loss for risk-acceptant actors. This is, of course, the opposite of what utility theory suggests.

Given these problems, the modification I suggest is as follows. Let $U_{si} = U_{ii} - U_{ij}$, $U_{fi} = U_{ij} - U_{ii}$, $U_{ii} = 1$, $-1 \leqslant U_{ij} \leqslant 1$, and $0.5 \leqslant ri \leqslant 2$ (where, like Bueno de Mesquita's proposition, a risk-averse actor is one for whom $ri > 1$, a risk-neutral actor is one for whom $ri = 1$, and a risk-acceptant actor is one for whom $ri < 1$).

First, we transform U_{ij} to U_{ij}^* such that $0 \leqslant U_{ij}^* \leqslant 1$, by:

$$U_{ij}^* = \tfrac{1}{2}(1 + U_{ij})$$

Second, we redefine V_{si} and V_{fi} as:

$$V_{si}^* = U_{ii} - U_{ij}^* = 1 - \tfrac{1}{2}(1 + U_{ij}) = \tfrac{1}{2}(1 - U_{ij})$$

$$V_{fi}^* = U_{ij}^* - U_{ii} = \tfrac{1}{2}(1 + U_{ij}) - 1 = -\tfrac{1}{2}(1 - U_{ij})$$

The value-utility transformation must satisfy the following conditions:

$$V_{si}^* \geqslant U_{si}^* \text{ and } V_{fi}^* \geqslant U_{fi}^* \quad \text{iff } ri \geqslant 1$$

$$V_{si}^* < U_{si}^* \text{ and } V_{fi}^* < U_{fi}^* \quad \text{iff } ri < 1$$

Thus, modified utilities are defined as follows:

$$U_{si}^* = (V_{si}^*)^{ri} = \tfrac{1}{2}(1 - U_{ij})^{ri}$$

$$U_{fi}^* = -(v_{fi}^*)^{1/ri}$$

Similarly, for costs of war (both tangible and intangible) we need to satisfy:

$$V(C_x) \leqslant U(C_x) \quad \text{iff} \quad ri \geqslant 1$$

$$V(C_x) > U(C_x) \quad \text{iff} \quad ri < 1$$

Thus, we first transform the relevant cost term to $V(C_x) = \frac{1}{2}C_x$, and the utility of tangible and intangible costs is defined as:

$$U(C_x) = (\frac{1}{2}C_x)^{1/ri}$$

APPENDIX 2

This appendix defines all payoffs in the conflict games presented in this paper in utility and expected-utility terms.

(a) The expected utility of simultaneous war without cost (EU_{ci0}):

$$EU_{ci0} = P_c U^*_{si} + (1-P_c)U^*_{fi} = P_c[\frac{1}{2}(1-U_{ij})]^{ri} - (1-P_c)[\frac{1}{2}(1-U_{ij})]^{1/ri}$$

(b) The expected utility of simultaneous war with costs included:

$$EU_{ci} = P_c[\frac{1}{2}(1-U_{ij})]^{ri} - (1-P_c)[\frac{1}{2}(1-U_{ij})]^{1/ri} - (1-P_c)^{1/ri}$$

(c) The expected utility of self-defense (EU_{di}):

$$EU_{di} = P_d U^*_{si} + (1-P_d)U^*_{fi} - U(C_d)^*$$

$$= P_c^2[\frac{1}{2}(1-U_{ij})]^{ri} - (1-P_c^2)[\frac{1}{2}(1-U_{ij})]^{1/ri} - [1+\frac{1}{2}P_c(1-3P_c)]^{1/ri}$$

(d) The expected utility of an aggressive war is:

$$EU_{ai} = P_i U^*_{si} + (1-P_i)U^*_{fi} - U(TC_i)^* - U(IC_i)^*$$

$$= P_c(2-P_c)[\frac{1}{2}(1-U_{ij})]^{ri} - (1-P_c)^2[\frac{1}{2}(1-U_{ij})]^{1/ri} - (1-P_c)^{2/ri}$$

$$-[P_c(2-P_c)(3+U_{ij})/4]^{1/ri}$$

(e) The utility of a nonviolent victory (when j yields):

$$U_{wi} = U^*_{si} - U(IC)^* = \frac{1}{2}(1-U_{ij})^{ri} - P_c(2-P_c)(3+U_{ij})/4^{1/ri}$$

(f)   The utility of yielding (U_{yi})

$$U_{yi} = U^*_{fi} = -[\tfrac{1}{2}(1-U_{ij})]^{1/ri}$$

(g)   The utility of the status quo

$$U_q = (U^*_{ij})^{1/ri} = [\tfrac{1}{2}(1+U_{ij})]^{1/ri}$$

NOTES

1.   One could convert the U_q term into a lottery containing several states of future relations among the parties (Bueno de Mesquita, 1985).

2.   It is easy to show that this game has either no Nash equilibrium or at least one Nash equilibrium on one of the two diagonal outcomes.

3.   See a similar treatment of standardized utilities derived from ordinal games in Brams (1985, Chap. 1).

4.   This applies to the revised expected-utility model as well.   Formally, treating the utility of the status quo as a variable whose values are a function of a nation's perceptions regarding the improvement or worsening of relations with the opponent implies that, instead of assigning a constant utility to the status quo (U_q in Figures 5.2 and 5.3), we should assign it an expected-utility value (EU, as suggested by Bueno de Mesquita, 1985).   Either way the status quo will get a single value whenever j does not initiate conflict.   Yet, Propositions 1 and 2 show that it is insufficient for determining whether an actor would indeed initiate conflict.   (For more elaborate discussion of this topic, see Maoz, 1984a.)

5.   The U_s and U_f terms are defined differently than in Bueno de Mesquita (1985).   The modifications are justified in Appendix 1.   In general, we have:

$$U_{si} = [\tfrac{1}{2}(1-U_{ij})]^{ri} \quad \text{and} \quad U_{fi} = -[\tfrac{1}{2}(1-U_{ij})]^{1/ri}$$

where U_{ij} is the utility of Actor i to j's policies (Bueno de Mesquita, 1981) and ri is a risk-propensity measure, as defined in Bueno de Mesquita (1985).

6.   The following discussion explores indicators of the various probability and cost terms of the game playoffs.   While some of the indicators may seem somewhat

ad-hoc, I believe nonetheless that they possess a considerable face-validity in the sense that they represent the logic used by actual decision makers to estimate such terms subjectively.

7. Surprise attacks pose a heavy strain on the defender, at least during the initial phase of the war. In addition, they create a relatively long period of regrouping and reorganization. Consider, for example, the cases of Pearl Harbor, the German invasion of the Soviet Union in 1941, the Yom Kippur war of 1973, and, more recently, the Iraqi attack on Iran.

8. In 1940, the French army was not surprised by the timing of the German attack. Yet the German drive through the Ardennes outmaneuvered the French defenses and put the latter in a strategically inferior position, forcing them to transfer forces from the eastern Maginot line to the north. Another example is Israel's attack on Egypt on June 5, 1967. By June 2 it was fairly obvious that such an attack was imminent. Yet its precise form and scope placed a heavy strategic burden on the Egyptian army, leaving it without aerial support. A similar case could be made regarding the Japanese attack of Pearl Harbor, whose timing was not unanticipated but whose form and locus were.

9. Imagine the following situation. A nation having eight ICBMs is attacked by a nation with only two. Assuming single warheads and perfect accuracy, the most that the defender can lose is two ICBMs. However, if the stronger nation were to attack the weaker, the latter would face a high prospect of being totally disarmed even if accuracy were less than perfect.

10. So do other power functions of P_c. I do not mean to argue that stating that $P_d = f(P_c)$ necessarily implies that $f(P_c) = P^2$. Rather, the emphasis here is on a logical argument relating the probability of victory in a self-defensive war to the baseline probability in a certain way which is consistent with substantive considerations. The key of this definition is the value of the D term, which, I think, should be of the general form $D = P_c - P_c^x$ where $x > 1$.

11. The reason for defining cost as a value-based discount rate, rather than utility-based, is that cost itself must be transformed into utility terms via exponentiation by the risk-propensity measure, as are the other terms in the expected-utility equations. This point is further explicated in Appendix 1.

12. This definition can also be derived from decomposed costs of winning and losing as follows:

$$TC_s = \frac{V_s - P_x V_s}{V_s} = 1 - P_x \tag{11.1}$$

$$TC_f = \frac{V_f + (1-P_x)V_f}{V_f} = 2 - P_x \tag{11.2}$$

$$TC_x = P_x TC_s + (1-P_x)TC_f = P_x(1-P_x) + (1-P_x)(2-P_x)$$

$$= 2(1-P_x) \tag{11.3}$$

13. The i (or j) subscript is meant to suggest that intangible costs of aggression are incurred by the initiator whether the opponent resists (aggressive war), or yields (nonviolent victory). See Appendix 2.

14. U_{ij}^* is defined in Appendix 1 as $\frac{1}{2}(1+U_{ij})$, and ranges between zero and one.

15. The third condition is essential in games that contain several Nash equilibria. Since the game starts at the status quo outcome, if that outcome were one of the Nash equilibria, no party could move from it. (This is true in both myopic and nonmyopic rationality senses.)

16. See also Zagare (1977, 1979) for applied models of deception in international negotiation games.

6 Moving Forward in Time: Paths Toward a Dynamic Utility Theory of Crisis Decisions

Recently, interest has renewed in an expected-utility approach to analyzing conflict decisions. Although the expected-utility approach is not new to the international conflict literature (see Ellsberg, 1961, and Russett, 1963, for two noteworthy early examples), attempts to actually estimate the actors' utility functions for the outcomes and their expected utilities for their strategies are. This empirical approach to expected-utility models has yielded interesting results on war initiation (Bueno de Mesquita, 1981a, 1985), crisis escalation (Bueno de Mesquita, 1984; Petersen, 1983), alliance formation and dissolution (Altfeld, 1984; Berkowitz, 1983; Morrow and Newman, 1983; Newman, 1982, 1983), the link between arms races and war (Morrow, 1984c), the costs of wars (Bueno de Mesquita, 1983), deterrence (Petersen, 1982, 1984; Huth and Russett, 1984), and the intervention of third parties into ongoing wars (Altfeld and Bueno de Mesquita, 1979). Related theoretical papers cover optimal alliance formation (Morrow, 1982), the link between the distribution of power and the onset of war (Bueno de Mesquita, 1981b), the ending of wars (Wittman, 1979), and war initiation and crisis escalation (Morrow, 1984a, 1984b, 1985). The expected-utility theory treats nations as unitary rational actors; that is, a utility function can be constructed which is consistent with a nation's foreign policy acts. However, because there is no decision system which can insure that groups of rational individuals can reach rational group decisions, the theory has focused on explaining those actions, such as wars and alliances, where the political leadership of a nation will share a common basis of values and will be certain to enforce their decision on the government they lead. Signal issues of national security are most likely to satisfy these conditions, and consequently research efforts have focused on these phenomena.

Expected-utility approaches to explaining conflict depend, not surprisingly, upon the definition of the utilities. According to the classic approach of von Neumann and Morgenstern (1953), utilities are calculated to fit an individual's preferences for gambles. In practice, utilities are estimated from actions of the individual prior to the decision to be explained. By the axiom of revealed choice, an individual's preferences are reflected in the decisions he reaches, and those preferences are recoverable from those decisions. This line of reasoning suggests that we need look no farther than an individual's actions to deduce his dynamic behavior; because those actions incorporate both timing considerations (is now an appropriate time to act?) and relative preferences for the future versus the present, an empirical utility theory is completely dynamic. This argument is reminiscent of Savage's (1972) idealization of utility theory in the concept of overall decisions, the idea that an individual makes one and only one decision his entire life--how to live--and that all his actions follow from that decision. Both arguments reduce many decisions into one, which can be explored completely through simple empiricism. Furthermore, both arguments suggest that detailed examinations of decisions to develop the rationales underlying those decisions are unnecessary.

Nevertheless, existing applications of utility theory to explain international conflict are almost entirely static in nature, an observation that seems paradoxical, given the inherent dynamic nature of empirically estimated utilities. However, what appears to be a paradox is not; there is a crucial difference between the utilities generated by von Neumann-Morgenstern experiments and those used in current empirical applications of utility theory. Because we cannot obtain a complete ranking of each actor's preferences over all possible gambles, von Neumann-Morgenstern experiments cannot be conducted to determine the utilities of those actors in international conflicts. Instead, the utility functions used to represent the actors' preferences in such models are a composite of assumption and approximation. Actors' utilities are theoretically assumed to be based on several factors, which vary from actor to actor, and the values of these factors are estimated for each actor from a set of prior actions commensurate with the decision to be explained. For example, in the spatial theory of voting behavior, each voter's utility function is determined by the weighted distance of each outcome from the actor's ideal outcome in an issue space, where the ideal outcome and weights vary throughout the electorate to represent differences in individuals' preferences. Consequently, the assumptions made about the nature of actors' utility functions will color the nature of the theory; if we assume utility functions which include only static elements, we will have a static theory of decisions. The questions then are: how can we build dynamic elements into a rational decision theory of international conflict and how can we estimate those dynamic elements to arrive at an empirically useful theory?

DYNAMIC FACETS OF EXISTING RATIONAL MODELS

Before proceeding to consider the above questions, a brief examination of dynamic elements of existing expected-utility models of international conflict is in order. This examination will suggest several ways dynamic elements can be built into estimable rational models. By considering existing models, we can also perceive what possible routes to developing a dynamic empirical rational model exist, what logical and empirical blocks exist on those routes, and what steps can be taken to open those routes. This consideration will also lead to a better understanding of what a dynamic rational model is and what it can explain.

Bueno de Mesquita (1981a) made the first extensive attempt to estimate an expected-utility model of international conflict. In The War Trap, he assumed that each nation would act as if it were an expected-utility maximizer. Bueno de Mesquita's theory argues that each nation embroiled in a conflict will see two components to its utility assessment of the possible outcomes of winning and losing, the change in the losing nation's policies that the winning nation will extract as its price for ending the war and the anticipated magnitude of changes in the differences between the two nations' policies that would occur in the absence of war.[1] The second of the two components captures the notion that war is less attractive to a nation if it expects that the policy differences between itself and its opponent will shrink over time and more attractive if those differences are likely to grow over time. In the former case, war is not necessary to change the other nation's policy toward a more acceptable policy; in the latter case, war becomes attractive to forestall those anticipated differences. Using these dynamic considerations, Bueno de Mesquita deduces that allies are more likely to fight than enemies and that detente reduces the probability of war in the short run but increases it in the long run. Both of these conclusions follow from the realization that the diplomatic relationship between close allies can only deteriorate over time, while a relationship between bitter enemies can only improve over time.

These are the only two conclusions that Bueno de Mesquita deduces about how changes in the utilities over

time affect the rational calculations. The primary
reasons for the paucity of dynamic conclusions from his
expected-utility model, which includes dynamic
considerations, is the complete inability to estimate
those considerations with existing data. Bueno de
Mesquita's measure of the utility each side attaches to
the outcomes of wars is based on the assumptions that
those utilities depend only on the differences in policy
outcome and that alliance decisions will be based on the
same policy preferences as conflict decisions. From the
latter assumption, we can analyze a nation's alliance
policy to derive estimates of its relative preferences
for other nations' policies and use those estimates to
calculate its utilities for conflict outcomes. Because
alliance formations and dissolutions are relatively rare,
this index changes only slightly for most dyads in most
years. These small, almost random, changes make it
impossible to determine a meaningful measure of change in
the relationship between two nations over time by
examining changes in Bueno de Mesquita's utility
indicator, and therefore, it is impossible to estimate
the dynamic components of Bueno de Mesquita's expected-
utility model from his utility indicator. Given Bueno de
Mesquita's commitment to empirical tests of his
propositions, it is not surprising that he did not choose
to develop additional dynamic propositions that he could
not test.

The above argument assumes that changes in the
utilities are the only source of possible dynamic
behavior within an expected-utility model. Obviously,
this assumption is not true; the probability terms
certainly vary over time as the military capabilities of
the two sides rise and fall. These variations can
increase or decrease the attractiveness of war for either
side in a sustained hostile relationship. An example of
an expected-utility model that examines the effects of
changes in the distribution of probabilities over time is
discussed in Morrow (1984c). That model links the
development of arms races to the occurrence of war by
seeing how arms races can change each racing nation's
expected utility for war over time. According to this
argument, arms races cause the ratio of capabilities of
the racing sides to vary as the race progresses because
each side cannot respond instantaneously to the other
side's new armament programs. Then each party's expected
utility for war will fluctuate as the ratio of
capabilities varies. If we assume that each side will
compare the expected utility of escalating a conflict to
its expected utility for conflict at a fixed time in the
future, then the side with a temporary military advantage
will want to escalate disputes before its advantage
fades. Faced with a threat to escalate, the target of

such a threat will stand firm only if its utility for doing so is greater than its utility for making the concessions which the threatener demands. It can be shown then that arms races which induce large swings in superiority are more likely to escalate to war than those which create relatively small swings in superiority. Because each side cannot immediately match the other side's additions to its arsenal, each side will gain temporary advantages when its own armament program is at peak production, and these temporary advantages give the side which possesses them an incentive to escalate disputes to war.

This arms race model is a true dynamic model because the escalating nation compares its utility for escalation now to its utility for war later. Assuming that the value of the status quo now is the value of conflict in the future, as this approach does, represents a simplification of each nation's consideration of the stream of benefits that flows from not fighting, because it ignores the possible gains from strategies short of conflict which will induce change in the opponent's position. Such a simplification can be justified when examining arms races where the two sides by definition are engaged in a long-term rivalry. Arms races require a long-term rivalry to serve as a justification for the race; the expectation of the continuation of this rivalry through time provides each side with an obvious reason to consider the relative attractiveness of war now to war later. However, most dyadic relationships are not characterized by a long-term rivalry between the nations of the dyad. This observation undermines the possibility of using this arms race model as a prototype for a more general dynamic utility theory of international conflict. If the parties to a dispute do not expect to find themselves in conflict in the future, why should they care about future benefits and costs?

The estimation of such future costs and benefits depends upon the theory which specifies those costs and benefits. If we are satisfied with not estimating the utilities and just deducing testable propositions from an expected-utility theory, then the specification of such costs and benefits is not as great a problem. For example, consider Wittman's (1979) model of how wars end. Wittman presents a basic expected-utility model of each warring party's decision whether or not to continue an ongoing war. Although Wittman discusses the effects of different time preferences (each side's discount rate) on the settlement each side will accept, he does not exactly specify the dynamic elements of the calculation. Instead, he argues that each side's utility for winning and losing is a combination of utilities during and after the war, both discounted for time. How each side's minimal acceptable settlement changes as its discount rate changes depends upon each of the components of the expected utility. Wittman concludes that sometimes nations will prolong wars even at the cost of reducing their probability of victory if they heavily discount the future. To test this conclusion requires a measure of a nation's discount rate, whose estimation requires the specification of the costs and benefits received over time. In some sense, this approach is a logical cul-de-sac; we can deduce interesting, testable propositions, but we cannot test those propositions without facing the same question of what costs and benefits each actor will receive over time. Although Wittman's model is dynamic, it faces the same empirical problem already presented in the introduction.[2]

One type of dynamic behavior that can be considered through a rational approach is each side's time preference, showing how different values attached to future versus present outcomes can lead to different decisions. Another type of dynamic behavior that can be examined with a rational model is the interactive play of crisis tactics. Existing rational models, like The War Trap model, are static in the sense that they do not consider the possible responses to each possible move. Part of the reason for the adoption of this static approach is a belief that the choice of strategy follows obviously from an actor's evaluation of the possible strategies.[3] This approach leads to conclusions that are very broad and general about the likely outcomes of crises. For example, Bueno de Mesquita concludes that war is impossible unless the initiator has positive expected utility; this statement, while powerful in the prediction of the final outcomes of crises, tells us next to nothing about how crises develop over time or how to manage them either to reduce the probability of war or to increase the chance of success. To reach conclusions about crisis management, a theory which predicts the efficacy of different management tactics is needed. If we view crises as periods of negotiation through the tactics of escalation and concession that each side adopts, we need a theory that accounts for each side's actions at the point in time that those actions are adopted. We would then have a rational model that accounts for all of the major decisions that each nation makes in a crisis, and consequently accounts for the unfolding of the crisis by predicting each decision in sequence.

Because we would also like to know that path of decisions in order to assess the usefulness of different crisis management tactics, we need to develop a structure which examines both the path of decisions throughout a crisis and the stability of the final outcome. Of course, tracing the path of decisions and finding the final outcome are facets of the same problem, because each interim point in a crisis is an unstable outcome which then is upset by another possible outcome until a stable outcome, namely one where none of the players has an incentive to changes its strategy with or without the support of other actors, is achieved. We need to specify how actors can change their actions and when they will want to change their actions and use that framework to specify which outcomes are then stable.

A preliminary attempt to build such a framework is presented in Morrow (1984a, 1984b). This model assumes that each stage in a crisis can be represented as a triad of two competing coalitions and a means of coercion that they are employing against one another, called a challenge. A crisis progresses from one challenge to another when one of the two coalitions either recruits additional members, compromises with the other coalition, or escalates the means of coercion. Given a utility function for each reactor which represents its preferences for all possible outcomes and a probability distribution that specifies the likelihood of each outcome given a particular challenge, each actor's expected utility for each possible move that its coalition can make (recruitment, compromise, or escalation) can be calculated. One challenge supercedes another when all of the members of one coalition are better off after the change than before, whether that change be the recruitment of a new member, reaching a compromise with the other coalition, or escalating the means of coercion. Crises are then sequences of challenges where each challenge supercedes the prior challenge in the sequence. Having the complete sequence of challenges that composes a crisis provides a complete description of the composition of each side to the dispute (and consequently where and how each side gained outside support), the position that each coalition advanced and how those positions changed over the crisis, and all the escalatory actions that each side made during the dispute. Consequently, this model can provide a detailed description of the dynamic unfolding of a crisis. From any one challenge within a crisis, there are many other challenges which supercede that challenge, and thus many different resolutions to a crisis from any challenge of that crisis. The unfolding of a crisis depends then upon which of the many possible superceding challenges the actors will choose at each point in he crisis. These choices are necessarily dynamic choices because each coalition must consider the other coalition's probable response to each move it makes. To solve this problem, we need a game-theoretic solution concept that will account for how far into the future each side projects the other side's expected countermoves and chooses the best course of action given that projection.

Empirically, the estimation of this model is not yet possible. Starting with the problem of estimating each actors' spatial utility function, an ideal outcome, a matrix of saliences, and a risk attitude for each actor must be estimated. Because the first two of these three quantities are issue-specific, they cannot be estimated until detailed information is available about the actors' preferences regarding the set of issues. This information could either be directly obtained or estimated from a history of actions based on that spatial utility function. Currently, there does not exist a data set sufficiently sophisticated for such an estimation. Additionally, statistical techniques do not presently exist to perform such an estimation even if the data did exist. Still, it once appeared that the estimation of spatial utility functions for individual voters would be impossible for the same reasons, but those obstacles have been overcome. Given a commitment to direct tests of expected-utility theories, such estimation is not out of the question.

WHAT DO WE MEAN BY DYNAMIC?

As should be clear from the previous survey, what we conceive as dynamic rational behavior covers several different approaches. Dynamic behavior, as opposed to static behavior, is placed within a context of change over time. Static decision making assumes either that behavior does not change because it is at equilibrium or that the decision process can be collapsed into one grand decision. Nash equilibria are an example of static decision making of the first type; none of the players will want to change strategy at a Nash equilibrium, so to find optimal decisions we need only look for Nash equilibria. Two examples of static decision making of the second type are Bueno de Mesquita's expected-utility model and the normal form of two-person game theory. Pure strategies in the normal form of a game reduce all of a player's choices within the extensive form of the game to just a single choice of strategy that will specify that player's move at each decision node in the game.[4] The first method of developing a dynamic theory, then, is to focus on the individual choices of moves within each strategy.

Such a dynamic theory would emphasize the interplay of the disputants' bargaining tactics in a conflict. It would capture the essence of the decisions that each side faces in a crisis; unlike the traditional game-theoretic approach which assumes that crisis decisions are dictated by the choice of a grand strategy at the beginning of a crisis, the rationales for individual decisions within crises would be examined and optimal moves could be determined at each turning point in a given crisis. This type of theory would allow us to draw conclusions about the efficacy of different crisis management tactics and offer advice on which actions will produce what outcomes at specific decision points of a crisis. For example, such a dynamic theory would allow us to judge the efficacy of low-level military escalation early in crises as a means to gain each side's desired ends. We could then analyze the effectiveness of military movements and mobilizations in different situations. It is reasonable to believe that in some situations such moves are unproductive because they provoke counter-escalation from the target, while in other situations they will intimidate the target and gain the desired ends before the target's political will to resist builds. So, the first type of dynamic theory focuses on the interaction of crisis bargaining tactics between the two sides.

This approach immediately presents us with an important question: given that actions may be taken that in the short run are unwise, but that in the long run produce benefits, how far into the future do actors project the consequences of their decisions when deciding? Do actors choose their actions in response to the current situation or do they anticipate changes in their opponent's actions? The former approach adopts a static view of decisions; each actor views the current situation as fixed and changes its actions to reach the best possible preferred outcome. The latter approach recognizes that the interplay of decisions is dynamic and interdependent, with each actor choosing the course of action that it believes will best help secure the most advantageous final outcome. Such an approach would include threats, decoys, and bluffs as desirable tactics because they induce changes in the other actor's behavior which are beneficial to the first actor. In games in the normal form, the opponent's strategy choice is considered in choosing an optimal strategy, but the dynamic interplay within the game is eliminated, since all the choices of moves are compressed into one choice of a strategy that specifies all those moves. N-person game-theoretic solutions only specify the set of outcomes that will compose the solution; they do not describe the path of coalition formation and negotiation that lead through the game to the final outcome. In a model where each choice of move is considered as an independent decision, an actor could simply choose the best response to the opponent's prior move or anticipated next move. The former rationale is referred to as Cournot rationality, the latter as Stackelberg rationality. These terms arise from economic models of duopoly in which each firm's choice of selling price and level of production depends upon the other firm's choice. An actor using Cournot rationality is like a chess player who only responds to the immediate positioning of pieces on the board without considering any countermoves by the opponent; an actor using Stackelberg rationality, then, would consider one and only one countermove by the opponent. Obviously, there are even more sophisticated levels of rationality where the actors project their opponents' actions even further into the future.

In conflicts, each nation's choice of action at each point in time will depend upon the other nation's actions, and consequently the question of Cournot versus Stackelberg rationality presents itself. Furthermore, there is no reason to believe that, if crisis negotiation is expected to occur over an extended period, an actor would not choose actions that are best response neither to the opponent's current actions or anticipated reactions, but rather to even later actions in the crisis. There should be a range of rationales from the short-sighted Cournot rationality to the patient, long-run maximizing rationality. Ideally, we might expect that all actors would adopt the latter form of rationality, choosing each act to maximize their final payoff at the termination of the conflict. However, it seems more plausible to believe that actors will adopt all of the possible ranges of anticipation in their deliberations, sometimes adopting a long-run perspective on their choice of tactics and other times looking only at the short-run responses to their actions.[5] Later in this paper, I will suggest some ideas of when actors will adopt these different rationales in their decisions.

The second method of developing a dynamic theory of international conflict is to model each actor evaluation of its future benefits from its actions. Unlike static models, this approach assumes that actors evaluate the streams of benefits and costs that flow from a decision rather than just the immediate net gain. To specify such a rational model, we need to identify the stream of outcomes that flows from each available action and each actor's relative preference for outcomes in the near future as opposed to outcomes in the far future, or, since the latter is better known, each actor's discount rate. To estimate such a rational model, we would also need to estimate both the stream of benefits that flow from different actions and each actor's discount rate. Given that the stream of benefits can be specified and quantified for the available actions, an actor's discount rate could be estimated from its chosen actions over time. At first glance, then, there appear to be few

empirical blocks to introducing dynamic elements into the
utility calculations, provided that the streams of
outcomes that flow from different actions can be
specified. However, such specification of a complete
stream of outcomes could be quite difficult, because
future outcomes will depend upon not only the action
under consideration but the future actions of other
nations. To specify a complete stream of outcomes over
all time would require estimating all expected future
actions. One way around this problem is to notice that
we can introduce considerations about future outcomes
without including all future outcomes in the calculation.
For instance, Bueno de Mesquita entered a limited
consideration of future outcomes in The War Trap model by
including the terms for the expected change in utilities
over a fixed period of time. No matter how the addition
of future expectations is done, their addition to the
estimated expected utilities will move the model into the
realm of dynamic decision making.

A third method of adding dynamic elements to a
rational choice model is to model decisions as
time-dependent calculations. This approach assumes that
the decision to be made is when to act, rather than how
to act. To pursue this approach, we must assume that the
actors always wish to carry out certain actions, like the
initiation of a crisis, but are simply waiting for the
most advantageous time. Axelrod's (1979) model of
surprise is exactly this type of dynamic model; each
nation determines when to spring its surprise by
comparing the advantage gained now to the expected value
of waiting to employ the surprise in the future. Games
of timing fall into this category of dynamic rational
models. In the prototypical game of timing, two actors
face off in a duel in which the longer an actor waits,
the higher the probability of hitting the opponent
becomes. Of course, if the opponent shoots first, there
is always a chance that he will hit and win the game.
Each player then must choose an optimal time to shoot by
comparing the advantage of waiting for a higher hit
probability to the advantage of firing first by shooting
sooner. Games of timing are useful models for
determining when actors will implement strategies that
they have already decided to employ. However, we must
assume that the question of when to enact the strategy is
the only decision to be reached. A more elaborate model
could attempt to integrate both the choice of strategy
and the choice of timing into one decision model. It
would be a "true" dynamic model in the sense that all
decisions would be functions of their timing, and thus be
time-dependent. Some actions would be preferable at
different times simply because the time was right. To
test such models, we would need to predict the time

dependence of different actions and be capable of estimating those time dependences.

Several of these different facets of dynamic rational behavior can be included in one model. However, the three facets are distinct in that each captures a distinguishable notion of what we think of as dynamic behavior. We can focus on the dynamics of interaction between two nations in crisis, or the dynamic effects of future versus present outcomes, or the idea of the dynamic timing of actions. What we need now is a better idea of how such models could be constructed.

SOME POSSIBLE DYNAMIC RATIONAL MODELS

The first type of dynamic model to be considered specifies the stream of outcomes that will flow from the different choices of a given decision and then selects the choice that will provide the "best" stream of present and future outcomes. The most general form of such a calculation is a present value calculation like that used in investment theory in economics. The present value of an alternative is the sum of the values of all the outcomes that result from that alternative discounted for the passage of time. For investments, this calculation is just the value of the income stream that flows from the investment; given a discount rate for the investor, the present value of an investment is just the sum of the income received from the investment, discounted by how far in the future the income is received.[6] (Normally, such calculations are performed on continuous income streams using integrals to sum the continuous payments received.) Present value calculations could be applied, for example, to explain alliance formation. Alliances are durable goods in the sense that the allies generally do not form an alliance solely for the immediate benefits it bestows, but rather to gain those benefits over a period of time, until the alliance is no longer in the interest of the allies. An alliance will then generate a stream of benefits (and costs) over time that each ally will have to evaluate when deciding whether or not to form the alliance. Given that we can estimate a nation's discount rate and the net benefits of each possible alliance, we can determine the alliance(s) that nation will form by comparing all alliances and choosing those which have positive net present value.

The problem with this approach to alliance formation is the difficulty of estimating the benefit streams that flow from each alliance. Traditionally, it has been assumed that security is the benefit that nations gain through their alliance policies. However, recent evidence suggests that security is not the sole motivation behind alliances (Newman, 1982; Morrow and Newman, 1983). First of all, not all historical alliances increased security for both parties to the alliance; if security was the sole motivation for alliances, alliances which reduce either ally's security would never form. Second, even those nations which form security-increasing alliances never form the complete set of alliances needed to maximize their security. The latter evidence suggests that even if security is the only benefit gained from an alliance, there are sufficient non-security costs to alliances to discourage nations from forming all the alliances needed to maximize their security. Rational-choice theoretical perspectives on alliance formation and dissolution drawn from the theory of the consumer (Altfeld, 1984) model alliance decisions as trade-offs between several "goods," of which security is only one (other possible alliance "goods" are political autonomy and control over one's allies' economic and domestic policies). Because these trade-offs vary with each nation's preferences, different nations will assign different values to the same alliance. Although the calculation of the present value is easy, given the value of the stream of outcomes, the determination of that value stream is not. Of course, we could have the actors maximize the present value of the utilities of the stream of outcomes, but as stated in the introduction, utility is a concept of limited usefulness unless we can account for it in terms of primitive quantities, like security. Unlike the investment example considered earlier, in which utility increases with the present monetary value of an investment, we cannot reduce the actors' utilities for the outcome streams to a single quantity for which more is always better. Unless we can find a way of estimating an actor's utility function (which cannot be done using static models presently), we cannot estimate an actor's present value for the different options.

The next approach to developing dynamic models is through greater explication of the dynamic setting of decisions. By analyzing individual decisions within the chain of events of a crisis, we can model how the sequence of decisions (and the events triggered by those decisions) unfold over the life of a crisis. Game theory, once we turn from the normal form of a game to the extensive form, provides the best possible framework for this approach to a dynamic rational model. A game presented in extensive form specifies each of the players' choices at each node of the game and the possible consequences that follow from those choices. Models of crises can be built that present a general extensive-form game for crises; obviously, no two crises are the same, but there are sufficient common elements among them that a general game of crises could be developed (otherwise, it would be pointless to study past crises). At the present, such models do not exist, and their development requires extensive theoretical and empirical work.

Still, there are possible approaches to this development that we can consider in detail. One way to build an extensive form game is to examine repeated applications of static decisions to see how the sequence of decisions unfolds over time. An example of this approach can be drawn out of Morrow's (1982) model of optimal alliance formation. This model defines a nation's security to be the sum of all other nations' expected utility for war against that nation, because each nation's expected utility gives the level of concessions that nation will demand not to go to war with the nation whose security is being determined. A decision rule for forming alliances is found by maximizing security with respect to the deciding nation's utility for each possible ally. Whenever nation pursues the strategy explicated by this decision rule, a Nash equilibrium which maximizes each nation's security results. Because the result is a Nash equilibrium, this theory of optimal foreign policy is inherently static; it is possible that a nation could gain in the long run by adopting other strategies than its Nash strategy in the hope that its new strategy would produce changes in other nations' strategies that it could exploit to its own advantage. For instance, one nation might choose to form an alliance with one of its enemies, reducing its security in the short run but possibly breaking up that other nation's other alliances and increasing the original nation's security in the end. Empirical work that has examined alliance formation and dissolution from the security-maximizing perspective (Berkowitz, 1983; Morrow and Newman, 1983; Newman, 1982) is also static in approach because it only considers the immediate security effects of alliances.

One way to build toward a dynamic security-maximizing theory of alliances would be to consider an iterated model based on the static decision rule. The Nash equilibrium could be calculated, and then the strategy of one nation could be changed away from its equilibrium strategy to see whether that move produces changes in other nations' strategies that are beneficial for the first nation. This procedure would determine which non-Nash strategies are advantageous in the long run and would allow the testing of possible counters to those strategies. By repeated application of static decision rules, a first approximation of the dynamic consequences of decisions could be developed.

Such an approach is best described as an enlightened Cournot rationality. An actor employing Cournot rationality will adopt the best response to the opponent's prior move, rather than evaluating the possible counters to each new move and adopting the course of action which is most difficult to counter. The above procedure is an enlightened Cournot rationality in that it assumes that actors judge the efficacy of their strategies by following the sequence of Cournot decisions that flow from each strategy and choosing the strategy which produces the most preferred final outcome. Optimal dynamic strategies are found by working backwards from the final outcomes and eliminating each strategy that produces an inferior outcome for that actor in the end.[7] After completing this elimination procedure for all possible alliances, we have left the structure of an extensive-form game for alliance formation. In a normal form of this game, the strategies would specify what patterns of alliances will maximize security; in the extensive form, optimal dynamic strategies would specify which alliances (if any) should be formed at each decision point.

The calculation of such optimal dynamic strategies depends upon the ability to project the opponent's actions into the future. The eventual consequences of each action must be deducible in order to determine which possible move has the best final consequences. When such consequences cannot be determined (even up to a probability distribution) or are uncertain, optimal dynamic strategies cannot be determined. This problem brings us to a third possible approach to dynamic rational models, limited information models. These models arise from games with incomplete information, where the players do not know all the moves available to their opponents, the probability distributions of the outcomes that result from each combination of moves, or each other's utility functions for the outcomes. These models eliminate the assumption of complete information, providing a more general model of the conditions under which crisis decisions are reached. Because little is known about games under incomplete information (Owen, 1982), existing limited-information models loosen one of the above three assumptions of complete information and then examine what optimal strategies exist in the resulting games. For example, Fudenberg and Tirole's (1984) model of market bargaining when both the buyer and the seller do not know the reservation price of the other eliminates the assumption that the players know each other's utility function. Limited information models examine how the flow of information affects an actor's estimates of the other actors' likely moves and, thus, its best moves. Actors are assumed to have prior probability distributions over the unknown parameters and use the available information to update those distributions in a Bayesian fashion. Then the order in which the actors receive information will have immense importance in what decisions they reach. This perspective raises two questions: one, how can one collect information in order to reach the "best" decision, and two, how can one manipulate other actors' information in order that the first actor receives "better" outcomes? If we view crises as extended bargaining periods through the escalatory and conciliatory actions of the actors where each actor is transmitting information about its preferences over the possible outcomes, then the choice of action is a matter of information flow. Because those actions and the resulting information flow change over time, limited-information models are inherently dynamic.

An example of a limited-information model can be developed out of the problem of war termination. From this approach, each warring party enters a war with a (subjective) probability distribution over the possible outcomes of the war (Wittman, 1970; Morrow, 1985). As the war progresses and each side faces military successes and failures on the battlefield, each side will revise its probability distribution of the final outcomes. Because each side's calculation of the attractiveness of continuing the war depends upon this changing probability distribution, if we could determine when and how this distribution changes over time with changes in the military fortunes of both sides, we could determine when wars should end and which types of military actions are most likely to end wars. The warring parties are assumed to be Bayesians when they re-estimate their probability distributions, but we would also need to know their prior distributions and their evaluations of each event in the war in order to calculate their posterior probability distribution of outcomes. Such calculations are even more complicated, because the actors not only have to update their probability distributions of the outcomes, but also their estimates of their opponents' utility functions for those outcomes, all from the same information gained from the battlefield and the negotiation table.

One interesting possibility that arises out of limited-information models is an ability to distinguish when actors will employ Cournot rationality and when they will employ more sophisticated forms of rationality in reaching their decisions. Because the more sophisticated forms of rationality require the ability to project the opponent's moves into the future in order to calculate the best possible move, those forms of rationality can only be employed when the opponent's moves can be easily projected into the future. When the opponent's future moves cannot be projected into the future because of a lack of information about its utility function, the calculations which underlie sophisticated rationality collapse. When information about the opponent, its capabilities, and its intentions is limited, we should expect actors to employ Cournot-like rationality, reacting only to their opponents' latest actions. Limited-information models can account for when actors will use the different kinds of rationality, because they specify what information actors have and when additional information will have a great impact on their calculations. An actor's decision of what degree of rationality to apply to an individual decision will vary in a limited-information model, allowing the actor to adapt to the available information and the degree of calculation that information permits. Limited-information models, thus, hold out not just the promise of a more general rational model, but also the hope of resolving the question of how extensively rational actors calculate.

CONCLUSION

This paper has discussed possible paths toward developing an estimable expected-utility model of international conflict. Dynamic aspects of existing expected-utility models were reviewed, the concept of dynamic rational behavior was explored for its different facets, and possible approaches to dynamic rational models that are estimable were considered. The development of a dynamic expected-utility model whose primitive quantities can be estimated is still a long way off. Given that there is not agreement at present on the proper form of a static expected-utility model, it is premature to jump into the full-scale development of a dynamic rational model. For instance, the question of what game-theoretic concepts should be added to existing static expected-utility models to account for the interdependence of the actors' strategy choices is completely unresolved. Nevertheless, some dynamic elements should be introduced into expected-utility models now, if only for the reason that static approximations of some types of dynamic behavior may be completely inappropriate. Further, some dynamic questions, such as the choice between Cournot rationality and more sophisticated degrees of rationality, are vital to the building of both static and dynamic rational models. Development of these models should proceed on both levels.

One problem confronting th further development of both static and dynamic rational models is a lack of appropriate data to estimate both the utilities and capabilities needed in the models. Currently, all the primitives used in the estimation of the utilities are derived from alliance data, following the idea that alliance decisions are based on security considerations similar to those of crisis decisions. Unfortunately, it is hard to see how additional primitive concepts, like discount rates or reactions to uncertainty, could be drawn from that data. Without more detailed data that will allow both a better estimation of present theoretical primitives and a possible estimation of yet-unmeasured primitives, direct empirical tests of future models may not be possible. Nevertheless, these problems, because of their ease of remedy, should not discourage the further development of both static and dynamic rational models.

NOTES

1. Bueno de Mesquita breaks each nation's expected utility for war into bilateral and multilateral calculations where the latter is a marginal adjustment to the former for the expected effects of third parties. Because both calculations contain both components, there is no need to consider the two calculations separately for our purposes.

2. It should be pointed out, however, that Wittman's approach does not require as complete a specification of the dynamic calculation as a complete estimation of the expected utilities would. If we can find empirical referents which are related to the underlying theoretical concepts (e.g., an indicator that is linked to a nation's discount rate without providing a measure of the latter), derived propositions can be tested even when it is unlikely that those empirical referents would provide sufficient information for the estimation of a dynamic calculation.

3. Wagner (1984) takes Bueno de Mesquita (1981a and b) to task for adopting an expected-utility approach instead of a game-theoretic approach, on the grounds that each actor's choice of strategy necessarily depends upon its opponent's strategy. Although Wagner is technically correct in this criticism, it would be extremely useful to determine how the actors evaluate the relative desirability of the different outcomes in order to determine what game they are playing. Such an evaluation is an expected-utility calculation very similar to the calculation that Bueno de Mesquita considers in detail.

4. If we examine the moves specified by each strategy, we can reach conclusions about the dynamics of those moves within the game. However, when strategies

are given in the normal form, it is rare that the link between those strategies and the moves within the extensive form of the game are presented. Instead, most work on games in the normal form starts with the strategies as given and analyzes what pure or mixed strategies are optimal for the players.

5. The long run here means the termination of the crisis, rather than some notion of outcomes in the distant future, with the short run being the immediate state of the crisis. Consequently, we cannot use discount rates, which measure a nation's relative preference for the present over the future, to assess the length of its vision in projecting its opponent's counters to its own actions.

6. Alternatively, the present value of a continuous stream of income is always equal to the discounted value at some point in the future by the mean-value theorem for integrals. How far in the future this point is located varies with the stream and the discount rate, but we could use these points to simplify the comparison between different options, provided that they do not vary greatly from one option to another. Under this approach, each actor would compare the value of each option at this future time, referred to as a time horizon, to determine which course is preferred. The main caveat here is that the time horizon varies from option to option because it depends upon the value of the present value integral. Still, time-horizon models often produce the same conclusions as present-value models and are easier to use.

7. This backwards-elimination procedure is very similar to the procedure used in the determination of sophisticated voting strategies, where the consequences of each possible voting strategy are examined and dominated strategies are eliminated.

_____ **Part 2**
Escalation Processes

7 Heuristic Decision Rules, the Dynamics of the Arms Race, and War Initiation

Previous analyses or models of military procurement or the arms race typically assume either that the process of arms acquisition is mechanistic and autonomous, and hence not explicitly limited to defense decision makers, as in the Richardson model of arms races, or that arms acquisitions are based on rational choices, given certain defense objectives and certain constraints with respect to arms production and the reaction of the opponent.[1] Modeling the arms race as either a mechanistic or an optimizing process, however, fails to account for the institutions of defense decision making. To the extent that these institutions are large, complex, bureaucratic organizations, as indeed they are, they tend to rely on neither passive mechanical responses nor on explicit optimization rules but rather on rules of thumb or heuristic decision rules with regard to weapons procurement. Thus, the defense bureaucracies establish certain rules to guide their conduct, specifically their choices with regard to arms acquisitions. These rules may be based, in part, on some optimizing behavior in the past or over a long-run horizon or on the part of certain components of the bureaucratic organization. They may, however, also be based on history, attitudes of decision makers, interservice rivalry, and other institutional aspects of the defense bureaucracy.

An example of such a decision rule is British naval policy in the period preceding World War I, when the navy was the principal component for projecting force world-wide. British naval policy at that time was to have a navy capable of defeating the combined fleets of the two next-largest naval powers. This decision rule was based on institutions, history, and some degree of analysis of

This research was completed under collaborative grants on "Behavioral and Economic Foundations of Arms Races" from the National Science Foundation, whose support is gratefully acknowledged.

the capabilities required for Britain to retain its naval preeminence and to meet its responsibilities. Another example is recent US policy on conventional force capabilities, which calls for forces sufficient to fight one and one-half wars at the same time, i.e., a major conflict plus a separate local conflict. A third example is US policy on strategic capabilities, which calls for sufficient force levels to enable the United States to survive a Soviet first strike and inflict unacceptable levels of damage on a second strike to the Soviet Union, the policy of deterrence by assured destruction. In all three cases decisions on weapons procurement can be described in a two-stage process involving, first, a bureaucratic-political decision to establish a certain rule or goal and, second, an economic decision on the rate of accumulation of weapons to achieve the rule or goal.

In this chapter we treat alternative decision rules with regard to weapons procurement and their implications for stability and war initiation in the context of a dynamic model of an arms race. The dynamic model of an arms race is one we have previously developed to study the interaction between two opposing superpowers, each of which is capable of striking at the homeland of the other, such as in the US-Soviet arms race. Each superpower chooses to build (or destroy) weapons according to a decision rule, and we investigate the implications of arms acquisitions not only for purposes of deterrence, as in the US strategic policy above, but also for purposes of attack, parity, and superiority. We are concerned with identifying whether there is a stable equilibrium or, alternatively, whether there is an unstable equilibrium or no equilibrium exists, and we find that all such cases are possible. We are also concerned with the implications of these alternative cases for the probability of nuclear war. The second section summarizes deterring and initiating regions in the weapons plane, based on an explicit model of a nuclear war. A third section identifies possible decision rules and the resulting "gaps" in weapons, comparing desired and actual levels. The fourth section derives optimal investment behavior on the basis of a given decision rule and gap. Section five uses the implied differential equations to study gaps relative to some target levels of arms and their implications for dynamic stability in terms of the nature of the arms race and for crisis stability in terms of the probability of war initiation. Our conclusions are then presented.

DETERRING AND INITIATING REGIONS IN THE WEAPONS PLANE

The decision rules we will analyze for their implications with regard to the dynamics of the arms race and war initiation will be studied in the context of deterring and initiating regions in the weapons plane. We treat the interaction between two superpowers, each of which has the capability of attacking the homeland of the other with weapons of mass destruction which can be targeted against enemy weapons or cities. The case is specifically the interaction between the United States and the Soviet Union, each of which has missiles and bombers capable of delivering nuclear weapons to the homeland of the other. We treat in our model Countries A and B, each of which has at any instant of time t a certain number of missiles, $M_A(t)$ and $M_B(t)$, representing a point in the weapons plane of all pairs (M_A, M_B). An arms race is the interactive acquisition of weapons by the two nations, and it is summarized by the paths over time of the numbers of weapons on both sides, given by a trajectory over a time interval in the weapons plane. In order to relate the arms race implied by alternative decision rules to stability against the outbreak of war it is necessary to specify the nature of war initiation. We do so by specifying a model of a missile war and applying this model to war initiation in order to identify deterring and initiating regions in the weapons plane.[2]

Our model of a missile war analyzes the causes of changes over time in the number of missiles and casualties in both countries during a possible war.[3] The model consists of a system of four differential equations with initial boundary conditions, and it determines the evolution over time of the war as a result of initial numbers of weapons on both sides, strategic decisions made by both countries, and the effectiveness of weapons against both counterforce targets (enemy weapons) and countervalue targets (enemy cities).

The variables of the model are $M_A(t)$ and $M_B(t)$, which, as already noted, represent the missiles in Countries A and B at time t. The model consists of the following differential equations for changes in each of these four variables and accompanying boundary conditions:

$$\dot{M}_A = -\alpha M_A - \beta' \beta M_B f_B \qquad \text{such that} \quad M_A(0) = M_A^0 \qquad (1)$$

$$\dot{M}_B = -\beta M_B - \alpha' \alpha M_A f_A \qquad \text{such that} \quad M_B(0) = M_B^0 \qquad (2)$$

$$\dot{C}_A = (1 - \beta')\beta M_B v_B \qquad \text{such that} \quad C_A(0) = 0 \qquad (3)$$

$$\dot{C}_B = (1 - \alpha')\alpha M_A v_A \qquad \text{such that} \quad C_B(0) = 0 \qquad (4)$$

The war starts at time t = 0, at which point, as shown in the boundary conditions, Country A has M_A^0 missiles, Country B has M_B^0 missiles, and there are no casualties on either side. Country A launches its missiles at rate $\alpha(t)$, so $-\alpha M_A$ in (1) represents the reduction in A missiles due to its decisions to launch some. Similarly, $-\beta M_B$ in (2) represents the reduction in B missiles due to launch decisions. The dependence of M_A, M_B, α, β, and other variables on time is omitted in equations (1)-(4) for convenience.

Missiles can be targeted counterforce at enemy missiles or countervalue at enemy cities. If A uses the counterforce proportion $\alpha'(t)$ at time t, then, of the αM_A missiles launched at this time, $\alpha' \alpha M_A$ are launched at B missiles while $(1-\alpha')\alpha M_A$ are launched at B cities. If $f_A(t)$ is the counterforce effectiveness of A missiles at time t, i.e., the number of B missiles destroyed per A counterforce missile, then $\alpha'\alpha M_A F_A$ represents the B missiles destroyed by A counterforce missiles, as shown in equation (2). Similarly, $\beta'\beta M_B f_B$ in equation (1) represents the A missiles destroyed by B counterforce missiles, where $f_B(t)$ is the counterforce effectiveness of B missiles. If $v_A(t)$ is the countervalue effectiveness of A missiles, i.e., the number of B casualties inflicted per A countervalue missile, then $(1-\alpha')\alpha M_A v_A$ represents the B casualties inflicted by A countervalue missiles, as shown in equation (4). Similarly, $(1-\beta')\beta M_B v_B$ in equation (3) represents the A casualties inflicted by B countervalue missiles, where $v_B(t)$ is the countervalue effectiveness of B missiles.

The evolution of the war over time, as summarized by the dynamic model (1)-(4), thus depends on the initial levels of missiles, M_A^0, M_B^0; strategic decisions on both sides regarding rates of fire, $\alpha(t)$, $\beta(t)$; strategic decisions on both sides regarding targeting, $'(t)$, $'(t)$; the effectiveness of missiles of both sides against enemy missiles, $f_A(t)$, $f_B(t)$; and the effectiveness of missiles of both sides against enemy cities, $v_A(t)$, $v_B(t)$.

From the viewpoint of either one of the countries, the problem of **grand strategy** is that of choosing both a rate of fire and a targeting strategy. For Country A, the rate of fire α can range between zero and some maximum rate $\bar{\alpha}$, determined on the basis of technical characteristics of weapons. Similarly, the counterforce proportion α' can range between 0 and 1, where $\alpha' = 1$ is pure counterforce targeting (no cities) and $\alpha' = 0$ is pure countervalue targeting (only cities). Omitting intermediate values, which, in fact, would never be used, the two extreme values for each of the two strategic variables for Country A yield four alternatives for grand strategy for A:

(1) **Maximum rate/counterforce,** where A fires its missiles at the maximum rate ($\alpha = \bar{\alpha}$) and targets only B missiles ($\alpha' = 1$), destroying as many enemy missiles as possible--a **first-strike strategy.**

(2) **Maximum rate/countervalue,** where A fires its missiles at the maximum rate ($\alpha = \bar{\alpha}$) and targets only B cities ($\alpha' = 0$), inflicting as many enemy casualties as possible--a **massive retaliation strategy.**

(3) **Zero rate/counterforce** , where A holds its missiles in reserve ($\alpha = 0$) and targets only B missiles ($\alpha' = 1$), threatening to strike enemy missiles--a **limited strategic war strategy.**

(4) **Zero rate/countervalue,** where A holds its missiles in reserve ($\alpha = 0$) and targets only B cities ($\alpha' = 0$), threatening to strike enemy cities--a **war of nerves strategy.**

Assuming that Country A treats the Country B strategy as fixed, rather than trying to influence it, and that A has the goal of maximizing a payoff function

$$P_A = P_A[M_A(T), M_B(T), C_A(T), C_B(T)] \ , \quad \frac{\partial P_A}{\partial M_A(T)} > 0, \quad \frac{\partial P_A}{\partial M_B(T)} < 0,$$

$$\frac{\partial P_A}{\partial C_A(T)} < 0, \quad \frac{\partial P_A}{\partial C_B(T)} \gtrless 0 \tag{5}$$

which depends on missiles and casualties in both countries at the end of the war, time T. It has been shown that Country A will select at any one time in the war t (where $0 < t < T$) one of these four grand strategies.[4] In particular, while A could choose some rate of fire intermediate between 0 and α, it is optimal for it to choose only one of these extreme values, firing missiles at either the zero or the maximum rate. Similarly, while A could choose some counterforce proportion intermediate between 0 and 1, it is optimal for it to choose only one of these extreme values, firing missiles at only enemy cities or enemy missiles. Thus, A is confined to the above four possibilities for grand strategy. Furthermore, given the payoff function in (5) and the differential equations and boundary conditions describing the evolution of the war in (1)-(4), it is optimal for A to make a single switch in its rate of fire, namely a switch from the maximum rate $\alpha = \bar{\alpha}$ to the zero rate $\alpha = 0$. Similarly, it is optimal for A to make a single switch in its targets, as summarized by the counterforce proportion, namely a switch from pure counterforce targeting $\alpha' = 1$ to pure countervalue targeting $\alpha' = 0$.

If Country A uses its optimal strategy the war proceeds in three stages: it starts the war with a first-strike strategy ($\alpha = \bar{\alpha}$ and $\alpha' = 1$), the situation in which it has not yet switched either strategic choice variable, and it ends the war with a war of nerves strategy ($\alpha = 0$ and $\alpha' = 0$), the situation in which it has switched both of the strategic choice variables. The middle stage of the war can be either one of massive retaliation strategy ($\alpha = \bar{\alpha}$ and $\alpha' = 0$) if the switching time for targets precedes that for the rate, or of limited strategic war strategy ($\alpha = 0$ and $\alpha' = 1$) if the switching time for the rate precedes that for targets. Country A thus starts the war using only counterforce targeting at the maximum rate of fire, so as to destroy as many as possible of the enemy missiles; ends the war by holding enemy cities as hostages, placing itself in the best possible position for extracting concessions or a desired settlement of the war; and, depending upon which switching time occurs first, during the middle stage of the war either inflicts massive casualties in Country B or holds its missiles in reserve, threatening enemy missiles.

To use this model to analyze heuristic decision rules, the arms race, and war initiation we reinterpret it in an essential way. It is treated not as a model of an actual war but rather as a model of a hypothetical or potential war, i.e., a war that might break out at any time. Thus, the model is treated not as a representation of actual missiles, casualties, strategic choices, etc., but rather as a representation of plans for a war, including expected missiles, casualties, strategic choices, etc., that are foreseen as possible situations by defense planners. The model is thus a representation of war simulations or war scenarios used by defense analysts, e.g., those in the Pentagon or the Kremlin.

From the vantage point of defense analysts in Country A the model can be used to simulate various possible scenarios. Of particular importance are two cases. The first case is that in which B attacks A. A then simulates the effect of the B attack and its own retaliation. In this case defense analysts in A would seek to have enough missiles to deter B by threatening it with unacceptable levels of casualties in its retaliatory strike. The second case is that in which A contemplates a first-strike attack on B. Its defense analysts would seek to destroy enough B missiles to disarm it and render a retaliatory strike ineffectual. These two cases represent Country A as a deterrer and an attacker, respectively.

In the first case, with Country A as a deterrer, its defense analysts should anticipate, as in the last section, that B will strike first, using a first-strike strategy ($\beta = \bar{\beta}' = 1$) over the time interval from 0 to θ_B, before A can retaliate. A would then respond with a massive retaliation strategy ($\alpha = \bar{\alpha}$, $\alpha' = 0$), inflicting casualties in B over the retaliation time interval from θ_B to $\theta_B + \psi_A$.[5] If defense planners in A simulate the result of this scenario they can solve the differential equations (1)-(4) using these strategic values, if we can assume for this simulated war outbreak that f_B is constant over the first-strike interval θ_B and v_A is constant over the retaliation interval ψ_A. These are reasonable assumptions if both intervals are relatively short, e.g., measured in minutes. The solution for the casualties in Country B at the end of the retaliatory interval is then

$$C_B(\theta_B+\psi_A) = v_A[M_A^0 - f_B(1-\exp(-\bar{\beta}\theta_B))M_B^0][1-\exp(-\bar{\alpha}\psi_A)], \quad (6)$$

showing explicitly the dependence of simulated casualties on initial number of missiles M_A^0, M_B^0; rates of fire $\bar{\alpha}$, $\bar{\beta}$; missile effectiveness ratios f_B, v_A; and the time intervals θ_B, ψ_A. If this expected number of casualties is sufficiently large, then A would deter B. In particular, if the minimum unacceptable number of casualties in B is $\bar{C}_B$ then solving

$$C_B(\theta_B + \psi_A) > \bar{C}_B \tag{7}$$

for M_A^0, the number of A missiles required to deter B (by threatening an unacceptable level of casualties) is given as

$$M_A > f_B(1-\exp(-\bar{\beta}\theta_B))M_B + \frac{\bar{C}_B}{V_A(1-\exp)(-\bar{\alpha}\psi_A))}, \tag{8}$$

where M_A^0 and M_B^0 have been replaced by M_A and M_B, respectively, since the model is one of a simulated war which can start at any time. This inequality shows the number of missiles required for A to deter B as an explicit function of the number of B missiles (and also the technical parameters $\bar{\alpha}$, $\bar{\beta}$, f_B, v_A; timing parameters θ_B, ψ_A; and the minimum unacceptable number of B casualties $\bar{C}_B$). Geometrically, this inequality is the area to the right of the line marked "A deters" in the weapons plane in Figure 7.1 with intercept $C_B/[v_A(1-\exp(-\bar{\alpha}\psi_A))]$ on the M_A axis and with slope $1/[f_B(1-\exp(-\bar{\beta}\theta_B))]$.

In the second case, with Country A as an attacker, defense analysts in A anticipate attacking B, using the first-strike strategy ($\alpha = \bar{\alpha}$, $\alpha' = 1$) over the time interval from 0 to θ_A before B can retaliate. They then have to consider the effects of B responding with a massive retaliation strategy ($\bar{\beta} = \bar{\beta}$, $\beta < 0$) over the retaliatory time interval from θ_A to $\theta_A + \psi_B$. Solving the differential equations (once again assuming that the time intervals are sufficiently short that f_A can be treated as constant over the first-strike interval and f_B can be treated as constant over the retaliation time interval), the casualties anticipated by defense planners in A in this simulated war outbreak are $C_A(\theta_A + \psi_B)$, a case similar to that of equation (6), interchanging the roles of A and B. If defense planners in A regard $\hat{C}_A$ as a maximum acceptable level of casualties, then, solving

$$C_A(\theta_A + \psi_B) < \hat{C}_A \tag{9}$$

for M_A (= M_A^0) yields

$$M_A > [\frac{1}{f_A(1-\exp(-\bar{\alpha}\theta_A))}] M_B - \frac{\hat{C}_A}{f_A(1-\exp(-\bar{\alpha}\theta_A))v_B(1-\exp(-\bar{\beta}\psi_B))} \tag{10}$$

This inequality shows the number of A missiles required for A to attack B as an explicit function of the number of B missiles (and also the technical parameters $\bar{\alpha}$, $\bar{\beta}$, f_A, v_B; timing parameters θ_A, ψ_B; and the maximum acceptable number of A casualties C_A). Geometrically this inequality is the area above the line marked "A attacks" in the weapons plane in Figure 7.1, with intercept $\hat{C}_A/[v_B(1-\exp(-\bar{\beta}\psi_B))]$ on the M_B axis and with slope $f_A(1-\exp(-\bar{\alpha}\theta_A))$.

Figure 7.1 also shows "B deters" and "B attacks" lines, indicating regions in which defense analysts in Country B, on the basis of their simulated war outbreak using the same model of a missile war, have enough missiles, respectively, to deter A from attacking (by threatening unacceptable casualties) and to attack A (suffering an acceptable level of casualties). If the technical and timing parameters are estimated to be the same in both countries, then the "B deters" line is parallel to the "A attacks" line and the "B attacks" line is parallel to the "A deters" line. For example, the common slope of the "B deters" and "A attacks" line is $f_A(1-\exp(-\bar{\alpha}\theta_A))$. If, however, defense planners in the two countries have different assessments of these parameters (f_A, f_B, $\bar{\alpha}$, $\bar{\beta}$, θ_A, θ_B), then the lines need not be parallel.

This model of war initiation allows us to identify parts of the weapons plane in Figure 7.1 as regions of deterrence and of war initiation.

The upper shaded cone bounded by the "A deters" and "B deters" lines is one of **mutual deterrence,** in which each country deters the other. This region above the point D of minimal mutual deterrence is one of stability against war outbreak, because in it each country has the

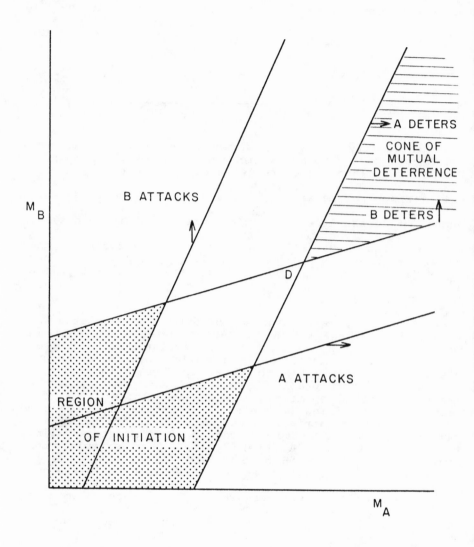

Figure 7.1   Regions of Deterrence and War Initiation

ability to inflict unacceptable damage on the other in a retaliatory attack.[7] In it each country has enough missiles to deter the other, and neither country has enough missiles to attack the other.

The lower shaded sawtooth-shaped area is one of **forced initiation**. In it neither country deters the other, and one or both can attack the other. In the middle portion of this area, the cone between the origin and the point of initiation I, A can attack B and B can attack A, while neither can deter the other. Thus, this portion is one of virtually forced preemption in which there is a great advantage to initiate rather than retaliate. The "reciprocal fear of surprise attack" based on the tremendous advantage in striking first virtually forces both sides to[8] initiate, each trying to preempt the attack of the other. The other portions of this area are ones of asymmetry; in one, on the lower right, A can attack B but B cannot attack A, while in the other, upper left, B can attack A but A cannot attack B. Thus, in these two asymmetric regions stability relies on the intentions of one side. The entire sawtooth-shaped area, however, is one of initiation. This region exhibits instability against war outbreak in that neither side has an adequate retaliatory capability to ensure deterrence and one or both countries have enough capabilities, relative to the missiles held by the opponent, to attack the other.

The deterring and attacking lines for both countries that define the upper cone of mutual deterrence and the lower sawtooth-shaped area of initiation are themselves defined in (8) and (10) in terms of:

f_A, f_B: the effectiveness of missiles in destroying enemy missiles, which depend on missile accuracy and yield and enemy missile dispersion and hardness against attack.

v_A, v_B: the effectiveness of missiles in inflicting enemy casualties, which depend on missile accuracy and yield and enemy civil defense and dispersion.

$\bar{\alpha}, \bar{\beta}$: the (maximum) rates of fire of missiles, which depend on missile characteristics and the command and control structure.

θ_A, θ_B: the time intervals during which one country can attack the other without a response from the other, which depend on detection capabilities and command and control.

ψ_A, ψ_B: the time intervals for a retaliatory strike, which depend on missile characteristics and command and control.

$\bar{C}_A$, $\bar{C}_B$:   the minimum unacceptable level of casualties which would deter each country, as estimated by the other country.

$\hat{C}_A$, $\hat{C}_B$:   the maximum acceptable level of casualties which each country could accept in a retaliatory strike, as estimated by itself.

To give a numerical example, if it takes two missiles to destroy an enemy missile ($f_A = f_B = 0.5$), each missile can inflict 250,000 casualties ($v_A = v_B =$ 250,000), the maximum rate of fire is 10 percent per minute ($\bar{\alpha} = \bar{\beta} = 0.10$), the first-strike interval is 15 minutes ($\theta_A = \theta_B = 15$), the retaliatory strike interval is 10 minutes ($\psi_A = \psi_B = 10$), the minimum unacceptable level of casualties is 40 million ($\bar{C}_A = \bar{C}_B = 40$ million), and the maximum acceptable level of casualties is 5 million ($\hat{C}_A = \hat{C}_B = 5$ million), then the deterrence point D in Figure 7.1, i.e., the minimum number of missiles required for mutual deterrence, is 414 missiles on each side, while the initiation point I in Figure 7.1, the maximum number of missiles in the area of forced preemption (where each can attack the other) is 52 missiles. Thus, in this symmetrical example if each side has more than 414 missiles there is the stability of mutual deterrence, and if each side has fewer than 52 missiles there is the instability of forced preemption.
Obviously all the numbers used in these calculations are subject to uncertainty, particularly the estimates of the minimum unacceptable/maximum acceptable level of casualties. Thus, it would be more appropriate to refer not to a cone of mutual deterrence and a region of initiation but rather to equal probability contours of war outbreak, showing relatively high probability of war outbreak in the region of initiation and relatively low probabilities of war outbreak in the cone of mutual deterrence. Alternatively, the lines of deterrence and attack in Figure 7.1 can be replaced by bands, reflecting the uncertainty in the values of the parameters defining deterring and attacking regions. For purposes of exposition, however, the lines, the cone of mutual deterrence, and the region of initiation will be used in

the next three sections to analyze the influence of
decision rules on the dynamics of the arms race and war
initiation.

DECISION RULES AND GAPS

As noted in the first section, decision rules with
regard to weapons procurement and their effects on the
stability of the arms race and war initiation can be
described as a two-stage process. The first stage is a
bureaucratic-political decision to establish a certain
rule or goal and the second is an economic decision, using
this rule, to determine how resources are allocated
between arms procurement and other uses, particularly
consumption and investment. This section treats the
bureaucratic-political decision rule and the implied
"gaps" in weapons levels, while the next section treats
the implications of optimizing behavior for a particular
decision rule.

The decision rule decided on the basis of
bureaucratic and political considerations can be
considered a rule defining a desired level of weapons as a
function of the level of weapons held by the opponent.
For Country A if M_A^* is the desired level of weapons, then

$$M_A^* = M_A^*(M_B) \qquad (11)$$

is the decision rule, indicating for each level of B
weapons a desired target for A weapons. The gap for
Country A is then

$$M_A^* - M_A = M_A^*(M_B) - M_A \qquad (12)$$

that is, the difference between the desired and current
stocks of weapons in Country A.

An example of such a decision rule is one for which
the desired number of missiles is that required to deter
the opponent, given, for Country A, as in (8), as

$$M_A^* = f_B(1 - \exp(-\bar{\theta}_B))M_B + \frac{\bar{C}_B}{v_A(1-\exp(-\alpha\psi_A))} \qquad (13)$$

In this case the desired number of missiles depends only
(and linearly) on the number of missiles held by the
opponent. The gap, $M_A^* - M_A$ in (13) is then the minimum
number of missiles that A needs to add to its stock of
missiles, given the missiles held by the opponent, in
order to deter B. Geometrically, it is the horizontal

distance in Figure 7.1 between any point to the left of
the "A deters" line and the corresponding point on this
line. This decision rule and its corresponding gap are
the **deterrence decision rule** and **deterrence gap,**
respectively. Symmetric decision rules and gaps and their
geometric interpretation also exist for Country B, the gap
being the vertical distance between a point and the "B
deters" line.

A second example of a decision rule is one for which
the desired number of missiles is that required to attack
the opponent, given, for Country A, as in (10), as

$$M_A^* = [\frac{1}{f_A(1-\exp(-\bar{\alpha}\theta_A))}]M_B - \frac{\hat{C}_A}{f_A(1-\exp(-\bar{\alpha}\theta_A))v_B(1-\exp(-\bar{\beta}\psi_B))} \tag{14}$$

Here again the desired missiles depend only (and
linearly--but with different slope and intercept than
before) on the number of missiles held by the opponent.

The gap $M_A^* - M_A$ is then the minimum number of missiles

that A needs to add to its stock of missiles, given the
number held by B, in order to attack B. Geometrically, it
is the horizontal distance in Figure 7.1 between any point
to the left of the "A attacks" line and the corresponding
point on this line. This decision rule and its
corresponding gap are the **attacking decision rule** and the
attacking gap respectively. Symmetric decision rules and
gaps and their geometric interpretation also exist for
Country B, the gap being the vertical distance between a
point and the "B attacks" line.

A third example of a decision rule is that for
parity, given, for Country A, as

$$M_A^* = M_B \tag{15}$$

where the desired level is simply the number of the
opponent's weapons. The gap is then simply the difference
$M_B - M_A$, and geometrically it is the horizontal difference

in Figure 7.1 between any point to the left of the 45°
line (not shown explicitly) and the corresponding point on
this line. For Country B the gap would be the vertical
distance between a point and the 45° line.

A fourth example of a decision rule is that for
superiority, given, for Country A, as

$$M_A^* = \alpha M_B \quad (a > 1) \tag{16}$$

where α is a measure of the degree of superiority desired.

If $\alpha = 1.10$, for instance, Country A would seek to have 10 percent more weapons than B. The gap is then $\alpha M_B - M_A$, measured geometrically as the horizontal distance between any point and the line with slope $1/\alpha$ passing through the origin. For Country B, if the target is M_A, where $\beta > 1$ is the degree of superiority desired, the gap would be, geometrically, the vertical distance between any point and the line with slope β passing through the origin.

OPTIMIZING BEHAVIOR

Having developed a general decision rule for target levels of weapons and the corresponding implied gaps, as established by bureaucratic-political decisions, the next step in the two-step process describing weapons procurement is to treat the economic decision, using this rule, on the rate of accumulation of weapons. This economic decision will be based upon optimizing behavior of the macroeconomic agent responsible for resource allocation. The acquisition of missiles in Country A is given by

$$\dot{M}_A = Y_A - C_A - \delta M_A \tag{17}$$

where Y_A is national income or product, C_A is consumption and (nonmilitary net investment) and δ is the depreciation rate for weapons. Thus, investment in military hardware is given as gross military investment, the difference between income and consumption (plus nonmilitary net investment), less depreciation to allow for the scrapping of obsolete weapons.

The economic agent in Country A optimizes relative to a given decision rule and the resulting gap, given in (12), by maximizing the welfare integral at time

$$W_A(\tau) = \int_\tau^\infty e^{-r(t-\tau)} [U_A(C_A) - D_A(M_A^*(M_B) - M_A)]\, dt, \tag{18}$$

representing the discounted utility, discounted at rate r back to time τ, of the utility of consumption less the disutility (or penalty for) failing to meet the goal embodied in the given decision rule. Here $U_A(C_A)$ is the utility of consumption, which satisfies the usual assumptions of strict concavity, with positive and diminishing utility starting from an infinitely negative utility at zero consumption:

$$U_A'(C_A) > 0, \quad U_A''(C_A) < 0, \quad U_A(0) = -\infty \tag{19}$$

D_A is the disutility (or penalty) function associated with not meeting the political target level of weapons. It is assumed to be asymmetric and to satisfy

$$D_A(M_A^*(M_B)-M_A) > 0, \quad D_A'(M_A^*(M_B)-M_A) > 0, \quad D_A(0) = 0 \text{ for all } M_A^*(M_B)-M_A > 0 \tag{20}$$

$$D_A(M_A^*(M_B)-M_B) = 0 \text{ and } D_A'(M_A^*(M_B)-M_A) = 0 \text{ for all } M_A^*(M_B) - M_A < 0 \tag{21}$$

where the argument of the disutility function is the gap between the desired level of weapons set by the decision rule $M_A^*(M_B)$ and the current level M_A. In addition to (20) and (21), rationality requires that the left-hand derivative of the disutility function satisfy

$$D_A'(0) > U_A'(Y_A + M_A^*(M_B) - M_A) \tag{22}$$

If not, the economic agent would never reach the target level of weapons.

The economic agent in A maximizes $W_A(\tau)$ in (18) in a myopic fashion by choice of a trajectory for $C_A(t)$ from time τ to ∞ subject to the economic constraint in (17). Once such a trajectory for consumption is selected it implies from (17) a trajectory for $M_A(t)$ for the same time interval, obtained by integrating the differential equation (17) forward from the historical level (boundary condition) for $M_A(\tau)$, given values for $Y_A(t)$ and for $\delta > 0$. The Hamiltonian associated with this problem is

$$H_A = U_A(C_A) - D_A(M_A^*(M_B) - M_A) + p_A(Y_A - C_A - \delta M_A), \tag{23}$$

where p_A is the costate variable associated with the differential equation for missiles, interpreted as the shadow value for A acquiring missiles.[9] The first-order conditions are

$$U_A'(C_A) - p_A = 0 \tag{24}$$

and

$$p_A - (r+\delta)p_A = D_A'(M_A^*(M_B)-M_A) \tag{25}$$

We can solve for C_A as a function of p_A to obtain the second differential equation

$$\dot{M}_A = Y_A - C_A(p_A) - \delta M_A \qquad (26)$$

which can be plotted in the phase diagram given in Figure 7.2, which uses the linear heuristic decision rule (as in the examples of the previous section)

$$M_A^*(M_B) = \alpha_1 M_B = \alpha_2 \qquad (27)$$

and where the optimal levels are denoted by a star $*$. For all $M_A < \alpha_1 M_B + \alpha_2$ equation (25) can be solved for the locus of points for which $p_A = 0$, given by the equation

$$p_A = -D_A'(\alpha_1 M_B + \alpha_2 - M_A)/(r+\delta) \qquad (28)$$

Differentiating with respect to M_A yields

$$\frac{\partial p_A}{\partial M_A} = D_A''(\alpha_1 M_B + \alpha_2 - M_A)/(r+\delta) \qquad (29)$$

Solving (26) for the locus of points for which $M_A = 0$ yields

$$C_A(p_A) = Y_A - \delta M_A \qquad (30)$$

and differentiating with respect to M_A yields

$$\frac{\partial p_A}{\partial M_A} = -\delta/C_A'(p_A) > 0 \qquad (31)$$

These points are plotted in a phase diagram in Figure 7.2. Note that there is a point of discontinuity at the equilibrium, which is caused by the fact that the derivative of the duality function is discontinuous at the target level of weapons.

We can also solve equation (26) for the locus of points where $dM_A/dt = \varepsilon$, a small change in the level of missiles. This locus is given by

$$C_A(p_A) = Y_A - \delta M_A - \varepsilon \qquad (32)$$

Differentiating with respect to M_A yields

$$\frac{\partial p_A}{\partial M_A} = \delta/C_A'(p_A) > 0 \qquad (33)$$

150

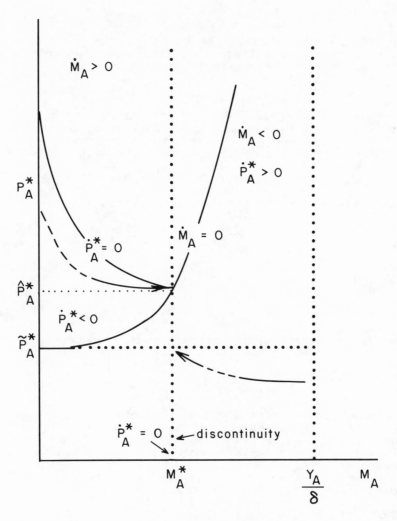

$\hat{P}_A^* = U'(Y_A - \delta M_A^*)$ is the steady state shadow price
will support the steady state M_A^*.

$\tilde{P}_A^* = U'(Y_A)$____ is the shadow price at which all income is consumed.

Figure 7.2   Phase Diagram for Optimizing Behavior

which is the same equation as (30). Thus, for any given level of weapons of Country B the economic agent in Country A can solve for the investment in weapons as a function of its own and its opponent's levels of weapons. This investment is given generally by

$$\dot{M}_A = F_A(M_A, M_B) . \tag{34}$$

If the utility function $U_A(C_A)$ and the disutility function $D_A(\alpha_1 M_A + \alpha_2)$ were both quadratic, then the solution of the resulting optimal control problem with a quadratic objective functional and a linear equation of motion yields a solution for the costate variable p_A, which is linear in the state variable M_A

$$p_A = \lambda M_A , \tag{35}$$

implying, from (24), that

$$\dot{M}_A = k_A[\alpha_1 M_B + \alpha_2 - M_A] , \tag{36}$$

a stock-adjustment model for which the acquisition of missiles is proportional to the gap between desired and actual levels of missiles.[10] The factor of proportionality k_A is the adjustment coefficient, which is assumed positive. This stock adjustment model, which is a special case of the general investment equation (34), will be used to study the stability of an arms race and its implications for war initiation.

GAPS, STABILITY, AND WAR INITIATION

We now consider various decision rules and their implications for stability and war initiation. We are particularly concerned with the stability of the arms race, that is, whether there is an equilibrium level of weapons held by both sides, at which neither will change the stock of weapons. Assuming such an equilibrium exists, we are also concerned with whether it is stable, in that small changes from the equilibrium lead to forces restoring the equilibrium, or alternatively, whether it is unstable, in that small changes from the equilibrium level lead to movement further and further away from this level. Finally we are also concerned with crisis stability in considering the implications of a particular situation for the probability of war initiation. These two types of stability are quite different, in that it is possible to have crisis stability but arms race instability. An example is continual movement up into the cone of mutual

deterrence of Figure 7.1. It is also possible, conversely, to have arms race stability but crisis instability. An
example is an arms race equilibrium in the initiation
region of Figure 7.2.[11] We will see that both examples
can, in fact, occur.

We will assume, as in the last section, that the
bureaucratic-political establishments in Countries A and B
each establish a certain linear decision rule for desired
levels of weapons (given the number held by the opponent)

$$M_A^* = \alpha_1 M_B + \alpha_2, \quad M_B^* = \beta_1 M_A + \beta_2 \tag{37}$$

These decision rules result in gaps between the desired
and actual values in each country

$$\alpha_1 M_B + \alpha_2 - M_A, \quad \beta_1 M_A + \beta_2 - M_B \tag{38}$$

The process of resource allocation in each country then
allocates between consumption and weapons acquisition
according to a stock adjustment model, as in equation (36)

$$\dot{M}_A = k_A [\alpha_1 M_B + \alpha_2 - M_A], \quad \dot{M}_B = k_B [\beta_1 M_A + \beta_2 - M_B] \tag{39}$$

where the adjustment coefficients k_A and k_B are both
positive. We will analyze the implications of alternative
decision rules.

If both countries use a deterrence decision rule, as
in (13), then (39) becomes

$$\dot{M}_A = k_A [f_B' M_B + \overline{C}_B' - M_A], \quad \dot{M}_B = k_B [f_A' M_A + \overline{C}_A' - M_B] \tag{40}$$

where, from (13),

$$\alpha_1 = f_B' = f_B(1 - \exp(-\overline{\beta}\theta_B)), \quad \alpha_2 = \overline{C}_B' = \frac{\overline{C}_B}{v_A(1 - \exp(-\overline{\alpha}\psi_A))} \tag{41}$$

and symmetric expressions define f_A' and $\overline{C}_A'$. An equilibri-

um exists for this pair of differential equations
at D in Figure 7.1, and the equilibrium is stable.[12] The
point of the stable equilibrium is one of (minimal) mutual
deterrence, so the equilibrium is stable against war
initiation as well. This situation is depicted in Figure
7.3, the arrows indicating the direction of motion and the
shaded stable arms race trap leading to the equilibrium at
D.

If both countries use an attacking decision rule, as
in (14), then (39) becomes

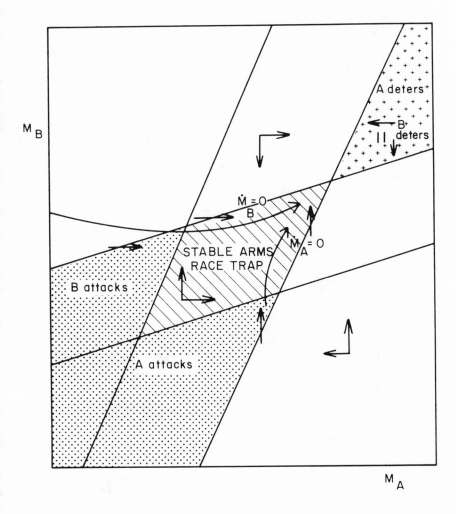

Note: If both sides use a deterrence decision rule the stable equilibrium is at D, the point of minimal mutual deterrence.

Figure 7.3   The Point of Minimal Deterrence

$$\dot{M}_A = k_A[f''_B M_B + \hat{C}''_A - M_A] , \quad \dot{M}_B = k_B[f''_A M_A + \hat{C}''_B - M_B] \quad (42)$$

where, from (14)

$$f''_B = \frac{1}{f_A(1-\exp(-\bar{\alpha}\theta_A))} , \quad \hat{C}''_A = \frac{\hat{C}_A}{f_A(1-\exp(-\bar{\alpha}\theta_A))v_B(1-\exp(-\bar{\beta}\psi_B))} \quad (43)$$

and symmetric expressions define f''_A and $\hat{C}''_A$. In this case the outcome depends on whether the starting point is in the region of initiation or above this region. As shown in Figure 7.4, in the (dotted) region of initiation the dynamics of the process drive levels of missiles down to the origin as each side attempts to move to a position where it can attack the other. By contrast, in the (shaded) region above that of initiation there is no equilibrium but rather an unstable arms race moving to higher and higher levels of weapons on both sides. Ironically, the equilibrium at the origin can be attained only by moving through regions of instability against war outbreak. On the other hand, the unstable arms race trap, where levels of weapons move to higher and higher values, occurs in regions with a relatively low chance of war outbreak. There can be a genuine dilemma in this case between seeking arms race stability at the disarmed point but at the cost of a relatively high probability of war outbreak and, alternatively, seeking stability against war outbreak but at the cost of a continuing arms race involving higher and higher levels of weapons on both sides.

A third case is the asymmetric one where one country, here A, attempts to deter, using a deterrence decision rule, as in (40) for A, while the other side, here B, attempts to attack, using an attacking decision rule, as in (42) for B. In this case, depicted in Figure 7.5, the result is an unstable arms race trap in the region of low probability of war outbreak, as in the last case where the starting point is above the region of initiation. If the process begins in the region of initiation, the direction of arrows indicates movement to the right as A attempts to deter, leading next to upward movement as B attempts to attack, and eventually to points in the shaded unstable arms race trap. Unlike the first two cases there is no equilibrium and unlike the last case there is no dilemma between an arms race and war initiation. This case leads eventually to an arms race trap with levels of weapons spiraling higher and higher but with a low chance of war outbreak.

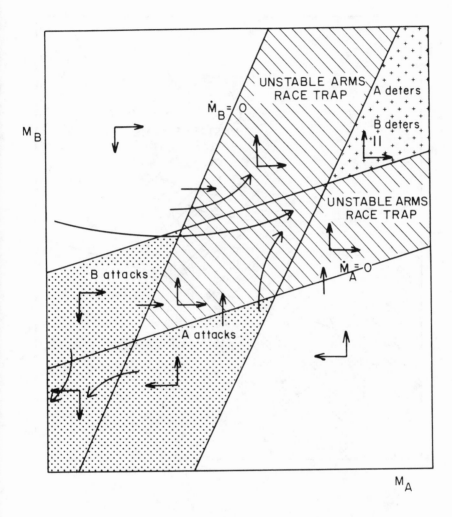

Note: If both sides use an attacking decision rule the outcome depends on whether the process starts in the region of initiation, leading to the disarmed point, or starts above this region, leading to an unstable arms race trap.

Figure 7.4   An Unstable Arms Trap

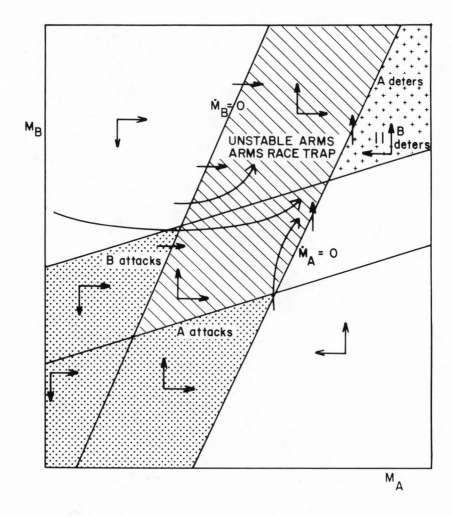

Note: If one side (A) uses a deterring decision rule and the other (B) uses an attacking decision rule the result is an unstable arms race trap.

Figure 7.5   Asymmetric Unstable Arms Traps

The next cases are those in which one or both of the countries seek parity, as in (15), or superiority, as in (16). Assume that A seeks parity or superiority, so the direction of movement above a 45° line (or above the line with slope $1/\alpha$ passing through the origin in the case of superiority) is rightward, and below this line it is leftward. If B seeks to deter, then the result is like that in Figure 7.3, with a stable equilibrium at the point where this line crosses the "B deters" line. The greater the degree of superiority A seeks the greater the chance the equilibrium will be one of mutual deterrence, where A deters B and B deters A. If B seeks to attack, then the result is like that in Figure 7.4, with an unstable equilibrium at the point where the line representing the A goal crosses the "B attacks" line. The result is either a spiral downward to the disarmed state, moving through regions of relatively high chances of war initiation, or a spiral upward to an arms race trap, involving higher and higher levels of weapons but a relatively low probability of war outbreak. This is the outcome also in the case of A and B each seeking superiority, an arms race trap leading to higher and higher levels of weapons but at least eventually resulting in configurations of weapons far above the region of initiation.

CONCLUSIONS

Our principal conclusion is that there can be a fundamental difference between arms race stability and stability against war outbreak. In several important cases, such as that of two attackers or that of one country seeking superiority and the other seeking to attack, the result is either arms race stability at an equilibrium point, usually the point of complete disarmament, or stability against war outbreak, usually in an arms race trap. Ironically, the stable equilibrium point of complete disarmament involves instability against war outbreak as the system passes through the region of initiation, while the unstable arms race trap involves stability against war outbreak as the system moves further and further away from the region of initiation. Although the contrast between arms race stability and crisis stability exists in certain cases, there are some situations where it is possible to have both types of stability, as in the case of two deterrers or in the case of one country seeking superiority while the other seeks to deter. In these cases there can be a stable equilibrium of mutual deterrence.

How does this analysis relate to the superpower arms race between the United States and the Soviet Union? While both sides profess to seek arms only to deter the

other, each believes the other is, or could be, seeking
weapons to attack it. The result is an asymmetric
situation, as in Figure 7.5, where each side assumes that
it is seeking to deter the other but that the other is
seeking to attack it. As each country seeks deterrence,
given its assumption that the other side is an attacker,
each side builds up its level of weapons, and the actions
of each side reinforce the suspicions of the other. The
result is an unstable arms race trap, escalating levels of
weapons to higher and higher levels, as has been the case
over the last twenty years, at the same time moving
further and further away from the region of initiation.
The result is crisis stability but arms race instability,
as each side acquires considerably more than enough
weapons to deter the other but continues, nonetheless, to
acquire yet even more weapons. From the viewpoint of arms
control the problem then becomes one not of incentives to
preempt, which have totally disappeared in view of the
overwhelming ability of each side to deter the other, but
rather of accidental initiation, e.g., by technical
mishap, delegation to undependable subordinates, or
through the action of third parties, including allies and
other nuclear weapons states. Given each side's
suspicions of the other, reinforced by the actions of the
other, there is little chance of bilateral agreements on
weapons reductions. On the other hand, there is value to
the stability of mutual deterrence, which is worth a
considerable investment in weapons. The major problem that
remains is that of even a small chance of initiation by
accident. A major (but not the only) example is one in
which either or both sides has in place a launch-on-
warning system (which each superpower is capable of
building) where the warning system is subject to technical
or human error. This type of problem and similar ones
relating to accidental initiation should be at the
forefront of arms control initiatives, including
unilateral, bilateral, and multilateral arms control
policies, rather than the present emphasis on negotiated
reductions, as in the START process; bilateral agreements
to the status quo, as in a negotiated freeze; or
unilateral defensive policies, as in the Strategic Defense
Initiative "Star Wars" approach.[13]

NOTES

1. Arms race models based on the mechanistic and
autonomous Richardson model are presented in Richardson
(1951, 1960) and Rapoport (1957) and discussed in
Intriligator (1975). For examples of arms race models
based on rational choices, using decision theory, control
theory, and game theory, see Schelling (1960, 1966),

Boulding (1962), Intriligator (1964), Brito (1972), Brito and Intriligator (1973), Brubaker (1973), Gillespie and Zinnes (1975), Simaan and Cruz (1975a and b, 1977), Gillespie et al. (1975, 1977a and b), and Brams et al. (1979). For further references on arms race models see Intriligator (1982), particularly Table 1, Column 1, "Arms Races."

2. We have previously used the same model to analyze the Richardson model of arms races in Intriligator (1975), to study whether arms races lead to the outbreak of war in Intriligator and Brito (1984), and to obtain policy conclusions relating to arms control initiatives in Intriligator and Brito (1985). See also Brito and Intriligator (1973, 1974, 1982), and Intriligator and Brito (1976, 1977).

3. See Intriligator (1967, 1968, 1975), Saaty (1968), Brito and Intriligator (1973, 1974), and Intriligator and Brito (1976, 1977).

4. See Intriligator (1967) for proofs of this result and the subsequent results reported in this paragraph.

5. This retaliation strategy is consistent with the switching strategy summarized earlier. In this case the switch in targets occurs at time θ_B, so after θ_B the A grand strategy is one of massive retaliation, with $\alpha = \bar{\alpha}$, $\alpha' = 0$.

6. For related diagrams see Kybal (1960) and Beaufre (1965).

7. The cone of mutual deterrence exists as long as the stability condition

$$f_A(1-\exp(-\bar{\alpha}\theta_A)) \ f_B(1-\exp(-\bar{\beta}\theta_B)) < 1$$

is met. This condition will always be met if it takes more than one missile to destroy an enemy missile, i.e., $f_A, f_B < 1$. Even if f_A and/or f_B exceeds unity, however, the condition could still be met. For example, if $\bar{\alpha} = \bar{\beta} = 0.10$ and $\theta_A = \theta_B = 15$, as in the numerical example in the second section, this stability condition is met as long as, in the symmetric case, both f_A and f_B are less than 1.28.

8. See Wohlstetter (1959).

9. For discussions of optimal control, the Hamiltonian, shadow values, etc., see Intriligtor (1971).

10. For discussions of the stock adjustment model and related models as well as references to this literature see Intriligator (1978).

11. Richardson (1960) confused these two notions of stability by identifying an unstable arms race with war initiation, a confusion shared explicitly or implicity by many later writers. For a further discussion of this point and an identification of certain arms races that lead to war and, conversely, arms races that reduce the probability of war, see Intriligator and Brito (1984, 1985).

12. The stability condition of Note 7, which can be expressed as

$$1 - f_A' f_B' > 0$$

is assumed to be met. The solution to the system of differential equations (30) is the sum of two exponential functions, where the two exponential growth rates are the characteristic roots of the matrix of coefficients

$$\begin{pmatrix} -k_A & k_A f_B' \\ k_B f_A' - k_B \end{pmatrix}$$

Assuming that k_A and k_B are positive and $1 - f_A' f_B' > 0$, this matrix is negative definite (since all leading principal minors are alternative in sign from negative to positive), so all the characteristic roots are negative, implying that the system is stable.

13. For a further discussion of arms control policies see Intriligator and Brito (1985).

8 Arms Races as Good Things?

"Not only does the arms race threaten the survival of mankind--it is also a terrible waste of resources!"

Such statements are often found in newspapers and periodicals, and with 5 to 10 percent of world income currently going to "defense" (however defined), the question should indeed be raised whether all this money is ultimately being squandered. Much the same point is frequently made on the scientific side, too. For example:

> From a global welfare point of view, an arms race clearly amounts to a suboptimal process: Heavier and heavier defense outlays will not in general buy more security or, in any case, the same levels of security could be obtained at a smaller economic and social cost. Of course, this is why the arms race phenomenon has elicited so much interest and concern. (Lambelet et al., 1979, p. 63).

It is one of the purposes of this chapter to suggest that such views are too simple and partial. As a first underpinning of this proposition, the following illustration, drawn from recent history, may be helpful. Fifteen or twenty years ago, it would have been risky to adduce this particular episode, which then was being mentioned rather too often. Today, almost fifty years after the event, there is perhaps a better chance that it will not cause too many allergic reactions.

A FIRST ILLUSTRATION

By March 1935 at the very latest, i.e., after Germany's urbi et orbi announcement that it was going to rearm, it was clear beyond any doubt that Adolf Hitler was bent on undoing the outcome of World War I--indeed, on realizing Germany's 1914-1918 war aims and possibly

more, and that he would not hesitate to use violent means
to that end. The potential losers were just as clearly
identifiable: Poland, Czechoslovakia, and the Soviet
Union in the East; France in the West; and England as
well, unless it agreed to give Germany a free hand on the
Continent. Assuming that a timely preemptive move was
not a feasible option, at least for the Western
democracies, the prudent and rational reaction on the
part of the potential "aggressees" then clearly consisted
in rearming just as quickly and fully as possible.

As is well known today, France and England did
rearm more and faster than many thought, either at the
time or in the immediate aftermath of 1940--for some
evidence see, for example, Luterbacher (1974). In the
spring of 1940, France had more tanks than Germany; they
were also qualitatively superior, except that they were
generally not outfitted with either radio sets or
operators and hence could not be deployed as effectively
as the German armor. As to England, all the world knows
that the RAF Hurricanes and Spitfires turned out to be a
fair match for Germany's Messerschmitts, Heinkels,
Dorniers, and Junkers.

Still, one cannot help feeling that the 1935-1939
rearmament effort in the West was often lukewarm and
halfhearted--that le coeur n'y était pas, particularly in
France. The latter's apparent helplessness in the air in
1939-1940 is often underlined. Yet, it is not as well
known that France did have a fighter plane, the Dewoitine
520, which was in the same league as the Hurricanes,
though the opportunity was not seized to produce it on a
time and quantity scale which would have made a
difference. As for England, the events of
August-September 1940 raise one of recent history's most
intriguing (if "iffy") questions: supposing that the
Luftwaffe had kept assaulting the British Fighter Command,
bombing its bases plus, perhaps, a few selected "civilian"
targets (e.g., power stations, communications), would not
the RAF ultimately have been overwhelmed--say, by
mid-September? The question never will receive a final
answer, but most specialists probably would agree that if
England eventually had not gone under, it would have been
by a narrow margin.

Be that as it may, there is no doubt--at least in
this writer's mind--that England and France would have
done well in 1935-1939 to rearm even more and faster than
they actually did.

Clearly, then, arms races can be good things--at
least from the standpoint of the potential aggressees.[3]
This suggests the following, initially static, typology of
bilateral arms races.

A SIMPLE STATIC TYPOLOGY OF BILATERAL ARMS RACES

Let us assume that in a two-country world, a country's fundamental posture can be characterized either as peaceful (P) or as aggressive (A). Let us further assume that the two countries (I and II) are engaged in an arms race. Then, the arms race configuration shown in Figure 8.1 obtains where the numbers 1, 2, 3, and 4 have no other purpose than to identify the various possible cases.

Nation I

		Aggressive	Peaceful
Aggressive	2	1	2
Nation II			
Peaceful	2	3	4

Figure 8.1   Peacefulness and Aggressiveness of Intentions in Arms Races

In a sense, case 4 is the most interesting one: both countries are fundamentally peaceful, yet they are engaged in an arms race. If the two countries distrust each other to the point of piling up arms for potential use against each other (presumably on some theory of the better-safe-than-sorry variety), it must be due to some correctible misperception or misunderstanding. Then--and, as will be seen, only then--can it be said that the arms race between I and II represents a waste of resources and hence a suboptimal process.

But what about case 1 and cases 2 and 3 (the latter two, being symmetric, really make up but a single theoretical case)? Are arms races of this type also a waste of resources? Indeed, does the very notion of optimality still have a sense in these cases?

Let us consider Pareto's definition of optimality, which, although it originated in economics, has since then penetrated most other social sciences. In this writer's experience, it is not always fully realized that the notion of Pareto optimality, and, indeed, much of economics in general, really makes sense only in a world of free agents engaging in voluntary exchanges, agents, that is, who of course remain subject to all sorts of

164

objective constraints (e.g., prices and endowments or, in partial equilibrium, income) but who are essentially immune from direct[4] "physical" encroachments and other forms of compulsion.

Take, for example, the simple "Economics I" pure-exchange situation of Figure 8.2, where it is assumed for illustrative purposes that two tribes (I and II) meet in the desert, each endowed with given amounts of two goods (say, camels and carpets).

There is no need to dwell on points E, ce, me, and me' in Figure 8.2 or on the CC contract curve, except to note that however the market may be organized (full competition, unilateral monopoly of the discriminating or non-discriminating sort, bilateral monopoly, oligopoly of one form or another), all agents are always assumed to be free not to part with their endowments if trading conditions and particularly relative prices are not to their liking.

Equlilibria A and B, however, are altogether different. Point A, for example, stands for a situation in which the Tribe II people, being physically stronger, would have pounced bare-fisted on Tribe I, simply taking away all their camels and carpets.[5]

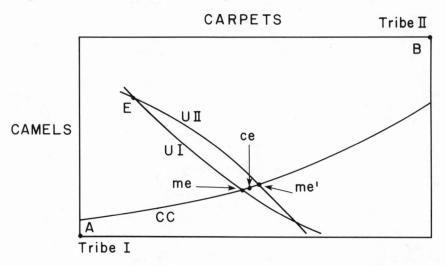

E   =   Initial endowment
CC   =   Pareto-optimal contract curve
ce   =   competitive equilibrium
me, me' =   Respective unilateral discriminating monopoly equilibria (limiting points)
A, B   =   unilateral predatory equilibria
U I, U II = The two utility curves of I and II which, on the usual convexity assumptions, pass through the endowment point

Figure 8.2   Of Carpets and Camels

Is point A (or B) Pareto-optimal? On the face of
it, this would seem to depend on whether the CC contract
curve passes through the lower-left (or upper-right) angle
of the Pareto-Edgeworth box of Figure 8.2, which in turn
hinges on the specific shape of the two utility maps.[6] If
the curve does not pass through the corners, point A or B
might appear Pareto-suboptimal. Yet, there of course is
no way in which the welfare of Tribe I could be increased
without decreasing the welfare of Tribe II; in other
words, the Pareto-optimal point is not part of the
feasible set and there is a "corner solution."

If the CC curve goes through the lower-left angle,
point A is technically Pareto-optimal. Yet, this would
hardly impress the Tribe I people who find themselves
entirely despoiled or, put differently, who must put up
with a rather extreme form of income (re)distribution.
Clearly, then, the notion of (Pareto) optimality cannot
be simply transposed into a world of predators and
(potential) victims.

In fact, equilibria like A or B can be evaluated,
in some welfare sense, only by reference to a higher
moral norm. For example, if one adheres to a broad
libertarian outlook, equilibrium A or B will be deemed
suboptimal, compared with any point enclosed by the U I
and U II curves, because freedom of choice and voluntary
exchange are held to be superior to compulsion.[7] But this
clearly is a philosophical matter. Suppose, for example,
that Tribe II is made up of self-proclaimed "true
believers" with a proselytizing bent, but who find they
are unable to make any impression on the Tribe I heathens.
In the view of the members of Tribe II, equilibrium A
would then be a just retribution for Tribe I's refusal to
embrace the true faith, i.e., they would see it as
optimal. It follows that the peaceful- aggressive
classification of arms races also rests--unavoidably and
unashamedly--on a specific normative view of the world, a
view whereby conflicts ought in general to be resolved by
nonviolent means and where aggression is defined as in
international law and particularly in the UN Charter.

Equilibria A and B in Figure 8.2 are related to
arms races in that they are the outcomes which will
obtain if--as assumed so far--the peaceful party has
failed to arm in order effectively to deter its aggressive
opposite number. However, if we now assume that both the
peaceful and the aggressive tribes have piled up a stock
of weapons, it is conceivable that their encounter in the
desert will result in a bloody fight, which, by analogy
with a full-scale nuclear exchange, could possibly lead
to well-nigh complete mutual destruction.[8] Is that,
then, not clearly suboptimal?

Broad suboptimality can indeed be surmised if this
radical outcome is a result of miscalculation or insuffi-

cient foresight by both parties. History suggests that
this can occur and has occurred, the famous (apocryphal?)
words of William II of Germany, "Das hab'ich nicht gewolt!"
("I did not intend that"), being an apposite illustration.

But what if the arms race leads to an actual fight
which is recognized beforehand by both sides as being
practically certain to cause mutual destruction? Then,
surely, the race must be a suboptimal process. Again,
the answer would seem positive only for arms races
between peaceful nations. Supposing that a way is found
to transcend the misperception or misunderstanding
underlying the arms race, both countries could then spare
the resources heretofore spent on defense while enjoying
the same level of external security.

In arms races between two nations, only one of which
is peaceful, however, the matter is open to discussion.
For the fundamentally peaceful party, certain or highly
probable destruction and death can be rationally preferred
to the loss of, for example, a free way of life. As a
matter of fact, deliberately and consciously choosing
(almost certain) death is a common form of behavior in
wartime. To that extent, there is an answer to the
famous "better red than dead" slogan: namely, the old
teaching which says that more important than life itself
are the reasons for living. As to the aggressive party,
it is probably prudent not to rule out the possibility of
a genuine longing for some orgastic Götterdämmerung.

One purpose of this section's discussion has been
to sketch a--currently almost nonexistent--scientific (or
at least somewhat rigorous) analysis of arms races from a
welfare or normative angle. Clearly, nothing more than
an outline is proposed. Yet, the importance of the
issues raised could hardly be overstated.

For example, it is arguable that what many
responsible Western military officials and analysts
really have in mind about the East-West arms race is an
asymmetric situation where only the West is considered as
fundamentally peaceful. Then, the race is seen as a good
thing, the West does nothing more than just defend
itself, and indeed the only real danger is that it might
not do enough to that end.[10]

Symmetrically, it is conceivable that many and
maybe most bona fide pacifists rather think of the arms
race as a case 4 phenomenon, i.e., a blatantly suboptimal
process which ought to be transcended somehow. This
basic view is often found in the scientific literature,
too. It is, for example, present in the asymmetric arms
race and war initiation model of Intriligator and Brito
(1984), which generates the so-called arms race trap and

where each of the superpowers assumes it is the deterrer and the other is the aggressor.[11]

THE DYNAMIC DIMENSION

"A world of predators and (potential) victims"--this is perhaps an acceptable characterization of the 1930s, or so many felt at the time and still feel today. But what about more recent and present times? The world in which we live nowadays of course is far from perfectly safe, but it hardly seems to have the same black-and-white quality, about which more further on. Consequently the preceding static typology may strike some as having little relevance for the sort of international conflict situations we seem to face today. Why?

The main reason probably is the typology's static character, whereas attitudes, and arms races as well, are dynamic phenomena. In other words, the runners' "fundamental postures" (aggressive or peaceful) may and usually do evolve over time, not necessarily in some autonomous fashion but conceivably and partly as a result of the arms race itself.

For example, it is easy to imagine that an (initially mild) arms race can start between two countries as a result of some "fundamental" underlying conflict which, in fact, is anything but fundamental, for example, difficulties in communicating across cultural and even linguistic barriers, internal politics, or exploitation by third parties for their own purposes. But as the dynamics of the arms race take hold, there may well be a feedback effect on the two sides' attitudes themselves. That is, a country which in the beginning was peaceful "at heart" could start becoming increasingly aggressive as the arms race gains in intensity. This need not be due solely to a psychological "getting-hooked" effect, but may also reflect an induced shift in perception: as the country watches the other side arming ever more, it may come to feel that this, in and of itself, is the main threat, thus progressively losing sight of the initial underlying motive for conflict. Faced with this increasing perceived threat, the country itself may start entertaining notions of such tactics as preemptive strikes, i.e., it may itself become increasingly aggressive.

Another example taken from the real world may illustrate how truly crucial this matter is.

A SECOND ILLUSTRATION

Simplifying perhaps too much, one could say that there was one image of the Soviet Union which was dominant in the West until perhaps 15 or 20 years ago, at least among the informed and nonfanatical. It was the image--which could fairly be called the Kennan (1945) image--of a fundamentally conservative, cautious, continental power intent above all on preserving the large European glacis acquired at great cost in the course of World War II. Maybe the 1962 Cuban crisis was the first indication that this image was becoming inaccurate, but the Soviet attempt to put missiles in Cuba could also be explained in a more benign manner.[12]

Today it is rather more difficult to defend this image of the Soviet Union. The main reason is not so much the invasion and partial occupation of Afghanistan, important though this episode is, since it represents the first time the Soviet Union has clearly overstepped its World War II security perimeter. Neither is it the influence gained by the Soviet Union in countries such as Angola, Ethiopia, or Syria, for such gains are generally emphemeral, as the case of Egypt shows. It is rather the Soviet buildup of a regular blue-water navy, complete with large aircraft carriers. In my opinion there is no way in which the recent Soviet naval programs can be reconciled with the image of a fundamentally nonexpansionary, continental power.[13]

In other words, the evidence seems rather strong to me that the Soviet Union has moved from a basically defensive, inward-looking, and--why not?--peaceful posture (at least as long as its vital interests were not threatened) to a rather more expansionary, outward-looking, world-wide strategy which the West lato sensu might understandably consider as ultimately aggressive.

The trouble, however, is that this shift from one posture to another can be explained, roughly speaking, in at least two ways, and, when it comes to reacting or adjusting to this change, it makes all the difference in the world which of the two explanations is the correct one.

A first view is to consider that, at least since World War II, the Soviet Union at bottom has not really changed at all. If, prior to the mid- or late 1960s, it refrained from any blatant outward push, it was only because it did not have the requisite means. But, as soon as it had reached anything close to strategic nuclear parity with the US, and as soon as it had become rich enough to afford large naval and assorted expenses, it embarked on a clearly expansionary course, profiting from the West's every false move and weakness, never retreating from any position once it was safely secured (i.e., once it was under direct Soviet military control), understanding no other language than that of firmness and strength, obstinately pursuing the old Tsarist dream of direct access to warm-water seas.

If this stylized characterization of the Soviet Union's supposedly unchanging real nature was correct, it would mean that the static typology illustrated in a previous section applies by and large today as it did in the 1930s. The West and particularly the US would then be fully justified, and indeed only prudent, in trying hard to keep ahead in the arms race.

On the other hand, it may also be that the Soviet Union's strategic evolution, over the last twenty years or so, from an inward-looking to an outward-looking posture, an evolution which to my mind is beyond question, was in fact largely induced. Faced not so much with blatant signs of direct Western aggressiveness (although a few episodes like the U-2 affair surely helped) as with the ongoing Western armament effort, particularly in the strategic field, the Soviet Union would have slowly changed its basic posture from "we are only making sure that you are leaving us alone" to "the best defense is a good offense."

Should this second explanation be closer to reality, it would then be in the West's best interest to try and find ways to reverse the process and endeavor to create an atmosphere of mutual confidence. Then the truly suboptimal and wasteful arms race could be slowed down and ultimately stopped altogether, about which more below.

MODELING ARMS RACES

If it is granted that induced shifts in fundamental postures are a real possibility, formalized models of arms races did not, until recently, include a feedback mechanism of this sort as a separate factor. In Richardson's original two-differential-equation model, which is too well known to need reproducing here, the fundamental underlying conflict between the two contenders is expressed by two "grievance terms," which, precisely, are the two equations' constants.[14] Basically the same is true of other formal arms race models, or at least of those known to this writer.[15]

Recently, however, an arms race model has been proposed (and applied to the 1946-1963 Cold War between the US and the Soviet Union) which, among several novel features, includes just such a feedback mechanism (Allan, 1983). In the Allan approach the equations accounting for each side's defense effort include "diplomatic climate" as a separate argument, where "diplomatic climate" is shorthand for both sides' attitudes towards each other. And as diplomatic climate evolves over time (in a way which need not detain us), the arms race will accelerate or decelerate, as the case may be.[16]

The Allan model certainly represents a major achievement. Still, it has its limitations, the main one being, in my opinion, that it--along with practically all other such models--is too highly aggregated or, if one prefers, too abstract and general to be really useful and operational when it comes to answering a number of practical, yet crucial questions in the East-West context. This is best shown by means of yet another illustration.

A THIRD ILLUSTRATION

As a first premise, let us assume that we do live today in a genuinely dangerous world, i.e., a world overloaded with nuclear weapons where some potentially very destabilizing technical developments lurk on the horizon, e.g., President Reagan's "Strategic Defense Initiative," or "star wars" program (see Bethe et al., 1984). Of course, nobody can really say today how likely it is that a hot "global" (i.e., East-West) war will eventually erupt some day in the more or less distant future, and whether nuclear arms will necessarily be used in such an event. Neither do we have a truly reliable picture of the damage a nuclear exchange would cause, particularly in the longer run--note the prudent language used in a recent survey on the prospect of a "nuclear winter" (Turco et al., 1984). Yet, even if the risk of a nuclear catastrophe is small, it exists and must be taken seriously.

Let us further assume that on both sides the fundamental conflict underlying the arms race is at least partly induced by the race itself. Allan's (1983, pp. 113-114, 120) empirical findings lend some support to this view, in the sense that the diplomatic climate is shown to have a significant influence on the military expenditures of both the US and the Soviet Union. Not too much, however, should be made of these results: first, they are valid, strictly speaking, only for the 1946-1963 Cold War era; second, Allan also shows that some of his parameters are highly sensitive to the choice of particular data sets. The answer to the question of the arms race's nature therefore remains, in my view, at least partly an act of faith.

If these two premises are granted, then a way should be found to lessen the likelihood of a nuclear catastrophe at some point in the future by exploiting the reversible nature of the arms race. The real problem, however, is how one should go about it.

As a much too simple illustration, one could imagine at least two approaches.

A first approach consists in negotiations of the SALT and MBFR variety, the aim being to implement disarmament, or at least to stop the armament escalation, in such a way as strictly to preserve parity between the two sides. As the record shows, the problem with this route is that parity is a rather elusive and fuzzy concept in a world where we know that different weapons systems are sometimes substitutes and sometimes complements, but where there is no widely shared consensus on the degree of substitutability or complementarity. The danger, therefore, is that difficult, drawn-out negotiations, in which everyone is obsessed with the idea of strictly preserving parity at all stages, will not help build up mutual confidence. Indeed, they might ultimately lead to even greater reciprocal distrust. In other words, the risk with this first approach is that it will fail to exploit the (presumed) reversible nature of the arms race.

Hence, a second approach would be for the West and, in particular, for the US to unilaterally adopt and implement a package which might look like the following one, which--it must be emphasized--is largely illustrative and does not represent a fully thought-out set of policy proposals:

(1) Complete and open dumping of the MX program, whose present shape has no relation to its original justification and whose current logic escapes me, along with many other analysts (see Bunn et al., 1983, and Steinbrunner, 1984).

(2) The withdrawal of the Pershings (but not the cruise missiles) from Western Europe, given that it seems to be the Pershings' high accuracy and closeness to Russia which, perhaps understandably, are so objectionable to the Soviet Union.

(3) A general but time-limited (see below) freeze on the production and deployment of other nuclear weapons, whether of a new or old type.

(4) Explicit renunciation of the "Strategic Defense Initiative" and all anti-satellite weapons (Garvin et al., 1984).

(5) Possibly, a declaration of "no first use" regarding nuclear weapons (see Gottfried et al., 1984).

(6) Instead, a buildup of Western conventional forces, but, as far as feasible, only in the defensive mode (e.g., anti-tank PGM's rather than tanks).

(7) Other defensive measures, such as civil protection or the hardening of preexisting ICBM silos.

This package should be limited in time--say, to the four years of an American presidential term--and it would have to be explicitly presented as a test of the other side's readiness to de-escalate. (The point is important since parts of this package have in fact been repeatedly proposed--but in good faith?--by the Russians themselves. Indeed, one could imagine a parallel announcement to the effect that no negotiations could be envisaged during the test period and before the other side had given concrete proofs of a similar nature. For it is arguable that, to the extent that the parties often try to use them to gain some advantage, early negotiations may actually make things worse. Put differently, negotiations are perhaps better left for the last stage of a genuine detente and disarmament process.

Compared with the first one, this second approach would take advantage of the presumed reversible and hence suboptimal nature of the arms race, in the sense that it would ultimately lead to a world with the same multilateral security level, but where the large amount of resources spent on defense could be used to other ends. Its disadvantage is, of course, that it entails a not inconsiderable risk for the West's safety (if, in fact, the Soviet Union's behavior were more akin to the static typology discussed earlier), although features 6 and 7 (above)--and conceivably others of a similar nature--could help lessen this risk.

It would therefore be highly desirable if formalized arms race models and, in general, formalized international conflict models could be developed further in this more finely disaggregated direction. However, such endeavors will likely run into a serious obstacle, namely and succinctly: in today's social sciences, we really have very little systematic knowledge about the conditions conducive to confidence (vs. distrust), cooperation (vs. confrontation), farsightedness (vs. myopia), socially oriented behavior (vs. selfishness), coalition formation (vs. infighting), and other similar behavior attributes.[1]

NOTES

1. Département d'économétrie et d'économie politique (DEEP), University of Lausanne, and Graduate Institute of International Studies, Geneva. Michael D. Intriligator's perceptive comments on a first version of this paper are gratefully acknowledged.

2. To take just one example, it crept up in almost all of Dean Rusk's utterances during and about the Vietnam War.

3. Of course, France's 1940 defeat and England's narrow escape cannot be ascribed exclusively to insufficient rearmament programs. Many other factors clearly played a role, e.g., the utter lack of imagination--not to say senility--of the French High Command, domestic decisions (Plutôt Hitler que Léon Blum!"), and general lassitude in the West ("This House will not fight for King and Country"). In the last analysis, it really all revolved around the will--or lack of will--to fight in self-defense.

4. Of course, the notion of "direct,'physical' encroachment and other forms of compulsion" is a great deal less clear-cut than might be thought. For example, what about moral intimidation? Or what about the gullibility of the innocent?

5. More realistically, one could imagine that, prior to crossing the desert, Tribe II had spent part of its camel-cum-carpet endowment on acquiring weapons while Tribe I remained entirely unarmed; this would be rational for Tribe II if the prospective booty, minus possible casualties, were worth more to it than what it had to give up to acquire its stock of weapons. However, one is then moving from a two-good to a three-good world--i.e., camels, carpets, weapons--which renders the analysis somewhat more complicated without adding anything essential. Hence, it is simpler to stick to the assumption that the Tribe II people are so much stronger that they can help themselves to the other tribe's riches, and thereby realize equilibrium A, without having to rely on weapons.

6. In many textbooks the contract curve is drawn so that it stops short of the sides of the box, which goes to show that economists instinctively tend to shrink away from extreme situations.

7. It is granted that the existence of public goods financed via compulsory taxation regrettably blurs the picture. In some instances, it is no doubt true that one is perilously close to the case of Tribe II robbing Tribe I, e.g., when education outlays are partly financed by taxes on childless (or rather, sterile) couples.

8. See Intriligator and Brito (1984), building on Lambelet (1975), for a penetrating discussion of the conditions under which an arms race may lead to war.

9. For example, during World War II, survival chances were small indeed for the crews of German submarines or for the flying personnel of the British Bomber Command. Of the approximately 40,000 who manned the German U-Boats, about 28,000 lost their lives, meaning that about 30 percent survived. For a thirty-mission tour of duty with the British Bomber Command, survival chances were no better than 40 percent, and 16 percent in case of a second tour of duty.

174

10.   For example, this comes through forcefully in Lord Zuckerman's critique of Freeman Dyson's 1984 book, published in the June 10, 1984, issue of The New York Review of Books.

11.   I owe--with thanks--this characterization of the Intriligator-Brito model to a direct communication from Michael D. Intriligator.

12.   In 1962 the "missile gap" myth was being exposed for just what it was, while the US was rapidly building up an arsenal of real ICBM's. Putting medium-range missiles on Cuba would then have been a way for the Soviet Union to compensate for the US's strategic headstart, while also salvaging some shreds of its former (though short-lived) image of strategic superiority.

13.   The expression "blue-water navy" is possibly misleading, in that it may suggest that the Soviets are trying to seize supremacy at sea from the US and its allies. At least so far as the Mediterranean is concerned, Soviet naval programs seem to have more limited aims, e.g., showing the flag, helping friendly regimes overseas, etc., during peacetime, and interfering with Allied communications during wartime. To this extent, the Soviet naval endeavors are reminiscent of the German naval ambitions prior to 1914. Thanks are due Albert Stahel for pointing this out.

14.   On this aspect of Richardson's model, see Lambelet et al. (1979, pp. 50-52).

15.   Not excepting the half dozen or so models for which he (Richardson) is wholly or partly responsible. On this point, see Allan (1983, pp. 64-65).

16.   Allan's model being very nearly a closed system, there is also a (roundabout) feedback effect from the arms race on the diplomatic climate. This feature, however, lies outside this chapter's purview.

17.   This probably somewhat contentious assertion ought to be justified in some detail. Such a discussion is, however, too long to be included here. It will be found in the working-paper version of this chapter and can be obtained from the author upon request. Author's address: Centre de Recherches Économiques Appliquées' ('Créa'), Université de Lausanne BFSH, CH-1015 Lausanne-Dorigny, Switzerland.

9 Transform Methods and Dynamic Models

ANALYTICAL STRATEGIES AND NUMERICAL STRATEGIES

Dynamic models representing processes which unfold over time are often formulated as systems of difference or differential equations, each equation expressing one or more hypotheses about how the process being modeled actually works. A famous example of a dynamic model in the social sciences is the pair of differential equations proposed by Richardson (1919, 1939, 1960) to represent bilateral arms races:

$$\frac{dX(t)}{dt} = \alpha_1 Y(t) - \alpha_2 X(t) + \alpha_3 \qquad (1)$$

$$\frac{dY(t)}{dt} = \beta_1 X(t) - \beta_2 Y(t) + \beta_3 \qquad (2)$$

where $X(t)$ and $Y(t)$ are functions of time giving the arms budgets (or arms stockpiles) of two mutually suspicious countries. These equations reflect three simple hypotheses: (a) arms spending by either country spurs arms spending by its competitor; (b) arms spending is a burden to the country undertaking it and tends to inhibit further arms spending; (c) cultural or psychological components have a fixed effect upon changes in a country's arms budget.

We shall soon return to this example, but for the moment let us consider the more general problem of how to deal with dynamic models formulated as difference or differential equations. Two strategies are available to the modeler: an analytic strategy and a numerical strategy. The essential idea of the **analytic strategy**

This paper could not have been produced without the assistance of Richard Cook, Robin Crews, Judy Fukuhara, Jani Little, Zeke Little, and Michael D. Ward.

is to derive a set of general functions which satisfy the equations defining the model, i.e., the general solutions of the equation system. Having derived general solutions for the original system of equations, the analytic strategy then chooses parameter values which achieve the best agreement (by some plausible criterion) between the solution functions and the available empirical evidence.

The **numerical strategy**, on the other hand, proceeds directly from the original equation system to a set of theoretical predictions circumventing the process of deriving a general solution. The numerical approach is based upon the methods of numerical analysis and has been made feasible by the development of high-speed computers. Instead of seeking a general solution to the given equation system, it makes a numerical approximation of the particular solution suitable for the conditions at hand. Thus, the two stages of the analytic strategy--solving the equation, and choosing parameter values--merge into one, because numerical approximation of a particular solution entails specification of parameters.

Use of the numerical strategy is often a matter of necessity, because general solutions of dynamic equation systems may be unknown or intractable. Thus, it greatly extends the horizons of dynamic modeling by rendering practical systems well beyond the purview of analytic methods. Nevertheless, without minimizing the importance of numerical approaches, we shall stress the value of the analytic strategy not only as a means of obtaining complete solutions to equation systems, but also as a way of summarizing the qualitative behavior of dynamic models.

What are the advantages of the analytic approach to dynamic modeling? As already indicated, an analytic approach usually requires working with quite simple models, but even so the mathematics required can be difficult and the symbol manipulations formidable. Why should we tolerate these hardships?

If an analytic solution to the equations defining a dynamic model is possible, it may illuminate the general meaning of the model. It should provide perspective on all possible solutions to the equation system, not merely the solution relevant for a particular application. The analytic approach helps distinguish **necessary** from **contingent** aspects of the model. By necessary we mean properties flowing from basic model structure (i.e., fundamental assumptions) that hold true in all particular versions of the system, and by contingent we mean features dependent upon particular parameter values, initial conditions, and the like, i.e., features which may change from one form of the model to another. An analytic solution to a dynamic model shows exactly how the predictions depend upon parameters, thus indicating the exact consequences of changing parameter values.

We may summarize these points by noting that analytic solutions to dynamic models help to provide theoretical insight into the substantive process being modeled. Sometimes these analytically generated insights will enable an investigator to detect previously unsuspected relationships in the empirical world.

Even though we cannot provide analytic solutions for highly complex dynamic models, analytic methods can be used to investigate the likely consequences of various possible model assumptions. Thus, they can act as a preliminary to (or in tandem with) a numerical strategy, suggesting which structural features should be incorporated into more complex dynamic systems.

Parsimony is usually recognized as a desirable attribute of dynamic models. The analytic strategy leans heavily towards parsimony if only because analytic solutions vanish or become impossibly complicated by significant departures from simplicity. Used in conjunction with a numerical strategy, analytic methods can clarify issues of parameter identification and redundancy, imparting greater parsimony (and thus greater interpretability) to numerical solutions of dynamic systems.

Analytic and numerical strategies are not in competition with one another, and the last few paragraphs are not brief on behalf of the former. Each approach can obviously strengthen and complement the other. But given the availability of high-speed computers, model builders may be tempted to neglect the analytic strategy in favor of exclusive reliance upon numerical methods.

TRANSFORM METHODS

Joseph Fourier (1768-1830) and Pierre-Simon de Laplace (1749-1827) proposed methods for solving difference and differential equations which are ingenious and powerful and relatively easy to use.[1] The main idea behind these methods involves transforming a given difference or differential equation into a simple algebraic equation. This latter equation is then solved by ordinary algebraic methods, and the result is transformed back into the original frame of reference, providing a solution to the difference or differential equation being investigated. Because Fourier and Laplace methods involve a transformation from dynamic equations to algebraic equations, and then an inverse transformation back again, they are referred to as **transform methods**.

Transform methods are not new to the social sciences. They have been used for some time in mathematical economics,[2] and Luterbacher (1974) has previously applied them to the analysis of arms race models. But, relative to their elegance and analytic power, the application of transform methods to dynamic problems in social sciences other than economics has been surprisingly meager. And even when applications have occurred, they generally use only the most elementary transform properties. By exegesis and by example, this chapter tries to motivate more extensive use of transform methods in the service of building analytic models.

We cannot provide anything approaching a complete exposition of transform methods--which have been elaborated greatly since the age of Fourier and Laplace and are the subject of an extensive mathematical literature--but we shall offer a very brief description of how they work.[3] Transform methods come in a number of different varieties, including Fourier transforms, Laplace transforms, Bessel transforms, Hilbert transforms, and operational calculus. The Laplace transform[4] of a function $f(t)$ is defined as

$$L[f(t)] \equiv \int_0^\infty e^{-st} f(t) dt \equiv L_f(s) \qquad (3)$$

Observe that $L_f(s)$ is itself a function of variable s.

Given the Laplace transform of function $f(t)$, this function itself can be recovered through an inverse Laplace transform defined as

$$L^{-1}[L_f(s)] = \frac{1}{2\pi i} \int_{r-i\infty}^{r+i\infty} \frac{e^{st}}{s} L_f(s) ds$$

$$= f(t) \quad \text{for } t > 0 \qquad (4)$$

where $i = \sqrt{-1}$ and r is a positive number such that the integral in (3) converges when $s = r$. It is usually unnecessary to perform the difficult integration indicated in expressions (3) and (4) because extensive tables of Laplace and inverse Laplace transforms are available. One simply consults these tables to find the Laplace transform corresponding to a given function or, conversely, to find the function associated with a particular Laplace transform.[5]

The Laplace transform is useful in solving differential equations because (a) it is a linear operator, and (b) it has a very simple effect upon the derivative of a function. The linear operator property of the Laplace transform may be expressed as follows: if α and β are constants and $f(t)$ and $g(t)$ are functions, then

$$L[\alpha f(t) + \beta g(t) = \alpha L[f(t) + \beta L[g(t)] \qquad (5)$$

The inverse Laplace transform is also a linear operator, simplifying work with Laplace transforms and their inverses. For example, if a standard table does not list the Laplace transform of a given function, one can often, using the linear operator property, decompose the function into additive components whose transforms are indeed listed. The transforms of the components are then merely added together, yielding the Laplace transform of the given function.

The Laplace transform of a function's derivative is simply

$$L\left[\frac{df(t)}{dt}\right] = sL_f(s) - f(0) \tag{6}$$

Applying this relationship to the second derivative yields

$$\left[\frac{d^2f(t)}{dt^2}\right] = s^2L_f - sf(0) - f'(0) \tag{7}$$

And applying (6) iteratively on the nth derivative yields the general relationship

$$L\left[\frac{d^nf(t)}{dt^n}\right] = s^nL_f - s^{n-1}f(0) - s^{n-2}f'(0) - \ldots - f^{(n-1)}(0) \tag{8}$$

A very simple connection exists between (a) the Laplace transform of a function and (b) the Laplace transform of the function's derivatives. This elementary relationship explains why Laplace transforms are so useful in solving an important class of differential equations.

Note that Laplace transforms of a function's derivatives depend upon the values of the function and of its derivatives at t = 0. Hence, transform methods are particularly suitable for handling what are often called "initial value problems," that is, differential equations where the initial value of the function being sought and the initial values of its derivatives are known.

The Richardson equations (1) and (2) illustrate the application of transform methods to systems of differential equations. In order to simplify the computations, set $\alpha_1 = 4$, $\alpha_2 = 1$, $\alpha_3 = 2$, $\beta_1 = 1$, $\beta_2 = 1$, $\beta_3 = 4$, X(0) = 20, and Y(0) = 10. With these specifica-tions, equations (1) and (2) become

$$X' = 4Y - X + 2 \tag{1a}$$

$$Y' = X - Y + 4 \tag{2a}$$

Now take the Laplace transform of both sides of these equations. Using the linear operator property (5), and the derivative property (6), and the fact that the Laplace transform of a constant c equals c/s, we get

$$sL_x(s) - 20 = 4L_y(s) - L_x(s) + 2/s \qquad (9)$$

$$sL_y(s) - 10 = L_x(s) - L_y(s) + 4/s \qquad (10)$$

where $L_x(s)$ is the Laplace transform of function X(t) and $L_y(s)$ is the Laplace transform of Y(t).

Observe that equations (9) and (10) are linear in L_x and L_y.[6] Therefore, they may be solved for L_x and L_y with the usual techniques of elementary algebra. In particular, Cramer's rule is helpful for solving the simultaneous linear algebraic equations arising when systems of linear differential equations with constant coefficients undergo Laplace transformation.

Solving for L_x and L_y in equations (9) and (10) yields

$$L_x(s) = \frac{20 \cdot s^2 + 62 \cdot s + 18}{s(s-1)(s+3)} \qquad (11)$$

$$L_y(s) = \frac{10 \cdot s^2 + 34 \cdot s + 6}{s(s-1)(s+3)} \qquad (12)$$

Both of these Laplace transforms are rational algebraic functions of s, and their inverse transforms are well known. Consulting a table of Laplace transforms we find that

$$X(t) = 25e^t + e^{-3t} - 6 \qquad (13)$$

$$Y(t) = 1/2 [25e^t - e^{-3t} - 4] \qquad (14)$$

These functions satisfy equations (1a) and (2a) and are the only functions which do so under the given initial conditions. In this example, the ratio X/Y starts at 2, asymptotes at 2, and remains very close to 2 for all t $\geq$ 0.

The transform method can be applied to all linear differential equations with constant coefficients provided that the necessary initial values are known. The method is quite simple to use and, if the number of differential equations is small (four or less), it accomplishes a dramatic simplification of the equation system. In systems with more than four differential equations, the linear algebraic equations generated by the transformation are themselves cumbersome, and Laplace transforms calculated by the above procedure may well be untabulated or even intractable.

Transform methods are also applicable to difference equations. The procedures are not essentially different from those outlined above. The Laplace transform, however, proves to be a cumbersome tool for working with finite difference equations. For these equations it is generally easier to use close relatives of the Laplace transform, like the Z-transform or the generating function.

This illustrates a fundamental point. Transform methods refer to the general procedure of transforming dynamic equations into algebraic equations, and then back again. These methods should not be exclusively identified with a particular transform. We will use Laplace transforms extensively, but the reader should recognize that they are not the totality of the transform method, and that, in principle, we could use a different integral transform.[8]

ALTERNATIVES TO THE RICHARDSON MODEL

Having discussed transform methods for working with dynamic models, and having applied these methods to hypothetical examples of Richardson arms race models, let us now use the transform approach to explore a few simple alternative arms race models.

A Second-Order Equation Model

An obvious alternative to the Richardson model would be a system in which both the forces goading and the forces restraining arms acquisition have the general nature hypothesized by Richardson; but instead of influencing the rate at which armament levels change--that is, the first derivative of the $X(t)$ and $Y(t)$ functions--they influence the armament level acceleration patterns, i.e., the second derivatives of $X(t)$ and $Y(t)$. The differential equations representing such a system are

$$\frac{d^2X(t)}{dt^2} = \alpha_1 Y(t) - \alpha_2 X(t) + \alpha_3 \tag{15}$$

$$\frac{d^2Y(t)}{dt^2} = \beta_1 X(t) - \beta_2 Y(t) + \beta_3 \tag{16}$$

These equations differ from (1) and (2) only in having second rather than first derivatives on the left side.

A second-order equation model of this sort might be prompted by the observation that, among nations involved in arms races, certain patterns of change become largely habitual (e.g., increasing armament levels) and only sluggishly responsive to external forces. However, these forces might govern the acceleration or deceleration of armament levels within the context of an enduring general change pattern. The first-order or classical Richardson model assumes that armament level change rates are instantaneously responsive to the pushes and pulls represented by the right sides of the model equations. By contrast, the second-order model treats these change rates as only indirectly and gradually responsive to the forces operative.

Transform methods are easily applied to equations (15) and (16). Transforming both sides of these equations and solving for the Laplace transforms yields

$$L_x(s) = \frac{(s^2 X_0 + sX_0' + \alpha_3)(s^2 + \beta_2) + \alpha_1(s^2 Y_0 + sY_0' + \beta_3)}{s[(s^2 + \alpha_2)(s^2 + \beta_2) - \alpha_1\beta_1]} \tag{17}$$

$$L_y(s) = \frac{(s^2 Y_0 + sY_0' + \beta_3)(s^2 + \alpha_2) + \beta_1(s^2 X_0 + sX_0' + \alpha_3)}{s[(s^2 + \alpha_2)(s^2 + \beta_2) - \alpha_1\beta_1]} \tag{18}$$

where $X_0 = X(0)$, $Y_0 = Y(0)$, $X_0' = X'(0)$, and $Y_0' = Y'(0)$.

Taking the inverse Laplace transform of (17) and (18)

$$X(t) = X_0[A_1 + A_2 \cosh \lambda_1 t + A_3 \frac{\sinh \lambda_1 t}{\lambda_1}$$

$$+ A_4 \cosh \lambda_2 t + A_5 \frac{\sinh \lambda_2 t}{\lambda_2}] \tag{19}$$

$$Y(t) = Y_0[B_1 + B_2 \cosh \lambda_1 t + B_3 \frac{\sinh \lambda_1 t}{\lambda_1}$$

$$+ B_4 \cosh \lambda_2 t + B_5 \frac{\sinh \lambda_2 t}{\lambda_2}] \tag{20}$$

where sinh t and cosh t are the hyperbolic sine and cosine,[9] A_k and B_k are constants determined by the model parameters and the initial values,[10] and

$$\lambda_1 = [1/2\{-\alpha_2 - \beta_2 + \sqrt{(\alpha_2 - \beta_2)^2 + 4\alpha_1\beta_1}\}]^{1/2} \quad (21)$$

$$\lambda_2 = i[1/2\{\alpha_2 + \beta_2 + \sqrt{(\alpha_2 - \beta_2)^2 + 4\alpha_1\beta_1}\}]^{1/2}.[11] \quad (22)$$

The most important properties of this model can be determined from the values of λ_1 and λ_2 (sometimes called roots or eigenvalues of the differential equation system). If α_1, α_2, β_1, and β_2 are positive, then λ_2 is imaginary, and λ_1 can be either real or imaginary.[12] If λ_1 is real and not equal to zero, then X(t) and Y(t) diverge   toward infinity. Here the equation system has an **infinite stability,** and the arms race which it presumably models exhibits explosive growth. This is true whether λ_1 is taken as positive or negative.[13]
On the other hand, if parameter λ_1 is pure imaginary (along with λ_2), then the hyperbolic sine and cosine in equations   (19) and (20) become the ordinary sine and cosine functions, and X(t) and Y(t) exhibit cyclical behavior fluctuating back and forth over a fixed course whose frequency depends on λ_1 and λ_2. The same is true if λ_1 equals zero. Under these circumstances the system is said to have a **cyclical instability.**
Given these general guidelines, we can see from inspection of (21) and (22) that an infinite instability occurs whenever $\alpha_1\beta_1 > \alpha_2\beta_2$. If all parameters are positive, then a cyclical instability occurs whenever $\alpha_1\beta_1 \leqslant \alpha_2\beta_2$. This criterion, the reader may recall, is also important in the classical Richardson model. There the equation system is stable if $\alpha_1\beta_1 \leqslant \alpha_2\beta_2$ and unstable otherwise (again assuming positive parameters). Here,

however, the same criterion distinguishes between two different forms of instability.

If we relax the assumption that all parameters are positive, then λ_1 and λ_2 can have both real and imaginary parts. In fact, this will occur if

$$(\alpha_2 - \beta_2)^2 + 4\alpha_1\beta_1 < 0 \tag{23}$$

a necessary condition for which is that α_1 and β_1 have different signs. If λ_1 and λ_2 are complex numbers (with both real and imaginary parts), $X(t)$ and $Y(t)$ exhibit yet another form of instability: **infinite cyclical instability.** As t grows large, $X(t)$ and $Y(t)$ fluctuate back and forth with an amplitude approaching infinity.

A dynamic system is considered **stable** if it converges to a finite and stationary limit as $t \to \infty$. The second-order equation model defined by equations (15) and (16) allows stability only for very special parameter values and initial conditions. A necessary but not sufficient condition for stability is that $\lambda_1 = \lambda_2 = 0$.

This occurs only if

$$\alpha_2 + \beta_2 = 0 \text{ and } \alpha_2^2 + \beta_2^2 = -\alpha_1\beta_1 \tag{24}$$

In fact, the set of parameter values for which the second-order model is stable has Lebesque measure zero within the space defined by possible parameter values.

An Asymmetric Model

Another alternative to the Richardson model arises from relaxing the assumption of symmetry between the countries involved in the arms race. Of course the Richardson model itself allows response parameters (i.e., α_k and β_k) to differ between the conflicting countries, but the structure of the response equations remains identical. We understand an asymmetric model as a system in which the response equations are not structurally identical. In light of our previous formulation, an obvious yet still intriguing asymmetric model might assume that the forces controlling armaments operate upon the second derivative for one country, and upon the first derivative for the other. An asymmetric model of this kind could be expressed by the following equations

$$\frac{d^2X(t)}{dt^2} = \alpha_1Y(t) - \alpha_2X(t) + \alpha_3 \tag{25}$$

$$\frac{dY(t)}{dt} = \beta_1 X(t) - \beta_2 Y(t) + \beta_3 \qquad (26)$$

There is no particular reason to assume structural symmetry in an arms race. The forces governing a nation's level of armaments appear to depend upon, among other things, its political and economic organization, and, regarding these, an assumption of symmetry is hardly unquestionable. Even similarity in observed patterns of armament is no guarantee of structural symmetry at the level of causation.

The model defined by (25) and (26) is only one possible asymmetric system, but it has the virtue of being asymmetric while preserving continuity with our previous formulations. Indeed, these equations offer an interesting blend of the Richardson and second-order systems, with (25) and (26) being identical, respectively, to (15) and (2).

We proceed exactly as before, by transforming the model defining differential equations and solving for the Laplace transforms. These prove to be

$$L_x(s) = \frac{s^3 X_0 + s^2[X_0' + \beta_2 X_0] + s[\alpha_3 + \alpha_1 Y_0 + \beta_2 X_0'] + [\alpha_1 \beta_3 + \alpha_3 \beta_2]}{s[(s^2 + \alpha_2)(s + \beta_2) - \alpha_1 \beta_1]} \qquad (27)$$

$$L_y(s) = \frac{s^3 Y_0 + s^2[\beta_3 + \beta_1 X_0] + s[\alpha_2 Y_0 + \beta_1 X_0'] + [\alpha_2 \beta_3 + \alpha_3 \beta_1]}{s[(s^2 + \alpha_2)(s + \beta_2) - \alpha_1 \beta_1]} \qquad (28)$$

Several features of these Laplace transforms deserve notice. They are once again rational algebraic functions, in which case the denominators become especially important because their roots express the main properties of the dynamic system represented. The denominators in (27) and (28) are identical. At first glance these denominators appear similar to those in the Laplace transforms of (17) and (18), but closer inspection reveals an important difference.

The asymmetry of the equation system may be seen in the numerators of (27) and (28). To understand this point, consider for a moment the numerators of the Laplace transforms in (17) and (18), which represent a completely symmetric system. Here one numerator may be changed into the other merely by changing α_k into β_k, X_0 into Y_0, and X_0' into Y_0', or vice versa. But this does not hold for the numerators of (27) and (28). In particular it does not hold for the coefficients of the s and s^2 terms in these numerators. These asymmetric coefficients express, in the mode of Laplace transforms, the asymmetric character of the system.

Taking the inverse transforms, the solution functions are found to be

$$X(t) = A_1 e^{\lambda_1 t} + A_2 e^{\lambda_2 t} + A_3 e^{\lambda_3 t} + A_4 \qquad (29)$$

$$Y(t) = B_1 e^{\lambda_1 t} + B_2 e^{\lambda_2 t} + B_3 e^{\lambda_3 t} + B_4 \qquad (30)$$

where λ_1, λ_2, and λ_3 are the roots of the third-degree polynomial.[14]

$$(s^2 + \alpha_2)(s + \beta_2) - \alpha_1 \beta_1 = 0, \qquad (31)$$

and A_k, B_k are constants whose values depend on the model parameters and initial values.[15] Because (31) is a third-degree polynomial, at least one of its roots must be real. Let λ_1 be a real root. Then the coefficients A_1 and B_1 will also be real (see note 15). The other two roots λ_2 and λ_3 are either both real (in which case A_2, A_3, B_2, B_3 are all real), or they can be complex conjugates. In the latter case, A_2 and A_3 are complex conjugates, as are B_2 and B_3. The constant terms A_4 and B_4 are always real. Thus, in the summation prescribed by (29) and (30), the imaginary parts cancel out, making $X(t)$ and $Y(t)$ real valued functions, as they should be.

If λ_1, λ_2, and λ_3 have negative real parts, then the asymmetric system will be stable; otherwise it is unstable. Because these roots are fairly complicated functions of the parameters, α_1, β_1, α_2, and β_2, we cannot give an elementary condition which is both necessary and sufficient for model stability. We can, however, state a simple necessary condition. Because

$$\lambda_1 + \lambda_2 + \lambda_3 = -\beta_2 \qquad (32)$$

it follows that β_2 must be positive if the asymmetric system is to be stable. And because

$$\lambda_1 \lambda_2 + \lambda_1 \lambda_3 + \lambda_2 \lambda_3 = \alpha_2 \qquad (33)$$

we see that α_2 must also be positive in order to have system stability.

Why is this so? Why isn't the asymmetric structure of the original equation system reflected in the solution functions? Two answers may be given to this question. On the one hand the structural asymmetries postulated by this model are not very great. Both equations remain linear and with constant coefficients. The right sides of the two equations are still structurally identical. Given these parallel assumptions, it is perhaps naive to expect much asymmetry in the solution functions.

But there is still a more fundamental reason for the surprising absence of asymmetry. The two equations defining this system are strongly interconnected. Neither can be solved without the other, and each equation contains both unknown functions. Even though the arms race equations are asymmetric, the fact of interconnection means that each function transmits the dynamic process by which it is created into both equations, thus at least partially negating the asymmetric structure.

An important lesson emerges from this. Observed similarities in the conduct of participants in an arms race may conceal major differences in motivation.

An Integrated-Lag Model

The stimulus that a country receives from the armament program of its opponent may depend not on the opponent's present armament level, but on its cumulative (i.e., integrated) weapons possessions. In other words, a country involved in an arms race may react to the entire history of its opponent's weapons acquisition process. The summation of previous experience may seem a more reliable guide to the opponent's intentions than is the fleeting present reality. A simple model embodying this assumption is the following:

$$\frac{dX(t)}{dt} = \alpha_1 \int_{t-a}^{t} Y(u)\,du - \alpha_2 X(t) + \alpha_3 \qquad (34)$$

$$\frac{dY(t)}{dt} = \beta_1 \int_{t-b}^{t} X(u)\,du - \beta_2 Y(t) + \beta_3 \qquad (35)$$

Note the limits of integration of these equations. Country X reacts to the armaments possessed by Country Y over the past a time units. It does not react to weapons possessed by Country Y more than a time unit ago.

Conversely, Y reacts to weapons possessed by X over the past b time units, but not to arms possessed earlier.

It may be asked why integrating on the right sides of equations (34) and (35) is limited to the opponent's armaments function. The reason for this is theoretical, not technical. A country is not in doubt about its own military intentions or weapons hardware. A summation of past experience is not necessary for a country to grasp the effect of its present armaments level on the rate at which this level changes. Hence, the rationale for integration is lacking.

Two additional facts about Laplace transforms are required in order to transform equations (34) and (35):

$$L[\int_0^t f(u)\,du] = (1/s)L_f(s) \tag{36}$$

$$L[f(t-a)] = e^{-as}L_f(s) \tag{37}$$

(36) gives the Laplace transform of an integral, and (37) the Laplace transform of a function whose abscissa has been shifted (in our context a time translation). From these two relations it follows that

$$L[\int_{t-a}^t f(u)\,du] = \frac{1 - e^{-as}}{s} L_f(s) \tag{38}$$

We can now transform equations (34) and (35) and solve for L_x and L_y in the usual way, yielding

$$L_x(s) = \frac{s(X_0 S + \alpha_3)(s + \beta_2) - \alpha_1(Y_0 s + \beta_3)(e^{-as} - 1)}{s^2(s + \alpha_2)(s + \beta_2) - \alpha_1\beta_1(e^{-as} - 1)(e^{-bs} - 1)} \tag{39}$$

$$L_y(s) = \frac{s(Y_0 s + \beta_3)(s + \alpha_2) - \beta_1(X_0 s + \alpha_3)(e^{-bs} - 1)}{s^2(s + \alpha_2)(s + \beta_2) - \alpha_1\beta_1(e^{-as} - 1)(e^{-bs} - 1)} \tag{40}$$

The exponential terms in the denominators make these Laplace transforms difficult to work with. Simplification can be achieved by substituting the quadratic approximation of the exponential functions

$$e^{-x} \sim 1 - x + 1/2\ x^2 \tag{41}$$

Using this approximation in the denominators (not the numerators) of (39) and (40), and then taking inverse transforms we get

$$X(t) \sim A_1 + A_2 t + A_3 e^{\lambda_1 t} + A_4 e^{\lambda_2 t}$$
$$+ \mu(t-a)[B_1 + B_2(t-a) + B_3 e^{\lambda_1(t-a)} + B_4 e^{\lambda_2(t-a)}] \tag{42}$$

$$Y(t) \sim C_1 + C_2 t + C_3 e^{\lambda_1 t} + C_4 e^{\lambda_2 t}$$
$$+ \mu(t-b)[D_1 + D_2(t-b) + D_3 e^{\lambda_1(t-b)} + D_4 e^{\lambda_2(t-b)}] \tag{43}$$

where

$$\lambda_1 = \frac{-(\alpha_2 + \beta_2) + \sqrt{(\alpha_2 - \beta_2)^2 + 4\alpha_1\beta_1 \; ab}}{2} \tag{44}$$

$$\lambda_2 = \frac{-(\alpha_2 + \beta_2) + \sqrt{(\alpha_2 - \beta_2)^2 + 4\alpha_1\beta_1 \; ab}}{2} \tag{45}$$

and $\mu(t)$ is the **unit step function** defined as

$$\mu(t) = \begin{cases} 0 \text{ if } t < 0^{16} \\ 1 \text{ if } t \geqslant 0 \end{cases} \tag{46}$$

For most possible parameter values this system will diverge towards infinity. The conditions for stability are the following:

$$\alpha_3 = \beta_3 = 0 \tag{47}$$

$$\alpha_2 + \beta_2 > 0 \tag{48}$$

$$\alpha_2\beta_2 > \alpha_1\beta_1 ab \tag{49}$$

If the parameter values are positive or zero, the arms race generated by this system would not exhibit cyclical behavior of any form.

The importance of the lag widths (i.e., a and b, respectively) is evident from (44) and (45). Assuming that α_1 and β_1 are both positive or both negative, then

the wider the lag widths the larger the weapons stock possessed by a country at any given time. This makes sense since, with wider lags, a longer stretch of the opponent's history--or more exactly, the opponent's weapons stocks summated over a longer stretch of history --goads a country's arms acquisition process.

According to (42) and (43), the nature of the solution functions change profoundly at t = a and t = b when the lag effects begin operating full force upon X(t) and Y(t) respectively. The distortions introduced by our quadratic approximation of the exponential function are apparent in two aspects of the solution functions (which are themselves approximations). According to (42) and (43), X(t) has a discontinuity at t = a, and Y(t) has a discontinuity at t = b. Thus X'(t) and Y'(t) cannot exist at t = a and t = b, respectively. However, the basic model equations indicate that the derivatives should indeed exist at these points.

A second distortion is the segregation of the lag effects. Although the equation systems are interconnected, the b-lag does not enter into X(t) and the a-lag does not figure into function Y(t). These distortions notwithstanding, the approximate solutions we have obtained express the main features of the more elusive exact solutions.

An Interrupted Model

Arms race interaction takes place in a rapidly changing political context. Major economic or political events may interrupt and temporarily alter the usual dynamic of the arms race. For example, Ward (1984) finds that the wars in Korea and Vietnam drastically altered the US military budget, and that both getting into and out of the Vietnamese conflict left definite traces on the time path of US military stocks.

How does a temporary but possibly intense disturbance affect the interactions postulated by Richardson-type arms race models? Let us suppose that an interruption occurs at time m_1 and continues until time m_2. During this interval the disturbance--it might be a regional war, an economic disaster, a temporary military alliance, etc.--is assumed to exert a constant effect upon the rate of weapons accumulation. Using the unit step function $\mu(t)$ defined in (46), we may specify a simple arms race model which has these properties:

$$\frac{dX(t)}{dt} = \alpha_1 Y(t) - \alpha_2 X(t) + \alpha_3 [\mu(t-m_1) - \mu(t-m_2)] \quad (50)$$

$$\frac{dY(t)}{dt} = \beta_1 X(t) - \beta_2 Y(t) + \beta_3 \quad (51)$$

where m_2 is assumed to be greater than m_1. This is clearly an asymmetric model because a disturbance occurs only in the first equation. Moreover, the disturbance only affects the constant term of the equation. It does not affect the cross-stimulus term, i.e., $\alpha_1 Y(t)$ in equation (50), or the feedback term, i.e., $\alpha_2 X(t)$. More advanced interrupted models might allow the disturbance to operate upon these terms, in which case solutions would probably require methods of approximation like those used in the previous section.

The Laplace transform of a step function is

$$L[\mu(t-m)] = \frac{e^{-ms}}{s} \tag{52}$$

Using this relationship, the standard transform procedure yields

$$L_x(s) = \frac{[X_0 s^2 + \alpha_1 Y_0 s + \alpha_1 \beta_3] + [\alpha_3(e^{-m_1 s} - e^{-m_2 s})(s + \beta_2)]}{s[(s + \alpha_2)(s + \beta_2) - \alpha_1 \beta_1]} \tag{53}$$

$$L_y(s) = \frac{[Y_0 s^2 + s(\beta_3 + \alpha_2 Y_0 + \beta_1 X_0) + \alpha_2 \beta_3] + [\alpha_3 \beta_1(e^{-m_1 s} - e^{-m_2 s})]}{s[(s + \alpha_2)(s + \beta_2) - \alpha_1 \beta_1]} \tag{54}$$

Taking inverse transforms

$$X(t) = X_0 [A_1 e^{\lambda_1 t} + A_2 e^{\lambda_2 t} + A_3] \tag{55}$$

$$+ \mu(t-m_1)[B_1 e^{\lambda_1(t-m_1)} + B_2 e^{\lambda_2(t-m_1)} + B_3]$$

$$- \mu(t-m_2)[B_1 e^{\lambda_1(t-m_2)} + B_2 e^{\lambda_2(t-m_2)} + B_3]$$

$$Y(t) = Y_0 [C_1 e^{\lambda_1 t} + C_2 e^{\lambda_2 t} + C_3] \tag{56}$$

$$+ \mu(t-m_1)[D_1 e^{\lambda_1(t-m_1)} + D_2 e^{\lambda_2(t-m_1)} + D_3]$$

$$- \mu(t-m_2) D_1 e^{\lambda_1(t-m_2)} + D_2 e^{\lambda_2(t-m_2)} + D_3]$$

where A_i, B_i, C_i, and D_i ($i = 1, 2, 3$) are constants depending upon model parameters and initial values,[17] and the roots λ_1 and λ_2 are the same as those for the general Richardson equations (see note 7).

It is clear from (55) and (56) that the stability of this interrupted model depends upon the values of λ_1 and λ_2. Since these depend upon model parameters in just the same way as in the original Richardson model, it follows that the stability conditions here are precisely the same as those for the Richardson model, being given by (48) and (49), with a = b = 1. According to this model a temporary disturbance does not influence the stability or instability of the system.

Nevertheless the disturbance has an enduring impact upon the arms accumulations of the interacting countries; an impact which continues and changes magnitude long after the disturbance is over. The effect of the disturbance is perpetuated over time because, during its duration, it has altered the character of the arms race. The consequences of this altered condition are then transmitted over time by the normal dynamics of the system.

APPLICATIONS TO THE SOVIET-AMERICAN ARMS RACE

The main purpose of this paper is to discuss the value of transform methods in developing dynamic models of international conflict. This purpose, strictly speaking, does not require application of conflict models to empirical data. Nevertheless, our argument will become more comprehensible (and hopefully persuasive) if the models presented in the previous sections are applied to a real situation of international conflict.

The most obvious and surely the most salient conflict to which these models apply is the ongoing arms race between the Soviet Union and the United States. Ward (1984) has calculated indices of both Soviet and American military stocks between 1951 and 1978. These indices are obtained by multiplying a conventional weapons index and a strategic weapons index.[18] Mainly for illustrative purposes, each of the four models discussed above, plus the standard Richardson model, has been fit to Ward's data on Soviet and American military stocks.

We proceed in three steps:

(1) Estimating the parameters contained in the differential equations defining a dynamic model.

(2) Specifying the previously obtained solution functions for the dynamic model by using the estimated parameters.

(3) Computing the predictions made by the model for Soviet and American military stocks by applying the specified solution functions.

Of these three steps, the first is by far the most difficult. Once parameters have been estimated, steps 2 and 3 are entirely straightforward from the formulae presented above.

Model parameters were estimated by use of MINUIT, a program developed at the Center for European Nuclear Research (CERN) to minimize the difference between the predictions of a theoretical model and a set of empirical data to which the model is applied (James and Roos, 1976). MINUIT contains three subroutines usable in various combinations, depending upon the nature of the model and data, to choose the optimal parameter values. Subroutine SEEK undertakes a Monte Carlo search process. Subroutine SIMPLEX uses the geometric concept of a simplex to undertake a more systematic search procedure. Subroutine MIGRAD employs the gradient of the function being minimized (i.e., the function chosen to measure the difference between observed and predicted values) to conduct a still more efficient--though less robust--search for optimal parameter values.

When the SIMPLEX or MIGRAD subroutines converge, they converge towards a local minimum, meaning the best parameter values in some particular region of the parameter space. This local minimum can also be the global minimum; but it need not be. The distinction between local and global minima, plus the fact that the subroutines do not always converge, means that using MINUIT is not entirely cut and dried.

Our standard procedure was to use the MINUIT subroutines in this sequence: SEEK, SIMPLEX, MIGRAD, SEEK. We used SEEK first in order to obtain a good starting point for the more sophisticated estimation procedures. SIMPLEX, described by the creators of MINUIT as "very 'safe' and reasonably fast when far from the minimum" (p. 2) was used next in order to approach the neighborhood of a local minimum. MIGRAD continued the parameter search process, hopefully carrying it towards convergence. Finally, we used SEEK to explore whether a better local minimum could be found.[19] When SIMPLEX or MIGRAD did not converge, we placed their last parameter estimates into the SEEK subroutine to obtain the results presented below. Estimates obtained in this manner may not be local minima.[20]

        As indicated above, Ward's data includes twenty-
eight yearly measurements of Soviet weapons stocks, and
twenty-eight parallel measurements of American weapons
stocks. The first measurements in each of the two
series--those for 1951--are both incorporated within our
models as initial values. This leaves twenty-seven yearly
weapons stock indices from 1952 through 1978 (for each
country) which our models can predict.
        We shall discuss the performance and interpretation
of all five arms race models (i.e., standard Richardson,
second-order,   asymmetric,   integrated-lag,   and
interrupted). Our concern is less with statistical
questions of model fit, than with more qualitative
appraisals of whether the distinctive feature embodied in
a model can help social scientists understand the Soviet-
American arms race.
        We begin by comparing empirical measurements of
weapons stocks with the theoretical predictions of our
five models. Table 9.1 presents this information for
United States weapons stocks, and Table 9.2 gives it for
the weapons stocks of the Soviet Union. To guide readers
through this daunting array of numbers, we indicate
whether each theoretical prediction falls above or below
the corresponding empirical observation.
        All five models are able to depict the general
movement of Soviet and American weapons stocks, but in no
case is a very high level of predictive accuracy attained.
Recalling that these models use between six and eight free
parameters to describe a mere fifty-four well-behaved data
points, this weakness seems especially evident. There is,
however, considerable variation in the predictive accuracy
of the five models. According to the chi-square index of
model fit used to select parameter values, the interrupted
model approximates the weapons data most closely, while
the integrated-lag model strays widest of the mark. We
will say more about these variations shortly.
        Lack of close agreement between data and models does
not disqualify the latter from further consideration. The
models were always recognized as quite elementary
formulations. Our interest focused on questions of
method, but also on whether the principles expressed in
simple form by these models should be incorporated into
more   elaborate   (and   hopefully   more   realistic)
representations of the arms race. On this account, at
least, these five models merit further attention.
        Perusal of Tables 9.1 and 9.2 yields some
interesting results. The deviations of predictions from
data are anything but random. Almost always we find long
stretches where a model's predictions consistently exceed
the empirical measurements, followed by equally lengthy
intervals over which measurements exceed prediction. The
pattern of deviations virtually never shows that unsys-

TABLE 9.1   United States Weapons Stocks 1952-1978:   Empirical
            Measurements and Theoretical Predictions

Year	Empirical Measure-ments**	I	II	III	IV	V
				Theoretical Predictions*		
1952	525	714(H)	568(H)	752(H)	2,790(H)	886(H)
1953	663	1,133(H)	815(H)	1,291(H)	3,114(H)	1,360(H)
1954	808	1,616(H)	1,110(H)	1,941(H)	3,471(H)	1,817(H)
1955	1,154	2,165(H)	1,470(H)	2,679(H)	3,862(H)	2,288(H)
1956	1,709	2,786(H)	1,905(H)	3,487(H)	4,291(H)	2,799(H)
1957	2,805	3,481(H)	2,425(L)	4,349(H)	4,762(H)	3,373(H)
1958	3,787	4,256(H)	3,039(L)	5,254(H)	5,278(H)	4,030(H)
1959	4,845	5,113(H)	3,755(L)	6,194(H)	5,846(H)	4,793(H)
1960	5,041	6,065(H)	4,580(L)	7,161(H)	6,469(H)	5,685(L)
1961	7,452	7,083(L)	5,522(L)	8,151(H)	7,152(L)	6,732(L)
1962	9,317	8,198(L)	6,589(L)	9,163(L)	7,902(L)	7,964(L)
1963	9,904	9,399(L)	7,790(L)	10,196(H)	8,726(L)	9,417(L)
1964	11,480	10,684(L)	9,132(L)	11,250(L)	9,629(L)	11,130(L)
1965	12,730	12,047(L)	10,622(L)	12,330(L)	10,621(L)	13,152(H)
1966	15,490	13,484(L)	12,265(L)	13,440(L)	11,710(L)	14,993(L)
1967	17,228	14,984(L)	14,063(L)	14,586(L)	12,904(L)	16,384(L)
1968	19,263	16,537(L)	16,015(L)	15,775(L)	14,215(L)	17,508(L)
1969	19,726	18,128(L)	18,109(L)	17,016(L)	15,654(L)	18,494(L)
1970	17,492	19,737(H)	20,324(H)	18,321(H)	17,234(L)	19,430(H)
1971	17,950	21,344(H)	22,617(H)	19,702(H)	18,967(H)	20,384(H)
1972	19,774	22,920(H)	24,920(H)	21,173(H)	20,870(H)	21,411(H)
1973	23,418	24,435(H)	27,120(H)	22,751(L)	22,957(H)	22,558(L)
1974	26,467	25,852(L)	29,042(H)	24,453(L)	25,249(L)	23,868(L)
1975	27,352	27,128(L)	30,419(H)	26,303(L)	27,764(H)	25,385(L)
1976	27,685	28,213(H)	30,843(H)	28,322(H)	30,523(H)	27,157(L)
1977	29,102	29,054(L)	29,708(H)	30,537(H)	33,552(H)	29,237(H)
1978	30,076	29,586(L)	26,106(L)	32,981(H)	36,876(H)	31,684(H)

  I: Standard Richardson model
  II: Second-order equation model
 III: Asymmetric model
 IV: Integrated-lag model
  V: Interrupted model

*(H) indicates that a theoretical prediction is higher than the
corresponding empirical measurement, while (L) indicates that the
prediction is lower than the measurement.

**Empirical measurements are taken from Ward (1984, p. 312).

TABLE 9.2   Soviet Union Weapons Stocks 1952-1978:   Empirical
Measurements and Theoretical Prediction

Year	Empirical measure-ments**	I	II	III	IV	V
1952	16	-22(L)	32(H)	16	34(H)	151(H)
1953	18	-42(L)	79(H)	27(H)	61(H)	268(H)
1954	20	-41(L)	157(H)	51(H)	99(H)	378(H)
1955	162	-16(L)	268(H)	93(L)	150(L)	488(H)
1956	309	38(L)	413(H)	158(L)	218(L)	606(H)
1957	432	126(L)	598(H)	251(L)	307(L)	737(H)
1958	533	253(L)	811(H)	375(L)	419(L)	886(H)
1959	650	425(L)	1,068(H)	536(L)	560(L)	1,058(H)
1960	824	649(L)	1,367(H)	739(L)	736(L)	1,259(H)
1961	1,002	930(L)	1,711(H)	990(L)	952(L)	1,494(H)
1962	1,037	1,276(H)	2,104(H)	1,294(H)	1,216(H)	1,771(H)
1963	1,072	1,694(H)	2,548(H)	1,658(H)	1,536(H)	2,097(H)
1964	1,252	2,191(H)	3,049(H)	2,090(H)	1,920(H)	2,482(H)
1965	2,014	2,776(H)	3,611(H)	2,599(H)	2,381(H)	2,936(H)
1966	2,439	3,456(H)	4,239(H)	3,193(H)	2,929(H)	3,459(H)
1967	3,838	4,238(H)	4,939(H)	3,884(H)	3,579(L)	4,058(H)
1968	4,790	5,131(H)	5,717(H)	4,682(L)	4,347(L)	4,750(L)
1969	5,857	6,143(H)	6,580(H)	5,603(L)	5,249(L)	5,560(L)
1970	7,028	7,280(H)	7,534(H)	6,660(L)	6,307(L)	6,509(L)
1971	8,471	8,549(H)	8,587(H)	7,872(L)	7,545(L)	7,626(L)
1972	9,200	9,955(H)	9,747(H)	9,258(H)	8,987(L)	8,943(L)
1973	9,851	11,504(H)	11,019(H)	10,841(H)	10,663(H)	10,495(L)
1974	10,976	13,198(H)	12,410(H)	12,645(H)	12,608(H)	12,327(H)
1975	13,235	15,038(H)	13,923(H)	14,699(H)	14,358(H)	14,489(H)
1976	16,494	17,024(H)	15,560(L)	17,085(H)	17,456(H)	17,041(H)
1977	20,317	19,152(L)	17,316(L)	19,691(L)	20,452(H)	20,054(L)
1978	26,594	21,417(L)	19,177(L)	22,708(L)	23,899(L)	23,611(L)

I: Standard Richardson model
II: Second-order equation model
III: Asymmetric model
IV: Integrated-lag model
V: Interrupted model

*
(H) indicates that a theoretical prediction is higher than the
corresponding empirical measurement, while (L) indicates that the
prediction is lower than the measurement.

**
Empirical measurements are taken from Ward (1984, p. 312).

tematic alternation between excessive and insufficient predictions expected from truly random error.[21] Model predictions more frequently exceed than lag below observations, a tendency particularly evident for the second-order and interrupted models.

As we all know, the 1960s were an unusual decade. This can be detected from Tables 9.1 and 9.2. In every year between 1962 and 1966, all five models overestimate Soviet military stocks. Conversely, in all but two years between 1962 and 1969, all models underestimate American military stocks. These uniform deviation patterns probably reflect the stabilization of Soviet weapon stockpiles during the early sixties, and the US buildup for the Vietnam war during the latter part of the decade.

These are not the only years when predictions deviate in a uniform direction from observations. All models overestimate US military stocks during 1952, 1953, 1954, and 1956, and again for 1971 and 1972, the former period being the aftermath of the Korean war, and the latter the wind-down phase in Vietnam.

Soviet weapons stocks fall beneath the predictions of all models during 1973-1975, and above their predictions in 1978 (the last year on which we have data). The shortfall in the former interval may reflect the effects of SALT-I and the so-called "detente" period, while the latter underestimation surely results from the recent Soviet weapons surge.

This sort of analysis could be carried further, but the main point is now fairly evident: theoretical structures can help identify distinctive phases of the arms race not entirely evident from scanning the weapons indices themselves. Such an identification procedure reduces the subjectivism associated with many historical judgments (Figures 9.1-9.5 present, in graphic form, the information given by Tables 9.1 and 9.2).

Application of the Standard Richardson Model

Table 9.3 summarizes the most salient information concerning application of the standard Richardson model to the Soviet-American arms race. Parameter estimates for this model make α_1 and α_2 negative, but set β_1 and β_2 positive. If this were the case, the Soviet Union would be animated by the classic Richardson dynamics, while American participation in the arms race would be propelled in exactly the opposite manner. That is, Soviet weapons stocks, instead of motivating further American armament, would create a tendency to disarm, while America's own arms accumulations would propel yet additional weapons acquisitions.

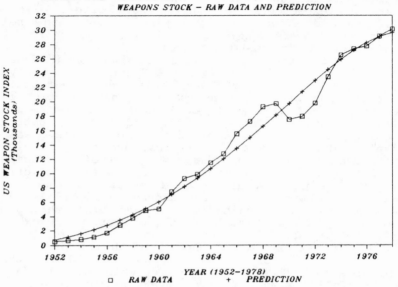

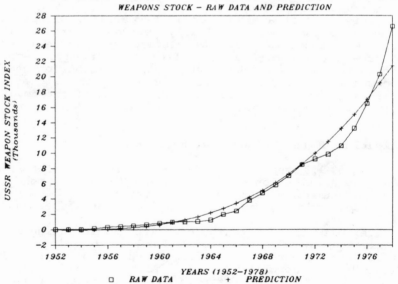

Figure 9.1   The Richardson Model of the Arms Race

UNITED STATES SECOND ORDER MODEL
WEAPONS STOCK – RAW DATA AND PREDICTION

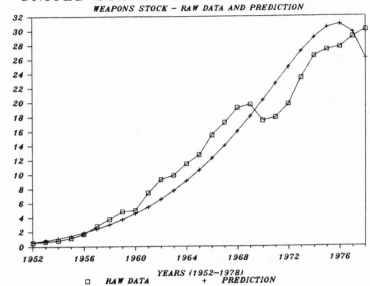

SOVIET UNION SECOND ORDER MODEL
WEAPONS STOCK – RAW DATA AND PREDICTION

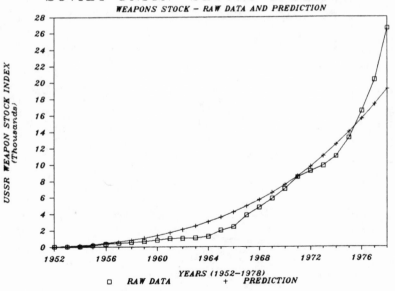

Figure 9.2   A Second Order Model of the Arms Race

UNITED STATES -- ASYMETRIC MODEL

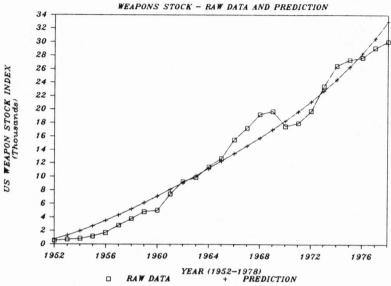

WEAPONS STOCK - RAW DATA AND PREDICTION

□ RAW DATA + PREDICTION

SOVIET UNION -- ASYMETRIC MODEL

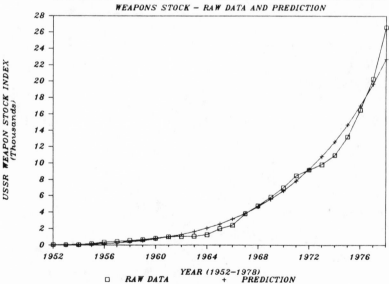

WEAPONS STOCK - RAW DATA AND PREDICTION

□ RAW DATA + PREDICTION

Figure 9.3   An Asymmetric Model of the Arms Race

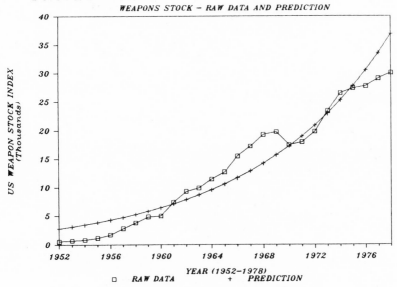

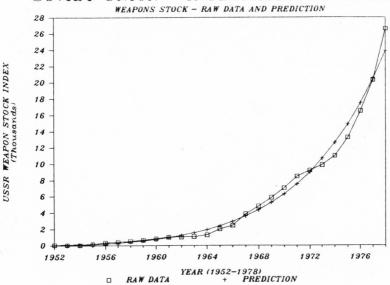

Figure 9.4   An Integrated Lag Model of the Arms Race

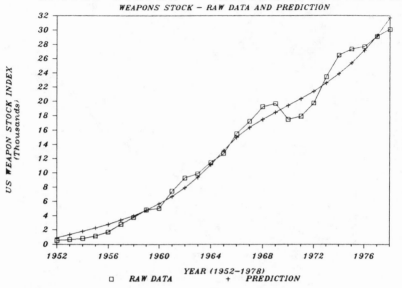

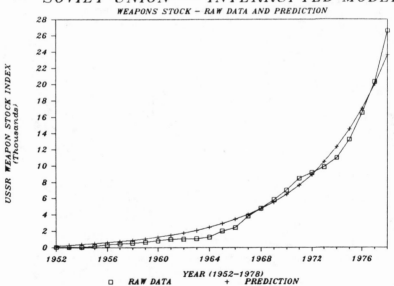

Figure 9.5   An Interrupted Model of the Arms Race

TABLE 9.3   Standard Richardson Model: Parameter Estimates, Model
            Equations, and Solution Functions

Parameter Estimates

Symbol	Possible Parameter Interpretations	Estimated Parameter Values
α_1	Effect of Soviet weapons stocks on American tendency to arm	-.1824
α_2	Effect of American weapons stocks on American tendency to disarm	-.1342
α_3	Intrinsic American tendency to arm	290.4
β_1	Effect of American weapons stocks on Soviet tendency to arm	.0465
β_2	Effect of Soviet weapons stocks on Soviet tendency to disarm	.0474
β_3	Intrinsic Soviet tendency to arm	-61.2

Model Defining Equations (in specified form)

$$\frac{dX(t)}{dt} = (-.1824)Y(t) + (.1342)X(t) + 290.4$$

$$\frac{dY(t)}{dt} = (.0465)X(t) - (.0474)Y(t) - 61.2$$

Solution Functions (in specified form)

$$X(t) = (263.8 - i \cdot (1766.4)) \cdot \exp\{t(.0908 + i(.0812))\}$$
$$+ (2.63.8 + i \cdot (1766.4)) \cdot \exp\{t(.0908 - i(.0812))\}$$
$$- 175.7$$

$$Y(t) = -(723.9 + i(538.1)) \cdot \exp\{t(.0908 + i(.0812))\}$$
$$-(723.9 - i(538.1)) \cdot \exp\{t(.0908 - i(.0812))\}$$
$$+ 1462.7 \qquad (i = \sqrt{-1})$$

Chi-square Index of Model Fit[*]

F = 13588

[*] See note 20.

A dynamic system of this sort is surprising, but not inconceivable. For example, it could arise if the economic well-being of a country depended upon progressively larger arms expenditures, yet citizens sensed that the resulting weapons acquisitions were dangerously provocative to the opponent.

According to the solution functions obtained from application of the standard Richardson model, the Soviet-American arms race should follow a cyclical course with a period of about 77 years and an exponentially increasing amplitude. Thus, the data cover only 35% of a complete cycle; an interval during which arms stocks are increasing. The system is unstable, with the amplitudes of the weapons cycles followed by the US and USSR approaching infinity. The ratio of the American to the Soviet amplitude approaches 2.0, showing that weapons acquisitions by the US would follow a more volatile course than those of the Soviet Union.

Since the Richardson model does not give a very accurate representation of our weapons data--and even if it did, the specified model could hardly remain appropriate for very long--these results may be of little scientific interest. But possessing only the predictions made by the model, and not the analytically derived solution functions, we would know almost nothing about the cyclical properties of this system.

Application of the Second-Order Model

The second-order model fits the data even more poorly than the standard Richardson formulation but, as can be seen from Table 9.4, it has some of the same properties.

Once again parameters β_1 and β_2 are positive (suggesting that the USSR responds to an arms race in approximately the manner hypothesized by Richardson), while parameters α_1 and α_2 are negative (suggesting that the US responds in the opposite or inverse manner). The weapons of the opposing side seems to have a stronger effect (either positive or negative) on the acceleration of weapons stocks than does one's own military hardware. This difference is particularly marked for the United States where (if the second-order model has any plausibility) a unit of Soviet military stocks has over two and one-half times the impact of a unit of American military stocks.

The solution functions for the second-order model indicate some thoroughly enigmatic long-term behavior. Soviet weapons stocks become infinite monotonically, while

TABLE 9.4   Second-Order Model: Parameter Estimates, Model Equations, and Solution Functions

---

Parameter Estimates

Symbol	Possible Parameter Interpretations	Estimated Parameter Values
α_1	Effect of Soviet weapons stocks on American tendency to accelerate arming	-.4079
α_2	Effect of American weapons stocks on American tendency to decelerate arming	-.1575
α_3	Intrinsic American tendency to accelerate arming	-46.3
β_1	Effect of American weapons stocks on Soviet tendency to accelerate arming	.0050
β_2	Effect of Soviet weapons stocks on Soviet tendency to decelerate arming	.0040
β_3	Intrinsic Soviet tendency to accelerate arming	27.6

Model Defining Equations (in specified form)

$$\frac{d^2X(t)}{dt^2} = (-.4079)Y(t) + (.1575)X(t) - 46.3$$

$$\frac{d^2Y(t)}{dt^2} = (.005)X(t) - (.004)Y(t) + 27.6$$

Solution Functions (in specified form)

$$X(t) = -8131 - (597)\cosh[t(.3791)] + (594.7)\sinh[t(.3791)]$$

$$+(9080)\cosh[t(.0989)] - (156.6)\sinh[t(.0989)]$$

$$Y(t) = -3253 - (20.1)\cosh[t(.3791)] + (20.1)\sinh[t(.3791)]$$

$$+(3287)\cosh[t(.0989)] - (56.7)\sinh[t(.0989)]$$

Chi-square Index of Model Fit*

   F = 20265.

---

*See note 20.

American weaponry, after increasing over a twenty-five-year interval, starts diminishing and ultimately approaches negative infinity (whatever that may mean in this context). As the reader can see in Figure 9.2, the model predicts that American military stocks reach a maximum by 1976 and decline thereafter. The problems posed by a model generating uninterpretable long-range predictions are considered in the final section of this paper.

Application of the Asymmetric Model

The asymmetric model, as explained in our earlier discussion, postulates an asymmetry at the level of causal dynamics, but not at the level of predicted outcome. This is evident in the solution functions presented in Table 9.5. We have arbitrarily named the United States as the country for which causal forces operate through the second derivative, that is, through the rate of acceleration in arms acquisition.

According to the estimated solution functions, the armament levels of both countries approach an exponential growth rate with doubling time of less than six years, and with Soviet armaments slightly more than 40% greater than American weapons stocks.

The asymmetric model, like the two models already discussed, represents the dynamics of American weapons acquisitions as exactly inverse to the process proposed by Richardson. Unlike the former models, however, it estimates parameter β_1 as positive and parameter β_2 as

negative. If this were actually so, then no structural factors would constrain the growth of Soviet weapons stocks: American weapons stocks would induce expansion of Soviet weaponry as would the existing accumulation of Soviet armaments. In all cases previously considered, own and enemy weapons stocks had opposing effects upon the acquisition of further armaments.

The asymmetric model, we note in passing, fits the 1952-1978 data better than the Richardson or the second-order model. This improvement has some connection with the flexibility introduced by treating the arms race participants differently. Political and military theorists should be cautioned against the sometimes automatic assumption of symmetry between competing nations.

TABLE 9.5 Asymmetric Model: Parameter Estimates, Model Equations, and Solution Functions

---

Parameter Estimates

Symbol	Possible Parameter Interpretations	Estimated Parameter Values
α_1	Effect of Soviet weapons stocks on American tendency to accelerate arming	-.0027
α_2	Effect of American weapons stocks on American tendency to decelerate arming	-.0236
α_3	Intrinsic American tendency to accelerate arming	212.2
β_1	Effect of American weapons stocks on Soviet tendency to arm	.0262
β_2	Effect of Soviet weapons stocks on Soviet tendency to disarm	-.1225
β_3	Intrinsic Soviet tendency to arm	0.2

Model Defining Equations (in specified form)

$$\frac{dX(t)}{dt} = (-.0027)Y(t) + (.0236)X(t) + 212.2$$

$$\frac{dY(t)}{dt} = (.0262)X(t) + (.1225)Y(t) + 0.2$$

Solution Functions (in specified form)

$$X(t) = 635.9 \exp\{t(.1243)\}$$
$$- 10^3 \cdot (9.4 + i(2809.4)) \cdot \exp\{-t(.1064 + i(.0003))\}$$
$$- 10^3 \cdot (9.4 - i(2809.4)) \cdot \exp\{-t(.1064 - i(.0003))\}$$
$$+ 18461.8$$

$$Y(t) = 911.5 \exp\{t(.1243)\}$$
$$+ 10^3(1.5 + i(336.8)) \cdot \exp\{-t(.1064 + i(.0003))\}$$
$$+ 10^3(1.5 - i(336.8)) \cdot \exp\{-t(.1064 - i(.0003))\}$$
$$+ 3948.9$$

$$(i = \sqrt{-1})$$

Chi-square Index of Model Fit[*]

$$F = 10213$$

---

*See note 20.

Application of the Integrated-Lag Model

Parameter estimates for this model once again suggest that the American weapons acquisition process obeys an inverse Richardson dynamic (see Table 9.6). They also suggest—as did the parameters estimated for the asymmetric model—that the Soviet Union functions with no structural constraints on the growth of its weapons stockpile (because β_1 is positive and β_2 negative).

The estimated length of American memory about Soviet weapons stocks is under 2 years, and thus much shorter than the estimated Soviet memory about American armaments which, at 28 years, reached the maximum length feasible, given the time span of our data set.

The reader will recall that the solution we gave for the integrated-lag model was not exact, but relied instead upon a crucial approximation which simplified the Laplace transform. This approximation, we suspect, has diminished the fit of the integrated-lag model by disrupting the initial value concordance (i.e., the agreement between model and data at time zero) which a full-fledged analytic solution using transform methods would possess.

The asymptotic properties of the model are perhaps more reliable, but of dubious meaning in view, among other things, of poor model fit. According to the estimated solution functions, Soviet weapons stocks will ultimately diverge towards infinity, while American stocks will become unboundedly negative.

Application of the Interrupted Model

The last of our five models is, by the chi-square criterion, also the one most congruent with the empirical data (see Table 9.7). In applying this model we have given the role of country experiencing interruption to the United States, and in this case the assignment was not entirely arbitrary. Our knowledge of the modern period, as well as certain properties of the data, suggest that the war in Vietnam was the most important "interruption" occurring between 1952 and 1978; and that, among the two contending superpowers, its impact fell primarily upon the United States. The estimation procedure recognized the presumed association between interruption and war in Vietnam, but could still select a different interruption interval should this improved model fit. As it happened, the estimation procedure selected an interruption interval running from 1965, the time of the major US escalation in Vietnam, through the end of the time period being modeled. The boundaries of the interruption were more or less what was expected, but a major surprise still lay in

TABLE 9.6   Integrated-Lag Model: Parameter Estimates, Model
             Equations, and Solution Functions

Parameter Estimates

Symbol	Possible Parameter Interpretations	Estimated Parameter Values
α_1	Effect of Soviet weapons stocks, summed over the past a time units, on American tendency to arm	-.0018
α_2	Effect of American weapons stocks on American tendency to disarm	-.0653
α_3	Intrinsic American tendency to arm	46.0
β_1	Effect of American weapons stocks, summed over the past b time units, on Soviet tendency to arm	.0136
β_2	Effect of Soviet weapons stocks on Soviet tendency to disarm	-.1287
β_3	Intrinsic Soviet tendency to arm	12.9
a	Length (in years) of American memory about Soviet weapons stocks	1.45
b	Length (in years) of Soviet memory about American weapons stocks	28.0

Model Defining Equations (in specified form)

$$\frac{dX(t)}{dt} = -(.0018) \int_{t-1.45}^{t} Y(u)\,du + (.0653)X(t) + 46.0$$

$$\frac{dY(t)}{dt} = (.0136) \int_{t-28.0}^{t} X(u)\,du + (.1287)Y(t) + 12.9$$

Solution Functions (in specified form)

$X(t) \sim - 683.8 - t(2.49) - (2096) \exp [t(.1001)]$
$\qquad +(5273) \exp [t(.094)]$
$\qquad + \mu(t - 1.45) \cdot \{ 155.5 + 2.49(t - 1.45)$
$\qquad +(1988) \exp[(t - 1.45)(.1001)]$
$\qquad -(2143) \exp [(t - 1.45)(.094)]\}$

$Y(t) \sim 1791 + t(66.5) + (18890) \exp [t(.1001)]$
$\qquad - (20600) \exp [t(.094)]$
$\qquad + \mu(t - 28)\{-1881 - (65.5)(t - 28)$
$\qquad -(18000)\exp [(t - 28)(.1001)] +(19950)\exp[(t - 28)(.094)]\}$

where $\mu(x) = \begin{cases} 0 & \text{if } x < 0 \\ 1 & \text{if } x \geqslant 0 \end{cases}$

Chi-square Index of Model Fit*

F = 21923.

*See note 20.

TABLE 9.7   Interrupted Model: Parameter Estimates, Model Equations, and Solution Functions

---

Parameter Estimates

Symbol	Possible Parameter Interpretations	Estimated Parameter Values
α_1	Effect of Soviet weapons stocks on American tendency to arm	.2152
α_2	Effect of American weapons stocks on American tendency to disarm	.1191
α_3	Effect of interruption (e.g., local war) on American tendency to arm	-69.6
m_1	Time in years at which interruption begins (1951 = time zero)	14.0
m_2	Time in years at which interruption ends	>27 (exact value is meaningless)
β_1	Effect of American weapons stocks on Soviet tendency to arm	.3875
β_2	Effect of Soviet weapons stocks on Soviet tendency to disarm	.1264
β_3	Intrinsic Soviet tendency to arm	15.6

Model Defining Equations (in specified form)

$$\frac{dX(t)}{dt} = (.2152)Y(t) - (.1191)X(t) - (69.6)\mu(t - 14.0)$$

$$\frac{dY(t)}{dt} = (.3875)X(t) - (.1264)Y(t) + 15.6$$

$$\text{where } \mu(x) = \begin{cases} 0 & \text{if } x < 0 \\ 1 & \text{if } x \geqslant 0 \end{cases}$$

Solution Functions (in specified form)

$$X(t) = (1287.7) \exp\{t(.1661)\} - (850.2) \exp\{-t(.4115)\} - 49.0$$
$$- \mu(t - 14.0) \cdot (10^3)[(114.0) \exp\{(t - 14)(.1661)\}$$
$$- 4.4 \exp\{-(t - 14)(.4115)\} + 15.8]$$

$$Y(t) = (289.8) \exp\{t(.1661)\} - (247.7) \exp\{-t(.4115)\} - 27.1$$
$$- \mu(t - 14.0) \cdot [(281.0)\exp\{(t - 14)(.1661)\}$$
$$+ (113.4) \exp\{-(t - 14)(.4115)\} - 394.4]$$

$$\text{where } \mu(x) = \begin{cases} 0 & \text{if } x < 0 \\ 1 & \text{if } x \geqslant 0 \end{cases}$$

Chi-square Index of Model Fit[*]
    F = 8742.

---

*See note 20.

store. The assumed effect of the interruption would be to increase American armaments, especially since the interruption began at the moment of expanded US involvement in Vietnam. This assumption proved false. The estimated effect of the interruption that began in 1965 on the growth of American weapons stocks (i.e., the effect measured by parameter α_3) turned out to be

negative!

How is such a result possible? Does it reflect an error of some sort, or is it perhaps the reductio ad absurdum of the integrated-lag model? The mathematical argument has been checked carefully and several different approaches to parameter estimation have been tried. The negative effect of the interruption on US arms accumulation is not an aberration. It shows up again and again in the various estimation routines. Keep in mind that the interrupted-lag model is the best fitting of our five theoretical structures.

We lack a persuasive explanation of this apparent anomaly. Perhaps the estimation procedure reacts to the temporary decline in US weapons stocks in 1970--the only departure from monotonic increasing armaments in the entire data set--rather than to the whopping increments between 1965 and 1968. But if so, why does the interruption interval contract to match the boundaries of this decline?

Consider several features of the integrated-lag model which may contribute to its relative success. The model's basic structure is asymmetric because it postulates an interruption to the arms acquisition process of one country, but not the other. This strengthens our hunch--not yet a hypothesis--that asymmetry contributes to predictive flexibility and hence to model success.

The notion of an interruption which can occur at any time implies that the arms race is not governed entirely by its own endogenous logic. Exogenous processes must have a strong bearing upon the weapons stocks of even those countries most intensely locked into arms races. The interrupted model barely scratches the surface of this important topic, but even this meager scratch suggests a useful direction for future inquiry.

The interrupted model, let us note in conclusion, alone among the five models here considered, suggests that the American weapons accumulation process obeys the normal Richardson dynamic (i.e., α_1 and α_2 both being positive), as does the Soviet process. For both countries the goading effect of enemy weapons appears much stronger than the retarding influence of one's own military stocks.

CONCLUSION

A summary of the long and involved arguments developed in this paper will not be attempted. The overriding purpose has been to present and defend the following major points:

1. Wherever possible it is advisable to give analytic solutions to dynamic models.

2. Transform methods offer a useful and relatively simple approach to obtaining analytic solutions.

3. In formulating dynamic models of international conflict, it is essential to move beyond the limitations of the standard Richardson model.

4. The analytic approach and the transform methodology allow elementary but informative exploration of dynamic relationships which, on this basis, can either be cast aside or incorporated into more elaborate formulations.

5. Arms race models might profit from relaxing assumptions of symmetry between arms race participants, and by recognizing the impact of exogenous processes on the growth of weapons stockpiles.

We conclude this paper with a warning about an error into which dynamic models of international conflict can easily fall. The danger we speak of is probably quite apparent to attentive readers of the previous section. Ability to present a pertinent data set is a necessary but not a sufficient condition for the plausibility of a dynamic model. Even when ability to represent empirical data is combined with reasonable theoretical assumptions, the union does not guarantee a plausible dynamic model. Why not?

The problem is most obvious when a data set exhibits a fairly simple pattern (e.g., monotonic increase or decrease), but the model estimated for it has a more complex trajectory (e.g., exploding cycles). If a very limited range of the model's trajectory is used to represent the data, a complex dynamic model can often reproduce a simple data set highly incongruent with the model's general nature.

For example, a model characterized by a general pattern of exploding cycles will have sectors over which it is monotonically increasing. These sectors can often be successfully fit to a data set exhibiting a generally increasing pattern. This is approximately what happened with the standard Richardson model considered in the previous section.

To assert that a dynamic model fits a set of empirical observations when the match has been achieved by considering only a narrow segment of the model's trajectory, and when the general nature of this trajectory is drastically at variance with the observed data (or even inconsistent with its meaning, as when weapons stocks are predicted to become negatively infinite) is highly misleading at best. Under these circumstances some might claim that the models in question detect and make evident tendencies implicit but obscure within the observed data. We regard such interpretations as exercises in self-deception, which only hinder the progress of dynamic modeling.

If a dynamic model is to be acceptable, its general nature (not merely its performance over a limited range) must be in harmony with empirical observations. If projecting the model forward in time produces results utterly different from the evidence presently in hand (and perhaps conceptually incompatible with the concept being measured), then the model is probably inappropriate. Phrases like "in harmony with" and "utterly different from" are inevitably imprecise. But they are clear enough to deliver a warning and identify a hazard to be avoided.

NOTES

1. Transform methods have also been successfully applied to integral equations, linear systems, probability theory, time series analyses, and mathematical communication theory, among other things.

2. See, for example, Samuelson (1947).

3. An elementary but reasonably thorough discussion of transform methods appears in Giffin (1975). Allen (1959) gives a brief and comprehensible account of how Laplace transforms are used to solve linear differential equations. Another elementary treatment of the same topic appears in The Differential Equations Problem Solver (Chapters 26-28). This book has the merit of providing numerous worked-out examples.

Ditkin and Prudnikov (1965) present a useful but non-elementary survey of transform methods for solving differential, integral, and difference equations of various kinds. Titchmarsh (1948) is a classic (but still widely used) account of Fourier transform methods. The use of transform techniques to solve partial differential equations is elaborated by Weinberger (1965). Van Der Pol and Bremmer (1955) develop an entire operational calculus on the basis of Laplace transforms. On the other hand Mikusinski (1983) uses the convolution integral to build his own versions of operational calculus. The reader who is interested in difference equations can consult the discussion of generating functions in Jordan (1947).

4. To facilitate exposition we shall ignore problems of convergence and divergence. These issues, however, are by no means routine, and place definite limits on the use of Laplace transforms in solving differential equations.

5. Roberts and Kaufman (1966) provide extensive tables of Laplace and inverse Laplace transforms. Ditkin and Prudnikov (1965) give an ample tabulation of the closely related Laplace-Carson transform.

6. But these equations are not linear in s.

7. The Laplace transform method gives the following solution to the general Richardson equations (1) and (2):

$$X(t) = A_2 e^{\lambda_1 t} + A_2 e^{\lambda_2 t} + A_3$$

$$Y(t) = B_1 e^{\lambda_1 t} + B_2 e^{\lambda_2 t} + B_3$$

where

$$\lambda_1 = -1/2 \ [(\alpha_2 + \beta_2) - \sqrt{(\alpha_2 - \beta_2)^2 + 4 \, \alpha_1 \beta_1} \ ]$$

$$\lambda_2 = -1/2 \ [(\alpha_2 + \beta_2) + \sqrt{(\alpha_2 - \beta_2)^2 + 4 \, \alpha_1 \beta_1} \ ]$$

$$\lambda_1 \neq \lambda_2$$

and

$$A_1 = X(0) \ [\frac{\lambda_1^2 + g_1 \lambda_1 + d_1}{\lambda_1 (\lambda_1 - \lambda_2)}] \ , A_2 = X(0) \ [\frac{\lambda_2^2 + g_1 \lambda_2 + d_1}{\lambda_2 (\lambda_2 - \lambda_1)}]$$

$$A_3 = \frac{X(0) d_1}{\lambda_1 \lambda_2}, \ B_1 = Y(0) \ [\frac{\lambda_1^2 + g_2 \lambda_1 + d_2}{\lambda_1 (\lambda_1 - \lambda_2)}]$$

$$B_2 = Y(0) \ [\frac{\lambda_2^2 + g_2 \lambda_2 + d_2}{\lambda_2 (\lambda_2 - \lambda_1)}] \ , \ B_3 = \frac{Y(0) d_2}{\lambda_1 \lambda_2}$$

and

$$g_1 = \beta_2 + \frac{\alpha_3 + \alpha_1 Y(0)}{X(0)} \ , \ d_1 = \frac{\alpha_1 \beta_3 + \alpha_3 \beta_2}{(X) 0}$$

$$g_2 = \alpha_2 + \frac{\beta_3 + \beta_1 X(0)}{Y(0)} \ , \ d_2 = \frac{\alpha_3 \beta_1 + \alpha_2 \beta_3}{Y(0)}$$

If the reader substitutes $\alpha_1 = 4$, $\alpha_2 = 1$, $\alpha_3 = 2$, $\beta_1 = 1$, $\beta_2 = 1$, $\beta_3 = 4$, $X(0) = 20$, and $Y(0) = 10$ into these formulae, she will obtain the results given in (13) and (14).

      8. Readers who want more information about the application of transform methods to finite difference equations may consult Giffin (1976), Goldberg (1958), Hildebrand (1968), Jordan (1947), or Miller (1960). An interesting discussion of the differences between discrete and continuous dynamic models appears in Kohfeld and Salert (1982).

      9. The hyperbolic sine and cosine are defined as

$$\sinh t = \frac{e^t - e^{-t}}{2}$$

$$\cosh t = \frac{e^t + e^{-t}}{2}$$

The reader should observe that

$$\lim_{t \to +\infty} \sinh t = +\infty$$

$$\lim_{t \to -\infty} \sinh t = -\infty$$

$$\lim_{t \to +\infty} \cosh t = +\infty$$

$$\lim_{t \to -\infty} \cosh t = +\infty \ .$$

Use will be made of the following relations

$$\cosh it = \cos t$$

$$\sinh it = i \sin t$$

where $i = \sqrt{-1}$.

    10. $A_1 = \dfrac{m}{\lambda_1^2 \lambda_2^2}$, $A_2 = \dfrac{\lambda_1^4 + h\lambda_1^2 + m}{\lambda_1^2(\lambda_1^2 - \lambda_2^2)}$, $A_3 = \dfrac{\lambda_1^2 g + k}{\lambda_1^2 - \lambda_2^2}$

$$A_4 = \frac{\lambda_2^4 + h\,\lambda_2^2 + m}{\lambda_2^2(\lambda_2^2 - \lambda_1^2)} \quad , \quad A_5 = \frac{\lambda_2^2 g + k}{\lambda_2^2 - \lambda_1^2}$$

with

$$g = \frac{X_0'}{X_0} \; , \quad h = \beta_2 + \frac{\alpha_1 Y_0 + \alpha_3}{X_0} \; , \quad k = \frac{\beta_2 X_0' + \alpha_1 X_0'}{X_0}$$

$$m = \frac{\alpha_3 \beta_2 + \alpha_1 \beta_3}{X_0}$$

The expressions for the B_k are exactly the same as those given above for the A_k except that g', h', k', and m' replace g, h, k, and m where

$$g' = \frac{Y_0'}{Y_0} \; , \quad h' = \alpha_2 + \frac{\beta_3 + \beta_1 X_0}{Y_0} \; , \quad k' = \frac{\alpha_2 Y_0' + \beta_1 X_0'}{Y_0}$$

$$m' = \frac{\alpha_2 \beta_2 + \alpha_3 \beta_1}{Y_0}$$

11. Solutions (19) and (20) assume that $\lambda_1 \neq \lambda_2$. If this assumption is false, that is, if $\lambda_1 = \lambda_2$, then the form of the solution will be slightly different. Both X(t) and Y(t) will equal functions of the general form

$$C_1 + [C_2 t + C_3] \cosh \lambda t + [C_4 t + C_5] \sinh \lambda t$$

12. If the α_k and β_k parameters are positive, then the A_k and B_k constants will be real valued.

13. Functions X(t) and Y(t) given in (19) and (20) are both even with respect to parameters λ_1 and λ_2. That is, they remain the same whether these parameters are positive or negative (provided they retain the same absolute value).

14. By Cardan's method of solving cubic equations, we have

$$\lambda_1 = U + V - \frac{\beta_3}{3}$$

$$\lambda_2 = -1/2[U + V - i\sqrt{3}(U - V)] - \frac{\beta_3}{3}$$

$$\lambda_3 = -1/2[U + V + i\sqrt{3}(U - V)] - \frac{\beta_3}{3}$$

where

$$U = [-\frac{g}{2} + \sqrt{R}]^{1/3}$$

$$V = [-\frac{g}{2} - \sqrt{R}]^{1/3}$$

and

$$p = \alpha_2 - \frac{\beta_2^2}{3} \quad , \quad q = 2[\frac{\beta_2}{3}]^3 - \alpha_1\beta_1 + \frac{2\alpha_2\beta_2}{3}$$

$$R = \frac{(p)^3}{3} + \frac{(q)^2}{2}$$

15. If $F(k, m, n, c, d, f) = \dfrac{k^3 + ck^2 + dk + f}{k(k - m)(k - n)}$

then

$$A_1 = F(\lambda_1, \lambda_2, \lambda_3, c_1, d_1, f_1) \quad , \quad B_1 = F(\lambda_1, \lambda_2, \lambda_3, c_2, d_2, f_2)$$

$$A_2 = F(\lambda_2, \lambda_1, \lambda_3, c_1, d_1, f_1) \quad , \quad B_2 = F(\lambda_2, \lambda_1, \lambda_3, c_2, d_2, f_2)$$

$$A_3 = F(\lambda_3, \lambda_1, \lambda_2, c_1, d_1, f_1) \quad , \quad B_2 = F(\lambda_3, \lambda_1, \lambda_2, c_2, d_2, f_2)$$

$$A_4 = \frac{-f_1}{\lambda_1 \cdot \lambda_2 \cdot \lambda_3} \qquad B_4 = \frac{-f_2}{\lambda_1 \cdot \lambda_2 \cdot \lambda_3}$$

where

$$c_1 = \beta_2 + \frac{X_0'}{X_0} \qquad c_2 = \frac{\beta_3 + \beta_1 X_0}{Y_0}$$

$$d_1 = \frac{\alpha_3 + \alpha_1 Y_0 + \beta_2 X_0'}{X_0} \quad , \quad d_2 = \alpha_2 + \frac{\beta_1 X_0'}{Y_0}$$

$$f_1 = \frac{\alpha_1\beta_3 + \alpha_3\beta_2}{X_0} \quad , \quad f_2 = \frac{\alpha_2\beta_3 + \alpha_3\beta_1}{Y_0}$$

16. The values of the coefficients in (42) and (43) may be computed as follows. Let

$$h_1 = X_0\beta_2 + \alpha_3, \quad g_1 = \alpha_3\beta_2 + \alpha_1 Y_0, \quad d_1 = \alpha_\alpha\beta_3$$

$$g_2 = -\alpha_2 Y_0, \quad d_2 = -\alpha_1 \beta_3, \quad h_3 = Y_0 \alpha_2 + \beta_3$$

$$g_3 = \alpha_2 \beta_3 + \beta_1 X_0, \quad d_3 = \beta_1 \alpha_3, \quad g_4 = -\beta_1 X_0, \quad d_4 = -\beta_1 \alpha_3$$

Then the coefficients of (42) equal

$$A_1 = \frac{\lambda_1 \lambda_2 g_1 + (\lambda_1 + \lambda_2) d_1}{\lambda_1^2 \lambda_2^2} \quad , \quad A_2 \quad \frac{d_1}{\lambda_1 \lambda_2}$$

$$A_3 = \frac{X_0 \lambda_1^3 + h_1 \lambda_1^2 + g_1 \lambda_1 + d_1}{\lambda_1^2 (\lambda_1 - \lambda_2)} \quad , \quad A_4 = \frac{X_0 \lambda_2^3 + h_1 \lambda_2^2 + g_1 \lambda_2 + d_1}{\lambda_2^2 (\lambda_2 - \lambda_1)}$$

$$B_1 = \frac{\lambda_1 \lambda_2 g_2 + (\lambda_1 + \lambda_2) d_2}{\lambda_1^2 \lambda_2^2} \quad , \quad B_2 = \frac{d_2}{\lambda_1 \lambda_2}$$

$$B_3 = \frac{\lambda_1 g_2 + d_2}{\lambda_1^2 (\lambda_1 - \lambda_2)} \quad , \quad B_4 = \frac{\lambda_2 g_2 + d_2}{\lambda_2^2 (\lambda_2 - \lambda_1)}$$

The coefficients of (43) equal

$$C_1 = \frac{\lambda_1 \lambda_2 g_3 + (\lambda_1 + \lambda_2) d_3}{\lambda_1^2 \lambda_2^2} \quad , \quad C_2 = \frac{d_3}{\lambda_1 \cdot \lambda_2}$$

$$C_3 = \frac{Y_0 \lambda_1^3 + h_3 \lambda_1^2 + g_3 \lambda_1 + d_3}{\lambda_1^2 (\lambda_1 - \lambda_2)} \quad , \quad C_4 = \frac{Y_0 \lambda_1^3 + h_3 \lambda_2^2 + g_3 \lambda_2 + d_3}{\lambda_2^2 (\lambda_2 - \lambda_1)}$$

$$D_1 = \frac{\lambda_1 \lambda_2 g_4 + (\lambda_1 + \lambda_2) d_4}{\lambda_1^2 \cdot \lambda_2^2} \quad , \quad D_2 = \frac{d_4}{\lambda_1 \cdot \lambda_2}$$

$$D_3 = \frac{\lambda_1 g_4 + d_4}{\lambda_1^2 (\lambda_1 - \lambda_2)} \quad , \quad D_4 = \frac{\lambda_2 g_4 + d_4}{\lambda_2^2 (\lambda_2 - \lambda_1)}$$

17. The coefficients in (55) and (56) are

$$A_1 = \frac{\lambda_1^2 + g \lambda_1 + d}{\lambda_1 (\lambda_1 - \lambda_2)} \quad , \quad A_2 = \frac{\lambda_2^2 + g \lambda_2 + d}{2 (\lambda_2 - \lambda_1)} \quad , \quad A_3 = \frac{d}{\lambda_1 \cdot \lambda_2}$$

$$B_1 = \frac{\alpha_3 (\lambda_1 + \beta_3)}{\lambda_1 (\lambda_1 - \lambda_2)} \quad , \quad B_2 = \frac{\alpha_3 (\lambda_2 + \beta_3)}{\lambda_2 (\lambda_2 - \lambda_1)} \quad , \quad B_3 = \frac{\alpha_3 \beta_3}{\lambda_1 \cdot \lambda_2}$$

where

$$g = \frac{\alpha_1 Y_0}{X_0} \quad , \quad d = \frac{\alpha_1 \beta_3}{X_0}$$

and

$$C_1 = \frac{\lambda_1^2 + h\lambda_1 + f}{\lambda_1(\lambda_1 - \lambda_2)} \quad , \quad C_2 = \frac{\lambda_2^2 + h\lambda_2 + f}{\lambda_2(\lambda_2 - \lambda_1)} \quad , \quad C_3 = \frac{f}{\lambda_1 \cdot \lambda_2}$$

$$D_1 = \frac{\alpha_3\beta_1}{\lambda_1(\lambda_1 - \lambda_2)}, \quad D_2 = \frac{\alpha_3\beta_1}{\lambda_2(\lambda_2 - \lambda_1)} \quad , \quad D_3 = \frac{\alpha_3\beta_1}{\lambda_1 \cdot \lambda_2}$$

where

$$h = \alpha_2 + \frac{\beta_3 + \beta_1 X_0}{Y_0} \quad , \quad f = \frac{\alpha_2\beta_3}{Y_0}$$

18. The conventional weapons index used by Ward is a modification and extension of that proposed by Lambelet (1973). Lambelet's index multiplies manpower by firepower by mobility, and combines the forces of the United States and West Germany. To achieve greater comparability, Ward has combined Soviet and East German conventional forces.

The strategic forces index was adapted from measures prepared by Tsipis (1975) and further developed by Allan and Luterbacher (1981). This measures total number of strategic weapons, each weighted by its lethality rating.

Ward explains his decision to multiply strategic and conventional weapons indices in generating an overall weapons index in this way (p. 302): "A multiplicative index not only answers the argument that both elements of the force structure are important, but also stresses that strategic and conventional forces are at some level substitutes for one another."

19. MINUIT has a special subroutine called IMPROVE designed exactly for this purpose. For our purposes, however, the SEEK subroutine proved to be quite a bit more effective.

20. A chi-square-like difference measure was used as the criterion for parameter estimation (i.e., the function minimized by MINUIT). In particular

$$F \equiv \sum_{i=1}^{n} \frac{(T_i - O_i)^2}{|T_i|}$$

where O_1 is empirical observation i, T_i is the theoretical prediction corresponding to observation i (a function of model parameters), and F is the overall measure of difference between prediction and observations (also a function of model parameters).

21. In other words, the errors are highly autocorrelated.

10 The Dollar Auction as a Model of International Escalation

Some of the basic problems of international conflict have been represented as mathematical games. The game of Chicken has the ingredients of extended deterrence and crisis bargaining (Snyder and Diesing, 1977) and the game of Prisoners' Dilemma represents an arms race in which the choice of building new weapons corresponds to the uncooperative move (Rapoport and Chammah, 1965; Axelrod, 1984). Crisis instability is structurally similar to the game known as the Stag Hunt (Jarvis, 1978; O'Neill, 1985). The games clarify the skeletal structure of their respective real world situations and sometimes generate laboratory experiments. Brams (1985) gives a two-by-two game modeling the decision to comply with an arms control agreement. Other specific games and further discussion are given by Brams (1985) and Wagner (1983).

Another conflict phenomenon of great importance is escalation. Several authors (including Shubik, 1971; Costanza, 1984; Teger, 1983; Rapoport, 1981; and Gorovitz, 1983) have suggested that the structure of escalation is well represented by the **Dollar Auction**. In a two-person game, the rules state that the high bidder will win the dollar but that both the high and low bidders must pay their respective bids.

The game generates the phenomenon so typical of escalation: players continue to commit resources well past the point where they could make a net profit, feeling they have "invested too much to quit." The bidders had hoped to win a dollar for a few nickels but competition develops and to their surprise the bidding almost always passes fifty cents. When bids reach the vicinity of one dollar

---

This chapter is an abridgement of a longer paper that was published in the Journal of Conflict Resolution. For details of proofs the reader should consult the latter. The author would like to thank Steve Brams, Mark Kilgour, Tom Mayer, Michael Intriligator, and Martin McGuire for helpful comments.

both realize that they are caught in a dilemma. They may hesitate at this point but most often they head upwards. The bidder now at 95 cents, say A, is willing to bid $1.05 even though that involves a loss--a net loss of a nickel is at least preferable to dropping out and losing 95 cents. But then B applies the same logic and bids $1.10 or more.

The game is often used in the classroom to demonstrate entrapment, but it has not appeared in the research literature as part of a clearly developed model of a specific escalatory situation. Perhaps the reason is that no one has identified what rational players should do. This gap in our understanding contrasts with the other games listed above--Chicken, Prisoners' Dilemma, and the Stag Hunt--where rational behavior has been specified, although sometimes controversially.[1]

My aim in this chapter is to give a rule for rational behavior in the dollar auction.

PAST SUGGESTIONS FOR THE RATIONAL STRATEGY

It has been suggested that the bidders should cooperate by bidding a nickel and splitting the gains later. This move is a good one if it is possible, but, as Shubik recognizes, in many situations cooperation is out: the bidders may not trust one another or be able to communicate. Likewise bidding a nickel and issuing a threat to bid up interminably if the other player does not drop out is an excellent strategy but is impossible if, as we assume here, players cannot communicate or cannot make themselves convincing.

Costanza states that the "only truly rational thing to do is not to enter the game in the first place. Once the game is entered by at least two bidders, their fate is sealed if they behave rationally from that point on." Those who have played the game and lost might agree, but this strategy is not an equilibrium: if you know your opponent would not bid you should clearly make some small bid. Thus, if the rational strategy for both is not to play and if you know your opponent is rational, then you can deduce that the rational strategy for you is to play, which is a contradiction.

Another suggested ploy is to bid 95 cents. Your opponent will not bid a dollar since there will be nothing to gain, so you are sure to win 5 cents. This strategy may be better than doing nothing but is not necessarily the best strategy: perhaps bidding less than 95 cents would also induce a rational opponent to drop out. Shubik suggested that bidding $1.00 at the outset is part of an equilibrium strategy, but I disagree that it is part of a perfect (or sensible) equilibrium for reasons just given.

THE SOLUTION

A difficulty in solving the Dollar Auction is that the game itself has not been well defined. To specify a game one must give a payoff for every pair of strategies, but if our players choose to bid indefinitely what payoffs do they receive? None are given in the usual statement of the game. Realistically speaking, bidding indefinitely is impossible since both have finite resources, and on these grounds I feel justified in incorporating into the game some upper limit on the amount the players can bid. These amounts will be b_1 and b_2, standing for 1 and 2's "bankrolls," respectively. The stakes, which in the present sample are $1, will be designated s.

Bidder 1, defined as the player able to bid first and selected by some chance mechanism, chooses either to pass or to bid some amount in integral multiples of some unit, up to a bid of b_1. If we assume for example that the the bids must be in nickels and that $b_1 = b_2 = \$2.50$, Bidder 1 can choose from 51 possible first moves. The second player can then respond with a higher bid not greater than $2.50 or drop out. Clearly the game must end, since at worst one or the other will reach the total bankroll. The game tree will be finite and we can work backwards, using the maximum value to a player of outgoing branches and assigning it to the branching point. Eventually every branching in the tree will be assigned a best move.

The backwards induction approach seems straightforward but it meets two difficulties. First, a player, say Bidder A, may face two outgoing branches of equal assigned value. This will present no problem to A since A can choose either branch arbitrarily, but it complicates the situation for Bidder B, since at some time previous to the branches of equal value B may need to know which move A will make at that future point. The Dollar Auction is not zerosum, so A's indifference at the branching point does not imply B's indifference.

I will add the assumption that a bidder confronting equally valued choices always chooses the one involving the least upward bid. The other bidder knows this. I am postulating a form of risk aversion in that a bidder never puts money in jeopardy without some positive reason to do so.

The second problem with the backwards induction approach is that the game tree is immense. A recursive formula in the parameters s and b can be calculated to show that for equal bankrolls b = $2.50 and bids in integrals of nickels the number of branching points in the game tree is about 2.2×10^{15}.

Fortunately there are shortcuts that render the calculation feasible, one based on the observation that when the two players have reached a given pair of bids, the path they took to reach those bids is irrelevant. So in fact there are only about 2500 strategically different possible positions of the game with the above parameters. In the case of equal bankrolls b one can calculate a simple formula for the best moves to make at the beginning of the game:

The first bidder should bid (b-1) modulo (s-1) + 1 and the second bidder should drop out.

The modulo function gives simply the remainder after dividing b-1 by s-1. This best first bid is measured in units of nickels since we have assumed that the possible raises are in multiples of nickels. In the case of our example the bankrolls b are 50 nickels ($2.50), the stakes s are 20 nickels ($1.00), and therefore the rational opening bid is 49 mod 19 + 1 nickels or 60 cents.

If somehow the players have already made bids in the game (they have suffered a lapse of rationality) but now trust each other's rationality, the best move is for i to bid $(b-x_i-1) \mod (s-1) + x_j + 1$ and for j to drop out, where it is assumed that Player i has the move and where x_i and x_j are the current bids.

Note that the best move by the above formula is always less than $b-x_i$ so that a player never makes a bid greater than or equal to the prize. This is a sensible rule, since even if the player were to win, the amount won would be no greater than the amount paid.

Note also that the best move is a function of $b-x_i$ so that it depends on how far i is away from the upper limit but not on i's previous investment x_i in any other way. This is an expression of the principle of irrelevance of sunk costs.

This prescription for a rational strategy seems to have no intuitive support at all. However, should we expect the answer to be intuitive? The strategic situation confronting the two players is much more complicated than the rules defining the game. The first bidder must look ahead to all of 2's responses, which

involves as a subtask calculating 2's evaluations of all
1's counter-responses, etc. This might involve a sequence
like the following: 1 thinks that 2 thinks that 1 thinks,
etc., up to 51 moves and countermoves.

Bidder 1 decides that 55 cents would be too low as
it would not be sufficient self-commitment for 1 to the
bidding contest to convince 2 to drop out. Also 65 cents
would be too high. Bidder 2 would respond by dropping
out, but the same goal could have been achieved for a
nickel less.

Likewise, it seems odd that the best move should be
influenced by the total available bankroll. The best
first bid as a function of bankrolls b follows a rising
sawtooth function according to the above formula, starting
at 5 cents for a bankroll of 5 cents, rising by nickels to
95 cents for a bankroll of 95 cents, then falling back to
5 cents again for b = $1.00, only to rise again to 95
cents when s reaches $1.90. Of course dependence on the
total available bankroll has its precedents in the normal
English auction where someone can win by having in pocket
the smallest amount more than the competing bidder.

ENRICHMENT OF THE DOLLAR AUCTION TO MODEL REAL ESCALATION

The Dollar Auction in its pure form does not
represent escalation well. In fact it suggests that
escalation never occurs. Governments do not behave this
way so the question becomes: What ingredients must we add
to the auction to produce escalation?

An important feature which must be added is
uncertainty. Real actors, governments and people, cannot
always foresee the consequences of their own actions, and
when they cannot they are usually optimistic. In
Kurosawa's movie The Seven Samurai two swordsmen meet in a
field and, to compare their skills, stage a mock battle
with bamboo poles. One claims victory but the loser
refuses to see the outcome that way. He insists on
repeating the contest with real swords, events follow the
same course, and he is killed.

Another type of uncertainty which might produce
escalation is incomplete information about the other's
values. Neither may know what the other wants in terms of
the relative value of the stakes and the goods committed.
Bids then become a form of communication which not only
perform the function of keeping a player in the game but
also try to convince the other player that the former is
serious about winning. Some simultaneous-move games of
this type have been analyzed in the context of wars of
attrition in the context of biology (Bishop and Cannings,
1978), although these games have been constructed to avoid

the possibility of communication and the resulting analytic difficulties.

Another difference between rational players and real players is that the latter have limited ability to look ahead and limited belief in the other's rationality. Real people seem to use a heuristic procedure by looking ahead a few moves and countermoves, making a rough evaluation of their position in the situation, and then playing as if those evaluations were their real payoffs at the end of those branches. They work backwards, maximizing and minimizing to select a present move. This heuristic can lead to unfortunate results: Pearl (1984) and Nau (1983) have shown that for a large class of zerosum extensive-form games the further one looks ahead the worse one does, in a sense of "worse" which they define.

The basic difficulty, as Pearl suggests, is the common statistical slip of failing to realize that the estimate of a function is generally different from the function of the estimates. In our case the max of a min of a max of estimates (which is what a player calculates by looking ahead three moves) is not the same as the estimate of the max of a min of a max (which is the proper statistic to calculate). A question for research is whether this difference systematically yields escalation, i.e., would players in a game of escalation be led to greater commitment of resources?

An important related question is the issue of Snyder's stability-instability paradox in international affairs. The worry is that when one makes the outcome of total conflict more disastrous, the conflict becomes more likely. Each player is confident that the other will back down and so feels freer to take risky action at lower levels of the escalation ladder.

Indeed it is sometimes stated that the existence of thermonuclear weapons has made the world a safer place now that war is unthinkable. The corresponding argument in a highway safety context is that seatbelts should be prohibited and accident victims should not be given aid. If we make the consequences more serious the probability of accidents will fall to give a net gain in benefit.

While this latter argument seems immoral and absurd, there is no clear evidence to suggest that it is wrong. In fact it has more face validity in the highway safety context than in the thermonuclear war context, since in the former there is no escalatory process that progressively induces people to have an accident. But escalation is common in international affairs, so one would expect that increasing the devastation of total war would be less effective in keeping nations off the bottom rungs and perhaps eventually the top rungs of the ladder.

The stability-instability paradox is thus tied in with the process of escalation and we would hope that a more realistic model growing out of the Dollar Auction would clarify when its thesis holds and when it does not hold.

A further topic is the question of how gaps along the ladder help or hurt escalation. It has been suggested that space-based battle stations and anti-satellite weapons are an impetus to escalation since both sides would hesitate less to strike at the other's satellites than to engage in acts of war now presently possible. In an anti-satellite attack, none of the opponent's personnel are killed, no foreign territory is invaded, and in fact one may conduct the operation over one's own territory. The existence of these weapons thus makes possible two small uppings of the bids (first an attack on satellites, then direct war), where previously the players had to make a single jump. Does this hurt or help the chances of entrapment and disaster? Implicit in this argument is that two small steps up the ladder are easier to take than one big one, and this thesis could be clarified by a good model of escalation.

A further difference between reality and our model is that real utilities change during the course of a conflict. Typically winning becomes an end in itself. Often people state that their desire to win is a function of amount invested, rather than, say, time spent, as in the declaration "Our dead shall not have died in vain." They act as if by winning the auction they would be winning back all the money they have bid. A general psychological basis for this tendency seems reasonable but, to my knowledge, has not been investigated.

A difference that helps to retard escalation in the real world is the possibility of quitting on even terms with the help of third party intervention. The Dollar Auction has been perversely constructed so that one bid cannot match the other's bid, with a sharing of the profits. If this were possible one would expect escalation to decrease. The mediating role of third parties can be to make a particular stopping point salient to the two bidders, in effect to restore communication between the bidders, if not trust.

The Dollar Auction is important largely because of the escalation features it lacks. Trying to add these features may clarify their workings and their interactions with each other.

NOTES

1. For the case of Chicken and Prisoners' Dilemma see Luce and Raiffa (1957) or Rapoport (1974). For the case of the Stag Hunt see Harsanyi and Selten (1980) and O'Neill (1985).

_____ **Part 3**
Simulation Approaches

11 Toward a Dynamic Theory of Conflict and Coalition Formation

TOWARD A RATIONAL THEORY OF CONFLICT

In order to develop a dynamic theory of conflict and coalition formation, it is important, in our view, to develop an approach that will account for the decisions of the international actors involved in them. We are convinced that rational decision-making frameworks, especially the ones presented by two- and N-person game theory, constitute potentially very powerful explanatory schemes which should be applied to all aspects of conflict and cooperative situations. Is it possible to develop such rational theories of conflict? Some authors (Taylor, 1975) have argued that voting and bargaining are the two main forms of social decision making amenable to rational analysis since they bear some relation to the preferences of the actors involved. The use of chance, contests, or combat to resolve social differences is considered by them as of little interest for the theorist because, in these cases, links with individual preferences are missing. In international political situations, however, voting does not have much importance. The votes at the UN General Assembly or Security Council have a very limited, mostly symbolic, impact. In any case, such votes cannot be compared to ordinary majority or plurality decision since they usually result from a complex negotiation process. Bargaining is therefore the dominant mode of collective decision making at the international level. In this context, however, the effects of combats and contests cannot be dismissed. Even if such events do not actually occur, their possibility must always be envisaged. The dismissal of combat and contests as theoretically interesting collective choice outcomes reflect some economists' prejudice against negative incentives,[1] forced decisions, and the use of power, violence, and extortions generally to explain social arrangements.[2] International actors, however, have to deal in the best possible way with such issues as potential combat and

229

contest situations and must take them into account when bargaining processes are conducted. In this context, cooperation and conflictual moves, diplomatic maneuvering, and coalition formations and dissolutions are of particular interest.

The purpose of this study is to elaborate a rational theory which will include all these aspects and will therefore be able to account for all the phases of the evolution of a conflict process. In this analysis, we apply the various constructs that have been proposed by game theorists and political scientists. Since for analytical purposes bilateral and multilateral cases are usually discussed separately in the literature, moving from the simpler context (bilaterel) to the more complex one (multilateral), we will proceed in a similar way. We begin with the examination of a two-actor situation, moving from there to the investigation of the three-actor case or triad, which presents more difficulty, and generalizing to N-actor situations.

THE TWO-ACTOR LEVEL

So far it has often been difficult to relate abstract considerations developed by game theorists to concrete models of international situations. This problem is due, among other things, to the fact that linkages are not easily established between the decision-making structures of game theory, which postulate equal and undifferentiated actors with fixed preferences, and the dynamic relations between unequal states with changing orders of priorities and objectives. Most often, empirical models of international interactions have tended to represent decisions about allocations of resources. This is certainly the case with most arms race formulations and even more so with more complex constructions, such as Guetzkow's (1963) Inter-Nation Simulation or Bremer's (1977) SIPER or the SIMPEST model (Luterbacher and Allan, 1982) developed in Geneva. Linkages between these and game-theoretical structures are virtually nonexistent. The reason for this absence of relationship between the two constructs does not lie so much in their alternative ways of formalizing human behavior[3] as in approaches that conceptualize actors and their preferences in different manners. In order to accommodate resource allocation models, game-theoretical conceptions should be able to deal with unequal actors and changing preference orders which result from different evolutions of resource potentials. Changes in resources, especially military potential, affect a nation's capacity to bargain and will therefore change its preference structure.

One of us (Allan, 1983) has emphasized these linkages between power potential and preference orders, relating game-theoretical concepts and resource allocation models. Essential political interactions between two international actors can be represented within a 2 x 2 game structure where the players each have two elementary strategies, cooperation and conflict or de-escalation and escalation. This point of view has been adopted implicitly or explicitly by many authors, such as Snyder and Diesing (1977) or Brams and Wittman (1983). Shifts from cooperation to conflict or from escalation to de-escalation can be explained within the framework of the 2 x 2 non-zero-sum game matrix presented in Figure 11.1.

In that matrix, a, a', b, b', c, c', BP_A, BP_B

represent utilities associated by each nation with the outcomes. It can be shown that for constant a, a', b, b', c, c', with a > b > c and a' > b' > c' >, the game

PLAYER A

	Cooperation (C)	Conflict (D)	
	b,b'	d,a'	C
	a,d'	BP_a,BP_b	D

PLAYER B

	$U(C)_a$,$U(C)_b$	d,a'	C
	a,d'	$U(D)_a$,$U(D)_b$	D

$U(C)_{a,b}$ = utility of mutual cooperation
$U(D)_{a,b}$ = utility of mutual confrontation

Figure 11.1   Generalized Matrices of 2 x 2 Games

structure varies fundamentally according to changes in BP_A, BP_B or the respective bargaining power of the protagonists. If BP_A and $BP_B < c,c'$, the matrix represents chicken (unstable cooperation). If c,c' $< BP_A$, $BP_B < b,b'$, the resulting game is prisoner's dilemma (conflict with cooperation possibility). The order b, b' $< BP_A$, $BP_B < a, a'$ produces the game of deadlock (stable conflict without cooperation). If the values of BP_A and BP_B are not situated within the same bounds, three asymmetric game structures obtain in which one of the players is in a weaker situation than the other one. These structures are called bluff (a combination of prisoner's dilemma and chicken), bully (a combination of deadlock and chicken), and weak deadlock (a combination of deadlock and prisoner's dilemma).

The two players will shift from cooperation to conflict or vice versa by maximizing their utilities according to the respective magnitudes of BP_A and BP_B.

Here these two variables represent utilities associated with mutual conflict or escalation. They express the power each player has to resist demands by the other one, or in other terms the bargaining power of A and B. For given values of BP_A and BP_B, either conflictual escalation, de-escalation, or temporary surrender to the request of the adversary can occur, as well as constant shifting among all these possibilities.[4] The terms BP_A and BP_B determine conflictual/cooperative reaction functions as they evolve over time.

A crucial assumption in the above game matrix concerned the ranking of the utilities a, b, c, and a', b', c', with a > b > c and a' > b' > c'. How were these determined? Four basic types of situations are represented in the game matrix:

(1) Each nation increases its conflict activity toward the other (escalation; BP_A, BP_B).

(2) Each decreases conflictual activity toward the other (de-escalation; b,b').

(3) The first is escalating while the second is de-escalating (the first is "winning"; a,c').

(4) The first is de-escalating and the second keeps escalating (the first is "losing"; c,a').

Each actor has a preference order, ranking these different outcomes from the most preferred ("4") to the least preferred ("1").
In a rational perspective, what can we postulate about the the ranking of the four different outcomes for states in a situation as described above? First, the most preferred one is winning, and second, compromise is preferred to losing.[5] These two postulates give rise to the two preference orders discussed. Including the utility associated with escalation we can derive the three possible preference orders of an individual actor:

I: 3 = de-escalation 2 = escalation   1 = losing

II: 4 = winning   2 = losing   1 = escalation

III: 3 = escalation   2 = de-escalation 1 = losing

Each international actor can have one of these preference orderings; thus, six combinations defining six different games are possible if we consider two actors producing the four different outcomes with respect to each other.[6]
In all these games, except deadlock and weak deadlock, non-escalatory outcomes are possible, especially in prisoner's dilemma, chicken, and their combination, called bluff, because they are characterized by some vacillation of both parties between coercive and accommodative moves. This results from the fact that common and conflicting interests are inextricably intertwined, a characteristic which explains their designation as mixed-motive games.
Changes in the utilities of a continued escalation will bring about the six different game structures seen before. These utilities depend directly upon the bargaining power of two parties, BP_A nad BP_B. Continuous changes in BP_A and BP_B at some points will induce structural changes whereby the game structure is radically altered. Whenever $BP_A \neq BP_B$, a more or less asymasymmetrical bargaining situation results. This situation is related to decision making through reaction functions, as pictured in Figure 11.2. The change in conflict behavior of one of he two protagonists is a function of the other conflict level. Actor B has more bargaining power than A in this case ($BP_B > BP_A$). This

means that B is willing to keep on escalating up to a higher conflict level than A (up to x = BP_B, whereas for A only up to a lower level of y = BP_A). For both states it is postulated that there exists some conflict level beyond which they will de-escalate, since, rationally, conflict is a means rather than and end in itself.

Figure 11.2 shows that the higher the utility of escalation or the bargaining power of a nation, the higher the conflict level of the adversary up to which it will continue to escalate, and also the larger its response. This response increases at first in intermediate conflict levels, corresponding to the probing states of a confrontation, and then becomes smaller as the adversary's conflict level comes closer to the maximum specified by the bargaining power available. Beyond that point de-escalation will occur for that side.

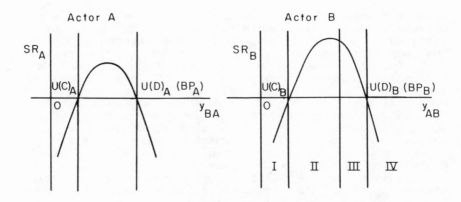

Figure 11.2 Stylized Reaction Functions

In Figure 11.2 an asymmetrical situation results from BP_B being significantly larger than BP_A. In Region I, conflict between the two parties is relatively low and decreasing, tending toward a compromise. In Region II, an action-reaction process leads into an acute crisis. Even though A's bargaining power is smaller, this is usually not clear to A, who will at first escalate. Both sides are probing each other. The critical comparison they have to make consists in weighing the costs of yielding against the expected costs of serious conflict, and "people will tend not to make this comparison realistically until they absolutely have to" (Synder and Diesing, 1977, p. 483), which is usually near the peak of the crisis. Here, it is A who will realize this and start de-escalating, as in Region III. Actor A's situation could thus be like a called-bluff game structure, the adversary being in prisoner's dilemma with respect to A while A is playing chicken. Actor B's preference order could even be like that of deadlock if $BP_B \gg BP_A$, giving rise to a game of bully. B would win even faster there as B's reaction would be much larger and B's conflict level accordingly greater took, thus prompting A to de-escalate sooner. Symmetric games are characterized by the same reaction functions for both protagonists, but with $BP_A = BP_B$. In chicken the maximum conflict levels x and y, determined by the bargaining power functions of the two sides, are of relatively low or intermediate conflict. In prisoner's dilemma these conflict levels do not preclude a possible war, and in deadlock the conflict levels implied are beyond the war threshold, that is, far along the right-hand side of the abcissa in Figure 11.2

The reaction functions described above (Figure 11.2), which we will call strategic reaction functions $(SR_{A,B})$, can be expressed in the most general way as:

$$SR_A = (Y_{BA} - U(C)_{AB}) \ (U(D)_{AB} - Y_{BA})$$

$$SR_B = (Y_{AB} - U(C)_{BA}) \ (U(D)_{BA} - Y_{AB})$$

where Y_{BA}, Y_{AB} represent conflict levels sent from B to A or A to B, and $U(C)_{AB}$, $U(C)_{BA}$ are respective utilities of cooperation between A and B, i.e., thresholds up to which either A or B is prepared to accept conflictual moves by the other without escalating. On the other hand $U(D)_{AB}$ and $U(D)_{BA}$ represent respective utilities of mutu-

236

al conflict between A and B. They represent thresholds
beyond which neither A nor B is willing to continue
escalating. In our conception $U(D)_{AB}$ and $U(D)_{BA}$ are

straightforward functions of the respective bargaining
powers (BP_A and BP_B).

While $U(C)_{AB}$ and $U(C)_{BA}$ can be measured terms of in

past conflict levels, the variations in $U(D)_{AB}$ and $U(D)_{BA}$

can be assessed in accordance with our description above,
through changes in the bargaining power levels BP_A and

BP_B.

What determines the changes in BP_A and BP_B? These

two variables can be conceived of as functions of two
elements: (1) the determination of each player to carry
out a threat, i.e. the player's resolve, and, (2) the
possibility of effectively carrying threats out, which is
given by the relative capabilities of a player vis-a-vis
another one. Both are necessary for bargaining power,
but neither is sufficient by itself. While capabilities
are easily measurable in terms of military and economic
resources, as given by an allocation model (cf.
Luterbacher, 1981), the concept of resolve is much more
difficult to evaluate. To deal with this problem Allan
(1983) considered this concept as a function of (a) past
successes or failures in confrontations with the other
nation, and (b) interests at stake for an actor. Past
successes or failures can be observed and measured. It
is more difficult to assess the importance of interests
which can change over time and depend in particular on
the fundamental strategic situation of each individual
actor, i.e., the size, shape, and location of territories
under his control. In an analysis of Cold War
interaction, Allan (1983) considered these interests
constant. Such a simplifying assumption can be made
about a situation where two very powerful actors such as
the US and the Soviet Union are involved. This
hypothesis is much more dubious in a multiactor situation
where geographical location may play a major role.

Resolve and reactive capabilities are substitutes
of each other, but not perfect ones. This structure can
be expressed by an multiplicative relationship:

$$BP_{A,B} = R_{A,B} \frac{PC_{A,B}}{PC_{B,A}}$$

where BP stands for bargaining power, R for resolve, and PC for power capabilities, all variables being positive by definition. A,B means Actor A with respect to Actor B.

All these relations can now be used within a dynamic model where shifts in conflictual or cooperative strategies over time are a function of bargaining power and past conflict levels. Bargaining power is itself a function of resolve (and thus past successes and failures) as well as of strategic interests and of relative capabilities, which can be determined by a resource allocation model. Finally, bargaining power is also influenced by the characteristics of the fundamental strategic situation. A particular bargaining power position can have an influence upon the resource allocations process. For instance, a state of weakness in current political capabilities could trigger a reallocation of resources to develop this power potential to a greater extent.[7] Such feedback loops are particularly important in a triadic situation.

This examination of the two-actor case and its fundamental characteristics sets the basis for an investigation of a three-player system.

ANALYSIS OF THE TRIAD

Studies of triadic situations go back to Von Neumann and Morgenstern's (1944) original work on game theory. However, as already mentioned, with a few exceptions these structures have not led to very interesting results even in simple cases. The main difference between two- and three- or N-person game theory lies in the constitution of coalitions. Game-theoretical analysis based uniquely on rational decision principles are not able to predict the exact composition of coalitions and their principles of formation. Also, characteristic game situations such as chicken or prisoner's dilemma in the two-player case are more difficult to visualize and to discuss in the triad. These and other problems are widely discussed in Guiasu and Malitza (1980). More meaningful analyses of the triadic case require the introduction of additional considerations beyond rational decision-making principles. The concept of bargaining power will be of particular importance in this context.

In order to examine the problems appearing in the triadic context, it is necessary to study the outcomes which occur in a 2 x 2 x 2 three-player game where the strategic options again are cooperating (C) and escalating, or "defecting" (D). Under these premises, eight possible outcomes obtain:

PLAYERS: A, B, C

Outcomes:
(1)	C,C,C	Total coalition	(A with B with C)
(2)	C,D,C	A + C → B	(A with C against B)
(3)	C,C,D	A + B → C	(A with B against C)
(4)	C,D,D	No coalition	
(5)	D,C,C	B + C → A	(B with C against A)
(6)	D,D,C	No coalition	
(7)	D,C,D	No coalition	
(8)	D,D,D	No coalition	

If this structure is interpreted as a coalition game, only five interesting situations emerge:

(1) The total or grand coalition where everybody collaborates.

(2) Coalition AC against B

(3) Coalition AB against C

(4) Coalition BC against A

(5) Various forms of the trivial coalition where players prefer to remain independent.

The problem that remains to be solved is: Which possibility is more likely to occur? Caplow's theory (1956, 1959) assumes an unequal distribution of power among members of the triad. Caplow's assumptions are the following:

1. Members of a triad may differ in strength. A strong member can control a weaker member and will seek to do so.

2. Each member of the triad seeks control over the others. Control over two others is preferred to control over one other. Control over one is preferred to control over none.

3. The strength of the coalition is equal to the strength of its two members.

4. The formation of coalitions takes place in an existing triad, so there is a pre-coalition condition in every triad. Any attempt by a stronger member to coerce a weaker member of the pre-coalition condition will provoke the formation of a coalition to oppose the coercion. This is a "balance of power" condition.

Basically, Caplow examines four possible situations:

1. An unequal power distribution A > B > C where B + C > A

2. An unequal distribution A > B > C where B + C > A, the so-called omnipotence case.

3. The situation A = B > C

4. The condition A > B = C where B + C > A. The B + C < A case is essentially the same as situation 2.

The main objective in Caplow's game is to maximize control over other players rather than over immediate outcomes. Such a power-maximizing behavior is most likely to emerge when the game situation lasts over a long time period and when the outcomes are not well defined in terms of concrete payoffs. Both of these conditions prevail in international political situations. What conclusions can be drawn from the power distributions presented above? In situation 2, no coalitions will form since A can control the two other players alone. In situation 3, the AB coalition is unlikely. In 4, no coalition can be excluded on a priori grounds. It can also be noticed that coalition AB in 3 and AB or AC in 4 are inefficient since they concentrate more than the necessary amount of power or control the game. The most interesting case is situation 1, where the following holds: C has control over no one. If C forms an alliance with B he will control A but will be dominated by B within the coalition. C is therefore indifferent between coalitions AC or BC. B will prefer a BC alignment, which allows him to control two players, A outside the coalition and C within it. For A, an AB or an AC arrangement is equally desirable. It should be emphasized that in no case will a grand coalition be formed: it does not provide players with the same possibilities of controlling other ones. Caplow's conclusion about his particular power structure is that coalitions AC and BC are equally likely. However, Gamson (1961), using essentially a size principle-type argument, considers that the BC coalition will prevail, a result that seems to be confirmed by experiments. Chertkoff (1970) argues that a BC alliance is more probable because B will not seek an AB alignment. A counterargument can be made if side payments are allowed: A, being the most powerful player, can offer C more than B to become a coalition partner. This would rather favor the formation of an AC configuration. In any case, the interesting fact is that C, the weakest element, is always in a coalition and is therefore a pivotal player in the game. This leads to the paradox noticed by Zinnes (1970) and Guiasu and Malitza (1980) that here the weak one is in a position of strength. Once a coalition is formed, the three-person game situation is reduced to a two-person situation. Caplow's approach has the advantage of showing ways in which some coalitions are more likely to emerge than others. Rather than using Caplow's conception of power and control, it seems more useful to reason with the help of the notion of bargaining power developed beforehand. If the goal of the players in a three-person structure is to maximize bargaining power, i.e., utilities associated with mutual confrontation or defection, the outcomes of a triadic situation can be described in terms of several two-stage games. The first stage will involve a series of potential two-player games which determine what coalition will be formed. The second stage will be a game between the resulting coalition and the remaining player. The decision function about which coalition to join can be expressed by each actor's choice of a combination of relative bargaining powers that will maximize independence within a coalition and effectiveness toward the outside. Such a choice can be formulated in the following way for Actor C:

$$\text{Max} \left\{ \underset{(1)}{(BP_{CA}, \ BP_{CB/AC})}, \ \underset{(2)}{(BP_{CA/BC})}, \ \underset{(3)}{(BP_{C/AB})}, \ \underset{(4)}{(BP_{CA}, BP_{CB})}, \right.$$

$$\left. \underset{(5)}{(BP_{CAB/ABC})} \right\}$$

Expression (1) represents the combination of bargaining powers that can be obtained in the AC coalition, i.e., C's bargaining power toward A within the coalition and C's bargaining power toward B as a member of the AC coalition. The second expression describes a similar combination for C within a BC coalition. Expression (3) describes a similar combination for C within a BC coalition. Expressions (3) and (4) represent C's position outside a coalition, (3) showing his bargaining power towards an AB coalition and (4) the combination of bargaining power C can master toward an isolated A and B, i.e., when each player stays independent. Finally, (5) determines what C can get out of the grand coalition ABC. If combination (1) yields the highest value for Player C, he will ally himself with A; otherwise he will either join B if (2) is highest or[8] remain independent if either (3) or (4) are greatest. Similar symmetrical decision functions can be established for the two other players. If Caplow's $A > B > C$, $B + C$

A triad is considered, only decisions[9] by C are relevant, since he is the pivot of the triad. Moreover, in this case, an AB coalition is unlikely. The above decision function for C reduces, therefore, to:

$$\text{Max} \left\{ (BP_{CA}, BP_{CB/AC}), \quad (BP_{CB}, BP_{CA/BC}), \quad (BP_{CA}, BP_{CB}) \right\}$$

$$\qquad\qquad (1) \qquad\qquad\qquad (2) \qquad\qquad\qquad (3)$$

In order to be able to decide, C has to evaluate (1), (2), and (3) via some trade-off functions between (a) maximizing bargaining power within the coalitions and towards the outside and (b) facing the two other players alone. These trade-off functions will represent the respective utilities for C of being in a coalition AC, a coalition BC, or unaligned.

Such trade-off functions could take several forms. The following simple ones will be proposed:

$$U_{AC} = (BP_{CB/AC} - E) \quad (F - BP_{CA})$$

$$U_{BC} = (BP_{CA/BC} - H) \quad (K - BP_{CB})$$

$$U_{C} = (BP_{CB} - I) \quad (J - BP_{CA})$$

All of these are double-threshold functions which have the following meanings:

(1) The utilities of coalitions AC and BC for C are both positive above thresholds E and H and below thresholds F and K. Below E and H, being in a coalition entails more liabilities than assets. Above F and K, C's bargaining power is high enough to render his staying in a coalition useless. E and H and F and K can thus be considered as intrinsic utility parameters of the inside (F,K) and outside (E,H) values of the coalition.

(2) The utility of staying alone is positive between two limits I and J. Between I and J, C finds it possible to allocate sufficient amounts of his bargaining power to either the weaker Player B or to the stronger Player A. Above J or below I not enough bargaining power can be allocated to counter either one or the other players, which makes staying alone less attractive than joining a coalition. For this outcome to obtain, it is necessary that the sum of I and J stay in some fixed relation like I + J = Q, where Q represents an upper constraint on C's resources. These trade-off functions are modified versions of the Nash solution (Luce and RAiffa, 1957, pp. 124-127). The second factor of either U_{BC} or U_C is the negative of the equivalent Nash term because C is arbitrating between advantages (first factor) and disadvantages (second factor) of a coalition or of allocating resources to one or the other opponent when staying alone.

The analysis of U_{AC} and U_{BC} are symmetrical, hence only U_{BC} and U_C will be discussed. Let us assume that:

$$BP_{CA/BC} = \frac{BP_B + BP_C}{BP_A}$$

and

$$BP_{CB} = \frac{BP_C}{BP_B}$$

$$U_{BC} = \frac{-BP_C - BP_B BP_C + K\,BP_B + K\,BP_B BP_C + H\,BP_C BP_A}{BP_A BP_B} - HK$$

If C tries to maximize U_{BC} with respect to BP_C (the only variable he controls) for given BP_A and BP_B one gets:

$$\frac{\partial UB_C}{\partial BP_C} = \frac{-2\,BP_C + (K-1)\,BP_B + H\,BP_A}{BP_A BP_B} = 0^7$$

and thus:
$$BP_C = \frac{(K-1)\,BP_B + H\,BP_A}{2} \tag{1}$$

On the other hand if

$$BP_{CB} = \frac{BP_C}{BP_B} \quad \text{and} \quad BP_{CA} = \frac{BP_C}{BP_A}$$

$$U_C = \frac{-BP_C + J\,BP_C BP_A + I\,BP_C BP_B}{BP_A BP_B} - IJ$$

Similarly:

$$\frac{\partial U_C}{\partial BP_C} = \frac{-2BP_C + J\,BP_A = I\,BP_B}{BP_A BP_B} = 0$$

and

$$BP_C = \frac{JBP_A + IBP_B}{2} \quad \text{or}$$

$$BP_C = \frac{(Q - I)\,BP_A + I\,BP_B}{2} \tag{2}$$

Formulation (1) expresses the idea that if K is smaller than 1 the bargaining power C obtains through its alliance with B is only due to the threat posed by A for a positive H.

This conclusion can be illustrated by the discussion of the two cases $K < 1$ and $K > 1$. The magnitude of K can be evaluated with respect to BP_{CB} by the ratio BP_C/BP_B. If the ratio is small (strong inequality), K can be relatively small. The higher K, the more equal C and B should be. If $K > 1$, C can get bargaining power from the coalition irrespective of A. The utility of the coalition is always positive.

One can derive a similar relation for the other coalitition member B:

$$BP_B = \frac{(K' - 1)\,BP_C + H'\,BP_A}{2}$$

If B is a much stronger member than C, K' should be superior to 1, while K is below 1. In other words, B's intrinsic coalition utility should be much greater than C's. However, in this case, C has much less incentive to stay in the coalition, whose existence will depend mostly on the threat posed by the outside Player A. Such a tendency will be accentuated if other weaker members are added to the arrangement as A's threat remains constant. Finally, one reaches a point where the adjunction of enough weak members renders the coalition useless for an additional one.

$$BP_{J+1} = \sum_{J+L}^{N} \frac{(K_{J+1i} - 1)\ BP_J + H_{J+1}BP_A}{2} \leqslant 0$$

Incentives to defect would become generalized in such a case, leading to a typical "public good" problem where the weak are in some sense exploiting the strong, who can then only either coerce the less powerful members into obedience and/or emphasize outside threats (cf. Olson, 1965). The above result is interesting in that it shows that the "public good" conception is embedded in our formulation if one assumes a particular relation among the various K parameters.

Formulation (2) determines for C how he should divide his attention in terms of bargaining power between A and B if he stays alone. If Q, C's upper constraint on resources is too low, the utility of staying alone is negative, and the incentive is to join a coalition. Both (1) and (2) are in a sense weighing schemes which establish how C should evaluate his costs and benefits for given values of the respective bargaining powers of A and B. For some values of H, K, I, and J an increase in BP_B for a fixed BP_A will result in a lower bargaining

power for C within the BC coalition and a higher one for staying alone. Eventually, an AC coalition will become attractive. The parameters E, F, H, K, I, and J are not necessarily constant. They could be considered as variables determined by C's resources or his specific situation vis a vis either A or B.

In particular, the value of the A parameter could be influenced by side payments from B to C. K would be represented as $K = K^* + X_{BC}$, where X_{BC} stands for side payments from B to C. The dynamics of K^* and the side payments would be expressed by the following structure:

$$X_{BC} = a \left\{ \log \frac{BP_B}{BP_C} + \text{Max } BP_{B/BC} \right\} \tag{3}$$

$$- bx_{BC}$$

$$K^*_{CB} = h \ (\text{Max } BP_{C/BC} - X_{BC} \qquad (4)$$
$$+ kx_{BC} - mix_{CB}$$

Equation (3) states that as long as B is superior to C and/or gets a positive maximum bargaining power out of the BC coalition, B has an incentive to provide side payments to C. B faces a cost constraint proportional to the size of the payments. The parameters a and b are constant.

Equation (4) indicates that C's K* parameter will increase in proportion to the difference between the maximum bargaining power he gets out of the BC coalition and the size of the side payments. If Max $BP_{C/BC}$ is high anyway, C's intrinsic coalition utility (without side payments), which is measured by K*, will tend to increase. Strong side payments with respect to Max $BP_{C/BC}$ will tend to decrease the intrinsic utility of the coalition, which is kept "alive" by side payments. On the other hand, some side payments are necessary to keep the intrinsic utility of the coalition high. Finally K* is diminished by possible side payments from C to B, and h, k, and m are constant parameters.

Symmetrical relationships could be envisaged in the evolution of B's intrinsic utility and C's side payments. In any case, the model outlined above shows how some evolution within a given power distribution can produce significant coalition shifts.

The above formulation can be extended to N-actor situations. Actor C would, however, be faced with a more complex choice. The would have to estimate the bargaining power he could get out of each dyadic coalition, each treadic coalition, and so on up to the grand coalition, and to compare all these to staying by himself. The stability of each coalition would have to be examined with respect to all other actors' similar calculations and the evolution of their respective bargaining powers over time.

Such a perspective can be expressed in terms of several bilateral reaction functions per country, similar to the ones defined above within the two-actor framework. However, in a multilateral situation, the various U(C)'s would shift according to the changing alignments of a particular actor and so of course would the U(D)'s. Whether the actor in question is aligned, opposed, or neutral toward another one would affect strategic response function accordingly:

$$SR_{J\ J+1} = (Y_{J+1\ J} - U(C)_{J\ J+1})\ (U(D)_{J\ J+1} - Y_{J+1\ J})$$

If J and J+1 are aligned we would have:

$$U(C)_{J\ J+1} = F_1 \quad \text{(Max BP obtained from the 1, ...J, J+1 alignment)}$$

$$U(D)_{J\ J+1} = F_2\ (-\sum_{i}^{J+1} (K_{Ji} - 1)\ BP_i)$$

that is, the liability term of the alignment. If J and J+1 are opposed these formulations would be reversed.

$$U(C)_{J\ J+1} = F_2$$

$$U(D)_{J\ J+1} = F_1$$

If J and J+1 are neutral toward each other

$$U(C)_{J\ J+1} = G_1\ (Q - \sum_{i}^{J-1} I_{Ji})\ BP_i$$

that is, J+1's interest as a potential ally against all other relevant actors

$$U(D)_{J\ J+1} = G_2\ I_{J+1}\ BP_{J+1}$$

that is, J+1's threat as a potential enemy.

A stability analysis of the above strategic reaction functions can be carried out for the specific case of the BC coalition which was examined beforehand. Dynamic strategic response formulations such as:

$$SR_{BC} = (Y_{CB} - U(C)_{BC})\ (U(D)_{BC} - Y_{CB})$$

$$SR_{CB} = (Y_{BC} - U(C)_{CB})\ (U(D)_{CB} - Y_{BC})$$

lead to four possible equilibrium points:

(1) $\quad Y_{CB} = U(C)_{BC} \quad Y_{BC} = U(C)_{CB}$

(2) $\quad Y_{CB} = U(D)_{BC} \quad Y_{BC} = U(D)_{CB}$

(3) $\quad Y_{CB} = U(C)_{BC} \quad Y_{BC} = U(D)_{CB}$

(4) $\quad Y_{CB} = U(D)_{BC} \quad Y_{BC} = U(C)_{CB}.$

A stability analysis leads to the following eigen values for each point:

(1) $\lambda_{1,2} = \pm \sqrt{(U(D)_{CB} - U(C)_{CB})\ (U(D)_{BC} - U(C)_{BC})}$

(2) $\lambda_{3,4} = \pm \sqrt{(U(C)_{CB} - U(D)_{CB})\ (U(C)_{BC} - U(D)_{BC})}$

(3) $\lambda_{5,6} = \pm \sqrt{(U(D)_{CB} - U(C)_{CB})\ (U(C)_{B} - U(D)_{BC})}$

(4) $\lambda_{7,8} = \pm \sqrt{(U(C)_{CB} - U(D)_{CB})\ (U(D)_{BC} - U(D)_{BC})}$.

These eigen values can either be real positive or negative in each case or complex. If they are real they lead to unstable dynamic paths (saddlepoints). If they are complex, they lead to stable cycles (so-called vortex points). The above results show that stability can only be achieved if (1) there is some asymmetry between the two allies or (2) one ally is at the cooperative equilibrium point while the other is at the conflictual one, another form of asymmetry. This shows that alliances between equals tend to be unstable.

However, in the case K > 1 for B and C the conflict equlibrium U(D) is really transformed into another cooperative outcome. Stability can therefore be achieved when the two allies see advantages in a coalition for different reasons, one against the outside and the other as an advantage inside the coalition. Diversity might therefore be an asset rather than a liability in coalition formations among relative equals.

Clearly, this formulation of the strategic response function can produce, as in the bilateral case, initiation, escalation, and termination of conflicts. Alignment shifts will affect the U(C)'s and U(D)'s in a significant way and thus increase or decrease the resulting willingness of an actor to escalate or de-escalate. For instance, the switch of alignment of the Soviet Union in 1936 increased Germany's conflict outcome utility tremendously, since it did not have to contemplate the perspective of a two-front war, and this bolstered its intentions to invade Poland. Similar moves in the other direction can occur when an ally defects, especially when the loss in bargaining power can not be compensated by an increased resolve.

SOME EMPIRICAL RESULTS

At this stage only some very preliminary operationalization of the above conceptions and the whole notion of bargaining power can be presented. Allan

(1983) obtained some interesting results with a formulation that is close to the one outlined above in the bilateral case of the Cold War. Is it possible to extend this analysis to a multilateral situation? In this context, an investigation of the application of the above model for the shifting alignments within the Washington-Moscow-Peking triangle--the three nations described within the SIMPEST model (Luterbacher and Allan, 1982)--seems particularly relevant.

The initial USSR-China alignment is understandable within the context of the early 1950s when the US, with its intervention in Korea and its support to Taiwan, appeared as a very threatening power to China. The power configuration US>USSR>China produces an alignment between the two weaker nations. However, if one takes the perspective expressed by formulations (1) and (2) it can be seen that this situation can evolve when the capabilities of the second-ranked nation increase. Such a development clearly took place between 1953 and 1963, when the ratio of US to USSR military expenditures went from about 1.8/1 to a little bit more than 1. The subsequent increase of Soviet military power, as well as the weakening of the US during the Vietnam war, precipitated this evolution. This historical context could explain the Chinese shift first to nonalignment and finally to "rapprochement" with the US.

however, the Chinese defection has important consequences for the USSR as well: given the uncertainty of the situation and its difficult strategic posture in case of a two-front war, the USSR is being pushed into "striving for omnipotence," a type of behavior where it tries to develop more and more its own military resources. Such Soviet moves have produced global American counter-reactions and thus fueled the international arms race. The present triadic situation results in a very unstable international environment.

Estimates of the Chinese resolve and security versus the US and the Soviet Union (Figures 11.3 and 11.4) show that China's position deteriorated at the end of the sixties but then improved over the seventies. China's position is, however, always better with respect to the US than it is with respect to the Soviet Union, which can explain why the Sino-American alignment became more likely. The numbers in Figures 11.3 and 11.4 also show, however, that China's position vis-a-vis the US has been worsening slightly since 1978, a circumstance which could explain current problems between the US and China.

Security figures were calculated on the basis of ratios of military indices as computed within the SIMPEST model (Luterbacher and Allan, 1982). Evaluations of resolves were derived from methods established by Allan (1983).[10] The resolve measurements are based on the

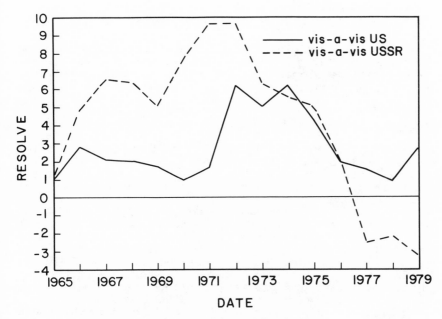

Figure 11.3   Chinese Resolve vs. US and USSR

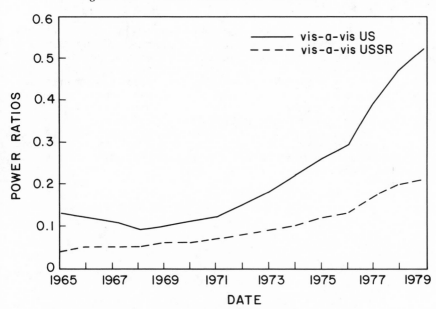

Figure 11.4   Chinese Military Power vs US and USSR

COPDAB events data set (cf. Azar, 1980, for a description).
    The data in Figures 11.3 and 11.4 should only be taken as a first attempt at validating the above theoretical developments. They nevertheless indicate that our approach has some explanatory potential.

NOTES

    1. An interesting attempt to deal with this problem has been made by Fenoaltea (1975).
    2. This is especially apparent in some economists' views about slavery (Fogel and Engerman, 1974) or feudalism (North and Thomas, 1971).
    3. This point has been made by Rapoport (1957, p. 285) commenting on Lewis F. Richardson's work. We do not think, however, that it resists a thorough examination of the problem.
    4. This latter outcome is especially likely in chicken and prisoner's dilemma where "non-myopic" equilibria (Brams and Wittman, 1981) occur.
    5. Thus, winning is preferred to losing.
    6. These six games are; **prisoner's dilemma** (both have preferences I), **chicken** (both II), **deadlock** (both III), **called bluff** (I,II), **weak deadlock** (I,III), and **bully** (II,III) .
    7. Such a model has been developed by Allan (1983) and is currently expanded to be included in the SIMPEST model of international interactions (Luterbacher and Allan, 1982).
    8. The grand coalition is excluded, as mentioned above.
    9. This represents a maximum, as can easily be seen by taking the second derivative.
    10. Allan's (1983) expression of change in resolve is the time integral of the difference between variations in conflictual moves (with respect to diplomatic time) between two actors.

12 Modeling External and Internal Conflict in Small Countries

SMALL COUNTRIES AND SIMULATION

Conflict behavior involving small countries attracts few investigations and is poorly understood.[1] Unlike the superpowers, these nations survive in situations where power is distributed in a fundamentally asymmetrical manner while simultaneously facing a series of internal constraints which smallness entails. This paper describes a dynamic simulation model, SIMSWISS, of a small nation-state and uses representative simulation results to illustrate the ability of the model to capture historical behavior and investigate hypothetical or counterfactual situations for policy purposes. A detailed discussion of the political sector reveals interesting structural properties which are partially explained by smallness. Several conclusions confirm previous research, but the case study approach limits the ability to generalize from the results. Nevertheless, we end with a series of suggestive hypotheses concerning the behavior of small countries. In keeping with the incremental strategy of this project, the paper considers how SIMSWISS could be extended to include a dynamic model of domestic conflict.

SIMSWISS (Luterbacher and Clarke, 1983) is a large-scale continuous time computer simulation model of Switzerland designed to form part of a global model consisting of interactive nation-states. Within the global modeling tradition, it is still unusual to start from the bottom up with separate nations as basic units, rather than disaggregating from a greatly simplified model of the world. However, this approach enables modelers to construct operational models containing much detailed structure of political and economic processes. For example, the SIMPEST superpower model (Luterbacher and Allan, 1982) goes beyond the study of resource allocation to look at a variety of politico-economic interactions and conflict processes.

Just as most of the dynamic modeling literature concentrates on interactions between the superpowers

(Allan, 1983; Ward, 1982), SIMPEST originally contained full models of only the United States, the Soviet Union, and China. This focus on major nuclear powers is usually justified by their central role in world politics and the potential threat their arsenals represent. Yet, recent work in the area of coalition formation repeatedly stresses the paradox that weak countries are often the pivotal members of an alliance and capable of bargaining from a position of strength (Luterbacher and Allan, 1983; Guiasu and Malitza, 1980). Thus, it is useful to model small countries such as Switzerland and investigate their reaction to a variety of conflict-producing situations.

As a large-scale simulation model intended for empirical analysis, SIMSWISS sacrifices the rigor and generality of approaches such as game theory for the realism and particularity necessary to analyze complex choice problems in concrete settings. This is not altogether an undesirable research strategy, as Roger Benjamin (1982) recently pointed out in a call for more contextual modeling in political science. As an applied model, SIMSWISS embodies particular occurrences of general theoretical principles as models of those principles, together with a set of auxiliary conditions necessary for the empirical application of these general theories. In particular, special care has been taken to construct compatible rational choice decision models as the basis for all sectors in the model. Although rationality criteria are not alone sufficient to define choices within the model, they comprise a unified model of human behavior applied to decision situations as disparate as gasoline consumption, fertility decisions, or voting choices.

The need for context and auxiliary conditions underlines the importance of building global models one nation at a time, so that the special structure and behavior of each society is adequately represented. A solid empirical grounding is provided for SIMSWISS by the use of historical time series data to estimate all of the equations in the model. The resulting model takes the general form of differential equations combined with logical switches and time delays to represent abrupt system changes due to policy switches or external events of an extreme nature. The model is then run in continuous time from a set of initial conditions using a dynamic simulation language called Dare-P (Wait and Clarke, 1976).

GENERAL STRUCTURE AND PURPOSE OF SIMSWISS

An interactive approach to modeling small countries is adopted here in two senses. First, because Switzerland is a small country characterized by an open economy and situated in a strategic location between the NATO and Warsaw Pact alliances, a number of international influences play an important role in SIMSWISS. These exogenous variables include population flows into Switzerland, the state of world trade and income, inflation rates for the industrialized nations, energy prices, and the degree of tension between the superpowers (see Figure 12.1). Second, the various sectors making up the model are highly interactive. This model structure reflects the tight institutional integration of many small countries and the spillover effects of crises anywhere in the social system.

SIMSWISS is designed primarily to investigate the effect of external crises on Swiss security and internal welfare. Security is defined in a broad sense to include military strength, government support, economic vulnerability, energy vulnerability, food embargoes, and population effects. Consequently, the model is structured into a series of separate modules, each with a limited number of linkages to the rest of the model. This strategy facilitates causal interpretation of simulation results, as well as the analysis of total system structure and the effect of sectoral interactions on system stability. Although Figure 12.1 is too simplified to show specific linking variables between sectors, it does indicate the great potential for dynamic interaction within the model.

SIMSWISS uses time series data covering the period between 1960 and 1980. Selected graphs, shown in Figures 12.2-12.4, illustrate how well simulation results agree with empirical data within the estimation period. The variables shown are generally more volatile than most political variables in the model.

Sensitivity tests indicate that the model is surprisingly stable across parameter changes for most variables, and a number of scenarios assuming exogenous external shocks to the system were adequately absorbed in the short-run. The model could be destabilized by relatively small changes in the parameter values for two domestic economic variables: the money supply growth variable in the consumption equation and the permanent income adjustment variable in the consumption equation. One external variable, relative foreign inflation, in the import equation also destabilized the model under certain assumed parameter values. In general, the model remained quite stable in spite of internal or external political crises. The vulnerability of Switzerland to outside pressures showed itself through major fluctuations in the simulated evolution of the model with changes in the values of exogenous variables used.

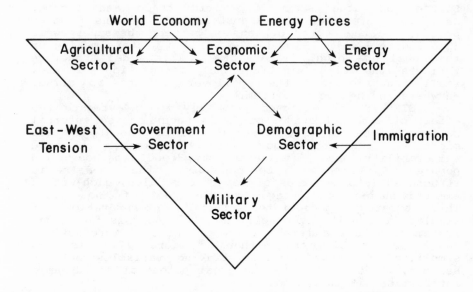

Figure 12.1   General Model Structure of SIMSWISS

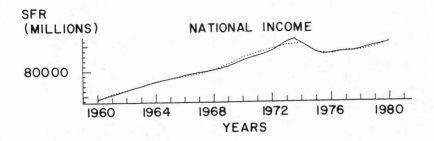

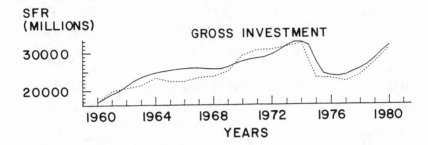

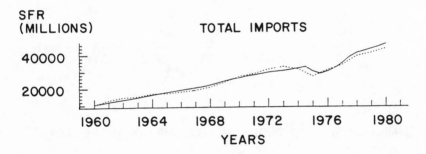

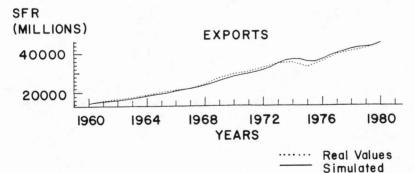

Figure 12.2   Selected Validation Graphs

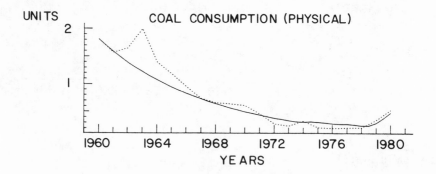

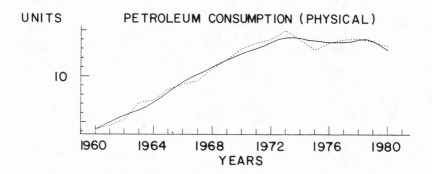

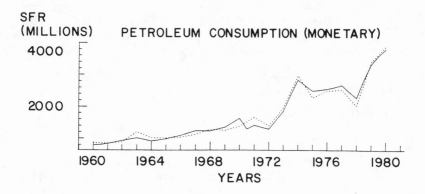

Figure 12.3   Selected Validation Graphs

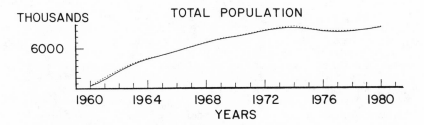

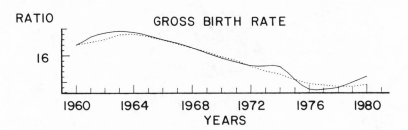

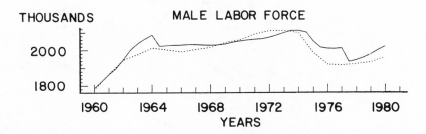

Figure 12.4   Selected Validation Graphs

The analytical emphasis in SIMSWISS is on external crises and their secondary effects on the country. This does not preclude the analysis of crises resulting primarily from domestic sources, as we shall see below. Nevertheless, the vulnerability of small countries leads us to expect special structures and strategies to compensate for weaknesses to which the superpowers are relatively immune. These special strategies will be a recurring theme in this chapter.

SIMSWISS produces simulation data which could be treated as forecasts. An example of such a forecast for gross domestic product between 1980 and 1983 is compared in Figure 12.5 with actual data for the time period. These simulation results cover a period outside the data set used for estimation, although the model simulates from initial conditions in 1960. The figure indicates that SIMSWISS can be used successfully to forecast, but it is improper to do so for several reasons. The model

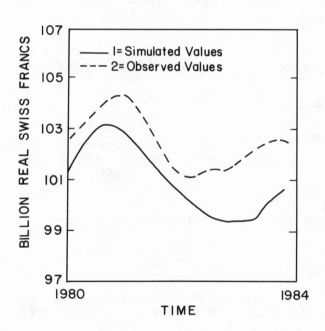

Figure 12.5   Gross Domestic Product, an Ex Ante Test

is far from being a closed system and many of the exogenous variables, such as oil prices or east-west tension,
are difficult to forecast accurately. Consequently, the
simulation results for the entire model are often strongly
dependent on the particular assumptions made concerning
these variables.

Widmaier (1984) discusses a series of technical
problems which arise when using large-scale simulation
models to forecast, and emphasizes that a good historical
fit is no guarantee that the model will forecast
accurately.[2] When the model is specifically designed to
simulate over a medium run of up to ten years into the
future, as SIMSWISS is, these forecasting problems must
be taken even more seriously.

SIMSWISS is primarily intended for theoretical and
scenario analysis rather than forecasting. The quality
of the results depends not only on the validity of the
model, but also on the appropriateness of the assumptions
upon which the scenarios are based. Although specific
numerical results should not be taken too seriously, the
analytical or qualitative results are often enlightening.
The structural effects of alternative assumptions or
parameter changes are easy to analyze, and the stability
properties of the model under dynamic simulation reveal
fruitful insights concerning small countries and the
operational versions of general theoretical propositions
embodied in models of such countries.

SIMSWISS simulations of a hypothetical energy
crisis scenario exposed a number of complicated net effects which could be analytically studied for policy purposes (Clarke and Luterbacher, 1984). For example, the
level of government support did not change significantly
because nominal wages, upon which it partly depends,
remained robust in the face of crisis. A larger inflation
effect would have induced more reaction via wages, but the
scenario demonstrated the basic stability of government
support in Switzerland. Thus, the government is free to
pursue strong stabilization policies without fear of
stimulating much political unrest. Figures 12.6-12.8
present some representative results from this crisis
simulation, comparing crisis values with base run values.
The unrealistically high jump in military expenditure,
shown in Figure 12.8, is a response to a major crisis in
east-west relations. Properly introduced lag structures
in the spending equation smooth out the curve with a
smaller increase extending over a longer time period.
However, even the dramatic increase in the original
version, shown here, produces only a minor change in the
evolution of military weapon stocks. The analytical use
of SIMSWISS is especially pertinent for the political and
military sectors to which we now turn.

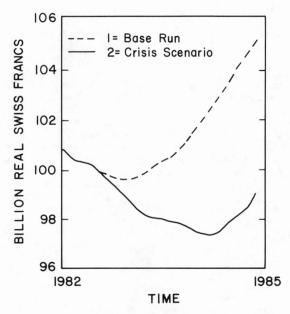

Figure 12.6   Gross Domestic Product during Crisis Scenario

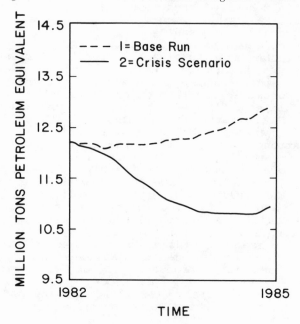

Figure 12.7   Real Demand for Petroleum during Crisis Scenario

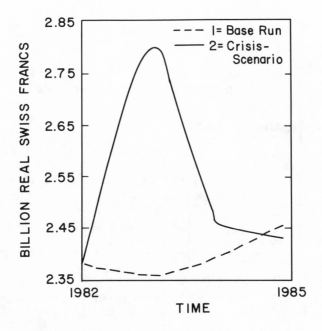

Figure 12.8   Military Expenditures during Crisis Scenario

THEORETICAL PRELIMINARIES CONCERNING POLITICO-ECONOMIC MODELS

In reality the government sector of SIMSWISS, shown in Figure 12.9, combines several political actors. The role of the electorate is represented by a measure of government support, which influences government expenditure along with other factors. Government spending is, in turn, differentiated by source (federal and local) and function (civilian and military). Within the federal government, the evolution of military weapon stocks is modeled partly as a function of expenditure. The governmental sector contains a number of internal relationships, as well as linkages to other sectors in the model. Figure 12.9 shows some variables (outside of the box) which influence political factors. Although not shown in the figure, the outputs from the government sector also affect economic and demographic variables, thereby forming feedback loops of a type frequently found in SIMSWISS.

Although conflict is the predominant interest here, it is worthwhile to first consider some aspects of the

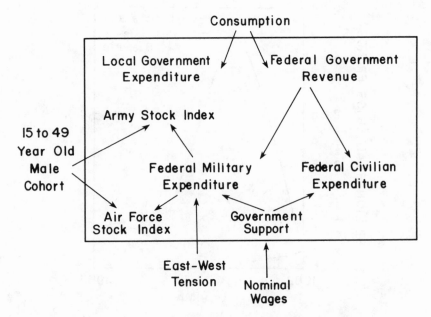

Figure 12.9   Government Sector of SIMSWISS

government sector in greater detail. The equations for
government support and expenditure rely on standard works
from the literature in politico-economic modeling with
appropriate modifications for institutional arrangements
in Switzerland (Frey, 1978; Schneider et al., 1981).
This literature builds on the seminal work of Anthony
Downs (1957), who defines rational political behavior as
behavior directed towards primarily selfish ends.   This
selfishness axiom, adopted uncritically from economics,
leads to many theoretical problems in politics, such as
why people bother to vote and why public-good problems
are not more severe.   In particular, the selfishness
axiom suggests that voters, when influenced by economic
criteria, should react only to the economic conditions
they personally experience.
    Theoretical and empirical work on the sociotropic
voter hypothesis (Sears et al., 1980; Kiewiet, 1983;
Kinder and Kiewiet, 1981) suggests strongly that voters
react to general economic conditions rather than their
personal situations.   Independent confirmation of this
hypothesis using time series data (Monroe, 1984) bypasses
methodological criticisms of previous work (Kramer, 1983;
Sears and Lau, 1983).   As Monroe notes, the possibility

that voters discount their own situations in favor of
national economic well-being strikes to the roots of
classic Downsian models based on rational choice. Monroe
rejects the sociotropic view for an alternative
explanation in which political judgments based upon
aggregate economic conditions are seen as rational
attempts to assess the managerial ability of presidents.
Thus, pocketbook voters still exist, but take a long-run
view of their economic prospects as affected by the
efficacy of chief executives.

Decision theorists are less hesitant to back away
from a narrow self-interest model of human behavior for
political phenomena. Harsanyi (1969) proposes that
social acceptance be added to economic gain as a dominant
interest entering into personal utility functions. While
this suggestion hardly moves beyond sketching how social
motives might be wedded to rational choices, Margolis
(1982) presents an elegant theory of altruistic or
group-oriented choice having the favorable
characteristics of a solid foundation in individual
psychology and the ability to subsume the standard
self-interest model as a special case. Margolis' theory
of the fair share (FS) provides a convincing rational
explanation for why people vote, extends Olson's theory
of groups and public goods to account for observed
behavior, and retains the important aspects of the
Downsian model without the limiting assumption of narrow
self-interest. For our purposes, the most interesting
aspect of this theory is its ability to provide a
rational explanation for the sociotropic voter that does
not rely on convoluted connections between managerial
ability and long-run benefits.

On the surface, Margolis justifies the use of
aggregate economic variables to predict political
popularity or government support. However, he also
suggests that voter preferences may be much more
complicated than assumed in standard politico-economic
models. Although the FS theory does not explain how
group loyalties, hence group preferences, are determined,
it does suggest that individual preferences toward the
allocation of group resources are interdependent with
general social standards. But these social standards may
be looked at as nothing more than satisfying rules of
thumb concerning the allocation of resources for social
welfare, which are adopted by so many people that they
become embodied as social rules of thumb. Thus, from a
dynamic social viewpoint, social rules come to
approximate the rational preferences of individuals
(Margolis, 1982, pp. 50-51). Perhaps a more important
implication is that changes in these social rules could be
dynamically modeled (Schotter, 1981).

POLITICAL SUPPORT

In the Swiss case, oversized or larger than minimal winning cabinets have ruled the government since 1945, a record for Western democracies (Lijphart, 1984). In addition, the members of these grand coalitions can usually look forward to automatic reelection, so that the major avenue for expressing discontent with government policy is through numerous referenda and initiatives rather than elections. Taking the voting results of these forms of direct democracy as indicators of government support equivalent to popularity polls in other democracies, our model shows that economic conditions do influence such support. We must explain, then, how a remarkably non-partisan and stable party system coexists with an electorate that still appears to punish the government for worsening economic conditions.

$$\text{GSUP} = 51.24 + 1.34 * \text{NW} \qquad (1)$$
$$\quad\;\; (.02) \quad (.63)$$

where GSUP = government support and NW = nominal wages. (The estimated symmetrical intervals for probability values of 99% are indicated below each parameter.)

We see from equation (1) that popularity is determined in the model by a constant and a variable representing nominal wages. Variables for unemployment and national income were not significant, with the former perhaps reflecting the historically low rates of unemployment in Switzerland. An inflation variable was significant, but with a positive sign. This counterintuitive result is explained by the high covariance between nominal wages and changes in the price level. Thus, nominal wages, a myopic indicator of income changes, are the only significant economic variable. We should not be too surprised by this result, since the only other dynamic model of popularity functions using a similar methodology does not find either inflation or unemployment to be significant determinants of popularity for the Federal Republic of Germany (Widmaier, 1984).

This leaves us with three related questions. Why are inflation and unemployment unimportant? Why is the nominal wage important? Why is a constant so important? The answer to the first question seems to be that voters rationally do not hold the government responsible for economic conditions. The government is extremely limited in its options toward macroeconomic policy in accordance with social preferences, and the small open Swiss economy is dominated by external forces. Voters clearly see these facts and neither reward nor punish the government inappropriately.

Then, why is another economic variable, nominal wages, important? If voters are so rational, why do they not at least judge nonmyopically on the basis of real wages? To solve these puzzles we must remember that the view of government support taken here is a dynamic medium-run perspective, and this stance calls for finer theoretical distinctions than ordinary static short-run models require. For example, researchers working on the GLOBUS dynamic model distinguish three levels of political support: for the current government, for the regime, and for the nation-state as an integrated political entity (Widmaier, 1984, p. 18). Consequently, the GLOBUS model contains three different political support equations, with economic conditions directly affecting only government popularity.

In the Swiss case this concept of multiple levels of support appears unnecessary. Because the model is designed to simulate only the medium-run future and national identity is quite stable, the equation for national integration drops away. At the other extreme, party stability and the ideology of a caretaker government remove most short-term fluctuations in popularity. The referenda yield information on a type of government support closer to regime approval. This use of the referendum instrument is especially rational in a system where government policy stems largely from an institutionalized negotiation process between mainly economic interest groups (Kriesi, 1980). But as Widmaier (1984) notes, since regime support responds to medium-run trends in economic and political processes, the distribution of economic resources should be the primary consideration.

The answer to our last question comes in two parts. The constant represents the high level of regime support given unconditionally to a trusted and stable government (Kerr, 1983, pp. 61-63). That is, most voters reward the government according to a social rule of thumb for exercising power in a manner matching their social preferences. The importance of nominal, as opposed to real, wage changes derives from the distributional effects of nominal increases. For the average male Swiss worker, a nominal increase often reflects a satisfactory real wage gain (OECD, 1983). This has not been the case for foreign and Swiss female workers, whose wages have not kept pace with those of Swiss males (Hoffman-Nowotny, 1973; Kriesi, 1980). This inequality of nominal wage increases changes the distribution of national income across social groups. The redistribution is politically popular because working females form a small fraction of the electorate (since women received the franchise in 1971) and foreign workers do not vote at all. In the section on domestic conflict we briefly discuss mechanisms which might account for the stable political consensus in Switzerland.

MILITARY AND CIVILIAN GOVERNMENT EXPENDITURE

Since the Margolis FS theory does not radically alter Downsian explanations of government expenditure, we may proceed in this area using a fairly conventional model. Because the central government of Switzerland absorbs the lowest share of total tax receipts of any Western democracy (Lijphart, 1984, p. 178), it is necessary to model local spending separately to obtain adequate results. As equation (2) shows, the determinant of local spending is theoretically uninteresting because local governments must respond primarily to a budget constraint.

$$\frac{dLG}{dt} = \frac{.15*CHCON}{(.003)} \tag{2}$$

where LG = local government expenditure and CHCON = change in total consumption.

Federal spending is more complex, responding to a number of influences, such as level of government support, a budget constraint, and, in the case of military expenditure, the level of east-west tension. A separate and more sophisticated model of Swiss military expenditure using dynamic specifications by Allan (1982) utilized adjustment parameters and memory decay functions to come to the same conclusion that east-west tension is an important determinant of changes in Swiss military spending.

$$FGG = 7.2*(GSUP-50) + .12*REV \tag{3}$$
$$(1.6) \qquad\qquad (.003)$$

$$FGM = 12.5*(GSUP-50) + 2*REV + .24*TEN$$
$$(6.4) \qquad\qquad (.01) \qquad (.06) \tag{4}$$

where FGC = federal government civilian expenditure, FGM = federal government military expenditure, REV = government revenue, TEN = level of east-west tension.

Notice that there is no trade-off or optimal allocation between civilian and military spending. Contrary to the popular notion concerning choices between guns and butter, the two spending categories do not compete directly in SIMSWISS. The level of expenditure in each category is proportional to government support and revenue, implying that each is fixed in relation to a total figure and not to each other. Domke et al. (1983) support this interpretation with data from the United States, the Federal Republic of Germany, France, and the United Kingdom, showing that defense and welfare expenditures for the four countries have separate sets of determinants. Furthermore, they found little generality in the causes and patterns of allocation across their sample, confirming the results of Cusack and Ward (1981) for the three superpowers. Even east-west tension is a significant factor for military spending only for the United States and the Federal Republic (Domke et al., 1983). Disparate patterns of government resource allocation provide another argument for the construction of global models one nation at a time. For Switzerland and other small countries there is presumptive evidence that budget allocations tend to be made by use of across-the-board or proportional rules of thumb to lower bargaining costs and avoid political conflicts that small or plural societies can ill afford.

MILITARY STOCKS IN SMALL COUNTRIES

The military sector of SIMSWISS is central to any investigation of conflict behavior in Switzerland. Even the government and demographic sectors are explicitly designed to facilitate analysis of Swiss military strength, an inherently difficult concept to quantify in a manner that is generally acceptable and useful for comparison with other nations. As the following discussion shows, definition and measurement of military strength depend partly on the strategic environment perceived by a particular country. Various problems connected with comparisons of military strength are identified and possible solutions presented, which have been implemented within SIMSWISS to the extent that our data sources allow.

Because the military sector is only one part of SIMSWISS, it is necessary to first decide in what way military weapon stocks should be related to the rest of the model. A very large literature on military spending and arms races has accumulated during the last twenty-five years, but much of this research has concentrated strictly on military expenditures without formulating theoretical or empirical connections to weapon stocks (see reviews by Luterbacher, 1975, and Allan, 1983). However, in the last few years several research groups have succeeded in formulating dynamic models which do link weapons and expenditure (Ward 1984;

Luterbacher and Allan, 1982), although empirical applications are still limited primarily to superpowers.

The latter models are generally based on the
assumption that each superpower sets goals for security
in relation to the weapon stocks of an opposing power.
Relative combat strength, measured by indices of weapons
and manpower, is assessed in the light of these goals and
each country then attempts to achieve or maintain its
ideal level of combat power. Sophisticated versions of
this basic approach include various domestic constraints
such as popular support for the government and budget
considerations, which modify the desired level of weapon
purchases stemming from purely military considerations.
The resulting quantity of desired new military investment
is then converted into a monetary value representing
defense expenditures.

A model of defense spending based on relative
levels of weapon stocks is convincing for the superpowers
and other countries whose economic and military power is
roughly equivalent to that of their potential enemies.
Rough equality insures that the military goals set by a
country are realistic in the sense that it is actually
possible to achieve the ideal level of weapons within
some "reasonable" period of time. In this case,
expenditure decisions primarily determined by reactions
to the combat power of an opponent are rational.
Although not superpowers themselves, Israel and its Arab
opponents set their military budgets according to this
logic because it is within the capabilities of these
nations to compensate for weapons purchases made by
enemies (with considerable aid from allied superpowers).
The case of Pakistan and India offers another example.

The mainstream model is a useful ideal type, but it
does not accurately reproduce the dynamics of defense
spending and military stock changes for all countries.
Many nations face hostile powers whose capabilities are so
much greater than their own that any hope of reaching
parity or dominance is illusory. By themselves, the
European members of NATO and the Warsaw Pact fall into
this category. For example, the Federal Republic of
Germany can never hope to match the military power of the
Soviet Union. The neutral countries of Europe have even
less chance of achieving parity since they must, at least
in theory, be capable of defending their sovereignty
against both superpowers and their formal allies. This
is the situation faced by Switzerland.

It makes no sense to react to fluctuations in
weapon stocks in this case. Defense spending must be
determined by other considerations, since the optimal
level of weapon stocks is out of reach. Desired military
spending has no upper limit from the military point of
view, so there can be no discernible reaction to the

opponent's investments. Logically, it is military expenditure which is first determined in these countries,
and the resulting sums are then converted into weapons.

If military spending is not determined by relative
weapon stocks, what does influence the level of
expenditure? It is reasonable to assume that the same
domestic considerations of popularity and budget limits
that are included in the stocks-to-spending model will
apply in the spending-to-stocks model. In SIMSWISS the
government expenditure equations incorporate these
domestic constraints, utilizing a model based on the work
of Schneider et al. (1981). Yet, it would be going too
far to say that these governments totally ignore external
influences when deciding how much to spend on the
military. This is especially true for European countries
strategically located in the "field of fire" between the
two superpowers.

In this case governments probably react not to
fluctuations in weapon stocks, but to changes in the
state of relations between the superpowers. When detente
is in full bloom, domestic pressure for more military
spending declines. When the superpowers pursue policies
of confrontation, support for military expansion grows.
Allan (1982) designed and tested a model of Swiss defense
spending, incorporating the variable of east-west
tension, and found that the external factor was a
significant determinant.

Now military spending must be transformed into
weapons. The corresponding equation cannot be estimated
until we have data on weapon stocks. The construction of
weapon stocks indices is a controversial and difficult
matter, but one for which we already have a
methodological model. The SIMPEST model (Luterbacher and
Allan, 1982) includes such indices for all NATO and
Warsaw Pact countries, together with explanations of how
they were constructed. These indices of combat power
have little meaning in isolation, since the point is to
compare the indices of different countries. For this
reason the indices in SIMSWISS are patterned after those
contained in SIMPEST, with some modifications. These
changes were based on the perception that the army in
Switzerland has a different function from equivalent
forces in some other countries, being designed
exclusively for territorial defense rather than any
offensive capacity.

Two equations transform military spending into
indices of combat strength for the army and air force,
respectively. The indices are distinguished to reflect
the different criteria with which the corresponding
weapon systems must be evaluated. Since the level of
overall spending is fixed prior to investment in stocks,
what is spent by the army is money which cannot be used

by the air force. Therefore, each index changes in proportion to total defense spending minus the share of expenditure flowing to the other index. The stock indices are also modified by variables representing the depreciation of stocks.

$$\frac{dAI}{dt} = \begin{array}{c} .07*FGM \\ (.002) \end{array} - \begin{array}{c} .5*CHAFI \\ (.03) \end{array} \tag{5}$$

$$\frac{dAFI}{dt} = \begin{array}{c} .04*FGM \\ (.002) \end{array} - \begin{array}{c} .63CHAI \\ (.03) \end{array} \tag{6}$$

where AI = army weapon stock index, AFI = air force weapon stock index, CHAI = change in AI, and CHAFI = change in AFI.

The equations of the military model were empirically estimated on the basis of time series data used to construct the combat power indices, yielding results that appear to roughly mirror the actual evolution of military stocks. However, the variables representing depreciation of weapon stocks in both of the equations proved to be insignificant. This result is theoretically interesting and may be interpreted in two ways. First, the data may be too inaccurate to pick up the depreciation in weapon stocks, a strong possibility in this case. The use of raw data representing net rather than gross investment increases the chances that the depreciation term might appear insignificant.

A second view is that the Swiss defense department may extend the life span of weapon systems otherwise considered obsolete for a considerable amount of time, obscuring the flow variables. This possibility could derive from the reliance on a militia army. Major weapon systems are less intensively used than in professional armies, since the artificial cheapness of labor skews investment away from new weapons as a means of maintaining combat strength. The retention of AMX-13 light tanks and DH-112 venom combat aircraft long past the time when neighboring defense forces utilized them may be examples of increasing deterrence by masking weapons depreciation, but a clear determination is difficult since the Swiss frequently retrofit their weapons to upgrade their performance.

This combat strength model was implemented within the context of SIMSWISS, although its full potential was not attained because of severe and ongoing data problems. Nevertheless, it represents an attempt to dynamically model the weapon stock decisions of a small country.

TOWARD A DYNAMIC MODEL OF DOMESTIC CONFLICT

The final section of the paper reviews and discusses some models of domestic conflict with the goal of
eventually incorporating such a model within SIMSWISS,
which already includes many variables of potential
interest.

A great many static cross-sectional models of
conflict exist, some of which are quite complex (Gurr,
1969; Johnson, 1966; Hibbs, 1973). A recent study by
Letterie and Bertrand (1982) typifies the statistical
techniques, broad scope, and worldwide samples of these
studies. Letterie and Bertrand try to explain variations
in the national use of violence, a composite variable
consisting of indicators such as collective protest and
internal war. The explanatory factors are also composite
variables representing broad concepts such as economic
development, type of democracy, and human rights policy.
Unlike more sophisticated examples of the genre, the
variance explained by this particular model is low, but
it does replicate other findings suggesting that
considerable regional variation in the causes of violence
apparently exists.

Such studies make a valuable contribution but do not
advance us very far because the level of aggregation is
too high, the variables are poorly understood, and the
models lack a temporal dimansion. Very few examples of
attempts to dynamically model domestic conflict in
individual countries exist in the literature, with
perhaps the most noteworthy case being the ongoing
GLOBUS project in Berlin. In an early research report on
GLOBUS, Widmaier (1981) tests a proposed linkage between
macroeconomic conditions and political conflict with a
sample of seven OECD countries. Specific hypotheses link
an expectations gap to a decline in political support,
which induces a disposition to engage in conflict
behavior. A number of complex variable transformations
fail to uncover any significant relationship between
economic conditions and the incidence of conflict across
the entire sample, although the inclusion of trend
variables and a variable representing government
sanctions noticeably improves the fit of the equations.
Not surprisingly, the pattern of economic factors which
are occasionally significant varies across countries.

In a later report Widmaier (1984) suggests that an
"insufficient" degree of regime support is a necessary,
but not sufficient, condition for increases in political
conflict. According to this formulation, changes in
economic conditions modify government popularity, which
in turn affects regime support. Political protests then
vary with the past rate of protest, the level of regime
support, and the rate of government sanctions. The

protest equation is written so that regime support and
government sanctions directly interact. Sanctions also
evolve in response to the past rate of sanctions and the
rate of protests.

When the model is operationalized, government
popularity replaces regime support, for which no time
series data exists. Because regime support can be
presumed to evolve slowly in most cases, the model
reduces in practical terms to an action-reaction or
tit-for-tat model of the type commonly found in the
literature on international conflict. Although equations
are again estimated for a sample of seven OECD countries,
the estimated parameters are allowed to vary across
countries and turn out to do so.

The estimated equations for sanctions and protests
in both countries for which detailed results are reported
are significant, although the economic variables in the
popularity functions are not. However, the fit between
the estimated and actual values is not very impressive
for either protests or sanctions, suggesting that the
model is on the right track but still excludes important
factors. When the model is simulated dynamically and
only the estimated parameters and a set of initial
conditions are used (as is done with both SIMSWISS and
SIMPEST), the results are extremely poor. This leads
Widmaier (1984, p. 41, author's translation) to conclude
that "an action-reaction model is scarcely in a position
to predict the historical-empirical variability and
instability of protest and sanction in the nations
studied."

Widmaier's study is reported in detail because it
points to a poverty in the theoretical foundations of such
models while serving as a positive example of how dynamic
models of domestic conflict might be specified. In a
theoretical model of how governments react to opposition
and crises, Lichbach (1981) points to accommodation as an
additional factor of some importance. Thus, the
protest-sanction model leaves out an important tool that
governments may use to reduce domestic conflict. Lichbach
also mentions the mediating effect of structural
conditions, such as inequalities of wealth and social
cleavages, but does not treat them in a formal way.

This last remark illustrates the immense gap which
currently separates the efforts of formal modelers and
historically oriented social scientists to explain
domestic conflict. For the latter group, collective
action (Tilly, 1978, 1975) or relative deprivation (Gurr
and Lichbach, 1979; Gurr, 1969; Hibbs, 1973) assume
central roles in the analysis. Eckstein (1980) shows that
these two approaches differ in their basic assumptions
Of the two, perhaps the work of Tilly, which emphasizes
competition for power, opportunity, mobilization, and

rational cost-benefit choices, is closer to the perspective of most formal modelers. In fact, Tilly (1978, p. 231) suggests that coalition and bargaining models should provide fruitful extensions of present explanations of political conflict. This view may stem from difficulties in operationalizing central variables of Tilly's model, such as power struggles and organizational strength (Zimmermann, 1980, p. 221).

That macrostructural conditions behind political protest vary across countries cannot be disputed. Date from Widmaier's (1981) seven-nation sample exhibit major differences, both in the range of political conflict and the peak values. We need ways of modifying the tit-for-tat model to incorporate such macrostructural conditions in a formal manner, since the importance of the basic model is not in doubt. A number of theorists have shown the rationality of tit-for-tat strategies in prisoner's dilemma supergames under certain conditions (Axelrod and Hamilton, 1981; Elster, 1979, p. 146), which include strong assumptions about information and a realistic possibility of defection (Brams, 1976; Taylor, 1976).

Dynamic prisoner's dilemma settings have been analyzed for two-player games by Schotter (1981), who formally demonstrates the possibility of two stable supergame strategies: cooperative, or tit-for-tat, and noncooperative. Allan (1983) independently extends this conclusion to show how oscillations between these two strategies depend upon the bargaining power of each player. Bargaining power is in turn a complex combination of relative power and expectations about the behavior of other players based on past actions.

Allan's analysis introduces two conditioning factors: expectations and relative power. Other authors have recently discussed the importance of expectations, calling it memory (Ward, 1982) or rules of thumb (Schotter, 1981; Margolis, 1982).[4] The moral stressed is that decisions to engage in conflict behavior depend not only on power capabilities and intentions, but knowledge about the intentions of other actors embodied in tacit conventions of behavior and expectations based on past behavior.

These models are meant to explain international conflicts where the actors are nation-states. Applying them to domestic conflicts is problematic because only the state is an easily defined actor. The assumption that all political protest can be treated as if it came from a single opponent as in a two-person game is highly questionable, and yet this is the theoretical implication of tit-for-tat models that oppose national events data for protests and sanctions. At the very least, we seem to require an n-person model of Allan's dynamic bargaining model and the identification of the relevant actors on the protest side.

The latter requirement has not been systematically attempted to my knowledge, but the former exists as a dynamic n-person coalition model of bargaining power (Luterbacher and Allan, 1983). When this model is generalized from triads to an n-person situation, a parameter representing intrinsic coalition utility emerges as a central determinant of potential conflict. Luterbacher (1983) suggests that the level of stability and cooperation in a society depends upon the intrinsic utilities of the principal actors, which in turn are based on factors such as social equality and consensus. But these favorable characteristics are functions of historical context, norms for collective behavior, and the evolution of cooperative institutions for alleviating political conflict. Switzerland is one of the most promising examples of the latter.

We may sum up the situation by describing what a dynamic model of domestic conflict should look like. To begin, it must incorporate some kind of action-reaction or tit-for-tat mechanism in a form sophisticated enough to move between cooperative and noncooperative modes of behavior. This implies that expectations are built into the model as norms of behavior, rules of thumb, resolve based on past behavior, or a memory filter. A feedback loop must cause expectations to evolve in response to outputs of the model over time. It also means that the relative power of each actor must be known, so that complete calculations of bargaining power are possible. Probably most difficult is the identification of the actors who potentially oppose the state and threaten political protest. Since coalitions may shift, we must also know which actors are presently allied to the state. Most events data on domestic conflict is unusable in this scheme because it lumps together all actors contemplating conflict behaviors. Finally, we must analyze macrostructural conditions to determine what the intrinsic utilities of these actors are and how they are likely to change.

Preliminary efforts with SIMPEST to carry out this agenda within the context of international conflict among the superpowers indicate the potential of such an approach (Luterbacher and Allan, 1983). Before domestic conflict can be successfully modeled within SIMSWISS, considerable efforts to collect data and operationalize the model discussed above must be carried out. Switzerland should be an interesting case to model not only because domestic conflict is admirably low and intrinsic utilities satisfyingly high, but also because it must evolve strategies which small countries can use to survive international conflicts.

A SET OF SMALL-COUNTRY HYPOTHESES

From the Swiss results, we may advance a number of tentative hypotheses about the behavior of small countries that are suggestive of further research. Some of these preliminary conclusions are clearly limited in relevance to the small rich countries of Western Europe, while others may apply to a wider universe with appropriate modifications.

The first point is somewhat surprising, if not paradoxical. Although Switzerland is very sensitive to external events, it is almost impossible to destabilize the country with external crises. Small countries are indeed vulnerable, but may not be critically so if there exists a series of institutions designed to respond to crises and keep the nation afloat. As a corollary, we should expect to find institutions specifically tailored to reducing domestic conflict and raising intrinsic coalition utilities. These mechanisms could take a wide variety of forms, depending upon actual domestic political constraints.

Contrary to a persistent and popular hypothesis in the literature, there need not be a guns-or-butter trade-off between defense and social spending. Both categories of expenditure may normally be proportional to total spending. This kind of rule-of-thumb budgeting probably reflects a conscious effort to lower bargaining costs and avoid potential sources of domestic conflict which small countries can ill afford. An additional consideration is the frequent impossibility of attaining ideal defense goals.

This brings us to the topic of defense spending and its determinants. In the Swiss case the obvious overriding strategic factor is east-west tension, and this variable exerts an expected influence on military expenditure. However, in keeping with the incremental and proportional nature of budgeting in small countries, the magnitude of government revenue is the dominant factor in spending decisions. In simple terms, the external political climate is not the most important influence, but it may be the most dynamic explanatory element.

The discussion of military stocks introduced an inconsistency in the definition of small countries implicitly used here. In earlier sections of the paper the phrase evoked an intuitive notion of relatively small geographical extent and perhaps a strictly reactive role in the international economy. However, the analytical distinction between situations leading to either a stocks-to-spending or spending-to-stocks model lacks any direct logical connection to small size. In fact, many small countries engage in arms races with neighbors of comparable size, suggesting that they are not "small" outside of their military reactions to the superpowers. Beyond Europe, the most common situation may be some combination of the two ideal types, as nations must make military decisions about local conflicts with global strategic implications.

Given a situation where the spending-to-stocks model applies, the most dramatic result is the extremely slow response of military stocks to major fluctuations in superpower tension. The dominant budget constraint appears to hold with a vengeance. In part, this result may merely reflect the long lead times associated with weapons procurement, and it suggests that stocks should be modeled by use of dynamic adjustment equations simulating the changing gap between desired and actual stocks.

Although SIMSWISS does not yet allow empirical work on domestic conflict, we may look forward to a similar series of hypotheses concerning the behavior of small countries when this new sector is implemented. If the extension of the model is based solidly on theories of coalitions, group behavior, and institutional evolution, the results should be equally suggestive of additional empirical and theoretical tests.

NOTES

1. The work upon which this paper is based was made possible primarily by a grant from the Swiss National Science Foundation, which is gratefully acknowledged. I wish to specifically thank Urs Luterbacher, Pierre Allan, Albert Stahel, and Jean-Christian Lambelet for providing technical advice, data, and computing facilities. Nicolas Kessler also contributed much time and effort to the SIMSWISS project. Stimulating and helpful comments on an earlier draft of this paper by the contributors to this volume were greatly appreciated. In this regard, I would be remiss not to thank Michael Intriligator, Charles Tilly, and Claudio Cioffi-Revilla, who still bear no responsibility for the final product.

2. A good discussion by Thomas Mayer of some potential problems with simulation models is contained in this volume.

3. Although Margolis bases his model of group behavior on an argument compatible with neo-Darwinian theory, he does not take the fatal additional step of postulating post hoc genetic explanations for behavior. Specifically arguing that his approach does not require a sociobiological or "selfish gene" underpinning, Margolis proceeds in a manner strikingly similar to the excellent essay by Axelrod and Hamilton (1981). Rather than expro-

priate the entire explanatory universe, Margolis explict-
ly points to the need for a complementary theory of group
preference formation.

    4. The empirical work on the dollar auction by
Barry O'Neill, also reported in this volume, emphasizes
the importance of learning and variable decision-making
horizons. The most interesting work in coalition
modeling has focused precisely on how expectations are
modified over time.

13 Simulation of Reliability Kinematics in Political Systems

Political breakdown and collapse are time-dependent phenomena that play a central role in a vast class of social systems, both domestic and international. For many political systems the probability that things will work, partially fail, or just collapse over time is the central focus of interest. Advances in political reliability theory provide some explanations for these phenomena. However, the large diversity of these systems and the difficulty of applying purely analytic or empirical approaches to many situations pose serious obstacles to advancing our scientific understanding of how political reliability behaves.

Deriving from a theory of political reliability, a taxonomy of political structures is presented here, and basic simulation methods are used to analyze reliability kinematics in a class of political systems. The results shed some light on the behavior of more complex political structures.

The **reliability kinematics** of political systems are interesting because they describe the likelihood of political systems working as a function of time, or along a time horizon. A theory of political reliability explains the causes of this behavior and reliability kinematics focus on the behavior of political reliability over time (without reference to the political forces causing these changes).[1]

_____

This study was supported by grant SES-84-00877 from the US National Science Foundation and by grants from the Research Board of the University of Illinois, Urbana-Champaign. I am grateful to Michael D. Intriligator and Michael D. Ward for their comments on the conference draft, to Gretchen Hower (Department of Political Science, University of Illinois) for conducting some preliminary tests of the simulation methods employed in this study, as well as to Greg Kessner (Computer Services Office, University of Illinois) for useful advice using the CMSAS.

POLITICAL RELIABILITY THEORY[2]

Political reliability theory is a positive theory which explains the likelihood of emergence, development, functioning, maintenance, and collapse of political systems. The theory is theoretically generic, formalized in its language, and probabilistic.[3] It focuses on both structural and process aspects of political systems. The following are fundamental ideas and some empirical applications of the theory.

Basic Concepts and Equations

Theoretical background useful for this simulation study is now reviewed.

The **probability reliability** R of a political system is the probability that the system will work, or function to the goals it is intended to carry out.
Let W denote the event that a given political system will work. Then

$$R \equiv Pr(W) \tag{1}$$

Two aspects of R should be noted. The first is the reliability of a political system as a function of its **structure,** as this term is defined below. The second, which is related to the first, is the reliability of a political system as a function of its **performance process,** as determined by empirical observations of partial or total failures through time. Here we focus only on the former, structural theory of political reliability.[4]

The **structure** of a political system is the configuration of subsystemic components (1) with regard to their condition of "necessity," and (2) with regard to their condition of "redundancy."

"Necessity" and redundancy" are defined below. There exist two types of structures within political systems, serial and parallel, corresponding to necesssary and redundant political components, respectively.

The **serial structure** of a political system is the set of "necessary" subsystemic components (or functional requirements) the system must have in order to operate.[5]

Let c, $1 \leqslant c \leqslant n$, denote the number of necessary components in the structure of a political system, and let W_1 denote the event that the ith of these components will work (i.e., will not fail). Then

$$R_s \equiv Pr\ W$$

$$= Pr\{W_1 \quad W_2 \quad W_3 \quad \ldots \quad W_n\} \tag{2}$$

Assuming events are independent, by the multiplication theorem for independent events (see, e.g., Bittinger and Crown, 1982, pp. 264-273), (2) can be written as

$$R_s = \Pr\{W_1\} \cdot \Pr\{W_2\} \cdot \Pr\{W_3\} \cdot \ldots \cdot \Pr\{W_n\} \tag{3}$$

$$= p_1 \cdot p_2 \cdot p_3 \cdot \ldots \cdot p_n \tag{4}$$

Finally, letting p denote the average probability across the n necessary components.

$$R_s = p^t \tag{5}$$

Equation (5) is the basic formula for the political reliability of a system having c necessary requirements to function.

The **parallel structure** of a political system is given by the set of "redundant" subsystemic components the system has.[6]

Let k, $1 \leq k \leq m$, denote the number of redundant components in the structure of a political system, and let W_j denote the event that the jth of these components will work. Then

$$R_p = 1 - \Pr \{ \bigcap_{j=1}^{m} W_j \} \tag{6}$$

Therefore, following similar conventions to those used before,

$$R_p = 1 - (1 - p_1) \cdot (1 - p_2) \cdot (1 - p_3) \cdot \ldots \cdot (1 - p_m) \tag{7}$$

$$= 1 - (1 - p)^k \tag{8}$$

Equation (8) is the basic formula for the reliability of a political system having k redundant components.

Some Empirical Applications

A large class of political systems exists in which the probability of failure is central, where structural complexity exists, and where both serial and parallel structures determine their political reliability. The following are some examples from this large class.

Strategic Nuclear Deterrence. Second-strike capabilities, in a deterrence relationship, are based on the fulfillment of a set of necessary conditions (Kaufman, 1954; Wohlstetter, 1959; Cioffi-Revilla, 1983), such as (1) the feasibility of safe, peacetime weapons systems, (2) survivability against attack, (3) post-attack C^3 capability, (4) launching, (5) penetration of active and passive defenses, and (6) targeting.

International Peace and Security. Peace and security in the international system are based on a set of requirements or "pillars" (Wilson, 1978), of which the lack of any one is likely to precipitate war (Cioffi-Revilla, 1985). In different historical periods these conditions might be fostered by formal commitments, sanctuary territories, acceptable norms of conduct, regime rules, and so on.

Government Coalitions. Government longevity--and thus governability--is based on the continued ability of a coalition to maintain the membership of pivotal actors, lacking any one of which the coalition fails (falls from power). This extends to international alliances and other systems of collective decision making based on coalition agreements (e.g., Central Committee of the Communist Party of the Soviet Union; see Casstevens and Ozinga, 1974).

Political Communication. Following Shannon and Weaver (1949), a communications channel contains, and the stream of political communication (messages-signals) passes through (1) encoders, (2) transmitters, (3) noise mergers, (4) receivers, and (5) decoders. The reliability of political communication is thus a function of these five requirements, each one of which may fail (Cioffi-Revilla, 1979; Cioffi-Revilla and Merritt, 1982).

Stable International Relations. These are generally based on high performance in a set of bilateral or multilateral international institutions (both governmental and nongovernmental) facilitating international cooperation. For example, the existence of a Standing Conference of Atlantic Organizations, based in London, indicates the existence of such a complex web within the western system. Some organizations are indispensable, others are redundant; all help maintain cooperative Atlantic relations.

Border Security and War. Security at each and every border is necessary for a nation to remain at peace with its neighbors. It is sufficient for a nation to be at war with one neighbor for that nation to be at war and for security to have failed. The border security system therefore has an n-component serial structure, where n is also the number of bordering nations.

Political reliability theory is a general theory of politics because its central concept--political reliability, as defined above--is vital in a large class of political phenomena, be these institutions, coalitions, or policies. Understanding the time-varying behavior of political reliability in these systems is clearly of scientific interest.

Equations (4), (5), (7), and (8) are the fundamental equations of structural political reliability. In many empirical cases their specification can be very complicated, since treating p as a time-varying probability--i.e., p(t)--may introduce considerable complications from an analytic viewpoint. When p(t) is anything but constant (trivial case) or linear (simplest case) the result can be mathematically cumbersome, making it difficult to see how political reliability R(t) will behave over time.

The focus here is on the set of relatively simple political structures called first-order serial and first-order parallel structures illustrated in Figure 13.1.[8] More complicated structures exist but fundamental understanding of reliability kinematics in this set is essential for understanding more complicated cases.

SIMULATION ANALYSIS

Three types of simulations were conducted. First, the static, time-invariant sensitivity of R, with respect to different values of component reliability p and different degrees of complexity (either c, for serial structures, or k for parallel structures), was explored. The range of p was set to $0 \leqslant p \leqslant 1.0$ and the numerical algorithm was run at increments of .01. The range for complexity (c or k, depending on the structural type) was set between 1 and 10 with increments of .10.

This resulted in two sets of outputs (one for the serial structure and one for the parallel structure). Each output plotted the corresponding surfaces R(p,c) and R(p,k).

Second, each type of structure (serial and parallel) was subjected to five different types of kinematic p(t) inputs to assess the extent to which qualitatively different patterns of change in p(t) affect R(t).

Each of the five inputs corresponded to a qualitatively different set of theoretical assumptions, as illustrated in Table 13.1 and Figure 13.2(a,b).

The first input (Figure 13.2a) was linear, simulating a drop in p(t) at a constant rate. This trajectory started at p(0) = 1.0, reaching p = 0 by the

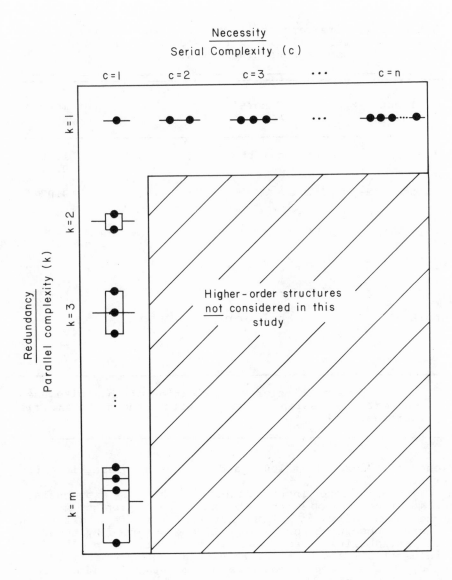

Taxonomy of structural complexity in political systems: the set of first-order serial and parallel political structures.

Figure 13.1   Taxonomy of Structural Complexity in Political Systems

Table 13.1   Time-varying input types for component
reliabilities p(t) used in simulation of
homogeneous kinematics.

Input Trajectory	General Equation	Parameters Used
linear	$p(t) = a + bt$	$a = 1.00$ $b = -0.01$
exponential	$p(t) = e^{-at}$	$a = -0.02$
logistic	$p(t) = \dfrac{1}{1 + \exp(a + bt)}$	$a = 10.00$ $b = -0.15$
parabolic	$p(t) = at^2 + bt + c$	$a = 0.00025$ $b = -.025$ $c = .6255$
spiked[1]	$pt = a[b - c\sqrt{2\pi}\ \exp[-(\dfrac{t - d}{c})^2]]$	$a = .05$ $b = 16$ $c = 5$ $d = 50$

1. This particular specification of the spike used
a   normal,   Guassian   curve,   with   known   symmetric
properties.

end of the run (t = 100), and was the simplest kinematic
run.
        The second input (Figure 13.2b) was exponential,
simulating a drop with rate negatively proportional to
the state of p(t).   Substantively, this is a situation
where subsequent drops in p(t) are governed by the rate
of reliability loss, and are asymptotic to p = 0.   The
value of a was set at .02 to simulate enough decay by t =
100, but at the same time to maintain a final loss
similar to the linear case.   Note, however, that the
assumptions underlying a linear drop are substantially
different from those associated with exponential decay.
        The   third   input   (Figure   13.2c)   was   logistic,
simulating a more complex loss pattern.   Substantively,
this simulates a loss of component reliabilities which is
governed by a rate that initially rises, reaches a
maximum (at the point of inflection in the logistic

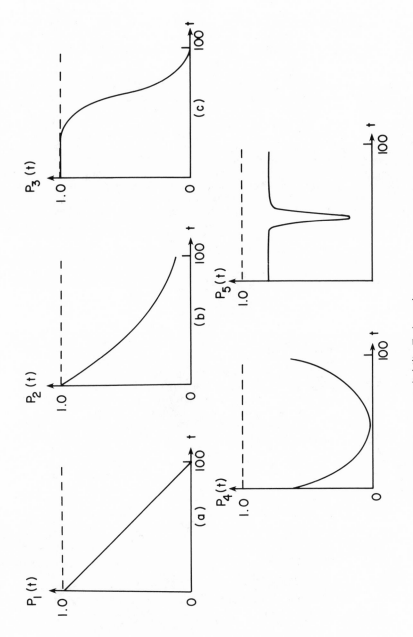

Figure 13.2   Input Reliability Trajectories

curve), and then tapers off.[9] The result is that
component reliability starts at p - 1, then drops off,
and settles slowly, asymptotically, to p = 0. Parameters
a = 10 and b = -0.15 were chosen to obtain a significant
drop beginning at about t = 35 and reaching p = 0.10 by
about t = 80.

The fourth input (Figure 13.2d) was parabolic,
simulating long-term loss and recovery in p(t). p(0) and
p(100) were chosen at slightly above 0.6 to simulate a
scenario in which there is better than 2:1 reliability in
the initial and final values of R(t). The parabolic
trajectory was made to drop all the way down to p - 0 (at
t = 50) to assess the effects of total loss and recovery
over the entire time horizon.

The fifth input (Figure 13.2e) was spiked,
simulating a steady state shocked by a sudden, sharp drop
in component reliability. Parameters were chosen to make
the spike relatively short-lived (compared with the time
horizon), and the spike was made to drop fairly deeply,
to approximately p = 0.15.

Third, the effects of mixed inputs on R(t) in both
serial and parallel structures were examined. Five
inputs for p(t) were chosen (see Figure 13.3a-e) and the
number of structural components was arbitrarily set to
5.[10]

The first input (Figure 13.3a) was linear, with
p(0) = 1.0 and p(100) = 0.60, simulating a steady loss in
the first component but still maintaining better than
0.50 reliability.

The second input (Figure 13.3b) was made to lose
reliability with an exponential pattern. The parameter
was chosen to reach the same approximate final value of
p(100) = 0.60 as in the first component. Note, however,
that the pattern differed from linear to exponential.

The third input (Figure 13.3c) was made to drop
only slightly, in a linear fashion, reaching a final
value of p(100) = 0.90, simulating only mild loss of
political reliability in the third component.

The fourth input (Figure 13.3d) simulated long-run
deterioration and recovery with parabolic trajectory,
starting with perfect reliability, dropping slowly to
p(50) = 0.60, and rising back to full reliability.

Finally, the fifth component (Figure 13.3e) was
made to follow a rising linear trajectory [p(0) = 0.80,
p(100) = 0.90], simulating a smooth, steady improvement
in a component which was, initially, already quite
reliable.

These five trajectories represent descriptions of
hypothetical scenarios for political systems having five
components. Note that in no instance was component
reliability p(t) below a value of 0.60.[11]

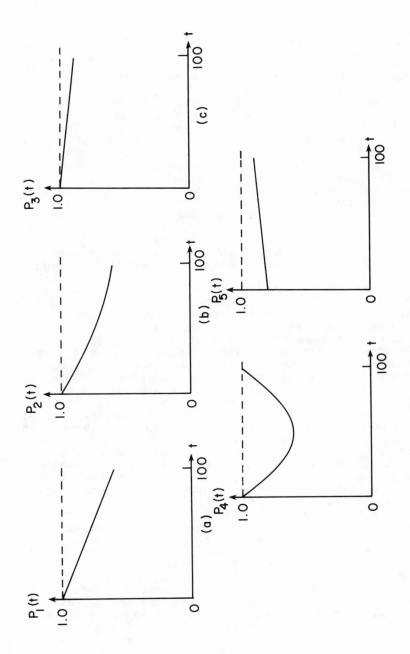

Figure 13.3 Input Reliability Trajectories

RESULTS

Results are divided into two classes, presented in the same order as they were described above.

Time-Invariant (Static) Effects of Complexity

Figures 13.4 and 13.5 present results for the simulation of (static) serial and parallel structures, respectively. In Figure 13.4 the darkest area (plotted by the * symbol in the contour chart) in the upper left marks the highest political reliability ($.944 < r < 1.000$), while the bottom right (plotted by the · symbol) shows the lowest political reliability ($0 < r < .556$). By contrast, Figure 13.5 shows that for parallel structures the area of highest political reliability ($.944 < r < 1.000$) lies in the upper right part (plotted by the * symbol), whereas the lowest political reliability ($0 < r < .055$) lies in the lower left corner (plotted by the · symbol). Both figures refer to static results of $\partial R_s / \partial_t$ (in Figure 13.4) and $\partial R_p / \partial k$ (in Figure 13.5).[12]

Figure 13.4 shows that for all but a small region in the $R^3(R,p,c)$ space, political reliability is quite low ($r \leqslant .500$) (see legend). The high-reliability region is bounded by very sharp slopes, so small drops in p, or even small increases in complexity c, cause large drops in R. (The slope toward lower p appears steeper than the slope toward higher c, but this is solely a function of scaling on the p and c axes.) Findings show that, in all but the simplest cases (i.e., when c equals 1, 2, or 3), R drops very quickly, even when p is moderately high.

Figure 13.5 shows somewhat opposite patterns in R, with almost exactly reverse symmetry.[13] Here the high-reliability region now occupies the largest proportion of $R^3(R,p,k)$ space. Contours show that this high-reliability region is in fact more like a plateau, and not a sharp peak (as in the high-reliability region for the serial structure in Figure 13.4). Both slopes, toward low p and low k, are steep.

Findings from these static runs thus show that the behavior of R in serial and parallel structures is qualitatively reverse, with virtually perfect symmetry. When complexity is high, in both cases changes in p cause changes in R. However, the intensity of this effect varies, depending on the structural type, with change in serial structures being most pronounced when p is moderately high to very high, while change in parallel structures is most pronounced when p is moderately low to very low.

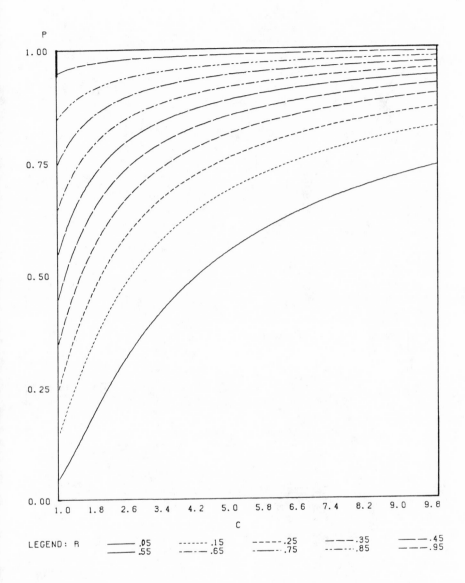

Figure 13.4   Serial Structure

290

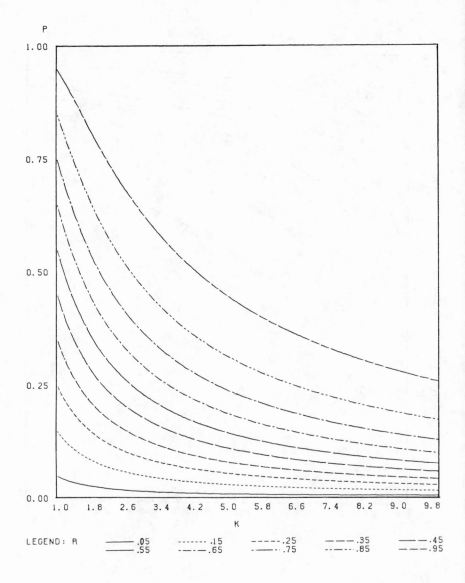

Figure 13.5   Parallel Structure

Kinematic Results: Homogeneous Trajectories

In the first set of kinematic runs, inputs p(t) p(t) were assumed to be homogeneous (both structurally and parametrically).

Serial Structures. Figures 13.6 through 13.10 refer to serial structures (1 ≤ c ≤ 10) with homogeneous inputs, each figure corresponding to linear, exponential, logistic, parabolic, and spiked inputs, respectively.

Findings for the first three inputs (linear, exponential, and logistic) show remarkably similar results. Particularly in the first two cases, R(t) drops far faster than p(t), with approximately the same pattern for both linear and exponential inputs. For moderately complex systems (c ≥ 6) both linear and exponential inputs yield a steep ridge dropping to its lowest range (0 ≤ r ≤ .056) rather quickly (t = 20 and t = 35 for linear and exponential results, respectively). For relatively simpler structures (c < 6) deterioration in R(t) is considerably slower, but always faster than deterioration in p(t).

Results for logistic inputs show that deterioration in R(t) can be delayed. However, when p(t) does drop, R(t) drops far faster, particularly when complexity is moderate to high. In fact, for the entire range of c, the ridge caused by logistic inputs has a gradient comparable to the steepest gradients caused by linear and exponential drops (compare Figure 13.8 with Figures 13.6 and 13.7).

Parabolic and spiked inputs yield distinctively different results. The former yields a reliability surface R(c,t) with two miniscule maxima (c = 1, t = 1 and 100), both far smaller than suggested by the parabolic input. The latter has two maxima (c = 1, 0 < t < 42 and 6 < t   100) separated by a deep ravine (occurring at about t = 50) with the lowest depth at approximately zero and with a maximum height of only approximately r = .20 when c is down to 1 (simplest serial structure). Figure 13.10 also shows that the effect of the spiked input is far stronger at the systemic level than at the component level (compare Figures 13.10 and 13.8).

Parallel Structures. Figures 13.11-13.15 show results from the five kinematic simulations of parallel structures (1 ≤ k ≤ 10) with homogeneous input, each figure corresponding to a different set of homogeneous inputs.

Figures 13.11, 13.12, and 13.13 (linear, exponential, and logistic inputs) again show approximately similar patterns for R(t), but with the

292

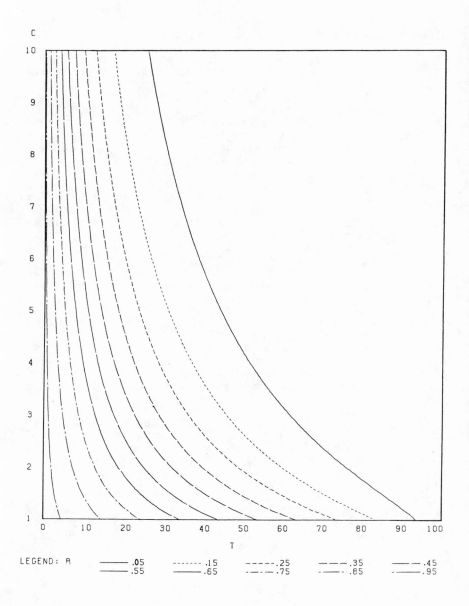

Figure 13.6   Serial Structure with Linear Components

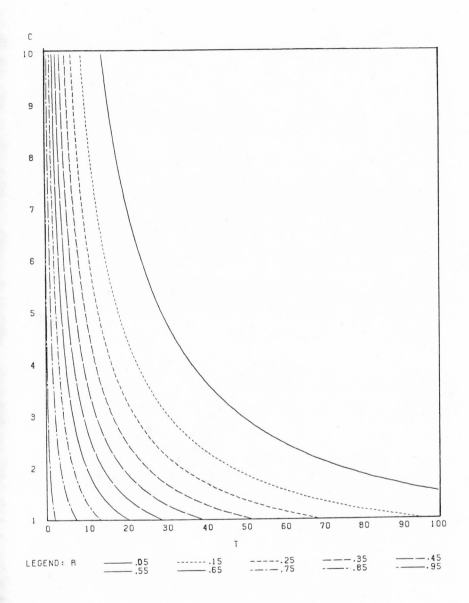

Figure 13.7 Serial Structure with Exponential Components

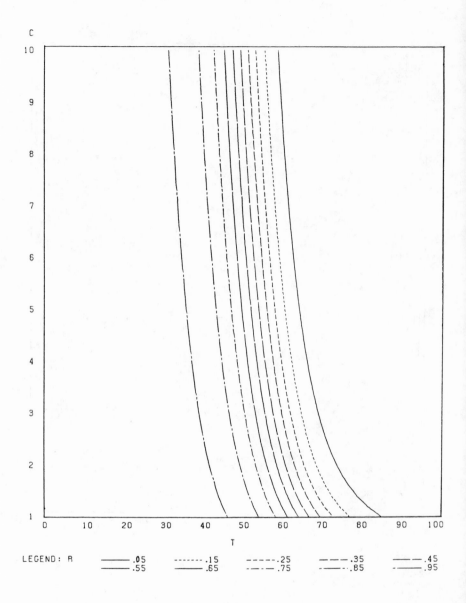

Figure 13.8   Serial Structure with Logistic Components

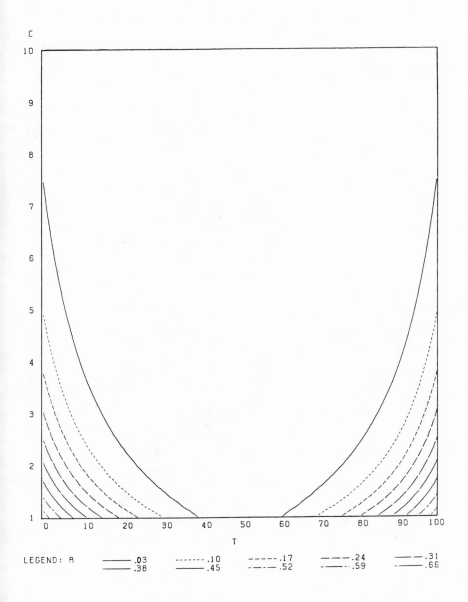

Figure 13.9   Serial Structure with Parabolic Components

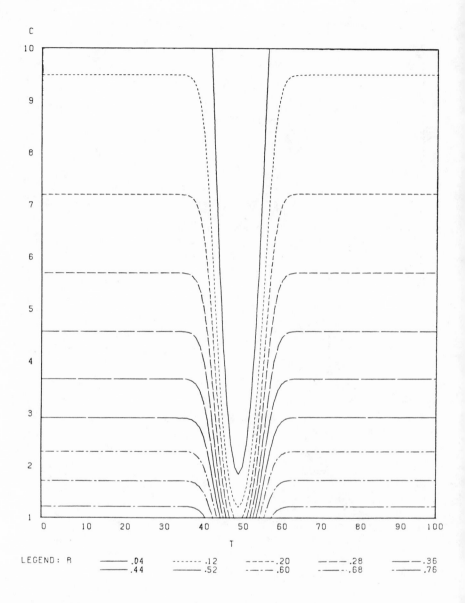

Figure 13.10 Serial Structure with Spike Components

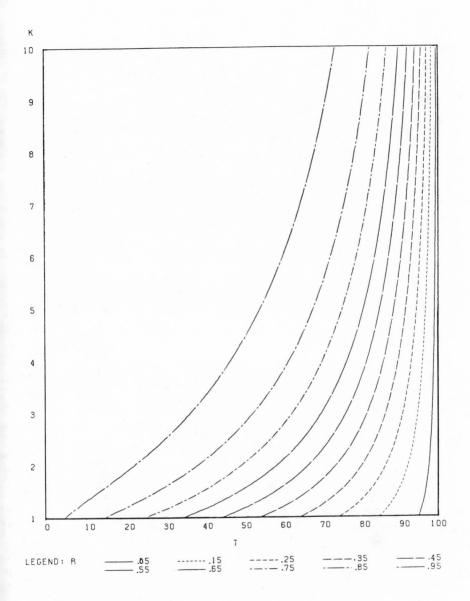

Figure 13.11 Parallel Structure with Exponential Components

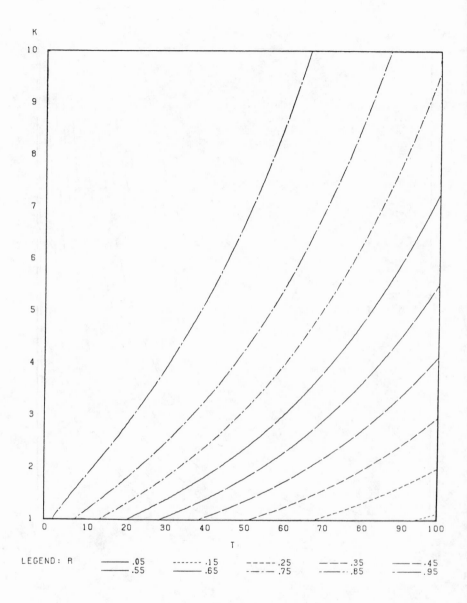

Figure 13.12 Parallel Structure with Exponential Components

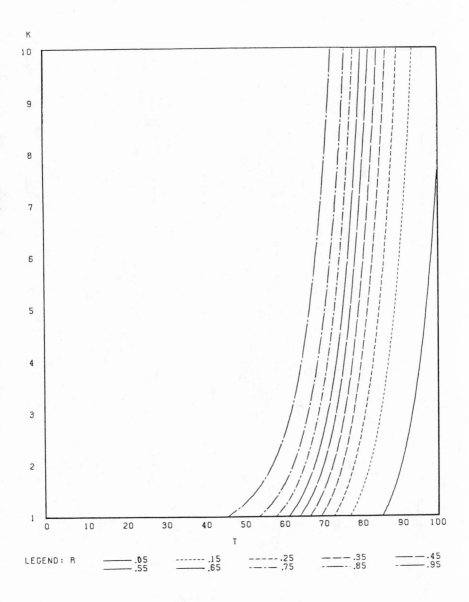

Figure 13.13 Parallel Structure with Logistic Components

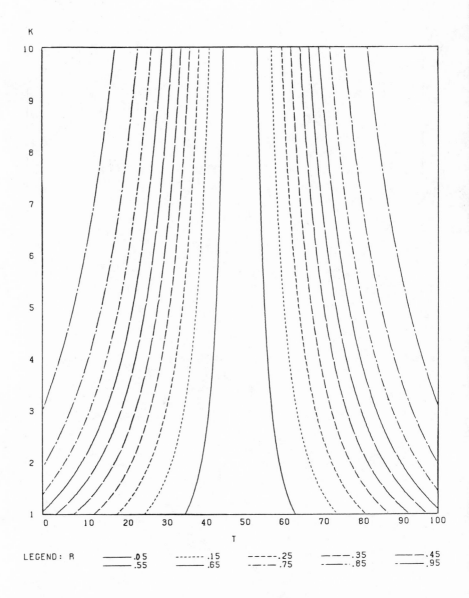

Figure 13.14 Parallel Structure with Parabolic Components

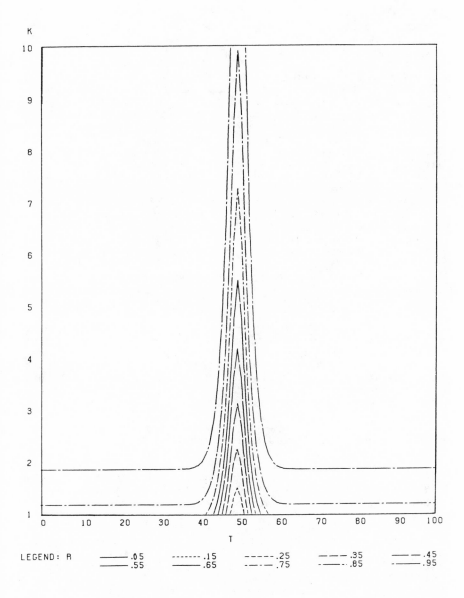

Figure 13.15 Parallel Structure with Spike Components

opposite effect of that found in serial structures. These systems are capable of maintaining approximately perfect R until very close to t = 100. In particular, the effects on R(t) are more akin to the logistic than to the exponential input. The effect of the three inputs is virtually the same when complexity is high, but when complexity is low the effects of linear and exponential inputs differ significantly from those of logistic inputs.[14]

Parabolic and spiked inputs cause qualitatively different behavior in R. Figure 13.14 shows that parallel structures of moderate complexity (k ⩾ 5) can maintain very high reliability (.944 ⩽ r ⩽ 1.00) even when p is at best modest (p ⩽ .600), as seen by the size of the maximum region ("*") in Figure 13.14.[15] Note also that the drop away from the plateau maxima (toward t = 50) is first convex (toward the top) but then concave (toward the bottom), unlike the strict concavity of the parabolic input. There is thus an interesting region where R(t) > p(t).

The effect of homogeneous spiked inputs on parallel structures is shown in Figure 13.15. Again, the topography of the ravine caused by the drop in p shows marked sensitivity to the level of complexity.[16] Here the ravine is very steep and narrow, having widths ranging from only t ⩽ 4 (when k = 10) up to t ⩽ 20 (when k = 2).[17] From k = 10 down to k = 2 the ravine drops from about r = .90 to about r = .35. Moreover, this drop, along t = 50, seems convex, with the highest gradient occurring after k = 4.

Kinematic Results: Mixed Trajectories

Figure 13.16a shows R(t) for the serial structure with five components. (Note that the scaling of the ordinate has the range [0.80, 0.25].) After an initial steep drop reaching a minimum at approximately t = 75, R(t) ends in a slight but noticeable recovery.

Figure 13.16b illustrates R(t) for the parallel structure. (Note that the scaling of the ordinate has the range [1.0000, 0.9997].) After an initial plateau, R(t) descends rapidly to a minimum and then recovers to full political reliability (1.0) at t = 100.

All seven trajectories--five p(t) inputs and two R(t) outputs--are superimposed in Figure 13.17 to show composite, comparative kinematic results. Clearly, in both serial and parallel structures outputs (whether R_s or R_p) differ from inputs (p). These differences between "the parts" and "the whole" are both quantitative and qualitative.

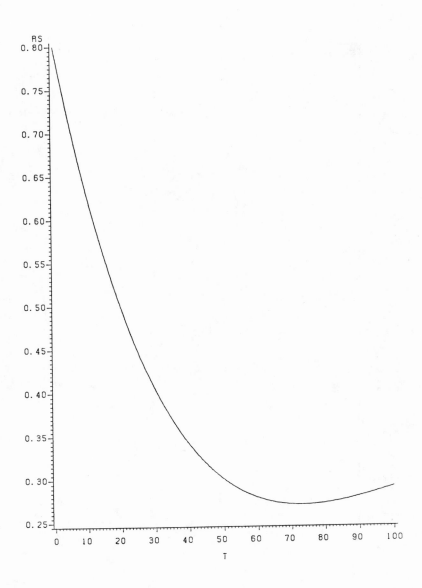

Figure 13.16a RSerial Trajectory

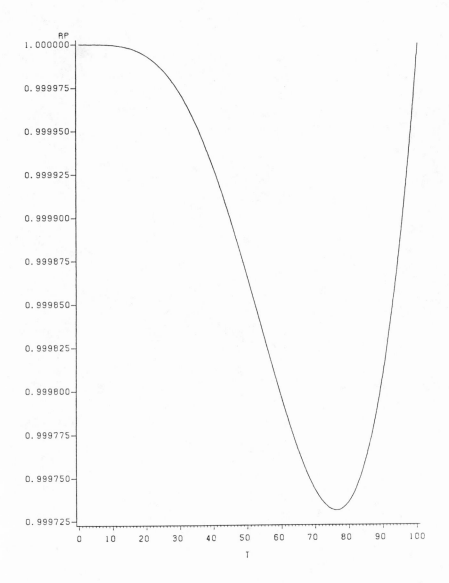

Figure 13.16b RParallel Trajectory

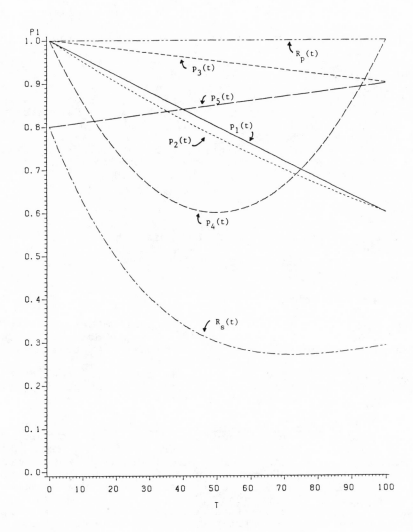

Figure 13.17 Overlay of Different Kinematic Results

Inputs and outputs also differ dramatically between serial and parallel structures. While the **serial output** R_s is never better than any of the component inputs--and in most cases runs at a far lower level ($R_s \ll p$)--the **parallel output** R_p is virtually indifferent, except for the negligible drop illustrated in Figure 13.17, to the behavior of component inputs. In particular, note that the recovery induced by the parabolic input $p_4(t)$, which starts rising up at approximately $t = 54$, has no noticeable effect on the serial output trajectory until about $t = 80$. That such a delay will arise at all is not obvious from plain inspection of the input trajectories. That the delay itself will be of approximately 26 units of time is even less self-evident.

DISCUSSION

Specific aspects of the simulation results are discussed, followed by some broader theoretical considerations and directions for future research.

Aspects of Specific Findings

Recall that results reported here refer exclusively to kinematic properties of first-order political structures (see Figure 13.1), and that empirical politi-cal systems are only rarely of first order.[18] With this With this caveat in mind, however, some aspects specific to the results reported above should be mentioned.

Symmetries in Comparative Statics. Reverse symmetries are quite noticeable in the comparative statics of R in serial and parallel structures. For instance, when c and k are large, changes in p have a strong effect on R_s, but a much milder effect on R_p. The effects of variations in complexity are also somewhat symmetric, but in reverse. With p held constant, R is positively proportional to complexity in parallel struc-tures, but is negatively proportional to complexity in serial structures.

Generally, therefore, the reverse symmetry of serial and parallel structures becomes more accentuated when (1) complexity (c and k) is high; (2) p is high; and (3) perturbations occur in either complexity or p. Under these conditions R in serial structures is greatly affected, whereas in parallel structures it is not. Clearly then, the reliability of political systems is significantly--and strongly--affected by their internal structure.

Topographic Variety of Homogeneous Kinematics. The
qualitative properties of inputs used in this analysis
varied considerably, particularly considering the
theoretical assumptions underlying each input. For
example, an exponential input assumes a change in p which
is negatively proportional to the existing state of p.
By contrast, for logistic inputs the theoretical
assumption is that dp(t)/dt first increases, then peaks
(at the point of inflection), and finally relaxes
asymptotically to p = 0. Clearly these are qualitatively
different scenarios for the kinematic behavior of p.

Likewise, outputs display considerable topographic
diversity. Clearly, even relatively simple political
structures (such as the first-order structures considered
here) can account for highly diversified kinematic
behavior in R. Plateaus, valleys, ridges, ravines, and
pronounced peaks in R can be generated by these simple
inputs. In a sense, therefore, the simple behavior of
components can aggregate into significantly more complex
systemic behavior. Complex systemic behavior, on the
other hand, can in some instances be accounted for by
simple component behavior.

Perceptual Heuristics for Heterogeneous Kinematics.
The analysis of heterogeneous inputs (third set of runs)
generated some findings with potential implications for
evaluating observers' subjective judgments about
political behavior.[19] Although this analysis considered
only five-component first-order serial or parallel
structures, each component varying according to linear,
exponential, and parabolic inputs, the resulting
trajectory for R, for either the serial or the parallel
structure, was far from intuitive. For the serial
structure R(t) was neither linear nor simply exponential
nor parabolic. R(t) differed qualitatively from any
component p(t). Much the same is true for the behavior
of R(t) in a parallel structure when subject to the same
inputs.

Substantively, an important conclusion is that
subjective estimates of the evolution of R(t) can be
grossly incorrect, even when the political structure is
simple (as in all first-order structures here). This has
broader theoretical implications about political decision
making and strategic planning. For instance, "observers
of the political scene" and others who fail to ground
predictions--or postdictions--on the appropriate
mathematical structures of political reliability, will
err (and often dramatically) in their estimates of real
world political reliability. These gross miscalculations
can be dangerous when strategic risk is being assessed;
they also explain many instances of political surprise.

Some Broader Theoretical Aspects

Further understanding of structures of general order (m, n) might depend on advances in the structural taxonomy referred to earlier. Nonetheless, these simulations point to several broader theoretical implications.

Mapping Generic Results onto Specific Theories. Political reliability plays a central role in a large class of specific theories of politics, both domestic and international. Some of these theories, such as balance of power theory, arms race theory, and theories of international communication and integration, contain significant kinematic aspects. Many empirical laws of politics, where political reliability plays a role, are also stated in kinematic form.[20] Therefore generic results from the general theory of political reliability can be incorporated into these specific theories, including results unveiled by simulation methods.

For example, in the theory of war it has been shown (Cioffi-Revilla, 1985) that the political reliability of the international security system is governed by a two-component first-order parallel structure, with one component obeying a Poisson process while the other obeys a strong-force process. Simulation results reported here should be useful in shedding some new light on the nature of war onsets, making it particularly clear that the political reliability of international security is robust (because it has a first-order parallel structure), but only on the condition that the serial structure of the Poisson component not be too complex. This implication is not intuitive, and difficult to see from direct mathematical analysis because the pertinent equations are somewhat complex.

Another specific implication of the simulation with heterogeneous inputs is for the theory of international security regimes. These are said to be grounded on a set of "pillars" for maintaining international order (Wilson, 1978). Results from this analysis show that observers' predictions about the stability of such regimes are almost surely--or very probably--incorrect. If the reliability of international regimes is based on "pillars" (i.e., first-order serial structures) then R(t) behaves substantially at odds with the kinematic behavior of the political reliability of the individual component "pillars" of the regime. The same can be said for the maintenance of conventional balances of power (when based on a set of balancing requirements), or for the credibility of strategic nuclear deterrence (when based on a set of indispensable conditions, viz. the classic "credibility of capability" and "credibility of intent").

In sum, the high level of abstraction portrayed by kinematic simulation analyses of political reliability is only apparent. Generic results from these simulations hold significant implications for specific theories where political reliability plays a nontrivial role.

Kinematics, Dynamics, and Statics of Political Reliability. Earlier a distinction was made among kinematics, dynamics, and statics of political reliability. The distinction is important for drawing theoretical implications from simulation results.

First, reall why it was originally necessary to conduct an analysis of comparative statics before analyzing kinematics. Statics govern some fundamental properties which affect all kinematic analyses. Whether time stands still or not, analysis shows that the basic equations for R are still such that in first-order structures R is strongly sensitive to changes in c, particularly when p is high. Likewise, R is strongly affected by changes in k, particularly when p is low. These and other qualitative properties stem from the comparative statics of R in $R^3(p,c,k)$ space and are thus independent of time.

Second, recall that political forces play no explicit role in reliability kinematics. However, it is desirable to introduce forces at some point, and these results are useful for modeling such forces. For example, when results of kinematic analyses of some structures point to significant complexity in R it might be initially assumed that the expected system of forces should also be complex. However, according to the general theory of political reliability, forces must satisfy certain conditions--e.g., $F(t) \geqslant 0$ for all values of t--and this limits substantially the set of permissible forces for explaining complex dynamic cases.

Third, although output R(t) trajectories can differ in complexity, it does not necessarily follow that the underlying forces must also be complex. Given what is known about the relationship between political forces and resulting political reliability, complex patterns of R can often be explained by much simpler forces. To confirm this, simulation of dynamic behavior in more complex systems is required.

A Theory of Perceptual Heuristics of Political Reliability. Subjective estimates of the kinematic behavior of R, based on the examination of component input behavior, will typically lead to gross misperception of actual reliability kinematics, making misperception of kinematic political reliability an empirically interesting phenomenon. This is important for explaining how political observers actually make predictions, and it is crucial for a better understanding of political decision making based on subjective assessments of kinematic political reliabilities.

How do political observers arrive at subjective estimates of R(t)? How do they estimate whether an international regime will maintain itself, whether a "window of vulnerability"[21] will open up, whether it will be short or long, whether the "pillars" of security will hold, whether an alliance will continue to be reliable?

There seems to be a set of **perceptual heuristics** employed by individuals in general, and by political actors in particular, when making subjective estimates of R in serial and parallel structures. For serial structures at least two heuristics exist: the "average" heuristic and the "weakest-link-in-the-chain (WLC)" heuristic. The former predicts R by considering the time path of the individual p(t)s, taking some sort of average, and producing an estimate for R which somehow "interpolates" the component p(t) reliabilities. The result is, in all but trivial cases (i.e., p = 0 or 1.0), grossly incorrect since R(t) will be too optimistic.

The WLC estimate is only slightly more sophisticated. However, that too is overly optimistic (and therefore incorrect) because the minimum of a set of numbers between 0 and 1 is always greater than the product of such numbers. Hence both hueristics are fundamentally wrong; they are not constructed on the basis of scientific knowledge about the behavior of R(t).[22] Unfortunately, politicians use them all the time!

Future Research Directions

A promising direction for future simulation research of reliability kinematics is in the area of higher-order structures. These, however, are very numerous. Lacking a clearly developed taxonomy, it remains unclear how best to approach the complexity of higher-order structures. Three directions for future research might be useful.

Empirically Recurrent Structures. The set of higher-order structures of political reliability is very numerous. In light of this difficulty it might be useful to focus on structures that have recurrent empirical relevance. For example, in international political phenomena in general, and in conflict and security systems in particular, third- or fourth-order parallels having serial complexity within each parallel component are quite common. One possible explanation is that

security, as described briefly earlier, is commonly
maintained by a set of redundant political arrangements;
these constitute a "regime" when taken together.
However, each component still depends on the successful
operation of a series of necessary, indispensable
requirements. These primary components (of first-order)
are often referred to as "the pillars of peace" (Wilson,
1978), but each of these "pillars" is hardly "solid" or
"seamless." They are more like chains or strings of
links, since to sustain order each "pillar" depends on
the maintenance of high political reliability across a
set of necessary requirements.

Another common higher-order structure is a three-
or four-component first-order serial where each component
is, in turn, first-order serial. This structure is still
first-order serial, but with an extremely large number of
components. Most security policies are of this type.
For example, consider three essential requirements for a
US policy toward Western Europe. This is "simply" R =
$r_1 \, r_2 \, r_3$. However, each component is, in turn, dependent

on a significant number of serial and parallel components
in the actual policy implementation. Therefore the
reliability of security policies is determined by a very
long serial structure, compounded by some parallel
sectors within some of the serial components in the long
chain.

Using Supercomputers. New possibilities for
advancing our understanding of reliability kinematics are
imaginable with the advent of supercomputers. Given
their vastly enhanced capabilities, it is still too early
to evaluate the full set of effects of this specific
future direction for the simulation of reliability
kinematics. Clearly, the variety of structures suggested
by the taxonomy presented earlier makes supercomputers
appropriate tools for handling the complexity within
reasonable computational time and cost. The analysis
reported here was limited to only five common input
trajectories with fixed parameters. It would clearly be
desirable to employ supercomputer capabilities to explore
the implications of higher-order structures of political
reliability in situations where the time horizon is long,
the components are heterogeneous, some parameters are
time-dependent, and some are also stochastic. In
particular, time-varying computer graphics, coupled with
supercomputer capabilities, would allow us to see, for
the first time, the evolution of reliability in highly
complex political systems such as historical security
regimes. This might also render possible the
reconstruction of significant historical processes in
considerable detail, as well as the prediction of

possible futures in complex political structures. Using existing mainframe technology for these more advanced analyses is too costly and slow.

Theoretical Organization. Evaluation of results from simulation analysis of political reliability presupposes the fullest possible development of the primary taxonomy presented in the earlier section. (Theory, after all, must still guide research!) In turn, the comparative analysis of simulation results for systems of all orders--which clearly also implies the application of techniques of mathematical induction--might well generate a new taxonomy, this time by qualitative similarity across different structural types in the primary taxonomy. A glimpse of this can be seen already from some of the results reported here. For example, it was shown earlier that for certain parameter values, linear and simple exponential input trajectories yield qualitatively similar patterns of R (cf. Figures 13.6 and 13.7), although the substantive properties or interpretations of linear and exponential inputs differ considerably. This was a very simple case, but it demonstrated that there exist sets of R(t) which are "similar"--with the specification of this similarity yet to be elaborated with precision--but where input trajectories can differ substantially. Given the difficulties encountered by direct analytic or mathematical solution of these problems, the application of simulation methods appears to be not only desirable, but also indispensable in advancing our understanding of political reliability.

NOTES

1. The forces causing changes in the state of political reliability are the subject of **reliability dynamics.** The relationship among these political forces, independent of changes in the state of political reliability, is the subject of **reliability statics.** Note that this is a rigorous use of the term "dynamics," unlike its widespread, but etymologically incorrect use in social science. "Dynamics" derives from "dinamis," meaning "force" in Greek. To mean simply "change in time" the term "kinematic" is the appropriate term, when forces are not explicitly introduced to account for movement.

2. This section reviews some fundamental ideas and empirical applications of political reliability theory and presents the framework for evaluating the results of kinematic simulations. The reader already familiar with the fundamental ideas of political reliability theory and

its applications may wish to skip this section without
loss of continuity, but not the next section (which
specifies the precise structure of those political
systems analyzed in this study).

3. The theory is positive in the sense that it
contains a set of theoretical concepts, derived
principles (theorems), empirical laws, and mathematical
models for the nomological explanation of the emergence,
functioning, and collapse of structures and processes in
political systems. It is generic because its principles
apply to a vast class of political systems in which the
likelihood of emergence and breakdown plays a central
role--i.e., the likelihood of political breakdown (or
emergence) in these social systems is what usually makes
them interesting from a scientific viewpoint. It is a
theory about generic properties of political systems.
The theory of political reliability is formalized, or
mathematicized, not in the sense that it refers only to
theoretical, abstract, or nonempirical political systems,
but in the sense that its fundamental concepts,
principles, and laws are stated in mathematical language.
Finally, it is fundamentally probabilistic, rather than
deterministic, because it views a vast class of political
phenomena in general, and the question of political
reliability in particular, as essentially indeterminate
in its behavior.

4. For applications of the theory to political
processes see Cioffi-Revilla (1984a and b, 1985).

5. A subsystemic component of a political system
is said to be "necessary," although not necessarily
"sufficient," if and only if its absence from the system
(or its failure) causes the system to fail or not work.
Necessary components can be thought of as "pivotal"
subsystemic components, in the sense of Riker (1962);
truly "pivotal" actors of a coalition are "necessary," in
the sense of political reliability theory.

6. A subsystemic component of a political system
is "redundant," although not necessarily "useless" or
"worthless," if and only if its absence from the system
does not cause the system to fail or not work. An
example of a redundant subsystemic component is given by
the land-based ICBM force (subsystemic component) in the
overall strategic triad (system) of the US and the USSR
(Smith, 1978). Winning coalitions which are not minimal
always contain some redundant actors (Cioffi-Revilla,
1984a).

7. A document of the Commission of the European
Communities, "prepared on the occasion of the high-level
consultations, held at Washington on 17-18 November 1980,
between the European Community and the United States,"
contains an introductory section entitled "Introduction:
Two Pillars of the Western System." It begins with the

following statement: "The European Community and the
United States of America are today the two principal
pillars of the western political and economic systems"
(EC Commission, 1980).

8. The name "first-order structure" is justified
because their complexity extends along either c or k, but
not along both dimensions. Analysis of second- and
higher-order structures is not reported here, although
some analyses of special cases of higher-order structures
have been previously published (Cioffi-Revilla, 1983).

9. There are several ways to model this S-shaped
decay. The logistic specification was chosen because it
has more appealing theoretical underpinnings than other
alternatives, such as the Gompertz curve.

10. Clearly, setting c = 5 in this set of runs does
not affect the qualitative results, only their numerical
detail. C = 6 is important in deterrence theory
(Wohlstetter, 1959); c = 2 is important in international
security regimes (Cioffi-Revilla, 1985); c = 4 is useful
for analyzing the case of borders and war as well as for
the case of international communications channels
(Cioffi-Revilla, 1979). These and other specific
applications are in the neighborhood of c = 5. However,
some reach very high values, such as c = 18 for
international mass communications systems (Cioffi-Revilla
and Merritt, 1982).

11. All simulation runs--i.e., static sensitivity,
kinematic homogeneous, and kinematic heterogeneous
analyses--were conducted with the CMSSAS version 82.3
operating on the IBM 4341 M2 (VMD) under VM/CMS at the
University of Illinois.

12. Time played no role in these two runs, although
changes in c and k can be interpreted as occurring over
time.

13. The imperfect reverse asymmetry can be seen
from a superposition of both surfaces, which is not shown
here. The reader can see this by holding both figures
against a light, reversing one of the two, and verifying
that the match is not exact.

14. Note also that the ridge caused by logistic
inputs has a significantly steeper gradient than the
gradient found in most of the other two surfaces.

15. Note from Figure 13.2 that the parabolic input
used for this run never surpassed p = .600.

16. The lower portion of Figure 13.12, i.e., the
region for which k < 2, can be ignored since parallel
systems are defined for k ≥ 2.

17. In fact, the low resolution of the SAS PROC PLOT
graphics was insufficient for showing every contour on
the walls of this ravine.

18. See the "bottlenecked" structure of a strategic
nuclear deterrence triad in Cioffi-Revilla (1983).

19. An interesting case in point is the "estimation" of the so-called "window of vulnerability" in projected US strategic capability.

20. An example of this case is Casstevens' law of legislative turnover, $L(t) = L_0 e^{-kt}$, where $L(t)$ denotes the number of existing legislators at time t, L_0 is the number of legislators initially elected, k is a constant controlling the cohort's rate of extinction, and t is time. Here k can be modeled as dependent on the political reliability of tenure in the legislature.

21. And indeed whether such a window will be "square," "rectangular," "round," or "oval "

22. The demonstrable deduction that both estimates are incorrect actually constitutes an important theorem in the general theory of political reliability, in the interest of space this is neither formally stated nor rigorously proved here. See Cioffi-Revilla (1979, 1983, 1985).

Models of War Fighting

Part 4

14 Lanchester Models of Battlefield Attrition and the Organization of Combat Forces

INTRODUCTION

Implicit in quantitative analyses of the evolution of warfare is the notion that opposing combat forces constitute a system in balance. This important idea was brilliantly elaborated on in an early study by Thornton Read, "The Nuclear Battlefield in Historical Perspective" (1964). "When a technical innovation unbalances the military system, tactical changes take place--often with some time delay--tending to bring about a new balance."[1] Ultimately the idea of balance will apply to the interplay among such tactical factors as firepower, mobility, dispersion, armored protection, span of control and communications, decentralization of command authority, target acquisition capability, logistic resupply ability, sustainable casualty rates, and many other variables.[2] The immediate, limited ambition of this paper is to demonstrate how the notion of military balance can be employed to clarify the relations among three of the foregoing variables considered especially crucial, namely loss rates, dispersion of troops, and decentralization of command on the battlefield.

One concern of a military historian desiring to explain the evolution of warfare should be the scale of losses suffered by opposing armies in relation to the technology and military organization of the time. And a military planner, given his technological environment, should want to know how the organization of forces influences power and vulnerability so he can make the best choice of organization. Two critical variables in the organization of an army are the density of troops over the combat zone and the degree of decentralization as measured by the size of independently operating units. The thesis

Department of Economics, University of Maryland, and Institute for Defense Analyses, Alexandria, Virginia. I am grateful to L. Bruce Anderson, Michael Intriligator, and Alan Karr for comments.

of this paper is that the historical evolution of
dispersion and decentralization is the result of a
tendency for military systems to reach a balance defined
by sustainable long-run average losses. If true, this
thesis suggests that in planning for future conflicts one
force design principle should be dispersion/decentraliza-
tion to maximize survival (minimize attrition).

TROOP DENSITY ON THE BATTLEFIELD

Numerous writers have observed the secular decline
since ancient times, in the density of troops on the
battlefield--in soldiers per linear mile, or soldiers per
square mile. B. H. Liddell-Hart (1960), for example, has
pointed out that from the Napoleonic epoch to the present,
troops per linear mile have declined from 20,000 to as
little as 1,000 at times in World War II. "For at least a
century and a half the number of troops needed to hold a
front of any given length securely has been declining
steadily. In other words, the defense has been gaining a
growing material ascendancy over the offense. Even
mechanized warfare has brought no radical change in this
basic trend."[3] Similar statistics on the historic trend
toward dispersion are reported by William G. Stewart
(1960), who noted that the average number of troops per
square mile in corps areas[4] in the U.S. Civil War was
4,700, in World War I was 930, and in World War II was 72.
The trend toward dispersion has been accompanied by
concomitant increases in mobility and firepower. Casual
empiricism suggests that these trends can be readily
extrapolated to encompass more recent guerilla wars, such
as the Vietnam war.[5] A further quantitative description
of this intuitively appealing argument has been attempted
by T. N. DuPuy (1964) (see Table 14.1).

How are such trends to be interpreted? Can we build
a general model of which these historical figures are seen
to be particular instances? The hypothesis of this paper
is that such alterations in the configurations of tactical
systems stem from adjustments necessary for both opponents
to strike a balance between their own ability to survive
by limiting their own casualty losses and their ability to
threaten the adversary's military survival by inflicting
losses.

The Tension Between the Need
to Concentrate and to Disperse

Numerous authorities have alluded to a historical
competition between firepower and mobility, or between
offense and defense. For any particular technology,

Table 14.1 Historical Lethality, Dispersion, and Mobility
           Characteristics of Armies[a]

Item	Napoleonic Wars	Civil War	World War I	World War II
Area of 100,000 men (square miles)	8.05	10.3	140	1,727
Average frontage of 100,000 men (miles)	5.7	6.4	11	38.4
Average diagonal for 100,000 men (miles)[b]	5.9	6.6	17	59
Lethality index totals (in millions)	5.5	14.3	232.8	1,280.5
Movement rate for major reserves (mph)[c]	2	2	2	15
Time to cross diagonal (hours)	2.95	3.3	8.5	3.9

[a] Figures are taken from DuPuy (1964), p. H-1 (Enclosure 10)

[b] Maximum distance from which reserves could be committed within area or sector.

[c] For the Napoleonic, Civil, and First World Wars, major reserves within the sector of a 100,000 man force were committed on foot at an average rate of 2 mph. For World War II, major reserves were committed within such a sector by truck at an average rate of 15 mph.

either too much concentration or too much dispersion will result in excessive casualties.

> So long as long range weapons are area weapons, there will be some balance between these and short range or line-of-sight weapons. And since the latter have to move about to establish local superiority at shifting points, maneuver will continue to be important. The threat of a local superiority of short range weapons, brought about by maneuver, is primarily what forces the enemy to concentrate sufficiently to form a target for indirect or area fire. . . . Too much concentration will lead to unnecessary losses from area fire. Too little concentration will lead to defeat in detail in small unit fire fights.[6]

Thus, "the degree of dispersal is a choice essentially constrained by technology. . . ." But, as Stewart has remarked:

> . . . of the three force characteristics being discussed, only fire power and mobility are really basic. Dispersion is simply the result of the other two. The enemy's fire power and mobility require us to disperse over a given area. Our own fire power and mobility permit us to disperse over an area probably different from the first. It is when our capabilities do not permit us to disperse as much as the enemy capabilities require of us that we are in trouble.[7]

There is scattered evidence that casualty rates for combat units in combat (corps) areas average out over extended periods at .2% per day and casualty rates for field armies average out at .1% per day (Wainstein, 1973). One explanation for this could be some inherent human limit in the ability of the human person to function in a violent environment. Another might be the limits on resupply capability. In any case, one might hypothesize that big, long wars enter a phase of steady state equilibrium, or of slowly moving equilibrium, during which intensity and style of combat adjust to allow both adversaries to make up losses and to resupply so as to sustain the process. Just how armies have been or should be organized to survive such a process must depend on a highly complex interplay between the tactical factors already mentioned--firepower, mobility, etc. We have singled out two of these factors, dispersion and granularity. We want to explore whether trends in these variables can be explained as the outcome of optimum equilibrating choices which were necessary to sustain long wars in the sense just explained.[8]

To demonstrate how this tension between the advantages of concentration and dispersion is resolved in the choice of densities is our next task. To this end, in Table 14.2 we will define certain terms relating to the geography, lethality, and timing of battles.

Although a precise notation is necessary to build a model of the tension between concentration and dispersion, weapon systems and force characteristics may not in fact be so easily classifiable into neat categories. Whether to categorize aircraft, mines, or mortars as direct- or indirect-fire weapons may be quite arbitrary. Moreover, some of the elements suggested as parameters may actually be variables determined by other battlefield inputs (e.g., r_i or the vulnerability factors) and not themselves inputs at all.[9]

Lanchester Attrition Processes and the Structural Relations Among Dispersion, Mobility, and Firepower

The interaction of these factors will now be used to illustrate balance on the battlefield in general, and more particularly the effects of troop density on losses or loss rates. Our demonstration of these effects will employ two further assumptions. First, we assume that combat losses are governed at least in part by approximately Lanchester-type relations among forces. Various alternative assumptions as to the precise relationships between force strengths and casualties might be made, as in Ling (1967), for example. Pending empirical test, the Lanchester assumption, therefore, is largely for heuristic purposes. Second, we assume that each opponent has a complex objective relating to its own and the opponent's battle losses. This objective may take on various forms. One plausible assumption might be that each adversary has an upper limit on the average casualty rates it can accept over the course of a campaign and that, subject to this limit, it desires to maximize the number of enemy casualties in the battle zone. As we said, the upper limit on our casualties might arise from technical limits in resupply, or from political, moral, or morale considerations. Whatever the cause, it has been repeatedly documented (e.g., Wainstein, 1973, or Yengst and Smolin, 1981) that front line divisions rarely incur casualties above 2 percent per month over extended periods.

Within a Lanchestrian framework, a desire to maximize the opponent's casualties might argue for packing as many troops as possible into the battle zone

Table 14.2 Definitions of Terms Relating to Battles

Symbol	Definition	Unit of Measure
$i =$	1 or 2; the two opponents in the war.	
$F_i =$	Total size of side i's combat forces.	Number of troops or weapons.
$A =$	Length of the battle front, or in some cases land area of the battle zone. This parameter depends on geography, on the technological epoch of the war, and the amount of resources deployed.	Miles or square miles.
$a_i =$	The distance (or area) over which troops can be spread out yet be available to be massed or concentrated under a single tactical command for a local attack or defense. This parameter depends in some complicated way on the span of control, speed of movement, and the communication capability. We would call "a_i" a "corps front" or "corps area."	Miles or square miles occupied by a corps.
$q_i =$	Number of corps in the entire battle zone.	$q_i = A/a_i$
$f_i =$	Size of the force deployed along a_i miles or within an area of "a" miles, i.e., force which can be concentrated under a single tactical command for local attack or defense. f_i therefore is a "corps" (of side i), in keeping with earlier terminology. The size or strength of this "corps" will be a decision variable to be explained by the model.	$f_i = F_i/q_i$
$d_i =$	Troop density in the battle zone.	Troops/ mile or mi. sq. $d_i = f_i/a_i$

Table 14.2 (cont'd.)

Symbol	Definition	Unit of Measure
h_i =	The firepower or lethality of side i's indirect fire weapons, such as artillery; depends on target acquisition and intelligence capabilities, as well as on arms characteristics.	Enemy casualties caused.
g_i =	The firepower or lethality of side i's direct-fire, line-of-sight weapons.	Enemy casualties caused.
v_i =	Side i's vulnerability to opposing indirect fire weapons; depends on intelligence, warning, mobility, morale, and other factors, including technologies.	Casualties prevented.
w_i =	Side i's vulnerability to opposing direct-fire weapons.	Casualties prevented.
r_i =	Tempo of battle measure. Percentage of time that the two opponents are concentrated for direct-fire attack/defense. May or may not differ for 1 and 2.	
$1-r_i$ =	Percentage of time that the two opponents are in passive low-level combat, each firing indirect fire at the other. May or may not differ for 1 and 2.	
L_i =	Total casualties per period.	Number of dead and wounded month.
ℓ_i =	Percentage of casualties per period.	$\ell_i = L_i / F_i.$

due to the advantage it confers in situations where troops
are massed for a concentrated coordinated attack or
counterattack. However, the disadvantage of high density
is a high casualty rate suffered from artillery exchange,
outpost patrol skirmishes, and routine target-of-
opportunity air strikes. To represent this tension or
conflict, we next assume that in the intensive phase of
combat, concentrated mass-attack-mass-defense casualties
depend upon force interactions in accordance with Lanchester square law, while the less intensive day-to-day
interaction between forces results in attrition according
to Lanchester linear law. The Lanchester square law
applies when all weapons on either side are aimed at
identified enemy targets (and continuously reaimed at new
remaining targets as old ones are destroyed), while the
linear law obtains when target locations are not precisely
known and each side therefore targets the general area of
the other's deployment.[10] As Karr (1976) shows, the
square and linear laws are only two of numerous alternatives which can be derived from careful specification of
underlying stochastic attrition processes. Moreover,
recent studies (Yengst and Smolin, 1981) as well as casual
empiricism suggest that wars are not smooth, continuous,
uniform-intensity, monolithic events, but rather consist
of repeated periodic phases of higher-intensity fights
interspersed[11] with recuperative low-intensity probing and
maneuvering. If this periodicity is characteristic,
then our assumption is realistic that over time total
attrition is a weighted average of Lanchester square and
linear laws. The total time rate of loss L_1 for Side 1

during some nominal time period (say, a week or month) can
be written as

$$L_1 = r\ [\frac{A}{a_2}\ g_2 w_1 f_2] + (1-r)\ [Ah_2 v_1\ \frac{f_2}{a_2}\ \frac{f_1}{a_1}\ ] \tag{1}$$

Equation (1) gives more precise expression to the idea
that during the more passive or less intense stages of a
campaign, opposing armies interact (on the average) on a
mile-for-mile basis; i.e., that along each linear mile (or
within each square mile) attrition depends on the
opposition forces only along (within) that mile. For this
reason, the second bracketed term in (1), which shows the
losses attributable to this linear law effect, has A

rather than A^2 entered. On the other hand, during the
more intense stages of the campaign, Side 1's losses depend on the full mobilization and coordination

capability of Side 2 (within the battle zone) and, consequently, on the total size of the force it can bring

to bear, namely F_2. The first bracketed term in equation
(1), therefore, indicates how the total number of 2's
corps ($q_2 = A/a_2$) generate losses for Side 1. Equation

(1) accordingly shows losses by Side 1 to be a weighted
average between these two types of battles, the dispersed,
passive, low-level Lanchester-linear combat, and the
intensely violent and active, concentrated,
Lanchester-square combat.

For contrasting the structure of battles at
different historical epochs, comparisons of total loss
rates L_i may be less useful than comparisons of
proportional loss rates. Dividing (1) by total forces
$F_i = f_i q_i$ yields

$$\ell_1 = rg_2 w_1 d_2/d_1 + (1-r)h_2 v_1 d_2 \qquad (2a)$$

and similarly for the proportional time rate of loss for
Side 2

$$\ell_2 = rg_1 w_2 d_1/d_2 + (1-r)h_1 v_2 d_1 \qquad (2b)$$

Thus, each side's absolute and proportionate loss rates
are seen to depend on troop densities on both dies and on
the parameters for firepower, lethality, vulnerability,
and tempo of battle.[12]

These parameters may depend on more fundamental
force characteristics. In fact, numerous efforts have
been made to relate them to such features as the
separation distance between opposing forces (Weiss, 1957),
the range of weapons and speed of movement (Bonder, 1967),
firepower potential (Fain et al., 1970), and mobility.
These factors may in turn be influenced by force density
so that the loss rate equations depend on densities in a
more complex fashion. For instance, suppose that the
tempo of battle depended in a systematic fashion on
densities, such that as the battlefield became more
crowded direct-fire combat occurred a greater percentage
of the time.[13] Then the loss function $L_1(d_1, d_2)$ could

reach a minimum in d_1 and/or a maximum in d_2. Even the

simplest version of combat losses as a function of troop
densities as in (2a) and (2b) suggests the beginnings of
an explanation for observed densities.[14] If we collapse
the firepower, vulnerability, and tempo of battle
parameters, assuming them to be constants for any given

situation, then (1) simplifies to

$$L_1 = \alpha_1 d_2 + \beta_1 d_1 d_2 \tag{3a}$$

and

$$L_2 = \alpha_2 d_1 + \beta_2 d_1 d_2 \tag{3b}$$

Evidently, from inspection of equations (3a) and (3b), if one side (say, i) has a maximum intolerable limit (technically, logistically, or politically determined) on the losses it can suffer, then an increase in the enemy's density d_j will force an opposite movement in its own density d_i. For example, an increase in d_1 by $+\Delta d_1$ should call for a decline in d_2 so as to maintain L_2 at a constant value. Clearly, $\frac{\Delta d_2}{\Delta d_1}$ that is, the marginal cost

to 2 (measured in terms of sustainable force density which 2 should have to give up so as to "pay") of an increase in 1's force density is an increasing function of d_2 and a

decreasing function of d_1. In the jargon of economic

theory the "marginal rate of technical substitution" between the two force densities is declining. Proceeding in a similar manner, the marginal rate of substitution between force densities in the "production" of casualties for Side 1 from equation (3a) is:

$$\left.\frac{\Delta d_1}{\Delta d_2}\right|_{L_1 = \text{Constant}} \qquad \frac{\partial L_1/\partial d_2}{\partial L_1/\partial d_1} = -\frac{\alpha_1 + \beta_1 d_1}{\beta_1 d_2} \tag{4a}$$

According to equation (3b) the required relationship between d_1 and d_2 is:

$$\left.\frac{d_1}{d_2}\right|_{L_2 = \text{Constant}} \qquad \frac{\partial L_2/\partial d_2}{\partial L_2/\partial d_1} = -\frac{\beta_2 d_1}{\alpha_2 + \beta_2 d_2} \tag{4b}$$

Again the marginal cost to 1 of an increase in d_2 is an

increasing function d_1 and a decreasing function of d_2

such that 1's marginal technical rate of substitution is

diminishing. Since the parameters α_1, α_2, β_1, β_2 are all positive and densities d_1 and d_2 must be positive, it is demonstrable that the absolute value of the slope of L_1^o exceeds that of L_2^o--which is to say that through any given point d_1^o, d_2^o) the L_1 casualty "production" contour is steeper than the L_2^o contour through the same point.[15]

Figure 14.1 gives an example of two such production contours L_1^o and L_2^o (with L_1^o being the steeper). Figures

14.2a, b, and c portray somewhat more complex loss function, such as might arise if battlefield density is a determinant of r, the tempo parameter; for example, if $r = (d_1 d_2)/[1 + (d_1 d_2)^2]$. These diagrams will be useful

for examining the behavioral interaction between Sides 1 and 2, each subject to attrition as per equations (1) or (2).

Interaction Between Adversaries

Force density on the battlefield is an important (intermediate) descriptive characteristic of combat configuration and battlefield dynamics and an important prescriptive characteristic for the design of military forces. Each side is constrained in the long run by some maximum sustainable loss rate, whereas force size and density strongly influence actual loss rates. The factors which explain these maximum casualty rates are highly complex, sociological, economic, geopolitical, ideological, and moral. But if losses on either side exceed this maximum over the long run, numbers and battlefield density will inevitably fall. The decline will continue until either (a) losses return to their critical sustainable level, (b) the battle front[16] or theater shifts so that higher losses can be sustained (a new ally enters the picture bringing fresh provisions, lines of communication are shortened by withdrawal, etc.), or (c) the battle breaks off or campaign ends through mutual exhaustion (see Helmbold, 1969). Figures 14.1 and 14.2 will be useful to illustrate these dynamics.

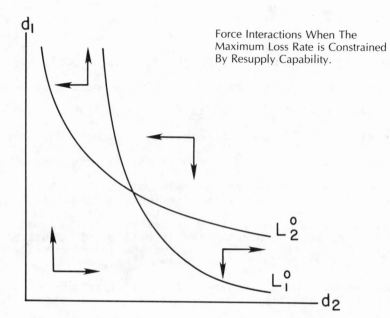

Force Interactions When The
Maximum Loss Rate is Constrained
By Resupply Capability.

Figure 14.1a   Unconstrained Force Interactions

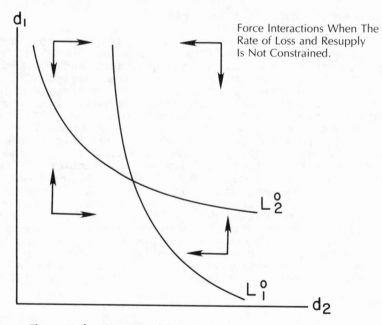

Force Interactions When The
Rate of Loss and Resupply
Is Not Constrained.

Figure 14.1b   Constrained Force Interactions

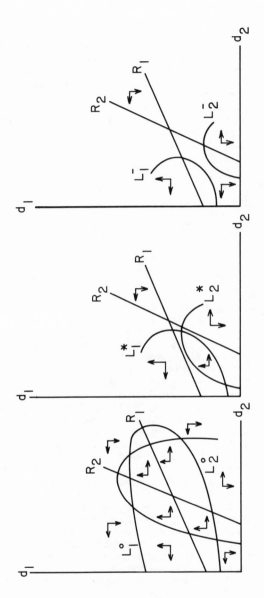

R̄₁ shows locus of choices of d₁ which minimize losses L₁ for different values of d₂.
R̄₂ shows locus of choices of d₂ which minimize losses L₂ for different values of d₁.
L_i^o, L_i^*, L_i^- show alternative Maximum Loss Constraint contours for i (1 or 2)
Arrows indicate direction of change when Maximum Loss constraint governs choice

Figure 14.2 Complex Objective Functions

Ecological Paradigm of
Interaction Between Opponents

Assuming that adversaries continuously add forces to their warring armies, and that they do so at a predetermined exogenous rate, then a maximum sustainable loss rate is also exogenously so determined, and the progress of the war is mechanistically or, as we might say, ecologically determined. Using S_1 and S_2 to indicate each opponent's maximum sustainable resupply rate, an ecological interpretation will imply two differential equations with an implied evolution of forces.

$$\frac{dF_1}{dt} = -L_1(d_1, d_2) + \bar{S}_1 \tag{5}$$

$$\frac{dF_2}{dt} = -L_2(d_1, d_2) + \bar{S}_2 \tag{6}$$

As Figures 14.1 and 14.2 then show, there may be potential equilibria between opponents, multiple equilibria may exist, these may be stable or unstable, and the characteristics of these equilibria will depend crucially on the shape and location of each opponent's maximum sustainable loss contour. Figure 14.1a illustrates the dynamic implications of our simplest model of losses, as specified in equations (3a) and (3b). The arrows in the diagram show the direction of change of the force variables over time. An intersection of the two loss rate contours represents an equilibrium, but it is unstable, attainably only by chance, and unlikely to be sustained. From points between the two curves, one opponent's losses will steadily mount in excess of its replacement capabilities while the other's will steadily decline, its forces growing and inevitably predominating.

Figure 14.1a represents only the simplest version of mixed Lanchester square and linear attrition processes. Allowing densities to influence the weights r_i, as between the two types of attritions (see note 13), or to influence lethality and vulnerability coefficients g, h, v, and w, will produce a greater range of potential outcomes. Figures 14.2a, b and c give examples mapping the equal loss contours for both adversaries which could arise in the more complex case. These contours differ from Figure 14.1 in that they show how each opponent could choose a force size and density to minimize its own losses--choices identified as stationary values at the peak of each loss contour. These peaks of each opponent's loss contour trace out a locus of loss minimizing force levels and densities. Again, arrows are drawn in the diagram to indicate directions of change over time. Evidently, semi-stable equilibria occur under these assumptions, multiple equilibria are more clearly in evidence, and the chances that confrontations will veer off in favor of one opponent or the other (as they do in Figure 14.1a) are higher where the maximum loss ratios are low and the critical contours are below the intersection of the reaction curves. Among Figures 14.2a, b, and c, for example, the chances of moving into a destabilizing region (and therefore the length of time that activity in the vicinity of equilibrium will persist) seem to be greater under configuration $(L_1^o L_2^o)$ than (L_1^*, L_2^*). As the diagram also

illustrates, if the critical loss/resupply ratio is very low, as with $(L_1^- L_2^-)$, force size/density will inevitably

drift toward the origin ending in mutual exhaustion or annihilation.

Behavioral Paradigm of
Interaction Between Opponents

Lanchester models and related explanations of combat are frequently criticized for being deterministic and mechanical. Adding stochastic elements to a pair of difference equations such as equations (4) and (5) may eliminate objections to determinism but not to the mechanical quality of the model. Meeting the criticism that the model is mechanistic would require that some human choice over alternatives by the planners, generals, or politicians be allowed to influence the evolution of combat. Whether such choice is deemed to represent optimizing behavior or the less demanding satisficing behavior (Simon, 1957), a model of the behavior requires an objective function. The simplest of such elaborations on a mechanistic set of differential equations might be to assume that each side sets a maximum attrition it can afford, L_i^o, and, subject to that condition, attempts to

maximize L_j. In Figure 14.1a, Side 1's objective would be

to move along L_1^o, therefore, as far to the southeast

as possible, since movement in that direction increases L_2.

Similarly, Side 2, with an objective to maximize L_1

subject to a constraint $L_2 = L_2^o$, will desire to move

northwest along L_2^o as far as possible. If we combine

these two objectives and the implied behavior by both
parties we see that only one point (where L_1^o and L_2^o
intersect) has compatible, stationary values of densities.
However, as the directions of the motion arrows indicate,
that particular combination of densities represents a
semistable equilibrium. That is, under this behavioral
assumption, any displacement northwest or southwest from
that equilibrium will lead to a progressive deterioration
for one side and a progressive improvement for the other.
Thus, the notion that decision makers act to maximize
enemy casualties subject to a constraint in their own
losses produces an evolution qualitatively similar to the
ecological model just discussed. If we accept this
underlying behavioral assumption, the analysis suggests
that battle is an inherently unstable process wherein
small advantages cumulate and multiply, forcing an enemy
to react at an increasing disadvantage. The evolution of
forces implied by Figure 14.1a also suggests the advantage
to be gained if one side could temporarily sustain an
extra high loss rate and thereby trap the opponent in a
downward spiral of declining force.

But is a choice criterion of maximizing enemy losses
subject to one's own long-term survival a plausible
objective function? Other candidates might include an
assumption that Side i has a minimum attrition rate it
must impose on j, and wishes to minimize its own
casualties, provided it reaches that target.
Simultaneously, it could be assumed that j has a minimum
attrition rate against i and wishes to minimize its own
casualties subject to a constraint of reaching its target.
We could characterize this objective as one of punishment
first, survival second. Under these assumptions, Side 1 in
Figure 14.1b will adjust d_1 so as to maintain L_2^o and Side
2 will adjust d_2 so as to maintain L_1^o. This set of
behavioral assumptions will now lead to a stable equilibrium (d_1^o, d_2^o). Compared with behavior when the objective
is long-run sustainability of forces, when a combatant's
primary objective is inflicting loss on an enemy it is not
driven from the battle by densely packed opponents,
whereas, if the object is survival, a slight imbalance
eventually causes one side to retire.

In addition to these two "basic" cases, other more
complex objective functions might be posited as deriving
the behavior of two adversaries. For instance, Side 1
might take as an objective some complicated function of L_1
and L_2 such as the difference $(L_1 - L_2)$, ratio L_1/L_2, or

some more complex variation. The objective function may involve force levels rather than losses or force ratios. And as objectives and models thereof become more detailed, the analyst may attempt to specify force momentum or geographical movement of the battle area. Similarly, one can envisage a complicated objective function for Side 2. Then a graphic display of the two, say $\Omega_1(d_1,d_2)$ and

$\Omega_2(d_1,d_2)$ might reveal further possibilities for multiple

equilibria, zones of stability, and other features characteristic of predator-prey, parasite-host population processes (see, for example, Lotka, 1956, or Pielou, 1969).

To summarize, this section of the paper suggests how alternative assumptions as to the objectives driving the decisions of planners, generals, politicians, etc., will produce systematically different types of evolutions of force configurations with particular positive or negative stability properties. For evaluating which of these assumptions are most plausible, it would be essential to know something about the real-world objectives of national and military leaders (although such objectives will often be highly variable and internally inconsistent) and to utilize other prior knowledge about the nature of equilibria in combat attrition processes. My own opinion is that extended middle periods of wars may well arise for which stable equilibrium concepts do apply to the evolution of the combatants' force configurations. For short periods such equilibria will be stable, due to the advantage which retreat confers by[17] shortening lines of communication, but over the long run will degenerate due to destruction of resupply capability. If this is true, we have in this essay the beginnings of a production-function approach to combat effectiveness and interaction between opponents.

Empirical Test of Force Density Effects

Could the combination of maximizing or satisficing behavior and the Lanchestrian attrition process form a theory for interpreting the historical trends of Table 14.2? We have the beginnings of the required theory. As an example of its application, the early stages of World War I suggest a high intensity but stable attrition trap--of the type illustrated by Figure 14.1b--which later was broken up by a change in parameters r, g, h, v, w, etc., and/or a shift in objective functions, which in turn produced instability in land battle, and finally by the retirement[18] (drift to zero intensity) of one side from the front.

If we have the beginnings of an intuitive theory to explain certain crucial variables in the configuration of armies, we might hope to proceed to more rigorous statistical tests of the processes. The decisions necessary for proceeding with empirical analysis fall into several categories.

1. Is it to be assumed that observed historical readings of losses or loss rates and of densities reproduce equilibrium or disequilibrium values in the equation set (2 or 3)? Rigorous procedures have been devised for estimating systems of differential equations over time (see, e.g., Ward, 1984, for discussion) as economists have recently focused on the statistical estimation of systems which are out of equilibrium. For individual engagements, combat processes are undoubtedly disequilibrium events. But for longer periods when resupplies make up for losses, "equilibrium" may be a superior assumption.

2. In addition to testing the general plausibility of a theory that densities influence loss rates, we might hope statistical estimation would evaluate the size and magnitude of the parameters r, w, v, h, etc. (if not each individually, then in combinations). For example, net estimates of "$g_i w_j$" might be obtainable. If such were the

objective, then battles should be grouped into similar kinds, in similar historical epochs. Baily (1970), for instance, used the following categories: (a) small meeting engagements, (b) large meeting engagements, (c) assault on fortified lines, and (d) attacks on hastily fortified positions. Other classifications would most probably be more appropriate for other wars, but some partitioning of engagements into homogeneous classes would be necessary to approximate repeated trials of the same attrition process. If accurate measures of firepower, lethality, vulnerability, target identification, and acquisition were available, similar types of engagements from different wars might be included in the same sample for regression analyses.

3. Still another issue in testing these hypotheses might be whether to estimate directly the "structural" equations $L_i = \phi_i(d_1, d_2)$ as postulated in (2) and (3), or

instead reduced forms, say, $d_i = \psi_i(L_1, L_2)$--assuming

identification problems to have been resolved. Since correlation between densities as explanatory variables and error terms--e.g., non-combat losses--seems probable, estimating the reduced form system is likely to be preferable.

To give an indication of how to proceed, suppose we assumed that observed outcomes occur approximately in the vicinity of the intersection of L_1^o and L_2^o curves. To solve equations (3a) and (3b) for realized outcomes, we must express each density as a function of attrition rates. First, we normalize loss rates on a per-mile or per-square-mile basis,

$$L_1 = \frac{L1}{A}; \ L_2 = \frac{L1}{A} \tag{7}$$

This should allow one to compare different epochs of warfare fought on different geographical scales. Then, to obtain troop strengths or densities as the dependent variables of choice, solving the two normalized "structural" attrition equations

$$L_1 = (e + fd_1)d_2 \tag{8}$$

and

$$L_2 = (g + hd_2)d_1 \tag{9}$$

gives the non-linear equation

$$d_1 = A_0 + A_1 L_1 + A_2 L_2 + A_3 L_2/d_1 \tag{10}$$

as a reduced form equation to be estimated. In a similar fashion, solving (8) and (9) for d_2 gives

$$d_2 = B_0 + B_1 L_2 + B_2 L_1 + B_3 L_1/d_2 \tag{11}$$

as a second reduced form. These two reduced form equations can then be estimated for battles for which one has reason to believe that the parameters $A_0 \ldots A_3$, $B_0 \ldots B_3$, etc., are constant. Of course, these two reduced form equations may be too simplistic. More elaborate structures may produce better estimates; basing the reduced forms on attrition equations using higher-order polynomials may prove desirable. If a loss rate equation such as

$$L_1 = a_0 + a_1 d_1 + a_2 d_2 + a_3 d_1 d_2 + \ldots \tag{12}$$

outperforms the simpler one the analyst ought to be able to infer something about the nature of the objective functions motivating the combatants—for example, whether optimizing or satisficing behavior obtains.

DECENTRALIZATION AND SIZE OF
INDEPENDENT OPERATING UNITS

This section of the paper takes up the second important feature of special significance to the maintenance of a balance within and among opposing forces, namely the degree of decentralization into tactically independent combat units. This problem is substantively distinct from the problem of explaining troop density just treated, since every density is compatible with different organizations, in terms of decentralization and hierarchy. For instance, a density of 1,500 troops per square mile is compatible with, say, two independent battalions, six companies, twenty-four tactically independent platoons, etc. Here we want to explore the structure and balance of relationships which tend to cause armies to be organized around different sized clusters of independent tactical action. Wintringham (1940) called attention to the long-run historical reduction in the size of the independent tactical unit. This tendency toward battlefield decentralization is well illustrated by Table 14.3. Figures are for the usual tactical unit in battle, and not for small outpost actions or exceptional battle conditions.

The optimum size of independent tactical units is of more than historical interest. One major concern of the United States and Soviet armies since the beginnings of the atomic era has been how to organize for tactical nuclear battle. There has been general consensus that tactical nuclear weapons require dispersal. But " . . . if the required dispersion is achieved by uniformly increasing the spacing between men, the result would be loss of that tactical integrity and mutual support which makes a trained unit much more than the sum of its parts . . . a force so dispersed would be vulnerable to defeat in detail in conventional small unit fire fights. . . . In other words, the dispersion required on the nuclear battlefield would destroy combat effectiveness if it were achieved by uniformly increasing the spacing between individual men."[19] Of course, the need for balance between vulnerability to piecemeal defeat in detail and mass destruction from larger weapons does not apply only to tactical nuclear combat± Rather, it is a general problem--of how to decentralize or structure independent operating units so as to maximize effectiveness of the whole. To describe this problem, we shall begin by augmenting the notation of Table 14.2 with the understanding that the notation continues to apply to the analysis of optimum granularity or decentralization. This notation will help us to formulate the basic tension between the risk of disastrous wipe-out from mass fire against too concentrated a target, and the risk of

Table 14.3 Battlefield Decentralization

Year	Tactical Unit	Men in Unit	Number of Men in a Whole Army Responsible For Tactical Decisions
1757	Army	15,000-50,000	1
1815	Brigade or Division	2,000- 6,000	20-30
1870	Battalion or Brigade	800- 3,000	100-200
1914-16	Company or Division	200-15,000	200-10,000
1917	Group (German)	8-16	100,000-200,000
1940-45	Platoon-Battalion	20-600	Hundreds of
1965-75	Fireteam	5-10	Thousands

repeated defeat in detail. To generate this tension, we postulate two characteristics of the decentralized battlefield. First, we shall assume that massed fires will completely destroy, during a standard time period, a certain number or a certain percentage of the granules (independent units) no matter what their size.[20] Second, we shall assume that the number of individual independent unit encounters between adversaries and, therefore, the number of opportunities for defeat in detail, depends on each opponent's number of independent units per square or linear mile (not number of troops per mile). We shall make the further assumption that once two opposing units make contact by approaching each other within a certain distance, a conventional firefight will necessarily ensue, and that each such one-on-one contact is governed by Lanchester square law attrition processes. Other assumptions could well be plausibly made, and thus ours must be regarded as largely heuristic. Table 14.4 introduces notation to express these features of battle.

   With the foregoing notation we can now express the total losses for say, side i, by equation (13) as comprised of two parts:

$$L_1 = K_{12}S_1 + E(e) \cdot w_1 g_2 S_2 S_1 \qquad (13)$$

First, the number of i units lost from massed fire, K_{ij} times the size of each unit S_i; second, the gross effectivness of each and every j soldier adjusted for i's vulnerability to direct fire, $w_i g_j$, times the number of j

Table 14.4   Notations Regarding Battle Features

Symbol	Definition	Unit of Measure
i	The two opponents in a war.	
C	Elemental battle area which defines a conventional encounter. Whenever two adversary units occupy such a "cell" or "linear element" simultaneously, they will engage in a Lanchester square law conventional battle: "C" is assumed to be independent of the sizes of the opposing granular units within the relevant range (this factor could also be a variable, at the cost of a more complex model).	Square or linear miles.
m	Number of battle "cells" or linear elements in area or frontage "A".	$m = A/C$
q_i	Same as defined in Table 14.2, assumed to be constant for this optimum-size-of-independent-unit problem.	$q_i = A/a_i$
$f_i q_i$	Total conventional forces available to 1 and 2 for the battle: assumed to be given for purposes of this analysis.	$F_i = f_i q_i$
S_i	Size of independent granular unit chosen by side i.	Number of troops
n_1, n_2	Consequent number of granules available to each side as a result of the decision on S_1, S_2	$n_i = f_i q_i / S_i$
K_{ij}	Number of i units which j can destroy per time period by means of massed fire. Assume that K_{ij} is independent of S_i, the size of the i unit brought under such massed fire. A further elaboration might allow K_{ij} to be an increasing function of S_i. A more elaborate model should incorporate search and concealment, target detection and acquisition, and probabilistic weapon effects into this parameter.	Number of units

Table 14.4 (cont'd.)

Symbol	Definition	Unit of Measure
g_i, h_i, v_i, w_i	Lanchesterian firepower rates and vulnerabilities in conventional combat; same as former definition in Table 14.2.	
S_i	The losses within one i unit (S_i chosen by i) during one conventional engagement, with one j unit. $S_i = w_i g_i S_j$; indicates that during a conventional encounter between individual granular units attrition proceeds in accord with Lanchester's square law.	Number of troops
$p(k)$	Probability that a cell will be occupied by one k unit of size S_k; k = i,j.	
$p(i \cdot j)$	Probability of an encounter; i.e., probability that one cell or linear element will be simultaneously occupied by one 1 unit size S_1 and one 2 unit size S_2. In this paper we assume that n_1 and n_2 are randomly assigned to the "m" cells and that no two units from one side are allowed to occupy one cell simultaneously. A more realistic model would incorporate reciprocal search and target acquisition operations to obtain estimates of "p".	
$p(e)$	Probability that e encounters will occur; e is now assumed to be a random variable which can be as high as the lesser of (n_1, n_2) and as low as zero. This probability distribution will depend on m, n_1 and n_2.	
$E(e)$	Expected number of cells or linear elements occupied simultaneously (i.e., during a conventional time unit) by one 1 unit and one 2 unit; this is expected number of encounters, since we have defined a cell as the space within which initial occupation necessarily results in a local battle.	Number
L_i	Total loss by side i during some notional period.	Number of troops

troops in an encounter S_j, times the expected or average number of encounters, $E(e)$. Since we have assumed that encounters are random, the probability that any cell or linear element will be occupied by a 1 unit is n_1/m

$$p(1) = n_1/m : n_1 = \text{number of 1 units} \qquad (14)$$

Similarly,

$$p(2) = n_2/m : n_2 = \text{number of 2 units} \qquad (15)$$

Since $p(1)$ and $p(2)$ are assumed to be independent, the probability that a cell is occupied by both is $p(1) \cdot p(2) = p(1 \cdot 2)$

$$p(1 \cdot 2) = n_1 n_2/m^2 \qquad (16)$$

Thus, the expected number of encounters is:[21]

$$E(e) = mp(1 \cdot 2) = n_1 n_2/m \qquad (17)$$

Substituting fq/S for n from Table 14.3 and rewriting equation (13) gives us an estimate of the total loss rate for Side 1.

$$L_1 = K_{12}S_1 + \frac{f_1 q_1 f_2 q_2}{S_1 S_2 \cdot m} \cdot w_1 q_2 S_2 \qquad (18)$$

which simplifies to

$$L_1 = K_{12}S_1 + \frac{\sigma_1 T}{S_1} : T = f_1 q_1 f_2 q_2/m .$$
$$\qquad (19)$$
$$\sigma_1 = w_1 q_2$$

A similar chain of reason will give an expected loss rate for Side 2

$$L_2 = K_{21}S_2 \quad \frac{\sigma_2 T}{S_2} \qquad (20)$$

Note that in these expressions the loss rate of each side does not depend on the degree of decentralization of the other, but only on its own size of unit. Note also that a particular value of S_1 may well exist which minimizes l's loss rate, L_1. In other words, selection of the degree of decentralization and the size of the independent tactical granule may be an optimizing problem for Side 1. This is precisely because the choice of S_i has no effect on L_j.

(In contrast, the troop density problem as formulated in the previous sections of this paper was a satisficing problem because the choice of d_i influences both L_i and L_j.)[22] One can determine the value of S_1 which minimizes L_1 by differentiating L_1 and setting the expression so obtained equal to zero.

$$\frac{\partial L_1}{\partial S_1} = \frac{\partial}{\partial S_1}[K_{12}S_1 + \sigma_1 T/S_1] = 0 \tag{21}$$

$$= K_{12} - \sigma_1 T/(S_1)^2 = 0$$

Thus, the optimum value of S_1^* becomes

$$S_1^* = [\frac{\sigma_1 T}{K_{12}}]^{\frac{1}{2}} = A[\frac{\sigma_1 d_1 d_2}{mK_{12}}]^{\frac{1}{2}} \tag{22}$$

In a similar manner for the optimum[23] value of S_2^*

$$S_2^* = [\frac{\sigma_2 T}{K_{21}}]^{\frac{1}{2}} = A[\frac{\sigma_2 d_1 d_2}{mK21}]^{\frac{1}{2}} \tag{23}$$

An examination of equation (22) or (23) indicates that our model predicts that as either side's total force within a space-constrained battlefield expands, the size of the optimum operating unit increases as the square root of that force expansion. This follows from the fact that T contains the product of Side 1 and Side 2 forces. (T = (Total 1 forces) $\cdot$ (Total 2 forces) per battle cell.) If either adversary increases its troop strength, both have an incentive to reorganize into larger granules. The symmetry stems from the fact that T figures identically in both optimum decentralization equations (22) and (23). A peculiarity of these two particular equations is to suggest that one combatant's small unit individual offensive capability, g_i, and its massed fire destruction capability, K_{ij}, perfectly offset each other in their influence on its enemy's organization, so that if both g and K were to increase by the same proportion the effect on the adversary's organization would wash out. This neutrality effect deserves closer scrutiny; detailed specification more firmly grounded in the technology of maneuver, command control, target acquisition effectiveness, and weapons lethality might suggest a technical bias toward decentralization.

Lastly, we should note that equations (22) and (23) imply a relationship between unit organization and battlefield density. The substitution $q_i = A/a_i$ gives the right-most expressions where optimum organization S* is shown to depend on densities. One finds that as density $d_i = f_i/a_i$ decreases so does the optimum size of the independent tactical granule. Comparison with the data on past wars suggests that this is not inconsistent with historical trends.

INTEGRATION OF DENSITY AND DECENTRALIZATION MODELS

Having built two models, each to explain a separate feature of the balance within a combat system, a natural question is whether the two models can or should be merged. To generalize the theory proposed in this paper, we have suggested that the time rate of casualties incurred in a given technical environment--i.e., given mobility, firepower, vulnerabilities, command-control, and intelligence capabilities, etc.--depends on the force densities, on decentralized unit sizes (or number of units), on the size of battlefield, A, and of course on the numbers of battle areas (say, N) in some systematic way. We can write this generalized relationship as

$$L_1 = N_1 \cdot \phi_1 [n_1, n_2 \ S_1, S_2, A_1 \rho_1] \tag{24}$$

$$L_2 = N_2 \ \phi_2 \ [n_1, n_2, S_1, S_2, A_2, \rho_2] \tag{25}$$

where ρ_1 and ρ_2 represent a vector of technological parameters such as those mentioned above. In effect, this paper has proposed an economic, production function approach to the representation and structural analysis of ϕ_1 and ϕ_2. Such an analysis should be complementary to Lanchester's theory of combat attrition, not competitive. Lanchester-type equations should continue to explain dynamics of attrition processes.

Among the gains to be sought from an extension of production theory along these lines should be an explanation of historical regularities. These are illustrated by data in Tables 14.1 and 14.3. The relationship over the past two centuries between decentralization and density is illustrated by the formula

$$S = \mu d^{3/4} \qquad (26)$$

That is, as densities have historically declined, each 1% reduction in d has correlated with 3/4% decline in the size of the independent unit. This relation suggests that somehow the need to disperse in response to technical evolution of weaponry has exceeded the ability to coordinate decentralized units with appropriate command and control mechanisms. In fact, such an inference also corresponds with the evidence collected by Yengst and Smolin (1981) that the proportion of losses due to small arms direct-fire action has been steadily diminishing over the past two centuries in comparison with the proportion due to indirect, artillery-type weaponry.

Proposed Merger of Density and Decentralization

These trends in the geographic organization of armies and in the composition and etiology of battle losses should motivate further study of the joint relationship among losses, densities, and decentralization. Our analysis is at most suggestive. The simplest approach would be to combine the two models on the assumption that the physical dimensions of battle (the variable A) have been predetermined. To accomplish this, substitute equation (22) into (19) to obtain the casualties of Side 1 once 1 has selected S_1 so as to minimize these casualties. The result is:

$$L_1^* = K_{12}\sqrt{\frac{\sigma_1 H}{K_{12}}} + {}_1 H\sqrt{\frac{\sigma_1 H}{K_{12}}} \quad : \quad H = \frac{A_2 d_1 d_2}{m} \qquad (27)$$

which simplifies to[24]

$$L_1^* \doteq 2[\sigma_1 HK_1]^{\frac{1}{2}} \tag{28}$$

Similarly

$$L_2^* = 2[\sigma_2 HK_1]^{\frac{1}{2}} \tag{29}$$

Here both opponents' minimum casualties are "produced" by almost identical technologies; the only difference is a scalar factor (i.e., $\sqrt{\sigma_1 K_{12}/\sigma_2 K_{21}}$). Next, suppose that either opponent's ability to concentrate fires and destroy its adversary's units en masse depends on the size of its own force; then the optimized loss equation very closely resembles the satisficing loss equations of the second section of the paper, namely equation (1) or (3). This further assumption is expressed by the formulas:

$$K_{12} = R_1 f_1 q_1 = AR_1 d_1 \quad : \text{ where } R_1 = \text{a unit effect-} \atop \text{iveness parameter} \atop \text{for 1's forces} \tag{30}$$

$$K_{21} = R_2 f_2 q_2 = AR_2 d_2 \quad : \text{ where } R_2 = \text{a unit effect-} \atop \text{iveness parameter} \atop \text{for 2's forces} \tag{31}$$

Now, substituting (30) into (28) and (31) into (29) gives two new minimum loss equations, expressed here for convenience as a function of densities, d_1-d_2 .

$$L_1^* = \lambda_1 d_2 \sqrt{d_1} \; : \; \lambda_1 = 2[\sigma_2 A^3 R_2/m]^{\frac{1}{2}} \tag{32}$$

and

$$L_2^* = \lambda_2 d_1 \sqrt{d_2} \; : \; \lambda_2 = 2[\alpha_1 A^3 R_1/m]^{\frac{1}{2}} \tag{33}$$

These satisficing equations imply that increasing one's own density on assumptions (30) and (31) is more productive of enemy casualties than of one's own. A plot of notional curves for L_1^* and L_2^* will show a point of unstable equilibrium similar to Figure 14.1a. Thus, our simplistic approach to integrating the decisions as to density and decentralization suffers from several deficits; first, it depends on one specific functional form of equation (1); second, it assumes the overall physical dimensions of campaigns, i.e., A, to be determined exogenously; and third, it therefore does not allow that the organization of armies as to both decentralization and density could be optimization problems.

A more satisfactory approach to merging density and decentralization decisions--representing both as problems in optimization--might begin by assuming that losses are comprised of three components, deriving from (1) the chance of unit wipe-out, (2) Lanchester square law combat, and (3) Lanchester linear law combat. Under these assumptions we can write the losses of Side 1 in a single A-sized area as

$$L_1 = \Sigma^{\cdot} S_1 + \Pi_1 n_1 F_2 + \Theta_1 S_1 S_2 \tag{34}$$

where $F_i = n_i S_i$ and Σ = expected number of 1 units detected and destroyed by 2's massed fires. If we assume depends on both the size S_1 (with $\partial \Sigma / \partial S_1 > 0$), and the number of units n_1 (with $\partial \Sigma / \partial n_1 > 0$), we might represent Σ as

$$\Sigma = \Gamma n_1^2 {}^{\cdot} S_1 {}^{\cdot} F_2 \tag{35}$$

which gives us a loss function

$$L_1 = \underset{\text{Massed Fire}}{\Gamma_1 (n_1 S_1)^2 F_2} + \underset{\substack{\text{Square} \\ \text{Law}}}{\Pi_1 n_1 F_2} + \underset{\substack{\text{Linear} \\ \text{Law}}}{\Theta_1 S_1 S_2} \tag{36}$$

With the number of battle fronts--each of size A--now a variable, Side 1 should want to minimize its proportional losses in any one area; an increase in total war effort could be most effectively achieved by increasing the number of areas. Thus, 1's decision problems for both decentralization and density now become optimizing problems with choice variables n and S

$$\underset{n_1, S_1}{\text{Min}} \left[\frac{L_1}{F_1} = \Gamma_1 n_1 S_1 F_2 + \Pi_1 F_2 / S_1 + \Theta_1 S_2 / n_1 \right] \tag{37}$$

Assuming   that   interior   solutions   for n_1 and S_1 are
functions of the specified parameters, it now would become possible to derive testable hypotheses concerning the connections between decentralization and densities under optimizing behavior,[25] to collect relevant data, and ultimately to infer whether a rationalistic, optimizing substructure can provide a foundation for quantitative analysis of military operations.

NOTES

1. See Read (1964), page 11.
2. Read (1964) has suggested a similar idea in his discussion of the balance between fire and maneuver, on the one hand, and between direct-fire weapons (such as rifles and machine guns) and indirect-fire weapons (artillery and missiles) on the other. In order to give a flavor of the idea of balance in a military system, we quote Read at length:

It is advantageous to be able to concentrate an intensive fire on a local area and thus achieve local fire superiority over the enemy. It is disadvantageous to concentrate men and equipment in a local area where they come under hostile fire. Increasing the range of weapons tends to break the connection between the concentration of fire (which is desirable) and the concentration of bodies (which is undesirable). The need for concentration, like the need for maneuver, comes from the limited range of weapons. If both sides had only long range weapons, neither would have to concentrate. But, if these weapons were area weapons, neither side would have any targets. Targets for weapons that cannot be used against individual men will tend to form under the threat of weapons that can be used against individual men. Thus, so long as long range weapons are area weapons, there will be some balance between these and short range or line-of-sight weapons. And since the latter have to move about to establish local superiority at shifting points, maneuver will continue to be important. The threat of a local superiority of short range weapons, brought about by maneuver, is primarily what forces the enemy to concentrate sufficiently to form a target for indirect or area fire. . . . Too much concentration will lead to unnecessary losses from area fire. Too little concentration will lead to defeat in detail in small unit fire fights. (pp. 6-7)

3. See Liddell-Hart (1960), page 3.

4. See Stewart (1960), page 28.

5. I am thankful to Michael Intriligator for this observation.

6. See Read (1969), pages 6-7.

7. See Stewart (1960), page 32. Stewart does not seem to have recognized that if the dispersion which my capabilities permit me is the same as the dispersion those same capabilities require of the enemy, and if the same is true of the enemy, then one of us is by definition "in trouble."

8. In speaking of equilibrium and of a tactical organization which minimizes attrition, I do not mean the hour-to-hour or week-to-week fluctuations of individual battles, but rather the much longer averages, as in wars pursued over several years, where losses in combat divisions on the order of 5% per month have been sustained on both sides for prolonged periods made up by compensating resupply rates.

9. I thank L. Bruce Anderson for pointing out these problems.

10. A succinct summary of Lanchester's differential equation approach to the evolution of battles may be found in Hall (1971). In essence, Lanchester proposed a pair of differential equations

$$\frac{dF_i(t)}{dt} = \gamma_1 F_j(t) \qquad\qquad j \neq i = 1,2$$

for units experiencing aimed direct fire from each other. This pair represents the square law—square because the solution includes squared terms $F_i(t)^2$. A second pair

of differential equations

$$\frac{dF_i(t)}{dt} = \tau_i F_i(t) \cdot F_j(t) \qquad\qquad j \neq i = 1,2$$

represents exchange of area fire, the linear law. Note also that this treatment of loss functions ignores certain dynamic possibilities of attrition processes which could allow them to represent conscious tactical decisions or planning. I have in mind such "investment" decisions as absorbing large losses at one point in time so as to avoid even larger losses later.

11. Michael Intriligator (1975) has suggested that nuclear war may have a similar mix of high-intensity and low-intensity phases.

12. The nature of this interdependency is dramatically different, however, as between absolute loss rate

and proportional loss rate functions. As a result, which measure might be driving the behavior of adversaries would make a major difference. Thus, if one of the two adversaries increases its own numbers or density, then its own absolute losses will increase but its proportionate losses will decline. Which of these two measures of loss is the more relevant is closely bound up with the nature of the constraint--whether physical or psychological. Consequently, if physical capacity to resupply is the governing constraint, greater absolute numbers will eventually press up against that limit. However, if morale factors and proportionate losses dominate, increasing numbers/densities lead to diminishing proportionate losses.

13. For instance, an assumption that tempo depends on densities according to

$$r(d_1 d_2) = \{ (d_1 d_2)^2 / [1 + (d_1 d_2)^2] \}; \quad \text{with } r(0,0) = 0; \ r(\infty, \infty) = 1$$

would produce loss functions L_1, L_2 or ℓ_1 and ℓ_2, which were polynomials in d_1 and d_2.

14. This distinction between total and proportionate losses raises the further question of what determines the size of the battle zone. The numerical and economic size of opponents must play a crucial role as well as either side's technical capabilities for maneuver, command-control communications, intelligence, speed of movement, and so on. In a context with all of these given factors, however, the question remains as to whether for a given size total force it is economical to pack that force into an area of size A, or divide it equally into, say, two such areas, each of size A. To those familiar with the theory of production and of the firm in economics, this question will be seen to hinge on the effects of a scalar change in the loss functions $L_i(A, F_1, F_2)$. If L_i was characterized by constant returns to scale, proportional increases in force size and area would produce equiproportionate increases in casualties. Then doubling (say) forces without enlarging the area of battle would be uneconomical in the sense that losses would be needlessly high. On the other hand, if $L_i(A, F_1, F_2)$ were homogeneous of degree zero, losses under a given technical regime would be totally insensitive to the size of armies, provided the geographic area for a war changed in proportion to force size.

15. The absolute value of the slope of L_2^O compares to the absolute value of the slope of L_1^O as follows:

$$\left| \text{Slope of } L_1^O \right| = \frac{\alpha_1 + \beta_1 d_1}{{}_1 d_2} \overset{>}{<} \frac{\beta_2 d_1}{\alpha_2 + B_2 d_2} = \left| \text{Slope of } L_2^O \right|$$

is equivalent to

$$\alpha_1 \alpha_2 + \beta_1 \alpha_2 d_1 + B_2 \alpha_1 d_2 \overset{>}{<} 0$$

Since the lefthand side is necessarily positive if all parameters are positive, L_1^O is steeper.

16. The dynamics of movement of the forward edge of the battle area (FEBA), that is, the line of contact between opposing armies, has been the object of intense study by operations research analysts for years.

17. In the modern era of nuclear weapons and ICBM the long run may arrive very suddenly.

18. This explanation is suggested by Read's analysis (1964, pp. 18-19).

By the middle of the 19th century the direct fire of infantry weapons had put an end to frontal attacks on even hastily prepared positions. Open warfare of maneuver remained possible and was characteristic of the American Civil War and the European Wars of 1866-1871 because the limited number of men in relation to the extent of the theatre of war meant that there were always flanks to turn or envelop. Even in World War I, the war remained fluid in the great spaces of the Eastern front. But the armies massed in the West formed a continuous flankless front extending from the Swiss border to the English channel. Thus neither flank nor frontal attacks were feasible. But the resulting situation of linear siege warfare favored massive indirect artillery fire, and the dispersion enforced by this fire eliminated the linear forward defense that had slaughtered frontal attacks from Gettysburg to Passchendaele. In short, artillery--which had been driven back out of range of improved infantry weapons--drove the bulk of infantry back out of range of indirect artillery fire, replaced static position defense by mobile defense, opened up the locked fronts and led to the reappearance, at the level of small unit tactics, of the fluid warfare of maneuver which had been banished from grand tactics by a combination of protected direct firepower and conscript armies massive enough to man a continuous, flankless front.

19. Read (1964), pages 8, 25. Elsewhere he observes

The earliest treatments of nuclear tactics recognized that . . . dispersion be achieved by increasing not the distance between men in a unit, but the separation between units that remain internally concentrated . . . that each side has to strike a balance between its vulnerability to nuclear weapons and its vulnerability to piece-meal defeat in small unit non-nuclear fire fights. (p. 9)

[since] we have to increase the spacing between units which remain internally concentrated enough to fight effectively in conventional engagements with similar units on the other side . . . the deployment of combat forces will be granular, or porous. The size of a granule will be determined by the number of men who can be put at risk to one enemy nuclear weapon. (p. 26)

20. This is a strong assumption. We might alternatively assume very high loss rates for concentrated units. The assumption of local destruction might be viewed as a limiting case.

21. See Feller (1960).

22. To cast the choice of density into an optimizing problem requires that we postulate a complex objective function as in Figure 14.2. The behavior of the rival combatants postulated in the section on troop density was satisficing rather than optimizing since an optimum level of one's own casualties was not postulated to influence behavior at all. Instead, we assumed that a satsifactory sustainable level of losses did. Even if the choic of number or density could minimize one's own losses (as $R_i R_i$

in Figure 14.2) there is no particular reason for choosing this minimum. Countries engage in wars to win them and minimum losses are desired only as instrumental variables. In the instant case represented by equation (19) choosing a value of S to minimize one's own losses makes sense because it entails no opportunity cost. The theory of satisficing behavior is due to Herbert Simon (1957).

23. We check that this is indeed a minimum value of

S_2^v by differentiating (23) a second time:

$$\frac{\partial^2 L_2}{\partial S_2^2} = 2\sigma_2 T / (S_2)^3 > 0$$

A positive value indicates a minimum.

24. I am thankful to Michael Intriligator for drawing my attention to the similarity between this square root result and an analogous result in inventory theory. By analogy with inventory theory the two terms of the loss equation represent holding cost and ordering cost, respectively. See Arrow et al. (1951), Churchman et al. (1957), or Masse (1962) for further elaboration.

25. For example, assume an equation for Side 2 symmetric to (37). Optimizing choice for Side i requires $(L_i/F_i) S_i = 0$ and $(L_i(F_i/n_i = 0.$ Joint Nash equilibria yield the following relationships, where * indicates joint loss minimizing choices:

$$\frac{S_1^*}{S_2^*} = \frac{\Pi_1/\Theta_1}{\Pi_2/\Theta_2} \; ; \; \frac{n_1^*}{n_2^*} = \frac{\Theta_1^2/\Pi_1\Gamma_1}{\Theta_2^2/\Pi_2\Gamma_2} \; ; \; \frac{F_1^*}{F_2^*} = \frac{\Theta_1/\Gamma_1}{\Theta_2/\Gamma_2}$$

15 Dynamic Models of Guerrilla Warfare

THE PRINCIPLES OF GUERRILLA WARFARE

In his historical analysis of the wars since 1775 where guerrilla warfare was used, Walter Laqueur (1977) reveals that we have to make a fundamental distinction between a guerrilla war with national aims and one with revolutionary aims. A war with national aims is defined as a conflict between a resistance movement in an occupied country and the occupation forces of an aggressor. In a war with revolutionary aims, a minority of a country, be it an ethnic (Basque), a religious (catholics in Ulster), or a social minority (minor party), uses guerrilla warfare against the government of the country in question. Whereas the aim of the national guerrilla war is to drive away the occupation forces, the revolutionary guerrilla war aims at overthrowing the government and taking over the power. The next aim they are driving at is a change of the social and economic system.

Mao Tse-tung developed operational conceptions for both types. In Mao (1969) he describes the conception of revolutionary warfare. A detailed description of the national guerrilla warfare can be found in Mao (1968). As, according to Mao, the national guerrilla war is a means of resistance against the Japanese aggression, he puts this conception in the wider conception of the war of resistance (Mao, 1938). The aim of this paper being the simulation of national guerrilla warfare, we will study the principles and hypotheses formulated by Mao, especially in his study about the lengthy war.

In this study, Mao presents five principles which, he says, if followed by the participants of a guerrilla war, will guarantee a successful ending of the war against occupation forces.

The first principle of a successful guerrilla war and a war of resistance (the Chinese against the Japanese) is the fact that guerrillas are supported by the population. The guerrillas should live among the population like fish in a populated sea. This support is

354

both active and passive. The support is called active
when the population covers the losses of the guerrilleros
with farmers who are fit to fight. According to Mao, the
capacity and willingness for recruiting among the
population is reinforced by reprisals of the occupation
forces, because these reprisals don't just frighten the
population but also intensify the population's hatred for
the occupation forces (for the Japanese). Passive support
lies mainly in the population handing information about
the enemy to the guerrillas. This support also includes
the logistical help, such as food supplies for the
guerrillas.

The second principle in guerrilla and partisan
warfare is the size of the population. The larger the
population, the less sensible is the substance of the
population to reprisals and the greater is the stock to
fill up the losses and to reinforce the strength of the
guerrillas. The successful example given by China shows
the plausibility of this thesis. At the same time,
historic examples reveal that a guerrilla war with a small
population has little chance of success.

In his third thesis, Mao refers to the importance of
the proportion of strength between the guerrillas and the
aggressors. The more, in the course of the war, this
proportion turns in favor of the guerrillas, the more the
success of the war will turn to the guerrillas and the
occupation forces will be destroyed. This development
again is a factor of the quantity of the population.
Apart from this proportion, the result of the war is also
determined by the proportion of the fighting power of the
two enemies.

The fourth thesis refers to the importance of the
dimension of the territory in which the guerrilla war is
fought. The larger the territory which serves the
guerrillas as a theater of operations, the more successful
they will be.

The fifth principle for a successful guerrilla
warfare is the efficiency of the intelligence service of
the guerrillas on the one hand and the inefficiency of the
intelligence service of the occupation forces on the other
hand. Whereas the guerrilla forces, by receiving
information from the population, are informed about the
organization, the bases, the movements, and the actions of
the occupation forces, it's not the case for the
occupation forces. Due to the missing support of the
population, the intelligence service of the occupation
forces has to rely on air reconnaissance and
reconnaissance in force. This difference in efficiency
between the intelligence services determines the
efficiency of the actions of both enemies. Whereas the
guerrillas can successfully attack the occupation forces
from ambushes and wear them out in different fights, the

occupation forces can't do this. As their results of reconnaissance are not exact enough, their cannonade and bombardment are aimed at area targets rather than specific ones. The most important targets in the guerrilla territory are only partly hit. Different operations carried out by German fighters on the Balkans during the Second World War can be quoted as a good example. A guerrilla war, made on the basis of these principles, is obviously a total dispute, where ideological, political, and psychological, as well as military, means are involved. The execution and the development of such a war is therefore a complicated and dynamic process. As the interaction in such a process can't be formulated and analyzed verbally, we shall examine the processes and results of some historical examples of guerrilla wars by means of a simple model consisting of ordinary differential equations and of the simulation technique.

Before taking up this model, we shall present a few models of warfare which illustrate similar problems by means of differential equations.

MODELS OF WARFARE

Lanchester's Models

The illustration of wars by means of formal models is not new. During the First World War (1916), the British engineer Lanchester illustrated fights between two enemies with the help of ordinary differential equations of first order (Stahel, 1973). In the literature the result of the first model is called Lanchester's square law, and the result of the second model, Lanchester's linear law. Both models are based on the assumption that the fight is carried out with homogeneous units. Furthermore the square law requires the two following assumptions:

(1) Each effective unit is informed about the remaining units of the enemy, so that after the destruction of an aim a change of target takes place immediately.

(2) The fire is spread homogeneously over the other units. The development of the fight in this model is described by the following model:

$$x_1 = -a \cdot x_2$$
$$x_2 = -b \cdot x_1$$

x_1 and x_2 are the units of 1 and 2 at the point of time t.

Furthermore, x_{10} and x_{20} are the strengths of 1 and 2 at the beginning of the fight, a is the destruction rate of a unit of 2 against the unit of 1, and b is the destruction rate of a unit of 1 against the unit of 2.

By means of the analytical solution we get the following condition of balance for this model:

$$\frac{\dot{x}_1^2}{a} - \frac{\dot{x}_2^2}{b} = \frac{\dot{x}_{10}^2}{a} - \frac{\dot{x}_{20}^2}{b}$$

The denouement of the fight depends on the square of the number of the originally engaged combat units. An increase in units has a bigger effect than an improvement in the effectiveness of a few units.

Lanchester validated this model on the grounds of Nelson's plan for the attack on the combined French and Spanish fleet off Trafalgar and on the grounds of the results of the battle. The combined fleet was split up into three parts and the center and the rearguard were destroyed by the concentrated operation of the British vessels.

As a marginal product of the first model, Lanchester developed the second model. The following assumptions determine this model:

(1) Each firing unit is only informed about the territory where the opposing units are, and it fires into this territory without knowing the consequences of its fire.

(2) The fire of the surviving units is spread homogeneously over the territory where the opposing units have been detected.

According to Lanchester and other studies, this model should illustrate the course of a flight carried out with mortars:

$$\dot{x}_1 = -A \cdot x_2 \cdot x_1$$
$$\dot{x}_2 = -B \cdot x_1 \cdot x_2$$

The destruction rates are determined by the following factors:

$$A = r_2 \cdot A_{e2}/A_1$$
$$B = r_1 \cdot A_{e1}/A_2$$

A_1 and A_2 are the areas where units of 1 and 2 have been located by the opposing side. A_{e2} and A_{e1} are the surfaces destroyed with a single shot and are therefore the surfaces in which a shot is certain to put an opposing unit out of action; r_2 and r_1 are the rates of fire of the weapons of 2 and 1 per combat unit and per unit of time.

Obviously, the two Lanchester models are excellent means to illustrate and analyze fights on the tactical level. Quite a few models of the Lanchester type to examine tactical problems have been developed. As the Lanchester models are typical microcombat models, they can't always be transferred to the analysis of strategic problems, i.e., guerrilla warfare as a whole. For this investigation we need a macrocombat model, where a few fights which cohere locally and temporally are aggregated into one single process. It is interesting to see that, in quite different fields, macrocombat models which have a certain relation to the problems described have been developed.

Volterra's Host and Guest Model

In his essay, Volterra (1931) presents a model with which, by means of differential equations, he describes the eating up of one species by another. The first species, the host, would grow in a positive constant way if he were not eaten up.

$$E_1$$

The second species, which is exclusively fed by the first, would grow in a negative constant way if there were not first species.

$$-E_2$$

Supposing the two species are in the same area, the first species grows more slowly if there exists a lot of specimens of the second species. On the other hand, the second species grows faster if there exist a lot of specimens of the first species. According to Volterra, this simple hypothesis leads to the following growth coefficients:

$$E_1 - \beta_1 \cdot N_1 \text{ and } -E_2 + \beta_2 \cdot N_2$$

$$(E_1, E_2, \beta_1, \beta_1 > 0)$$

Volterra illustrates the development of the two species by means of the following equation:

$$\dot{N}_1 = E_1{}^\cdot N_1 - \beta_1{}^\cdot N_1{}^\cdot N_2$$
$$\dot{N}_2 = -E_2{}^\cdot N_2 + \beta_2{}^\cdot N_1{}^\cdot N_2$$

This model leads us to the macrocombat model of guerrilla warfare.

A MODEL FOR THE SIMULATION OF GUERRILLA WARFARE

With the help of Mao's hypothesis and a few structures of Volterra's model, the course of the actions in a guerrilla war between the partisan forces and the occupation forces can be illustrated by the following equation system (Stahel, 1980):

(1) dGUER/dt = (UEBLR*POP)-(VER21*GUER*CONV)

(2) dCONV/dt = (-VER12*GUER)+(MOBIL*CONV)

(3) dPOP /dt = (ZUWR*POP)-(DPMDR*POP)-(UEBLR*POP).

This model represents the interaction of three groups: (1) the guerrillas GUER, (2) the population POP, and (3) the regular occupation forces CONV.

The war structure of this model reflects the asymmetrical nature of a guerrilla war without fronts. While the losses on the regular side are directly proportional to the strength of the other side, the losses of the guerrilla forces are proportional to the strength of both. The more intense the fighting is, the higher are the losses of the guerrilla forces. But guerrilla fighters are like fish in the water. The exact position of their base is unknown to their enemy. The latter has to bomb the guerrilla territory or cover it with artillery fire without exact target data, and thus the losses of the guerrilla forces are proportional to their own strength. According to this, we have the following combat parameter in the first equation:

VER21 = R2*AE2/A1.

R2 is the rate at which the air-raids are carried out, A1 is the surface which is bombed, and AE2 is the destruction efficiency of a single operation. The first equation represents the change over time in the strength of the guerrillas who are fighting the regular occupation forces. Their strength is increased by the recruits coming from the population (UEBLR*POP) and diminished by their losses (VER21*GUER*CONV). The second equation describes the strength of the regular occupation forces as a function of their losses and their reinforcement and of the replacing of their losses by people from their own country (MOBIL*CONV).

As the intelligence service of the guerrillas is very good and as they are informed about every operative or tactical action of their enemy, the losses of the occupation forces are directly proportional to the strength of the guerrilla forces (-VER12*GUER).

The third equation describes the development of the population. This third equation is a function of (a) the natural growth of the population (ZUWR*POP), (b) the fact that members of the population join the guerrilla forces (UEBLR*POP), and (c) the genocide done to the population by the occupation forces (DPMDR*POP).

This simple a priori model has been used to analyze three examples of guerrilla wars:

(1) The guerrilla war in South Sudan against the government of the North from 1963-1972.

(2) Tito's partisan war against Germany, Italy, and the Utaschas from 1941-1944.

(3) The guerrilla war of the Mujaheddins in Afghanistan against the Soviet forces since 1979.

THE GUERRILLA WAR IN SOUTH SUDAN

This was a national guerrilla war insofar as, during the independence of Sudan in 1956, two different social groups were united in one state, two groups which had nothing in common and which belonged to different races and religions. Very soon the North imposed itself as an occupation force in the South. As the racial and occupation war of the military government of the North became more and more intense, a South Sudanese guerrilla movement called Anya-Nya was founded in 1963. The war, which caused heavy losses among the population, could only be ended by an armistice on February 26, 1972. Among other things the South Sudanese were promised, by virtue of treaty, the establishment of a federation of the Sudan with extensive autonomy for the South. In order to examine the development of this guerrilla war, the three equations of the a priori model have been used:

$$dGUER/dt = (UEBLR*POP) - (VER21*GUER*CONV)$$

$$dCONV/dt = (-VER12*GUER) + (MOBIL*CONV)$$

$$dPOP/dt = (ZUWR*POP) - (DPMDR*POP) - (UEBLR*POP)$$

For this war, the following values can be attributed to the parameters and to the initial conditions:

Initial conditions: GUERO = 5,000, CONVO = 18,000, POPO = 4,029,150

Parameter: VER21=0.0000042, VER12=0.025, UEBLR=0.00038
MOBIL=0.065833, ZUWR=0.028, DPMDR=0.027501

Here the two combat parameters VER21 and VER12 are of especial importance. Both were determined on account of other historic examples. The parameter VER21 was determined on the basis of data taken from the guerrilla war in Malaya from 1948-1960. For Malaya we get VER21= 0.000016. Taking into consideration the guerrillas' area

Al=105,100 km^2 of Malaya, this value has to be converted

to the South Sudanese guerrillas' area Al=399,100 km^2. The loss parameter VER12 of the regular Sudanese army and of the Soviets piloting combat helicopters (they flew the missions) was established on the basis of the losses the counter-guerrilla forces had in Malaya, and this parameter was validated on the basis of the losses the Americans suffered in Vietnam in 1966. With these values for the parameters of the model, by applying the simulation language MIMIC (Halin, 1974), we receive the following results for 1972: GUER = 10,859; CONV = 29,978; POP = 4,033,470; DMBEV = 997,785. The actual results of the war were GUER = 12,000; CONV = 30,000; POP = 4,050,000; DMBEV = 1,000,000. The usability of this model to analyze guerrilla wars is clearly confirmed.

And we mustn't forget that this model is based on a priori assumptions and that it is calculated endogenously from the start. By means of sensitivity analyses it is also possible to examine different strategies of the guerrillas and the regular troops of North Sudan. This leads to confirmation of Mao's thesis on the importance of the population reinforcing the guerrillas.

THE PARTISAN WAR IN YUGOSLAVIA (1941-1944)

Tito's partisan war started after German, Italian, Hungarian, and Bulgarian troops attacked Yugoslavia in April 1941. After the conquest, Yugoslavia was split up as follows:

(1) The independent state of Croatia, consisting of parts of Croatia and Bosnia-Herzogovina, was formed and dominated by the fascist organization Utascha.

(2)   The western part of today's republic of Slovenia as well as Dalmatia was occupied and annexed by Italy.

(3)   The eastern part of the republic of Slovenia was occupied and annexed by Germany.

(4)   The western part of Voivodina was annexed by Hungary.

(5)   The eastern part of Voivodina and the central area of today's republic of Serbia was occupied by Germany and controlled with the help of a quisling government.

(6)   Montenegro and Kosowo were occupied by Italy and annexed to Albania.

(7)   Macedonia was occupied and annexed by Bulgaria.

The resistance forces used the time between the destruction of the Yugoslavian army and the end of June 1941 to prepare and organize their war. We have to distinguish between two movements: the panserb monarchic movement led by the former colonel Draja Mihailovitch, whose members called themselves Chetnics and the communist movement led by Josip Broz Tito. Due to the ideological difference, the Chetnics turned against Tito's partisans and worked more and more for the occupation forces against the partisans. Being numerically inferior and limited to the territory of Serbia, the Chetnics fell behind and degenerated as a guerrilla movement. Tito succeeded in convincing Churchill that the Chetnics actually collaborated with the occupation forces. In January 1944, Churchill stopped supporting the Chetnics and started supporting the partisans. In March 1944, the United States approved of the British politics towards Yugoslavia. At the same time, the Soviets started supplying the partisans.
Two events during these three and a half years of partisan war in Yugoslavia (June 1941 to the end of 1944) are of the utmost importance:

(1)   The collapse of the Italian army in Yugoslavia in September 1943 as a consequence of the armistice between Italy and the allied forces.

(2)   The advance of the Soviet front towards Yugoslavia and the engagement of the Red Army in the eastern part of Yugoslavia to support the partisans when retaking Belgrade and Voivodina (October 1944). After having accomplished this operation, the units of the Red Army left Yugoslavia according to the agreement made with the Soviet government on September 28, 1944.

On the basis of the data available from the partisan war from June 1941 to the end of 1944 (3.5 years) and the surface of Yugoslavia (Al = 255,804 km^2) we have the following values for the simulation model:

Initial conditions: GUERO=80,000, CONVO=620,000, POPO=15,000,000

Paramter: VER21=0.00000089, VER12=0.85418, UEBLR=0.024629,
                     RESER=404,214, ZUWR=0.012, DPMDR=0.025749.

Apart from the fact that the partisan area of Yugoslavia and the one of South Sudan give different values, the two combat parameters have been adjusted to the greater brutality in this war. To give an example: until September 1944 all prisoners were executed by the Germans and the Utaschas. On the other hand, captured officers of the enemy didn't have to expect much mercy, either. Furthermore, to simplify things, the structure of the model war is reduced, and MOBIL * CONV is replaced by RESER. The simulation of this model leads to the following results for the end of 1944:

Partisans (GUER) = 528,948

Germans/Italians/Utaschas(CONV) = 378,296

Population (POP) = 14,295,300

Genocide (DMBEV) = 1,319,810

In reality we have the following figures for the end of 1944:

Partisans = 650,000

Germans/Italians/Utaschas = 400,000

Population = 13,605,000

Genocide = 1,395,000

Again, the results of this simulation point to the importance of the population's support of the partisans.

Concerning the Italian collapse in September 1943, it was taken into consideration by means of a function-switch which, from this date, had stopped to fill up the German and Italian losses as well as the reinforcement of the occupation forces. This simulation, too, is an indication of the solidity of the model for analyzing guerrilla wars.

THE GUERRILLA WAR OF THE MUJAHEDDINS IN AFGHANISTAN

The Model

The guerrilla war in Afghanistan, which has been going on since 1979, is a total resistance against the Soviet armed forces (Allan and Stahel, 1983). After five years of war, the Soviets still have to limit their control to the towns. All the bigger ethnic groups are at war against the Soviet divisions. Local commanders, heads of tribes, and mullahs are the leaders of the resistance. In order to analyze this war, a simulation model has been developed, starting with the model described above, and taking into consideration the interactions among the five most important groups of this war: (1) the guerrillas (mujaheddins), (2) the potential guerrillas (potential mujaheddins), (3) the remaining population, (4) the Soviet divisions and brigades, (5) the Afghan army. These factors determine the development of the size of these groups, especially by means of two interactions:

(1) The interaction between the guerrillas and the potential guerrillas as a rate at which the latter join the active guerrillas.

(2) The combat interaction between the guerrillas and their enemies, the Soviet and Afghan forces. The result of this interaction represents the losses on both sides.

The combat relationships reflect the asymmetrical nature of a guerrilla war without fronts. While the losses on the conventional side (USSR or Afghan army) are directly proportional to the number of opposing troops, the losses of the guerrillas are proportional to the size of both their own and the conventional divisions. The more the Soviets and regular Afghans are fighting, the higher the guerrilla losses, but the guerrillas are like fish in a population sea. Their exact position is not known to their enemies, who need to bombard more or less blindly over the guerrilla region, and thus the losses of the resistance are also proportional to their own number. The initial conditions are for February 1, 1980, approximately a month after the invasion, when the stage for the next years was set. The model consists of five ordinary differential equations representing the evolution of the five groups during the six-year period 1980 to 1985. The parameters are on a monthly basis. The basis of the data is the period 1980 to 1982. The first equation explains the change over time in the number of guerrillas actually fighting the Soviet and Afghan armies. Their number is increased by reinforce-

Table 15.1 The A Priori Model

155,000	guerrillas	:	$\dfrac{dGUER}{dt} =$	$0.01*GUERPOT - 0.00000035*GUER*(USSR+AFGH)$
				Fighters joining $\qquad$ losses
				the guerrillas
1,470,000	potential guerrillas	:	$\dfrac{dGUERPOT}{dt} =$	$- 0.01*GUERPOT$
10,850,000	rest of population		$\dfrac{dPOP}{dt} =$	$- 1500 \quad - \quad 0.0011*POP - REF$
				Afghan $\qquad$ genocide $\qquad$ refugees
				army $\qquad$ leaving
				recruits
0	Soviet army		$\dfrac{dUSSR}{dt} =$	$2*(85,000 \quad - \quad USSR) - 0.003*GUER$
				Soviet $\qquad$ Soviet $\qquad$ losses
				objective $\qquad$ troops
35,000	Afghan army		$\dfrac{dAFGH}{dt} =$	$1500 \qquad - \qquad 2*0.003*GUER$
				recruits $\qquad$ losses

reinforcements from the potential guerrillas and diminished by their losses. These depend on the size of the fighting forces. The assumption is that the antiguerrilla troops do not know the exact position of the different guerrillas and, as a result, fire and bomb blindly over the region where the guerrillas are suspected. Helicopters' operations are mainly of the countervalue type (bombing to punish the supportive population). The guerrilla losses are proportional both to the number of targets (guerrillas) and to the size of the combined forces of the adversaries (the Soviet and Afghan regular armies).

The evolution of the potential guerrillas is described by the second equation, where potential guerrillas joining the fighting guerrilla forces are subtracted. The transition rate from potential to actual is a simple function of the number of potential guerrillas.

The relationship was retained because of its logical simplicity. It means that with the passage of time, there will be potential guerrillas joining the fight as a part of the whole process, notably guerrilla losses to be replaced and weapons to be obtained by the potential fighters who are trained.

The rest of the population is explained by the third equation. Three factors decrease the size of the population:

(1)   Recruits into the Afghan army (at a rate of 1,500 per month).

(2)   Deaths resulting from the war (genocide factor).

(3)   Migrants leaving Afghanistan, almost exclusively for Pakistan and Iran.

The size of the Soviet divisions and forces was more or less constant from the beginning of the invasion up to the end of 1982, when it increased from 85,000 to 110,000. The Soviet equation describes the continuous adjustment between a Soviet objective of 85,000 men and their losses, which are regularly replaced.

The fifth equation describes changes in the size of the Afghan regular forces. They increase at the rate of 1,500 recruits per month and decrease due to losses in the same fashion as the Soviet army, but at double rate.

The Strengths and the Parameters

The available information is too fragmented for a good assessment of the guerrilla forces in Afghanistan by region (Stahel and Bucherer, 1984).   This is why we proceed deductively, starting from the total population and making conservative estimates of the potential and actual guerrillas.   On the basis of primitive demographic statistics we assume after the deduction of the refugees (before the invasion) and the nomads for the population of Afghanistan 1980 the number of 13 million people.   For the initial condition of February 1, 1980, we estimate and deduct 500,000 refugees in Pakistan and 100,000 refugees in Iran.   So we have 12.4 million people in Afghanistan February 1, 1980, nomads not included.

The potential guerrillas are men aged 15 to 60. Many adolescents and older men are fighting.   We estimate the proportion of all men between 15 and 60 at one-quarter of the total population.   We assume that only one-half of these are able men willing to fight.

For the number of guerrillas in February 1980, we make the assumption that only 155,000 guerrillas were fighting.   To the number of the potential guerrillas we add one-eighth of the total refugees because many men in refugee camps participate in the war.   So we receive as an initial condition for the potential guerrillas 1,470,000 men.   The combat parameters were taken from the analysis of the guerrilla war in South Sudan from 1963 to 1972.   We used the same parameters, correcting the one for guerrilla losses in proportion to the larger combat area in Afghanistan (we are estimating the guerrillas' area at

$400,000 \text{ km}^2$ of the $650,000 \text{ km}^2$ of Afghanistan), in our simulation of the Afghan war, because of certain similarities between South Sudan and Afghanistan. In both cases, the combat area is quite inhospitable and the guerrillas can count on a great deal of support from the population.

An important assumption is the 1% figure for potential guerrillas who join the fighting ranks each month. We have taken this figure on an a priori basis. Though this rate seems high, it is not: it is lower by about a third than the rate at which reinforcements were coming in for the Yugoslav partisans during World War II. In the equation for the rest of the population the second term represents civilian deaths from the war, notably from the Soviets bombing villages to punish guerrilla supporters. The rate of 0.11% used here is lower than the genocide rates in Yugoslavia and those in the South Sudan.

The third term in the population equation represents the refugee flow. This is based on both official Pakistani figures that are accepted by international humanitarian organizations and on estimations about the refugees in Iran.

Soviet troops reached the number of 85,000 only in February 1980 because the invading divisions were not at full strength from the start. Their number increased to 110,000 only toward the end of 1982. The factor of 2, multiplying the difference between Soviet goals and the effective number of Soviet troops in the fourth equation, implies a two-week adjustment between the situation and the goals that appears to be realistic, and that also generates plausible figures for Soviet forces.

According to The Military Balance, the Afghan regular army had 100,000 men in July 1978. A year later, it was estimated to have approximately 80,000, due to internal troubles. Two weeks after the Soviet intervention, estimates dropped to only 40,000 to 50,000. Whole units sometimes fought the Soviets and joined the resistance. We put the strength of the Afghan army at 35,000 on February 1, 1980. In January 1981 the government announced the general conscription for all men age 20 and over and a year later for age 16 and over. Forced conscription has induced many youngsters to hide or to leave government-controlled regions--mainly towns--and (partially) to join the resistance. Voluntarily or involuntarily, the Afghan regular army has been the greatest source of weapons for the guerrillas. In addition, soldiers and officers who help the guerrillas are not atypical.

The Results of the Simulation

The a priori model describes the evolution of the military situation within Afghanistan from February 1, 1980, to the end of 1985. The main results trace the evolution of the strength of the guerrilla, Soviet, and Afghan army forces.

The number of guerrillas increased to 249,000 in January 1983, before decreasing to 198,000 at the end of 1985. The Soviet army remained constant according to the postulate made, and the level of Afghan regular army forces increased very slightly to 45,000. This run seems to replicate events in the period from 1980 to 1982 quite well. These were combats limited to a few towns and some regions in early 1980, followed during the summer of 1980, and especially since 1981, by more intense combat involving more and more Afghan regions and towns. Thus, the war seemed to be escalating through 1982. In addition, the size of both the Soviet and Afghan armies did not change significantly.

Since the combat loss parameters have been determined a priori, the predictions for the losses generated by the full model running endogenously from the start can be compared with the actual losses in Afghanistan. This allows us to validate the model. There are, of course, diverging estimates about these losses, but a certain consensus among analysts enables us to judge the performance of the model. The potential guerrilla population decreased from 1,470,000 to 723,000, showing very heavy losses for the guerrillas of 712,000 over the six years. These losses represent approximately half of the potential guerrillas and nearly 6% of the prewar population. They seem much too large but some experts estimate the losses of the guerrillas at 5,000 deaths per month.

The Soviet losses are quite important. Numbering 49,000 over the six years, they are comparable to US losses in Vietnam. The Afghan army losses are, as prescribed in the model, double the Soviet ones. What are the estimates for Soviet losses? Since the coffin factory in Kabul has an output capacity of 4,000 coffins per year the Soviet losses are calculated to 7,280 deaths in one year. Thus it appears that our predicted Soviet losses are very precise.

In summary, our model cannot be rejected because its predictions are quite good for the first years of the war. It needs to be emphasized that these results were obtained on the basis of a priori assumptions for a dynamic model running endogenously from the start. The model predicted (1) the intensifying combat of 1981 and 1982, (2) the difficulties in building up the Afghan army, and (3) the high Soviet casualties. The guerrillas held out, bolstering our confidence in this basic result of our analysis. The conditions for the resistance imposed by our conservative assumptions still allow for development of a resistance.

How sensitive are these results to varying assumptions? Since the data are not quite good this is an important question to ask, because the results may depend to a critical extent on one or more false assumptions, or at least on empirical evaluations that may err considerably. The overall answer to this question is negative: the results are quite robust and do not appear to depend on a few crucial assumptions. Even when parameters range very widely, the mujaheddins are holding more or less well. They are never annihilated in any case, while the Soviets are still enduring appreciable losses and the development of the Afghan army remains a problem.

CONCLUSIONS

The model used in these three examples is still an a priori model, because not enough cases of guerrilla wars have been examined with it to be sure that this model could also be used as an a posteriori model. Subsequent papers will aim at extensive application to more examples of war. Although reservations have to be made, we can already say that this model leads to better analyses and simulation of guerrilla warfare than the Lanchester models did.

Artificial Intelligence Approaches

16 Adaptive Precedent-Based Logic and Rational Choice: A Comparison of Two Approaches to the Modeling of International Behavior

The purpose of this chapter is to explore the possibility of a dynamic precedent-based model of decision making in international relations. I will do so by way of a more general critique of a dominant cognitive (or at least rational) model of foreign policy decision making, the rational choice model. My basic argument is that the rational choice model, however well suited for explaining economic behavior in market systems, and perhaps in explaining political behavior in quasi-market systems such as elections, misses many of the key features of decision making in international relations. At the same time, it is clearly desirable to have a formal model of foreign policy decision making. I argue that models developed in the field of artificial intelligence (AI) may be an appropriate source of such models.

The original (and longer) version of this paper (Schrodt, 1984b) dealt with three categories of formal models--statistical models, dynamic models, and rational choice models--and looked at the strengths and weaknesses of each. However, in conference discussion it became clear that the comments on statistical and dynamic models were relatively uncontroversial and the battle was only joined over the issue of rational choice models. This is, in retrospect, unsurprising since AI models, by emphasizing cognitive processes, paradigmatically challenge homo oeconomicus in a manner that statistical and dynamic models do not. Therefore, in revising the paper it seemed sensible to elaborate on these points of disagreement at the expense of appearing to criticize only the rational choice model.

My alternative model uses two concepts from artificial intelligence: a knowledge base and pattern matching. The model assumes that foreign policy decision-making, far more than most forms of decision making, is heavily based on historical precedent. Precedent is incorporated into decisions by pattern-matching "theories" which relate current events to past events.

373

These pattern matching theories are dynamically altered by the decision making structure on the basis of their success or failure. I argue that recent advances in formal modeling of complex cognitive systems may make it possible to formalize these general characteristics into a testable model. An example of such a model--adaptive precedent-based logic--is given, and the results of some initial attempts to implement a critical part of the model are reported.

RATIONAL CHOICE MODELS

The "economic" or "rational choice" paradigm utilizes models in economics to explain individual and microeconomic behavior. This approach expanded dramatically in political science during the 1970's; Riker and Ordeshook (1973) and Frohlich and Oppenheimer (1978) provide book-length introductions to this approach. These models are characterized by the not-unreasonable assumption that political processes are the result of individual decisions, and that these decisions are at least partially determined by some form of "rational" calculation, usually expressed in terms of expected utility. In some fields of international relations, notably defense-related applications, these models have been extensively employed since the early 1960's; in other areas their application if fairly recent.

Game Theory

Since the genesis of game theory was in the analytical problems of World War II, it is not surprising that it has seen extensive use in the study of military problems in international relations. Military problems tend to be zero-sum and two-person, which are the type of game where complete results exist; cooperative and N-person games have been extensively applied to the problem of negotiation, though with less success due to the ambiguity of the results in this field. There is a wide variety of books on game theory, most of which provide examples of military/diplomatic applications: Luce and Raiffa (1957) is still an excellent survey; Schelling (1960) specifically addresses the conflict issues; Hamburger (1979), Brams (1975), and Davis (1983) provide good text-level introductions. Brewer and Shubik (1979) provide a survey of the use of these techniques (and models) in the Department of Defense.

Expected Utility

The expected utility model, based on the assumption that individual decision making involves the calculation of expected loss or gain across a stochastic set of outcomes, is the dominant model of human decision making in microeconomics and has been extensively applied to the study of voting behavior. Since it is, for the most part, a model of mass behavior in an uncertain world rather than elite behavior in a competitive world (this assumption is implicit in most applications; it is not usually explicit), there have been fewer applications of the approach in IR than in fields such as public policy and voting behavior, but nonetheless some efforts have been made in this direction. The most notable work in this field is Bueno de Mesquita (1981); the approach has been extended by others (e.g., Berkowitz, 1983; Altfeld and Bueno de Mesquita, 1979).

Economic Competition and Maximization

The possible convergence between the competition of the marketplace and the competition among nations has been a theme of international relations theory for centuries (see Parkinson, 1977) and it is not surprising that the extensive formal theory of economic competition and the results of that competition--some sort of optimized allocation of benefits based on resources--should be applied to international affairs. The bulk of this work has been concerned with arms races and two-nation competition, but more detailed work in the "balance of power" framework also exists. Intriligator (1971) provides a survey of the techniques; he has been one of the more prolific scholars in applying the methods (e.g., Intriligator, 1964; Brito and Intriligator, 1974; Intriligator and Brito, 1984). Busch (1970) and McGuire (1965) also take this approach.

* * *

Since the bulk of my critique will concern weaknesses of the rational choice approach, I should emphasize from the beginning that this approach has made some major contributions to the formal study of international relations, which in my opinion remain valid even if my criticism of the approach as an overall model of foreign policy behavior is accepted. These contributions are briefly summarized below.

The Introduction of Concepts

In my opinion, the most important contribution of the rational models has been conceptual rather than empirical: the augmenting (or perhaps updating) of the conceptual armory of international relations theory to include modern formal concepts of possible determinants of behavior. The concepts "rational," "zero-sum," "game," "strategy," "utility," "expected utility," "Arrow's theorem," "Prisoners' Dilemma," "risk adverse," and so forth have proven very useful in characterizing certain international situations, and clearly our theoretical understanding would be poorer without them. What is interesting is that in many cases the concepts are introduced but frequently the formal mathematics is not used: Rapoport (1974) and Snyder and Diesing (1977) provide examples of this. Both books use game-theoretic concepts extensively but don't have nearly the mathematical content of works of comparable level in microeconomics. This cross-fertilization has allowed IR theory to keep pace with conceptual developments in economics, as it has for centuries, but it is not converging with economics in terms of methodology.

The Existence of Mixed Strategy Solutions and Multiple Equilibria

The early results of game theory provided two related results which fixed a limit on predictability in international relations: multiple equilibria and mixed strategy solutions. Both of these results provide formal grounding for what most observers had suspected all along: international events are in many cases highly unpredictable and involve a lot of guesses, hedging, feints, and so forth. With the game-theoretic results, we now know that these behaviors are consistent, rather than inconsistent, with the assumption of rational behavior, and that in many circumstances predictable behavior would be irrational.

The Prisoners' Dilemma/Chicken Analysis of War Initiation and Arms

The single most widely analyzed game in international relations is Prisoners' Dilemma and its variants, particularly Chicken. This cooperative game appears to have wide applications in IR, and is particularly important in the analysis of nuclear deterrence and military affairs in general. The existence of the dilemma is simple to demonstrate, a wide literature on solutions exists, and it is probably the formal model most likely to show up in an introductory international relations course.

The Axelrod Altruism Results

Axelrod (1984) uses the Prisoners' Dilemma to show that tit-for-tat behaviors are selected in evolutionary situations. While this result is quite recent, I suspect that in the long term it will have a place in the IR literature comparable to that of the mixed strategy. Axelrod's results show why the world is not, for the most part, a war of all against all, and why life is not nasty, brutish, and short for most people, most of the time. Since the existence of high levels of order in an essentially anarchic situation has always presented profound problems for international relations theory, Axelrod is providing a solution to a core problem. Moreover, this result has the simplicity and elegance one expects of a breakthrough, and deals with a fundamental problem in political behavior generally.

The Game-Theoretic Analysis of Deterrence

The problem of nuclear deterrence has been extensively studied under the principles of game theory, and game theory has probably contributed substantially to our understanding of that problem. The nuclear deterrence problem has thus far been a two-actor game, and it is of sufficient importance that there is greater reason to believe that nations will behave as if they were unitary actors. Nuclear deterrence is also a counter-factual situation, and hence history provides less guidance than it does in other foreign policy decisions, opening a niche for the more hypothetical analyses of game theory.

PROBLEMS WITH THE RATIONAL CHOICE APPROACH

Despite the contributions of the rational choice approach, there is a large jump from assuming that the rational choice approach can make some contributions to our understanding of international behavior to assuming that it should be the model of international behavior. I will argue that the rational choice approach is, for the most part, unsuitable for the study of international politics, and that our efforts would be better spent elsewhere.

To those unacquainted with the intellectual debates surrounding this topic, I may appear to be setting up a straw man. Most political scientists outside of the formal models area consider political behavior so obviously distinct from economic behavior that arguments showing that the two are different are regarded as mere sophistry. Economists and rational choice theorists, in contrast, bristle at the suggestion that economic models might not be appropriate for describing political behavior and regard failure to accept this premise as ideological or ignorant.

More generally, the assertion that economic and political behavior require fundamentally different models has elicited a very predictable response when I have proposed it. Economists, and political scientists in the rational choice tradition, almost without exception feel that this assertion indicates my lack of appreciation of the full breadth of contemporary mathematical economics. For every example I propose of behavior which is primarily political rather than economic, the proponents of the universality of the economic model construct what is to them a convincing economic model to explain the phenomenon. Political scientists outside the rational choice tradition, again virtually without exception, tend to agree with the assertion and express concern that in attempting to fit political behavior into the Procrustean bed of homo oeconomicus, much of what passes for contemporary political science is not only divorced from real world politics, and hence useless, but also frequently downright silly.

Yet the issue, I contend, is more than a purely rhetorical one. If it is the case that international relations functions in its important features according to axioms similar to those used to model economic behavior, then there are good reasons to pursue that approach. These range from the practical utility of being able to apply results obtained from a half-century of work in mathematical economics to the theoretical objective of finding a set of "universal" laws governing human behavior. As one who is proposing that modelers of international relations look elsewhere for those models, and in particular look to a field which is new and not highly developed, it is incumbent upon me to make an argument for rejecting that approach.[1]

There is no single definition of what constitutes the economic approach, and definitions in books explicitly following the rational choice approach (e.g., Riker and Ordeshook, 1973; Bueno de Mesquita, 1981) are very diffuse and occupy entire chapters. The following two definitions would seem to capture the key points, however. First, from an excellent review paper by Bruno Frey (1983, p. 2):[2]

The homo oeconomicus as dealt with here is certainly not the one found in the traditional micro-economic textbooks, where it is assumed that economics actors are fully informed or where the problem of uncertainty is defined away by postulating certainty equivalents. Rather, the homo oeconomicus here considered is the much more advanced and generalized model currently used in non-market economics, particularly in the economic theory of politics, or Public Choice [Footnote: See in particular the works by Downs (1957), Buchanan and Tullock (1962) and Olsen (1965).] This approach follows the methodological individualism, it strictly distinguishes between preferences and constraints; takes the preferences to be stable and explains changes in behavior by changes in the constraints (e.g., in relative prices); considers marginal changes and stresses substitution; and finally assumes that individuals behave in a consistent ("rational") way. Economic man is thus considered to be resourceful (he searches for and finds solutions, he learns and is inventive), restricted (he is confronted with scarcity and has to choose between alternatives), expectant (he attaches subjective probabilities to future events), evaluating (he has ordered and consistent preferences) and he is maximizing his utility.

Gary Becker's (1976, p. 5) innovative work in applying the economic model to various sociological phenomena, such as marriage, crime, and fertility, uses a definition which is quite similar:

The combined assumptions of maximizing behavior, market equilibrium and stable preference, used relentlessly and unflinchingly, form the heart of the economic approach.

My critique will focus on four major reasons why I think that the economic approach is inapplicable to the study of international behavior. These are: the lack of testable theory, the inappropriateness of the major results, the irrelevance of methodological individualism, and the inefficiency of international history.
Following Frey (1983), I take as given that some of the classical assumptions of linear expected-utility maximization are simply wrong: a large--and growing-- empirical literature indicates that humans do not make decisions in the fashion assumed by the expected-utility model, even under most controlled laboratory situations. Kahneman et al. (1982) provide a thorough introduction to this literature, as does Frey. The actual behavior

appears to be nonlinear, information- rich, socially influenced, and generally far more complicated than expected utility. While many models of political behavior have yet to catch up with this fact, I will accept, following Frey, that these problems could be fixed without fundamentally altering the homo oeconomicus approach, and focus instead on other issues.

Lack of Testable Theory

One of the fundamental tenets of the positive economic school is that incorrect (empirically false) assumptions are legitimate, provided they lead to empirically correct results. Given that those assumptions do, in fact, seem to be inaccurate, which is to say they don't describe actual human decision-making behavior, one would infer that much would rest on the empirical verification of the results. This, however, is not a dominant characteristic of the rational choice literature. In fact, of the three fields of formal models, rational choice models are by far the least tested (with some exceptions, notably Bueno de Mesquita, 1981[3]). As Leontief (1982) has rather forcefully pointed out, neoclassic economics generally has an institutionalized disregard for the real world. This seems to carry over to the rational choice literature.

The basic rational choice model defined by preferences and constraints is in many ways nonfalsifiable, in the sense that preferences effectively provide infinite degrees of freedom and that for any behavior one can construct a set of preferences which will predict that behavior. This contrasts, for example, with the Richardson model, which will only fit certain patterns of arms expenditures (e.g., it will not fit the USA/USSR for the post-World War II period by most accounts). The ability to explain everything, of course, explains nothing--the models are simply tautologies.

It is only in the operationalization of preferences and constraints that a rational choice model becomes falsifiable, and here one generally finds that a large number of additional assumptions are required. Preferences are not, of course, directly measurable and require a great deal of specification--far more, for example, than might be required to define a war or an alliance or a defense budget. They must be inferred from other information and this in turn adds a large overburden of additional assumptions to what was initially a rather parsimonious model. For example, Bueno de Mesquita (1981), in constructing a measure of utility, uses a complex set of measures involving congruence of interests, national capabilities, probability of winning or losing a war, a loss-of-strength gradient, and other factors. It is legitimate to do this, but some of the universality of the model is lost at that point: presumably there exist equally justifiable measures that would yield different results.

The international system is also a hostile environment for obtaining information on the basis of the principle of "revealed preference." In an election or a consumer choice situation, revealed preference is a rather innocuous assumption: the voters vote or the consumers buy and considerable information is obtained. In international affairs, the scope of possible activities is substantially more complex, and the pace of international decision making is sufficiently slow that it is very likely that only a fraction of the preferences of many leaders are ever expressed because circumstances are such that an action is not possible at a given time. In other words, once an action has occurred, one may be able to use revealed preference information to explain why it occurred, but in the absence of revealed preference information, it is impossible to answer "what if" questions with any certainty. The War Trap provides just such an example: Bueno de Mesquita is able to correctly identify utility conditions which will obtain if a war breaks out (necessary conditions), but is unable to identify those other conditions which prevent war from breaking out.

I am not arguing that it is inherently impossible to develop a model of international behavior based on rational choice principles and provide a thorough empirical test of that model. I am simply arguing that this is going to be very difficult, and I'm not optimistic about the prospects. But such empirical validation is a necessity: formalism alone is all but useless, or at best of heuristic value. We have long ago shown that it is possible to create mathematical structures that at least vaguely resemble human behavior; the challenge is to find those that accurately model that behavior, and this requires empirical tests. This observation is hardly novel; Simon made the same point thirty years ago:

> Mathematical social science is first and foremost social science. If it is bad social science (empirically false), the fact that it is good mathematics (i.e., logically consistent) is of little comfort. (Simon, 1954, p. 388)

Inappropriateness of Results

The most important and most complete result in game theory deals with the two-person zero-sum game under minimax conditions. A variety of economic situations have those characteristics, as do a variety of military situations, and game theory is quite useful in those situations. Game theory becomes less clear when one introduces any of the following complications: more than two persons, cooperation, multiple objectives or multiple decision criteria. The bulk of the game theory literature is, in fact, devoted to trying to deal with games with combinations of these characteristics. The problem with this literature is that it has not converged. If anything it has expanded exponentially. The clean results of the two-person, zero-sum situation are not found in more complex situations. Outside of the US-Soviet confrontation (and decreasingly even there), most interesting problems in IR involve N actors. Outside of purely military situations (and rarely even there, as Schelling and Axelrod have pointed out), most IR "games" have cooperative elements. And finally, unlike many economic situations, negotiation in IR usually involves multiple objectives and is very difficult to reduce to a single dimension, such as price. As a consequence, most IR problems hit game theory where it is mathematically weak and the applicability of the technique is limited.

Might it then be possible to construct political models utilizing only those types of behavior where existing techniques provide results? I am skeptical, and suggest that there are fundamental differences between the behavior that we call economic and the behavior we call political and that these differences will, in the end, limit the utility of any theory of economic behavior in the study of political behavior. This assertion goes to the core of innumerable contemporary debates, but in outline I would suggest that economics deals primarily with production and exchange where the dominant constraints are physical, whereas politics deals primarily with the development of coalitions ("coalitions" defined as groups of individuals who are collectively engaging in some activity) where the dominant constraints are social and historical.[4] In economic activity, the single individual can be a viable unit; in political activity the individual, alone, is by definition without political power. Political power is achieved only when groups of individuals act in concert. The physical requirements of production and consumption required for survival vary little between individuals, across time, or within limits even across cultures, and therefore the assumption that these may be held constant and dominant in determining economic activity is, prima facie, not unreasonable. But to assume that same consistency in the highly mediated (both culturally and historically) behavior of political coalition formation is a major step. Economic behavior exists to provide more efficiently the basic goods which individuals require to exist; political behavior exists to solve the public goods and Prisoners' Dilemma problems which must be solved in order for organizations to exist. Economics in the end is a physical process; politics is a social process.

It is clearly the case that virtually all civilizations have distinguished between behavior that is economic and behavior that is political, more so than, for example, the differentiation between behavior that is religious and behavior that is political: Jaynes (1976) argues for a psychological convergence of these two in early history, for example. We can also recognize political behavior occurring at various levels: the term "office politics" has a meaning to anyone who has worked in a large organization, and office politics shares some characteristics with politics at higher levels. Political behavior can also be identified cross-culturally. A priori, then, there is at least some reason to think that economic and political behavior may be different at some fundamental level. If that is the case, the models of these types of behavior will have to be different, though they will undoubtedly share some characteristics.

The Irrelevance of Methodological Individualism

With very few exceptions, international behavior is the behavior of organizations, not individuals. In this respect, the problems of interest in IR are very different from those of an individual deciding how or whether to vote, or a farmer deciding how to price grain. As both the formal (e.g., Arrow, 1963) and bureaucratic-psychological (e.g., Allison, 1971; Janis, 1982) literatures show, the decision behavior of groups is potentially very different from the decision behavior of individuals. Therefore even if individuals behaved according to rational models, there is little reason to assume that aggregates of those individuals would do the same. In this regard IR is profoundly limited in the extent to which it can use models rooted in the assumption of methodological individualism, in contrast with theories of voting behavior, for example.

A related issue is whether the individual is the appropriate unit of analysis for an international relations theory. Granted, international relations is, in the end, the result of individual human behavior. But

it does not necessarily follow that the best way to study
international behavior is by studying individuals: if it
is the case that some aggregate of individuals (e.g., the
bureaucracy or nation) has sufficiently predictable
behavior that a theory can be constructed, parsimony
would argue for dealing at the level of that aggregate.

An excellent analogy to the role of the analysis of
groups even in a world where we know the actions are
determined by individuals is found in the field of
organic chemistry. As Brodbeck notes:

> The reduction of chemistry to physics is by now a
> fairly well-accomplished fact. . . . Once _the laws
> of quantum physics_ were known, it turned ⁻out that
> the (chemical) laws⁻ by which molecules combine could
> be derived from them. Yet, organic chemistry
> appears to be here to stay. In principle, the
> interactions of the complex molecules can be
> derived from the laws of physics about the
> fundamental particles. However, the mathematics of
> the relevant composition laws is so involved that
> it is much simpler to study directly the behavior
> of these organic complexes. (Brodbeck, 1968, p.
> 302)

The untangling of operation of the hemoglobin molecule
(Perutz, 1978) provides an example of this: despite the
fact that the function of the hemoglobin molecule was
known (and fairly simple) and, of course, the relevant
physical laws governing the atoms within that molecule
were known, many years of experimentation with the
aggregate of these atoms was necessary to ascertain how
the molecule functioned.

The situation facing students of international
politics is, arguably, more complicated than that of
organic chemistry, hence there is even less reason to
expect that analysis of international relations on the
basis of the uniform individual will yield results. All
but the most naive observer of international affairs
would reject the hypothesis that

> Preferences are assumed not to change substantially
> over time, nor to be very different between wealthy
> and poor persons, or even between persons in
> different societies and cultures. (Becker, 1976, p.
> 5)

Instead, much of the traditional study of IR deals with
the effects of the clash of cultures, histories, and
personality. Even in the rational choice literature,
Bueno de Mesquita (1981, p. 33), for example, rejects
this hypothesis of uniformity.

International relations is generally dealing in that awkward area where there are more than two actors (ruling out two-person approaches) but not so many that theories of mass behavior (e.g., markets or elections) can be used. Attempts to model the preferences and constraints facing even a single decision maker, e.g., the "operational code" literature or the related "cognitive mapping" literature (see Holsti, 1976, for a review), require information vastly more complex than that used in most economic models and in no cases that I know of has the operation of an international system containing multiple, real (as opposed to hypothesized) actors been simulated using such models. While the assumption of methodological individualism and individual uniformity may be quite useful in predicting market behavior, and perhaps even quasi-market behavior such as that observed in elections, it is irrelevant to the modeling of international relations.

This point is, in a sense, conceded by virtually all rational choice models of international behavior. In these models, the nation (or decision-making structure) is assumed to be a unitary actor behaving as if it were an individual. This is at best a very shaky assumption in light of the literature on foreign policy decision making. It may be the case, as Bueno de Mesquita (1981, 1984) asserts, that this assumption can be defended on positivist grounds so long as no other formal theory provides better predictions, but I would unquestionably urge caution in building too large a structure on such foundations of sand. Observers of foreign policy from Thucydides to Kissinger may have overlooked, in their emphasis on bureaucracy, faction, competition for leadership, and the intricacies of negotiation, the profound simplification that nations behave in most fundamental aspects no differently than a Valley Girl deciding whether to purchase a Big Mac or a Whopper, but this is not self-evident. The historical, anecdotal and theoretical literature on foreign policy argues for a substantially more complicated calculus than that assumed by game theory, expected-utility models, or the rational choice model generally. The behaviors described in that literature have not, and, I will suggest, for the most part cannot, be derived from the assumptions of economic approach given above.

Inefficiency of History

My final argument against building on the rational choice model deals with the issue of maximization, which Frey, Becker, Bueno de Mesquita, and game theory in general all find central to the economic approach. I suggest that however valid this assumption may be in the fast-paced competitive world of the market economy, it is quite inappropriate in the slow, inefficient, information-poor world of international affairs.

Maximizing behavior by individuals is a strong assumption, particularly given that individuals frequently do not consciously maximize. Still, the argument can be made that even if individuals or organizations do not consciously behave according to the assumptions of economic models, they will still behave as if they did because behavior not in accordance with those assumptions will be selected against. In the words of Veblen:

> A gang of Aleutian Islanders slushing about in the wreck and surf with rakes and magical incantations for the capture of shell-fish are held, in point of taxonomic reality, to be engaged in a feat of hedonistic equilibration in rent, wages and interest. (Lerner, 1948, p. 20)

In IR, this runs up against a fundamental problem that March and Olsen (1983) call "the inefficiency of history"--the fact that many social processes change so slowly that even if equilibrium behaviors exist, they are never reached. International behavior clearly falls into this category; institutions and policies can exist for decades as historical anomalies (the Ottoman Empire, US policy towards the PRC prior to 1970, and Berlin come to mind) without any particular pressures for their change. When changes do occur, they are frequently the result of catastrophic transformation of the system (e.g., World Wars I and II) rather than the smooth movement towards an equilibrium. A related problem occurs with respect to the applicability of expected-value calculations in one-time decision: many of the key decisions in international behavior are made only once, and the assumption that expected utility is used in such circumstances becomes questionable.

Related to the inefficiency of the historical process is the lack of information and feedback in the international system. As proponents of the rational model point out, the lack of information by itself does not invalidate the model--if anything, the recognition of the importance of the cost of information and the consequences of imperfect information have been among the more important contributions of this theory. Still, I think that one can reach a point where so little information is available--particularly information directly relevant to the assumptions of the model--that any model assuming such information is rendered useless. As noted earlier, if the source of preference information is revealed preference, international affairs reveals little, and individuals go in and out of the system at a rate which is much more rapid than the change in international affairs. The overall stability of international relations--the preservation of policies over generations or even centuries--must have a basis somewhere other than the mortal individual.

KEY FEATURES OF THE CLASSICAL APPROACH

The preceding discussion has made occasional reference to the "classical" or "traditional" approach to international relations, taking as a given that the reader knows what is being referred to (if not, Dougherty and Pfaltzgraff, 1981, is the now-standard reference). This approach is, of course, not a single approach but a set of approaches sharing some common characteristics which place them at variance with formal models. Since one of the potential advantages that I see in the artifi- intelligence model is greater compatibility with the traditional approach, in this section I will briefly outline these key characteristics.

In doing this, I am accepting the general legitimacy of the traditional approach as a means of studying international behavior, even coexisting with a fully developed formal theory of international relations (which we currently do not have), much as engineering coexists with physics and management coexists with formal economics. Many problems exist which need a solution in the near term that formal methods cannot provide. Just as a physicist in a skidding car does not pause to work out the Newtonian mechanics of the situation, so a diplomat in an unforeseen crisis situation can hardly be expected to use regression analysis. The problem is that existing formal theories of IR show considerably greater divergence from informal theory than does engineering from physics. I would suggest that, given the somewhat dubious pedigree of many of those IR models, born as they are from physics, economics, and whole cloth, more attention to the characteristics of the classic theories might be useful.

Small-N, Large-N Analysis

If statistical studies tend to look for large numbers of cases on a small number of variables, traditional theories do the opposite--a small number (sometimes one, usually a few more) of cases is extensively analyzed with respect to a large number of characteristics. Furthermore, these characteristics usually have some sort of hierarchical ordering--for example, "power" is composed of military, economic, and diplomatic power, each of which can be defined in more specific terms With few exceptions (factor and cluster analysis perhaps) this hierarchical structuring is not a characteristic of formal models, which tend to use only a few simple variables.

Use of Precedent and Analogy

Traditional theory makes extensive use of precedent and analogy in theory construction. The underlying model is a sophisticated version of "If X happened in the past under conditions $C_1 C_2, \ldots, C_n$, then if conditions similar to $C_1, C_2, \ldots C_n$ occur again, X is likely to happen again." The most common evidence provided for any argument in international relations is an historical example, and much of international relations theory consists of explicating a theory by a survey of historical precedent in the context of the theory. With the possible exception of some of the international law literature, IR theory without reference to history is rare.

The formal modeling literature runs against this grain in two ways. First, both the rational and dynamic models are frequently presented in the abstract, without any empirical grounding. To the traditional scholar, this renders them as mathematical abstractions with no a priori claim for relevance to human behavior. Second, most empirical tests of formal theories deal with central tendencies (usually expressed numerically) rather than with the identification of specific discrete sets of conditions.

Flexible Assumptions about Cognition

The traditional literature usually assumes that cognition of some sort is involved in international behavior, except in a few theories of historical determinism (e.g., Toynbee and some variants of Marxism). Furthermore, in most of these theories something resembling self-interest is assumed to be dominant; this assumption is perhaps most clearly made in realist theory. In both these respects traditional theory is similar to rational choice theory. Where the two differ is in the richness of allowable modes of cognition--traditional theory allows great scope for individual idiosyncracies and diffuse types of decision making (and the bureaucratic-psychological literature explores this in detail), whereas rational choice decision

making is highly structured and limited in its assumptions
In addition, few traditional theories would accept the
rational choice assumption that preferences are similar
across actors and time--in fact the emphasis on cultural
characteristics in the traditional literature argues for
the opposite.

The Sentient Organization
as Primary Actor

With the exception of the "Great Man" [sic]
theories, most traditional theories use the organization
as the unit of analysis, or more generally the nation as
a set of interacting organizations. While the nation can
be treated as a unitary actor with respect to some
limited questions (e.g., in the cruder aspects of
balance-of-power theory) few theories go very far without
studying the decision-making parts of that
entity--foreign offices, military bureaucracies,
executives, business organizations, social classes,
political parties, and so forth. These bureaucracies are
assumed to be sentient--that is, they react to their
environment--and they are usually assumed to have
objectives, but they are rarely assumed to be omniscient
or omnipotent, or able to achieve optimal or maximizing
behavior. In addition to starting with the organization,
most traditional theory stops there as well--specific
individuals may be important in determining specific
decisions of an organization in the short term, but rare
is the theory that tries to infer organizational behavior
solely on the basis of individual behaviors.

Massive Data Bases as the
Source of Inductive Theory

A final characteristic of traditional theory is
that it is incredibly data-intensive, and in that sense
highly empirical. The data for a traditional theory is
the historical or case study, and this data is studied in
great detail. As a consequence, the traditional theories
tend to be largely inductive rather than
deductive--historical studies are used to discern general
characteristics, which are then applied to other
historical cases to ascertain their validity. While some
general processes are invoked deductively--the elusive
balance of power being the most common--the bulk of the
literature is an inductive effort. The only major
exception to this is the literature of counter-factuals
(e.g., the study of nuclear war or the world in the year
2050) where deductive principles provide the only means

of study. Not suprisingly, counter-factuals are also the area where formal methods (game theory and simulation, respectively) have made the greatest inroads.

While there are clearly major differences in the traditional and formal approaches, I think these are often differences of language and technique rather than objective. Clearly both approaches are empirical--the objective of international relations research is the study of the real world, not the creation of abstract mathematical or philosophical structures. Both approaches would, in the long term, like to be able to make predictions, and in general both seek to be policy-relevant. Both approaches seek simplifications of the total historical experience into a few principles of behavior. Both have reasonably similar definitions (within paradigmatic variations) of what constitutes international behavior and generally what are and are not interesting problems (e.g., international conflict and international economic inequality are major concerns in some areas of both approaches). The key differences are in the type of approach taken (historical versus statistical), the type of language used (natural versus mathematical) and, out of those, the types of tools available and the types of problems that can be considered.

A DYNAMIC MODEL EMPLOYING ARTIFICIAL INTELLIGENCE METHODS

In light of the differences between the analytic techniques of the traditional IR scholars, and the problems of existing formal techniques (dynamic and statistical models as well as the rational choice model: see Schrodt, 1984b), it would be useful to have some methods which bridge the gap. In my opinion, various developments in the past decade or so in the broad set of computer-oriented techniques[5] known collectively as artificial intelligence (AI)[5] provide some tools for bridging this gap. In this section I will briefly outline such a model, and in the next section demonstrate a simple empirical application of it.

The decision-making model I propose is a fairly straightforward adaptive system based on the use of precedent. In this model, individuals or organizations are assumed to have a base of past experiences. When a new situation arises, a data base is searched for a past experience which matches the situation as closely as possible according to some pattern-matching criterion. That experience is used as a template for the current action: on the basis of past experience one applies a set of rules to determine what should be done. Depending on the outcome of the decision, the data base is either modified or reinforced. I term this model "adaptive precedent-based logic," or APBL.

A simple example of APBL would be: "I am at a red stop light at 3 a.m., with no one in sight. In previous situations like this when I drove through the light, nothing happened and I got where I was going more quickly. Therefore I will drive through the light. If a cop appears from behind a billboard and tickets me, I will think twice next time; if I get away with this, I will probably continue to do it." The model is summarized in Figure 16.1.

Consistent with traditional and rational choice approaches, an APBL model assumes that the decision maker has preferences and constraints, as well as the "common sense" to relate those preferences to the real world. In addition, however, the decision maker has a very large historical data base which may be changing rapidly or slowly, depending on circumstances. This base of experience is largely beyond the decision maker's control except in situations where the decision maker can actively experiment. Pattern-matching rules or theories are used to match the contemporary situation to analogous historical situations. The choice of these rules and their modification is where most of the adaptation in decision-making behavior occurs: changes of behavior are usually due to changes in means and interpretation. Changes in preferences or constraints, and the decisions provided by pattern-matching are frequently suboptimal (in the sense of not maximizing) and inefficient, due to the lack of an adequate base of experience from which to determine behavior.

This emphasis on the knowledge base in the model follows a general trend in AI, the discovery that human-like cognition seems to depend far less on axiomatic reasoning than on information:

> The first principle of knowledge engineering is that the problem solving power exhibited by an intelligent agent's performance is primarily the consequence of its knowledge base, and only secondarily a consequence of the inference method employed. Expert systems must be knowledge-rich even if they are methods-poor. This is an important result and one that has only recently become well understood in AI. For a long time AI focused its attentions almost exclusively on the development of clever inference methods; almost any inference method will do. The power resides in the knowledge. (Feigenbaum, 1983)

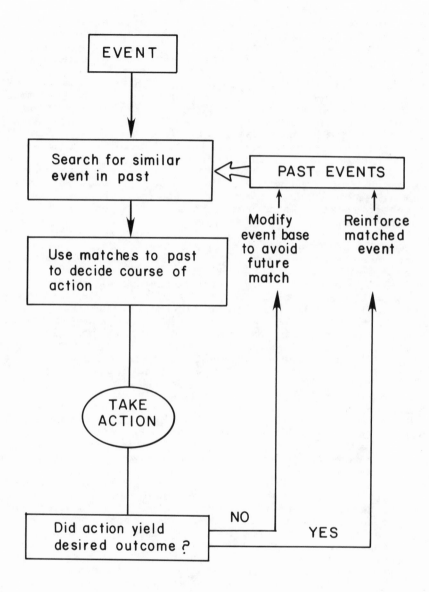

Figure 16.1 Adaptive Precedent-Based Logic Model

The APBL model is also consistent with the observa-vation that the human brain and human organizations are considerably more efficient at storage and recall of information than at the logical manipulation of information. For example, most evidence indicates that chess experts use large amounts of pattern recognition as shortcuts to problem solving, and their performance slows considerably when they actually have to solve problems. Mathematicians work the same way, and most research in expert systems points in this direction. In other words, a lot of our "thinking" is simply recall masquerading as logical processing.

In a similar vein, an organization may depend largely on precedent and standard operating procedure when dealing with day-to-problems, and a mature organization may develop sufficient experience that actual analytical problem solving is virtually eliminated, until such time as an unprecedented crisis occurs. If this is in fact the typical pattern of organizational behavior, then any attempt at the construction of a political reasoning model primarily out of logical principles (e.g., expected values operating on indifference curves) will at best only crudely approximate actual behavior, because, in effect, it is capturing only the rule-based parts of cognition and not the data base itself. The key question for homo politicus is not "what do I want?" but rather "what is attainable and how?"--politics as the art of the possible. The single strongest argument for a policy is to show that it has been successful in the past, and to use whatever method was used in the past as a guide, with suitable transformations. That in turn means that behavior will be driven by information at least as much as by rules, and, for example, the same set of rules could potentially produce either extremely conservative or extremely radical behavior depending on the event base, a behavior swing which otherwise requires a shift in rules.

The second major component in the model which derives from AI is the concept of pattern matching. In the context of traditional IR, pattern matching rules are essentially theory: a means of organizing history and experience, connecting seemingly unrelated events, and filling in the gaps between events where insufficient information is known. For example, an unreformed naive international relations realist, confronted with the fact that a war has broken out, will assume that there must have been a breakdown in the balance of power; an unreformed naive Leninist, given the same information, would assume that somewhere capitalists saw that there was money to be made from the event. Individuals are more likely to change their theoretical approach than their preferences and logical rules, as the same events might be explainable by several theories with roughly equal effectiveness. As this event base changes, individual behavior could be expected to change in response to it, so the model provides a mechanism whereby changing the information base of the decision maker rather than changing the rules of decision making could alter behavior. This is in line with Simon's approach of modeling cognitive behavior as a set of simple rules operating in a complex environment, rather than complex rules operating in a simple environment.

It could be argued that there is nothing in the APBL model that could not be subsumed in the rational choice framework: I've acknowledge that preferences and constraints exist, that the historical base is an example of incomplete information, and that the adaptive characteristics are not inconsistent with Frey's definition of homo oeocnomicus. If this is the case, then nothing except empty rhetoric has been gained in the previous critique.

I would differentiate the APBL model from the rational models on three grounds. First, as I define the model, the maximization is quite different from that assumed in most rational choice theories. Maximization occurs only with respect to pattern matching against an imperfect data base, rather than with respect to some set of all possible outcomes. Decision making in this model is primarily constrained by the availability of information.

Second, the methods by which the model reacts to past events must be explicitly specified in the definition of the pattern-matching model. The pattern matching constraints what the model can do, in the sense that a pattern-matching system which matches everything would be meaningless. This makes the model; more directly falsifiable, while still preserving the possibility that different decision-making units might (and undoubtedly do) employ different types of pattern matching.

Finally, and most importantly, the model (when fully specified) can be tested against the information which is available to decision makers: history. A fully specified model can change in response to changes in directly observable information, rather than waiting for the trickle of information provided by the revealed preference.

AN EXAMPLE OF A FORMAL MODEL OF
HISTORICAL PATTERN MATCHING

While it is easy to construct the hypothetical characteristics of a precedent-based system, this is clearly stupid until one has been constructed. The following discussion will give one example of an element of such a system, based on Schrodt (1984a), to indicate that such a system appears possible.

The basic issue that was addressed in this model was whether it is possible to design a process to "recognize" specific patterns of past behavior based on information which is similar to the historical information available to decision makers. Briefly, the objective was to compare the relations between two dyads during the year 1983 to determine whether dyads which had similar relations during that period (e.g., both conflictual or both cooperative) could be distinguished from dyads where the relationships were different (e.g., one cooperative and one conflictual). "History" in this instance was approximated by use of a WEIS-like events data set, and more specifically a simplified WEIS code which used only the first two digits of the three-digit WEIS code. This coding scheme yields 22 categories of behavior, ranging from "Yield," "Comment," "Consult," "Approve," "Promise," and "Grant" at the cooperative end of the scale to "Threaten," "Demonstrate," "Reduce Relations," "Expel," "Seize," and "Force" at the conflictual end of the scale. Details of the WEIS coding scheme can be found in McClelland (1976).

The pattern recognition was done with Levenshtein metrics, a general technique for sequence comparison which is described in detail in Sankoff and Kruskal (1983). The Levenshtein metric provides a quantitative measure of the distance between two sequences of items by a weighted total of the number of insertion, deletion, and substitution operations necessary to make one sequence match the other. In the pilot study of this method, the insertion and deletion weights were approximated by the rank of the frequency of the events (i.e., rare events were more "costly" to insert and delete than frequent events) and the substitution weights were simply the differences between the WEIS scores, which are roughly ordinal. The smaller the Levenshtein distance, the greater the similarity between two sequences.

In order to get around the problem of parsing the total set of event sequences into discrete sequences, a statistical bootstrap technique was used to find the approximate distribution of the Levenshtein distances between randomly chosen ten-event sequences. Figure 16.2 shows the probability distribution of the Levenshtein

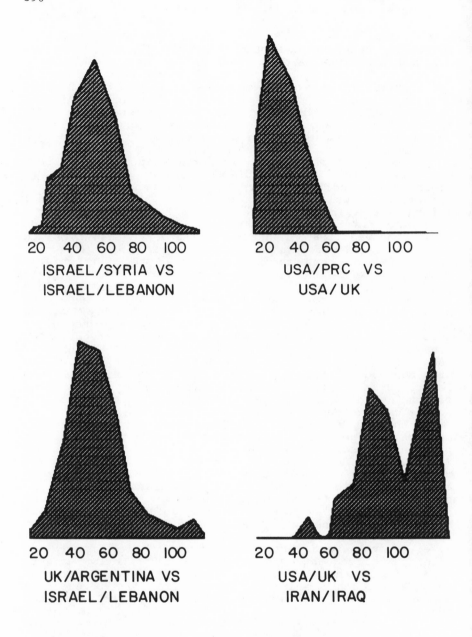

Figure 16.2 Distribution of Levenshtein Distance

distances between randomly selected ten-event sequences for four dyad pairs, based on 100 or more Monte Carlo experiments. In each experiment, a ten-event sequence was chosen for the event history of each dyad in the pair, and the Levenshtein distance between those two ten-event sequences was computed using the metric described above. The resulting distribution of those distances for each dyad pair is given in Figure 16.2. The results for additional dyad pairs are reported in the original paper.

As indicated in Figure 16.2, the system more or less functions as intended, and does particularly well, given the rough approximations used in both the coding and the Levenshtein metric. In general, like dyads have lower Levenshtein scores than unlike dyads. At one extreme, the comparison between the USA/UK dyad and the USA/PRC dyad, both characterized during 1983 by intense but generally cooperative negotiations (over Argentina and Taiwan, respectively), shows a distribution highly skewed to the left, indicating that most sequences were similar. At the other extreme, the comparison between the USA/UK and Iran/Iraq dyads (the latter being almost exclusively conflictual) shows a skew to the right. The comparison between dyads which were engaged in conflict again shows general agreement, though the scores are much more dispersed due to the bootstrapping technique used. The scores indicating high disagreement usually arise when a sequence taken from a period when the dyads were actively engaged in conflict is compared with a sequence from the other dyad which occurred either before or after the active stage of the conflict.

Where does this get us? The point of this exercise was simply to indicate the feasibility of the pattern-recognition techniques required in the APBL model. It is only a feasibility study, but nonetheless a successful feasibility study. In particular, it indicates that it is possible to do the following:

(1) Utilize discrete historical events directly rather than aggregate numerical summaries of those events.

(2) Use a previously coded set of events, rather than an artificial set of events or one requiring elaborate recoding.

(3) Recognize similar sets of events based on an a priori measure of similarity.

(4) Do this using methods developed in the AI literature for other purposes.

This is not to argue that the Levenshtein method is unique or even the best way to specify such pattern recognition. In fact, based on more recent research (Schrodt, 1985), I suspect that syntactic pattern-recognition methods (see Fu, 1974) provide a richer set of techniques. However, this does indicate that some AI techniques could be directly applied to modeling international relations decision making.

CONCLUSION

The APBL model I have introduced in this paper and the feasibility study of the Levenshtein metric as a pattern-matching technique are intended only as introductions to the type of models possible with AI techniques: neither is intended as the final word on the subject. With the exception of the work of Hayward Alker (e.g., Alker and Christensen, 1972; Alker and Greenberg, 1976) and studies done since 1980, there is little actually available in this area, and hence AI does not have the track record of the techniques I have been criticizing. Warts and blemishes will doubtlessly emerge on this newborn baby, if the infant itself survives, much as they have in game theory and the Richardson model.

At the same time, AI allows us to extend formal modeling into areas which are inaccessible to existing models by transcending the intrinsic limitations of those techniques. As I have argued here and elsewhere (Schrodt, 1984b), the study of international relations poses major problems for existing modeling techniques--whether rational choice, dynamic or statistical--and to move beyond those constraints will require new methods. The techniques developed in AI appear to answer many of those problems, without raising disproportionate numbers of new problems.

By definition, AI techniques are computer-intensive This has a couple of implications. First and most obviously, it is possible to use existing computing resources, and to use the techniques developed in other fields using computers, when dealing with a new problem. Thus, the existing investment in machine-readable data sets can be maintained, existing hardware can be used (perhaps with an additional expenditure in software), and developments in other fields can be borrowed, just as existing techniques borrow from mathematics, physics, and economics. For example, the Levenshtein metric uses methods developed for the analysis of DNA sequences in biochemistry.

On a more subtle level, the use of computer-intensive models enables one to experiment with models and explore the implications of complexities with greater ease than one can with analytical techniques.

This is an advantage that simulation and statistical models have always had in comparison with differential equation and rational choice models; AI is similar to the former in this regard. The importance of easy experimentation should not be discounted: one of the reasons that differential equation and rational models have not moved very far from their roots is the frequent difficulty of obtaining meaningful results when even minor changes are made in their assumptions. The flip side of this is that AI could encourage the social science variation of hacking--a problem to which simulations and statistical studies are not immune--but this problem is a matter of discipline rather than an intrinsic drawback to the technique.

Because AI models are already implemented on computers, there is little reason why they cannot incorporate computationally extensive estimation techniques. In this regard, AI is following a general trend in statistics away from analytically simple stochastic structures (e.g., the Normal family) towards whatever stochastic structures the data may demand. This is convenient for IR, since the stochastic distributions we encounter are rarely well behaved.

The ability to use computationally intensive statistical technique also means that a model is likely to be tested, or at least estimated, provided that some data set is available to provide a test case. Given that one has created a model on the computer, going to the additional effort of testing the model in some form requires little additional effort. As a consequence it is less likely that AI models will succumb to the trap into which rational choice models have fallen: the generation of a self-referential literature largely devoid of empirical validation (Leonteif, 1982).

The cognitive structures available in AI techniques are far richer than those available in the rational choice literature, and as a consequence a wider variety of types of cognition can be explored. Much of this richness extends from the fact that AI models do not have to be analytically solvable, but some also stems from the fact that the data structures and data bases themselves are more complex. Even the simplest AI model of decision making is usually far more complex than the average model of homo oeconomicus, and modifications of the decision strategies can be made without difficulty.

I am fully aware that AI has a history of unfulfilled promises--the fabled "typewriter which takes dictation" ranks right next to "nuclear power too cheap to meter" in the list of much-heralded nonachievements of the twentieth century. At the same time, models (programs) using AI techniques are diagnosing medical problems with success rates comparable to that of human experts;

credible chess-, poker-, and backgammon-playing computers, once grandly proclaimed to be cognitive impossibilities, are available for $50 at the local toy store. AI may be over-hyped, but there is fire beneath the smoke.

NOTES

1. Criticisms in this same vein of the two other major fields of formal modeling in international relations--statistical models and dynamic models--are found in Schrodt (1984b).

2. Editors' note: Unfortunately, conflicting obligations prevented Bruno Frey from attending the Boulder conference.

3. Bueno de Mesquita (1981) (and work of his students) provides one of the few rational choice models that have been empiricially tested, and thus is of necessity a target of my criticism. This should not be taken as indicating disapproval of Bueno de Mesquita's efforts in this direction. By actually testing his theory, Bueno de Mesquita has at least gone beyond the bulk of the rational choice literature, whose primary empirical contribution lies in proving that people don't vote, public goods aren't provided, coalitions are minimal, and candidates take equal positions on issues. In contrast with this literature, Bueno de Mesquita's efforts seldom stray below the bounds of common sense. But, as the saying goes, pioneers can be recognized by the arrows in their backs.

4. Frey (1983, p. 3) also notes the postulated existence of two variations of homo sociologicus which challenge the dominance of homo oeconomicus as a universal model of behavior, though neither is the coalition builder that I propose here as homo politicus.

5. Barr et al. (1982) provide an encyclopedic survey of AI, and Sylvan and Chan (1984) have written the only book discussing AI with respect to academic international relations. Anderson and Thorson (1982), Schrodt (1984a and b), and Mefford (1984) also provide surveys of some applications to international relations. It should be noted that AI is a set of techniques rather than a single technique or model, much as statistics is a set of techniques, and many of these techniques do not involve directly simulating human cognitive processes.

17 Changes in Foreign Policy Across Time: The Logical Analysis of a Succession of Decision Problems Using Logic Programming

From differential equation models to game theory, this volume provides examples from the full range of formal approaches to modeling political conflict. The present chapter marks a departure. In terms of substance, it addresses the perennial issue of the use of force in the pursuit of interest in opposition to right. More specifically, it examines how that question is formulated and reformulated by a political community over time in the face of war and internal crisis. In terms of method, the work reported here relies on the formal but essentially qualitative mechanisms of logic. The predicate calculus is used to render the assertions and inferences that shape and determine the decision to respond to a provocation or opportunity in one way rather than another. The purpose is not only to inspect the rationales behind those courses of actions that are seriously entertained, but to explore the set of meaningful options in its entirety. The object of study is political argument and inference, but the theoretical interest is focused not on individual arguments or examples of reasoning, but on systems of arguments. Our purpose is to probe and record the changes in the options that a system of argument will sustain. To do this requires examining the boundary between options or criteria which are seriously considered and possibilities or principles which are not. The assumption is that this boundary changes over time as a complex function of the makeup of the community and the world around it.

To anticipate the empirical case to be explored in the later sections of this chapter, an example of a changing universe of argument is documented in Thucydides's history: in the first years of the war, while self-interest is the paramount consideration, Athens's policies toward rebel cities are complex, due to additional considerations of right and retribution. As the war progresses, the appeals to such norms carry less and less weight until, ultimately, at Melos, the decision problem for the Athenians has undergone a radical simplification: all considerations except that of naked

401

power have been purged. A political community, whether it takes the form of a cloistered elite or an open forum, can be viewed as a system that collectively reasons, argues, and rationalizes on the basis of what it has experienced and what it believes. The dynamics of change in the structure of how a community collectively reasons ranks, or should rank, as one of the foremost concerns of formal and empirical political theory. The purpose of the formal approach introduced here is to track such fundamental change in political imagination and reasoning.

The approach to be introduced overlaps with game theory and its extensions. Game theory, despite the variety of abstract situations it investigates, is a limited case of the more general problem of political inference and decision. It is restricted to decision problems in which options are given and well defined. A predefined structure is assumed. Our concern is with both the prior question of how options are identified and interpreted and the subsequent, game-theoretical question of how given options are ranked or combined into strategies. In short, our concerns are related to, but logically prior to, those of game theory. Options and the criteria for the evaluation of options are not given a priori, but must be constructed through a process involving reason, imagination, and rhetoric. Using Marc Kilgour's distinction between the established concept of "game" and the more fundamental notion of "gameboard" or universe of games which the concept of game presupposes,[1] our interest is in how the gameboard itself is structured and, more generally, how it is reorganized through time.

The predicate calculus offers several advantages for a project of this sort. Though limited in some important respects (McCawley, 1981; Sowa, 1984), first-order logic is a descriptively adequate formalism for systematically expressing much of what political analysts and theorists study. This is to be expected, given the intertwined history of logic and classical rhetoric (Kneale and Kneale, 1962; Perelman and Olbrechts-Tyteca, 1969). A second advantage, and one vital for our purpose of examining systems of argument and what they will and will not sustain, is the proof-theoretical concept of "consistency," which provides a basis for circumscribing a universe of debate. There are additional advantages in the use of logic as a modeling language. These will become apparent as we program and simulate a political community and trace the structure of its argumentation. By modeling the logic of debate, it is possible to reconstruct and then watch the evolution of the patterns of reasoning that determine the purposes and actions pursued by a community. The attempt will be to replicate the activity of a political community as it reasons, calculates, and debates policies on the basis of what it believes to be true or possible in a world in which it competes with other communities.

There are several reasons for choosing Thucydides's history as a laboratory for testing the approach. Thucydides's account remains the most penetrating and most complete examination of the master theme of the use of force in the pursuit of interest. It initiates the theoretical and the descriptive treatment of political power (Cornford, 1971; Halle, 1955). Thucydides records and reconstructs the evolution of this theme in Athenian policy under the pressure of protracted war. He preserves the full complexity of the issues as he documents the thought and speech of the spokesmen and leaders of the communities locked in the struggle for dominance. Thucydides' purpose, like ours, is not only to reconstruct the reasoning behind the actions, but to trace out the fundamental changes in the thought and character of Athens as manifest in its motives and behavior.

Thucydides's account, in particular his dramatizations of crucial debates, provides windows on the political mind of Athens. Everything, including the deepest motives, is open to view. In this Thucydides exhibits a quality of exposition which Eric Auerbach identifies with the Homeric legends: in the hands of the narrator light penetrates into every corner and crevice of motive and assumption. In Auerbach's characterization, the Hellenic tradition is marked by a style in which "externalized, uniformly illuminated phenomena, at a definite time and in a definite place [are] connected together without lacunae in a perpetual foreground. . . ." " . . . Like the separate phenomena themselves, their relationships--their temporal, local, causal, final, consecutive, comparative, concessive, antithetical, and conditional limitations--are brought to light in perfect fullness. . . ."[2] While it may lack the mystery and suspense that Auerbach prizes in other traditions, a history written in this literary form is an ideal source of evidence for the type of analysis introduced here. It exposes the thoughts and motives behind events; it supplies the material from which the operative logic of a political community can be extracted.

In addition to its themes and its transparency, The History of the Peloponnesian War is a natural choice for a study of how a system of political calculation changes in the face of events, because Thucydides is concerned with changes of the most fundamental kind in the character of a community and its capacity to act. The history records the steady loss of civic virtue and the growing corruption of the leadership and public alike, which results, ultimately, in the loss of that community's capacity to recognize and pursue its true interest. This protracted change over the span of a generation is revealed in changes in the universe of debate. Not only is there a change in policy following the death of Pericles, there is a change in the community's very capacity to conceive and execute policy. The change involves the character and constitution of Athens as a political entity. The story of Athens and its empire is not only a story of hubris and ensuing nemesis, but is one of the steady erosion and eventual collapse of a state's ability to formulate and judge courses of action. Structural change of this order is the object to be analyzed and put on display in the model.

The question of change in the character and capacity of a policy community is in no way restricted to epic histories. It applies generally to all political communities, including our own. A recurring theme in the present debate over US foreign policy centers on the claim that the United States has lost the capacity to act decisively in pursuit of its interest. This claim asserts in effect that options which were not only considered but acted upon in the past are, at this point in time, no longer recognized as possible or justified. A fundamental change has taken place which is not necessarily a reflection of change in strategic power; the shift is explained in terms of loss of nerve or will. Perhaps the starkest recent example of this line of argument is Jeane Kirkpatrick's remarks in <u>Commentary</u> in December 1979. Kirkpatrick outlines what she sees as the progressive loss of nerve in American policy toward Latin America. The immediate object of her criticism is President Carter's passive response to the election of a leftist coalition in Bolivia. According to Kirkpatrick, Carter's preoccupation with legality marked just one more backward step in the United States's progressive abdication of power in the region. To Carter's unwillingness to oppose the new regime she contrasts the activist steps which earlier, more confident administrations would have taken if faced with a government containing "a significant Communist/Castroite component." She asserts that if confronted with such a government five years earlier, "the US would have welcomed a coup," and ten years earlier "the US would have sponsored it," while fifteen years earlier "we would have conducted it."[3]

The truth of Kirkpatrick's claim, and the validity of any comparable generalization as to the changing character of foreign policy, cannot be ascertained by examining actions that are a matter of historical record. The claim is not a statement of fact. It is more encompassing, involving a political community's capacity to act. The issue entails not only behavior observed, but the set of all possible actions seriously recognized as options by a political community at a point in time. The generalization Kirkpatrick advances implies counter-factuals, such as the assertion that actions that were expected or automatic at some point in the past have now been pushed to the periphery of what is considered realistic. No recounting of the facts of American involvement or noninvolvement would suffice to disprove an assertion of this order. What is required is a full reconstruction of the system of argument and inference that determines which options are deemed realistic and which ones are perceived as anachronistic, naive, or utterly foolish. To confirm or disconfirm claims like that which Kirkpatrick puts forward requires an analysis of the order we will undertake.

Arguments of this type present a number of issues for systematic inquiry that go well beyond standard questions of data collection and hypothesis checking. While students of foreign policy can assemble and classify events, perhaps ordering them into time series, it is an open question whether methods exist for conceptualizing and measuring fundamental change in the "character" of policy which is, by definition, only partially expressed in the events on record. Change in, for example, the observed conduct of interventions is at best incomplete evidence for change in a state's propensity to intervene. The problem for the theoretically minded analyst is to penetrate to the reasoning that underlies the recognition that certain courses of action, including, possibly, intervention scenarios, are live options, while other policies are unthinkable. Recording and arraying observed behavior or policy outcomes is but a first step in the theoretical investigation of the evolution of policy. Such analysis must ultimately scrutinize the universe of debate and discourse. Changes in that universe determine what is conceivable, what is worthy of serious consideration, and what is, on the other hand, implausible, ridiculous, or simply beyond present understanding.

The effort to reconstruct the reasoning and perception from observed behavior, e.g., the actual use of force, is difficult not only because of the complexity of the linkage, but because the empirical record is inevitably too sparse and too uneven to adequately mirror underlying changes in the formulation of policy. The mismatch between the complexity of the problem of reconstructing the formulation of policy and the limited leverage that the record of events can provide is illustrated in accounts of Soviet and American interventions (Hosmer and Wolfe, 1983; Kaplan, 1981). The richness of the interpretations imposed contrasts starkly with the motley sample of cases. The historical data, rather than supplying the patterns, is assigned the secondary role of illustrating generalizations or trends. Just as with Kirkpatrick's insights, the interpretations

typically far exceed the information that the data
contains. It is as if the questions the interpretations
pursue are of a wholly different scale from the questions
the empirical evidence collected can answer even in
principle. This same mismatch between the question that
motivates an analysis and the answers that the evidence
collected can support is endemic in the field of
international relations. It afflicts a large body of
work, including studies concerned with war initiation,
crisis management by international organizations, and
similar investigations. The questions are out of scale
with the evidence.

FROM THE LOGIC OF EXPLANATION TO THE
LOGIC INHERENT IN A UNIVERSE OF DEBATE

In a number of respects our efforts to represent a
policy community as a system of logical inference
generalizes that work in historiography which has explored
the connections among logical inference, historical
explanation, and the structure of historical narrative.
The step from the event to the reasoning behind the event
is consonant with the characterization of the historian's
research program as one involving the reconstruction of
intentional actions (Dray, 1957; Collinwood, 1947; Croce,
1923). In a fair but not overly generous summary of the
program by one of William Dray's critics, the analysis of
historical change is resolved into the analysis of a
sequence of intentional acts viewed as decision problems:

> . . . given a particular social situation--one or
> more individuals [identify] goals to be pursued;
> then, given the ensuing state of affairs, it is once
> again asked what human agents might be expected to
> set themselves to do, etc. etc. Thus history is
> interpreted as a linear sequence of intelligible
> human actions, and tracing the course of these lines
> of action is regarded as constituting a proper
> reconstruction of the past. (Mandelbaum, 1967, 416)

This view, perhaps best expressed by William Dray,
has been criticized on grounds that other forces,
including those that shape situations, are immediately
involved as determinants in any historical episode.
Critics object that Dray overestimates the role of
purposive behavior in the determination of events
(Mandelbaum, 1967). Keeping this in mind, the notion of
an underlying decision problem, with its overly rational
connotations, can be replaced with the larger notion of a
universe of policy or a universe of discourse that resides
within a community of policy makers, critics, and other

players. This universe contains not only the goals and objectives of the aggregate of individuals in their various corporate identities, but also contains the constraints and situational factors that enter into the formulation and evaluation of courses of action. The function of the individuals acting within this universe of information and imagination is to collectively, perhaps via various coalitions, hammer out scenarios that orient and justify policies.

Schematically, the activity of constructing scenarios on the basis of the information and beliefs resident in a policy universe must proceed according to a logic much like that employed by historians, who, in many ways, are engaged in the same activity of explaining and justifying through the construction of narratives.[4] Recognizing that efforts to conceptualize the structure of historical explanation excites as much skepticism as acceptance (Mandelbaum, 1967; Gruner, 1969; Dray, 1969; Ely, 1969), the work by Dray, Danto, and others does provide an initial sketch of what is entailed in the historian's activity. Arthur Danto presents the activity of historical narration as one of chaining together a succession of significant changes that lead from some initial situation or set of conditions to some subsequent event. In his notation, an episode or "atomic unit" within an historical narrative entails three propositions: roughly, some situation obtains at a given time, a new situation that differs in some important respect obtains at a later point time, and some act, cause, or process intervenes that is responsible for the change. A succession of such units, linked one to the next, forms a series. In Danto's depiction the actions or points of change are represented by slashes, each of which is labeled by a capital letter. Dots are used to represent the causes of these changes. A sequence of episodes takes the form of a succession of slashes and dots, e.g.,

$$F\ G\ H\ I\ J\ K$$
$$.../././././.../...$$

The purpose of rendering an historical account in this reduced form is to emphasize that it consists essentially of a chain of inferences, each of which takes the logical form

(x)	Fx --> Gx	[inference rule]
	Fa	[given or consequence of prior inference]
Therefore:	—————————— Ga	[consequence or conclusion]

This syllogism closely resembles Hempel's "Covering Law" model of scientific explanation, which assumes that modus ponens is the core form of inference used in scientific argument (Hempel, 1965).

Danto's effort to depict the logic of historical explanation can serve to relate the analytic purpose of the historian to that of the foreign policy theorist. Only the events that are a matter of record properly belong to Danto's scheme. But these actions and events are, at least in part, the product of calculations and debate. In going beyond a strict chronicle, the historian is engaged in reconstructing this reasoning. If we pursue the question of change further, it is clear that the structure of the decision problems gives rise, at another level, to a second time series. Though it is theoretically possible that exactly the same set of judgments and inferences underlie an entire sequence of actions, it is more likely that the set of assumptions and the rules of inferences that prefigure and guide decisions are themselves changing over time. This second time series is pictured in Figure 17.1, along with that which Danto depicts. In this way the analytic problem for the political theorist is juxtaposed to that of the historian.

The foreign policy analyst interested in the changing structure of the decision problem associated with changes in policy is concerned with a time series not of events but of perceptions and reasoning. To give this notion substance and to flesh in the diagram in Figure 17.1. Danto's undefined predicates can be replaced by events and episodes in Thucydides's history. This is pictured in Figure 17.2. The boxes, left empty for the time being, represent the universe of debate and calculation associated with Athenian policy and actions in each of these cases. The boxes symbolize moments in the evolving universe of debate and discourse out of which policy emerges.

RENDERING THE LOGIC OF ATHENIAN POLICY ON REBELLIOUS CITIES CIRCA THE FIFTH YEAR OF THE PELOPONNESIAN WAR

In keeping with the initial sketch of the research problem, we distinguish between an action taken and the reasoning and assumptions that motivate it. This distinction is between policy in the narrow sense of an observable action, and the universe of alternatives and rationales that comprise the decision problem out of which individual policies emerge. The policy actually pursued is but one of a universe of alternatives that are, in principle, both possible and plausible. While much of the work in policy analysis is concerned with the operation of decision rules, voting rules, and the like, which rank or

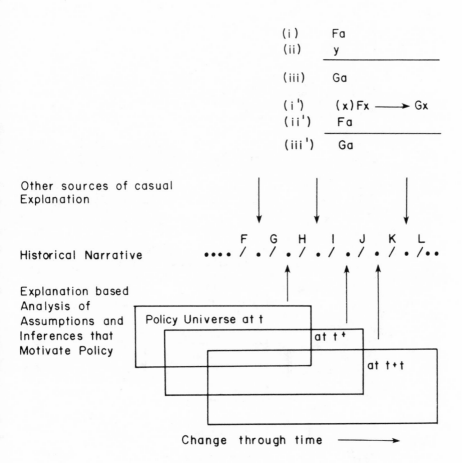

(i)   Fa

(ii)   y

(iii)   Ga

(i')   (x)Fx ⟶ Gx

(ii')   Fa

(iii')   Ga

Other sources of casual Explanation

F   G H I J K L

Historical Narrative

Explanation based Analysis of Assumptions and Inferences that Motivate Policy

Policy Universe at t

at t'

at t'+t

Change through time ⟶

(Danto's predicate symbols, F, G, etc., represent, roughly, states of the world at points in time; the dots represent transitions which carry one state of the world into a subsequent state. Each such transition involves a logical inference of the form represented in the left-hand corner (i,ii,iii), which is a relaxation of Hempel's use of modus ponens (i',ii',iii'); an historical narrative is a series or chain of such forms. (Danto, Ch. XI) In principle, the middle terms in each of these transitions signifies a cause or action and requires an explanation. An explication of the changing policy universe, represented by overlapping boxes, provides one source of explanation.)

Figure 17.1: Expanding Danto's "Logical Map" of the Structure of Historical Explanation.

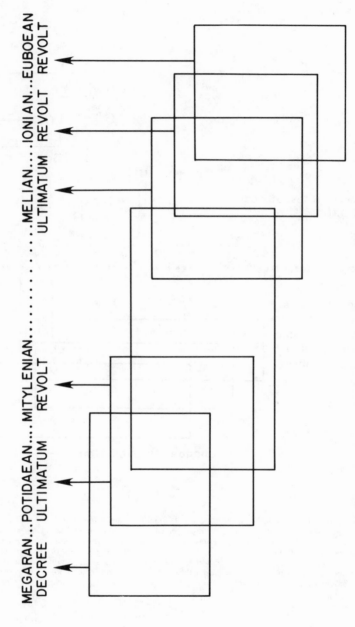

Figure 17.2 Sequence of Cases Involving Rebellion against Athens

MEGARAN...POTIDAEAN...MITYLENIAN..................MELIAN....IONIAN...EUBOEAN
DECREE   ULTIMATUM   REVOLT   ULTIMATUM   REVOLT   REVOLT

select among possible courses of action, the concern here
is with the prior question of what bounds the universe of
choice. This question concerns not simply the options
considered, but the set or space of all options that might
have been considered given the inferences that govern the
selection and evaluation of courses of action. In
explaining a decision the task for the analyst is
ultimately to recover this universe of debate and
calculation.

Given the sheer number of options and variations on
options that might theoretically exist, the space of
alternatives is too large for enumeration. For this
reason, in the effort to identify the bounds of the
universe of policies and to explore its internal
structure, we adopt a standard tactic in such situations
and substitute for the task of enumeration the task of
specifying the discriminate or generating function that
characterizes the set of interest. The set of options can
be defined as that universe of candidate policies which is
consistent with the assumptions and rules of inference
that can be shown to be operative at a point in time. A
substantial number of these assumptions and rules are
introduced implicitly as specific policies are advocated
or criticized. The justification for a policy, or the
debate over the advisability of one policy over another,
invokes criteria that belong to some governing universe of
discourse. In short, in making the case for a particular
course of action, arguments are advanced that may
adumbrate ranges of possible options. These arguments and
appeals, taken in aggregate, constitute the constraints
and requirements against which options are measured.

In Thucydides's history, these assumptions are
frequently recorded in the reconstructed speeches. In
other histories or accounts such evidence is sought in the
memoranda, remembered conversations, records of debate,
and the like, which historians sift through in their
efforts to explain the actions and objectives of an actor
or regime. The effort is to reconstruct that universe of
perception and reason. A strategy for extracting and then
examining such a universe can be illustrated by use of the
speeches Thucydides reassembles. Specifically, the purpose
is to reconstruct the progressive change in Athenian
thinking on the question of what steps should be taken in
the face of rebellion within the empire. This question is
selected because of its resonance with present-day foreign
policy issues like those Jeane Kirpatrick addresses in her
abbreviated history of policy of intervention.
Thucydides's history is used because Thucydides is a keen
observer of the changing universe of policy that marks the
erosion of Athenian politics. The debate over Mitylene,
as one of the best documented cases in the series of
Athenian responses to revolt or the threat of revolt, will

serve as an experimental case on which to apply a new form of analysis. That debate, recounted below, presents a catalogue of essential assumptions, constraints, and rules of inference that frame the search for a viable policy. The arguments that comprise the debate represent a sample from the policy universe that obtained in Athens at that time. The problem for the analyst who would reconstruct this universe is one of rendering the sample in a form that permits systematic examination. A proposal for how this might be accomplished is outlined and demonstrated in the section on the modeling strategy. Before presenting that technique, the case to which it is to be applied is introduced.

ONE CASE IN THE SERIES: THE EVIDENCE THUCYDIDES PROVIDES

Breaking into the narrative in the fourth year of the war, the cities on the island of Lesbos, including the largest, Mitylene, are in revolt against the Athenians. Athens sends a force to besiege Mitylene, which capitulates the following year on the condition that its case be heard before the assembly in Athens. On the arrival of the Mitylenians in Athens, the Athenians "in the fury of the moment [are] determined to put to death not only the prisoners . . . but the whole adult male population of Mitylene, and to make slaves of the women and children" (III, 36).[5] The following day they repent the harshness of this sentence and reopen the question for debate. The case for butchering the population is made by Cleon, who argues that Athens's imperial interest is best served by the deterrent value of summary execution. In opposition to Cleon, Diodotus asserts that the value of the deterrent is questionable, and that Athens's interest is better served by a more discriminating policy.

For Thucydides, the arguments voiced by Cleon and Diodotus constitute the range of options that were seriously under consideration at this point in time. Both spokesmen proceed from the assumption that matters of right and justice are of no relevance; policy is to be predicated solely on what can be shown to be in the best interest of the Athenian state. Following Cleon's plea that the original policy be executed as commanded, Diodotus advances the alternative course of action, which is subsequently adopted, one in which the conspirators are to be executed and the innocent left unharmed. In support of this policy, Diodotus repeats Cleon's initial assumptions regarding the injury that Mitylene has committed against Athens through its revolt; he furthermore adopts Cleon's premise that the Athenian response should not be determined on the basis of justice or right, but solely on grounds of expediency. After asserting that deterrents, no matter how brutal, generally fail to serve their purpose, he proceeds to argue that if Cleon's policy is adopted, Athens's imperial interest will suffer. He draws two scenarios. The first argues that, should a city rebel and then reconsider its action, if all that can be expected from Athens is a sentence of death, then it would have no motive to negotiate or surrender. As a necessary consequence, then, once rebellion commences, Athens will be forced to undertake a costly siege that results inevitably in a decimated city which is of no value to the empire. The second scenario introduces the assumption that all rebellious cities are composed of factions, one of which is the natural ally of Athens. Again positing that Athens follows Cleon's recommendation, Diodotus follows out the implications of such a policy:

> Only consider what a blunder you would commit in doing as Cleon recommends. As things are at present, in all the cities the people is your friend, and either does not revolt with the oligarchy, or, if forced to do so, becomes at once the enemy of the insurgents; so in the war with the hostile city you have the masses on your side. But if you butcher the people of Mitylene, who had nothing to do with the revolt, . . . first you will commit the crime of killing your benefactors; and next you will play directly into the hands of the higher classes, who when they induce their cities to rise, will immediately have the people on their side, through your having announced in advance the same punishment for those who are guilty and for those who are not. (III, 47, pp. 179-80)

The debate between Cleon and Diodotus illustrates how Thucydides assembles and recreates decision problems at crucial points in history. As in similar moments throughout the account, Thucydides uses the device of dramatized speeches to present the reasoning and assumptions which motivate a course of action. In effect he freezes the narrative of events and, through the reconstructed arguments, opens a window on the thought and calculations that underlie policy. He records only the epitome of the considerations entertained, stripping away what is redundant or irrelevant. While he strives for veracity, it is the thrust of the most essential arguments and not a verbatim record that interests him. As he states at the outset of the history in his justification of the device, " . . . my habit has been to make the speakers say what was in my opinion demanded of them by the various occasions, of course adhering as closely as

possible to the general sense of what they really said"
(I, 22, p. 13). Thucydides uses the device sparingly; it
is employed only at those critical turning points in the
course of events where a decision is to be made or a
policy initiated which portends significant consequences.
Often, the speeches recorded are those of individuals
whose remarks are of importance by virtue of their rank,
for example, the speeches of Archidamus and Sthenelaidas
at the first congress of the Peloponnesian Confederacy (I,
66-88) or Pericles's funeral oration at the conclusion of
the first year of the war (II, 35-46).

But Thucydides does not restrict his attention to
the words of notable individuals; his intent in recording
statements and debates is not simply to compile a complete
record but to penetrate to the reasons behind the actions
taken. The dramatizations serve not only to record a
decision but to portray the composition of assumptions and
reasoning out of which the decision to engage in an action
emerges. In some instances this analytic and explanatory
purpose appears to take precedence over historical
verisimilitude. If the context requires it, Thucydides
seems prepared to invent an anonymous spokesman so that
the issues and information that are deemed essential to
the deliberation at a point in time are adequately
represented. For example, this is clearly the function of
the nameless Athenian merchants who step forward at the
Peloponnesian Congress to provide a succinct history of
the Athenian empire complete with an inventory of
justifications in terms of right and interest that
explains Athens's policy toward its allies. In rapid
order these spokesmen itemize a number of considerations
that justify or explain the Athenian position, including
reference to the prerogative to intervene that
Lacedaemonia had long enjoyed vis-a-vis the affairs of
other Hellenic communities. Through the creation of these
Athenian spokesmen Thucydides balances the case brought by
the Corinthian envoys and the Spartan leaders. For
Thucydides it is clearly so vitally important that the
essential parameters of the debate be fully articulated
that he is justified in conveying the points of view
through characters, some of whom are historical
individuals and others of whom are composites and
surrogates. In terms of the factual narrative, the
coincidental presence of Thucydides's merchants is on a
par with the appearance of Rosencrantz and Guildenstern in
Shakespeare's Hamlet.

Thucydides's use of this device is of great service
for implementing the design of the project we have
undertaken. The break in the narrative signaled by the
interjection of the dramatized speeches announces that the
historian is reading into the record those perceptions and
convictions that, while the sources of action, are not

adequately expressed in a mere chronicle of events. These arguments will serve as primary data. After making explicit the tensions and the range of choice that underlie Athenian policy in the fifth year of the war, as evidenced in the Athenian response to the revolt of Mitylene, it is possible to proceed to Thucydides's characterization of Athenian policy on this same issue at points earlier and later in the history. What results is a series of decision problems, each of which can be subjected to further logical dissection.

LOGIC PROGRAMMING AS A MEDIUM FOR RECONSTRUCTING THE UNIVERSE OF DEBATE AND DECISION

A universe of debate and decision, like that which has been described, can be rendered as a system of inference and argument informed by facts and beliefs. Such a system can be constructed by extracting the propositional content and structure of verbatim accounts and similar records and texts. These are converted into formulae in the predicate calculus, or into the formally equivalent form required by the clausal syntax of the logic programming language, PROLOG. The purpose of this conversion is to reconstitute the facts and inferences of the text as a program that will permit the systematic analysis of the bounds and structure of the decision problem as understood by the Athenian spokesmen. The steps in this conversion involve a series of translations and paraphrases, each of which is, like all translations, problematic. In defense of the effort to encode the critical arguments into predicate calculus and the subsequent conversion into an equivalent clausal form, it can be pointed out that the activity of translating and paraphrasing, with all its attendant dangers, is endemic to any scholarly treatment of documents or textual accounts.

Rendering the text in a logical form converts it into an object that can be subjected to systematic analysis. In effect, the text becomes a system composed of objects and relations that, taken together, define a world. More than an inventory, this system imposes requirements and constraints through the relations among propositions. As a formal object and--once rendered in PROLOG--as a program, this system can be examined for what it says about the semantic interpretations or possible worlds that satisfy it. This is desirable because these properties of the system are precisely the properties of the reconstructed decision problems or policy spaces that the theorist of policy change wants to explore. In short, this formal object makes possible a systematic investigation of the structure and bounds of the option space induced from the textual evidence of a history. Worked examples of how this proceeds must wait until the steps in the encoding are motivated, but the theoretical objective can be sketched.

Rendered in PROLOG, the collection of assumptions and rules of inference contained in the text now constitute an inference system. This operationalizes the notion of a universe of policy alternatives. A course of action lies within this universe if and only if it is provable on the basis of this inference system. Beyond this useful definition of "admissibility," which defines the boundary of the policy space, there are additional analytical advantages that accompany the conversion of the text into a logic program. These include procedures for reconstructing justifications for policies and methods for establishing measures for reconstructing the distribution of options within the policy universe in terms of the similarity and overlap in the subsets of rules and assumptions used to construct or prove a policy. The well-defined concept of policy universe plus the notion of distributions of policies within such universes provide the conceptual equipment to chart change through time in the breadth, complexity, and composition of a policy space.

The steps in translating the historical text into program form can be illustrated by use of an argument extracted from the set of arguments that Thucydides recreates in the debate over the fate of Mitylene. In the process of rebutting Cleon, after asserting that deterrents fail to deter, Diodotus proceeds to attack the specifics of Cleon's policy. He first establishes that if a rebel city has no motive to come to terms with Athens, then it will fight to the death. In this event Athens not only incurs the cost of the siege, but is deprived of a source of revenue. In the predicate calculus these propositions might be rendered as the following set of formulae:

```
(FOR ALL x) {(REVOLTS-FROM(x, ATHENS)
 IMPLIES (BESIEGES (ATHENS, X)))}

(FOR ALL x) {(REVOLTS-FROM(x, ATHENS)
AND NOT (SURRENDER-TO(x, ATHENS))))}
 IMPLIES (DESTROYED (x))

(FOR ALL x) {(REVOLTS-FROM(x, ATHENS)
 IMPLIES (BESIEGES (ATHENS, x)))}

(FOR ALL x) {BESIEGES (ATHENS, x)
 IMPLIES INCURR-COST (ATHENS)}
```

```
(FOR ALL x) (FOR ALL y) {(CITY(x) AND EMPIRE(y)
AND CONTAINS (y, x) AND NOT(DESTROYED(x)))
IMPLIES SOURCE-OF-REVENUE-FOR (x, y)}
```

To cinch his argument, Diodotus introduces a third line of reasoning that turns on the roles of factions within rebellious cities. Since this part of his argument has been quoted at length, it can serve to illustrate the correspondence that is established between the text and its rendering as a set of propositions in the predicate calculus.

TEXT: ". . . in all the cities the people is your friend, and either does not revolt with the oligarchy, or, if forced to do so, becomes at once the enemy of the insurgents; so in the war with the hostile city you have the masses on your side." (III, 47, pp. 179-180)

TEXT IN THE PREDICATE CALCULUS:

```
(FOR ALL x)(FOR ALL y)(FOR ALL z) {CITY(x) AND CONTAINS(x,y)
AND PEOPLE(y) AND CONTAINS(x,z) AND OLIGARCHS(z)
AND FRIENDS-OF(x, ATHENS)
AND ((REVOLTS-FROM(z, ATHENS) AND NOT(REVOLTS-FROM(y, ATHENS))
    OR ENEMIES-OF(y,z)))
    IMPLIES (REVOLTS-FROM(x, ATHENS) IMPLIES HELPS(y, ATHENS))}
```

Diodotus's next statement hypothetically applies Cleon's policy to the particular case of Mitylene, implicitly generalizing the single case to the entire class of cases involving rebellious cities.

TEXT: "But if you butcher the people of Mitylene, . . . who as soon as they got arms, of their own motion surrendered the town, first you will commit the crime of killing your benefactors; and next you will play directly into the hands of the higher classes, who when they induce their cities to rise, will immediately have the people on their side, through your having announced in advance the same punishment for those who are guilty and for those who are not." (III, 47, p. 180)

Replacing the constant or individual "Mitylene" with a variable denoting the class of rebellious cities, the compound sentence becomes . . .

TEXT IN THE PREDICATE CALCULUS:

```
(FOR ALL x)(FOR ALL y)(FOR ALL z) {(PEOPLE (x)
AND BUTCHERS(ATHENS, x))
IMPLIES (BUTCHERS(ATHENS,y) AND FRIENDS-OF(ATHENS,y))
IMPLIES (REVOLTS-FROM(z,ATHENS) AND OLIGARCHS(z))
        IMPLIES REVOLTS-FROM(x,ATHENS)}
```

These propositions, along with the propositions that are understood but not expressed, suffice to define an inference system. Examples of propositions that are understood include the implication that costly campaigns and the loss of revenue-generating client cities injure Athenian interests; other implicit propositions reside in the meanings of terms or in the state of the world, e.g., in the Hellenic world circa fifth century B.C. the citizenry of a city is divided into people and oligarchs.

The first step in capturing the reasoning implicit in Diodotus's speech is to assemble and translate the assumptions and inferences upon which his argument depends. The second step is to reduce this collection of predicate calculus formulae into their equivalent clausal form. Clausal form is a subset of the set of formulae that can be constructed in the syntax of the first-order predicate calculus. In some instances this translation involves a loss in the degree to which the formalism appears to correspond to the natural language text, but this loss in expressibility is compensated for by the increased facility it provides for manipulating the information contained in a collection of statements. Proof of the equivalence between the conventional predicate calculus and what is expressed in accordance with clausal syntax, along with the unification algorithm that is efficiently implemented in this form, figure among the major discoveries in formal logic that power the work in automatic theorem proving (Robinson, 1965; 1979; Chang and Lee, 1973). Robinson established that a set of formulae in the predicate calculus is consistent if and only if the corresponding set of formulae in clausal form is consistent. For the general algorithm that carries predicate calculus formulae into clausal form, see Kowalski (1979), Clocksin and Mellish (1981), or Clark and McCabe (1984).

Presented in its entirety, the syntax of clausal form is as follows:

A "clause" is an expression of the form

$$B1,\ldots,Bm \; < -- \; A1,\ldots,An$$

where $B1,\ldots,Bm, A1,\ldots,An$ are atomic formulae, n =0 and m =0. The atomic formulae $A1,\ldots,An$ are the joint "conditions" of the clause and $B1,\ldots,Bm$ are the alternative "conclusions." If the clause contains the variables $x1,\ldots,xk$ then interpret it as stating that

for all $x1,\ldots,xk$
B1 or ... or BM   if A1 and ... and An.

If n = 0 then interpret it as stating unconditionally that

```
        for all xl,...,xk
        Bl or ... or Bm.
```

If m = 0 then interpret it as stating that

```
        for all xl,...,xk
        if is not the case that
        Al and ... and An.
```

If n = 0 then write it as   and interpret it as a sentence which is always false.

An "atom" (or "atomic formula") is an expression of the form

```
        P(tl,...,tm)
```

where P is an m-place predicate symbol, tl,...,tm are terms, and m =1. Interpret the atom as asserting that the relation called P holds among the individuals called tl,...,tm.
A "term" is a variable, a constant symbol, or an expression of the form

```
        f(tl,....,tm)
```

where f is an m-place function symbol, tl,...,tm are terms, and m = 1   (Kowalski, 1979, 5-6).

Implementations of the clause-based programming language PROLOG impose the additional restriction that the expressions be Horn clauses, which requires that the conclusion or left half of an expression contain a single atomic formula rather than a set of disjoint formulae. Informally, the translation of a statement from English or the predicate calculus into clausal form entails rendering that statement as one or more implications in which the conclusion consists of a single expression, while the condition is composed of a conjunction of one or more expressions. To illustrate, using the conventions of the implementation of PROLOG by McCabe et al. (1984), the statement

"Cities that revolt from Athens, which are besieged by Athens, are destroyed unless they capitulate."

can be rendered as:

```
        ((destroyed X)
         (revolts-from X Athens)
         (besieges Athens X)
         (NOT capitulates X))
```

The algorithm for converting a statement into clausal form insures universal quantification across variables, hence the absence of a leading term specifying quantification as in the predicate calculus. The conclusion comes first, followed by one or more conditionals that are understood to be related by conjunctions. The statement is circumscribed by parentheses.

Programming in this language amounts to recording rules and assumptions. In contrast to such languages as FORTRAN or LISP, in which the purpose is to fully specify a sequence of steps that carries some input into a desired output, PROLOG, or logic programming more generally, essentially describes the relation between the input and output, i.e., what is true about it. The correspondence, or rather the effort to identify an interpretation that satisfies the correspondence, is performed by an efficient pattern matcher that implements the process of resolution, perhaps with the aid of additional control structure introduced by the programmer. This language, and its underlying philosophy, serves the purpose of capturing the issues intrinsic to the study of change in the formulation of policy. This can be demonstrated by programming a part of the argument attributed to Diodotus. The program is listed in Figure 17.3.

The program is composed of assumptions and inferences extracted from the key passages in Book III, Section 47 of Thucydides's history. Put to the purpose of the present analysis, it can be used to determine whether a proposition of interest, e.g., a statement of policy, is consistent with the universe embodied in the program, and, if not, in what ways it contradicts what is known or believed. Proceeding in this fashion allows scrutiny of the bounds on the universe of policy. Through the trace it produces, e.g., Figures 17.5 and 17.6, the program also reveals the structure of reasoning within this universe, i.e., the sets of facts and inferences that are germane to the validity of a given proposition or question. Remarkably, the sequence of assertions and inferences that the program generates, as displayed in the trace, takes a form very much like that of a scenario. Starting with a hypothetical statement regarding the state of the world, it unpacks the implications of this statement vis-a-vis what is known to be true of the world, and displays the cascade of consequences. (Editors' note: Examples have been deleted by the editor; they may be obtained directly from the author of this chapter.) In attempting to prove that a proposition of interest is consistent with the propositions that comprise the data base, the program in effect reconstructs an argument or set of arguments. Equipped with such a working version of the policy universe as extracted from historical or contemporary sources, the analyst is in a position to reconstruct and

```
((not-injured-by X Y)
  (not-butchers Y X))
((revolts-from Mitylene Athens))
((friends-of XY)
  (not-injured by X Y))
((besieges X Y)
  (revolts-from X Y)
((surrenders-to X Y)
  (besieges Y X)
  (contains X Z)
  (friends-of Z Y)
((benefactors-of X Y)
  (citizens Y)
  (not-butcher X Y))
((people Mitylene))
((citizens people))
((citizens oligarchs))
((citizens Mitylene))
((city Melos))
((city Mitylene))
((serves-interest-of X)
  (source-of-revenue-for Y X)
  (city Y)
  (NOT destroyed Y))
((serves-interest-of X Y)
  (source-of-revenue-for X Y))
((destroyed X)
  (besieges Y X)
  (NOT surrenders-to X Y))
((contains X people)
  (city X))
((contains X oligarchs)
  (city X)
((contains Athens Mitylene))
((source-of-revenue-for X Y)
  (empire Y)
  (contains Y X)
  (NOT destroyed X))
((oligarchs Mitylene)
((not-butchers Athens people)
(empire Athens))
  &.
```

Figure 17.3 PROLOG Program Based on Diodotus's Rebuttal
to Cleon.

cross-examine not just the arguments which the historical record contains but the universe of arguments and considerations that underlie policies.

The operation of the program in effect asks whether the policy advocated by Diodotus, viz., the policy of executing rebellious oligarchs but sparing the commoners, serves the long-term interest of the Athenian empire, given the world of Hellenic politics circa 426 B.C. The motivating question appears as the first line of the trace. The policy, introduced hypothetically as a fact asserted to be true in this world, appears as simply one more assumption. The program, which applies the unification algorithm built into the programming language, seeks to establish the consistency of the entire set of assumptions. That is, it attempts to find an interpretation which makes all the assumptions simultaneously true. In effect the program asks whether Athens's interest is served by a policy that does not discriminate between oligarchs and people. This is answered in the negative.

The programs in these figures illustrate a probing tactic which determines whether a hypothetical option is within, or excluded from, the universe of recognized alternatives. By testing for the inconsistency of each of a range of hypothetical options, it is possible to establish the extent of the universe of alternatives to a desired degree of specificity. This procedure provides a means for monitoring change in the policy universe, for example the shifting logic of Athenian policy toward rebellious cities as evidenced in the succession of cases that lead from Mitylene to Melos (cf. Figure 17.2). The degree and direction of change in the universe of options considered is measured in terms of the inclusion or exclusion of a set of options. By successively testing whether given alternatives are consistent or inconsistent with the beliefs and inferences of a community, it is possible to systematically chart shifts in the working logic and perception that underlie policy.

CONCLUSION

The approach introduced in this chapter is specifically designed for the systematic portrayal of the system of beliefs and inferences that underlie foreign policy. The conceptual strategy centers on the formal definition of a policy universe of discourse and debate. Such a universe is defined as the collection of semantic interpretations that satisfy the beliefs and assertions which comprise that universe. A policy or alternative lies within that universe if it is consistent with it, otherwise not. An effective procedure in programmed form

is described which makes possible the exploration of the
limits of a policy universe as well as its internal
structure. In addition to capturing the extent of the
policy universe that obtains for some political community
at some point in time, the purpose in introducing the
approach is to initiate an order of analysis which is
capable of reconstructing the evolution of foreign policy.
Stated in terms of the case example used, this involves
reconstructing the logic of Athenian response to rebellion
and revolt within its empire over the course of the
Peloponnesian War. The objective is not only to render the
reasoning that results in the individual actions as
recorded in the historical narrative, but to capture the
change in the reasoning that results from the internal
erosion of Athenian leadership and judgment under the
pressure of events. To effect this, arguments are
rendered in the predicate calculus and programmed in the
logic programming language, PROLOG. In this way the
universe of candidate policies, and not simply the
individual policies enacted, becomes the object of analysis. This conception of a policy universe as a system of
argument and inference, as implemented in first-order
logic, makes possible the systematic investigation of
questions which, to this point, have resisted scientific
treatment. The approach is rigorous, qualitative, and
dynamic.

NOTES

1. Remarks by Marc Kilgour in his oral presentation
of the paper, "Anticipation and Stability in Two-Person
Non-Cooperative Games," at the conference, "Dynamic Models
of International Conflict," Boulder, Colorado,
October 31, 1984.
2. Eric Auerbach, Mimesis. The Representation of
Reality in Western Literature, translated from the German
by Willard R. Trask, Princeton, Princeton University
Press, 1953, pp. 11, 6.
3. Cited in Orville H. Schell, "Carter on Rights--A
Reevaluation," The New York Times, October 25,
1984, p. 29.
4. See Mefford, "The Debate Over the Logic of
History, the Logic of Explanation, and the Logic of
Narrative," working paper.
5. All references are to the Modern Library edition
of the revised Crawley translation of Thucydides, The
Peloponnesian War, revised with an introduction by T. E.
Wick, New York, Modern Library, 1982.

Part 6

Empirical and Theoretical Frontiers

18 A Visual Approach to International Conflict and Cooperation

A new method for displaying information about international conflict and cooperation is described in this chapter. Color displays of ongoing and historical international conflicts portray the evolution of crisis behavior, geographic and temporal diffusion, and the multilateral operation of alliances. With this technique it is possible to go beyond the bilateral perspective that typifies most quantitative international relations research without at the same time abandoning a rigorous, analytic perspective. This visual display technique leads to several interesting findings, including a new method of defining power that is not dependent on standard capability scores.

Recently there has been interest in the graphical display of quantitative information in the social sciences. The year 1981 marked the publication of the State of the World Atlas, a volume of color cartograms (Kidron and Segal, 1981) in which distortion is used to equate the areal size of a nation-state, with an attribute such as population or arms imports, while at the same time preserving the rough geographical relation among nation-states. To our knowledge, Brown's 1982 article contained the first three-dimensional display of quantitative information to appear in the American Political Science Review. Most visible has been Tufte's (1984) fascinating book of examples and illustrations of display principles for those who have access to graphic artists.

Paper presented at the 1985 Annual Meetings of the International Studies Association, March 5-9, Washington, D.C. We would like to thank Rose Reynolds, Andrew Stanger, and Sandra L. Ward for their help in assembling the graphic displays described in this chapter. Michael Intriligator and Barry O'Neill were especially helpful in making useful suggestions about the final presentation of the data set, as were Kenneth Boulding and Dwain Mefford. Kun Park provided a useful survey of major events.

This chapter reports on an ongoing project that uses image-processing techniques to display quantitative information about the dynamic, bilateral political interactions of contemporary nation-states. In particular, this project uses color graphics to represent event-interactions among fifty nation-states over the period from the close of World War II to the end of the 1970s. Color displays of quarterly aggregations of the ongoing bilateral interactions are linked together to make a 16mm color movie or video portraying the kinematic evolution of international conflict and cooperation. Unfortunately full display of this movie is not possible in printed format, however in this presentation we do display several selected gray scale frames from contemporary international crises with the goal of providing the flavor, if not the hue, of the visual analysis.

WHY GRAPHICS?

Feasibility is coterminous neither with worth nor meaning. Why is it that people like to look at graphics, especially color graphics, instead of tables of more precise numbers? Psychologists are beginning to address this question, and an informative and interesting survey of the topic is Wainer's 1981 article. There are no well-substantiated answers to this question that we have been able to uncover. Nor, despite the inherent belief that has sustained the efforts we report on in this chapter, is there an abundance of scientific evidence that graphic display is more significant, easily understood, or elegant than tables of numbers. While we are convinced that catastrophe theory would not have reached as many without the physical and graphic models of Zeeman's presentations, the equational form is equally elegant and perhaps more practical. The sparse experimental data on graphics does tend to suggest that, for example, correlation coefficients may have greater perceptual efficacy than do scattergrams (Wainer, 1981, p. 235). In spite of this line of reasoning, our project has proceeded on the working assumption that good graphics should provide easy (to the viewer) access to information and patterns that are difficult to otherwise recognize or demonstrate. However, in the physical sciences such techniques are commonplace and well established, if not required, as the succinct way of presenting analytic and numerical results.

Graphics has proved useful in displaying vast quantities of data in a parsimonious way. Ward (1982a) has experimented with displaying simulation trajectories using three-dimensional graphics and in presenting correlational summaries of data on international politics

(1982b). In each application, the basic problem addressed was to display hundreds of thousands of pieces of discrete information. Whether condensing one-half million event-interactions or evaluating the outcomes of several thousand computer simulations, contours provided one useful summary of results.

The major goal of the conference from which the present contribution emerged was to explore dynamic approaches to examining and explaining international conflict behavior (Ward, 1983; Luterbacher, 1984). The stochastic and episodic nature of certain aspects of day-to-day international conflict serves to characterize much of what scholars of international politics analyze. One of the many so-called plus ca change phenomena of global politics is bilateral and multilateral conflict. One of our first goals, therefore, was to elaborate a method for describing these varied interactions. While helpful, statistical techniques, deriving in the main from correlational underpinnings, themselves do not well summarize the data. In a world of 160 nation-states, each interacting with or ignoring one another every day, one could easily imagine as many correlation coefficients as data points. On the other hand, tables of the actual data, even if aggregated into yearly or quarterly periods, are cumbersome and difficult to synthesize, present, or digest, not to mention lug around.

Thus, in exploring graphic representation of these data, we sought not so much to create a technicolor social science, but to present the numerical information about interactions in a topological form that could change visually to reflect changes in the so-called real world. As our colleague Kenneth Boulding has pointed out, numbers are an important and convenient crutch invented to correspond to a topological world.[1] Whatever the true topology of international conflict (if any), it seems important to explore whether techniques and topologies created in other contexts or invented here could be a useful, complimentary method for viewing international conflict in a dynamic context.

THE DATA BASE

We chose to first concentrate our efforts on the most densely packed data set available in quantitative international politics. These are the data taken from the COPDAB (Conflict and Peace Data Bank) that has been assembled through the stewardship of E. E. Azar (1980a,b). The procedures employed in aggregating this data set of some one-half million events are described elsewhere (Ward, 1982b), but will be recapitulated here for completeness.

The basic model undergirding this data set is what we call the Actor-Action-Target (who did what to whom, when) framework, wherein an initiator of the action, whether it is high or low conflict or cooperation, is specified by a coder from publicly available news reports. The type of action and the intended or unintended target is then identified. The COPDAB data set contains ". . . about 500,000 event records which have been systematically coded from about 70 international sources between January 1, 1948 and December 31, 1978, which describe the actions of about 135 countries in the world toward one another" (Azar, 1980a, p. 3). These data primarily include information on symbolic political relations, economic relations, military and strategic interactions, cultural and scientific contacts, environmental interactions dealing with the physical environment, demographic affairs, law and political order, and diplomatic relations.

Pioneering work was done by Azar and colleagues in deriving a scale for these data based on the ratings of eighteen experts who weighted the fifteen basic event types by perceived intensity. For the purposes of our investigations these intensity scores were not employed. Instead, we concentrated on the simple frequency counts of events into four basic categories demonstrated to be substantively and empirically meaningful in earlier work (Hopple et al., 1980). Mintz and Schrodt (1983) use this same categorization. These four basic categories divide the data set into those event types that are conflictual and those that are cooperative, while at the same time focusing on event types that require resources. Thus, we have both conflictual and cooperative words and deeds. Our analysis in this paper concentrates on the major part of the data set, the utilization of words by international foreign policy makers in their relationships with one another.[2] While the analysis presented in this paper is, in a sense, limited to who said what to whom, when, its exclusion of wars and other resource-intensive forms of conflict does not exclude the verbal conflict that goes along with nonverbal engagements. As we shall show below, major international wars of the 1948-1978 period show up in these data.

It should be pointed out that these event-interaction data are not without controversy regarding their ability to accurately represent the ebb and flow of international conflict and cooperation. A recent symposium in the International Studies Quarterly addressed this general problem (Howell, 1983; Vincent, 1983; and McClelland, 1983).

The visual presentation of these data on international conflict also required using only a subsample of the 135 possible actors and targets. For convenience, we decided to use a symmetric matrix, with the same list of actors and targets. The fifty nation-states that were selected are taken from Ward (1982b) and comprise the twenty-five nations of the GLOBUS Project--a global modeling project under way at the International Institute of Comparative Social Research at the Science Center Berlin--plus an additional twenty-five selected to include important foreign policy actors not included in the GLOBUS project (such as Israel). These fifty nation-states (listed in Appendix 1) represent a large portion of the total amount of foreign policy activity that is reported in the COPDAB data set, but this proportion consistently declines from the high of between 80% and 90% that existed in 1950 to around 50% in 1975, for example. It should be pointed out that this list significantly underrepresents African nation-states, a site of considerable international conflict during the 1960s and 1970s.

THE DISPLAY

Several issues required resolution in designing the format of the visual display.[3] The first is the overall layout that is presented in Figure 18.1. Note that to keep the price of this volume under $100, this display is presented in discrete gray scale, rather than in the color produced. Fifty actors are arrayed along the rows of the matrix, and these same fifty nation-states correspond to the fifty rows of targets. The intersection of any row and target (except for the diagonal that is left blank) corresponds to the total quarterly verbal conflict or cooperation that was initiated by the row actor toward the column target. The label in the upper right indicates the year followed by the quarter and whether the data represent verbal conflict (CONF) or verbal cooperation (COOP). Rather than numbers in the display, color or gray scale provides the quantity of exchange.

The gray scale bar on the left of the display represents a scaled, logarithmic transformation of these data. The quarterly frequency data were scaled to range between 1 and 256, the possible range of color choices available to us through the configuration of hardware and software. Once scaled, we examined the histograms of many frames to determine how many packets of information, in general, existed in the data. From histograms we determined that six discrete levels will adequately represent the data. We found six such packets, with exponentially declining frequencies. That is, quarterly summations of bilateral (in this case) verbal conflict yielded six different levels of excitation. The numbers of verbal conflict events per quarter for these levels are: 1-2, 3-4, 5-8, 9-14, 15-22, and 23-49.

432

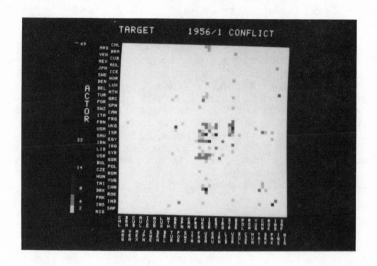

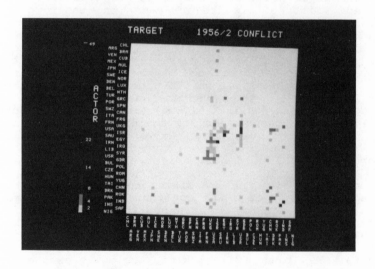

Figure 18.1 Verbal Conflict in 1956, alliance ordering

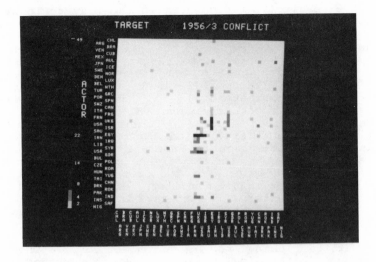

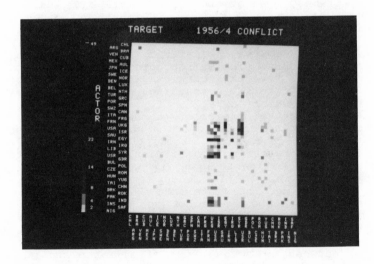

Figure 18.1 Verbal Conflict in 1956, alliance ordering

Because of the difficulty the human eye has in distinguishing among more than five grays at one time, only five levels are represented in the gray scale bar at the left margin of our displays (the two lowest categories being combined). Figure 19.1 presents the verbal conflict exchanged during each quarter of 1956. A verbal conflict message sent from actor X to target Y will have a gray level at the X,Y intersection that corresponds to the level (summation) of scaled quarterly interaction. The first frame, corresponding to the months January, February, and March, includes US suspension of arms shipments to Israel during a continuing escalation of fighting between Israel and Egypt as well as a continuation of conflict in Kashmir. The third quarter, or frame, encompasses the conference on the Suez and the end to British occupation of the Suez Canal. In the last three months of 1956, conflicts among these nations continued to center on fighting in the Middle East, including a Soviet threat to end the fighting, as well as a French/British ultimatum and considerable economic pressure on Egypt. It also includes the outbreak of the 1956 war, including the invasion of Egypt. The light background in the display square shows no recorded verbal conflict interaction between the given actor and target for the quarter in question. Like many, but not all, display frames, most of the world is at peace with itself and not involved in active conflict at any given point. This is true even in periods that are conflictual, such as 1956. Darker gray shows more conflict and, conversely, lighter tones portray bilateral relations of a less conflictual nature. The darkest areas, or black spots, in this portrayal of verbal conflict tend to correspond, in this frame and others, to ongoing hostilities, typically involving the use of force.

While not a topic of utmost salience in this discussion, choice of appropriate colors to represent the level of conflict and the ordering of the nation-states proved to be interesting and difficult tasks. In order of most intensity to least intensity we employed: hot red, light magenta, hot yellow, deep emerald, hot blue, hot cyan, and white (no interaction). The ordering of the nation-states, along the actor and target axes, however, was an even more challenging task. An initial ordering was provided that pinned down the United States at the top of the image plane and the Soviet Union at the bottom. Arrayed between in rough order of alliance and geography were the other forty-eight nation-states. Cluster analysis (Späth, 1980) was employed to examine this ordering via the bond-energy algorithm. We found that this initial ordering represented a local minimum. However, it forced all the information to be located away from the diagonal toward the edges of the display plane.

One ordering presented in this paper is a folded version of that initial ordering in which the US and USSR are located toward the center of the list, separated by the Middle East nation-states; the allies of the United States and the Soviet Union are displayed respectively above and below these pivotal nation-states. Asia falls at the bottom of the list and Latin America toward the top. An alternative is also used that presents an order based on rank orderings of quarrelsomeness, per the suggestion of Kenneth Boulding. This is discussed in more detail below.

LOOKING AT THE RESULTS

Figure 18.2 portrays the evolution of verbal conflict in 1962. This year is particularly important in many analyses of US-Soviet foreign policy since it includes episodes focused on the then newly proclaimed Marxist government in Cuba. In particular, the Bay of Pigs invasion of Cuba brings forth considerable US-Cuban conflict. During this time there is some conflict over the newly constructed Schutzmauer separating the Soviet sector of Berlin from the French, British, and American occupation sectors, although the conflict over Berlin was muted in comparison with 1961. DeGaulle and Adenauer agreed that German reunification was the only solution to the so-called Berlin question. The major conflict of 1962 dealt with Cuban-US relations. Argentina severed relationships with Cuba and there was an ongoing US economic blockade of the new regime in Havana. The last quarter frame illustrates the transmission of considerable verbal conflict from virtually every nation-state in the sample directed toward the United States. This is shown by the vertical line of tones in the middle of the display and represents the Cuban Missile Crisis and its immediate aftermath. China also invaded India and the Algerian civil war ended.

It is illustrative to look at the corresponding representation of cooperation during this same period (Figure 18.3). Cooperation in 1962 was extensive and highly organized. The Latin American nation-states show a high degree of cooperation evidenced by the two quasi-symmetric triangles in the upper left-hand corner of the display for the first quarter of 1962. Similarly, toward the middle of the display one sees the square representing intra-NATO cooperation. The last two frames illustrate the strong organization of intra-WTO cooperation as well as the continuation of a high degree of cooperation in Latin America--excluding, of course, Cuba. Similarly, the US is the target of a considerable amount of unorganized

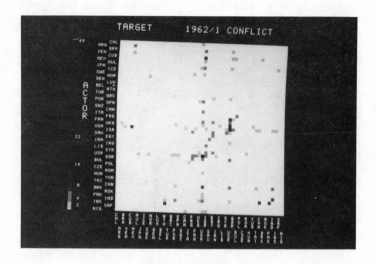

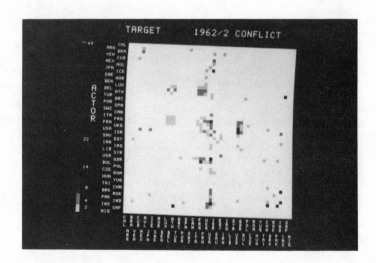

Figure 18.2   Verbal Conflict in 1962, alliance ordering

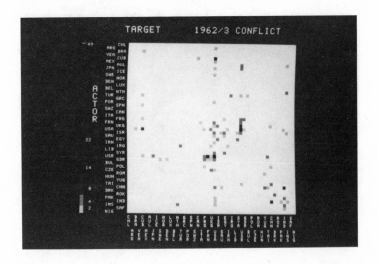

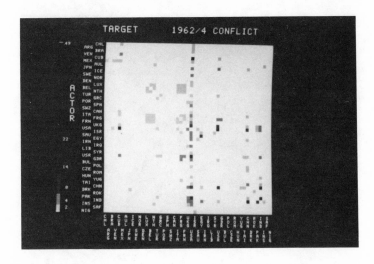

Figure 18.2 Verbal Conflict in 1962, alliance ordering

438

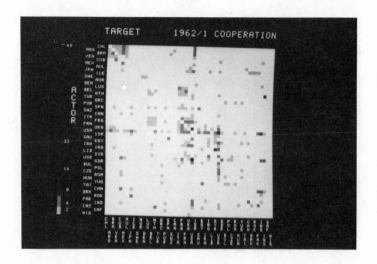

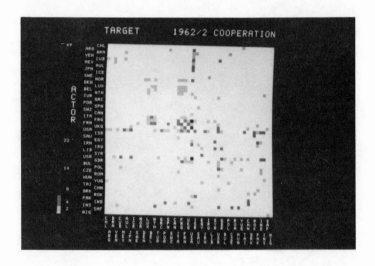

Figure 18.3   Verbal Cooperation in 1962, alliance ordering

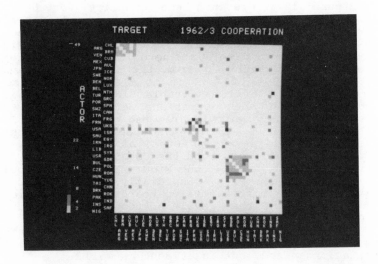

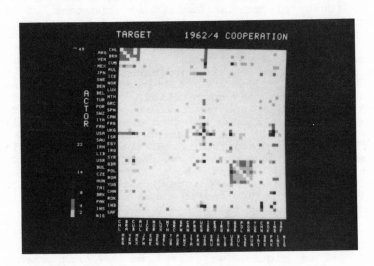

Figure 18.3   Verbal Cooperation in 1962, alliance ordering

cooperation from most every nation-state in the sample, excluding the Warsaw Pact nation-states.

Figure 18.4 presents the conflict for the 1967 period, and Figure 18.5 illustrates the cooperative patterns in the same era. This year witnessed the intensification of the war in Vietnam (not included in the subset of nations displayed here), a coup d'etat in Greece, French withdrawal from the military aspects of NATO, and the visit of Kosygin to the United States. It was also a period of considerable Sino-Soviet hostility, including Chinese demonstrations outside the Soviet Embassy in China, which were reciprocated by Soviet demonstrators. Once again, the dominance of conflict between Israel and Egypt is noted, as is the involvement, at a similar level, of both the US and USSR. The spread of the conflict beyond the Middle East is particularly noted in this example. Especially striking is the comparison of the multilateral patterns of cooperation and conflict. First, the level of cooperation abounding during this year is high, considering there is a war going on. This is evident both in the intra-American interactions, and among the WTO nation-states. NATO cooperation is not as organized, but is evident as well.

While the actual movie of the evolution of these must be seen to be appreciated, there are several salient characteristics regarding this form of analysis. First, the emptiness of the data matrix is important in itself. Although this is one of the most dense data sets available for the analysis of international relations, most of our display is white, illustrating no interaction--either conflictual or cooperative. Second, it is easy to identify the operation of coordinated interactions, beyond the bilateral level. Alliances and alignments, particularly involving cooperation, are clearly evident in the displays. Thus, one positive attribute of this form of display is that although the data are inherently bilateral by virtue of the actor/action/target framework, the multilateral characteristics of international relations become readily apparent when presented visually. The symmetry of the images above and below the downward sloping diagonal also points to the basic reactivity (action-reaction) involved in the conflict interactions of contemporary nation-states.

As suggested above, the order in which the nation-states are arranged is important for organizing the quantitative information into a display. The order used in the above figures was based on an arrangement that sought to highlight the operation of alliances in world politics. Adjacent placement of NATO nation-states permitted an organization to their interactions to be more readily apparent, as it did for the members of the Warsaw Treaty Organization. Kenneth Boulding (1985) suggested to

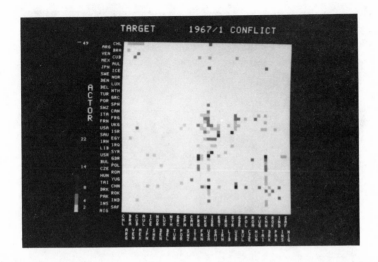

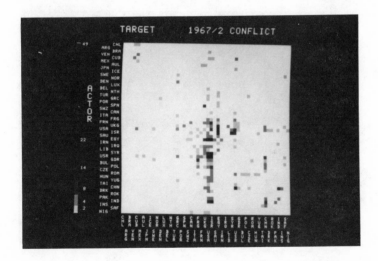

Figure 18.4 Verbal Conflict in 1967, alliance ordering

442

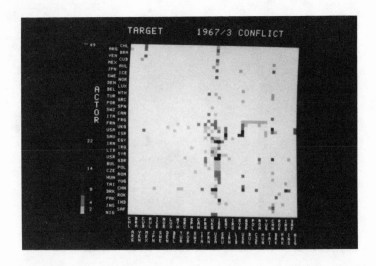

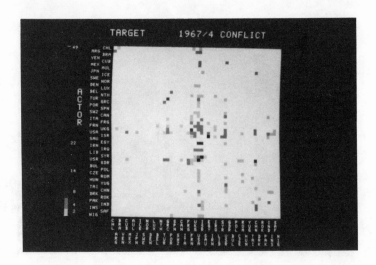

Figure 18.4   Verbal Conflict in 1967, alliance ordering

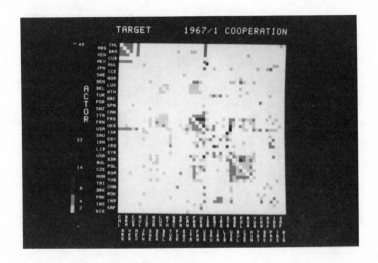

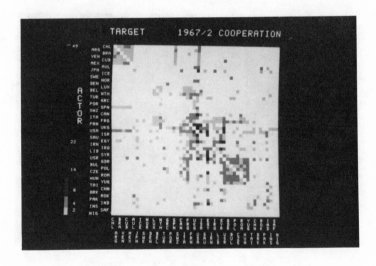

Figure 18.5   Verbal Cooperation in 1967, alliance ordering

444

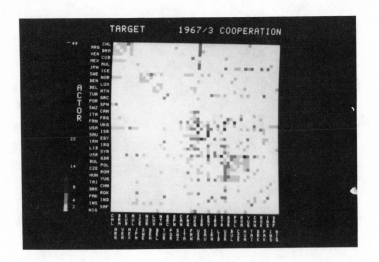

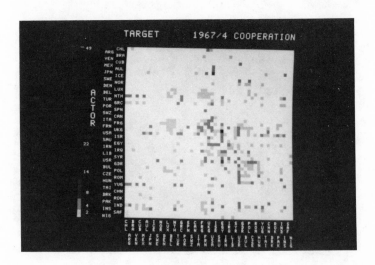

Figure 18.5   Verbal Cooperation in 1967, alliance ordering

us that we explore a rank ordering of nation-states that highlighted their quarrelsomeness. In implementing this suggestion we ordered the fifty nation-states in descending order of the amount of verbal conflict sent over the entire period from 1948 to 1979. Thus, at the top of the y-axis in Figure 18.6, the least conflictual nation-states are arranged (respectively, Iceland, Switzerland, Nigeria, Australia, Norway, Denmark, Mexico, Venezuela, Sweden, . . .) and at the bottom one finds those nation-states that have sent the most verbal conflict over the period (respectively, United States, USSR, Israel, Egypt, Britain, China, France, West Germany, . . .). In displays ordered by quarrelsomeness, the lower-left quadrant represents the space in which one expects the most conflict activity. The extent to which activity spreads to those nation-states not so frequently involved in conflict represents the diffusion and spread of conflict through time and space. Figure 18.6 shows this diffusion for the 1956 period. By the end of the year, many of the least quarrelsome nation-states are sending conflict to the participants in the Suez Crisis. Figure 18.7 shows the same pattern for the evolution of the crisis-prone twelve months of 1962. Note that in each of these displays, the operation of alliances is not so evident, although the data displayed are identical, simply ordered differently. The 1967 war in the Middle East especially highlights the spread of conflict throughout the world, as illustrated by Figure 18.8. Cooperation about the so-called June War evinces the same pattern, as shown in Figure 18.9.

The final graphic of this presentation illustrates the power of organization. Figure 18.10 presents the cooperative data for the second quarter of 1978. During 1978, two Popes died in office, the New York Times was unavailable owing to a strike lasting three months, and peace in the Middle East dominated international affairs. The beginning of the year saw both Israeli and Egyptian peace initiatives, as well as visits by Begin and Sadat to Israel, Egypt, the US, and Austria to negotiate a settlement to the ongoing conflict in the Middle East. The Camp David Accords were signed in September, and by October the Nobel peace prize had been jointly awarded to these two statesmen. The first frame corresponds to the ordering of nation-states by quarrelsomeness. The second frame displays the same data using the alliance ordering. While the first presents a seemingly random display of information, the second provides clear evidence of organized cooperation within and to some extent across NATO and WTO alliances.

446

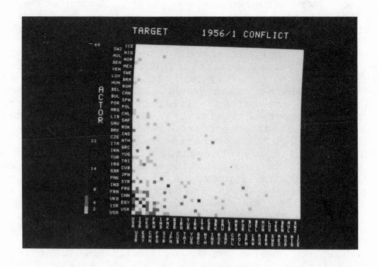

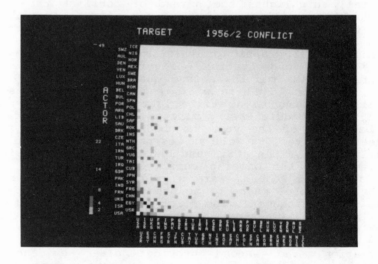

Figure 18.6   Verbal Conflict in 1956, quarrelsome ordering

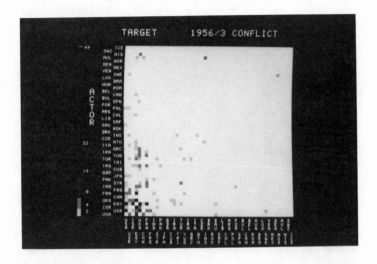

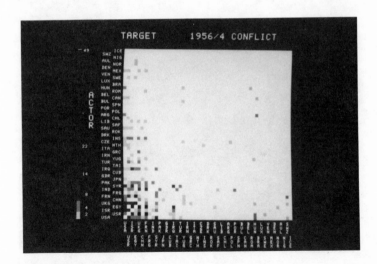

Figure 18.6 Verbal Conflict in 1956, quarrelsome ordering

448

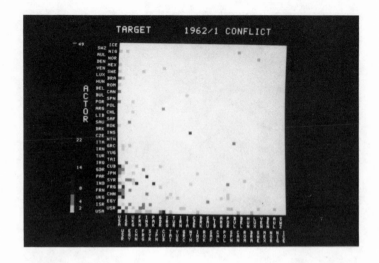

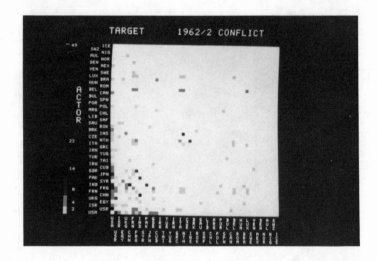

Figure 18.7   Verbal Conflict in 1962, quarrelsome ordering

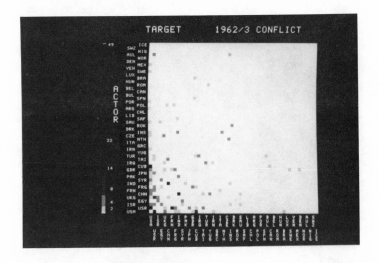

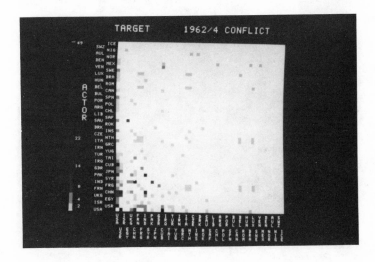

Figure 18.7 Verbal Conflict in 1962, quarrelsome ordering

450

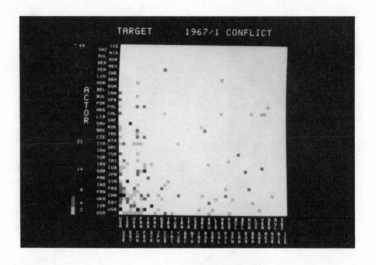

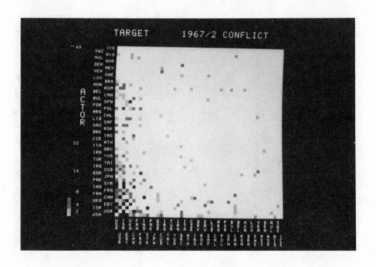

Figure 18.8   Verbal Conflict in 1967, quarrelsome ordering

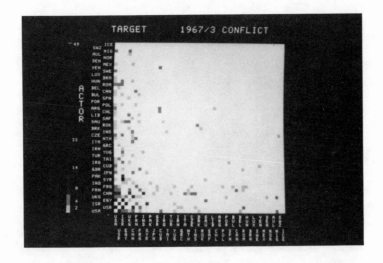

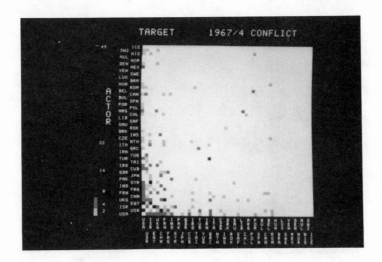

Figure 18.8   Verbal Conflict in 1967, quarrelsome ordering

452

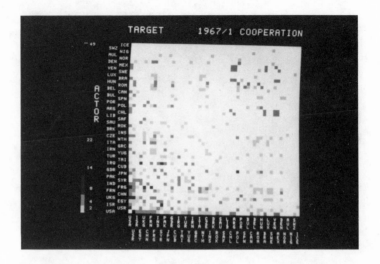

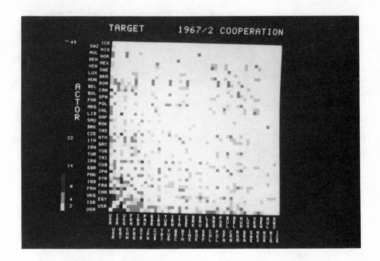

Figure 18.9   Verbal Cooperation in 1967, quarrelsome ordering

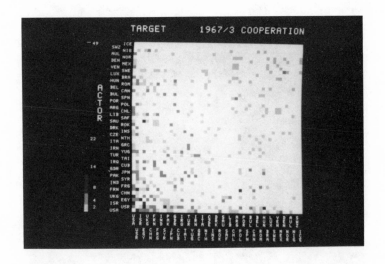

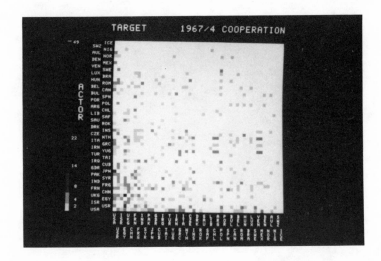

Figure 18.9   Verbal Cooperation in 1967, quarrelsome ordering

454

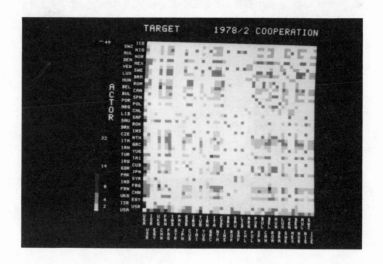

Figure 18.10   Data Organization, Second Quarter of 1978

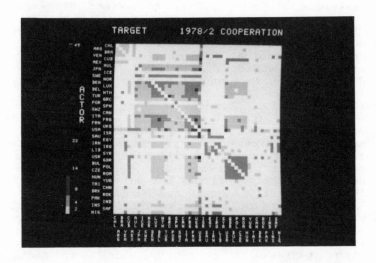

Figure 18.10   Data Organization, Second Quarter of 1978

MATHEMATICAL ANALYSES AND CONCLUSION

The graphic display of international conflict and cooperation is not an end in itself, and constitutes only part of our investigation of these data and the processes and behaviors they putatively represent. However, the graphic display has been an integral part of that investigation. We have taken a bilateral data set of considerable density and organized and displayed it in a coherent and economical format. In doing so a number of characteristics emerged, including the diffusion and spread of both conflict and cooperation, and the organized activity of blocs of nation-states, especially in the cooperation domain. Symmetry and reciprocity are also evident in these data. When viewing the movie, or slides of both the cooperation and conflict displays, one hypothesis that merits investigation is that organized cooperative activity within alliances often precedes the outbreak of a war or crisis. Thus, cooperation may be a leading indicator of conflict, but only when viewed from a unilateral perspective (House and Ward, 1985c).

As this summary suggests, the visual analysis is simply part of the systematic study of international conflict and cooperation. In addition to our study of cooperation as a leading indicator of conflict, two other specific studies are currently under way that were directly stimulated by our focus on the visual display of these data on international interactions. A full elaboration of these studies and their methods is outside the scope of this presentation. However, a brief overview may serve to illustrate the analytical directions that our visual display has stimulated.

The first of these is a Markov analysis of international conflict using the COPDAB data. While there have been several (e.g., Duncan and Siverson, 1975 and 1982; Leavitt, 1972; and Zinnes, Zinnes, and McClure, 1972) Markovian analyses of international conflict and cooperative behaviors, to our knowledge these have all been oriented to a bilateral form of analysis, generally focusing on the Markovian properties of the conflict states of a particular dyad. Similarly, Midlarsky (1981) and others have used Markovian assumptions to examine whether the entire international system is at war. Our analyses start with the assumption that you need to look at the entire system, but to do so in the context of the myriad of bilateral and multilateral interactions of which it is composed. Thus, our fundamental probability matrix is similar to our display matrix, with actors comprising the rows and targets representing the columns.

To illustrate the outline of this project that analyzes the Markovian properties of interactions among the fifty nation-states described above (House and Ward,

1985a), consider the top three conflict senders, US, USSR, and Israel, as a simple subset for analysis. Using the frequency data over the entire period, 1948-1979, to calculate the probability matrix we find that the US has a probability of .81 of sending any particular conflict message toward the Soviet Union, while the Soviet probability for sending any of its verbal conflict to the US is .88. Israel, on the other hand, distributes about 65% of its conflict in this subset to the US and the other 35% to the Soviet Union. These data permit a more or less classic Markov analysis to be undertaken in which mean first passage times--the average number of events it takes the system to return to any given initial state--are calculated. Table 18.1 provides the mean first passage times for this illustrative, three-nation subset.

TABLE 18.1
MEAN FIRST PASSAGE TIMES FOR VERBAL CONFLICT, 1948-1979

MEAN FIRST PASSAGE TIME:			
Actor:	USA	USSR	Israel
USA	[2.2]	1.3	6.3
USSR	1.7	[2.4]	6.6
Israel	1.4	1.97	[7.4]

Mean first passage illustrates that this subsystem is more or less dominated by US conflict directed toward the Soviet Union. The diagonal elements are also interesting in that they tell that if the US, for example, sends a message anywhere in the system, it will propagate throughout the system and return (i.e., conflict will be reciprocated) within 2.2 events, on average. While the Soviet Union has a similar reciprocal mean first passage time, it is interesting to speculate why this figure is so much higher--about 7 events--for Israel. Evidently, it takes the US and the Soviet Union considerably more time to respond to Israel than to each other.

To examine cycles of behavior it is also possible to examine the absorbing states of the system. Thus, if one assumes that a given conflict will end up with the US as its target, what states will the conflict visit before being first absorbed by the US? By expanding our subset to a somewhat larger number, a variety of intriguing findings are evident. While we do not report the specifics here, much conflict that starts in the Middle East gets absorbed by the US and USSR. In short, our visual analysis led us to investigate these cycles of international behavior involving not just two, but many important international actors.

A second track of visually inspired research revolves around our attempts to derive a new way of measuring power. Our reasoning has proceeded from the simple premise that if power exists, it is behavioral. This implies that capability data such that available from the good efforts of the Correlates of War project may need augmentation. We were interested in behavioral power simply defined as the ability to provoke a behavioral response. If the US sends a threat to Cuba and provokes a great many responses, whereas a threat from Belgium to Cuba is ignored not only by Cuba but also by the rest of the world, this permits an inference about relative, behavioral power. Based on mathematical models of the statistical equilibrium of thermodynamic systems in physics, we assumed that an equilibrium in power relationships exists at any given time. This permits us to calculate the relative, behavioral power of any given subset of nations and to derive solutions for these over periods of time. In the example above, if the US's behavioral power index is 1.0, the Soviet Union's is .91, and the Israel score is .29.[4] It is hoped that such calculations and conceptualizations may ultimately augment the capabilities approach now dominant in quantitative international relations. House and Ward (1985b) describe the results of this line of research in more detail.

We end this contribution in the hope that visual analysis of quantitative information may become a more accepted and widely used tool in the analysis of international relations. We are not advocating a return to the era of so-called arm-chair theorizing. Nor do we promote a situation that avoids the generation and use of quantitative information dealing with world politics. Instead, we seek to prove that visual display of quantitative information can be an integral part of rigorous international relations scholarship.

NOTES

1. We are indebted to Kenneth Boulding's insightful comments on an intermediate version of our slides. His own work on turning numbers into knowledge will no doubt be the source of further inspiration.

2. The four categories are (1) nonverbal conflict behavior, corresponding to COPDAB event types 15, 14, 13, 12, 11; (2) verbal conflict behavior, comprising event types 10 and 9; (3) verbal cooperation, including event

types 7, 6, and 5; and (4) nonverbal cooperation, indicated by event types 4, 3, 2, and 1. Only verbal cooperation and conflict are studied in this chapter.

3. A brief summary of the hardware-software configuration used to produce the visual displays is described in Appendix 2.

4. It is shown in House and Ward (1985b) that these indices are equivalent to the solution in the Markov analysis.

APPENDIX 1

The 50 Nation Subset

Abv.	Nation	Abv.	Nation
USA	United States	CAN	Canada
CUB	Cuba	MEX	Mexico
VEN	Venezuela	BRA	Brazil
CHL	Chile	ARG	Argentina
UKG	United Kingdom	NTH	Netherlands
BEL	Belgium	FRA	France
SWZ	Switzerland	SPN	Spain
POR	Portugal	LUX	Luxembourg
FRG	Federal Republic of Germany	POL	Poland
GDR	German Democratic Republic	HUN	Hungary
CZE	Czechoslovakia	ITA	Italy
YUG	Yugoslavia	GRC	Greece
BUL	Bulgaria	RUM	Rumania
USR	Soviet Union	SWE	Sweden
NOR	Norway	DEN	Denmark
ICE	Iceland	ISR	Israel
NIG	Nigeria	SAF	South Africa
LIB	Libya	IRN	Iran
TUR	Turkey	IRQ	Iraq
EGY	Egypt	SYR	Syria
SAU	Saudi Arabia	CHN	China
TAI	Taiwan	DRK	Democratic Republic of Korea
JPN	Japan	IND	India
PAK	Pakistan	ROK	Republic of Korea
INS	Indonesia	AUS	Australia

APPENDIX 2

The tools used to create our displays were developed in the study of the solar atmosphere as observed from satellite experiments, such as the Solar Maximum Mission Coronagraph/Polarimeter telescope. This study, operated by the High Altitude Observatory of the National Center for Atmospheric Research, employs three-dimensional and color displays to analyze the evolution of solar corona (see House et al., 1981, for an early description). The quantity of data for a single frame exceeds one million bits. Movies and other image-processing techniques of the explosive ejection of massive quantities of matter from the sun (a billion tons at one million miles per hour) have evolved as a standard tool for identifying and studying such events. Enormous quantities of data are involved. Some 30,000 frames of data (of about 1.6 million bits each) are collected, collated, organized, and displayed in a typical nine-month period of SMM operation.

The hardware/software configuration consists of a Digital Electronics Corporation 11/750 running BSD UNIX version 4.2. It is configured with a Grinnel Data Systems high-resolution color display monitor. An image-processing language called ZODIAC and several specially written C programs transform the actual data into colors on the screen. Connected to this is a Videoprint 5200 unit onto which either a 16mm Bolex film camera or a Nikon 35mm SLR may be mounted. The screen of the Grinnell is not flat and cannot be directly photographed without introducing distortion. Thus, it is necessary for the Videoprint to produce a flat image plane that can be photographed. The Videoprint produces this image in gray scale that is then exposed through three primary color filters to produce the full range of visible color on the film. However, because screen technology is based on a standard of 30 frames per second while film technology relies on a different standard (24 fps), synchronization is required to prevent rolling of the image plane in any film that is made. A physical controller, under software control, synchronizes the writing of the image plane with the opening and closing of the aperture. Once a 16mm film is produced, a visual internegative is made and at least 24 copies of each frame must be developed and copied onto a positive to produce a moving picture.

19 Cycles of General, Hegemonic, and Global War

For those of us who feel the need to make a case for repetitive regularities in the occurrence of warfare, or at least certain types of warfare, the following two passages should be comforting.

> Confronted with what might otherwise be a mysterious conundrum or a vast buzzing welter, we have devised all sorts of models and metaphors as a means of imposing coherence. . . . When it comes to war--a type of social event that is clearly the result of complex and interdependent processes--the tendency to fall back on one or another of these simple models is particularly acute. . . . From among the inexorable trend (toward or away), the cyclical and the stochastic models, modern man seems to prefer the cyclical. The trend model seems too teleological and the stochastic model seems too nihilistic, whereas the cyclical one has a certain aura of a priori plausibility in the twentieth century. After all, who amongst us is eager to embrace the implicit assumption of a largely beneficent, or essentially malevolent, or utterly capricious cosmos? Somehow, the notion that war comes and goes with some regularity seems to be the assumption that is least offensive to contemporary sensibilities (Singer and Cusack, 1981, pp. 404-06).

> As widely held as the belief that war is on the increase is the belief that war comes and goes in some clear and recurrent cyclical pattern (Small and Singer, 1982, p. 143).

Yet if it is really true that the belief that war is cyclical is widespread and that the twentieth century prefers the plausibility of the cycle to the teleology of the trend or the nihilism of the stochastic perturbation, why then are empirically grounded cyclical models and

462

analyses of war so rare? For that matter, why is there
so much skeptical resistance to the idea that certain
cyclical rhythms may be fundamental to the unraveling of
world politics? Cyclical analyses are hardly the norm
and academic skepticism is sufficiently abundant to make
it easy to argue that the following summary comes closer,
in comparison to the ones above, to capturing the
prevailing outlook on cycles of war and peace.

> History seems to be neither as monotonous and
> uninventive as the partisans of the strict
> periodicities and "iron laws" and "universal
> uniformities" think; nor so dull and mechanical as
> an engine making the same number of revolutions in
> a unit of time. It repeats its "themes" but almost
> always with new variations. In this sense it is
> ever new, and ever old, so far as the ups and downs
> are repeated. So much for periodicity, rhythms,
> and uniformity (Sorokin, 1937, pp. 359-60).

While it is possible to contend that Sorokin's view
is more representative of the academic community than the
views expressed by Singer, Small, and Cusack, it is
equally important to point out that Sorokin's conclusion
was made nearly inevitable by one of his fundamental
premises. Cycles require precise periodicities according
to Sorokin. A 50-year war cycle, therefore, could not
have a 45-year length in one period and then last for 55
years in the next sequence. The two waves might average
50 years but averages are meaningless in the Sorokin
view. To require such precision of social and political
rhythms seems both unreasonable and naive. Many
observers of economic processes, for example, accept the
existence of business cycles. While those same observers
may disagree about their causal mechanisms, few, if any,
believe that business cycles are or must be characterized
by precise periodicities.

Although Sorokin is often cited approvingly by
cyclical skeptics, his insistence on unwavering precision
is consistently ignored. This trait--the tendency to
overlook central premises--also seems characteristic of
much of the literature on cycles of war and peace. On
the one hand, we have a sparse empirical literature that
has attempted to model war cycles along fairly inductive
lines. If or when evidence for a cycle (or cycles) is
uncovered, some effort may then be made to account for
the discovery. But, generally, the support for the
existence of cycles of war produced by these efforts has
been uneven and often amorphous. We also have a
theoretical literature on cycles of what are variously
referred to as general, hegemonic, or global wars. This
second literature, of fairly recent origin, is often

either overlooked as a source of hypotheses, or, more
simply, misinterpreted. Yet many analysts give the
impression that the inductive modeling efforts somehow
address the empirical validity of arguments pertaining to
the repetition of systemic wars. To the contrary, as
will be argued in this paper, the evidence produced by
the first group has little bearing on the claims of the
second group. Moreover, from the perspective of the
second group, the inductive modeling efforts have been
looking for cycles of war and peace in all the wrong
places. In order to elaborate on these assertions, we
need to first review the nature of the inductive evidence
for cycles of war and peace and then contrast this
evidence with the types of arguments put forward by the
analysts of repetitive systemic wars. It should become
clear that there is an important conceptual gap between
what has been modeled and what historical-structural
analysts would like to see modeled.

WRIGHT

Any discussion of warfare can hardly overlook the
work of Quincy Wright (1942/1965), who touched upon the
subject of cyclical oscillations. While his observations
are often cited as justification for analyzing cycles of
war, the nature of his basic generalization on this topic
is less than straightforward in meaning.

> In addition to these three periods--the normal
> battle period of a day, the campaign period of a
> season, and the war period of four or five years--a
> longer period may be detected. There appears to
> have been a tendency in the last three centuries
> for concentrations of warfare to occur in
> approximately fifty-year oscillations, each
> alternate period of concentration being more
> severe. The period is not discernible in the
> sixteenth century and is scarely noticeable in the
> seventeenth century. The War of the Spanish
> Succession (1701-14) occurred less than a century
> after the Thirty Years' War (1618-48), but there
> were several important wars initiated by Louis XIV
> between these two great wars. The War of the
> Spanish Succession was followed in about a century
> by the Napoleonic Wars, which were followed in about
> another century by the Napoleonic Wars, which were
> followed in about another century by the World War
> (1914-18, renewed in 1939). In the mid-eighteenth
> century a concentration of wars centered about the
> Seven Years' War (1756-63) and in the mid-nineteenth
> century about the Crimean War and the wars of

Italian and German nationalism (Wright, 1942/1965, p. 227).

Taken at face value, the passage seems to suggest the following sequence: the Thirty Years' War, the wars of Louis XIV, the War of the Spanish Succession, wars centered around the Seven Years' War, the Napoleonic Wars, the Crimean War and the Italian/German wars of nationalism, World War I, World War II. But to accept this sequence as meaningful, at least one of two conditions would first have to be satisfied. Either this listing would have to exhaust the system's inventory of warfare (or that of a significant group of actors such as the great powers) during the period encompassed by the observation or Wright would have to have made a case for these wars as being of special categorical interest. It is clear that the first condition is not satisfied. Wright provides a detailed list of the warfare between 1480 and 1940, which includes a number of unmentioned wars for the post-Thirty Years' War period.

It seems also clear that Wright was not thinking of great power warfare as a separate class. Elsewhere in his encyclopedic tome, Wright presents a list of fifteen "general wars" which are reproduced in Table 19.1. Wright does not define the concept of general war but he appears to be isolating periods of concentrated great-power warfare in which all or most of the great powers participate for at least 2 years or more. While he does specifically name the fifteen wars listed in Table 19.1, Wright muddies the issue a bit by identifying other great-power wars on more or less simultaneously with these events, of which only some can be linked as directly or even indirectly related.

In any event, most of the wars mentioned in the quoted paragraph can be found in Table 19.1, but not all of them are there (i.e., the Italian/German wars of nationalism are missing). Yet there are also wars listed in Table 19.1 which are missing from the paragraph on the 50-year periodicity (e.g., the War of the Quadruple Alliance, the War of the Polish Succession). Examining the chronological sequence found in Table 19.1, it also becomes clear that there is no 50-year pattern discernible. Up to the mid-nineteenth century, each successive war is separated by no more than 15 years and often less. Moreover, if we assign each ongoing war to the appropriate 50-year aggregations, beginning in 1600, no alternating sequence of more or less warfare is apparent.

Wright did advance a variety of other conceptual distinctions between types of warfare (e.g., balance-of-power wars versus imperial wars), but most of these types would produce far greater frequencies and more continuous

Table 19.1 Wright's General Wars

General Wars	Dates	Fifty Year War/Ongoing Aggregations
1. Thirty Years' War	1618-1648	1600-1649
2. Franco-Spanish War	1648-1659	2
		1650-1699
3. First Coalition against Louis XIV	1672-1679	
4. Second Coalition against Louis XIV	1688-1697	3
		1700-1749
5. War of the Spanish Succession	1701-1714	
6. War of the Quadruple Alliance	1718-1720	
7. War of the Polish Succession	1733-1738	
8. War of the Austrian Succession	1740-1748	
		4
		1750-1799
9. Seven Years' War	1756-1763	
10. American Revolution	1778-1783	
11. French Revolutionary Wars	1792-1802	
		3
		1800-1849
12. Napoleonic Wars	1805-1815	2
		1850-1899
13. Crimean War	1854-1856	1
		1900-1949
14. World War I	1914-1919	
15. World War II	1939-1945	2

Source: Based on Wright (1942-1965, pp. 647-49).

durations than the set of great-power general wars. The
one possible exception is Wright's (1942/1965, pp. 359-
367) discussion of "political trends" in European
international politics, which he asserted were
characterized by four successively different ways of
dealing with instability (territorial sovereignty,
balance of power, concert of power, and nationality).
Each of these four epochal conceptions was "successively
recognized in the treaties terminating the great wars."
In turn, the "great wars" (also referred to as the great
transitional wars) to which Wright alluded are the Thirty
Years' War (1618-48), the 1688-1714 period of warfare
leading to the Peace of Utrecht, the French
Revolutionary/Napoleonic Wars (1789-1815), and World Wars
I and II (1914-45).

The system's "great wars" are therefore
recognizable in terms of their impact on what Wright
refers to as the system's constitution. Distinguishing
wars according to their effect on the system's game rules
is a theme to which we will return at later points in
this paper. It suffices for the moment to observe that
Wright's great wars are no more subject to a 50-year
periodicity than are his general wars. The first great
war is separated from the second by some 40 years while
the last three are separated by roughly 100-year
intervals.

Wright's perodicity claim evidently then is not in
reference to the frequency of wars in general or of
particular types of war, whether it be great power wars,
general wars, or great transitional wars. Rather, it
turns out that Wright is actually referring to the
intensity of war as measured by the number of battles.
If the number of battles engaged in by Wright's ten
principal powers (England/Great Britain, France, Spain,
Austria, Prussia/Germany, Russia, Turkey, the
Netherlands, Denmark, and Sweden) are aggregated by year,
the following clusters of battles are said to emerge:
1618-48, 1672-90, 1701-15, 1740-63, 1789-1815, 1854-78,
and 1914-41.

Since Wright (1942/1965, p. 626) provides battle
frequency data only in decennial aggregations, the precise
duration of his asserted clusters cannot be replicated.
But if one inspects the decennially plotted data (see
Figure 19.1) it is possible to detect spikes of varying
magnitudes in the vicinity of the following decades:
1630-1649, 1670-1679, 1700-1719, 1740-59, 1790-1819,
1860-1879, 1910-1919, and 1930-1940. These decennial
spikes do tend to overlap with Wright's clusters of battle
concentration. It is the timing of these battle clusters,
presumably, that led Wright (1942/1965, p. 232) to put
forward his one elaboration on the fifty-year oscillation:

468

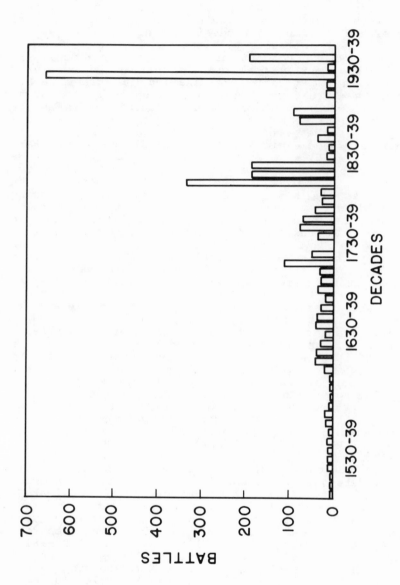

Figure 19.1 Wright's Estimates of Battles, by Decades 1480-1940

The alternating periods of predominant war and predominant peace have varied in length, but there has been a tendency for each to approximate twenty-five years during the [post-Thirty Years' War era].

Given this interpretation, it is possible to visually appreciate the accuracy of Wright's assertion. But it is another matter entirely to ask whether the number of battles has a great deal of theoretical significance or operational reliability. One might consider, for example, how many land battles are equivalent in systemic significance to a Trafalgar or a Midway. In some other cases, the relative absence of battles (e.g., the small number of naval battles in which the Germans participated in World Wars I and II) may be more significant than many of the land battles that did take place. Alternatively, in an examination of any compilation of battles (see Harbottle, 1975, or Dupuy and Dupuy, 1977), one cannot avoid being struck by the subjectivity involved in deciding which battles are included or excluded. Major battles tend to be included but so are a number of minor battles of interest for a variety of reasons (for instance, following the course of a campaign or illustrating the tactics of an individual general or admiral). Invariably, certain periods of time and/or certain regions are slighted. The sixteenth century, for example, is always poorly covered and, of course, prior to the twentieth century, non-European areas are frequently ignored unless European armies are involved in some way.

All of these threats to validity and reliability are not of equivalent significance. But they do suggest that we need to be careful in according too much importance to findings based on battle frequency data. Perhaps the most appropriate commentary is suggested in the following evaluation.

. . . no class of military incidents has the same significance in all periods of history. The battle has been the most persistent type of military incident. It has meant a concentrated military operation between armed forces on a limited terrain for a limited time, usually a day or less. At some periods, however, battles have been isolated events from which flowed important political consequences. At other times a battle has been but an incident in a campaign consisting of complicated strategic operations over a season or in a siege or maritime blockade. In such circumstances political conse-quences cannot be attributed to the single battle battle but only to the whole campaign. Campaigns themselves have sometimes been but incidents in a war waged on many fronts with a number of distinct armies over a series of years. Neither the battle, the campaign, nor the war is entirely satisfactory as a unit for statistical tabulation.

The author of the above paragraph was none other than Quincy Wright (1942/1965, p. 102).

RICHARDSON AND MOYAL

Towards the end of World War II, another major figure in the empirical study of conflict, L. F. Richardson, published his finding that the 1820-1929 outbreaks of war with magnitudes of 3.5 to 4.5 were characterized by a Poisson or random distribution. Similar results shown in Table 19.2, were obtained when Wright's data for the 1500-1931 period were examined.

Table 19.2   Number of Outbreaks of War per Year

	0	1	2	3	4	5+	Total
Observed Distribution	223	142	48	15	4	0	432
Poisson Prediction	216.2	149.7	51.8	12.0	2.1	0.3	432.1

Source: Richardson, 1960, p. 129.

Although Richardson demonstrated little direct interest in the question of cycles and periodicities, and had even less use for the validity of Wright's data, it is frequently assumed that a war cycle would be likely to produce a nonrandom distribution with more years of frequent outbreaks of war than is expected by chance. Richardson's evidence would seem to contradict this expectation.

However, the Poisson distribution of war outbreaks appears to depend on how analysts treat calendar time. Both Richardson and Moyal (1949) demonstrated that the random distribution is observed as long as each year is treated separately. If years are clustered in various ways, the probability of event independence becomes more doubtful. For example, Moyal (1949) found statistically significant autocorrelations in the frequency of Wright's war outbreak data at 5- and 15-year lags. Moyal then went further and calculated a 50-year moving average of war outbreaks per year which disclosed, in Richardson's words, "a conspicuous oscillation" with peaks in 1625 and 1880 and a trough in 1745.

Moyal's finding does not seem to have inspired any further research into its implications. As Wilkinson (1980, p. 30) has remarked recently:

> What might account for such a periodicity? The question takes on additional significance in that the maximum probability of outbreak is larger than the minimum by an impressively large factor of five, which suggests that whatever accounts for the historic variation may be worth examining if we wish to minimize the probability of war outbreaks for the future. Were there fewer war crises at the bottom of the cycle? Was there a better mechanism of crisis resolution, a more pacific world view, greater general satisfaction with the status quo, a more centralized power structure? Investigation is warranted.

Further exploration may no doubt be warranted. But two factors are probably most responsible for the absence of direct reexamination to date. Although it is usually referred to as a 200-year cycle, as many as 255 years separate the two Moyal peaks at 1625 and 1880. How are we to account for such a long-term fluctuation? Without some substantive clue, it is difficult to know how to proceed. In addition, the finding is based on Wright's war data, which are vulnerable to a host of criticisms pertaining to debatable rules about which events are included and excluded, and for what time periods (cf. Singer and Small, 1972, pp. 17-19; Wilkinson, 1980, p. 122). Alternative data bases of comparable length (e.g., Beer, 1974; Levy, 1983) have only become available in the past few years.

DENTON AND PHILLIPS

Denton and Phillips (1968) sought evidence for the data that the level of violence in the international system was characterized by 25-year and 80- to 120-year upswings. Since these upswings could be brought about by increases in either the frequency of warfare and/or the scope/intensity of warfare, a composite "amount of violence" index was created by combining information on the following indicators for the Wright war data set: (1) the frequency of war, (2) the number of belligerents, (3) the number of belligerents divided by the number of states in the system, (4) the total number of belligerent years of war per time interval, and (5) the number of battles fought. No distinction between intrastate and interstate violence was made. No attempt was made to capture the number of lives lost in warfare. Nor were any distinctions made about the status of the war participants. All actors, including revolutionary groups, were treated equally. Despite the fact that the five indicators were not very highly intercorrelated (mean correlation = .499), a single composite index was then created employing factor-analytic techniques. It is the battles indicator that is primarily responsible for depressing the level of intercorrelation. In addition, the 1480-1900 time period that they chose to analyze was divided into five (for the 25-year cycle) and twenty (for the 80- to 120-year cycle) year aggregations for the indicators described above. This procedure implies that (a) the emphasis is on war ongoing as opposed to war outbreaks, and (b) war duration is considered to be of some importance as well since long-running wars would be likely to be counted in successive intervals.

The reported findings for a 25-year cycle are difficult to interpret. The authors report the number of periods above and below the mean for 20-, 25-, and 30-year intervals. Their interpretation is that violence increases about every 20 years between 1495 and 1680 and about every 30 years between 1690 and 1900. However, knowing the distribution of periods above and below a mean does not tell us to what extent the temporal pattern is one of cyclically alternating periods of higher and lower levels of violence. A visual examination of their plotted data is not particularly reassuring on this score.

In contrast, the findings for the 80- to 120-year cycle are easier to evaluate. Denton and Phillips (1968, pp. 190-91) report that the data do indeed support the generalization that:

(1) Periods of high violence in the system will be followed by a decrease in the level of violence.

(2) Periods of low systemic violence will be followed by an increase in violence.

These hypotheses imply a system in which conflict (manifested in violence) grows in scale until a reaction against violence per se occurs. This reaction results in lower conflict in the system until conditions permit the growth of new conflict.

To test these hypotheses, the authors asked how frequently a period with high or low violence (defined in distance from the mean terms) was followed by an increase or decrease in violence. When "high" violence is defined as half a standard deviation above the mean, periods of high violence are followed by periods with a decrease in violence 5 of 6 times, and periods of low violence are followed by periods with an increase in violence 13 of 14 times.

The statistically significant distribution of 20-year intervals is interesting but the connection to an 80- to 120-year cycle is less clear. The appropriate question would seem to be not whether adjacent periods of time alternate between high and low levels of violence but whether violence builds up to a high level before crashing to a low level and then beginning anew the build-up to another high systemic level. In Denton and Phillips' (1968, p. 191) plot (see Figure 19.2) of the 1480-1900 intervals the basic pattern is not quite as temporally uniform as the calculated distribution implies. The level of violence rises in successive intervals between 1481-1500 and 1561-1580, 1581-1600 and 1641-1660, 1661-1680 and 1701-1720, and 1721-1740 and 1821-1840. After the Napoleonic Wars, the direction of movement reverses itself and the level of violence declines gradually from 1821-1840 to 1881-1900. Hence, we have the following sequence: a 100-year rise and abrupt decline, an 80-year rise and abrupt decline, a 60-year rise and abrupt decline, a 120-year rise, and an 80-year decline.

Clearly, these findings raise a number of questions, all of which go unanswered. First, the 80- to 120-year cycle is actually a 60- to 120-year cycle. There is no need to resurrect Sorokin to wonder why the cycle is sometimes fairly short (half the length of the longest interval) while at other times it is quite long (twice as long as the shortest interval). Second, the temporal pattern that is created by 20-year intervals is substantially different from the profile established by 5-year intervals (and the cyclical findings reported for the shorter cycle). As is often the case with cyclical analysis, investigators must be sensitive to the risk of creating the very cycles they are hypothesizing through the data manipulations employed to examine a given series.

Twenty-year intervals, furthermore, are fairly broad periods of time for aggregation purposes. Consequently, it is difficult to know just what event or events in a score of years are responsible for establishing that interval's level of violence, at least without replicating the creation of the violence index. Nevertheless, one cannot help but wonder why the 1821-1840 interval is twice as violent as the preceding

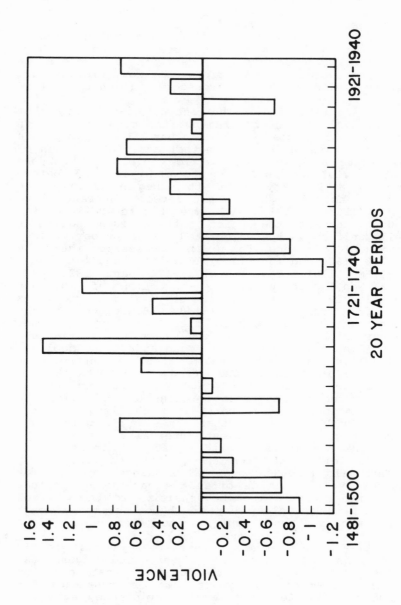

Figure 19.2 Denton & Phillips Long Violence Cycle, 1480-1940

1801-1820 interval that encompasses the Napoleonic Wars. It also seems curious that the first half of the nineteenth century, often celebrated as an unusually peaceful era (at least in terms of European interstate warfare), appears so much more violent than the entire eighteenth century. On the same note, what are we to make of an index that informs us that the 1641-1660 interval was the most violent period in the system's modern history? Interestingly, Denton and Phillips suggest some values for 1901-1920 and 1921-1940 which they estimated from Richardson (1960) data. The violence score for 1901-1920 is roughly equivalent to the level of systemic violence in 1861-1880. The 1921-1940 level of violence is at least twice as high as the level recorded for 1901-1920 but still only on a par with the violence attributed to the 1821-1840 interval. In light of these puzzling anomalies, it seems only fair to speculate that the amount-of-violence composite index may not be functioning as accurately as the authors assume.

Accordingly, it is difficult to know just what to make of Denton and Phillips' long violence cycle. We are never told why an 80- to 120-year cycle should have been expected in the first place. Nor can we be sure how much of a role the techniques (e.g., the composite index or the 20-year aggregations) have played in shaping the cyclical fluctuations that emerge. In sum, Denton and Phillips' procedures and evidence are less than fully convincing. One, however, is forced to concur with the authors' concluding statement: "The possible effects of improved data are, of course, not known."

THE CORRELATES OF WAR

Empirical analyses of war periodicities naturally require, at a minimum, information on the frequency and duration of warfare. Not surprisingly, each of the three major war data sets in the quantitative analysis of international relations has been associated with the quest for periodicity in some way. After all, periodicity is or can be treated as if it is a basic descriptive question. Having touched upon the pertinent work of the developers of the first two sets (Wright and Richardson), it is appropriate to turn to the third, the Correlates of War project headed by J. David Singer. Most analysts should be sufficiently familiar with the many differences in data collection procedures among the three main war data sets that we need not devote time and space to that topic at this juncture. From a periodicity perspective, however, it is important to stress that the Correlates of War project's focus is limited to the post-Napoleonic Wars era (1816 on) and that much of the relevant analysis has been centered on international (excluding intranational) warfare.

Essentially, Singer and Small (1972) pick up the analysis of periodicity where Richardson and Moyal left it. Richardson's finding of a Poisson-distributed outbreak of war with 1-year intervals is replicated separately for the frequencies of 1816-1965 international and interstate war, with 6-month intervals. The randomly distributed outcome is quite similar to Richardson's finding. Moyal's examination of autocorrelation patterns is also replicated at this time through the technique of spectral analysis. No systematic fluctuation (limited to a periodicity of 40 years or less) was observed in the annual amount of international war begun. However, some evidence suggesting 20- and 40-year cycles is generated when the same technique is applied to international war under way (as measured in normalized nation-months). Similar results are obtained when 1816-1965 interstate and 1816-1919 central system wars are analyzed separately.

In a recent update of this analysis, Small and Singer (1982) extend their war series through 1980 and find no empirical reason to adjust their earlier findings on the Poisson distribution of war outbreaks or the absence of cyclical fluctuation traces in the international war begun series. Moreover, the spectral analysis of war under way again generated support for a war periodicity, now described as residing in the 20- to 30-year range. But, as the authors note, the peaks of war under way for the twentieth century's two world wars (1917 and 1943) happen to be 26 years apart. The possibility that their 20- to 30-year cycle might be the product of the two outliers led them to recalculate the analysis without the two world wars. Once the outlier values are removed, the 20- to 30-year cycle evidence tends to disappear, but the reanalysis still produces support for a 14- to 21-year cycle. As Small and Singer (1982, pp. 150-56) conclude:

> This range of 14-21 years is, of course, often treated as the interval between political generations, lending some modest support to certain inter-generational hypotheses built around age, learning, and forgetting.

In a related but much more complicated analysis, Singer and Cusack (1981) confine their attention to the 101 wars engaged in by major powers between 1816 and 1965. Basically, the question they address is whether any periodicity can be detected in the intervals between the termination of one war and the onset of another. Using a battery of techniques ranging from the Poisson through correlations to spectral analysis, Singer and Cusack are unable to discern any systematic periodicity that cannot be accounted for by outlier problems. Yet they do find relationships (see also Levy and Morgan, 1984) that suggest that when major powers

> suffer military defeat, and pay a high price in battle deaths per month of war, they tend to avoid war for a longer time, and the longer they wait, the more intense the next war experience will be (Singer and Cusack, 1981, p. 417).

They are also careful to make explicit what one could say is probably the major weakness of the Correlates of War project's approach to the question of periodicity.

> Having addressed the proposition that national war experiences come at regular intervals in time with some periodicity--foreordained or otherwise--all we have demonstrated is that the probability of the major powers getting into war is independent of when and with what effects they experienced their prior wars. Does this absence of periodicity permit us to infer that there is no underlying regularity, and that war experiences are randomly occurring responses to randomly occurring conditions? Clearly not, since it is quite possible that war requires the concatenation of several conditions, each of whose appearance is cyclical, but with different intervals. This <u>could</u> produce a periodicity in the war experiences of nations, but the concatenation of as few as three such cycles, even if they show (for example) three-, ten-, and fifty-year periodicities, would occur only once every 150 years. Thus the war cycle would be so long as to make its occurrence barely visible in the span under scrutiny here (Singer and Cusack, 1981, p. 419).

Whether Singer and Cusack regard this qualification as a serious constraint on their analysis' ability to tap cycles of war is not a critical issue here. The fundamental point is that it is possible that the Correlates of War (COW) data set, restricted as it is to the post-1816 period, may not be capable of capturing longer-term cycles. With "only" 150 to 165 years of data, short-term, generational cycles may certainly be tackled, but cycles that require the passage of several generations are probably beyond the scope of the COW project. Evidence generated by analyses dependent on COW data, therefore, cannot be regarded as the final word on the presence or absence of cyclical periodicities in war.

LEVY

Finally, some mention of one of the most recent examinations of the war cycle question is in order. Jack Levy's (1983) assembly of data on the 1495-1975 war experiences of some 14 great powers contributes still another data set to the realm of empirical conflict analyses. As a new data set, it possesses at least three explicit advantages over the others that have been employed in tackling hypotheses about fluctuations in warfare. It avoids Wright's legalistic biases in collecting data on war frequency and duration, it concentrates on a specific group of important actors rather than trying to encompass multiple levels of analysis, and it offers a much longer time span than the Correlates of War data set.

However, as in the case of most of the other studies reviewed here, the question of war cycles is only one of many treated by Levy. He initiates his analysis by observing that the work done by Sorokin, Wright, Denton and Phillips, Richardson, Singer and Small, and Singer and Cusack has not generated much empirical support for the notion of cyclical trends. He then visually inspects a set of scattergrams charting the serial history of great power warfare as measured in terms of frequency, duration, extent (the number of great power participants), magnitude (the summary duration for all participating great powers), severity (the number of battle deaths), intensity (the number of battle deaths divided by the population of Europe), and concentration (the severity divided by the magnitude). He concludes:

> There are no hints of any cyclical patterns in either the occurrence of war or in any of its other dimensions. For each of the war indicators, the highest peaks in war as well as the periods of no war appear to be scattered at random. . . . In the absence of any hints of the existence of cyclical trends either in the scattergrams or in earlier studies, however, it is very unlikely that sophisticated statistical techniques could uncover any patterns that are sufficiently strong to have any substantive significance. For this reason these tests are not applied here (Levy, 1983, p. 137).

LOOKING FOR CYCLES OF WAR AND PEACE

This selective review of the empirical literature for and against war periodicities has not been intended to examine every facet or component of the pertinent literature. Rather, it has been intended to illustrate certain distinctive features of the literature. Most clearly, the evidence for specific war periodicities is less than compelling. Each time a researcher uncovers some form of cycle, it has become customary that more questions are raised than are answered. Such a state of affairs, admittedly, is not uncommon in the empirical study of world politics. But in this particular case, many of the questions that are raised have to do with precisely what activity is thought to be cycling and why, with whether the techniques and/or procedures utilized to detect the cycle are actually most responsible for the appearance of a cyclical fluctuation in the data. The ultimate outcome is a great deal of uncertainty about what has been found and whether what has been found has any meaning.

Should we then adopt the prudent strategy that advises that if previous empirical researchers have experienced so many problems in uncovering war cycles, they probably do not exist in any systematic fashion? I would suggest that such a conclusion is premature, not in spite of the evidence accumulated but, in part, because of its very nature. Prudence, as well as skepticism, have crucial roles to play in the (war) research process. But the often nebulous literature on war periodicity reveals several interrelated features, so far left implicit, that may actually be responsible for many of the amorphous findings.

First, most if not all of the analyses reviewed here have violated what should be the first rule of periodicity research:

> Any search for periodicity in the incidence of war is likely to be informed by some theoretical framework which seeks to account for the hypothesized or observed periodicity (Singer and Small, 1972, p. 208).

If we change the phrase "is likely to be informed" to "must be informed," it is likely that the earlier researchers on periodicity might have produced much different results if they had followed this maxim. As it is, a peculiar empirical tradition has been established that encourages inductive searches for periodicities. Only if some type of cycle emerges is it incumbent upon the researcher to struggle with an explanation for it. Indeed, the mere existence of earlier examinations of periodicity will frequently suffice as justification for continued searches in the same inductive spirit. But if the earlier examinations lacked strong justification in the first place, an entire subliterature gradually emerges on a very shaky substantive foundation. We need to reverse the tradition and insist on the statement of specific reasons to search for periodicities in war. Without specific and a priori justification, it is unlikely that we or its midwives will be able to make much sense of what emerges in its absence.

Second, a veritable melange of indicators--frequency, duration, magnitude, severity, intensity, number of battles, and so forth--have been examined at various levels of analysis. Rather than simply picking an indicator, or several indicators to hedge our bets, or some composite index to hedge our bets even better, the specific and a priori justification should clarify in what form the cycle is to be anticipated. If, for instance, the hypothesized cycle is predicated to exist at the systemic level, introducing information on intranational civil wars may either be essential (if the premise makes it necessary to aggregate the system's total sum of violence) or confusing (if the premise focuses only on certain major power wars fought to settle systemic leadership struggles). Only when we know exactly what the hypothesis is about can we judge whether the data, and the tests conducted on those data, correspond to the original premise. This second rule is particularly critical if there is some reason to suspect that all wars and all actors are not of equivalent significance, either to world politics or to cyclical fluctuations of war and peace.

Third, analysts of cyclical periodicities, particularly those of the longer persuasion, need to develop a keener sensitivity for the history of the series they are examining. If one is going to examine a 400- or 500-year series, for example, it helps to know whether it makes sense from an historical perspective to simply divide the series into two segments of equal length. It also helps to know whether it is appropriate to give equal weight to the squabbles of Central European principalities, the frequently peripheral clashes of Russia and the Ottoman Empire, and the major clashes of the system's strongest powers. Alternatively, if an index of violence is constructed that indicates that the worst conflict occurred in the middle of the seventeenth century, the distant clamor of validity alarm bells should be heard at some point before the analysis is completed.

In sum, what is needed are theoretically and operationally justified and historically sensitive analyses. Satisfying these preconditions for the analysis of war and peace cycles will not, by any stretch of the imagination, resolve once and for all the periodicity question (or questions). But the extent to which the preconditions are satisfied should assist in narrowing the extent and nature of disagreement.

The goal of narrowing academic disputes about the periodicity of war can be taken one step further. As noted above, most of the empirical periodicity literature has treated war in a relatively undifferentiated fashion. To be sure, distinctions are sometimes made about international and intranational conflict. The wars of great powers have also been examined as a special case. Nevertheless, it has been an underlying premise of this chapter that the differentiation must proceed even further if we are to capture what historical-structural analysts regard as the most salient war periodicity in the world system. In brief, this further step requires differentiating wars according to the role(s) they perform in the functioning of the system. From this historical-structural vantage point, most of the wars of the past 500 years or so are not unimportant by any means but a few wars have far greater systemic significance than the others. It is these few wars with the greatest significance that tend to recur in cyclical fashion. Consequently, it is their periodicity with which we should be most concerned.

In the past decade or so, a relatively new, historical-structural approach has emerged in the analysis of world politics. The distinguishing characteristics of historical-structural analyses include the presumptions that (a) the present world system is the product of evolutionary and discontinuous historical developments, (b) the system's past must be taken into explicit account in unraveling its present and future, and (c) a major key, if not the major key, to understanding the historical development process and the operational principles of the world system is linked to structural fluctuations in the distribution and concentration of power. More specifically, the fundamental systemic dynamic is the structural movement to and from capability concentration and deconcentration. Periods of unipolarity and systemic leadership are followed by periods of multipolarity and increased competition, which, in turn, devolve into periods of intensive global warfare. Global war resolves the question of systemic leadership and ushers in a new period of unipolarity and systemic rule creation that once again erodes into multipolarity and eventually a renewal of global war.

The unipolar-multipolar-global war sequential process is a common denominator of what is being referred to as historical-structural analyses. But the alleged existence of a common denominator does not imply the absence of a great deal of diversity within the historical-structural format. There is ideological diversity. Left, right, and center are all represented. Terms of reference will differ. For example, the system leader may be labeled the hegemonic power, the dominant power, or the world power. The connotations overlap, but they also conceal different perspectives on what systemic leadership entails. Emphasis on the nature of the motors that drive systemic processes will also vary, with some analyses stressing the predominance of "economic" factors while others promote the significance of "political" and "military" variables. Rapkin (1983), Thompson (1983a, b, c, and d), and Chase-Dunn and Sokolovsky (1983) provide a more extensive discussion of these points.

Most of these differences are not trivial. They reflect differences in assumptions and, not surprisingly, often lead to different conclusions about the same subject matter. It is also difficult, if not epistemologically incorrect, to dismiss one school of thought's assumptions and concepts as false or erroneous. Some degree of tolerance for differences of opinion must be accepted if the historical-structural perspective is to develop into full fruition. Ideally, the best ideas will win out. But, at the same time, some of the disagreements are more susceptible to objective empirical inquiry than others. And, in the interest of maximizing cumulation, we should work towards broadening the number of common denominators whenever and wherever possible. Within this context, a promising area of investigation is the historical identification of the critical and periodical global war punctuations in the systemic concentration-deconcentration process.

Table 19.3 provides an interesting illustration by bringing together and contrasting three different perspectives on the tempo of what is variously labeled general war, hegemonic war, and global war. Whatever the terminology, the most interesting feature of Table 20.3 is the impressive degree of overlap in the asserted cyclical phases.

Of course, the overlapping phases are not addressing the exact same systemic processes. Toynbee's (1954) perspective is closely linked to the classical balance of power conceptualization.

> . . . the most emphatic punctuation in a uniform sequence of events recurring in one repetitive cycle after another is the outbreak of a great war in which one Power that has forged ahead of all its rivals makes so formidable a bid for world dominion that it evokes an opposing coalition of all the other Powers. . . (Toynbee, 1954, p. 251).

Table 19.3 Three Interpretations of General, Hegemonic, and Global War Cycles

Toynbee		Farrar		Modelski	
General War	1494-1525	Probing War	1494-1521	Global War	1494-1516
Breathing-space	1515-1536	Adjusting Wars	1521-1559	World Power	1517-1540
Supplementary Wars	1536-1559			Delegitimation	1541-1561
General Peace	1559-1568	Probing Wars	1559-1568	Deconcentration	1562-1579
General War	1568-1600	Hegemonic Wars	1568-1588	Global War	1580-1609
Breathing-space	1609-1618	Probing Wars	1588-1618	World Power	1609-1634
Supplementary Wars	1618-1648	Adjusting Wars	1618-1659	Delegitimation	1635-1661
General Peace	1648-1672	Probing Wars	1659-1688	Deconcentration	1662-1687
General War	1672-1713	Hegemonic Wars	1688-1714	Global War	1688-1713
Breathing-space	1713-1733	Probing Wars	1714-1740	World	1714-1738
Supplementary Wars	1733-1763	Adjusting Wars	1740-1763	Delegitimation	1739-1763
General Peace	1763-1792	Probing Wars	1763-1789	Deconcentration	1764-1791
General War	1792-1815	Hegemonic Wars	1789-1815	Global War	1792-1815
Breathing-space	1815-1848	Probing Wars	1815-1848	World Power	1816-1848
Supplementary Wars	1848-1871	Adjusting Wars	1848-1871	Delegitimation	1849-1880
General Peace	1871-1914	Probing Wars	1871-1914	Deconcentration	1881-1913
General War	1914-1918	Hegemonic Wars	1914-1945	Global War	1914-1945
Breathing-space	1918-1939				
Supplementary Wars	1939-1945				
General Peace	1945-	Probing Wars	1945-1973	World Power	1946-1973
				Delegitimation	1973-

Sources: Toynbee (1954), Farr (1977), Modelski and Thompson (1981), and Modelski (1984).

According to Toynbee, the combination of cumulative tensions and the disproportionate increase in the relative strength of one of the great powers seeking world dominion leads to the engulfing explosion of a general war. The challenger is defeated by the temporary coalition brought together by the challenger's threat. A patched-up peace, the "breathing-space," is improvised so that the system may recover from its exhaustion. But the problems that were left unresolved in the general war eventually lead to another burst of supplementary warfare which produces more constructive settlements of the outstanding issues and brings about an interlude of "general peace."

In partial contrast, Farrar (1977) assigns wars to three general categories according to their relationship with the existing distribution of power's status quo. Probing wars are the least violent and bring about little change. Adjusting wars create a moderate amount of violence and either bring about some changes in the status quo or else indicate that some changes have already taken place. Still, adjusting wars fall short of disturbing the overall structural distribution. Hegemonic wars, however, do bring about fundamental changes in the system's structure and are associated with a high level of violence. The system's essential war dynamic is thus viewed as first testing, then adjusting or modifying, and then testing again the prevailing status quo. As the pressures for change accumulate and coincide with the attempt of a great power to dominate the system, a hegemonic war establishes a new status quo.

While Farrar's view is fairly compatible with Toynbee's, Modelski's (1978, 1983) perspective is that a single world power emerges from the struggle for systemic leadership, the global war, with a preponderant control of the resources essential to global reach. As this resource base erodes, the world power phase, a period of systemic leadership and politico-economic rule creation, gives way to the phases of delegitimation and deconcentration. Structural power deconcentration proceeds until challengers for the role of world power are encouraged to initiate a new struggle for systemic leadership.

Yet, even though these interpretations are different, markedly similar periodicities are produced and a fairly high level of agreement is obtained on the critical general/hegemonic/global war punctuations in the systemic cycles. This is not meant to imply that Table 19.3 is necessarily representative of the much broader historical-structural school (or schools) of thought. But if we survey the various identifications of general/hegemonic/global wars, there is perhaps much more agreement than is frequently thought.

Table 19.4 summarizes the level of agreement and disagreement among nine major authors. Strong agreement is found on the League of Augsburg and Spanish Succession Wars (1688-1713), the French Revolutionary/Napoleonic Wars (1792-1815), and World Wars I and II (1914-1918 and 1939-1945 or 1914-1945). Another five wars are advanced only by Wright (1942/1965) as part of his general war set: the Franco-Spanish, Quadruple Alliance, Polish Succession, American Revolution, and Crimean Wars. These wars, it is suggested, can be safely regarded as unlikely candidates for special cyclical consideration.

Table 19.4   Level of Agreement in Identifying General, Hegemonic, and Global Wars

Strongest Candidates	Number of Citations	%
French Revolutionary/ Napoleonic	10	100.0
World War I	10	100.0
World War II	8	88.9
League of Augsburg	8	80.0
Spanish Succession	8	80.0
Disputed Candidates		
Thirty Years	7	70.0
Dutch War	5	50.0
Italian	3	30.0
Dutch Independence	3	30.0
Jenkin's Ear/Austrian Succession	3	30.0
Seven Years	3	30.0
Weakest Candidates		
Franco-Spanish	1	10.0
Quadruple Alliance	1	10.0
Polish Succession	1	10.0
American Revolution	1	10.0
Crimean	1	10.0

Note: The number of citations and proportions are based on the ten identifications: Mowat (1928), Wright A (1942/1965), Wright B (1942/1965), Toynbee (1954), Farrar (1977), Modelski (1978), Gilpin (1981), Wallerstein (1982), Midlansky (1984), and Levy (1985).

In between the ten strongest and weakest candidates
are another six candidates with varying degrees of
support: the Italian, Dutch Independence, Thirty Years',
Dutch, Jenkin's Ear/Austrian Succession, and Seven Years'
Wars. Of these six, two--the Thirty Years' War (70.0%)
and the 1672-1678 Dutch War (50.0%), which is often
linked to the 1688-1713 wars as an opening prelude--
receive more support than the remaining four. But while
we can appreciate the virtual absence of disagreement on
the 1688-1713, 1792-1815, and 1914-1945 frays, it seems
unlikely that the status of the disputed candidates can
be resolved by a poll of the relevant literature. Nor do
I agree with Levy's (1985) argument that the issue can be
resolved by definitional fiat:

> Each of the following defining characteristics of
> hegemonic war is a necessary criterion and together
> constitute sufficient criteria. First, the conflict
> must at some point involve the leading military
> power in the system. Hegemony over the system is
> conceivable only through a major victory by the
> leading power or its decisive defeat by a rising
> challenger. The second and third criteria are that
> (2) the war must involve the active participation of
> most of the great powers in the system, and (3) that
> they be allied against a state threatening hegemony.
> . . . Finally, a fourth criterion is that this be a
> substantial war involving sustained and intense
> combat.

Levy (1985) proceeds to specify this definition
even further. A minimum threshold of great power
participation--(N + 1/2N)--is suggested. A minimum intensity of 1000 battle deaths per European population is
also advocated. Yet, while this empirical approach is
certainly in tune with the canons of contemporary
international politics and does represent an improvement
over the often vague assumptions underlying the
identifications summarized in Table 19.3, it overlooks
certain disagreements that continue to plague
historical-structural analyses. We do not fully agree on
the identity of the world system's elite, variously
referred to as great powers, major powers, core powers,
or global powers. We do not agree on how best to
conceptualize military power; thus, there are
disagreements on which states are leading at any given
time. We do not fully agree on whether the theoretical
focus should be the balance of power, hegemony, or power
concentration and deconcentration. Evidently, we also do
not agree on whether the number of battle deaths really
matters from a definitional perspective as long as other,
more important, criteria are satisfied.

As long as we continue to disagree, it is unlikely that we will be able to generate a single set of critical systemic wars. And if we cannot agree on a common set of critical systemic wars, the debate over the timing of war and peace periodicities will continue as well. But this debate, I would suggest, is an improvement over the questions addressed in the literature reviewed in the first part of this paper. The question is not whether some periodicity can or cannot be coaxed from--let alone explain--the welter of statistical information available on deadly quarrels. Rather, the historical-structural question is: which theoretical interpretation of the cycle of war and peace is best supported by the evidence (assuming any are) and which one provides the most rewarding theoretical insights on the functioning of the world system's key processes?

At the same time, Levy's (1985) call for more explicit definitions in the identification of system transforming wars is well taken. The empirical challenge that I would propose, however, is to distinguish between those wars that transformed the system in some theoretically significant way from those wars in which the key players may have tried to transform the system but failed. Table 19.4 gives some useful clues about which bouts of war are most likely to pass this test (e.g., 1688-1713, 1792-1815, and 1914-1945) but more work needs to be done.

For example, Modelski's long cycle approach calls attention to those wars that bring about a reconcentration of the capabilities of global reach. After several years of data collection and index construction, Modelski and Thompson (in progress) are currently working on a series measuring annual changes in the concentration of seapower that encompasses the 1494-1983 period. Within this context, it is possible to examine whether or not, as well as the extent to which, the global wars identified in Table 19.3 have the theoretically predicted impact on the level of concentration. It is also possible to determine whether the other candidates have any discernible impact. These tests can be conducted by use of the venerable eyeball technique or with more sophisticated impact-assessment, time-series techniques. Other historical-structural modelers could do the same. Analysts who contend that the wars that count most are the ones that usher in new eras of economic hegemony simply need to develop a longitudinal measurement of economic hegemony upon which the impact of different war candidates could be assessed. Unfortunately, the focus that is least amenable to this type of dynamic modeling is the emphasis on the balance of power.

Will these analyses, if executed, make some difference to our understanding of international conflict patterns? I think the answer is definitely yes. An appreciation for the periodicity of cycles of war and peace is fundamental to a better understanding of what I have elsewhere (Thompson, 1983a) called "world system time." In brief, it is argued that important political, social, and economic processes proceed according to a clock (in the probabilistic sense) measured not in calendar time but in terms of structural change at the global level. To accurately model the processes of system transformation, war, and peace, we need to be able to tell time according to the appropriate clock. For an alternative view on dealing with different versions of time, see Allan's (1985) chapter in this volume. Moreover, recent research (Rasler and Thompson, 1983, 1984, 1985a and b) suggests that the implications of war and peace cycles and world system time are by no means restricted to the global arena but also influence such processes as state building and the political economy of decline as well. In point of fact, we simply do not yet know just how far an understanding of the fundamental periodicity in war and peace cycles will take us in deciphering the way in which the world works.

20 Forecasting East-West Diplomatic Climate: A Politometric Approach

EAST-WEST POLITICO-DIPLOMATIC CLIMATE: DOES IT MATTER?

Quantitative, empirical political science has not as yet succeeded in adequately coping with the seemingly erratic swings in the East-West politico-diplomatic climate, particularly as reflected in events-interaction data. There is a tendency to dismiss the complete problem of politico-diplomatic climate as "the froth thrown up by the currents of history" (McClelland, 1983, p. 176). According to Pipes, who is hardly sympathetic with quantitative political science, efforts of "taking regular readings of the East-West climate as manifested in the level of rhetoric emanating from Washington and Moscow, the prevalence or absence of dialogues and negotiations, and the intensity of their competition in regions outside their immediate control" are useless exercises in "meteorology." What counts are allegedly internal factors (Pipes, 1984, p. 47). No wonder that many scientists "moved on to greener pastures" (McClelland, 1983, p. 176).

There can be little doubt that politico-diplomatic climate still is one of the crucial variables because in shorter (than eternal) perspective it affects either directly or in a mediated fashion most aspects of East-West relations, including arms control, trade, and human rights (this can be demonstrated empirically; c.f. Frei and Ruloff, 1983, p. 231ff.)--even if so only via psychological mechanisms. What people perceive as real tends to become reality, if we like it or not. Therefore, East-West politico-diplomatic climate must remain on the agenda of empirical research.

IMPLICIT MODELS OF EAST-WEST DIPLOMATIC CLIMATE

A selected bibliography was published in 1980 by Schwarz and Lutz (1980) that lists about 1,000 books and articles dealing with East-West relations in general and,

notwithstanding Pipes's reservations cited above, politico-diplomatic climate is one of the crucial variables
in East-West relations. Without any doubt, the body of
academic literature on this subject has grown considerably since. Looking from a methodological point of view
at a more or less "representative" selection of books and
articles that deal with East-West politico-diplomatic
climate, we find that one interesting feature is that the
majority of approaches hardly point at one or more
"independent" variables that might explain the variations
in East-West climate. This is understandable, since it
would only raise new questions regarding those determinants that the "independent" variables depend on.
Rather, most explanations of East-West climate contain
some more or less precise ideas about the internal logic
of the process.

Regarding the nature of the "mechanisms" that are
to be praised or blamed for what happened, respectively,
four general approaches may be distinguished. In the
first group, **trend models** are preferred. The second
group points at **cycles** or **periodicities** that allegedly
explain the ups and downs in East-West
politico-diplomatic climate. The third group still
favors **stimulus-response models** (S-R) of interaction,
while the fourth group of explanations apparently
perceive East-West climate as a process that
statisticians would call **stochastic**. In most cases, the
choice of the model is implicit. Only a minority of
authors explicitly contemplate their basic model of the
East-West climate.

Trends

Speculation about longer or shorter trends in East-
West climate is particularly popular in socialist
countries. Allegedly, the detente of the seventies was
primarily due to a major shift in the "correlation of
forces" in favor of the socialist countries: catching up
gradually in military terms with the West, the East was
(in its own perspective) capable of virtually forcing the
West to mitigate its "aggressive" policy and to adopt a
more cooperative attitude toward the socialist countries
(Lebedev, 1978, Chapter 2; Cherkasov and Projecktor,
1978, p. 370; Koloskov, 1978, p. 27ff.; Pastusiak, 1978;
Arbatov, 1981, p. 84f.). From the perspective of
Historical Materialism, there is a secular trend toward
peaceful coexistence of East and West, although, in the
long run, only the socialist system is supposed to
prevail, of course, while the capitalist system is
allegedly doomed to extinction.

Since the decline of detente during the late seventies, analysts of East-West relations from the socialist world had increasing difficulties in explaining Western noncompliance with these laws of history, particularly the efforts undertaken by the current US administration to restore the American military capability. These attempts by the West to reverse the "historic dynamics of the change of the correlation of forces" (Samoschkin and Gantman, 1980) are interpreted as a last dogged and desperate attempt to withstand the iron law of history (Zagladin, 1982, p. 43f.; Kortunov, 1979, p. 271). Still, in East and West there appears to be a growing conviction (even among politicians) that there is no reasonable alternative to a policy of coexistence and cooperation among the major powers. No matter what the rationale may be, besides avoiding a nuclear holocaust--whether the "decline of capitalism" and changes in the "correlation of forces" (Arbatov, 1981, p. 87) or the increasing need of the socialist countries to import Western technology and know-how (Bell, 1977, p. 6; Thalheim, 1980; Simes, 1980)--there is agreement that the secular trend (at least) is toward increasing cooperation and decreasing conflict between the United States and the Soviet Union.

Cycles

Other observers of East-West relations appear to be puzzled by what might be called its **cyclical properties**. In an apparent look back in anger, the former Chancellor of the Federal Republic of Germany, Helmut Schmidt, explained at a so-called Atlantic Alliances Conference (organized by _Time_ magazine in Hamburg in April 1983) that "Europeans want continuity and no upheaval every fourth year at every change of administration in the U.S." Not only might the European allies be irritated by such change, but also, according to Schmidt, the Russians "find it difficult to forecast what comes next" (_Time_, 1984). Since the sixties "revisionist" American historians, such as Gar Alperovitz, David Horowitz, and William Appleman Williams, have argued that the American attitude toward the Soviet Union was determined largely by shifts in domestic politics rather than changes in Soviet conduct (cf. Maddox, 1973). Commenting on the decline of detente and the current new "cold war" in US-Soviet relations, one of them (Wolfe, 1979) argues that "U.S. perceptions of hostile Soviet intentions have increased, not when the Russians have become more aggressive or militaristic, but when certain constellations of political forces have come together within the United States to force the question of the Soviet threat onto the American political agenda" (p. 2). Wolfe sees three peaks and two

valleys in US hostilities toward the Soviet Union (p. 8):
the first peak during the beginning of the Cold War, the
second peak in the late 1950s, and the third peak in the
late 1970s, with "valleys" of detente in between. The
blame is put not on the Soviet conduct of foreign affairs
but rather on "peculiar features of the American political
system" (p. 2). Speaking about cycles in East-West
climate is one thing and empirical evidence another, of
course. The first author of this article has recently
demonstrated by means of spectral analysis (Ruloff, 1983)
that both American and Soviet behavior toward each other
does contain some periodicities. Regarding the causes of
these cycles, one is confined to mere speculations,
however.

Interdependence

Particularly popular among students of East-West
relations are the more or less sophisticated
stimulus-response (S-R) models. According to these
views, East-West relations are a process of mutual give
and take, of actions (friendly or hostile) stipulating
reactions (friendly or hostile) that will lead to further
reactions, and so on. The concept of escalation is not
really new in conflict research and strategic thinking.
More interesting but still not new, either, is the idea
of turning the escalation ladder upside down, which would
lead to a process of mutually stimulating cooperative
actions and reactions (for a detailed discussion of the
approach see Frei, 1980). In the seventies, detente led
to a comeback and sophistication of the S-R approach, for
example in the work of Keohane and Nye (1977). It is
perhaps true that the web of interdependence between East
and West has become both tight and complex in certain
areas. As a consequence, Keohane and Nye (1977: 30-32)
expected the emergence of **linkage diplomacy**, a more
complex type of S-R relationship: one party exchanges
concessions in one or more issue areas for concessions of
the other party in still other issue areas, and so on.
Linkage diplomacy did work for a brief period between
1972 and 1974. But hopes that the process of detente
would develop its own momentum through mutually
stimulating and reinforcing cooperative actions and
reactions (Haftendorn, 1975, p. 231) proved premature.
Gamson and Modigliani (1971) and Sullivan (1976, pp.
277-300) have demonstrated empirically that in certain
cases the process works both ways--up and down the ladder
of conflict and cooperation. The question remains,
however, under what precise conditions the process starts
and how it comes to a halt. This is exactly the point
made by the adherents of the stochastic model.

Stochastic Properties

Stochstic processes are those in which arbitrary "inputs" or "shocks" on a system produce specific impacts. It is quite obvious that events beyond the direct or even mediated influence of top decision makers in East and West (such as the downing of a civilian air liner by Soviet interceptors in September 1983) have had an impact on US-Soviet diplomatic climate. Still, even if a certain amount of control by top decision makers over East-West politico-diplomatic climate is admitted, the resulting process, it could be argued, will be stochastic. As McClelland (1983, p. 176) recently pointed out on the occasion of the International Studies Association (ISA) symposium on events data, " . . . there are no highly-determined patterns of international interaction which foreign policy decision-makers are compelled to pursue." According to McClelland, they are "free to decide to start a train of action tomorrow morning, but they also may exercise the option to wait until next year." Hence, it comes as no surprise that the literature on East-West relations is full of rather controversial suggestions as to who started certain initiatives and who spoiled them. According to Schwarz (1979, p. 53), for example, detente was allegedly started by the Soviets. This is certainly true for the Conference on European Security (CSCE) process. Other authors maintain that Western "Ostpolitik" was the crucial factor in starting detente. Also, views regarding responsibility for the chill in East-West relations during the late seventies and early eighties differ strongly. According to the Reagan administration, it was Soviet misbehavior that stipulated the crisis in East- West relations: " . . . hopes that the Soviets would imitate our example of restraint, or that detente would discourage aggression, had all but disappeared" (Secretary of Defense, 1984, p. 19f.); hence the attempts to "rebuild U.S. military capabilities." Stochastic processes have a serious shortcoming from the point of view of the scientist, however. The historic behavior of a stochastic system may be explained to a certain extent, but since the impacts on the system are arbitrary in shape, size, and timing, its _future_ behavior cannot be forecasted.

There are certainly a large number of good arguments in favor of and also against each of the four models of the driving forces that shape East-West political climate. As McClelland pointed out very aptly in his article cited above, the "domain of action and response in international politics has a breadth and complexity that we may have been underestimating" (McClelland, 1983, p. 176). Consequently, the approach

of this chapter is not to prove one of these models or to
falsify the other; this would be naive. Rather, it is to
identify patterns by statistical means. The focus is on
US-Soviet interaction as the core part of East-West
relations. Since attempts to uncouple other parts of
East-West relations from the major power relationship
have failed repeatedly, this appears to be fully
justified. We will first develop a general model of
US-Soviet politico-diplomatic climate. This general
model incorporates trend components, cyclical components,
interaction components (taking into account possible S-R
relationships), and stochastic components. Using
events-analytical data, the exact structure of the model
is then determined and its parameters are estimated.
This will shed some new light on what forces really shape
East-West climate--trends, cycles, S-R relationships, or
exogenous disturbances. Finally, with the estimated
values for the parameters plugged back into the model, it
is employed to simulate US-Soviet politico-diplomatic
climate and compute a forecast up to the end of this
decade.

THE DATA

        Politico-economic conflict and cooperation between
nation-states may be perceived within the framework of
events analysis (cf. Azar and Ben-Dak, 1975, p. 2ff.) as
an actor-action-target relationship. The identification
and coding of events reported in appropriate source
material (most newspapers and other periodicals) proceeds
in principle as follows: actors and targets (in most
cases states) receive a code; the action reported is then
classified (cooperative or conflictive and according to
one or more of eight issue types) and finally scaled with
respect to intensity (applying a specially developed
yardstick). The data of this analysis come from Azar's
Conflict and Peace Data bank (COPDAB) that consists
presently, as he describes it (Azar, 1980, p. 3), of
" . . . about 500,000 events records which have been
systematically coded from about 70 sources between
January 1, 1948 and December 31, 1978. . . ." These
event records contain information about "which source
reported who did what to whom about what issue-area(s)
and when."
        Recent research (Howell, 1983; Vincent, 1983) has
detected significant differences between the findings of
the two currently most advanced events-analytical data
banks, COPDAB and World Event Interaction Survey (WEIS).
This in turn has cast some shadows on the
events-analytical approach in general. Events analysis is
of course far from perfect in its methods, but most of the

objections to it seem to arise simply from the fact that there are no generally agreed-upon ways of collecting events data. In any case, without events data the research reported in this chapter would be impossible Regarding the selection of approaches, it appears that appears that COPDAB is superior to WEIS for at least two reasons: source coverage and robustness of the coding and scaling procedure.

In this analysis, four of Azar's variables are employed: quarterly aggregated index values for total cooperation (Y1 and Y2) and total conflict (Y3 and Y4) with the United States and the Soviet Union as actors and targets, respectively, from 1950 through 1984 (second quarter). Currently, data from COPDAB are available only until 1978. The remaining data (1979 to 1984, second quarter) were collected by the authors according to Azar's coding rules and scaling procedure (sources: New Your Times Index, Kessing's Contemporary Archives, and other chronologies of political events).

MODEL AND METHODS

The traditional model for a time series includes a trend component, seasonal fluctuations and irregular or random variation (Fuller, 1976, p. 387). Sometimes the trend component is decomposed into cyclical and long-term components. In this analysis, we only refer to the so-called long-term component as the trend and introduce a separate component denoting cycles. Seasonalities need not be taken into account. Since there are four time series variables (Y1, Y2, Y3, and Y4) in this analysis that represent US-Soviet politico-diplomatic climate, four equations may be employed to model these variables. With the introduction of a further component I into the model, which accounts for the interaction between each series and the rest of the four, the complete general model is:

$$Y_i t = T_i t + C_i t + I_i t + Z_i t \ldots i=1,\ldots 4 \qquad (1)$$

In this set of equations, the components I_i represent the respective time series Y as a function of values of the other time series:

$$I_1(t) = f(Y2, Y3, Y4) \qquad (2)$$
$$I_2(t) = f(Y1, Y3, Y4) \qquad (3)$$
$$I_3(t) = f(Y1, Y2, Y4) \qquad (4)$$
$$I_4(t) = f(Y1, Y2, Y3) \qquad (5)$$

Because Y_1, Y_2, Y_3, and Y_4 are mutually dependent endogenous variables, this is a system of **simultaneous equations**.

The system of equations provides for the possibility that all time series contain all four components: trends, cycles, interactions with other time series, and stochastic properties. In practice, however, only the statistical analysis of the data will tell whether there is evidence for trends, cycles, interactions, and stochastic properties.

Trends are usually modeled as lower-order polynomials where the dependent or endogenous variable is a simple function of time. Simple OLS techniques will suffice to fit one of these trend lines to any series of data. However, only if all other components of the model are controlled will a real trend possibly emerge.

The identification of cyclical patterns in data is not as simple. One possible approach is spectral analysis. In principle, spectral analysis works as follows: any finite realization from a time series, for example, Y1 in the case of this analysis, with t = 1, 2, 3...n observations (even a series of random numbers) may be represented by a trigonometric polynomial of degree m = n/2, or, if n is odd, m = (n-1)/2. The formula of this trigonometric polynomial is:

$$Y1(t) = (a0/2) + a1 \cdot \cos(w1 \cdot t) + b1 \cdot \sin(w1.t) + \qquad (6)$$
$$a2 \cdot \cos(w2 \cdot t) + b2 \cdot \sin(w2 \cdot t) +$$
$$a3 \cdot \cos(w3 \cdot t) + b3 \cdot \sin(w3 \cdot t) +$$
$$\dots\dots$$

$$am \cdot \cos(wm \cdot t) + bm \cdot \sin(sm \cdot t)$$

where

$$wk = 2 \cdot Pi \cdot k/n \quad (k = 1, 2, 3 \ . \ . \ . \ m)$$

In other words, a function that consists of n/2 or (n-1)/2 pairs of cosine and sine waves with different amplitudes a and b and frequencies ranging from 1/n to m/n = 1/2 may be fitted to any set of n time series data. The cosine and sine coefficients can be computed by means of a finite Fourier transform. As with ordinary polynomials, the fact that a geometric polynomial may be fitted to a specific time series variable is still not an indication that the data actually reveal significant cyclical patterns. Rather, as results of the spectral analysis, certain periodicities must be selected for further investigation, with the possible impacts of other model components under control, of course. The periodogram I that indicates the individual contribution of each of the k = 1...m pairs of cosine and sine waves to the overall shape of the curve is defined as:

$$Ik = (n/2) \ (ak^2 + bk^2) \ (k = 1, \ 2, \ 3 \ ... \ m). \qquad (7)$$

A suitable basis for interpretation, however, are spectral density estimates rather than periodogram ordinates. In principle, spectral density estimates are smoothed periodograms. In this analysis, a so-called rectangular lag window was used for smoothing. For an introduction to spectral analysis see Fuller (1976, pp. 275-301).

Interdependent endogenous variables in a set of equations (that is, "dependent" and "independent" variables from one equation that swap sides in other equations) require a special treatment. OLS regression of each equation separately, in this case, could lead to inconsistent estimators for reasons that need not be discussed in this context. The usual cure is the two-stage generalized least-squares procedure. In principle, a preliminary regression is made to predict all endogenous variables that turn up on the right-hand side of any of the equations in the system. Then, a regression is made by use of these predicted endogenous variables as "independent" variables in the structural equations of the system. A three-stage least squares procedure, furthermore, takes into account correlations among errors across the equations of the system. This approach allows us to perform significance tests for the complete system of equations, rather than only for separate equations or single estimators of parameters.

The stochastic components will be identified by means of a technique developed by Box and Jenkins (1976, Part V; cf. also Pindyck and Rubinfeld, 1976, Part 3, for an introduction). In principle, the procedure tries to model the behavior of a time series variable as a function of lagged values of the same variable or/and lagged errors. The first is the "autoregressive" part of the model (AR); the second is the "moving average" part (MA). In some cases, an integrated version (ARIMA) is required to model a time series variable adequately.

Both ARIMA techniques and spectral analysis require a stationary time series. Most time series, including those of this analysis, are not stationary, however. In principle there are three reasons for this: (a) the mean of the series is a function of time, (b) the variance is a function of time, and (c) the time series is generated by a third type of nonstationary stochastic mechanism (Fuller, 1976, p. 387). Nonstationarity may be detected

by inspecting the autocorrelation function of a series
(Pindyck and Rubinfeld 1976, p. 440ff.). The time series
of this analysis were corrected for variance
nonstationarity by use of logged values. Nonstationarity
due to changes in the mean of the series over time may be
corrected in various ways. Linear filtering (computation
of moving averages or exponential "smoothing") is a very
simple method of removing the mean function from the time
series and should be used only for the purpose of a
preliminary inspection (Fuller, 1976, p. 402ff.).
Differencing of first or higher order is a popular way of
removing nonstationarity in time series and is
incorporated in most ARIMA software packages, but it will
only remove nonstationarity due to locally polynomial
trends of the mean (Fuller, 1976, p. 413). Successive
differencing would also reduce the number of data points
available for further analysis. A way out of these
diffculties is to estimate the trend component T in the
model (assuming that the mean function is "smooth," a
low-order polynomial is used) and employ the residuals
from the trend for further analysis (Fuller, 1976, pp.
393, 398f.). In this study, a cubic trend was employed
for this purpose.

STATISTICAL RESULTS

Following the general model, possible components
(trends, cycles, interdependences among endogenous
variables, and stochastic properties) were identified in
the four time series variables of this analysis. Then all
single components were tested in a regression (OLS) for
their separate impact on the time series variables. The
results (significant R^2, significance level at least 10
percent are presented in Table 20.1.
All four variables apparently contain trends,
provided that other model components are not controlled.
US cooperation with the Soviet Union increased from the
1950's to its climax during 1973 and decreased again. A
linear trend can hardly be fitted, but both quadratic and
cubic trend lines would model this course of events with
some accuracy. Up to 28 percent of the variable's
variance could be "explained" by a trend. To a lesser
degree, the same pertains to Soviet cooperation. A
quadratic trend could be fitted onto the data, but it
"explains" less than 10 percent. As much as 25 percent
of the variance in US conflictive behavior could be
"explained" by a linear declining trend; a cubic trend
(which would take into account also the peak in US
conflictive behavior during the early sixties) would
account for as much as 28 percent of the variable's
variance. The trend in Soviet conflictive behavior is

Table 20.1 Direct Impact of Model Components on Endogenous Variables (R-square)

Model Components:	Y1: cooperation USA-USSR	Y2: cooperation USSR-USA	Y3: conflict USA-USSR	Y4: conflict USA-USSR
Trends				
linear	n.s.	n.s.	0.25	0.13
quadratic	0.21	0.09	n.s.	0.18
cubic	0.28	n.s.	0.28	0.20
Periodicities				
cycle 1	0.18 (15)*	0.04 (6.5)	0.08 (10)	0.06 (12.5)
cycle 2	0.04 (5)	0.04 (2.25)	n.s. (2.25)	0.05 (4)
cycle 3	0.04 (2.25)	n.s. (1)	0.05 (1.25)	n.s. (2)
Interdependence				
Y1: coop. USA-USSR	.	0.23	0.07	n.s.
Y2: coop. USSR-USA	0.23	.	n.s.	0.02
Y3: conf. USA-USSR	0.07	n.s.	.	0.15
Y4: conf. USSR-USA	n.s.	0.02	0.15	.
Autoregression				
first-order	0.33	0.03	0.25	0.24
second-order	0.28	0.02	n.s.	0.16

n.s.: one or more parameters of the component are not significant
* in ( ) length of cycle in years

declining lightly. Still, the characteristic feature of the variable's behavior is its extraordinary peak in 1962 (Cuban missile crisis). The relatively high R^2 values reported for nonlinear trends are largely due to this property of the data.

Using spectral analysis, the three most important periodicities in all four variables were identified and tested in regression equations; plots of spectral density estimates for all four endogenous variables of the model are presented in Figures 20.1-20.4. US cooperation shows a strong cycle of 15 years' length; less important but still significant are shorter cycles. Also, Soviet cooperation contains two significant shorter cycles of 6½ years and 2¼ years, respectively. Both the US and the Soviet conflictive behavior contain a longer and a shorter cycle.

The explanation of cycles and periodicities is a difficult task. More advanced disciplines such as macroeconomic theory have not fully solved the problem; business cycles are an established fact and well explained, but long waves still appear to be a major subject of discussion in economics. Regarding the causes of cycles, endogenous and exogenous factors are distinguished. One possible endogenous cause of periodicities (those "produced" within the system) is the lags, in higher-order feedback loops. Diplomatic processes certainly contain these kinds of lags which could be responsible for the shorter cycles. Among the exogenous causes of cycles, periodic changes in the environment of the foreign policy-making process such as elections are perhaps most important. A theory of diplomatic cycles is still, of course, beyond the scope of this article. The results presented in Figures 20.1-20.4 clearly show that there are indeed cycles in US-Soviet diplomatic climate (or at least certain behavioral traits that might be conceptualized as cycles). This information can be used to model the variables' behavior. Anything more remains speculation.

Interdependence among the model's endogenous variables is somewhat less evolved than might have been expected. Both US and Soviet cooperation appear to be closely related ($R^2 = 0.23$). To a lesser extent, the same pertains to US and Soviet conflict ($R^2 = 0.15$). There are also indications that both the United States and the Soviet Union coordinate conflictive and cooperative behavior, respectively. However, cooperation apparently will not exclude conflict, and vice versa. Correlation coefficients for lagged relationships among the system's endogenous variables are in all cases much weaker than simultaneous interdependences and consequently need not be taken into account.

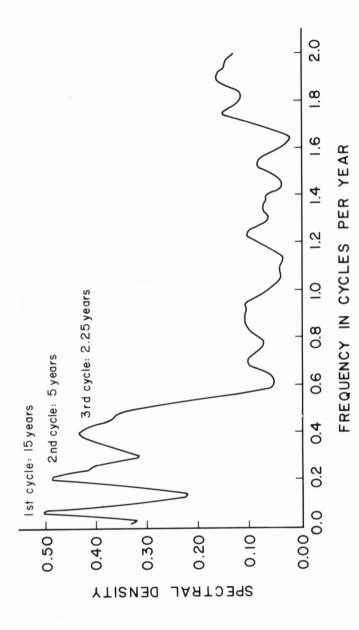

Figure 20.1   Spectral Density Estimates for U.S. Cooperation with Soviet Union

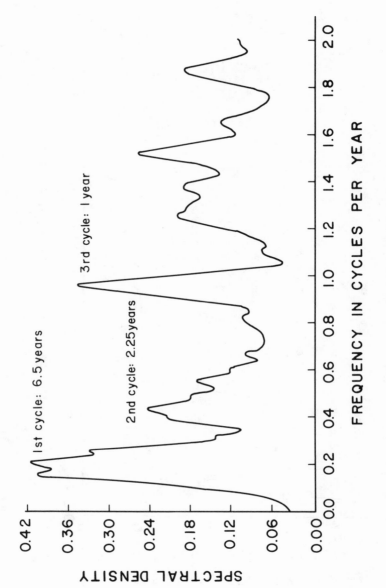

Figure 20.2 Spectral Density Estimates for USSR Cooperation with U.S.

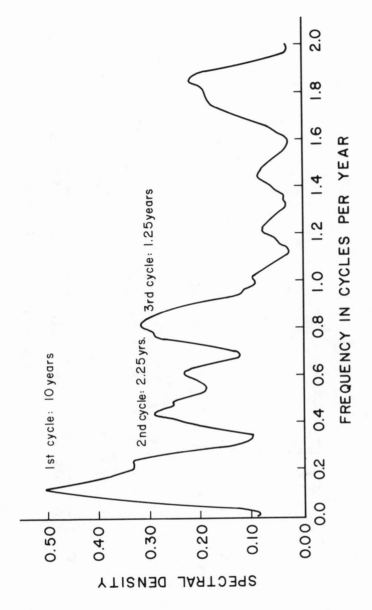

Figure 20.3 Spectral Density Estimates for U.S. Conflict with the Soviet Union

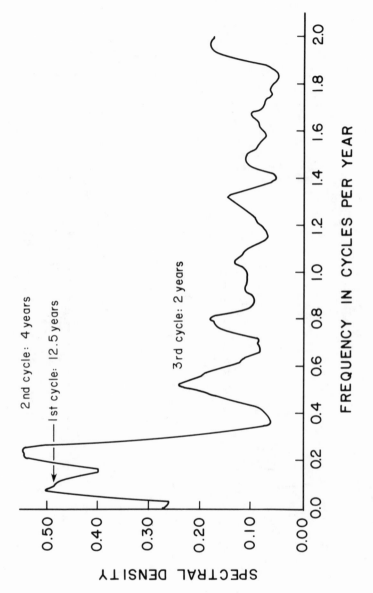

Figure 20.4 Spectral Density Estimates for Soviet Conflict with the U.S.

Using Box/Jenkins techniques, all four time series variables were tested for possible autoregressive and/or moving average patterns. Three out of four variables could be modeled as autoregressive processes (one of first order, two of second order); only Soviet cooperation contains neither autoregressive nor moving-average patterns nor combinations of both.

Hence, to some extent, all four endogenous variables contain trends, periodicities, and stochastic characteristics. To a lesser degree than might have been expected, the endogenous variables are interdependent. Reconstructing the model, however, requires more than simply linking together all components. Rather, in this second step, the model was constructed "bottom up" with OLS, two-stage GLS, and three-stage GLS techniques, i.e., by using those components that proved most important in the first step as a core, and then carefully adding further components as long as the impact of all components on the endogenous variables remains significantly large. This is an iterative process of "trial and error" that yields a Pareto-optimal or "best fit" representation (in terms of "explained" variance) of the four time series variables by trend components, cycles, stochastic (autoregressive) components, and interdependences among the endogenous variables. Results of the estimation for the complete model are presented in Table 20.2

$$Y1(t) = a0 + a1 \cdot \sin(2 \cdot pi/15) \ t + a2 \cdot \cos(2 \cdot pi/5) \cdot t + \quad (8)$$
$$a3 \cdot \sin(2 \cdot pi/2.25) +$$
$$a4 \cdot Y1(t-1) + a5 \cdot Y1(t-2)$$

$$Y2(t) = b0 + b1 \cdot t + b2 \cdot \sin(2 \cdot pi/6.5) \ t + b3 \cdot Y1(t) + \quad (9)$$
$$b4 \cdot Y4(t)$$

$$Y3(t) = c0 + c1 \cdot t + c2 \cdot \cos(2 \cdot pi/10) \ t + \quad (10)$$
$$c3 \cdot \cos(2 \cdot pi/1.25) \cdot t +$$
$$c4 \cdot Y3(t-1) + c5 \cdot Y1(t)$$

$$Y4(t) = d0 + d1 \cdot \cos(2 \cdot pi/4) \cdot t + d2 \cdot Y4(t-1) + \quad (11)$$
$$d3 \cdot Y4(t-2) + d4 \cdot 1(t)$$

It emerged in the analysis that US cooperation is a simple second-order autoregressive process with three cycles superimposed. For simplicity, the lagged version of the respective endogenous variable was employed on the right-hand side of the equations in order to model auto regression. Trends become insignificant in their impact on this variable's behavior when autoregression is controlled for. US cooperative behavior is related to both Soviet cooperative behavior and, to a smaller

Table 20.2 Parameters Estimated for the Final Model

	beta	t-ratio	prob. of t	R-square	F-ratio	prob. of F
[8]	(DF=130, Method=OLS)			0.43	19.43	0.00
a0	0.01	0.20	0.84			
a1	-0.13	-1.71	0.09			
a2	-0.11	2.10	0.10			
a3	0.14	2.10	0.04			
a4	0.35	4.18	0.00			
a5	0.30	3.52	0.00			
[9]	(DF=131, Method=OLS)			0.35	18.05	0.00
b0	0.03	0.42	0.68			
b1	0.25	2.82	0.00			
b2	0.21	3.03	0.00			
b3	0.51	7.40	0.00			
b4	0.15	2.02	0.05			
[10]	(DF=130, Method=OLS)			0.47	23.50	0.00
c0	-0.11	-1.76	0.08			
c1	-0.44	-4.93	0.00			
c2	0.25	3.55	0.00			
c3	-0.18	-2.76	0.01			
c4	0.25	3.18	0.00			
c5	0.25	3.92	0.00			
[11]	(DF=131, Method=OLS)			0.34	16.75	0.00
d0	0.00					
d1	0.12	1.69	0.10			
d2	0.30	3.59	0.00			
d3	0.19	2.30	0.02			
d4	0.23	3.07	0.00			

Weighted R-square for complete system with DF=522: 0.40
(Method: Joint generalized least squares)

degree, US conflictive behavior. In second-stage and three-stage (GLS) regression it became evident that impacts of other endogenous variables of the model on US cooperative behavior become insignificant if interdependences among the model's endogenous variables are controlled. Consequently, US cooperation has an impact on both US conflict and Soviet cooperation, but not vice versa. Still, more than 40 percent of the variable's variance could be "explained"; this is, of course, largely due to the impact of the autoregressive part of the regression equation.

Soviet cooperation apparently has four important determinants. These are (in order of importance): US cooperation; a negative (linear) trend that clearly emerged when other determinants were controlled; a cycle of 6½ years' length; and Soviet conflictive behavior. These four determinants "explain" 36 percent of the variable's variance.

US conflictive behavior toward the Soviet Union appears to be influenced most of all by a linear (declining) trend. Equally important, then, are, a 10-year cycle, a first-order autoregression, and the impact of US cooperation. A shorter cycle of 5 quarters' length also has an important influence on the variable's dynamics. This part of the model "explains" 47 percent of the variance in US conflictive behavior.

Soviet conflict appears to be determined by first-order and second-order autoregression, with additional influence from US conflict and a 4-year cycle. Equation (11) would "explain" 34 percent of the variable's variance. In sum, stochastic properties are most important for the model's overall behavior, followed by interdependence among the endogenous variables. The structure of these interdependences still is no feedback relationship, but a recursive (hierarchical) sequence of impacts: Soviet cooperation depends on both US cooperation and Soviet conflict, while US cooperation influences US conflict, which in turn further affects Soviet conflict. In general, cycles are important, but more so for the US than the Soviet Union. Finally, those theorists who argue in favor of trends in the US-Soviet climate have some reason to do so: US conflictive behavior is decreasing, while Soviet cooperation is increasing. The weighted R^2 for the complete system that corresponds to the approximate F test on all nonintercept parameters is 0.40. This leaves 60 percent of the variance in US-Soviet politico-diplomatic climate (as far as reported in events-analytical data) "unexplained"; but the fact that the simple model presented before "explains" 40 percent of the variance is more than what might have been expected, particularly with McClelland's remarks on the complexity of patterns in diplomatic processes in

mind. As tests show, the residuals of all four endogenous variables must be regarded as "white noise: from
the point of view of statistics. The conclusion is not
necessarily that mere chance or arbitrary decisions largely rule in the US-Soviet climate. We simply cannot
explain the remaining 60 percent of the variance by
referring to trends, cycles, interdependences, or
autoregressive properties. Probably, further independent
(exogenous) variables are required.

SIMULATING AND FORECASTING THE US-SOVIET
POLITICO-DIPLOMATIC CLIMATE

Finally, the model may be employed to simulate and
forecast the US-Soviet politico-diplomatic climate--as
far as represented in the four variables of this
analysis. Up to the point where data on all four
variables are available (second quarter of 1984) the
simulation is **static.** With the reduced form of the
system's equation, estimated values assigned to each
parameter and **real** (measured) values are plugged into the
endogenous variables on the right-hand side. For the
period to be forecasted (second half of 1984 to 1990), the
simulation is **dynamic.** With the reduced form of the
system's equations, previously computed values for
right-hand-side lagged endogenous variables are fed in,
with time as the only "exogenous" variable remaining.

The most important aspect of the crisis in US-Soviet
relations during the late seventies/early eighties was the
complete breakdown in cooperation while the general level
of conflict remained conspicuously at a very low level.
Both sides were obviously very anxious to avoid any
dangerous confrontation (see Figures 20.5-20.8). The
simulation reproduces the characteristic feature of the
US-Soviet climate, namely the seemingly erratic ups and
downs in the curves. A more detailed comparison of
measured values and computed values shows that the simulation also reproduces the major turning points in the US-
Soviet climate. For the coming years, up to the end of
this decade, the forecast is hardly a new detente, despite
increasing values for cooperation. Rather, a return to
normalcy in the US-Soviet climate after the breakdown in
cooperation is apparently in sight. The agreement to
resume arms control talks shortly after the US election
day in late 1984 corroborates this finding. But more
cooperation also includes the possibility of increased
conflictive interaction (particularly on behalf of the
US). As the case of detente in the early seventies shows
clearly, this appears to be the normal course of events.
Regarding the strong impact of autoregressive components
on three out of four endogenous variables, forecasts

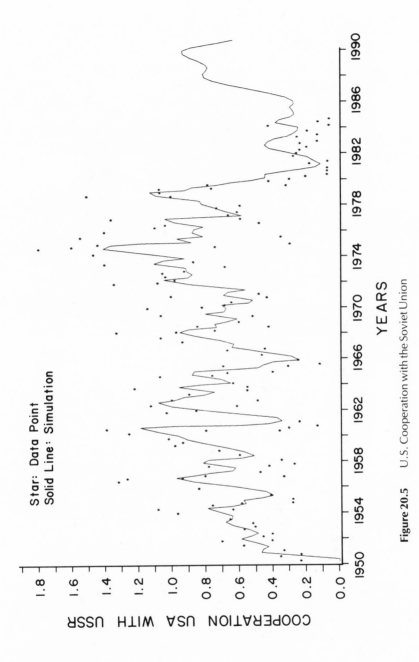

Figure 20.5   U. S. Cooperation with the Soviet Union

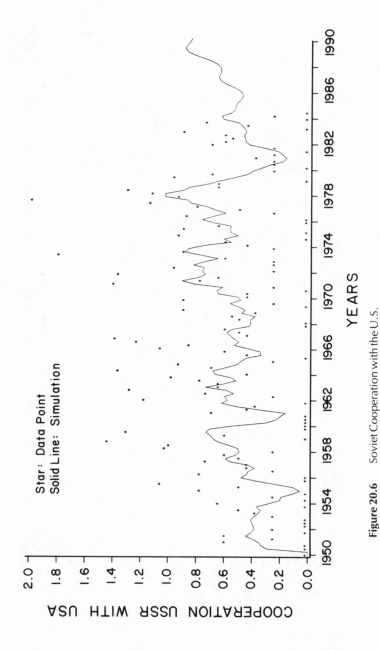

Figure 20.6   Soviet Cooperation with the U.S.

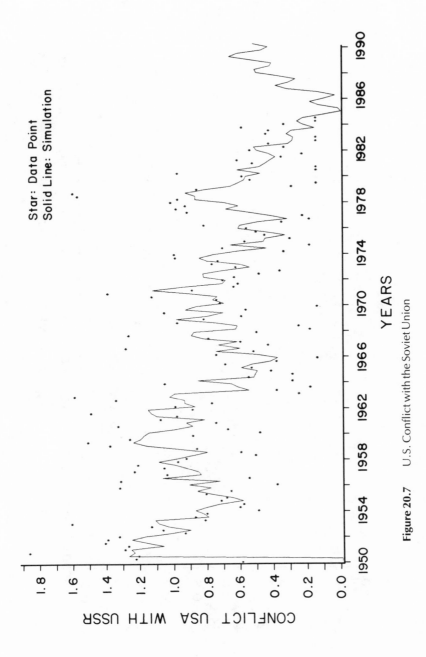

Figure 20.7   U.S. Conflict with the Soviet Union

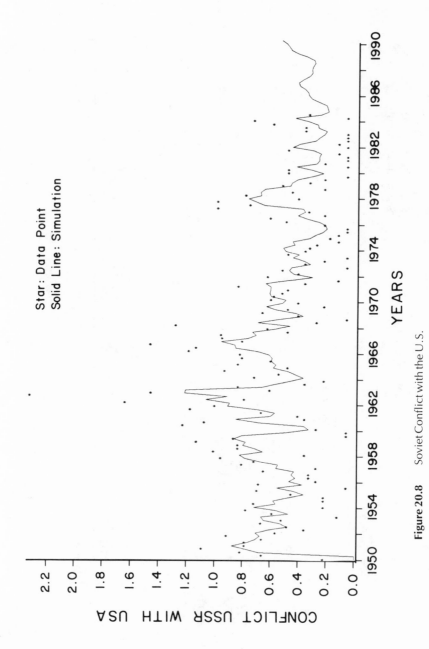

Figure 20.8   Soviet Conflict with the U.S.

should be treated with caution. The complete system is apparently highly sensitive to exogenous shocks and/or deliberate initiatives on the part of the actors themselves, be they conflictive or cooperative. Since US cooperative behavior assumes a central position in the model, US cooperative initiatives would certainly cause reactions on behalf of the Soviet Union. Continuity is not the most notable trait of US behavior toward the Soviet Union. In this the European critics of American conduct in foreign policy are correct. But if the forecasts presented above are apt, the time appears to be ripe for a change in the US-Soviet climate, beginning with the second half of this decade; as a result, the entire picture of US-Soviet relations could improve, particularly the field of arms control and trade.

SUMMARY AND CONCLUSIONS

Based on the expert literature on East-West relations that has been reviewed and tested empirically in a previous study by the authors (Frei and Ruloff, 1983), a quarterly model of politico-diplomatic climate between the US and the USSR was developed. This model explains the behavior of four endogenous variables (US conflictive and cooperative attitude toward the Soviet Union; Soviet conflictive and cooperative attitude toward the US) in terms of trend components, cyclical components, stochastic components, and interaction among endogenous variables. Parameters were estimated by use of events-analytical time series data (from COPDAB) for the period 1950 to 1984 (second quarter). The weighted R^2 for the complete system that corresponds to the approximate F test on all nonintercept parameters is 0.40. Considering the simplicity and parsimony of the model, this is certainly an amazing result.

Still, the research presented in the preceding pages "explains" the US-Soviet climate only in the statistical sense (and not the more substantive theoretical meaning) of the term. The behavior of time series variables is modeled mathematically by fitting four equations to the data while treating the structure of the system that produces this behavior as a **black box.** In general terms, the dynamics of the US-Soviet politico-diplomatic climate may be explained as a result of superimposed trends, cycles, stochastic components, and interactions among both powers. This is the only interesting result from a theoretical point of view. More important, however, the model was employed to simulate and forecast the US-Soviet climate.

Data and forecasts show that the relationship between the United States and the Soviet Union has always been and will likely remain a variable mixture of conflict and cooperation. The crisis in East-West relations since the latter days of the Carter administration has been characterized by a near-complete breakdown in cooperation, while at the same time both sides have been very anxious to constrain their conflictive behavior. The very modest US policy during the KAL 007 incident and the Polish crisis is an example. The euphemism of detente is definitively gone and replaced by a more sober view both in East and West. A comeback of detente is not in sight. But, from the forecasts presented here, the prospects for a return to normalcy in US-Soviet relations are good. The fact that new talks on arms control were announced shortly after the presidential election in the US is a promising start. Still, whether "business as usual" in East-West relations would provide a sufficiently solid basis to jointly overcome more extreme strains on the system (possibly originating in a controversy over a Third World crisis) is a different matter.

The strong impact of stochastic components (first- and second-order autoregression) on the model's behavior supports the assumption that exogenous shocks on the systems (i.e., events of all kind) do play a crucial role. These phenomena are not taken into account in the model, but must be considered when interpreting the forecasts. Hence, if these phenomena could be traced sufficiently and incorporated into the model, the precision of explanations and forecasts would increase considerably. Further research by the authors, employing the impact-assessment techniques of Box and Tiao (1975), will focus on this problem.

_____ **Part 7**
Commentary

21 Connecting Domestic and International Conflicts, Past and Present

VIOLENT CONFLICT WITHIN AND AMONG STATES

Violent conflict is dynamic, but most models of it are static representations of conflicting interests and capacities, set into motion only with the jerky rhythm of a slide show. The lack of effective dynamic models is clear enough for international conflict. In the case of conflict within states, however, it is nearly absolute. At least in international conflict analysts generally begin with the assumption that they are dealing with interactions among two or more parties. When it comes to conflict within states, observers, authorities, and theorists alike commonly perceive the conflict as "protest," "rebellion," "disorder," "collective behavior," and the like. Such ideas attribute the action to a single--generally irrational--actor. Such ideas badly distort the continuous interactions among organized parties that actually constitute the bulk of larger-scale conflicts, violent or not, within states. Clearly, students of domestic conflict have something to learn from current analyses of international conflict.

This chapter makes two sorts of connections with efforts to build dynamic models of contemporary international conflict. The first connection runs from international conflict to conflict within states. Conceptually, to what extent can we consider the two categories of conflict to be variants of the same basic phenomenon? Empirically, to what degree and how does international conflict shape conflict within states, and vice versa? The second connection links present to past conflicts. In what ways, if any, do the dynamics of present conflicts, both within and among states, resemble those of the past? What are the critical differences? From the perspective of modern European history, this chapter offers thinly documented speculations on these questions, in hopes of inciting others to undertake research more firmly connecting past and present.

517

As idea and as fact, the sharp distinction between international and domestic conflict is a fairly recent creation. Consider national states: relatively centralized, autonomous, differentiated organizations exercising control of the major concentrated means of coercion in substantial and well-bounded contiguous territories. Various states and empires have waxed and waned in different parts of the world for 5,000 years or so, but national states, as such, have only become common in the world since 1500. Depending on how we count colonies and empires, we might place the mapping of most of the world into national states as late as 1850, or even 1950.

Nor did the states established before 1850 sit securely in their positions. Until recently, would-be sovereigns regularly faced major rivals within their territories. Even in England--that paragon of stability--Tudor, Stuart, and Orange monarchs had to contend with the princes, pretenders, and other potentates who repeatedly claimed the right to rule England before 1714. So long as that was true, the lines among intergroup conflict, revolution, civil war, and international war remained blurred. One of the most important consequences of state formation was to separate the types of conflict from each other, and thereby to establish a distinct arena of conflict within the state's perimeter, an arena limited and monitored by agents of the state.

The construction of national states centered on two major clusters of activity: the organization of coercive force and the control of goods and services. The two reinforced each other. The building of effective force consumed substantial goods and services, while giving statemakers the means of controlling more goods and services. Each cluster consisted of several overlapping activities; the organizational differentiation of those activities from each other resulted from the very process by which states became powerful. Defined from the perspective of persons controlling states, the activities break down as shown in Table 21.1.

In the early stages of European state formation, the production and distribution processes remained secondary both in organizational bulk and in salience for the managers of states. Warmaking, statemaking, protection, and extraction were the primeval state activities, with war at their very core. Warmaking, statemaking, and protection, furthermore, overlapped greatly at the start. So long as national boundaries were porous, so long as most soevereigns ruled indirectly, leaving considerable autonomy and armed force to regional magnates, and so long as alliances between "domestic" and "foreign" opponents of the same ruler remained common, the lines among warmaking, statemaking, and protection were blurred.

Table 22.1   Activities Leading to the Formation of
National States.

Organization of Coercive Force

Warmaking
Eliminating or neutralizing their rivals outside the territories in which they have clear and continuous control.

Statemaking
Eliminating or neutralizing their rivals inside those territories.

Protection
Eliminating or neutralizing the enemies of their clients, both inside and outside the territory in which they, the agents, exercise clear and continuous control.

Control of Goods and Services

Production
Creating goods and services (both individual and collective) by transforming labor, land, capital, and/or raw materials.

Distribution
Allocating goods and services, both individual and collective.

Extraction
Acquiring the means of carrying out the previous five activities.

To a lesser degree, the three activities also overlapped with extraction; when armies lived directly off the land, for example, the line between warmaking and extraction blurred. Only the imposition of continuous territorial control by the managers of states and the creation of a distinctive state apparatus--which were themselves outcomes of warmaking, statemaking, protection, and extraction--made them clearly separate.

In more recent phases of European state formation, states have broadened their range of protection, have separated warmaking from statemaking and protection, and have devoted increasing energy to production and distribution. All three of these changes have resulted largely from the changing character of extraction. In the process of seizing the wherewithal of warmaking, statemaking, and protection from their subject populations, state managers have bargained out agreements: guarantees of public debt, representation of the taxed, rights in exchange for military service, extensions of

protection from the few to the many, provision of services, sometimes even redistribution of income.

An effective income tax, for example, depends on
three conditions: (1) an economy in which money wages
constitute a large share of national income, and in which
those wages are accessible to governmental scrutiny, (2)
relative immobility of labor and labor-employing capital
across national boundaries, and (3) broad cooperation from
the taxed population. No western state has been able to
meet the third condition without extensive concessions of
rights and protections to its citizenry. Immediately
after its revolutions of 1640 and 1688, Great Britain
installed head taxes graded by social category in crude
correspondence to the likely income of each category.
War-pressed France tried a similar rough experiment in
1695. But all these efforts soon suffered widespread
evasion, slipped back toward fixed property taxes, and
disappeared. Britain first installed a system approaching
a genuine income tax in the war year of 1799, and
maintained it until 1816. Only in 1842, however, did
Great Britain establish a permanent general income tax.
That was two decades or more earlier than other major
European states. By 1842, Britain was ten years past its
Parliamentary Reform of 1832 and had a labor force of
which over three-quarters were wage-earners. Britain was
no doubt the first large European state to meet the three
basic conditions: commercialized wage-economy, relative
immobility of capital and labor, consent of the taxed.
And that consent ran through powerful, relatively
representative national institutions.

The balance among warmaking, statemaking,
protection, extraction, production, and distribution remained delicate into our own time. Over the last 400
years, for example, the rhythm of warmaking has driven the
cadence of extraction in almost all western states.
Taxation and other forms of extraction have risen with
preparation for war and have tended to reach a new
threshold with each major war. The same has been true of
national debt. Yet, the ability of a state to extract the
means of war has depended on an interaction between the
state's resource base and its extractive strategy. The
Dutch state, for instance, was able to summon significant
armed forced without building a large fiscal apparatus by
applying customs and excise taxes to a highly
commercialized economy. Neighboring Prussia, relying more
heavily on land taxes and applying its excise to a less
commercial economy, created a massive governmental
organization that twinned fiscal with military structures.

The interplay of warmaking and extraction had a
paradoxical effect. The vast growth of military
organization led to the "civilianization" of western
states. Although the requirements of warmaking continued

to set the rhythm of governmental expansion, the early
establishment of a division between the supporters and the
executors of warmaking--between financiers and generals,
for example--gave civilians control not only of extraction
but also of statemaking, protection, production, and
distribution.

In western states, on the whole, military men
eventually lost the power to make the major strategic
decisions, including the decision to start or end a war.
They found themselves surrounded and contained by the very
civilians whose predecessors had taken office to serve
military purposes. Kings withdrew from all but the
symbolic trappings of warfare and the major strategic
decisions. Military leaders lost their once-intimate
access to kings, especially in times of peace.

Meanwhile, kings and their servants were striking
bargains with their subject populations in order to assure
the flow of goods and services to their armed forces.
Those bargains further constrained the autonomy of
military action; within the territories of their own
states, for example, generals lost their rights to billet
soldiers on the civilian population, requisition supplies
directly, impress new troops, or establish police forces
to control whole communities. As the personnel and
organization of government civilianized, furthermore, the
simple logic of conquest and defense started giving way to
considerations of national politics and policy. To put it
differently, national politics and policy veered away from
conquest and defense toward the protection and advancement
of civilian interests defined as urgent by civilian-
operated organizations. The expansion of warmaking power
led indirectly to the civilianization of state power.

All along the way, extraction often caused conflict.
State attempts to gather the wherewithal of war from
reluctant citizens, and in the presence of organized
competitors for state power, provided the most frequent
occasions for major rebellions and for the far-reaching
successful rebellions we call revolutions. The expansion
of war in seventeenth-century Europe thus incited
rebellion after rebellion, including France's Fronde and
England's two revolutions. State managers who could not
balance warmaking, statemaking, protection, and extraction
lost control of their states.

Up to now, however, no state has ever gained an
effective monopoly of violence within its territory. So
far, in every state some bandits, sadists, private police,
brawlers, and vandals have always evaded state control.
But successful states did acquire control over the
principal concentrated means of coercion inside their
boundaries, and managed to dissolve or absorb those
concentrations that were large enough to coalesce into
effective rivals to state power. The establishment of

state-controlled police forces that were clearly distinct from armies did not occur generally in western states until after 1800. Their appearance marked the victory of states over other sorts of organizations.

Thus, over much of history international and domestic conflict have been not merely similar but overlapping, even indistinguishable phenomena. Our own age has differentiated them. Even in our era, we might reasonably expect very general models of conflict to apply equally to both categories.

Nevertheless, the emergence of a worldwide system of national states has itself created differences in the qualities of conflict within and among states. By and large, states have far more lethal force at their disposal than do any other sorts of organizations; struggles among them therefore entail the possibility of more lethal outcomes. Despite great disparities among the world's states, furthermore, the homogenization of the state system has produced far more resemblances among states than among the range of groups (including states) that sometimes engage in domestic conflict. Finally, domestic conflicts take place within limits set by national states, and often involve those powerful actors as monitors, mediators, repressors, objects, or initiators; today's superpowers do not approach the relative position in the world as a whole that almost every state occupies on its own terrain. Models of international conflict that do not give a significant place to lethal force are likely to be inadequate, just as models of domestic conflict that do not allow for great inequalities among the actors and for the intervention of powerful third parties are likely to be of little value.

INTERACTIONS BETWEEN DOMESTIC AND INTERNATIONAL CONFLICT

States face in two directions, toward other states and toward their own populations. Because of that, international conflicts commonly have strong repercussions on domestic conflicts, and vice versa. Sometimes those mutual influences are enormous. Consider the string of wars involving France, Great Britain, and other European powers from 1756 to 1815. Attempts to pay for the first of them, the Seven Years' War (1756-63), by means of stamp taxes and similar imposts in Britain and its colonies incited strong resistance within Great Britain; they also played a major part in aligning colonists against British rule in North America. Domestic opponents of the British crown took up the American cause enthusiastically; symbols and slogans of opposition flowed easily across the Atlantic in both directions. French efforts to finance their participation in the American War of Independence,

in their turn, led to great standoffs between France's
sovereign courts and the crown, then to the calling of the
Estates General, which became the vehicle of revolution.
When France declared war on Great Britain in 1793, both
states began large drives to raise troops, taxes, and
supplies.
In France, that mass mobilization precipitated
multiple rebellions, including the great counter-
revolution of the Vendee. In Great Britain, the massive
increase of taxes during the Revolutionary and Napoleonic
Wars encountered surprisingly little resistance. Military
service was another matter; of the 617 "riots" John
Bohstedt has catalogued in England and Wales from 1790
through 1810, 133 concerned military affairs, especially
recruiting (Bohstedt, 1983, p. 14).
Within France, the revolution and military history
intertwined. Armies and militias played important parts
in all the major revolutionary transitions, from the
defection of royal troops to the popular opposition in
1789 to the consolidation of Napoleon's successive coups
d'etat by military force. From 1789 onward, city-based
militias, national guards, and revolutionary armies cowed
the French countryside, commandeered grain and other
supplies for the urban population, and provided the
cutting edge of the Terror.
The mobilization of France's enemies for war
similarly aroused struggles against tax increases,
conscription, impressment, and restrictions on trade in
country after country; not only in Great britain, but
also in the Netherlands, Spain, Prussia, and elsewhere.
From 1799 onward, expanding French forces frequently
encouraged or organized movements of opposition to existing governments before they displaced those governments.
As a consequence of Spanish and Portuguese involvement in
the French wars, much of Latin America acquired de facto
or de jure independence from its colonial masters. And
the successive settlements of the war not only redrew the
European map, but also transmuted domestic politics in
every state of western and central Europe--a textbook
case, we might say, of interaction between domestic and
international conflict.
Nor have such interactions disappeared from the
contemporary world. Because of struggles over fiscal,
military, and industrial policies, every industrial state
now finds its domestic politics locked to international
conflicts, and the current government of every industrial
state faces at least one vociferous opposition that calls,
directly or by implication, for a significantly different
approach by the state to international conflict.
In the Third World, a different sort of interaction
seems to be going on. Since World War II, the provision
of arms, military training, and related technical advice

to Third World governments by the US the USSR and a few other western states has increased enormously. At the same time, the proportion of Third World states under military rule has risen to a majority, and the military coup has become the most frequent form of governmental succession in Latin America, Asia, Africa, and the Pacific. Although the precise relationships among these changes are open to debate, most likely a disproportionate expansion of military power and effectiveness relative to all other organizations in many Third World countries results from the postwar military buildup, facilitates military takeovers, and encourages those who seek power to work with and through the armed forces. Once again, domestic and international conflict interact.

EXTRACTION AND REPRESSION AS LINKS BETWEEN DOMESTIC AND INTERNATIONAL CONFLICT

It is not hard, then, to find instances of plausible ties between domestic and international conflict. The difficulties begin with the efforts to generalize and to model such instances. Two bundles of relationships merit special attention: **extraction** and **repression.** Extraction we have met before. Repression is simply a name for those aspects of statemaking, protection, and extraction which entail the application of coercion within the state's zone of domestic control.

The first bundle connects the extractive activities and capacities of states to their involvement in and preparation for war. Judging from western historical experience, preparation for war through military organization, taxation, conscription, construction, manufacture, requisition, and purchase outweighs all other activities in determining the size and shape of national states. In 1500, Europe contained about 500 nominally autonomous political entities, only a few of which--England, France, Sweden, Poland, Russia, and perhaps the Ottoman Empire--resembled national states as we know them. Those principalities, free cities, bishoprics, city-states, and other entities averaged about 3,800 square miles of land area and 125,000 people each. By 1890, the roster stood between 20 and 30 (depending on how one counts the 9 members of the German Empire), almost all of which had the recognizable characteristics of national states. They averaged some 63,000 square miles and 7.7 million people, not including colonies outside of Europe. Almost all of that radical reduction in number and increase in scale resulted directly from wars and war settlements.

Each war entailed an organized increase in the state's extractive efforts. In the course of these activities, states not only created armies and navies, but also incurred debt, established treasuries, built bureaucracies, elaborated systems of surveillance and repression, and bargained out arrangements for negotiation with their subject populations.

The effectiveness of these activities, and thus of the preparation for war, depends on (a) the volume and character of resources under the control of the subject population, and (b) the fit between the state's means of extraction and the subject population's organization. Between 1790 and 1808, the British state drove up its taxes from about 24 to 36 percent of national income, while the French state may have moved from 12 to 13 percent (Mathias and O'Brien, 1976) The establishment of the income tax in Britain, to be sure, helped make the remarkable increase possible. The British state could only accomplish that feat because it was dealing with a highly monetized economy, because a large proportion of its labor force already consisted of wage earners, and because an exceptional share of its revenues came from customs, excise, and other taxes on trade rather than on land, capital, or movable property.

Thence, however, a strong connection between international and domestic conflict arises. Subject populations always have other uses for the land, capital, movable property, and labor that states covet for warmaking, and often have strong commitments to use them in those ways. These commitments commonly have bases in law and social organization. Efforts to extract the wherewithal of war from subject populations therefore always engender resistance. Depending on the character and intensity of the state's demands, the organization of the subject population, and the means of negotiation employed, the resistance is sometimes fierce, even revolutionary. Almost all major seventeenth- and eighteenth-century rebellions (emphatically including the English and American Revolutions of 1640 and 1776) began with the effort of financially pressed states to draw the means of war from reluctant populations.

The second bundle of relationships between international and domestic conflict that deserves special attention concerns governmental repressive capacity and activity. By "repression" I mean any activity that makes nongovernmental mobilization or collective action more costly. Although visible increases in governmental repression sometimes incite strong action from well-organized groups, in general higher repression means less collective action. When governments facilitate mobilization or collective action by lowering its costs or increasing its benefits, they usually do so quite selectively, action by action and group by group; nevertheless, facilitation ordinarily increases overall levels of mobilization and collective action. A weak government --one that does little repressing or facilitating-- is vulnerable to attack and seizure by organized segments of its subject population.

These truisms matter because involvement in international conflict inevitably affects a state's repressive capacity and activity. Drawing on western experience of the last few hundred years, let us hazard some empirical generalizations:

(1) A state that mobilizes successfully for war increases its capacity to repress domestic collective action.

(2) A state that is mobilizing for war characteristically attempts to increase its repressive activity. It typically aims that repression at (a) resistance to the extraction of warmaking resources from the subject population, and (b) opposition to warmaking activity.

(3) To the extent that mobilization for war builds up the power and coherence of military organizations relative to all others, it gives military personnel the incentive and the opportunity to control the state as a whole.

(4) Insofar as a warmaking state has increased its repression, deferred commitments to organized groups within its subject population, and drawn a high proportion of the population into warmaking activity, war-ending demobilization increases the likelihood of strong demands on the state.

(5) Insofar as warmaking depletes a state's resources, its capacity to meet or repress strong demands declines.

(6) A state's loss of a war generally lowers its subject population's shared estimates of the state's repressive capacity and of the likelihood that other states will defend it against popular demands.

(7) For these reasons, the end of a war--especially a lost war--usually increases a state's vulnerability to popular opposition, including attempts to seize state power.

(8) A winning state, however, commonly reduces the vulnerability of a losing state by occupying its territory, temporarily dissolving its sovereignty, and organiz-

ing an international compact for the reestablishment of a state with ample extractive and repressive capacities.

All these generalizations imply significant relationships between the form and intensity of a state's involvement in international conflict, on the one hand, and the rhythm and character of its domestic conflict, on the other. They imply, for example, a concentration of revolutionary movements around the ends of wars, especially within states that have lost wars. They also imply a tendency for collective action that is not initiated and controlled by the state to decline in wartime. Those implications deserve investigation.

DYNAMICS OF DOMESTIC CONFLICT

Before we can investigate those relationships effectively, however, we need a much better understanding of the dynamics of domestic conflict. There, alas, existing work leaves a great deal to be desired. In international relations, a large share of all theories are purposive: they state how an actor or set of actors with a given array of orientations and a given set of means might be expected to behave. The literature of domestic conflict contains relatively few purposive theories, especially theories sufficiently specified to yield predictions about real events. Instead, theories of domestic conflict are largely causal: they aim implicitly at stating the necessary and sufficient conditions for different sorts of action, such as nationalist movements, revolutions, or strikes. Such an emphasis has its advantages; it encourages analysts to work through the sorts of connections between large-scale governmental changes and shifting forms of conflict we explored earlier. But it makes dynamic analysis extraordinarily complex. How can we line up necessary and sufficient social conditions in causal chains?

In fact, most empirically grounded work on domestic conflict (including my own) concentrates on description. Its models lack precision, elegance, and coherence; either they are crude but serviceable or they take the form of post hoc rationalizations of quantitative results. Furthermore, although standards of measurement are sometimes quite high, the evidence analyzed rarely tracks strategic interactions as such. Instead, it generally concerns a population, or a set of populations, considered to be at risk to action. The analysis, essentially epidemiological in conception, then consists of accounting for the actual pattern of action among the populations at risk.

Consider, for example, the well-designed research of Hanspeter Kriesi and collaborators on "political activation" in Switzerland from 1945 to 1978. Kriesi and his colleagues went through a series of sources--two social histories, a news agency's annual summary, three series of cantonal yearbooks, a national political yearbook, a newpaper's annual index, special serials concerning initiatives, referenda, petitions, and strikes, plus a few other sources, for reliability checks. They identified nonroutine events involving ordinary people which publicly committed those people to positions concerning specific problems of shared concern.. These events were their <u>Aktivierungereignisse</u> (activation events).

With these definitions and data, Kriesi and associates did a number of simple but revealing analyses of Swiss popular politics--showing, for example, that during a period of declining electoral participation the frequency of these nonelectoral actions was rising and that the resort to illegal forms of action was becoming more common. However, although one can learn a good deal about Swiss politics from such analyses, they have two obvious drawbacks. First, the very form of the evidence obscures the interaction among groups, including groups of ordinary people and of authorities, that provides the rationale of such "activation." Second, even the best analyses of the evidence remain fundamentally static. We are a long way from dynamic models of domestic conflict.

The dynamic models of domestic conflict that do exist almost uniformly treat it as the work of a single actor or a single type of actor: a society as a whole, a social movement, protest groups, dissatisfied people. The dynamics result not from strategic interaction, but from transformation of the actor's state. That is obviously true of the stage and trajectory models that clutter contemporary sociology and political science. It is also true of learning and diffusion models, such as those of Robert Hamblin, in which the course of a revolution, a strike, or a social movement depends on rates of adoption of a new behavior within populations of varying permeability.

Those models of domestic conflict that treat interaction explicitly have the virtue of greater realism. They permit, for example, direct consideration of coalition formation, of repression, of inequalities among antagonists. But they are also almost unrelievedly static. One of the best, for example, appears in the work of Gamson et al. (1982) on the "micromobilization" of rebellions against unjust authorities. They postulate three mutually reinforcing processes which occur in the course of interaction with unjust authorities: changes in organizational capacity, alterations of ties with authorities, and transformations of shared definitions. **Organizing** acts increase organizational capacity, **divesting** acts acts neutralize ties to authorities, and **reframing** acts redefine the actions of authorities as unjust.

A successful rebellion against unjust authority, in this model, results from a series of acts of organizing, divesting, and reframing. The rebellion gets this far by thinning the interaction drastically; in the model and in the experiments conducted to test it, the unjust authority has little room for maneuver; he simply reveals and reinforces his unjustness. Thus, the model ends up like many other insufficiently dynamic models of conflict (including my own): at best a statement of preconditions for alternative outcomes to interaction.

BORROWING FROM INTERNATIONAL RELATIONS

What could students of domestic conflict learn from specialists in international relations (IR)? That question is valuable for unexpected reasons. On close inspection, it turns out that relatively few standard international relations models will apply to domestic conflict without serious modification, and that the essential modifications point up significant problems for theory and research. In order to apply to domestic conflict the wide array of game-theoretical models now at large among students of international relations, for instance, researchers will have to shift away from their favored causal analyses to the analysis of strategic interaction. There, they will have to either (1) accept the usual limitation to a small number of actors, but allow for very large inequalities among the actors, as in the characteristic encounters between domestic challengers and states (or between workers and owners), or (2) devise N-party models in which the number, identities, and boundaries of the parties change as a function of the action.

Again, even after the fact, the payoffs of domestic conflict are hard to define, hard to allocate, and harder to measure. Analysts of the American civil rights movement, for example, are still debating what difference, if any, civil rights activism made to the positions of American blacks in the 1950's and 1960's. These problems, and others like them, are no less soluble in principle for domestic conflict than they are for international conflict. But in practice the lack of any viable solution reveals a discouraging fact. Outside of highly ordered arenas such as elections and budget-making, students of domestic conflict have done little of the prefatory political analysis: identifying the actors, the stakes the alternative means, the outcomes, the rules of the game.

Over the last decade or so, nevertheless, studies of domestic conflict have been changing in ways that make a rapprochement with dynamic analyses of international conflict a bit easier (for recent surveys, see Gurr, 1980; Jenkins, 1983; and Zimmerman, 1983). First, analysts of conflict have been abandoning the "collective behavior" preoccupation with inchoate crowds and masses in favor of the identification of concrete, organized groups of actors. Second, they have placed the actions of those groups in streams of interaction with allies and enemies instead of treating them as the sort of instantaneous, self-contained event connoted by such words as "riot," "disturbance," and "disorder." Third, they have frequently substituted rational-action models for the irrationalist treatments of crowds and masses that once prevailed. All these steps bring students of domestic conflict closer to analysts of international relations.

RETURNING THE FAVOR

Current analyses of domestic conflict therefore have some modest rewards to offer students of international struggles. For one thing, specialists in domestic conflict have developed a rich sense of the variety of means that enter into conflict: the differentiation in organization, personnel, and likely effectiveness among strikes, demonstrations, protest meetings, electoral rallies, insurrections, boycotts, occupations, petition drives, and other forms of collective action with respect to different targets, demands, and political situations. To some extent, the specialists have systematized the description and measurement of these alternatives.

For another thing, the causal analyses that dominate studies of domestic conflict have some merits. As the time span under consideration lengthens, reallocations of resources, transformations of production, changes in the organization of states, alterations in the coalitions, and power relations among crucial actors all become more important. Even in short-run analyses, students of international relations gain from integrating game-theoretical models with models of resource allocation. These changes in structure are the terrain of many accounts of domestic conflict. To be sure, in order to adapt the causal arguments of domestic conflict analysts to their international sphere, IR specialists will have to do some of the same sorts of preparatory work that will precede the serious application or IR models to domestic conflict. Yet that work will serve both sides.

Finally, some of the apparent superiority of international relations models of conflict probably comes at the price of ignoring problems that students of domestic conflict have faced directly. In those regards, IR specialists have something to gain from examining the solutions, however stumbling, the domestic conflict analysts have devised. The division between interstate and intrastate conflict, as we saw earlier, is itself a historical creation, not an eternal given. An extension of the earlier analysis to the present and future suggests the likelihood that new actors and new sets of actors are becoming relevant: not only a roster of national states, but a network of states connected by flows of arms, persons, goods, and capital. Not just states, but also blocs of states, coalitions of terrorists, multinational corporations, religious organizations, blocs of commodity producers, clusters of arms merchants, mercenaries, and/or purveyors of drugs. To the extent that such structures themselves acquire coercive power, they become significant actors in the international arena. To that extent, the neat mapping of that arena into a set of mutually exclusive turfs, each inhabited by a single calculating actor, loses its value. Students of domestic conflict have a lot of experience in dealing with that sort of world.

References _____

Alker, Hayward R., Jr. and C. Christensen (1972). "From Causal Modeling to Artificial Intelligence: The Evolving UN Peace-Making Simulation." In Experimentation and Simulation in Political Science, edited by J. A. LaPonce and P. Smoker. Pp. 177–224. Toronto: University of Toronto Press.

Alker, Hayward R., Jr. and William Greenberg (1976). "On Simulating Collective Security Regime Alternatives." In Thought and Action in Foreign Policy, edited by Matthew Bonham and Michael Shapiro. Pp. 263–306. Basel: Birkhauser Verlag.

Allan, Pierre (1982). "Determinants of Swiss Military Expenditures." In Small Countries and International Structural Adjustment, edited by I. Dobozi, C. Keller, and H. Matejka. Geneva: Graduate School of International Studies.

Allan, Pierre (1983). Crisis Bargaining and the Arms Race. Cambridge, Mass.: Ballinger.

Allan, Pierre (1984). "Towards Building Social Clocks." Paper presented at the Joint U.S.-Swiss N.S.F. Conference on Dynamic Approaches to Modeling International Conflict, Boulder, Colorado.

Allison, Graham T. (1971). The Essence of Decision. Boston: Little, Brown.

Altfeld, Michael F. (1984). "The Decision To Ally: A Theory and Test." Mimeographed. East Lansing: Michigan State University.

Altfeld, Michael F. and Bruce Bueno de Mesquita (1979). "Choosing Sides in Wars." International Studies Quarterly 23:87–112.

Ames, Edward and Richard T. Rapp (1977). "The Birth and Death of Taxes: A Hypothesis." Journal of Economic History 37:161–178.

Anderson, P. and Stuart Thorson (1982). "Artificial Intelligence Based Simulations of Foreign Policy Decision-Making." Behaviorial Science 27:176–193.

Arbatov, Georgji A. (1981). Der sowjetische Standpunkt. Uber die Westpolitik der UdSSR. Munich: Rogner & Bernard.

Ardant, Gabriel (1975). "Financial Policy and Economic Infrastructure of Modern States and Nations." In The Formation of National States in Western Europe, edited by Charles Tilly. Princeton: Princeton University Press.

Arrow, Kenneth (1963). Social Choice and Individual Values. New Haven: Yale University Press.

533

534

Arrow, Kenneth, Theodore Harris, and Jacob Marshak (1951). "Optimal Inventory Policy." Econometrica 19:250–272.

Aubert, Jacque et al. (1979). L'Etat et sa police en France (1789–1914). Geneva: Droz.

Auerbach, Eric (1953). Mimesis: The Representation of Reality in Western Literature. Translated by Willard R. Trask. Princeton: Princeton University Press.

Axelrod, Robert (1979). "The Rational Timing of Surprise." World Politics 31:228–246.

Axelrod, Robert (1984). The Evolution of Cooperation. New York: Basic Books.

Axelrod, Robert and W. D. Hamilton (1981). "The Evolution of Cooperation." Science 211:1390–1398.

Azar, Edward E. (1980a). "The Codebook of the Conflict and Peace Data Bank (CODAB): A Computer-Assisted Approach to Monitoring and Analyzing International and Domestic Events." Mimeographed. Chapel Hill: University of North Carolina.

Azar, Edward E. (1980b). "The Conflict and Peace Data Bank (COPDAB) Project." Journal of Conflict Resolution 24:143–152.

Azar, Edward E. and Joseph Ben-Dak, eds. (1975). Theory and Practice of Events Research. New York, London, and Paris: Gordon & Breach.

Badie, Bertrand and Pierre Birnbaum (1979). Sociologie de l'Etat. Paris: Bernard Grasset.

Bailey, Martin J. (1970). "Tactical and Lanchester Analysis of Combat in the U.S. Civil War." Unpublished manuscript, University of Rochester.

Barr, Aaron, Paul R. Cohen, and Edward A. Feigenbaum (1982). The Handbook of Artificial Intelligence. Los Altos, Calif.: William Kaufmann.

Basar, T. and G. J. Oldser (1982). Dynamic Noncooperative Game Theory. New York: Academic Press.

Baumol, William J. (1965). Economic Theory and Operations Research. Englewood Cliffs, N.J.: Prentice-Hall.

Bean, Richard (1973). "War and the Birth of the Nation State. Journal of Economic History 33:203–221.

Beaufre, A. (1965). Deterrence and Strategy. Translated from the French by R. H. Barry. New York: Praeger.

Becker, Gary S. (1976). The Economic Approach to Human Behavior. Chicago: University of Chicago Press.

Beer, Francis A. (1974). How Much War in History: Definitions, Estimates, Extrapolations and Trends. Beverly Hills, Calif.: Sage.

Bell, Coral (1977). The Diplomacy of Detente. The Kissinger Era. London: Martin Robertson.

Benjamin, Roger. "The Historical Nature of Social-Scientific Knowledge: The Case of Comparative Political Inquiry." In Strategies of Political Inquiry, edited by E. Ostrom. Beverly Hills, Calif.: Sage.

Bennett, P. G. (1980). "Hypergames: The Development of an Approach to Modeling Conflicts." Futures 12:489–507.

Bergesen, Albert (1980). Official Violence During the Watts, Newark, and Detroit Race Riots of the 1960s." In A Political Analysis of Deviance, edited by Pat Lauderdale. Minneapolis: University of Minnesota Press.

Bergstrom, A. R. (1966). "Non-recursive Models as Discrete Approximations to Systems of Stochastic Differential Equations." Econometrica 34:173–182.

Berkowitz, B. (1981). "Stability in Political Systems: The Decision To Be Governed." Ph.D. dissertation, University of Rochester.

Berkowitz, B. (1983). "Realignment in International Treaty Organizations." International Studies Quarterly 27:77–96.

Best, Geoffrey (1982). War and Society in Revolutionary Europe, 1770–1870. London: Fontana.

Bethe, H. A., R. L. Garvin, K. Gottfried, and H. W. Kendall (1984). Space-based Ballistic-Missile Defense." Scientific American, October:37–47.

Bishop, D. and C. Cannings (1978). "A Generalized War of Attrition." Journal of Theoretical Biology 70.

Bittinger, Marvin L. and J. Conrad Crown (1982). Mathematics: A Modeling Approach. Reading, Mass.: Addison-Wesley.

Blainey, J. (1973). The Causes of War. New York: Free Press.

Bohstedt, John (1983). Riots and Community Politics in England and Wales, 1790–1810. Cambridge, Mass: Harvard University Press.

Bonder, S. (1967). "The Lanchester Attrition-Rate Coefficient." Operations Research 15:221–232.

Boulding, Kenneth E. (1962). Conflict and Defense: A General Theory. New York: Harper and Row.

Boulding, Kenneth E. (1985). Communication with Michael D. Ward and Lewis L. House, February 1.

Box, G. E. P. and G. M. Jenkins (1976). Time Series Analysis: Forecasting and Control. San Francisco: Holden-Day.

Box, G. E. P. and G. C. Tiao (1975). "Intervention Analysis with Applications to Economic and Environmental Problems." Journal of the American Statistical Association 70:70–92.

Brams, Steven J. (1975). Game Theory and Politics. New York: Free Press.

Brams, Steven J. (1976). Paradoxes in Politics. New York: Free Press.

Brams, Steven J. (1977). "Deception in 2 x 2 Games." Journal of Peace Science 2:171–203.

Brams, Steven J. (1983). Superior Beings: If They Exist, How Would We Know? New York: Springer-Verlag.

Brams, Steven J. (1985). Superpower Games: Applying Game Theory to Superpower Conflict. New Haven: Yale University Press.

Brams, Steven J., M. D. Davis, and P. D. Straffin, Jr. (1979). "The Geometry of the Arms Race." International Studies Quarterly 23:567–588.

Brams, Steven J. and Marek Hessel (1982). "Absorbing Outcomes in 2 x 2 Games." Behavioral Science 27:393–401.

Brams, Steven J. and Marek Hessel (1983). "Staying Power in Sequential Games." Theory and Decision 15:279–302.

Brams, Steven J. and Marek Hessel (1984). "Threat Power in

536

Sequential Games." International Studies Quarterly 28:23–44.
Brams, Steven J. and D. Marc Kilgour (1985a). "Optimal Deterrence." Social Philosophy & Policy, forthcoming.
Brams, Steven J. and D. Marc Kilgour (1985b). "Rational Deescalation." Mimeographed.
Brams, Steven J. and Donald Wittman (1981). "Nonmyopic Equilibria in 2 x 2 Games." Conflict Management and Peace Science 6:39–62.
Braun, Rudolf (1977). "Steuern and Staatsfinanzierung als Modernisierungsfaktoren. Ein deutsch–englischer Vergleich." In Studien zum Beginn der modernen Welt, edited by Reinhard Koselleck. Stuttgart: Klett–Cotta.
Bremer, Stuart (1977). Simulated Worlds. Princeton: Princeton University Press.
Brewer, Gary D. and Martin Shubik (1979). The War Game: A Critique of Military Problem–Solving. Cambridge, Mass.: Harvard University Press.
Bright, Charles and Susan Harding, eds. (1984). Statemaking and Social Movements. Ann Arbor: University of Michigan Press.
Brito, Dagobert L. (1972). "A Dynamic Model of an Armaments Race." International Economic Review 13:359–375.
Brito, Dagobert L. and Michael D. Intriligator (1973). "Some Applications of the Maximum Principle to the Problem of an Armaments Race." Modeling and Simulation 4:140–144.
Brito, Dagobert L. and Michael D. Intriligator (1974). "Uncertainty and the Stability of the Armaments Race." Annals of Economic and Social Measurement 3:279–292.
Brito, Dagobert L. and Michael D. Intriligator (1982). "Arms Races: Behavioral and Economic Dimensions." In Missing Elements in Political Inquiry: Logic and Levels of Analysis, edited by John A. Gillespie and Dina A. Zinnes. Beverly Hills, Calif.: Sage.
Brodbeck, May, ed. (1968). Readings in the Philosophy of the Social Sciences. London: Macmillan.
Brown, Courtney (1982). "The Nazi Vote: A National Ecological Study." American Political Science Review 78:285–302.
Brubaker, Earl R. (1973). "Economic Models of Arms Races: Some Reformulations and Extensions." Journal of Conflict Resolution 17:187–205.
Buchanan, James M. and Gordon Tullock (1962). The Calculus of Consent. Ann Arbor: University of Michigan Press.
Bueno de Mesquita, Bruce (1980). "An Expected Utility Theory of International Conflict." American Political Science Review 74:917–931.
Bueno de Mesquita, Bruce (1981a). The War Trap. New Haven: Yale University Press.
Bueno de Mesquita, Bruce (1981b). "Risk, Power Distributions, and Likelihood of War." International Studies Quarterly 25:541–568.
Bueno de Mesquita, Bruce (1983). "The Costs of War: A Rational Expectations Approach." American Political Science Review 77:347–357.
Bueno de Mesquita, Bruce (1984a). "A Critique of `A Critique of The War Trap.'" Journal of Conflict Resolution 28:341–360.

Bueno de Mesquita, Bruce (1984b). "The Expected Utility of Conflict Escalation: A Preliminary Analysis." In The Dynamics of Conflict Processes in Inter-state Relations, edited by Dina A. Zinnes. Denver, Colo.: University of Denver Monograph Series in World Affairs.

Bueno de Mesquita, Bruce (1985). "The War Trap Revisited." American Political Science Review, forthcoming.

Bunn, M. and K. Tsipis (1983). "The Uncertainties of a Preemptive Nuclear Attack." Scientific American (November):32–41.

Busch, Otto (1962). Militarsystem und Sozialleben im alten Preussen 1713–1807. Die Anfange der sozialen Militarisierung der preussisch-deutschen Gesellschaft. Berlin: de Gruyter.

Busch, Peter (1970). "Appendix on Mathematical Models of Arms Races." In What Price Vigilance, by Bruce M. Russett. New Haven: Yale University Press.

Button, James W. (1978). Black Violence. Political Impact of the 1960s Riots. Princeton: Princeton University Press.

Caplow, Theodore (1956). "A Theory of Coalitions in the Triad." The American Sociological Review 21:489–493.

Caplow, Theodore (1959). "Further Developments of a Theory of Coalitions in the Triad." The American Sociological Review 55:488–493.

Casstevens, Thomas W. and J. R. Ozinga (1974). "The Soviet Central Committee Since Stalin." American Journal of Political Science 18:559–568.

Chang, Chin Liang and Richard Char-Tung Lee (1973). Symbolic Logic and Mechanical Theorem Proving. New York: Academic Press.

Chapman, Brian (1970). Police State. London: Pall Mall.

Chase-Dunn, Christopher and J. Sokolovsky (1983). "Interstate System, World-Empires and the Capitalist World-Economy: A Response to Thompson." International Studies Quarterly 27:357–67.

Cherkasov, P. P. and D. M. Projektor (1978). "The Problem of Deepening the European Detente." In European Security and Cooperation, edited by the Soviet Committee for European Security and Cooperation. Pp. 306–346. Moscow: Progress.

Chertkoff, Jerome M. (1970). "Socio-psychological Theories and Research on Coalition Formation." In The Study of Coalition Behavior, edited by S. Groenings, E.W. Kelley, and M. Leiserson. Pp. 297–322. New York: Holt, Reinhart and Winston.

Childs, John (1983). Armies and Warfare in Europe, 1648–1789. New York: Holmes & Meier.

Churchman, Charles West, Russell L. Ackoff, and E. Leonard Arnoff (1957). Introduction to Operations Research. New York: John Wiley.

Cioffi-Revilla, Claudio (1979). "Diplomatic Communications Theory: Signals, Channels, Networks." International Interactions 6:209–265.

Cioffi-Revilla, Claudio (1983). "A Probability Model of Credibility: Analyzing Strategic Nuclear Deterrence." Journal of Conflict Resolution 27:73–108.

538

Cioffi-Revilla, Claudio (1984a). "European Political Cooperation (EPC): An Application of Political Reliability Theory to Integration." International Studies Quarterly 28:467–492.

Cioffi-Revilla, Claudio (1984b). "The Political Reliability of Italian Governments: An Exponential Survival Model." American Political Science Review 78:318–337.

Cioffi-Revilla, Claudio (1985). "Political Reliability Theory and War in the International System." American Journal of Political Science 29:47–68.

Cioffi-Revilla, Claudio and Richard L. Merritt (1981/82). "Communication Research and the New World Information Order." Journal of International Affairs 35:225–245.

Cipolla, Carlo (1965). Guns, Sails, and Empires: Technological Innovation and the Early Phases of European Expansion 1400–1700. New York: Pantheon.

Clark, K. L. and F. G. McCabe (1984). Micro-PROLOG: Programming in Logic New York: Prentice-Hall.

Clark, Sir George (1969). "The Social Foundations of States." In The New Cambridge Modern History, Vol. 5, The Ascendancy of France, edited by F. L. Carsten. Cambridge: Cambridge University Press.

Clarke, T. Michael and Urs Luterbacher (1984). "Energy Crises and the Small State: An Analysis of Swiss Security." Paper presented at the Annual Meeting of the International Studies Association, Atlanta, Georgia.

Clausewitz, Carl (1832). On War. Edited by Anatol Rapoport. New York: Penguin, 1966.

Clocksin, W. F. and C. S. Mellish (1981). Programming in Prolog. New York: Springer Verlag.

Collingwood, R. G. (1946). The Idea of History. Oxford: Oxford University Press.

Connelly, Owen (1965). Napoleon's Satellite Kingdoms. New York: Free Press.

Cornford, Francis M. (1971). Thucydides Mythistoricus. Philadelphia: University of Pennsylvania Press.

Costanza, R. (1984). "The Nuclear Arms Race and the Theory of Social Traps." Journal of Peace Research.

Crawley, C. R., ed. (1969). The New Cambridge Modern History IX. War and Peace in an Age of Upheaval, 1793–1830. Cambridge: Cambridge University Press.

Croce, Benedetto (1923). History, Its Theory and Practice. New York: Harcourt-Brace.

Cronin, James and Jonathan Schneerm, eds. (1982). Social Conflict and the Political Order in Modern Britain. London: Croom Helm.

Cusack, Thomas R. and Michael D. Ward (1981). "Military Spending in the United States, Soviet Union, and the People's Republic of China." Journal of Conflict Resolution 25:429–69.

Davis, Morton D. (1983). Game Theory: A Nontechnical Introduction. New York: Basic Books.

Deitchman, Seymour J. (1962). "A Lanchester Model of Guerrilla Warfare." Operations Research 10:818–827.

Denton, F. H. and W. Phillips (1968). "Some Patterns in the History of Violence." Journal of Conflict Resolution 12:182-95.

Dessert, Gabriel (1984). Argent, Pouvoir et Societe au Grand Siecle. Paris: Fayard.

Dickson, P. G. M. (1967). The Financial Revolution in England: A Study in the Development of Public Credit, 1688-1756. London: St. Martin's.

Domke, W., R. Eichenberg, and C. Kelleher (1983). "The Illusion of Choice: Defense and Welfare in Advanced Industrial Democracies, 1948-1978." American Political Science Review 77:19-35.

Dougherty, James E. and Robert L. Pfaltzgraff. (1981). Contending Theories of International Relations. New York: Harper and Row.

Downs, Anthony (1957). An Economic Theory of Democracy. New York: Harper.

Dray, William H. (1957). Laws and Explanations in History. Oxford: Oxford University Press.

Dray, William H. (1969). "Mandelbaum on Historical Narrative: A Discussion." History and Theory 8:287-294.

Duffy, Michael, ed. (1980). The Military Revolution and the State 1500-1800. Exeter Studies in History, No. 1. Exeter, England: University of Exeter.

Duncan, George T. and Randolph Siverson (1975). "Marakov Chain Models for Conflict Analysis: Results from Sino-Indian Relations, 1959-1964." International Studies Quarterly 19:344-374.

Duncan, George T. and Randolph Siverson (1982). "Flexibility of Alliance Partner Choice in a Multipolar System." International Studies Quarterly 26:511-538.

Dupuy, R. E. and Trevor N. Dupuy (1977). The Encyclopedia of Military History. Revised edition. New York: Harper and Row.

Dupuy, Trevor N. and Associates (1964). "Historical Trends Related to Weapon Lethality." Washington, D.C.: Historical Evaluation & Research Organization.

Dyson, F. (1984). Weapons and Hope. New York: Harper and Row.

Eckstein, Harry (1980). "Theoretical Approaches to Explaining Collective Political Violence." In Handbook of Political Conflict, edited by Ted R. Gurr. New York: The Free Press.

Ellsberg, D. (1961). "The Crude Analysis of Strategic Choices." American Economic Review 51:472-478.

Elster, Jon (1979). Ulysses and the Sirens. Cambridge: Cambridge University Press.

Elton, G. R. (1975) "Taxation for War and Peace in Early-Tudor England." In War and Economic Development, Essays in Memory of David Joslin, edited by J. M. Winter. Cambridge: Cambridge University Press.

Ely, Richard G. (1969). "Mandelbaum on Historical Narrative: A Discussion." History and Theory 8:275-283.

Emsley, Olive (1983). Policing and its Context, 17501-1870. London: Macmillan.

Fain, J. B., W. W. Fain, L. Feldman and S. Simon (1970). Validation of Combat Models Against Historical Data. Professional Paper No. 27, Center for Naval Analyses.

Farrar, L. L., Jr. (1977). "Cycles of War: Historical Speculations on Future International Violence." International Interactions 3:161-79.

Feigenbaum, Edward A. (1983). "Knowledge Engineering: The Applied Side." In Intelligent Systems, edited by J. E. Hayes and D. Michie. Chichester, England: Ellis Horwood.

Feller, William (1960). , An Introduction to Probability Theory and Its Applications, Vol. 1. Second edition. New York: John Wiley.

Fenoaltea, Stefano (1975). "Authority, Efficiency, and Agricultural Organization in Medieval England and Beyond: A Hypothesis." The Journal of Economic History 35(4):693-718.

Finer, Samuel (1962). The Man on Horseback: The Role of the Military in Politics. London: Pall Mall.

Fogel, Robert W. and Stanley L. Engerman (1974). Time on the Cross. Boston: Little, Brown.

Fraser, N. M. and K. W. Hipel (1979). "Solving Complex Conflicts." IEEE Transactions on Systems, Man and Cybernetics SMC-9:806-816.

Fraser, N. M. and K. W. Hipel (1984). Conflict Analysis: Models and Resolutions. New York: North-Holland.

Frei, Daniel (1980). Evolving a Conceptual Framework of Intersystems Relations. New York: UNITAR.

Frey, Bruno S. (1978). Modern Political Economy. Oxford: Martin Robertson.

Frey, Bruno S. (1983). "The Economic Model of Behavior: Shortcomings and Fruitful Developments." Mimeographed. University of Zurich: Institute for Empirical Research in Economics.

Friedmann, David (1977). "A Theory of the Size and Shape of Nations." Journal of Political Economy 85:59-78.

Frohlich, Norman and Joe E. Oppenheimer (1978). Modern Political Economy. Englewood Cliffs, N.J.: Prentice-Hall.

Fu, K. S. (1974). Syntactic Methods in Pattern Recognition. New York: Academic Press.

Fudenberg, D. and J. Tirole (1984). "Sequential Bargaining with Incomplete Information." Review of Economic Studies 50:221-247.

Fueter, Edward (1972). Geschichte des europaischen Staatensystems von 1492-1559. Reprint of 1919 edition. Osnabruck: Zeller.

Fuller, W. A. (1976). Introduction to Statistical Time Series. New York: John Wiley.

Gamson, William. (1961). "A Theory of Coalition Formation." The American Sociological Review 26:373-382.

Gamson, William and Andrew Modigliani (1971). Untangling the Cold War: A Strategy for Testing Rival Theories. Boston: Little, Brown.

Gamson, William, Bruce Fireman, and Steve Rytina (1982). Encounters with Unjust Authority. Homewood, Ill.: Dorsey.

Garvin, R. L., K. Gottfried, and D. L. Hafner (1984). "Antisatellite

Weapons." Scientific American (June):27-37.

Gause, G. F. (1964). The Struggle for Existence. New York: Hafner Publishing.

George, Alexander L. (1971). The Limits of Coercive Diplomacy: Laos, Cuba, Vietnam. Boston: Little, Brown.

Gillespie, John V. and Dina A. Zinnes (1975). "Progressions in Mathematical Models of International Conflict." Synthese 31:289-321.

Gillespie, John V., Dina A. Zinnes, and G. S. Tahim (1975). "Foreign Military Assistance and the Armaments Race: A Differential Game Model with Control." Peace Research Society Inter-national) Papers 25:35-51.

Gillespie, John V., Dina A. Zinnes, and G. S. Tahim (1977). "Deterrence as Second Attack Capability." In Mathematical Systems in International Relations, edited by John V. Gillespie and Dina A. Zinnes. New York: Praeger.

Gillespie, John V., Dina A. Zinnes, G. S. Tahim, Philip Schrodt, and R. M. Rubison (1977). "An Optimal Control Model of Arms Races." American Political Science Review 71:226-244.

Gillespie, Judith and Dina A. Zinnes, eds. (1982). Missing Elements in Political Inquiry: Logic and Levels of Analysis. Beverly Hills, Calif.: Sage.

Gilpin, R. (1981). War and Change in World Politics. Cambridge: Cambridge University Press.

Gooch, John (1980). Armies in Europe. London: Routledge & Kegan Paul.

Gorovitz, S. (1983). "When Both Bidders Lose at a Stupid Game." International Herald Tribune, April 16.

Gottfried, K., H. W. Kendall, and J. M. Lee (1984). "'No First Use' of Nuclear Weapons." Scientific American (March):23-31.

Granovetter, Mark (1978). "Threshold Models of Collective Behavior." American Journal of Sociology 83:1410-1443.

Grillo, R. D. (1980). "Nation" and "State in Europe: Anthro-pological Perspectives. New York: Academic Press.

Gruner, Rolf (1969). "Mandelbaum on Historical Narrative: A Discussion." History and Theory 8:283-287.

Guetzkow, Harold, Chadwick Alger, Richard Brody, Robert C. Noel, and Richard Snyder (1963). Simulation in International Relations. Englewood Cliffs, N.J.: Prentice Hall.

Guiasu, Silviu and Mircea Malitza (1980). Coalition and Connection in Games. Oxford: Pergamon Press.

Gurr, Ted R. (1969). Why Men Rebel. Princeton: Princeton University Press.

Gurr, Ted R. and Mark Lichbach (1979). "A Forecasting Model for Political Conflict Within Nations." In To Augur Well: Early Warning Indicators in World Politics, edited by J. David Singer and M. D. Wallace. Beverly Hills, Calif.: Sage.

Gurr, Ted R., ed. (1980). Handbook of Political Conflict. Theory and Research. New York: Free Press.

Haftendorn, Helga (1975). "Versuch einer Theorie der Entspannung." Sicherheitspolitik Heute 2:223-242.

542

Haig, Alexander (1984). Caveat: Realism, Reagan and Foreign Policy. New York: Macmillan.

Hale, J. R. (1968a). "Armies, Navies, and the Art of War." In The New Cambridge Modern History, Vol. 2, The Reformation 1520–1559, edited by G. R. Elton. Cambridge: Cambridge University Press.

Hale, J. R. (1968b). "Armies, Navies, and the Art of War." In The New Cambridge Modern History, Vol. 3, The Counter-Reformation and Price Revolution, 1559–1610, edited by R. B. Wernham. Cambridge: Cambridge University Press.

Hall, Garrett S. (1971). Lanchester's Theory of Combat: The State of the Art in Mid-1970. U.S. Naval Post Graduate School Thesis. Alexandria, Va.: Defense Documentation Center.

Halle, Louis J. (1955). Civilization and Foreign Policy. New York: Harper.

Hamburger, Henry (1979). Games as Models of Social Phenomena. San Francisco: Freeman.

Hamilton, Earl J. (1950). "Origin and Growth of the National Debt in France and England." In Studi in onore de Gino Luzzato, Vol. 2. Milan: Giuffre.

Harbottle, T. (1975). Dictionary of Battles. Revised and updated by G. Bruce. New York: Stein and Day.

Harris, Richard J. (1972). "An Interval-Scale Classification System for all 2 x 2 Games." Behavioral Science 17:371–383.

Harsanyi, John (1969). "Rational Choice Models of Political Behavior vs. Functionalist and Conformist Theories." World Politics 21:513–38.

Harsanyi, John and R. Selten (1980). "A Non-cooperative Solution Concept with Cooperative Applications." Mimeographed. Berkeley: University of California.

Hechter, Michael and William Brustein (1980). "Regional Modes of Production and Patterns of State Formation in Europe." American Journal of Sociology 85:1061–1094.

Heirich, Max (1971). The Spiral of Conflict: Berkeley, 1964. New York: Columbia University Press.

Helmbold, Robert L. (1969). "Probability of Victory in Land Combat as Related to Force Ratio." October (P-4199). The Rand Corporation.

Helmbold, Robert L. (1971). "Decision in Battle: Breakpoint Hypotheses and Engagement Termination Data." June. The Rand Corporation.

Hempel, Carl G. (1965). Aspects of Scientific Explanation and Other Essays in the Philosophy of Science. New York: The Free Press.

Henderson, J. M. and R. E. Qiuandt (1971). Microeconomic Theory: A Mathematical Approach. Second edition. New York: McGraw-Hill.

Hibbs, Douglas A., Jr. (1973). Mass Poltiical Violence: A Cross-National Causal Analysis. New York: John Wiley.

Hoffmann-Nowotny, Hans-Joachim (1973). Soziologie des Fremd-arbeiterproblems. Stuttgart: Ferdinand Enke.

Holsti, Ole (1976). "Foreign Policy Viewed Cognitively." In Structure of Decision, edited by Robert Axelrod. Princeton: Princeton University Press.

Hopple, Gerald W., Paul J. Rossa, and Jonathan Wilkenfeld (1980). "Threat and Foreign Policy Analysis." In Sage International Yearbook of Foreign Policy Studies, edited by Patrick J. McGowan and Charles W. Kegley, Jr. Beverly Hills, Calif.: Sage.

Hosmer, Stephen T. and Thomas W. Wolfe (1983). Soviet Policy and Practice Toward Third World Conflicts. Lexington, Mass.: Lexington Books.

House, Lewis L. and Michael D. Ward (1985a). "A Markov Analysis of International Conflict and Cooperation." Mimeographed.

House, Lewis L. and Michael D. Ward (1985b). "Behavioral Power in International Politics." Mimeographed.

House, Lewis L. and Michael D. Ward (1985c). "International Cooperation as a Leading Indicator of International Crises." Mimeographed.

House, Lewis L., W. J. Wagner, E. Hildner, C. Sawyer, and H. U. Schmidt (1981). "Studies of the Corona with the Solar Maximum Mission Coronagraph/Polarimeter." The Astrophysical Journal 244:117-121.

Howard, Michael (1976). War in European History. Oxford: Oxford University Press.

Howard, Michael (1984). The Causes of Wars. Cambridge, Mass.: Harvard University Press.

Howard, N. (1971). Paradoxes of Rationality. Cambridge, Mass.: MIT Press.

Howell, Llewellyn D. (1983) "A Comparative Study of the WEIS and COPDAB Data Sets." International Studies Quarterly 27:249-159.

Huth, Paul and Bruce M. Russett (1984). "Why Does Deterrence Work? Cases from 1900 to 1980." World Politics: 496-526.

Intriligator, Michael D. (1964). "Some Simple Models of Arms Races." General Systems Yearbook 9:143-147.

Intriligator, Michael D. (1967). Strategy in a Missile War: Targets and Rates of Fire. Security Studies Paper No. 10. Securities Studies Project. Los Angeles: University of California.

Intriligator, Michael D. (1968). "The Debate Over Missile Strategy: Targets and Rates of Fire." Orbis 11:1138-1159.

Intriligator, Michael D. (1971). Mathematical Optimization and Economic Theory. Englewood Cliffs, N. J.: Prentice-Hall.

Intriligator, Michael D. (1975). "Strategic Considerations in the Richardson Model of Arms Races." Journal of Political Economy 83:339-353.

Intriligator, Michael D. (1978). Econometric Models, Techniques, and Applications. Englewood Cliffs, N.J.: Prentice-Hall; Amsterdam: North-Holland.

Intriligator, Michael D. (1982). "Research on Conflict Theory: Analytic Approaches and Areas of Application." Journal of Conflict Resolution 216:307-327

Intriligator, Michael D. and Dagobert L. Brito (1976). "Formal Models of Arms Races." Journal of Peace Science 2:77-88.

Intriligator, Michael D. and Dagobert L. Brito (1977). "Strategy, Arms Races, and Arms Control." In Mathematical Systems in

544

International Relations Research, edited by John V. Gillespie and Dina A. Zinnes. New York: Praeger.

Intriligator, Michael D. and Dagobert L. Brito (1984). "Can Arms Races Lead to the Outbreak of War?" *Journal of Conflict Resolution* 28:63–84.

Intriligator, Michael D. and Dagobert L. Brito (1985). "Non-Armageddon Solutions to the Arms Race." *Arms Control*, forthcoming.

Isaac, Larry and William R. Kelly (1982). "Developmental Modernization and Political Class Struggle Theories of Welfare Expansion: The Case of the AFDC 'Explosion' in the States, 1960–1970." *Journal of Political and Military Scoiology* 10:201–235.

Janis, Irving (1982). *Groupthink*. Boston: Houghton-Mifflin.

Janowitz, Morris and Jacques Van Doorn, eds. (1971). *On Military Intervention*. Rotterdam: Rotterdam University Press.

Jaynes, Julian (1976). *The Origin of Consciousness in the Breakdown of the Bicameral Mind*. Boston: Houghton Mifflin.

Jenkins, J. Craig (1983). "Resource Mobilization and the Study of Social Movements." *Annual Review of Sociology* 9:527–553.

Jervis, R. (1979). "Cooperation Under the Security Dilemma." *World Politics* 30:167–214.

Johnson, Chalmers (1966). *Revolutionary Change*. Boston: Little, Brown.

Johnson, John J. (1962). *The Role of the Military in Underdeveloped Countries*. Princeton: Princeton University Press.

Kahn, Herman J. (1965). *On Escalation*. New York: Praeger.

Kahneman, Daniel, Paul Slovic, and Amos Tversky (1982). *Judgement Under Uncertainty: Heuristics and Biases*. Cambridge: Cambridge University Press.

Kaplan, Stephen S. (1981). *Diplomacy of Power: Soviet Armed Forces as Political Instrument*. Washington, D.C.: Brookings Institution.

Karr, Alan F. (1974). "Stochastic Attrition Processes of Lanchester Type." Arlington, Virginia: Institute for Defense Analyses.

Karr, Alan F. (1976). "A Class of Lanchester Attrition Processes." Arlington, Virginia: Institute for Defense Analyses.

Kaufman, William (1954). "The Requirements of Deterrence." Research Memorandum No. 7. Center for International Studies. Princeton: Princeton University.

Kennan, George F. (1967). "Russia's International Position at the Close of the War with Germany (May 1945)." In *Memoirs 1925–1950*. Appendix B. New York: Pantheon.

Kennedy, Gavin (1974). *The Military in the Third World*. London: Duckworth.

Keohane, Robert O. and Joseph S. Nye (1977). *Power and Interdependence*. Boston: Little, Brown.

Kerr, Henry (1983). "Swiss Electoral Politics." In *Switzerland at the Polls: 1979*, edited H. R. Penniman. Washington D. C.: American Enterprise Institute.

Kidron, Michael and Ronald Segal (1981). The State of the Atlas. New York: Simon & Schuster.

Kiewiet, D. R. (1983). Micromotives and Macropolitics. Chicago: University of Chicago Press.

Kilgour, D. Marc (1984). "Equilibria for Far-sighted Players." Theory and Decision 16:135-157.

Kilgour, D. Marc (1985). "Anticipation and Stability in Two-Person Non-cooperative Games." In this volume.

Kilgour, D. Marc, K. W. Hipel, and N. M. Fraser (1984). "Solution Concepts in Non-cooperative Games." Large Scale Systems 6:49-72.

Kinder, D. R. and D. R. Kiewiet (1981). "Sociotropic Politics: The American Case." British Journal of Political Science 11:129-61.

Kneale, William and Martha Kneale (1962). The Development of Logic. Oxford: Clarendon Press.

Kolkowicz, Roman and Andrzej Korbonski, eds. (1982). Soldiers, Peasants, and Bureaucrats: Civil-Military Relations in Communist and Modernizing Societies. London: Routledge & Kegan Paul.

Koloskov, I. A. (1978). "Prerequisites for a Security System in Europe." In European Security and Cooperation, edited by the Soviet Committee for European Security and Cooperation. Pp. 27-47. Moscow: Progress.

Korpi, Walter and Michael Shalev (1980). "Strikes, Power and Politics in the Western Nations, 1900-1976." In Political Power and Social Theory, edited by Maurice Zeitlin. Greenwich, Conn.: JAI Press.

Kortunov, Vadim (1979). The Battle of Ideas in the Modern World. Moscow: Progress.

Kowalski, Robert A. (1974). "Predicate Logic as Programming Language." Proceedings IFIP 74. Pp. 569-574. Amsterdam: North Holland.

Kowalski, Robert A. (1979). Logic for Problem Solving. Amsterdam: North Holland.

Kramer, G. H. (1983). "The Ecological Fallacy Revisited: Aggregate Versus Individual-Level Findings on Economics and Elections and Sociotropic Voting." American Political Science Review 77:92-111.

Kriesi, Hanspeter (1980). Entscheidungsstrukturen und Entscheidungsprozesse in der Schweizer Politik. Frankfurt: Campus.

Kriesi, Hanspeter (1981). AKW-Gegner in der Schweiz. Eine Fallstudie zum Aubau des Widerstands gegen das geplante AKW im Graben. Diessenhofen: Verlag Ruegger.

Kriesi, Hanspeter et al. (1981). Politische Aktivierung in der Schweiz, 1945-1978. Diessenhofen: Verlag Ruegger.

Kronus, Carol L. (1978). "Mobilizing Voluntary Associations into a Social Movement: The Case of Environmental Quality." Sociological Quarterly 18:267-283.

Kybal, D. (1960). "Remarks." In Proceedings, National Security Seminar, Asilomar, California, April 24-30.

546

Lambelet, Jean C. (1975). "Do Arms Races Lead to War?" Journal of Peace Research 12:123-128.

Lambelet, Jean C. and Urs Luterbacher with Pierre Allan (1979). "Dynamics of Arms Races: Mutual Stimulation vs. Self-Stimulation." Journal of Peace Science 4:44-66.

Lanchester, F. W. (1916). Aircraft in Warfare, the Dawn of the Fourth. London: Constable.

Lane, Frederic C. (1950). "Force and Enterprise in the Creation of Oceanic Commerce." The Tasks of Economic History. Supplemental issue of the Journal of Economic History 10:19-31.

Lane, Frederic C. (1958). "Economic Consequences of Organized Violence." Journal of Economic History 18:401-417.

Leavitt, Michael (1972). "Markov Processes in International Crises: An Analytical Addendum to an Events-Based Simulation of the Taiwan Straits Crisis." In Experimentation and Simulation in Political Science, edited by John A. Laponce and Paul Smoker. Toronto: University of Toronto Press.

Lebedev, Nikolai I. Eine neue Etappe in den internationalen Beziehungen. Berlin: Staatsverlag der DDR.

Leontief, Wassily (1982). "Academic Economics." Science 217:104-107.

Lerner, Max, ed. (1948). The Portable Veblen. New York: Viking.

Letterie, J. W. and A. F. Bertrand (1982). "Social Welfare, Its Economic and Political Determinants: A Comparison of 115 Countries." Paper presented at the International Political Science Association Congress, Rio de Janeiro. Levi, Margaret (1983). "The Predatory Theory of Rule." In The Microfoundations of Macrosociology, edited by Michael Hechter. Philadelphia: Temple University Press.

Levy, Jack S. (1983). War in the Great Power System, 1495-1975. Lexington: University Press of Kentucky.

Levy, Jack S. (1985). "Theories of General War." World Politics 37:344-374.

Levy, Jack S. and T. Cliff Morgan (1984). "The Frequency and Seriousness of War." Journal of Conflict Resolution 28:731-749.

Lichbach, Mark (1981). "An Economic Theory of Governability: Choosing Policy and Optimizing Performance." International Institute for Comparative Social Research Discussion Paper IIVG/dp 81-123. Berlin: Science Center.

Liddell-Hart, B. H. (1960). "The Ratio of Troops to Space." Military Review (April):3-14.

Lijphart, Arend (1984). Democracies. New Haven: Yale University Press.

Ling, Rufus C. (1967). "Generalization of Lanchester's Combat Model—Forces with Nuclear and Fire Adjustment Capabilities." Staff Memorandum RAC-S-1934. McLean, Va.: Research Analysis Corporation.

Lotka, Alfred J. (1956). Elements of Mathematical Biology. New York: Dover.

Luce, R. Duncan and Howard Raiffa (1957). Games and Decisions. New York: John Wiley.

Ludtke, Alf (1980). "Genesis und Durchsetzung des modernen Staates: Zur Analyse von Herrschaft und Verwaltung." Archiv fur

Sozialgeschichte 20:470-491.

Luterbacher, Urs (1981). "Negociation et coalitions." In L'Historien et les relations internationales: Recuil d'etudes en hommage a Jacques Freymond, edited by S. Friedlander, H. Kapur, and A. Reszler. Geneva: Institut Universitaire des Etudes Internationales.

Luterbacher, Urs (1983). "Public Good Theory and Coalition Theory: A Reformulation." Paper presented at Annual Disentis Meetings, Disentis.

Luterbacher, Urs (1984). "Approches dynamiques dans la representation et la modelisation des conflits internationaux." Mimeographed. Geneva: Institut Universitaire des Etudes Internationales.

Luterbacher, Urs and Pierre Allan (1982). "Modeling Politico-Economic Interactions Within and Between Nations." International Political Science Review 3:404-433.

Luterbacher, Urs and Pierre Allan (1983). "Simulating the Initiation, Escalation, and Termination of Conflict." Paper presented at the Summer Institute for the Study of Conflict Theory and International Security, Los Angeles.

Luterbacher, Urs and T. Michael Clarke (1983). "Simulation of International Politico-Economic Influences on Switzerland." In Wirtschaftliche Landesversorge im Rahmen der Sicher-heitspolitik, edited by Paul Staehly. Stuttgart: Paul Haupt.

McAdam, Doug (1982). Political Process and the Development of Black Insurgency, 1930-1970 Chicago: University of Chicago Press.

McCabe, F. G., K. L. Clark, and B. D. Steel (1984). Micro-PROLOG 3.1 Programmer's Reference Manual, CP/M and MSDOS Versions. Fourth edition. London: Logic Programming Associates Ltd.

McCawley, James D. (1981). Everything That Linguists Have Always Wanted To Know About Logic but Were Ashamed To Ask. Chicago: University of Chicago Press.

McClelland, Charles A. (1976). World Event/Interaction Survey Codebook (ICPSR 5211). Ann Arbor: Inter-University Consortium for Political and Social Research.

McClelland, Charles A. (1983). "Let the User Beware." International Studies Quarterly 28:169-177.

McGuire, Martin. Secrecy and the Arms Race. Cambridge, Mass.: Harvard University Press.

McNeill, William H. (1982). The Pursuit of Power: Technology, Armed Force, and Society Since A.D. 1000. Chicago: University of Chicago Press.

McPhail, Clark and David L. Miller (1973). "The Assembling Process: A Theoretical and Empirical Examination." American Sociological Review 38:721-735.

Maddox, Robert James (1973). The New Left and the Origins of the Cold War. Princeton: Princeton University Press.

Mandelbaum, Maurice (1967). "A Note on History as Narrative." History and Theory 6:413-419.

Maoz, Zeev (1982). "Games and Decisions in International Conflict."

Paper presented at the Annual Meeting of the American Political Science Association, Denver, Colorado.

Maoz, Zeev (1984a). "The Expected Utility of International Conflict." Mimeographed. Haifa: University of Haifa.

Maoz, Zeev (1984b). "Games and Decisions in International Conflict" (in Hebrew). State, Government and International Relations 23.

Maoz, Zeev (1984c). "Peace by Empire? Conflict Outcomes and International Stability." Journal of Peace Research 21:227-241.

March, James G. and Johan P. Olsen (1983). "The New Institutionalism: Organizational Factors in Political Life." Paper presented at the Annual Meeting of the American Political Science Association, Chicago, Illinois.

Margolis, Howard (1982). Selfishness, Altruism, and Rationality. Cambridge: Cambridge University Press.

Masse, Pierre (1962). Optimal Investment Decisions. Englewood Cliffs, N.J.: Prentice-Hall.

Mathias, Peter and Patrick O'Brien (1976). "Taxation in Britain and France 1715-1810: A Comparison of the Social and Economic Incidence of Taxes Collected for the Central Governments." Journal of European Economic History 5:501-650.

Mefford, Dwain (1984). "Formulating Foreign Policy on the Basis of Historical Analogies: An Application of Developments in Artifical Intelligence." Paper presented at the Annual Meeting of the International Studies Association, Atlanta, Georgia.

Midlarsky, Manus I. (1981). "Equilibrium in the Nineteenth Century Balance of Power System." American Journal of Political Science 25:270-296.

Midlarsky, Manus I. (1984). "Some Uniformities in the Origins of Systemic War." Paper delivered at the Annual Meeting of the American Political Science Association, Washington, D.C.

Mintz, Alex and Philip A. Schrodt (1983). "Distributional Patterns of Regional Interactions." Paper presented to the Roundtable on Global Communication of the International Political Science Association, Urbana, Illinois.

Modelski, George (1978). "The Long Cycle of Global Politics and the Nation State." Comparative Studies in Society and History 20:214-235.

Modelski, George (1981). "Testing Cobweb Models of the Long Cycle of World Leadership." Paper delivered at the Annual Meeting of the Peace Science Society (International), Philadelphia, Pennsylvania.

Modelski, George (1983). "Long Cycles of World Leadership: An Annotated Bibliography." International Studies Notes 10:1-6.

Modelski, George (1984). "One Long Cycle or a Family of Long Cycles?" Mimeographed. Seattle: Department of Political Science, University of Washington.

Modelski, George and W. R. Thompson. Seapower and Global Politics, 1494-1983. In progress.

Monroe, Kristen R. (1984). Presidential Popularity and the Economy. New York: Praeger.

Morris, Aldon D. (1984). The Origins of the Civil Rights Movement: Black Communities Organizing for Change. New York: Free Press.

Morrow, James D. (1982). "A Theory of Optimal Foreign Policy." Paper presented at the Annual Meeting of the International Studies Association.

Morrow, James D. (1984a). "A Spatial Theory of International Conflict." Paper presented at the Annual Meeting of the International Studies Association, Atlanta, Georgia.

Morrow, James D. (1984b). "Some Tests of a Spatial Theory of International Conflict." Paper presented at the Annual Meeting of the Midwest Political Science Association.

Morrow, James D. (1984c). "A Twist of Truth: A Re-examination of the Effects of Arms Races and the Occurrence of War." Paper presented at the Annual Meeting of the American Political Science Association, Washington, D.C.

Morrow, James D. (1985). "A Continuous-Outcome Expected Utility Theory of War." Journal of Conflict Resolution, in press.

Morrow, James D. and David Newman (1983). "The Quest for Security: Some Evidence from Domestic and International Coalitions." Paper presented at the Annual Meeting of the American Political Science Association, Chicago, Illinois.

Mowat, R. B. (1928). A History of European Diplomacy. London: Edward Arnold.

Moyal, J. E. (1949). "The Distribution of Wars in Time." Journal of the Royal Statistical Society 115, ser. A, pt. 4:446–49.

Mueller, Carol McClung (1978). "Riot Violence and Protest Outcomes." Journal of Political and Military Sociology 6:46–63.

Nash, John (1950). "Equilibrium Points in n-person Games." Proceedings of the National Academy of Sciences of the U.S.A. 36:48–49.

Nash, John (1951). "Non-cooperative Games." Annals of Mathematics 54:286–295.

Nau, D. (1983). "Pathology on Game Trees Revisited and an Alternative to Maximizing." Artificial Intelligence 21:221–244.

Newman, D. (1982). "Security and Alliances: A Theoretical Study of Alliance Formation." Mimeographed. Rochester, N.Y.: University of Rochester.

North, Douglass and Robert Thomas (1971). "The Rise and Fall of the Manorial System: A Theoretical Model." Journal of Economic History 31:777–803

O'Donnell, Guillermo (1980). "Comparative Historical Formations of the State Apparatus and Socio-Economic Change in the Third World." International Social Science Journal 32:717–729.

O'Neill, Barry (1985). "A Measure for Crisis Instability." Mimeographed. Evanston, Ill.: Northwestern University.

Oberschall, Anthony (1978). "Theories of Social Conflict." Annual Review of Sociology 4:291–315.

Olson, Mancur (1965). The Logic of Collective Action. Cambridge, Mass.: Harvard University Press.

Organization for Economic Co-operation and Development (1983). OECD Economic Surveys: Switzerland. Paris: OECD.

Organski, A. F. K. and Jacek Kugler (1980). The War Ledger.

550

Chicago: University of Chicago Press.

Owen, G. (1982). Game Theory. Second Edition. N.Y.: Academic Press.

Parkinson, F. (1977). The Philosophy of International Relations. Beverly Hills, Calif.: Sage.

Pastusiak, Longin (1978). "Objective and Subjective Premises of Detente." Polish Round Table 8:53–72.

Peacock, Alan T. and Jack Wiseman (1961). The Growth of Public Expenditure in the United Kingdom. Princeton: Princeton University Press.

Pearl, J. (1984). Heuristics: Intelligent Search Strategies for Computer Problems Solving. Reading, Mass: Addison-Wesley.

Perelman, Chaim and L. Olbrechts-Tyteca (1969). The New Rhetoric: A Treatise on Argumentation. Translated by John Wilkinson and Purcell Weaver. London: University of Notre Dame Press.

Perutz, M. F. (1978). "Hemoglobin Structure and Respiratory Transport." Scientific American 239:97–105.

Petersen, W. J. (1982). "Conflict Resolution and the Status Quo." Paper presented at the 1982 Annual Meeting of the International Studies Association.

Petersen, W. J. (1983). "International Conflict Resolution: An Expected Utility Approach to the Analysis of Decisions During Crisis." Ph.D. dissertation, University of Rochester.

Petersen, W. J. (1984). "Deterrence versus Compellence: A Critical Assessment of Conventional Wisdom." Paper presented at the Annual Meeting of the International Studies Association, Atlanta, Georgia.

Pielou, E. C. (1969). An Introduction to Mathematical Ecology. New York: Wiley.

Pillar, P. (1983). Negotiating Peace. Princeton: Princeton University Press.

Pindyck, R. S. and D. L. Rubinfeld (1976). Econometric Models and Economic Forecasts. Tokyo: McGraw-Hill/Kogakusha.

Pipes, Richard (1984). "Can the Soviet Union Reform?" Foreign Affairs 63:47–61.

Pounds, Norman J. G. and Sue Simons Ball (1964). "Core-Areas and the Development of the European States System." Annals of the Association of American Geographers 54:24–40.

Quester, George H. (1982). "Six Causes of War." The Jerusalem Journal of International Relations 6:1–23.

Rapkin, D. P. (1983). "The Inadequacy of a Single Logic: Toward an Integration of Political and Material Approaches to the World System." In Contending Approaches to World System Analysis, edited by W. R. Thompson. Beverly Hills, Calif.: Sage.

Rapoport, Anatol (1957). "Lewis F. Richardson's Mathematical Theory of War." Journal of Conflict Resolution 1:249–299.

Rapoport, Anatol (1960). Fights, Games, and Debates Ann Arbor: University of Michigan Press.

Rapoport, Anatol (1974). "Verbal Maps and Global Politics. Et Cetera 37:297-313.

Rapoport, Anatol and A. Chammah. (1965). The Prisoners' Dilemma. Ann Arbor: The University of Michigan Press.

Rapoport, Anatol, Melvin J. Guyer, and David G. Gordon (1966). The 2 x 2 Game. Ann Arbor: University of Michigan Press.

Rasler, Karen A. (1983). "Global Wars, Public Debts and the Long Cycle." World Politics 35:489-516.

Rasler, Karen A. (1984). "Longitudinal Change in Defense Burdens, Capital Formation and Economic Growth." Paper delivered at the Annual Meeting of the International Studies Association, Atlanta, Georgia.

Rasler, Karen A. (1985). "Global War and Major Power Economic Growth." American Journal of Political Science 28.

Rasler, Karen A. and W. R. Thompson (1985). "War Making and State Making: Governmental Expenditures, Tax Revenues, and Gloibal Wars." American Political Scienced Review 79.

Read, Thornton (1964). "The Nuclear Battlefield in Historical Perspective." Unpublished paper. Murray Hill, N.J.: Bell Telephone Laboratories.

Read, Thornton (1969). "Problems of Strategy and Tactics." Unpublished paper. Murray Hill, N.J.: Bell Telephone Laboratories.

Richardson, Lewis F. (1951). "Could An Arms Race End Without Fighting?" Nature 29:567-8.

Richardson, Lewis F. (1960). Statistics of Deadly Quarrels. Pittsburgh: Boxwood Press.

Riker, William H. (1962). The Theory of Political Coalitions. New Haven: Yale University Press.

Riker, William H. and Peter Ordeshook (1973). An Introduction to Positive Political Theory. Englewood Cliffs, N.J.: Prentice-Hall.

Robinson, J. A. (1965). "Machine-oriented Logic Based on the Resolution Principle." Journal of the ACM 12:23-41.

Robinson, J. A. (1979). Form and Function. Edinburgh: Edinburgh University Press.

Rokkan, Stein and Derek W. Urwin, eds. (1982). The Politics of Territorial Identity: Studies in European Regionalism. Beverly Hills, Calif.: Sage.

Rosenberg, Hans (1958). Bureaucracy, Aristocracy and Atuocracy: The Prussian Experience, 1660-1815. Cambridge, Mass.: Harvard University Press.

Ruloff, Dieter (1983). "Ursachen 'klimatischer' Schwankungen in den Ost-West-Beziehungen. Zyklen von Konflikt und Kooperation zwischen den USA und der UdSSR 1950-1978. Eine Spektralanalyse." Politische Vierteljahresschrift, Sonderheft: 141-162.

Russell, Diana (1974). Rebellion, Revolution, and Armed Force. New York: Academic Press.

Russett, Bruce M. (1963). "The Calculus of Deterrence." Journal of Conflict Resolution 7:97-109.

Russett, Bruce M. (1970). What Price Vigilance? The Burdens of

National Defense. New Haven: Yale University Press.

Saaty, Thomas L. (1968). _Mathematical Models of Arms Control and Disarmament_. New York: John Wiley.

Salert, Barbara and John Sprague (1980). _The Dynamics of Riots_. Ann Arbor: Inter-University Consortium for Political and Social Science.

Samoschkin, Juri and Wladimir Gantman (1980). "Die marxistische Konzeption der Ideologie, Ethik und Aussenpolitik in den fuhen achtziger Jahren." _Wissenschaft und Frieden_ 4:4-13.

Sankoff, David and Joseph B. Kruskal, eds. (1983). _Time Warps, String Edits and Macromolecules: The Theory and Practice of Sequence Comparison_. New York: Addison-Wesley.

Savage, L. J. (1972). _The Foundations of Statistics_. Second edition. New York: Dover.

Schelling, Thomas C. (1960). _The Strategy of Conflict_. Cambridge, Mass.: Harvard University Press.

Schelling, Thomas C. (1966). _Arms and Influence_. New Haven: Yale University Press.

Schneider, F., W. Pommerehne, and B. Frey (1981). "Politico-Economic Interdependence in a Direct Democracy: The Case of Switzerland." In _Contemporary Political Economy_, edited by D. Hibbs ·and J. Fassbender. Amsterdam: North-Holland.

Schotter, Andrew (1981). _The Economic Theory of Social Institutions_. Cambridge: Cambridge University Press.

Schrodt, Philip A. (1985). "Pattern Recognition of International Events Using a Natural Language Data Base." Paper presented at the Annual Meeting of the International Studies Association, Washington, D.C.

Schrodt, Philip A. (1984). "Artificial Intelligence and International Crisis: An Application of Pattern Recognition." Paper presented at the Annual Meeting of the American Political Science Association, Washington, D.C.

Schrodt, Philip A. (1984). "Artificial Intelligence and the State of Mathematical Modeling in International Relations: A Survey." Paper presented at the Conference on Dynamic Models of International Conflict, Boulder, Colorado.

Schwarz, Gunter and Dieter S. Lutz (1980). _Sicherheit und Zusammenarbeit. Eine Bibliographie zu MBFR, SALT, KSZE_. Baden-Baden, West Germany: Nomos.

Schwarz, Hans-Peter (1979). "Supermacht und Juniorpartner. Ansatze amerikanischer und westdeutscher Ostpolitik." In _Entspannungspolitik in Ost und West_, edited by Hans-Peter Schwarz and Boris Meissner. Cologne, West Germany: Heymanns.

Sears, D. and R. Lau (1983). "Self-interest vs. Symbolic Politics in Policy Attitudes and 1976 Presidential Voting." _American Political Science Review_ 74:670-84.

Secretary of Defense (1984). _Annual Report to the Congress for the FY 1985 Budget_. Washington, D.C.: U.S. Government Printing Office.

Selten, Reinhard (1975). "Reexamination of the Perfectness Concept for Equilibrium Points in Extensive Games." _International_

Journal of Game Theory 4:25–55.

Shubik, Martin (1971). "The Dollar Auction: A Paradox in Non-cooperative Behavior and Escalation." The Journal of Conflict Resolution 15: 545–547.

Shubik, Martin (1981). "Perfect or Robust Noncooperative Equilibrium: A Search for the Philosopher's Stone?" In Essays in Game Theory and Mathematical Economics, edited by R. J. Aumann et al. Mannheim: Bibliographisches Institut.

Shubik, Martin (1982). Game Theory in the Social Sciences: Concepts and Solutions. Cambridge, Mass.: MIT Press.

Simaan, M. and J. B. Cruz, Jr. (1975a). "Formulation of Richardson's Model of the Arms Race from a Differential Game Viewpoint." Review of Economic Studies 42:67–77.

Simaan, M. and J. B. Cruz, Jr. (1975b). "Nash Equilibrium Strategies for the Problem of the Armaments Race and Control." Management Science 22:96–105.

Simaan, M. and J. B. Cruz, Jr. (1977). "Equilibrium Concepts for Arms Race Problems." In Mathematical Systems in International Relations Research, edited by John V. Gillespie and Dina A. Zinnes. New York: Praeger.

Simes, Dimitri K. (1980). "The Death of Detente?" International Security 5:1–25.

Simon, Herbert A. (1957). Models of Man. New York: John Wiley.

Singer, J. David and T. Cusack (1981). The Wages of War, 1816–1965: A Statistical Handbook. New York: Wiley.

Small, Melvin and J. David Singer (1982). Resort to Arms: International and Civil Wars, 1816–1980. Beverly Hills, Calif.: Sage.

Smith, Harvey A. (1978). "Nuclear Deterrence." UMAP 327.

Snyder, David (1976). "Theoretical and Methodological Problems in the Analysis of Governmental Coercion and Collective Violence." Journal of Political and Military Sociology 4:277–293.

Snyder, Glenn H. and Paul Diesing (1977). Conflict Among Nations: Bargaining, Decision-Making, and System Structure in International Crises. Princeton: Princeton University Press.

Sorokin, P. A. (1937). Social and Cultural Dynamics: Fluctuation of Social Relationships, War, and Revolution. New York: American Book Company.

Sowa, John F. (1984). Conceptual Structures: Information Processing in Mind and Machine. Reading, Mass.: Addison-Wesley.

Spath, Helmuth (1980). Cluster Analysis Algorithms for Data Reduction and Classification of Objects. Chichester, England: Ellis Horwood.

Stein, Arthur A. and Bruce M. Russett (1980). "Evaluating War: Outcomes and Consequences." In Handbook of Political Conflict. Theory and Research, edited by Ted R. Gurr. New York: Free Press.

Steinbrunner, J. (1984). "Launch Under Attack." Scientific American (January):23–33.

Stewart, William G. (1960). "Interaction of Firepower, Mobility, and Dispersion." Military Review (March):26–33.

Stohl, Michael (1976). War and Domestic Political Violence: The

554

American Capacity for Repression and Reaction. Beverly Hills, Calif.: Sage.

Stone, Lawrence (1947). "State Control in Sixteenth-Century England." Economic History Review 17:1043-120.

Sullivan, Michael P. International Relations: Theories and Evidence. Englewood Cliffs, N.J.: Prentice-Hall.

Sylvan, Donald A. and Steve Chan (1984). Foreign Policy Decision Making. New York: Praeger.

Takahashi, M. A., N. M. Fraser, and K. W. Hipel (1984). "A Procedure for Analysing Hypergames." European Journal of Operational Research 18: 111-122.

Tarrow, Sidney (1983). Struggling To Reform: Social Movements and Policy Change During Cycles of Protest. Western Societies Program, Occasional Paper No. 15. Ithaca, N.Y.: Center for International Studies, Cornell University.

Taylor, Michael (1975). "The Theory of Collective Choice." In Macropolitical Theory, edited by Fred I. Greenstein and Nelson W. Polsby. Pp. 413-481. Reading, Mass.: Addison Wesley.

Taylor, Michael (1976). Anarchy and Cooperation. London: Wiley.

Teger, A. (1980). Too Much Invested To Quit. New York: Pergammon.

Thalheim, Karl C. (1980). "Wirtschaftliche Beziehungen im Wandel." In Ost West: Erfahrungen und Perspektiven, edited by Alfred Domes. Pp. 183-204. Munich: Hanns-Seidel-Foundation.

Thomis, Malcolm I. and Peter Holt (1977). Threats of Revolution in Britain, 1789-1848. London: Macmillan.

Thompson, W. R. (1983a). "The World-Economy, the Long Cycle, and the Question of World System Time." In Foreign Policy and the Modern World-System, edited by Patrick J. McGowan and Charles W. Kegley, Jr. Beverly Hills, Calif.: Sage.

Thompson, W. R. (1983b). "World System Analysis With and Without the Hyphen." In Contending Approaches to World System Analysis, edited by W. R. Thompson. Beverly Hills, Calif.: Sage.

Thompson, W. R. (1983c). "Uneven Economic Growth, Systemic Challenges, and Global Wars." International Studies Quarterly 27:341-55.

Thompson, W. R. (1983d). "World Wars, Global Wars, and the Cool Hand Luke Syndrome: A Reply to Chase-Dunn and Sokolovsky." International Studies Quarterly 27:369-74.

Thucydides, Erklart von Johannes Classen (1982). The Peloponnesian War. The Crawley Translation, Revised (1910), with an Introduction by T. E. Wick. New York: Modern Library.

Tilly, Charles (1975). "Revolutions and Collective Violence." In Macropolitical Theory, edited by F. Greenstein and N. Polsby. Reading, Mass.: Addison-Wesley.

Tilly, Charles (1978). From Mobilization to Revolution. Reading, Mass.: Addison-Wesley.

Titchmarsh, E. C. (1948). Introduction to the Theory of Fourier Integrals. Second edition. London: Oxford University Press.

Toynbee, A. J. (1954). A Study of History, vol. 9. London: Oxford University Press.

Tufte, Edward. R.(1983). The Visual Display of Quantitative

Information. Chesire, Conn.: Graphics Press.

Turco, R. P., O. B. Toon, P. T. Ackerman, J. B. Pollack, and C. Sagan (1984). "The Climatic Effects of Nuclear War." Scientific American (August):23-33.

Vincent, Jack E. (1983). "WEIS vs. COPDAB Correspondence Problems." International Studies Quarterly 27:161-168.

von Neumann, John and Oskar Morgenstern (1953 and 1944). Theory of Games and Economic Behavior. New York: Wiley.

von Stackelberg, H. (1934). Marktform und Gleichgewicht. Vienna: Springer.

Wagner, R. H. (1980). "The Theory of Games and the Problem of International Cooperation." American Political Science Review 77: 330-346.

Wagner, R. H. (1984). "War and Expected Utility Theory." World Politics: 407-423.

Wainer, Howard (1981). "Graphical Data Analysis." Annual Review of Psychology 32:192-241.

Wainstein, Leonard (1973). "Some Allied and German Casualty Rates in the European Theater of Operations." Paper P-989. Alexandria, Va: Institute for Defense Analyses.

Wait, J. and D. Clarke (1976). Dare-P User's Manual. Tucson: University of Arizona.

Wallerstein, Immanuel (1982). "The Three Instances of Hegemony in the History of the Capitalist World-Economy." Mimeographed. Binghamton, N.Y.: Fernand Braudel Center for the Study of Economics, Historical Systems and Civilizations.

Walton, John (1984). Reluctant Rebels: Comparative Studies of Revolution and Underdevelopment. New York: Columbia University Press.

Waltz, Kenneth (1958). Man, the State and War. New York: Columbia University Press.

Ward, Michael D. (1982a). "A Model of Conflict and Cooperation Among Contemporary Nation-States. International Institute for Comparative Social Research Discussion Paper IIVG/dp 82-109. Berlin: Science Center.

Ward, Michael D. (1982b). "Utilizing the COPDAB Data Set for the Globus Model To Measure International Conflict and Cooperation." IIVG dp 82-101. Berlin: Science Center.

Ward, Michael D. (1983). "Joint Seminar on Dynamic Approaches to Modeling International Conflict: A Proposal to the NSF." Mimeographed. Boulder, Colo.: Institute of Behavioral Science, University of Colorado.

Ward, Michael D. (1984). "The Differential Paths to Parity: A Study of the Contemporary Arms Race." American Political Science Review 78:297-317.

Weiss, Herbert K. (1957). "Lanchester Type Models of Warfare." Proceedings of the First International Conference, Conference on Operational Research. Pp. 82-99.

Widmaier, Ulrich (1981). "Economic Development, Government Resource Allocation, and Poltiical Conflict." Pp. 81-119.

International Institute for Comparative Social Research Discussion Paper IIVG/dp. Berlin: Science Center.

Widmaier, Ulrich (1984). "Konstruktion, Simuilation, und Schaetzung kontinuierlicher dynamischer Modelle." International Institute for Comparative Social Research Discussion Paper IIVG/dp. Pp. 84–129. Berlin: Science Center.

Wijn, J. W. (1970). "Military Forces and Warfare 1610–1648." In The New Cambridge Modern History, Vol. 4, The Decline of Spain and the Thirty Years War, edited by J. P. Cooper. Cambridge: Cambridge Univeristy Press.

Wilkinson, D. (1980). Deadly Quarrels: Lewis F. Richardson and the Statistical Study of War. Berkeley: University of California Press.

Wilson, E. Raymond (1978). "The Pillars of Peace." World Affairs 141:165–176.

Wintringham, Tom (1940). Deadlock War. London: Faber and Faber.

Wittman, D. (1979). "How a War Ends." Journal of Conflict Resolution 23:743–763.

Wohlstetter, Albert (1959). "The Delicate Balance of Terror." Foreign Affairs 37:211–234.

Wolfe, Alan (1979). The Rise and Fall of the 'Soviet Threat': Domestic Sources of the Cold War Consensus. Washington, D.C.: Institute For Policy Studies.

Wright, Q. (1942/1965). A Study of War. Chicago: University of Chicago Press.

Wymer, C. R. (1972). "Econometric Estimation of Stochastic Differential Equation Systems." Econometrics 40:565–577.

Yengst, W. C. and T. Smolin (1981). Conventional Warfare Damage and Casuality Trends. La Jolla, Calif.: Science Applications, Inc.

Zagare, Frank C. (1977). "A Game Theoretic Analysis of the Vietnam Negotiations: Preferences and Strategies." Journal· of Conflict Resolution 21:663–684.

Zagare, Frank C. (1979). "The Geneva Conference of 1954: A Case of Tacit Deception." International Studies Quarterly 23:390–411.

Zagare, Frank C. (1981). "Nonmyopic Equilibria and the Middle East Crisis of 1967." Conflict Mangement and Peace Science 5:139–62.

Zagare, Frank C. (1982). "A Review of 'The War Trap.'" American Political Science Review 76:738–739.

Zagare, Frank C. (1983). "A Game Theoretic Evaluation of the Cease-Fire Alert Decision of 1973." Journal of Peace Research 20:70–86.

Zagare, Frank C. (1984a). Game Theory: Concepts and Applications. Beverly Hills, Calif.: Sage.

Zagare, Frank C. (1984b). "Limited Move Equilibria in 2 x 2 Games." Theory and Decision 16:1–19.

Zagare, Frank C. (1984c). "Toward A Reformulation of the Theory of Mutual Deterrence." Mimeographed.

Zagare, Frank C. (1985). "Toward a Reconciliation of Game Theory and the Theory of Mutual Deterrence." International Studies Quarterly, forthcoming.

Zagladin, Vadim (1982). "Peace and Human Progress." Peace and
    Disarmament: Academic Studies. Pp. 34-50. Moscow: Progress.
Zimmermann, Ekkart (1980). "Macro-Comparative Research on Political
    Protest." In Handbook of Political Conflict, edited by Ted R.
    Gurr. New York: The Free Press.
Zimmermann, Ekkart (1983). Political Violence, Crises and Rev-
    olutions. Cambridge, Mass.: Schenkman.
Zinnes, Dina A. (1970). "Coalition Theories and the Balance of
    Power." In The Study of Coalition Behavior, edited by S.
    Groenings, E. W. Kelley, and M. Leirserson. New York: Holt,
    Rinehart and Winston.
Zinnes, Dina A., Joseph L. Zinnes, and Robert D. McClure (1972).
    "Markovian Analysis of Hostile Communications in the 1914
    Crisis." In Crisis in Foreign Policy Decision Making, edited
    by Charles F. Hermann. New York: The Free Press.
Zolberg, Aristide R. (1980). "Strategic Interactions and the
    Formation of Modern States: France and England."
    International Social Science Journal 32:687-716.

About the Editors
and Contributors_____

CO-EDITORS

Urs Luterbacher is a professor at the Graduate Institute of International Affairs, Geneva, Switzerland, where he is director of the Center for Empirical Research on International Relations.

Michael D. Ward, a professor of political science at the University of Colorado, Boulder, is a member of the Program on Political and Economic Change in the university's Institute of Behavioral Science and a founding member of the Center for International Relations, where he directs the Program on International Conflict and Cooperation.

CONTRIBUTORS

Pierre Allan is a professor of political science at the University of Geneva, Switzerland. Involved in the construction of the SIMPEST models, he has written on arms races, international conflict, and social time.

Steven J. Brams is a professor of political science at New York University. He is one of the foremost international authorities on the application of game theoretic models to social issues.

Dagobert L. Brito is the Peterkin Professor of Political Economy in the Department of Economics at Rice University, Houston, Texas. He is widely published in the area of national security.

Claudio Cioffi-Revilla is a professor at the University of Illinois, Urbana, where his research focuses on the development of a mathematical theory of political reliability.

T. Michael Clarke is an associate of the Center for Empirical Research on International Relations at the Graduate Institute of International Affairs, Geneva, Switzerland.

Daniel Frei, a professor in the Department of Political Science at the University of Zurich, Switzerland, has worked extensively on the evolution and dynamics of East-West interactions, particularly detente and deterrence.

Lewis L. House is a senior scientist at the National Center for Atmospheric Research, Boulder, Colorado. He is currently conducting research on international conflict and cooperation as related to power in the international system.

Michael D. Intriligator is a professor of political science and economics at the University of California, Los Angeles, where he is the director of the Center for International and Strategic Affairs. He has written extensively on international relations, focusing on national security issues, and in the areas of econometric theory and practice.

D. Marc Kilgour is chairman of the Department of Mathematics at Wilfrid Laurier University, Waterloo, Ontario, Canada. His research concentrates on non-cooperative games and utilizes formal mathematics to represent "far sightedness" and anticipation.

Jean-Christian Lambelet, one of the leading macroeconomists in Switzerland, is in the Department of Economics at the University of Lausanne. Much of his research has dealt with the topic of arms races.

Zeev Maoz is a professor in the Department of Political Science at the University of Haifa, Israel. His research has concentrated on the initiation and escalation of serious international disputes.

Thomas F. Mayer is a professor in the Institute of Behavioral Science and the Department of Sociology at the University of Colorado, Boulder. His major interest is the analysis of significant social problems, such as the nuclear arms race.

Martin C. McGuire is a professor of economics at the University of Maryland, College Park. His writings have focused on the arms race, alliance behavior, and the general problems surrounding the allocation of resources.

Dwain Mefford is a professor in the School of International Relations at the University of Southern California. His research is organized around the application of logic programming and artificial intelligence.

James D. Morrow, a professor at Michigan State University, has written widely on the topic of utility theory as applied to national security policies.

Barry O'Neill is a professor in the Department of Industrial Engineering and Management Science at Northwestern University. The role of escalation in social processes stands at the center of many of his recent writings.

Dieter Ruloff is a privat dozent at the University of Zurich in the Department of Political Science. His research focuses on the politics of East-West diplomatic interactions, particularly cooperation.

Philip A. Schrodt is a professor of political science at Northwestern University. An expert on the application of formal techniques to the study of political phenomena, he is currently at work on pattern matching.

Albert A. Stahel works in the Military Studies Section of the Federal Institute of Technology in Zurich, Switzerland. He is one of the world's leading authorities on guerrilla warfare as studied through the use of simulation.

William R. Thompson is a professor in the International Relations Department at the Claremont Graduate School. His recent research has focused on the investigation of cyclical properties of international conflict.

Charles Tilly is the Distinguished Professor of History and Sociology at the New School for Social Research, New York. He is best known for his seminal work on domestic political conflict behavior.

Frank C. Zagare, a professor at Boston University, has concentrated his research on the application of game theory to the study of historical and ongoing international security problems, including war and deterrence.

OTHER PARTICIPANTS IN THE CONFERENCE

Francis A. Beer, Department of Political Science, University of Colorado.
Wilmont Hess, Director, National Center for Atmospheric Research.
Manus I. Midlarsky, Department of Political Science, University of Colorado.
Karen Rasler, Department of Political Science, Arizona State University.
Lynne Rienner, Lynne Rienner Publishers.